Gaylaw

GAYLAW

Challenging the Apartheid of the Closet

William N. Eskridge, Jr.

HARVARD UNIVERSITY PRESS
Cambridge, Massachusetts
London, England

For Wendy Webster Williams

First Harvard University Press paperback edition, 2002

Library of Congress Cataloging-in-Publication Data

Eskridge, William N.
    Gaylaw : challenging the apartheid of the closet / William N.
    Eskridge, Jr.
        p.   cm.
    Includes bibliographical references and index.
    ISBN 0-674-34161-9 (cloth)
    ISBN 0-674-00804-9 (pbk.)
    1. Homosexuality—Law and legislation—United States.
    2. Gays—Legal status, laws, etc.—United States.
    3. Lesbians—Legal status, laws, etc.—United States.
    I. Title.
    KF4754.5E84   1999
    342.73'087—dc21   99-26321

contents

acknowledgments

The chapters in this book reflect my ongoing effort to understand the history of American regulation of sexual and gender variation, the ways in which challenges to that regulation fit into and destabilize constitutional doctrine, and what American culture and law can learn from gay theory and experience. All of the chapters have profited from the ongoing institutional support of Georgetown's Dean Judith Areen; her Deputy Deans Steven Goldberg, Wendy Webster Williams, Mark Tushnet, and Anita Allen; Georgetown's fabulous library staff, particularly Yalli Fang, Joan Marshall, Mabel Shaw, and Karen Summerhill; and wonderfully helpful student research assistants, including Kristi Bailey, Jonathan Beyer, Stewart Chang, Glenn Edwards, Amy Foote, David Fromm, Julie Harris, Judith Holibar, Jennifer Johnson, Bret Leas, Matt Michael, Justin Murphy, Jason Oyler, Amy Persapane, and Thaddeus Pope. I finished the book at the Yale Law School, where Dean Anthony Kronman has given me valuable support. Librarian Gene Coakley and research associates Sarah Light and Brent McIntosh have enabled me to finalize the research and most of the thinking. The historical research would not have been easily possible without the time provided by a fellowship from the Simon Guggenheim Foundation, to which I am especially grateful.

Individual chapters in the book have been presented at faculty workshops or public lectures at the law schools of the University of California at Berkeley, the University of California at Los Angeles, Columbia University, Duke University, Florida State University, Georgetown University, Harvard University, Hofstra

University, the University of Illinois, the University of Indiana, the University of Iowa, the University of Maryland, the University of North Carolina, the University of Pennsylvania, Temple University, William and Mary University, and Yale University. I received valuable comments from students and faculty at all these institutions and from members of the GAYLAW Reading Group.

The historical chapters in Part One profited enormously from detailed critical feedback from various historians, particularly Allan Bérubé, George Chauncey, Mary Dudziak, John D'Emilio, Jonathan Ned Katz, and Mark Tushnet. Chapter 4's evaluation of *Bowers v. Hardwick* benefited from detailed critiques by Katz and Tushnet, as well as Michael Seidman. Chapter 5 grew out of an article I coauthored with David Cole and owes its best ideas to our collaboration. Chapter 6 benefited from Hans Johnson's insistence that I think more deeply about the relationship between law and cutting-edge theories of prejudice, and from Andrew Koppelman's insistence that the miscegenation analogy provides the best argument for same-sex marriage. The three doctrinal chapters (4 through 6) have been generally informed by an ongoing collaboration with Nan Hunter. The final three chapters (7 through 9) have had the benefit of exchanges I have enjoyed with Gayle Rubin and Wendy Webster Williams; their influence is most apparent in Chapter 7. Chapter 8 has developed in response to my experiences defending same-sex marriage. I have learned the most from feminist critics Paula Ettelbrick, Marcia Kuntz, and Nancy Polikoff and from gay defenders Carlos Ball, Marc Fajer, Tom Stoddard, and Evan Wolfson. Alison Anderson, Stephen Bainbridge, Jack Balkin, Evan Caminker, Julian Eule, Kent Greenawalt, Alan Hyde, Christine Littleton, Warren Schwartz, Stephen Sugarman, Kendall Thomas, and Mark Tushnet gave me most helpful comments on Chapter 9.

The historical chapters and the appendixes draw from archives across the country. Arrest records in Appendix C1 were compiled from annual police reports readily available at the municipal libraries for the following cities: Baltimore, Boston, Chicago, Cleveland, Los Angeles, Miami, Philadelphia, Richmond, St. Louis, San Francisco, and Washington, D.C. The New York Public Library has not only the best collection of police reports but also houses the private papers of the Committee of Fourteen and other antiprostitution groups. I appreciate the warm cooperation of the municipal librarians at all these cities. Similarly helpful were the librarians at the Library of Congress and the National Archives. Richard Boylan of the National Archives was critical in pointing me toward materials relevant to the military exclusion of gay people during World War II, and Immigration and Naturalization Service historian Marian Smith was even more important in guiding me to the relevant immigration materials. For nineteenth-century municipal ordinances, I relied on the substantial collections in the libraries of the University of Illinois, the Yale Law

School, the Harvard Law School, and Florida State University School of Law; the librarians at all the institutions were helpful, but David Warfield and Gene Coakley went way beyond the call of duty to facilitate my use of materials at Harvard and Yale, respectively. The "historical core" of the Georgetown University Law Center's Library is the best collection of nineteenth- and early twentieth-century state codes, and I appreciate the cooperation of Bob Oakley and his staff, both during and after my happy tenure at Georgetown. The Florida State Archives in Tallahassee made the Johns Committee files available to me, which provided invaluable context for my understanding of the antihomosexual Kulturkampf of the 1950s. The Lesbian Herstory Archives in Brooklyn gave me important insights into materials of lesbian history; I also benefited from examining the archives on lesbian and gay history at the New York Public Library, the San Francisco Public Library, and various private collections.

I dedicate this book to Wendy Webster Williams, one of the founders of feminist legal theory and a pioneer in feminist litigation and legislation. I owe her a special debt because she brought me to Georgetown when she was chair of its appointments committee, funded my gaylegal work as deputy dean, guided me as a faculty mentor, embraced me as a friend, and lent me her copy of *Macho Sluts*.

introduction

Gaylaw is the ongoing history of state rules relating to gender and sexual non-conformity. Its subjects have included the sodomite, the prostitute, the degenerate, the sexual invert, the hermaphrodite, the child molester, the transvestite, the sexual pervert, the homosexual, the sexual deviate, the bisexual, the lesbian and the gay man, and transgendered people. For most of American history, there was no state regulation of "gay" people—people not conforming to rigid sexual and gender roles[a]—because the categories of sexuality and gender were not well conceptualized until after the Civil War. This book starts with a legal history of the state's post–Civil War treatment of people who violated norms of gender or sexuality (Part One). Once the state was alerted to gender and sexual nonconformity as a prominent social phenomenon, the state sought to discourage the nonconformity and ultimately to erase the nonconformers. The law was a chief mechanism for the 1950s Kulturkampf, or state-sponsored culture war, against homosexuals and other gender-benders, yet simultaneously became the hunted's chief refuge from that assault. Since 1969 the law's hostility to gay people has relented, and today the law sometimes protects gay people against private violence and discrimination.

a. This book uses the term "gay people" to include both sexual orientation minorities—lesbians, gay men, bisexuals—and transgendered people—transsexuals and transvestites. This terminology reflects the conceptualization offered in William N. Eskridge, Jr., and Nan D. Hunter, *Sexuality, Gender, and the Law* (1997), that issues of sexual nonconformity should not be separated from issues of gender nonconformity.

Gaylaw is, also, reconceiving law from a more gay-friendly or gay-neutral perspective, the project of Part Two of this book. Although it is not illegal to be gay in the United States, the law continues to treat gay people as second-class citizens. The admitted lesbian cannot serve in the United States armed forces, cannot legally marry the woman she loves, commits a felony or a misdemeanor every time she has oral sex if this occurs in any of eighteen states, is subject to male violence and rape that the state will usually not investigate, in most juris-dictions has no legal remedy when she is fired from her job because her employer hates lesbians, and is subject to state confiscation of her biological children and in some states cannot adopt children (see Appendix B3 to this book). This level of formal inequality is morally indefensible and politically imprudent. Gaylaw insists that it be changed. Part Two shows how change is directed or supported by existing legal principles and precedents.

Gaylaw is, finally, derived from insights of the gay experience in America and its theoretical sibling, "queer theory" (Part Three). Some gaylegal ideas provide new arguments for old notions. The anticensorship principle is an example. In addition to the traditional liberal reasons, such as the value of personal auton-omy and of the marketplace of ideas, a gay-theoretical reason the state should not censor sexual or gender expression is that censorship not only fails to sup-press the targeted expression but produces a discourse that is likely to be more deviant than the uncensored one. Sexuality and gender are like heads of a hydra: the more the law cuts against them, the more multifarious they become. Other ideas are more distinctive to gaylaw: gender and sexual orientation are not natural forms but are instead "socially constructed" categories reflecting a system of power relations; the social creation of disapproved forms of gender and sexuality generates social travesty, and the invocation of law to direct social travesty generates an apartheid of the closet, where gay people are psychically as well as socially isolated; and the categories and the closet have not been produc-tive and should be ameliorated by law's acceptance of the idea of benign sexual variation. Consider each of these ideas in greater detail.

The Construction of Gender and Sexuality

Mary McIntosh and, later, Michel Foucault suggested that the "homosexual" is not a natural category, and that "homosexuality" is a concept peculiar to the West after 1892.[1] People of the same sex have engaged in all forms of human intimacy over the centuries, but modern Western culture is distinctive in ana-lyzing that intimacy around the concept of sexual orientation and stigmatizing the desire for such intimacy as well as the acts themselves. In America, as in Europe, homosexuality at the beginning of the twentieth century was not just a scientific classification but was also a "social dividing practice" embedded in a web of particular anxieties.[2] Precisely the same points could be made for transgendered behavior: cross-dressing is as old as the West, but it was not until 1900 that the "transvestite" emerged as a scientific classification. The "transsexual" and "intersexual" came even later.[b] The naming of these new categories of people was in part a displacement of new anxieties.

Many of the anxieties arose out of increased social and economic opportunities for women outside the home, which fueled not only a robust feminist movement but also a reaction that emphasized rigid gender lines and roles. Faced with the newly independent woman, middle-class men grew obsessed with cultural reinforcements for their manliness. Concepts of gender inversion and sexual perversion were part of a medicalized discourse that responded to men's, and often women's, concerns about the loss of stable expectations about male and female roles. The new discourse of sexuality was a system of knowledge that gave men a new venue for masculinity. The new discourse of sexual deviance reinforced that venue as a prohibitory discipline.

Other cultural anxieties concerned children, who immediately became a situs for the discourses of sexuality and deviance. With manhood being reconceived in terms of sexual aggression and with newspapers reporting examples of that aggression deployed toward children, society grew increasingly worried that asexual children would be "corrupted" by sexualizing male adults. By World War I, Americans' understanding of childhood was changing: children were sexual beings undergoing a fragile developmental process that could easily be derailed by adult predation. That derailment could occur not only through penetrative intercourse but also through other means of stimulation, including fondling and obscene pictures. The derailment could turn children into sexual or gender deviates themselves. Particularly in urban areas, where families were having fewer children but focusing more attention on them and their psyches, the new discourses of sexuality and sexual deviance constituted a system of knowledge that helped parents order family life and that warned against adult interference with childhood sexual and gender development.

The law both reflected and contributed to these systems of knowledge. Once the invert, transvestite, pervert, child molester, or homosexual was identified as a menace, and once social stigmas proved inadequate to contain communities of nonconformists, old legal rules were adapted and new rules created to regulate or suppress the menace. The legal prohibitions served positive as well as

---

b. A *transvestite* is someone who derives pleasure from dressing in the garb of the "opposite" sex. A *transsexual* is someone whose self-perceived gender does not match her or his biological sex. Biological sex itself is a newer point of inquiry: *intersexual* people, hermaphrodites, have physical characteristics of both sexes.

negative functions. The rules normalized what they did not prohibit, and working together various rules formed a normalizing regime. For example, the sodomy, prostitution, and other sex regulations of 1900 reconfirmed procreative marriage as the norm for Americans. To the extent that the prohibitory rules focused, at times hysterically, on homosexuality as a surrogate for all gender deviation or for child molestation in general, the rules further made heterosexuality the norm for all. Once heterosexuality became compulsory, the homosexual became a universal scapegoat. Although fondling and intercourse with children were overwhelmingly by men with girls, often fathers and daughters, society and the law focused disproportionately on the homosexual as the predatory child molester. Already a symbol against whom bourgeois men could define themselves as masculine as well as straight, the homosexual male conveniently served as a cover for the underside of compulsory heterosexuality—men who fondled, had intercourse with, or raped girls, including their daughters and nieces. Additionally, the rules created new power relationships, whereby police, doctors, family members, and even complete strangers were given authority to control members of the stigmatized group. The law impelled these people to interrogate suspected deviates, and their interrogations stimulated an intensified discourse of normal-versus-deviate sexuality and gender. The modern state of this century carried out this interrogation in many venues, detailed in Chapters 1 and 2.

In particular, the unprecedented state-sponsored discourse about sexual deviation during World War II helped create not only specific "perverted" identities but also facilitated awareness of a group identity focused by the state around homosexuality. The postwar state-sponsored Kulturkampf against gay people was a frightened reaction to the greater visibility of gender-bending subcultures, with an intent to renormalize around the family headed by the masculine, working dad and the feminine, housekeeping mom that had been disrupted by the war. The terror, which intensified discourse about sexual deviation, not only victimized tens of thousands of gay people but assured them a greater group solidarity beyond what the war had accomplished. If homosexuals were content to be objects of fear before the war, they were on the verge of reclaiming their status as subjects after bombardment during the postwar Kulturkampf.

The homophile movement that began in earnest after the war became the gay rights movement of the 1960s, which turned into a gay liberation movement in the 1970s. The role of law has come full circle: originally, law was a necessary supplement to social suppression of nonconforming gender and sexual performances; at the peak of the state's suppression, nonconforming subcultures turned to constitutional law and rights discourse as a means of resisting the positive law; after escaping most efforts at state suppression, the gay rights movement in the 1970s and 1980s turned them around, as the state started to prohibit private discrimination and violence against gay people. The legal struggle was part of the larger gay struggle for social recognition that gender role or sexual orientation ought not be a dividing practice stigmatizing and setting gay people off from the rest of Americans.

The developments described above can be situated along lines of sex, class, and race as well as sexual orientation. Although the social and legal rules against gender and sexual nonconformity operated on all people, they operated differently against men than women, working class than middle class, and white people than people of color. Although men and women were both exposed to police enforcement of antiprostitution regulations, the rules were more harshly but less pervasively enforced against inverted men; the goal of such rules was primarily to keep women in their accustomed gender roles and to deny their sexuality, while the goal as it pertained to men was primarily to control their easily deranged sexuality. When working-class people or people of color intruded into white middle-class spaces, the law became particularly harsh. Middle-class white offenders were often harassed and were more likely to be embarrassed by exposure than working-class and nonwhite offenders, but they were less likely to go to jail for long periods and were more likely to invoke legal rights to resist state action. Although the loci of legal battles over gay rights—libraries and universities, bathhouses and bars, automobiles, public restrooms and subway stations, parks, and other cruising areas—have been almost as much working class as middle class and female as male, gaylegal struggles have been dominated by white middle-class male perspectives. One project of this book is to initiate a legal conversation about where gaylaw is going now that voices of women and, to a lesser extent, those of people of color and the working class are being considered.

The Apartheid of the Closet

Eve Kosofsky Sedgwick identifies the "closet" as a metaphor characteristic of sexuality and gender in America.[3] Sedgwick treats the closet as a diacritical concept that helps us understand gender- and sexuality-normative discourse. The closet enables a series of "double binds" (lose-lose scenarios) for sexual and gender nonconformists. The lesbian teacher, for example, loses her job whether she admits her sexual orientation (fired because the bureaucracy fears parental reaction) or denies the same (fired because she lied on a bureaucratic form). This book explores the conceptual and legal history of the discourse Sedgwick describes. For law's purposes, the main limitation of her analysis is that double binds are not problematic per se. The drug-dealing teacher, after all, faces the same double bind as the lesbian teacher. A goal of this book is to develop normative political and legal arguments about the regime of the closet, which I provocatively describe as an "apartheid."

An archaeology of the closet begins with travesty and masquerade. Early modern society and literature were fascinated with masquerade as a means of playing with gender, sex, class, and other identity features. The masquerades that both shocked and titillated Western culture the most were ones where women "passed" as men.[4] In the era surrounding the Civil War, numerous men and women renounced the roles traditionally associated with their sexes, donning attire of the opposite sex and sometimes becoming intimate with persons of their own sex. Gender became a key organizing precept for these people as well as their neighbors in the mainstream. By constructing a set of characteristics associated with each sex, both society and its rebels recognized and supercharged the idea of *gender deviance:* the person's gender did not match her sex. That construction was closely followed by the idea of *sexual deviance:* the person's sexual preferences did not match those associated with his sex and gender. As society became more focused on, and alarmed by, sex and gender deviance, it assumed an increasing air of exotic secrecy, like a masquerade. Indeed, secrecy about gender and sexuality was called "wearing a mask."

Social pressure alone could not suppress gender and sexual nonconformity. Groups of nonconformists formed in big cities, newspapers reported their behavior, and doctors analyzed them and their press accounts. Especially after such nonconforming conduct hit the streets, middle-class society was shocked and alarmed. Municipal, then state, government was enlisted as an ally to stamp out or discourage gender and sexual nonconformity. Government responded, but the early instances of legal discipline yielded dramatic events—notably Oscar Wilde's 1895 trials for gross indecency and Alice Mitchell's 1892 sanity hearing—whose publicity increased curiosity about nonconforming gender and sexual feelings. More people came to see themselves as wearing a mask, and more people were willing to drop the mask in urban subcultures where their nonconformity found a receptive audience, and an increasing number of fellow nonconformists.

Although American law became increasingly interested in regulating gender or sexual "inverts" and "homosexuals" (to use the contemporary terms), regulation had little direct effect. For those increasing numbers who chose to "come out" (as it was put by the 1930s) to others in the subculture, the law in the first third of the twentieth century posed little impediment to what came to be known as the "double life": the gender or sexual "pervert" would wear the mask among her or his family, coworkers, and "straight" friends, but would drop the mask within the subculture.[c] For various reasons explored in Chapter 2, the accommodation collapsed in many urban areas during the 1930s, and the state came to be much more aggressive in regulating gender and sexual deviation. At the same time, the closet started to become a metaphor for secrecy about sexuality and gender.

The closet took form as a response to three legal conundrums in the 1940s and 1950s: the increasing use of sexual orientation as an important regulatory category, which fanned and nationalized society's obsessional discourse about minority sexualities; the insistence of legal republicans to command state apparatus to hunt down and destroy deviant minorities, especially homosexuals, countered by the insistence of legal libertarians that such minorities should be left alone; and the conflicting desires of gay people to hide behind traditional libertarian barricades while at the same time becoming more inclined to make their presence known in republican public culture. The idea of the closet, therefore, is not just the idea that deviant gender or sexuality must be secret—that was entailed in the masquerade and then the double life—but is more centrally a complex product of society and the law, which in the 1950s sought to enforce compulsory heterosexuality as a pervasive public policy. This is an "apartheid of the closet," because it insisted on segregating and hiding one's gender or sexual nonconformity as a condition of citizenship, freedom, and employment.

But the closet was an unstable construction, in part because of its ambiguity for gays and straights alike.[5] The closet could be *protective:* for gays, as a refuge from social or legal persecution; for straights, as a means of secluding offensive sexuality and gender-bending, the proverbial skeletons in the closet. So long as gays and straights considered the closet mutually protective, the closet was stable: don't ask, don't tell. But such a closet could not be stable if either straights (ask!) or gays (tell!) breached its security. This was always possible, as the closet could simultaneously be *threatening:* for straights, because the closet could be a hiding place for predatory and subversive criminals; for gays, because the seclusion was an identity prison and an insulting denial of their integrity and dignity. Law contributed to the instability of the closet, at first by empowering homophobes to throw open closet doors in antihomosexual witch-hunts, and

c. This book will generally use then-contemporary terms in discussing each historical period. Chapter 1, for example, uses the terms "invert" and "fairy" for the period from 1880 to 1900 and then "homosexual," "sex pervert," and "transvestite," which supplanted the previous terms after 1900. By the 1930s the term "coming out" meant a homosexual's dropping her "mask" and revealing her sexual identity to another person she believed to be homosexual. The "closet" did not emerge as a common metaphor until after World War II (Chapter 2), and the term "coming out of the closet" not until the 1960s (Chapter 3). The best early glossary of subcultural terms is Gershon Legman, "The Language of Homosexuality," in George Henry, *Sex Variants: A Study of Homosexual Patterns,* 1149–79 (1941).

then by empowering gay people not only to resist the witch-hunts but also to express nonconforming ideas through publication, association, and speech and even to aspire, as African Americans and women did, to formal equality. The antihomosexual Kulturkampf of the 1950s cast many gay people out of their closets, but by the 1960s others were "coming out of the closet" voluntarily. Coming out did not end the regime of the closet; most gay people remain closeted, and new closets have formed around AIDS, for example. But coming out has rendered the closet even more unstable and subject to strong public contention.

One by-product of the collapsing closet is the increasing legalization of gay and antigay discourse. One hundred years ago, gender and sex were understood along lines of religion or natural law: man and woman were made by God for procreative intercourse within the institution of marriage; women and men who departed from that model were immoral, threatening to the natural order. Fifty years ago, gender and sex were understood along lines of medicine and psychiatry as well: masculine man and feminine woman were considered sexual beings, with needs that could only be met by bonding with one another; women and men who departed from that model were mentally ill, perhaps psychopathic, and sexually threatening to children in particular. Today, the religious and medical discourses have been supplemented by legal discourse. Progay assaults on the closet are mounted along lines of constitutional and legislative rights, and those assaults are countered by arguments that fearful straight people have a right not to be exposed (or have their children exposed) to openly gay people or even knowledge about disapproved forms of sexuality and gender-bending.

Part Two of this book argues that law's perpetuation of the sexual closet is in need of reevaluation. The judiciary's traditional refusal to recognize full rights of privacy, equality, and free expression for gay people is incoherent with the overall constitutional jurisprudence the Supreme Court has developed under the due process clause, the equal protection clause, and the first amendment. Factual misunderstandings, antigay prejudice, and squeamishness about sexuality itself may explain persisting inequalities—but such explanatory factors cannot justify the inequalities. Doctrinally, the Supreme Court's decision in *Romer v. Evans* (1996),[6] overturning an antigay initiative, provides an occasion for rethinking antigay constitutional jurisprudence. *Evans* can be understood as a criticism of the apartheid of the closet. The purpose of the antigay initiative was to discourage gay people from coming out of the closet and participating in the workplace and in politics as openly gay citizens. If, as the Court held, silencing of sexual orientation minorities is not a legitimate state policy, many other policies are also vulnerable. Part Two of this book will argue that, after *Evans,* the Supreme Court should reconsider its refusal to extend the right of privacy to same-sex intimacy (Chapter 4); the state cannot censor identity speech and even sexual expression without a neutral justification (Chapter 5); and most gender- and sexuality-based state discriminations are questionable for equal protection reasons (Chapter 6).

Benign Sexual Variation

Gay equality is a shocking idea to most Americans, but much that was shocking to earlier generations is considered a civil right today. At the beginning of the twentieth century, many WASP (white Anglo-Saxon Protestant) Americans considered non-English immigrants, Roman Catholics, and African Americans filthy and lewd peoples. The idea of a WASP marrying or even having to associate with an immigrant, a Catholic, or an African American was shocking. It was also prejudiced, and experience with ethnic, religious, and racial groups in America has taught us not just to tolerate but also to value ethnic, religious, and racial diversity. There are three dimensions to the earlier experience. One is self-interest: once minorities became politically active, it would have been disastrous for the WASP majority to suppress their rights, for a coalition of minorities could have retaliated against the WASPs. A second is political pragmatism: a society divided along ethnic, religious, and racial lines is in trouble; a healthy pluralism accommodates the different groups and keeps them from warring. A third is moral reality: minority peoples were human beings just as worthy as the WASP majority; working and associating with minority people taught WASPs that perceived differences were less important than the real similarities. Experience with openly gay people may, similarly, teach America not just to tolerate but also to value sexual and gender diversity for the same reasons of self-interest, pragmatism, and morality. Just as the law played an important role in accommodating ethnic, religious, and racial diversity and in making it productive rather than divisive, so too can the law contribute to accommodating sexual and gender diversity and making it productive rather than divisive.

Consider this. At the turn of the twentieth century, religion was an identity trait that was morally divisive and was stigmatizing for minority identities, namely, those outside of the Protestant mainstream. At the turn of the millennium, America has productively internalized the idea of *benign religious variation,* that there are a number of equally good religions, and one's religion says little or nothing about one's moral or personal worth. The opposite is true of sexual orientation. The sexual orientation concept barely existed at the turn of the century but is charged with normative meaning at the turn of the millennium. Most Americans do not believe there is *benign sexual variation,* Gayle

Rubin's term for the idea that there are a number of equally good sexual orientations and one's sexuality says little or nothing about one's moral or personal worth.[7] Some of the legal propositions in Part Two of this book may depend, entirely or in part, on this country's movement from the idea of *malign* to *tolerable* or *benign* sexual and gender variation.

Such movement can be facilitated by legal experiments at the local level, what Chapter 9 terms "equality practice." The gaylegal history developed in Part One suggests that we should be skeptical about apocryphal claims that equality for a minority would imperil majority values. Racists opposed equal rights for African Americans on the grounds that they would offend white people and would undermine white institutions such as marriage. Thus blacks were segregated in schools and the armed forces lest their unwanted association be thrust onto fearful whites, and different-race marriage was prohibited to prevent what the Virginia Supreme Court termed a "mongrel breed" of citizens. Integrated schools, armed forces, and marriages have shown that white and black people can get along fine and benefit from one another. People today oppose equal rights for gay people on the ground that they would offend straight people and would undermine heterosexual institutions such as marriage. If the closet door were completely opened, straight people would find gay people remarkably easy to work with, and the institutions would flourish.

A leading heterofear is that gays in the military, same-sex marriage, and gay families with children would unleash weirdness upon the country. Greater weirdness has been built up by state campaigns against gay people, for such campaigns drive people away from mainstream values and create unproductive anger, as well as empower society's worst bigots. If gay people were treated equally, the weirdness would in fact diminish. Gay people already inhabit all the institutions of the American middle class—career, family, faith—and legal recognitions, such as same-sex marriage, would incrementally but positively reinforce those allegiances. Part Three of this book argues that open recognition of the presence of gays in families, careers, and faiths would be educational for America. Gaylaw, in brief, can contribute to mainstream legal and policy discourse. The final three chapters examine issues of sexual consent, family, and identity politics from gaylegal experience and theory. Feminist theory has already questioned key normative choices made within the liberal state about consensual sex, marriage and family, and the value of free speech. While generally contributing to the feminist project, gaylaw questions some normative choices made by feminism, including norms as to which many feminists and traditionalists agree.

The most significant normative theme of gaylaw is that the United States overregulates sexuality and gender, and that this excessive regulation creates new closets and discourses that undermine both traditionalist and feminist goals. The gay experience has been systematically different from the straight experience. Because same-sex intimacy is disconnected from procreation, it is more purely connected to other values, such as self-expression, bonding with another person, and pleasure. Without an anchor in procreation, same-sex intimacy is more openly committed to sexual diversity than different-sex intimacy is. This feature of gay experience critically notices how America is both sex obsessed and sex negative, puritanical and prurient. Neither feature is productive or morally admirable. Gaylaw would urge that the legal stakes of sex law be lowered and that the law give wider latitude to sexual variation.

Chapter 7 develops this theme as part of a positive and normative critique of the idea that "consent" is and should be the liberal litmus test for legal sex. Laws prohibiting consensual sodomy are obvious targets of gaylaw, but one should also be more critical of laws prohibiting prostitution, fornication, incest, sex between teenagers, and consensual sadomasochism. A radical gaylegal agenda would be to remove sex as a special case in American law altogether: sexual assaults (rapes) would be treated like other physical assaults (punching), incest and intergenerational sex would be legal, and workplace sexual harassment would be treated like any other unfair employment practice. I cannot go that far, for the feminist reason that sex remains a potent weapon of patriarchy, a way in which women are subordinated in relationships, the workplace, and society. If sex remains special for that or other reasons, public policy is then caught in this intractable paradox, however: state intervention is needed to protect the vulnerable against the predatory, but in most cases makes a bad situation worse by the discourse and closets that it engenders. This paradox is as tragic as it is inexorable.

A second regulatory implication of gaylaw involves the reconfiguration of family—de-emphasizing blood, gender, and kinship ties and emphasizing the value of interpersonal commitment. In our legal culture the linchpin of family law has been the marriage between a man and a woman who have children through procreative sex. Gay experience with "families we choose"[8] delinks family from gender, blood, and kinship. Gay families of choice are relatively ungendered, raise children that are biologically unrelated to one or both parents, and often form no more than a shadowy connection between the larger kinship groups. This is a social fact, and law in the post-closet era has no choice but to tolerate gay families of choice.

Should the law take the next step and give legal protection and recognition to gay families on the same terms as straight ones? Like the diversity of sexual preferences, diversity of family groups is potentially a good thing. It requires us to reconsider what it is that is good about family. Consistent with feminist critiques of marriage, Chapter 8 maintains that what best defines family is interpersonal commitment rather than gender, blood, or kinship ties. By denying gay people legal recognition, and reinforcement, of their interpersonal commitments, the law denies the relational features of gay personhood. This is to be regretted. The reasons given for this denial are analytically questionable, but the underlying cultural anxieties are genuine, even if factually underinformed.

The final chapter considers the chief public law complexity arising out of laws protecting against sexual orientation discrimination: the potential clash between gay equality and religious liberty. Although religious and gay communities have much in common and antigay and antireligious prejudices arise from similar destructive impulses, religious and gay ethics diverge, and their divergence has spawned controversies over application of antidiscrimination statutes. Drawing from a case where Georgetown University, a Roman Catholic school, was sued by gay student groups for recognition, the chapter sketches principles the law should apply in accommodating both communities even while resolving specific clashes. The judicial debate in the Georgetown case is a model of judicious accommodation, teaching us, among other things, that institutions need some equality practice before full equality can be achieved. Consistent with both gay experience and the precepts of most religions, mutual tolerance and cooperation notwithstanding different values should be law's guiding light in addressing future culture clashes.

part one

THE APARTHEID OF THE CLOSET

The homosexual was not created overnight nor was the apartheid of the closet. The three chapters in this part try to tell the story of their construction over several generations, with both coming into vivid display after 1947 and under attack after 1969. The changing legal regulation of same-sex intimacy is this part's focus and original contribution, but it draws from the pathbreaking work of feminist and gay historians. Most important have been the works of Carroll Smith-Rosenberg, John D'Emilio, Estelle Freedman, Allan Bérubé, Jonathan Katz, George Chauncey, Ruth Rosen, and Lillian Faderman. They have developed the outlines for shifting social and regulatory attention for the period examined (1880–1980) and have given flesh to the social constructionist vision originally suggested by Mary McIntosh.

The earliest locus of regulation was the city, and urban concern before 1900 focused strongly on gender inversion (Chapter 1). Women and men who transgressed increasingly hardened gender lines were harassed by the law and sometimes destroyed by it. The characteristic rules used to police gender nonconformity were laws prohibiting cross-dressing and prostitution. The former were widely adopted in cities all over America; in an ironic and unintended anticipation of the closet, police also interpreted state masquerade laws to outlaw attire not of one's sex. Although the cross-dressing rules are the most fascinating, they were less significant than the laws and ordinances prohibiting public lewdness, sexual solicitation, indecent assignation, disorderly conduct and degeneracy, lewd vagrancy, and indecent exposure. Except for the last, these laws were adopted to control prostitution, itself a gender inversion (the sexual-ized, entrepreneurial woman). Also significant were sodomy laws, originally adopted to prohibit disgusting acts, mainly anal sex, but transformed in this period to cover oral sex and to target "female impersonators," as degenerate men were called.

World War I is one watershed. Just as middle-class Americans were turning on to oral sex and companionate marriage, they cast a disapproving eye on the increasingly visible subcultures of "homosexuals." The regulatory concern shifted again. Just as gender inversion had superseded (but by no means dis-placed) disgusting acts as the chief concern with same-sex intimacy, so sexual deviation superseded (but by no means displaced) disgusting acts and gender inversion as the focal concern. The homosexual was not just a disgusting per-son or a gender-bending rebel, but was now a creature whose uncontrollable libido posed a momentous social danger to children's budding sexuality. The vampire lesbian and the predatory child-molesting (male) homosexual replaced the mannish lesbian and the female impersonator as the object of popular and legal concern and, starting in the 1930s, hysteria.

The next watershed was World War II. The military's exclusion of homosex-uals from service intensified the discourse of sexual deviation at the same time that homosocial service, both in and out of the military, made same-sex inti-macy commonplace. The tolerance of such intimacy during the war snapped back into an intense intolerance after the war, when America renormalized with a vengeance. Homosexuals became, after Communists, the chief enemy of the people. The federal government, and secondarily state and local governments, took the lead in mounting an antihomosexual Kulturkampf, a state campaign to erase homosexuality. Since the condition was not apparent to the naked eye, this reign of terror mainly succeeded in driving frightened homosexuals into the closet. The rules created by America's antihomosexual Kulturkampf between 1946 and 1961 bear eerie congruence to those adopted during Nazi Germany's antihomosexual Kulturkampf between 1933 and 1945.

The main difference is that America's campaign to extinguish public homo-sexuality and its subculture was markedly less successful than Germany's. This was mainly because Americans could not sustain the commitment of resources to hunting homosexuals that would have been required, given the ease of pass-ing as heterosexual and the decentralized structure of American government and society. Dismayingly, the rule of law played but a minor role in saving homosexuals from their persecutors, as judges usually went along with the per-secution during the terror period. After the terror, judges became more recep-tive, as did legislators and executives. What they were receptive to, however, was the *mutually protective closet:* so long as homosexuals operated within the privacy of the closet, the state would not open the door. This was an acceptable deal for most homophiles in the 1950s.

A final turning point occurred in the 1960s, arguably either in 1961, when Frank Kameny founded the Mattachine Society of Washington, or in 1969, the year of the Stonewall riots. It was during the 1960s that gay rights thinkers and leaders insisted that the mutually protective closet was a bad deal for gay people—nothing more than an "apartheid" (my term) that intrinsically denies equal citizenship and human dignity. This move was momentous: regulatory objects were reclaiming their subjectivity. The overriding political goal, around which gay people of all ideologies agreed after 1969, was to end the tyranny of the closet.

This, in turn, involved three overlapping struggles. The initial struggle was to protect *private gay spaces* against spying and intrusion of the police. These private spaces certainly included the home, but also the automobile, and for many gay people the enclosed toilet stall and sex club booth. A second struggle was for gays to assert control over the *institutions of gay subculture:* gay bars and restaurants, social and educational organizations, and literature, including erotica. The intruders here were not just the police but also liquor control agents, censors, and university administrators. A third struggle was for *equal gay citizenship.* Like African Americans who had long been insisting on their civil rights as equal citizens, openly gay people for the first time insisted on public equality and equal treatment on their merits as employees, soldiers, immigrants, and parents.

1. Masquerade and the Law, 1880–1946

Among the denizens of the "Gay 1890s" were Elvira Mugarietta, a Californian adventurer; Ralph Werther, a college student in New York City; and Alice Mitchell, a Memphis belle. All were gender-benders who ran afoul of the law.[1] Mugarietta, a biological female, passed as a man between 1892 and 1936. She was thereby able to enjoy experiences as a soldier, a journalist, and a philanthropist that were typically closed to women; the enjoyment was periodically interrupted with official detentions. Werther's autobiography describes himself as a "fairie" or "androgyne," namely "an individual with male genitals, but whose physical structure otherwise, whose psychical constitution, and *vita sexualis* approach the female type." Attracted only to virile men, Werther suffered from repeated run-ins with police and soldiers. Mitchell's single encounter with the law was the most tragic. She proposed to marry Freda Ward by passing as a man; after Ward demurred, Mitchell stabbed her to death on the streets of Memphis. The Shelby County Criminal Court adjudged her insane in 1892; she died six years later in an asylum.

There was nothing new about Mugarietta, Werther, or Mitchell. Fairies had cavorted in New York City before 1890; women passed as men and married other women throughout the modern era. What was new was the publicness and self-consciousness of their deviation from male and female roles, and society's anxious perception that many people shared their inclinations. That perception fueled a social discourse about same-sex intimacy that evolved from a focus on theology-based unnatural acts to medically based gender inversion and then to deviant sexual orientation. The discourse created specific categories of disapproved people—the sodomite, the sexual invert, the homosexual—who fit into yet broader stigmatized groups—the heretic, the degenerate, the psychopath.

Historians have developed a rich account of the late Victorian social construction of the "sexual invert" and the transformation of the invert into the modern "homosexual." This chapter draws from their work, particularly that of Carroll Smith-Rosenberg, Allan Bérubé, Lillian Faderman, George Chauncey, Estelle Freedman, and Jonathan Katz,[2] to demonstrate how the new regulatory categories affected the evolution of law between 1880 and 1946. These categories transformed the enforcement of sodomy laws and stimulated the creation of new laws to regulate same-sex intimacy and gender-bending. Several themes emerge from the account that follows: the different operation of these laws according to sex, class, and race; the interconnections between same-sex intimacy and laws regulating prostitution, cross-dressing, and indecency with children; and the evolution of law's regulation of same-sex intimacy from severe criminal sanction to mild criminal penalties and civil exclusion and suppression.

The most striking theme, however, inverts the previous one: just as social developments drove legal evolution, so legal developments affected social evolution. In 1900 most suppression of sexual and gender variation was accomplished outside the state, through family and social pressure. Gender-benders like Mugarietta engaged in a "masquerade" or "wore a mask," as contemporaries termed the socially impelled secrecy. Once subcultures of like-inclined "inverts" formed in major cities in the late nineteenth century, the mask could be selectively removed, and inverts like Werther could and did live what they called the "double life." Because social pressure was insufficient to quell the subcultural communities that made the double life possible, concerned citizens increasingly turned to the law. By World War II, legal officials in big cities outside the South were vigorously arresting cruising homosexuals, censoring homoerotic publications, closing down meeting places, and excluding gender-benders from admission to this country and its armed forces. This new legal regime represented society's coercive effort to normalize human relationships around "heterosexuality." Its actual effects were more complex and highly ambiguous. One was to transform travesty into tragedy, a process that was rhetorically captured by the emergence of "the closet" as the operative term for sexual secrecy.

Legal Regulation of Unnatural Acts and Inverted Gender, 1880–1921

New York's Penal Code of 1881 exemplified the post–Civil War state morals codes.[3] It prohibited as "crimes against the person and against public decency and good morals" rape, abduction, carnal abuse of children, abortion, bigamy, incest, sodomy, indecent exposure, possession or publication of obscene materials, and keeping a disorderly house. Section 887(4) of New York's Code of Criminal Procedure, also enacted in 1881, included prostitution in the misdemeanor of vagrancy.[4] Other states had less elaborate but similar criminal codes. Just as important were municipal codes of criminal offenses, summarized in Appendix A2 of this book. The 1881 Chicago Code, for example, prohibited vagrancy and loitering, prostitution and keeping a disorderly house, lewd acts or words, and indecent dress and exposure of the body.[5]

Some of the criminal prohibitions indirectly penalized sexual or gender variation, but none targeted consensual erotic activities between people of the same sex. Even sodomy laws were rarely applied to consenting same-sex adults. Thus, although thirty-six of the thirty-nine states criminalized sodomy or the "crime against nature" in 1881,[6] there were few prosecutions. The Census Bureau reported in 1880 that only sixty-three prisoners were incarcerated for crimes against nature in the entire country.[7] Thirty-two of the prisoners were males of color in the South, and a third of the white prisoners were foreign (European) born. Pre-1881 prosecutions overwhelmingly focused on male-female, adult-child, or man-animal relations rather than adult same-sex intimacy (see Chapter 4). To the extent crime against nature laws were mechanisms of social control, their objects were either predatory men assaulting children, women, and animals, or were people of color and foreign-born individuals, all "alien" to middle-class WASP America.

The lack of focused legal regulation does not mean that erotic activity between people of the same sex was unknown or socially approved in the nineteenth century. It was known, especially in big cities and among seafaring folk.[8] Although society gave same-sex intimacy no sanction, neither did it impose legal penalties. Eminent Bostonians tried to dissuade Walt Whitman from publishing the homoerotic *Calamus* poems as part of the 1860 edition of *Leaves of Grass*, but there was no effort at legal censorship of his "love of comrades" until 1882. Sarah Seelye not only passed as a man to serve in the Union Army during the Civil War but published an account of her masquerade, also without censorship.[9] After the Civil War, however, middle-class urban society became increasingly concerned with people who departed from society's increasingly rigid view of appropriate gender roles—including passing women such as

Mugarietta, fairies such as Werther, and women-obsessed women such as Mitchell.[10] Urbanization, which accelerated during America's post–Civil War industrialization, concentrated in small places large numbers of people with heterogeneous sexual tastes and afforded them many opportunities for satisfying those tastes. As Werther discovered in the 1880s, New York City's diverse mix of peoples offered many partners for unconventional sex and dress; over time, communities of like-feeling people could and did form. Demand then would follow supply in a synergism of sexual variety.

The main phenomenon was the enormous expansion of prostitution after the war, which was in turn met with a "purity movement" aiming to extinguish it.[11] The purity movement reflected heightened middle-class desire to reinforce traditional female gender roles in the face of a generation of "new women," educated and economically independent of men.[12] "True womanhood," from this perspective, was supportive of husband and children, nonsexual, and private. The prostitute, who was entrepreneurial, sexual, and public, was the antithesis of true womanhood—as were women who "inverted" gender. Alice Mitchell was bourgeois culture's nightmare example of the new woman, for she was not only wealthy, independent, and uninterested in men, but she proposed to appropriate the male role in a gender-bending marriage to feminine Freda Ward. When her plans were thwarted, she appropriated the classic male response, jealous battery.

Also disturbing were fairies, such as Werther, who renounced the male gender role as they renounced the male sex role, and women passing as men, such as Mugarietta, who lived as Babe Bean in the 1890s, served in the Spanish-American War as Jack Bean, and lived most of her life as Jack Garland in San Francisco. All of these figures were peripheral to nineteenth-century America, but they were a periphery increasingly irritating to the middle-class core. Americans had seen cross-dressing men and women before the Civil War, and drag shows became a staple of popular urban entertainment no later than the 1890s. New and disturbing in the post–Civil War period were the greater incidence of cross-gender attire and behavior that seriously flaunted natural gender roles; the formation of communities of gender inverts in eastern, midwestern, and western cities; and the creation of a discourse specifying the "invert" or "degenerate" as an object of medical study and social concern, and as a self-conscious subject aware of a difference in her or his constitution.

Americans after the Civil War increasingly noticed gender and sexual nonconformities and their possible connections. One early writer complained that cross-gender attire and "unnatural lust" between persons of the same sex were "practised, not in rare or exceptional cases, but deliberately and habitually in the great cities of our country."[13] By the turn of the century, sexologist Havelock

Ellis reported that "[t]he world of [male] sexual inverts is, indeed, a large one in any American city, and it is a community distinctly organized—words, customs, traditions of its own," as well as meeting places, clubs, and welcoming churches.[14] Accounts by gender-benders themselves as well as by contemporary observers suggest that by 1881 male subcultures existed in New York City, San Francisco, St. Louis, Philadelphia, Chicago, Boston, New Orleans, and Washington, D.C., to which by 1900 could be added Milwaukee, Denver, Louisville, and Portland as "homosexual capitals."[15] These accounts suggest the following generalizations about such subcultures.

Their most significant feature was a conscious interconnection of cross-gender dress and sexual desires. Women who dressed as men often married other women, appropriating male sexual as well as professional roles, as Mitchell tried to do.[16] While cross-dressing women typically tried to pass as men, whole communities of men sexualized gender-bending with their transparent impersonations of the opposite sex. Dr. Frank Lydston's 1889 description of Chicago's "colony of male sexual perverts" emphasized both the "abnormal sexual impulses" of the men and their "effeminacy of voice, dress, and manner." Ralph Werther claimed that from 1870 onward there were saloons in New York's Bowery where female impersonators (fairies) could go and flirt with working-class toughs. By the 1890s "Paresis Hall," with its drag shows and same-sex dancing, had become the center for New York's gender-bending "Cercle Hermaphroditos."[a] As in New York, San Francisco had saloons frequented by female impersonators, the best known being the Dash on Pacific Street. Male cruising in the Barbary Coast saloon district and near the Presidio (where soldiers could be had for a price) earned San Francisco the nickname "Sodom by the Sea."[17] In places like New Orleans, Washington, St. Louis, Harlem, Chicago, Los Angeles, and Seattle, female impersonators and fairies naturally gravitated toward periodic drag balls and burlesques that were becoming popular by the 1890s with mainstream as well as gay audiences.[18]

The connections between gender-bending subcultures and prostitution were multifarious. For women, the main community associated with unnatural acts and gender deviance was that of prostitutes. Many female sex workers, especially women of color, offered oral sex to their male customers and found sexual or emotional solace in one another. New Orleans' community of prostitutes was held up as a center of female inversion, contrasted with the reputable "smashes" middle-class girls had for one another and their teachers.[19] The most famous

a. "Cercle Hermaphroditos" linguistically reflects the blending of the male (Hermes) and the female (Aphrodite). "Paresis Hall" was a derogatory popular name, derived from the medical term for psychopathic interest in sex.

San Francisco cross-dresser was prostitute Jeanne Bonnet, described as a "man-hater," with "short cropped hair, an unwomanly voice, and a masculine face which harmonized excellently with her customary suit of boys' clothes." In 1875 she organized a gang of prostitutes who renounced their male pimps and supported themselves by petty theft. Lying in bed waiting for her lover, Bonnet was murdered in 1876, probably by a vengeful pimp.[20] Male fairies hung out with female prostitutes in bawdy houses and used these houses as places of solicitation and assignation much as prostitutes did. Indeed, many males were themselves commercial "trade"—soldiers, youths, and working-class men willing to receive oral sex or give anal sex in return for money. Like the culture of female prostitution, male communities brought middle-class fairies like Werther together with trade from a subordinate economic, social, or racial group.[21]

At the same time the nation was noting an increasing visibility of people who were violating gender norms, a new secularized vocabulary was developed to categorize these people.[22] Rather than criticizing prostitutes and sodomites for unnatural acts that violated religious ideals, the "sexologists" spoke of prostitutes and androgynes in terms of their inverted status, with bodies or minds that took on the gender traits associated with the opposite sex. This new emphasis originated in the writings of European authors, principally Karl Ulrichs, who saw himself as a female soul trapped in a male body, and Richard von Krafft-Ebing, whose *Psychopathia Sexualis* (English translation, 1892) argued that the strong contrast between aggressive male and passive female was a product of the progressive development of the human race and that role inversion by masculinized females or feminized males represented a "degeneration," or reversion to a prior evolutionary status.[23] Several European doctors seized upon Mitchell's story as an inversion tragedy.[24]

These ideas were simplified by American sexologists into a rigid science of gender role, at the same time European doctors such as Ellis and Krafft-Ebing were finding a broader range of natural and functional variation. Typical of the Americans, Dr. George Beard wrote in 1884 that when people's "sex is perverted, they hate the opposite sex and love their own; men become women and women men, in their tastes, conduct, character, feelings and behavior."[25] American doctors considered this sort of gender inversion a dangerous sickness.[26] They were most absorbed by the idea that any departure from strict binary gender roles (man = masculine, woman = feminine) represented a degeneration to more primitive forms. According to Lydston, all vice and crime could be traced to "the degenerate classes," those "persons of low grade and development, physically and mentally." Prostitutes (with inordinate sexual desire) and sexual inverts (with inappropriate sex and gender roles) were the chief degenerate classes, and they contributed in urban areas to a dramatic surge in "perverted" sexual practices. Lydston believed in "evolutionary reversion," whereby the prostitute and invert abandon the inhibitions of civilization and revert to sub-human, animalistic desires. His degeneracy theory was explicitly racist, as he linked the many "sexual crimes among the blacks of the south" with their "[p]hysical and moral degeneracy."[27] Other doctors reasoned from early drag balls in black Washington and St. Louis that cross-dressing was imported from Africa.[28]

Following Krafft-Ebing, most American degeneracy theorists believed that these inversions had a "constitutional" basis in the person's biological makeup. The worst perversions were the consequence of "psychopathic" problems that disabled the person from controlling her or his impulses. These theorists understood constitutional psychopathy to be the basis for sexual assaults on children, which in the late nineteenth century were perceived to be alarmingly high. In 1894 Dr. Charles Chaddock, Krafft-Ebing's American translator, published a pioneering account of "sex crimes" in the textbook *A System of Legal Medicine*. He opined that rape, pederasty (anal sex), and manual molestation of children were the most frequently reported sex crimes, by a large margin. Chaddock asserted that this "unnatural preference for children" arose out of a "constitutional psychopathic deficiency," much like the other "sexual perversions" cataloged in his article.[29]

Medical and press accounts of sexual and gender deviation triggered social responses in cities all over America in the late nineteenth century. In most major cities, civic groups formed to combat vice, mainly prostitution, but also other forms of degeneracy. In New York City, to take the most dramatic example, the Society for the Prevention of Cruelty to Children and the Society for the Suppression of Vice (the Comstock Society), both founded in 1872, pressed police to enforce sodomy laws against "child molesters" and male "prostitutes," respectively. In the 1890s the Comstock and other groups alerted the police to the degenerate affairs transpiring at Paresis Hall. By the turn of the century, New York City had half a dozen or more major citizen groups assisting the police in monitoring clubs, parks, subways, and public baths for illicit sexual activities among men. Other early antivice groups that focused on sexual and gender inversion included Boston's Watch and Ward Society and Chicago's Law and Order League. Later Chicago's Vice Commission reported vaudeville performances at bawdy houses where "men impersonate women and solicit men for 'perverted practices'" and urged regulatory responses. California muckrakers noisily objected to communities of inverts interspersed within vice districts. Such alarm was not limited to big cities. The Lancaster, Pennsylvania,

Vice Commission reported "[c]onsiderable evidence (impossible to print) of the practice of perversion in Lancaster by inmates of [bawdy] houses, by street walkers, by charity girls, and by men perverts or 'fairies,' and degenerates."[30]

Citizen reformers vented an outrage more intense than the concerns raised by ivory tower sexologists. Anthony Comstock, founder of the Society for the Prevention of Vice, had this to say when he read Werther's autobiography: "These inverts are not fit to live with the rest of mankind. They ought to have branded in their foreheads the word 'Unclean,' and as the lepers of old, they ought to cry 'Unclean! Unclean!' as they go about, and instead of the [crime against nature] law making twenty years imprisonment the penalty for their crime, it ought to be imprisonment for life."[31] Fueled by this kind of thinking and cognizant that social pressure was insufficient to erase degeneracy, private groups such as Comstock's continued to pressure the state to police inverted actions. For example, in New York City most of the police action against fairies between 1881 and World War I was the direct consequence of pressure by the Society for the Prevention of Cruelty to Children (alerting police to sodomy committed on youth), the Comstock Society and the Vigilance Society (female impersonator hangouts), and the Society for the Prevention of Crime (gay baths).[32] This wedding of social disgust and state mobilization was played out at the municipal, state, and national levels between 1881 and 1921 and resulted in an array of criminal and civil penalties to suppress gender and sexual variation.

New Specifications of the Crime against Nature

Sodomy statutes were an unwieldy mechanism for state response to citizens' demands for suppressing gender and sexual nonconformity. As a felony, sodomy prosecutions entailed jury trial and other legal rights for the accused, including a significant evidentiary advantage. Because a person could not be convicted of sodomy based only upon a willing adult accomplice's testimony, it was usually impossible to prove sodomy when between consenting adults (Chapter 4). Moreover, "sodomy" was anal sex, and the common law did not consider oral sex to be a crime against nature.[33] Accordingly, these laws were not clearly applicable to sex between two women, oral sex between two men, and mutual masturbation. At about the same time that England augmented its sodomy law with a "gross indecency" law prohibiting oral sex between two men in the famous Labouchere Amendment to an 1885 antiprostitution bill, the American states updated their sodomy laws, as Chapter 4 describes in greater detail.

Pennsylvania was the first state to respond formally, by enacting a new sodomy statute in 1879:

[T]he terms sodomy and buggery . . . shall be taken to cover and include the act or acts where any person shall wilfully and wickedly have carnal knowledge, in a manner against nature, of any other person, of penetrating the mouth of such person; and any person who shall wickedly suffer or permit any other person to wickedly and indecently penetrate, in a manner against nature, his or her mouth by carnal intercourse.[34]

The Pennsylvania statute ambitiously included women as well as men and the receiver as well as giver of oral sex. Following the Pennsylvania approach of specifying the crime against nature more precisely and broadly by statutory amendment were such big-city states as New York (1886), Ohio (1889), Louisiana (1896), Wisconsin (1898), Iowa (1902), Washington (1909), Missouri (1911), Virginia (1916), and Minnesota (1921). Following the English approach of creating a separate crime for oral sex, other states adopted entirely new statutes prohibiting "gross indecency" (Michigan [1903]) or "lewd and lascivious acts" (Massachusetts [1887], Maryland [1916], Florida [1917]) or "private lewdness" (New Jersey [1906]) or, most directly, "oral copulation" (California [1915, 1921]). Some states, such as Illinois (1897) and Georgia (1904), achieved the same result through judicial construction of crime against nature laws. By 1921 all of the states containing big cities, except Texas, had updated their criminal laws to make consensual oral sex a felony. (Appendix A1 provides references for each state.) Accompanying this legal shift was a boom in arrests for the crime against nature.

Where the 1880 Census had identified sixty-three prisoners for this crime, the 1890 Census identified 224,[35] a fourfold increase fueled by arrests in northeastern cities (Appendix C1). New York City, which had prosecuted a total of twenty-two sodomy cases between 1796 and 1873,[36] was arresting that many men each year by 1890, and double that number by 1900; arrests in Philadelphia, Boston, and Chicago were in the double digits by 1900. Other large cities, such as Baltimore, St. Louis, Cleveland, Los Angeles, and San Francisco, did not have regular double-digit arrests until the years 1911 to 1921, when sodomy records were set all over the country, and southern cities like Richmond and Nashville recorded their first sodomy arrests. Notwithstanding these records, sodomy arrests remained a tiny portion (a fraction of 1 percent) of total arrests in all cities.

A more subtle feature of the sodomy arrest statistics is their tie to legal reform: once oral sex came under the formal ambit of a state crime against nature law, the number of arrests in the state's urban center shot up. Link the figures in Appendix C1 with sodomy law expansion: Philadelphia's arrests jumped from two to thirteen after its 1879 law went into effect; arrests in New York and Baltimore did not reach double digits until their states explicitly criminalized oral sex in 1886 and 1916, respectively; St. Louis's arrests for the crime hit double digits at about the time the legislature amended the law to include oral sex in 1911, and then bounced upward after that; arrests in Los Angeles for crimes against nature zoomed up from seven per year before California's statutory liberalization (1915, 1921) to 123 for the first year after liberalization for which data are extant. The most direct evidence is for Boston: arrests for "unnatural and lascivious conduct" (oral sex) immediately hit double digits, greatly overshadowing sodomy (anal sex) arrests for each year the arrests were separately reported.[37] For the cities in Appendix C1, controlled for population increases, a comparison of arrests before oral sex was expressly illegal with arrests after illegality yields a statistically significant difference under both an Independent Samples T-Test and a Trivariate Regression.[38]

Once they covered oral as well as anal sex, sodomy laws were also regularly applied against women, at first mostly prostitutes. The 1880 Census reported only one woman incarcerated for sodomy; that changed in the next generation. New York's records regularly reveal female sodomy arrests after 1900; for example, thirty-one of the 601 persons arrested between 1901 and 1910 were women. In Boston and Baltimore women were regularly arrested, albeit in small numbers, after oral sex became a crime. Women as well as men were becoming responsible actors in the theater of perverted sexuality, and they sometimes went to jail for their roles.[39]

The legal process by which sodomy laws were updated entailed an analytical discourse specifying with much greater particularity what was forbidden and what was acceptable sexual conduct. The 1879 Pennsylvania law identified for the first time precisely what was involved in the crime against nature, and that became the norm as states revised their sodomy laws. Judicial opinions reviewing sodomy convictions began to describe the circumstances of the crime and the relationship of the parties rather than just announcing that "unmentionable" conduct had occurred. Most of the opinions engaged in a reasoning process rather than just denouncing the "abominable" nature of the conduct and the crime. (These developments occurred later in the South.) Treatises and practice manuals discussed the crime against nature. This legal discourse paralleled the more important medical and popular discourse that was creating the idea of "gender" and "sexuality" in the West during this era.

New Municipal and State Criminal Regulations

Even though arrests increased, sodomy was not the chief regulatory weapon against sexual or gender inverts. Just as prostitutes were usually arrested for public solicitation or for inhabiting a bawdy house and not for sex-with-pay or oral sex, so other gender-benders were usually arrested for public behavior and not for private sodomy. Symbolically, the most interesting legal regulation was the tidal wave of laws against cross-dressing. Practically, the chief regulations were the ones adopted as part of local purity campaigns—public lewdness, indecency, vagrancy, disorderly conduct, and solicitation laws, some of which were tailored to target same-sex intimacy.[40] Because they were either state misdemeanors or municipal offenses (in contrast to sodomy, a state felony), these laws carried with them few procedural protections, such as indictment or trial by jury. Proof was much easier than it was for sodomy laws because all that was required was some unusual public conduct, such as exposure of one's genitals or a lewd statement to a public or private vice officer. In terms of the future, the key regulations were those aimed at preventing the corruption of children.

Laws against Cross-Dressing. In 1851 Chicago adopted an ordinance making it a criminal offense, "[i]f anyone shall appear in a public place in a state of nudity, or in a *dress not belonging to his or her sex,* or in an indecent or lewd dress, or shall make an indecent exposure of his or her person, or be guilty of an indecent or lewd act or behavior" [emphasis not in original]. Similar prohibitions of cross-gendered attire or dress were adopted in Columbus, Ohio, in 1848; Charleston, South Carolina, in 1858; Kansas City in 1860; Houston in 1861; St. Louis in 1864; San Francisco in 1866; and dozens of cities in the South, Midwest, and West after 1870. Appendix A2 provides precise dates for fifty-eight cities and reveals that cities of every size and in every part of the country adopted gender-normative sumptuary rules.

At least two states had laws that were construed to regulate cross-dressing. New York in 1845 made it a crime to assemble "disguised" in public places, but in 1876 amended the law to allow "masquerade or fancy dress ball[s]" if police permission were obtained (the approach followed in Europe).[41] No later than 1890, and probably well before, police were applying this disguise law to cross-dressers.[42] In 1874 California amended its penal code to prohibit people from "masquerading" in another person's attire for unlawful purposes.[43] Mugarietta was detained under this law in 1897.

What was the purpose of these laws? Nan Hunter argues that cross-dressing laws were aimed at *gender fraud,* usually by women seeking the advantages of manhood by passing as men.[44] Certainly, her thesis is applicable to New York's disguise statute and California's masquerade law, both of which emphasized illegal deception as part of the crime. Conversely, the lack of fraud was sometimes a reason not to apply these laws. Randolph Milburn of Washington, Ohio, was arrested in 1906 for wearing women's clothing, but charges were dropped when he agreed to wear a silver breastplate saying, "Randolph Milburn. I am a man."[45]

The gender fraud explanation does not account for the fact that laws like Chicago's, which was the model for ordinances in most other cities, made no link with deception. For laws thus phrased, *gender deviance* was the greater concern. Such laws may have been, in part, responses to feminist demands for equality. Elizabeth Cady Stanton asserted, "When we have a voice in the legislature we shall dress as we please," that is, in the more comfortable garb limited to men.[46] Accordingly, the laws were applied to people who violated gender roles. Outlaw Jeanne Bonnet was arrested twenty times for "wearing male attire," even though no one was fooled into thinking her a man. The gender fraud theory also does not account for the fact that men as well as women were arrested.[47] Because it was rare for men to pass as women, these arrests were more for gender deviance than fraud. The application of cross-dressing laws to Werther, who solicited sex from male trade, and to Bonnet, who had a female lover, suggests that these laws were also rationalized around a third concern, *sexual deviance*. The Chicago prohibition was part of a general rule against public lewdness and indecency and can be read as a comprehensive regulation of desire: the state was urging proper sexual roles by prescribing dress, reading material, and behavior.[48] The pre–Civil War legal context suggests that inversion was a weighty concern with some citizens long before the sexologists popularized the concept.

The rationales for cross-dressing laws were dynamic as well as multifarious. When in 1897 Mugarietta, a/k/a Babe Bean, was detained by police in Stockton, California, for dressing as a man, the authorities were persuaded that she did not violate the state masquerade law because she conspired to commit neither crime nor deceit. But the urban middle class at the turn of the century grew more threatened than bemused by gender-bending such as Mugarietta's. Whereas Babe Bean could dress as a male with little harassment in 1890s Stockton, Jack Garland felt compelled to carry on a complete charade in post-1900 San Francisco, which was the first city to enact an ordinance directed specifically and exclusively against cross-dressing (1903).[49] By the beginning of the twentieth century, gender inappropriateness was no longer just a feminist curiosity—it was increasingly considered a sickness and a public offense.

In the next generation, cross-dressing's association with various forms of sexual deviance was reinforced. Magnus Hirschfeld in *Die Transvetitien* (1910) described people who had strong sexual urgings to cross-dress. Although Hirschfeld carefully distinguished between transvestism (erotic stimulation from cross-dressing) and homosexuality (erotic attraction to a person of the same sex), the American sexologists considered the two phenomena related. The image of degeneracy associated with deviant women was dramatically displayed by the Mitchell case, which was widely reported in the news and medical media.[50] By the early twentieth century, the male androgyne such as Werther was as much a threat as the passing woman in urban areas.

Laws against Public Indecency and Sexual Solicitation. Most American jurisdictions between 1881 and 1921 broadened their criminal codes to reach a wider array of public indecencies. The rules mainly targeted different-sex prostitution, but many of them were written broadly enough to include indecencies between people of the same sex. In the wake of its vice commission report, Chicago's 1911 Code added new criminal offenses for "disorderly conduct," defined to include "all persons who are idle or dissolute"; nightwalking, applicable to "all persons of evil fame or report" who walked the streets; and a broader vagrancy law targeting "[a]ll persons who are idle and dissolute" or "lewd, wanton or lascivious in speech or behavior."[51] In addition to vagrancy, disorderly conduct, and loitering laws, those against public indecent exposure and lewdness were similarly broad in other cities. Appendix A2 lists municipalities with indecency and solicitation laws that were broadly enough written to apply to overtures between persons of the same sex.

Urbanizing states similarly expanded their public indecency laws after the Civil War in ways that swept gender-benders within their ambit. Massachusetts was the first state to make it a crime to be a "lewd, wanton, or lascivious person[]," [52] but the most sustained state regulatory attention came in New York and California. In the former, changes to the state prostitution laws targeted male inverts and prostitutes as well as female prostitutes and their pimps. In 1900 the legislature added a new section 887(9) to the Criminal Procedure Code, expanding the definition of illegal "vagrant" to include "[e]very male person who lives wholly or in part on the earnings of prostitution, or who in any public place solicits for immoral purposes."[53] While the obvious purpose was to provide a criminal sanction against pimps, another was to provide a legal basis for police action against male inverts. The legislature's Mazet Committee had just conducted an investigation of New York City's police force. Among its objects of inquiry were the "male harlots," "fairies," and "degenerates" who hung out in dance halls or hotels. Citizens representing the City Vigilance League testified in 1899 that "what we call male degenerates frequent [Paresis Hall], and it is a nightly occurrence that they solicit men for immoral purposes," including propositions by "male prostitutes" who "act effeminately" to commit "that unmentionable crime" with Vigilance League spies.[54] The Mazet Committee's lengthy report calling for suppression of vice, including male degeneracy and prostitution, was submitted to the legislature on January 15, 1990; eleven weeks later, the legislature added section 887(9) in partial response to the committee's alarm.

The New York legislature returned to the issue repeatedly. Pressed by the Committee of Fourteen, the legislature in 1915 expanded section 887(4) to define a vagrant as a person "(c) who loiters in or near any thoroughfare or public or private place for the purpose of inducing, enticing or procuring another to commit lewdness, fornication, unlawful sexual intercourse or any other indecent act."[55] A 1919 law added further language to section 887(4) to assure that male as well as female "degenerates" were covered by the public indecency law.[56] As variously amended, section 887(4) was regularly applied to harass or arrest male inverts.

For New York City the most important regulatory device for policing sexual inversion was an 1882 law that empowered magistrates to punish "disorderly conduct" as a criminal offense. Sometime before 1915, the New York Police Department established a category in their arrest records for "Degenerates" (under the larger category of "Prostitutes"). The annual number of defendants fingerprinted for "disorderly conduct-degeneracy" grew from ninety-six in 1915 to 756 in 1920 (Appendix C3). A third of the arrests came through the efforts of undercover police officers who staked out or posed as decoys in public restrooms and parks; New York's Comstock Society played a role in a majority of the arrests in 1921. More than half of the arrests involved nothing more than fondling or being fondled by someone of the same sex. Most strikingly, degenerates had an 83 percent conviction rate in 1922, and more than a third of those convicted were incarcerated in the workhouse.[57]

In 1922 a local court declared this common law process of expanding the disorderly conduct law insufficiently precise or legislatively authorized to satisfy the due process clause.[58] A coalition of prosecutors and citizen groups immediately obtained a new disorderly conduct law, applicable only in New York City. New section 722(8) of the Penal Code made it illegal when "[a]ny person who, with intent to provoke a breach of the peace, or whereby a breach of the peace may be occasioned . . . [f]requents or loiters about any public place soliciting men for the purpose of committing a crime against nature or other lewdness."[59] As Appendix C3 shows, section 722(8) facilitated a boom in degeneracy arrests and convictions during the 1920s and 1930s.

California's regulation followed a pattern similar to that of New York. California's 1872 vagrancy law, as amended in 1891, made it a criminal offense to be an "idle or dissolute person . . . who wanders about the streets at late or unusual hours of the night," as well as to be a "lewd or dissolute person who lives in and about houses of ill-fame."[60] Both obviously referred to prostitutes but could be read more broadly. The vagrancy law was simplified and broadened in 1903 to make it a criminal offense to be simply an "idle, lewd, or dissolute person," the terminology pioneered by Massachusetts. The lewd vagrancy (colloquially, "vag lewd") provision became the most deployed criminal sanction against same-sex intimacy.[61] Together with the state's 1872 law against indecent exposure and a 1903 law criminalizing acts "outraging public decency,"[62] the vag lewd law was applied in the same broad way that New York applied its disorderly conduct law—to permit police to harass and sometimes arrest people who seemed deviant or gender-bending. Although I do not have the detailed enforcement data for pre-1921 California that I have for New York, there is evidence that some cities in that state used these laws to harass cross-dressing women, female impersonators, male inverts looking for partners, and male as well as female prostitutes.[63] Based on scattered accounts, police in cities ranging from St. Louis to Philadelphia to Toronto to Chicago to Portland to Washington, D.C., episodically invoked these kinds of laws as the basis for harassing, spying on, and entrapping gender-benders and homosexuals.[64]

That police were going undercover and cooperating with other groups in locales outside New York is illustrated by the prosecution of Reverend Samuel Kent, the YMCA chaplain in Newport, Rhode Island, the home of the Newport Naval Training Station.[65] Kent was arrested in 1919 for lewdness, based upon evidence gathered by undercover sailors deployed in a 1919 Navy investigation of inversion around the naval station. A former state policeman, Ervin Arnold, ran the naval investigation. Several of Arnold's agents provocateurs befriended Kent and received caresses and oral sex from him. Denying the charges and presenting evidence of his own rectitude, Kent was acquitted in state court but then reindicted in federal court for violating a statute making it a federal crime to "receive any person for purposes of lewdness . . . or prostitution" in the vicinity of a military installation.[66] The federal trial saw Kent's attorney turn the tables completely on his accusers, indicting them, by their own account, of engaging in illegal sodomy. The jury took only a few hours to acquit.

Child Molestation Laws. Old seduction statutes criminalized penile-vaginal intercourse by an adult man with prepubescent girls, and sodomy laws criminalized anal intercourse by men with either girls or boys. As post–Civil War America grew increasingly alert to the ways adult males were deploying the bodies of children, new kinds of sex crimes were invented, mostly at the state level. Almost all the new laws sought to protect boys as well as girls. In 1876 New York made it a crime to use children for any "obscene, indecent or immoral purpose, exhibition, or practice."[67] Immoral use laws such as this one focused on public abuse of children, but most of the other regulatory responses focused on private abuse, including exposing minors to indecent materials and practices, as Michigan did in 1881,[68] or enticing minors "to commit masturbation," as Indiana did the same year.[69] Michigan created a separate crime for sodomy with boys in 1897.[70] Each of these statutes reflected intensified regulatory attention on sex between men and boys; each was copied by other jurisdictions.

The turn of the twentieth century saw states develop two new forms of regulation that were to be of great consequence. In 1897 Wisconsin created a new crime of taking "improper liberties" with minors of either sex.[71] Similar laws were adopted in seven other states before World War I (Appendix A3). Particularly elaborate was Illinois' 1907 law making it a crime to take "any immoral, improper or indecent liberties with any child of either sex, under the age of fifteen years, with the intent of arousing, appealing to or gratifying the lusts, passions or sexual desires" of either person or to commit a "lewd and lascivious act" upon a child. (Note how the law explicitly recognized the sexual feelings of the child as well as the adult.) Illinois in 1915 expanded the law to criminalize lewd and lascivious conduct committed in the presence of a child.[72] Immediately more popular were statutes making it a crime to "contribute to the delinquency of a minor." The first major law was adopted in 1906 by Massachusetts, and most of the urbanizing states of the North, Midwest, and West adopted similar laws before World War I (Appendix A3).

The most comprehensive regulatory regime in place by World War I was that in California. In addition to seduction, sodomy, and fellatio laws, the California legislature created new crimes of committing a lewd act with a child under age fourteen (1901), sending a minor to an "immoral" place (1905), committing "degrading, lewd, immoral" practices in front of a child (1907), or contributing to the delinquency of minors (1915) (Appendix A3). This regulatory regime not only protected boys as well as girls, but defined the arena of sexual violation more broadly than seduction and sodomy laws had done, to include sexual touching, fondling, and even just observing sexual activities. The wide adoption of such regulations is evidence that law as well as bourgeois society was tangibly interested in the deployment of male sexuality toward the bodies of adolescent and prepubescent minors, both boys and girls, well before World War I.

Obscenity Laws. Before the Civil War many states had adopted laws making the possession or distribution of obscene or indecent materials a crime.[73] Most of the remaining states adopted some kind of obscenity law before the beginning of the twentieth century, and states with laws expanded them to include new media. Wisconsin, for example, amended its obscenity law in 1899 to criminalize the advertisement of any "indecent, lewd or immoral show, play or representation."[74] As Appendix A2 documents, municipal indecency ordinances of the period frequently extended to obscene publications and plays. Chicago's 1851 indecency ordinance, for example, banned the distribution or sale of "any indecent or lewd book, picture or other thing whatever of an immoral or scandalous nature."[75]

Obscenity was never defined in these laws, but Americans subscribed to the British rule of banning a publication if any part of it tended "to deprave and corrupt those whose minds are open to immoral influences and into whose hands a publication of this sort may fall."[76] Any direct description of same-sex intimacy was probably obscene during this period. For example, Walt Whitman's celebration of male camaraderie and sexuality in *Leaves of Grass* went legally unchallenged during the Civil War but was prosecuted as obscene by Boston and Philadelphia authorities in 1882.[77] Generally speaking, before 1900 same-sex eroticism in American literature was depicted either with the utmost indirection and euphemism, as in Herman Melville's *Billy Budd* (written in the 1880s), or with extreme distance, as in Charles Warren Stoddard's *South-Sea Idyls* (1873), which was nonetheless suppressed for its depiction of a South Sea romance between two men.[78] It is no coincidence that one of the first openly erotic male love stories by an American author, Edward Stevenson's *Imre* (1906), was privately published under a pseudonym in Naples, Italy, and an early female love story, Gertrude Stein's *Q.E.D.* (1903), was not published at all until 1950 (under the title *Things As They Are*). Stevenson's *The Intersexes* (1908), a systematic defense of homoerotic attraction by an American author, was also privately printed in Europe. Publishers' fear of suppression contributed to the absence of early American translations of leading European sexologists—Ulrichs and Hirschfeld, who were themselves inverts—although the sympathetic Ellis was published here in 1901.[79]

Plays were covered by many state obscenity laws and by 1921 were the focus of an increasing number of special ordinances (Appendix A2). For an early example, Baltimore in 1879 prohibited the "performance of any indecent or blasphemous play, farce, opera, public exhibition, show or entertainment."[80] Few productions tested the application of these laws to sexual inversion. The clearest test was the play *Sapho* by Alphonse Daudet and Adolph Belot. In 1900 the police closed down this play about a romance between a Paris prostitute and her female lover, but the play reopened when the jury acquitted its star of indecency.[81] Broadway's first explicit lesbian love scene, in Sholom Asch's *The God of Vengeance*, did not fare so well in 1923. Indictment and conviction (later overturned) of obscenity closed the show.[82]

The first generation of American movies (such as *The Gay Brothers* [1895] and *Spit Ball Sadie* [1915]) depicted gender-bending characters relatively freely. Responding to traditionalists' objections, Detroit adopted a law in 1907 that required a license from the police to show any movie and prohibited licenses for "indecent or immoral" films.[83] The regulation-by-licensing idea was immediately followed in Chicago (1907), Los Angeles (1908), San Francisco (1909), and other cities (Appendix A2). Los Angeles, the home of Hollywood, later particularized its ban to include movies depicting "any immoral, indecent, lewd, lascivious or unlawful act."[84] State legislatures followed suit, and the Supreme Court in 1915 upheld Ohio's licensing scheme on the ground that "the exhibition of moving pictures is a business" and not protected by the first amendment as one of the "organs of public opinion."[85] Afterward, a new wave of cities, from Atlanta to Kansas City to Houston, adopted similar permit-and-prohibition schemes (Appendix A2), as did many urbanized states. In 1921, New York, the biggest movie market, prohibited the licensing or showing of any film deemed by its censors to be "obscene, indecent, immoral, inhuman, sacrilegious, or is of such a character that its exhibition would tend to corrupt morals."[86] The censorship movement discouraged Hollywood from making films depicting minority sexual orientations and distributors from importing such films from Europe, where they were being made. *Anders als die Anderen* (1919) and *Gesetze der Liebe* (1927), German films sympathetically depicting the "third sex," never reached the United States. Exceptions were made for mainstream movies, such as *Manslaughter* (1922) and *The Soilers* (1923), that depicted same-sex intimacy as depraved.[87]

Nationwide Exclusions

Most regulation of sexual or gender variation was through local enforcement of criminal prohibitions, but there emerged a surprising degree of national regulation as well. Although federal policy was sometimes carried out in the military context through criminal prosecutions and court-martials as in the Newport cases, its main weapons against degeneracy were *exclusions*—of degenerate materials from the U.S. mail, of inverts from entering the country, and of inverts from serving in the armed forces. All of these federal policies took firm shape around 1921.

Federal Censorship. There was no general federal obscenity statute, but several laws sought to regulate obscene materials pursuant to national authority over the mails and commerce. An 1865 statute required that "all obscene publications . . . discovered in the mails shall be seized and destroyed."[88] The Comstock Act prohibited the Post Office from mailing "[e]very obscene, lewd, lascivious, indecent, filthy, or vile article."[89] The Tariff Acts of 1922 and 1930 prohibited the Customs Service from allowing "obscene" materials from coming into the United States from another country.[90] These statutes had little if any effect on gender-bending materials before World War I, as they were applied mainly against birth control materials. Still, they put in place a regulatory regime that complemented state and municipal obscenity laws. Hence, publishers or distributors handling such materials could be harassed or even put out of business at any of three different levels of government—local boards and police, state boards, and the United States Postal Service or (if imported) Customs Service.

Immigration. National standards for immigration were first developed after the Civil War. From the beginning, a major focus was the exclusion of degenerates: prostitutes (the first major statute, enacted in 1875) and people procuring them; "persons suffering from a loathsome or a dangerous contagious disease" (1891); and "persons who have been convicted of a felony or other infamous crime or misdemeanor involving moral turpitude" (1891).[91] These prohibitions were carried forward by subsequent immigration laws, culminating in the Immigration Act of 1917, which synthesized all the established exclusions and added a new one for persons suffering from "constitutional psychopathic inferiority."[92]

As the Commissioner-General of Immigration put it in 1909, "[n]othing can be more important than to keep out of the country the anarchistically and criminally inclined and the degenerate in sexual morality."[93] Although he was referring mainly to prostitutes, the exclusionary policy was repeatedly applied to the new kinds of sexual degenerates as well. A representative case was that of Nicholas P.[94] The youth was interviewed by Immigration Service investigators, who readily extracted casual admissions that he had frequented houses of prostitution, had been in the "habit of abusing [him]self, committing masturbation" since age twelve, and had engaged in "unnatural intercourse with men" both in Greece and St. Louis. Based upon these admissions, Nicholas P. was deported to Argentina in 1912 as a "public charge." This reflected the Service's policy of excluding sexual nonconformists on the ground that their degeneration would ruin them and leave them to the public welfare system. The 1885 immigration law and each subsequent one excluded "public charges."[95]

Working-class immigrants who engaged in male or female prostitution or sex with boys were most likely to be deported; well-to-do immigrants were typically able to stay. In the case of the Reverend Parthenios Colones, accused of having sex with "bad boys," the Solicitor of Labor ruled in 1917 that "moral perverts" were not "public charges" under the immigration laws, absent tangible proof of pauper status.[96] Although Colones got to stay, the Service simply shifted its grounds for excluding "perverts." If convicted of sodomy, gross indecency, or public lewdness or even if just admitting such conduct, noncitizens could be excluded or deported under the "crimes of moral turpitude" exclusion. The case of Ludwig W. is an early example.[97] He was arrested in 1915 for sodomy in Atlantic City and admitted that he was "a degenerate prior to his arrival" and was "addicted to this practice [of degeneracy]." The Immigration and Naturalization Service (INS) ordered him deported for being a public charge and having committed a crime of moral turpitude. Before he could be deported, however, he was institutionalized for "constitutional inferiority with manic tendencies" and then escaped.

After the 1917 statute created the category of "constitutional psychopathic inferiority" as a basis for exclusion or deportation, Ludwig W. could have been deported for this medical reason as well. Congress added this category "to prevent the introduction into the country of strains of mental defect that may continue and multiply through succeeding generations," but the medical experts in the Public Health Service charged with enforcing the exclusion saw it as an instrument to exclude "sexual perverts" and others who "because of eccentric behavior, defective judgment, or abnormal impulses are in repeated conflict with social customs and constituted authorities."[98] Three were debarred for psychopathic inferiority in 1917 and dozens per year after that (Appendix C6).

Military Service. Ervin Arnold's undercover investigation that unmasked Samuel Kent also uncovered a subculture of fairies among the Newport sailors themselves. At a Naval Court of Inquiry in March 1919,[99] the subculture was described as a "coterie of so-called moral degenerates whose pastime and pleasure is given to lewd purposes." The fairies were prosecuted as "inverts," defined as someone who "is extremely effeminate and does not care for the opposite sex," that is, "who is morally degenerated."[100] Defendants such as David ("Beckie") Goldstein not only took on women's names but also dressed and made themselves up as women, walked and minced in girlish ways, warmly embraced one another in public, and played the woman's role in sex. A favorite social activity was "drags," or "parties where the different men dressed in female attire and offered themselves in the same manner which women do."[101] If the fairies of Newport were feminized men, they were feminized in a particularly disapproved (i.e., degenerate) way, socializing more like prostitutes than like nice middle-class girls. The gang regularly hung out at the Newport YMCA, soliciting "trade," or "straight" men who would allow the fairies to perform oral sex on them.

The fairies in the Newport investigation were the *summum malum* of American turn-of-the-century anxieties about sex. Although the formal charges against them were "sodomy" and "scandalous conduct," the regulatory community was mostly electrified by the fairies' status as "moral degenerates" who committed the triple crime of abandoning their male role, shedding inhibitions about sex, and aggressively soliciting normal men to join in their perversions. Most of those investigated were dishonorably discharged and jailed; several were left in prison for long periods of time without pending charges. Court-

martialed for consensual "oral coition" and "scandalous conduct," Beckie Goldstein was sentenced to thirty years in prison, a sentence overturned after Goldstein had been imprisoned for two years.[102]

The Newport investigation triggered several regulatory responses. Congress
and the War Department quietly updated the Articles of War in 1920–21 to
criminalize the oral sex Goldstein and company had been imprisoned for
committing.[103] A subcommittee of the Senate Naval Affairs Committee in
1921 recommended "arbitrary and wholesale discharge" of any and all "suspected perverts." According to the subcommittee, "if perversion is known or
believed to exist in the Navy, even the suspicion of such a condition should
immediately lead to the undesirable discharge of the accused."[104] Thus
encouraged, the Army determined not only to discharge sodomites and inverts
but also, for the first time in its history, adopted a mechanism for screening
them out in the first place.

In 1921, Army Regulation 40-105 announced that Army recruits would be
examined and could be rejected for evidence of medical defects or diseases,
including "serious nervous affections." The first nervous disease identified was
"degeneration," which was to be diagnosed by both anatomical and functional
"stigmata." "The degenerate physique as a whole is often marked by diminished
stature and inferior vigor; males may present the general body conformation of
the opposite sex." Functional stigmata included "moral delinquencies, such as
willfulness, deceitfulness, indecency; . . . sexual perversion."[105] The regulation
also excluded recruits who showed signs of a "constitutional psychopathic
state," including "sexual psychopathy," which made them "incapable of attain-
ing a satisfactory adjustment to the average environment of civilized society."[106]
Just as immigration policy toward gender-benders was moving from a focus on
morality to a focus on medicine, so too was military policy.

Legal Regulation of Unnatural Acts, Inverted Gender, and Perverse Sexuality, 1921–1946

World War I's mobilization generated a great deal of same-sex intimacy and talk
about it. The war marked not only an accelerated movement toward municipal,
state, and federal regulation of sexual and gender inversion but also marked a
second regulatory shift. The Newport investigation was not only the first national
focus on inversion but revealed society's increasingly heterogeneous concerns
about same-sex eroticism. After Reverend Kent's acquittal, there was a reverse
court of inquiry into the Arnold investigation. The charge was "[t]hat young men,
many of them boys, in the naval service have been compelled under the specific
orders of officers attached to the office of naval intelligence to commit vile and

nameless crimes on the persons of others in the navy service or have suggested these acts be practiced."[107] The court of inquiry swept the charges under the rug, but the Senate Naval Affairs subcommittee in 1921 condemned the undercover activities as "deplorable, disgraceful, and unnatural."[108]

It is notable that Arnold's operatives did not consider it unthinkable to submit to oral sex from Kent and the other targets. Perceiving sex through the lens of gender role rather than unnatural acts, the men did not view oral sex as morally problematic so long as they were playing the man's part, the inserter, and the degenerate was playing the woman's part, the insertee. The Senate subcommittee saw the matter from a more traditional and middle-class perspective: the working-class operatives were engaging in unnatural acts, and the government must not allow the sailors' bodies to be used for immoral purposes. Old objections to same-sex intimacy retained much of their power, especially for the middle class, and the operatives were victims of heterogeneous perceptions about acceptable sexual practices.

The anxiety surrounding Newport ran deeper, however. The critics were worried not just about unnatural acts but also about natural and dangerous feelings of sexuality that are present—or can be aroused—in all of us. One operative said: "I had never had any dealings with a fairy before. He then started to rub my chest and belly and play with my cock. Human nature then took a hand and of course like any other fellow let him go to the limit." And another testified that, when Kent "[p]ut his arms around me, kissed me, began rubbing my penis . . . Nature took a hand and I discharged."[109] This testimony suggested that oral sex could be "natural" for human beings, and "straight" men could enjoy it just as fairies or degenerates could.

Was there cause for worry about this? The Council of Ministers in Newport thought so; they emphasized that "[t]he people of the United States are entitled to the assurance that hereafter no boy who enlists in the Navy will be consigned to a career of vice." The Senate subcommittee thought so; its report was shocked that "boys" were being sent into Newport "as a sacrifice to, and the prey of every degenerate and sexual pervert, male and female, in the city and at the training station."[110] The underlying fear was that, once fellated, a "boy" might himself become "inverted," bent for life. Even Dr. Erastus Hudson, the only medic involved in the affair, thought about this possibility. A body of literature accessible in 1919 to a popular as well as medical audience maintained that this should have been a concern, notwithstanding Hudson's lame excuse that the literature nowhere mentioned contagion by "any man in the status of an investigator or spotter."[111]

Sigmund Freud's writings about sexuality offered a perspective different from that of either degeneracy or natural law theory.[112] His most important idea, anticipated by Ellis, was that "sexual orientation" is a critical part of a person's identity, distinct from biological sex or gender character. Contrary to Ellis and Krafft-Ebing, Freud understood sexual orientation to be the result of an emotional-developmental, rather than hereditary, process. All of us have bisexual potential but can be expected to develop a "normal" heterosexual orientation so long as nothing goes wrong in the course of emotional and sexual development. If the process is "arrested," the individual develops in "perverse" ways; the most common "perversion" is "homosexuality."

Freudian theory, which was popularized to a receptive United States during the decade beginning in 1910, helps explain why the Newport investigators included men such as Thomas Brunelle, the "husband" of "Salome" Hughes, who were penis-inserters and not fairies, but who were attracted only to other men. That is, Brunelle was not "degenerate" in his gender for he played the male role physically and psychologically, but he was a Freudian "homosexual" because of his attraction to other men. It does not fully explain why Americans were so hysterical about sexual perversion, however. The "American Freudians" followed Freud in criticizing Victorian repression of sexual feelings even in children, rejecting biological origins of perversions in favor of environmental ones, and urging therapeutic rather than punitive approaches toward sexual dysfunctions such as homosexuality, but many did not share Freud's view of natural bisexuality and few shared his prosex hedonism.[113] Also, most American psychiatrists remained eclectic, assimilating Freudian ideas within degeneracy-based theories. For example, Dr. Paul Bowers of the Indiana State Prison observed that sexual perverts are typically "psychopathic," unable to control their sexual emotions (old school). Because "inverse and perverse sexual habits may be acquired early in life by the association with vicious and depraved individuals" (pseudo-Freudian), Bowers concluded that "sexual perverts are at any rate an exceedingly dangerous and demoralizing class which should be permanently isolated to prevent their mingling with others" (contrary to Freud).[114]

Bowers' idée fixe that homosexuals and other sex perverts are sexually out of control and predatory was shared by many Americans in the period between the World Wars. American public culture was nervous about the alarming number of Americans acknowledging their attraction to people of the same sex[115] and forming visible subcultures in cities all across the country.[116] This anxiety was, in part, a response to increased middle-class concern for the psychological well-being of their children and, in part, a cyclical reaction to the sexual and gender nonconformities tolerated during World War I. Most of all, though, the regulatory focus on sick, predatory homosexuality reflected a drawing of new lines for sexual morality. America was in the midst of a sexual revolution, with many people rejecting procreation as the only legitimate sex in favor of sex, including oral sex, for enjoyment and sociability. The easing of taboos against nonprocreative sex put pressure on the liberationists to defend new limits, and most of them chose adultery, homosexuality, and intergenerational sex—all associated with predatory men—as the new taboos.[117]

These ideas were assimilated by state officials, to whom society increasingly turned to control homosexuals, demonized as threatening to children whose sexual development was so easily derailed. Echoing the views of the popular press, an Ohio judge in 1922 described "sexual perverts" as "wild ferocious animals" who engaged in a "degenerate sexual commerce with little boys or little girls."[118] Inspired by such attitudes, the state became both more focused on and more aggressive against sexual as well as gender deviates. The state's goals were to control and punish the psychopathic homosexual, to harass and drive underground homosexual communities and their expression, and to exclude homosexuals from citizenship—all in the name of protecting children from a dangerous force threatening their development into heterosexuals. This regulatory shift did not mean that the state relaxed its disapproval of unnatural acts between adults or of gender deviance, for cross-dressers and sodomites continued to be arrested and harassed wherever they formed visible communities.

Criminal Sanctions against Homosexual Psychopaths

Estelle Freedman maintains that American regulation of sexuality shifted after World War I from a focus on female corruption to a focus on male sexual aggression, reaching an apex after 1935 when child molestation became a national hysteria.[119] As a matter of law enforcement, this meant a de-emphasis on prostitution and an emphasis on crimes by men against women and children: rape, sex and indecent liberties with minors, white slavery, corruption of minors, and forcible sodomy. Freedman's overall point is well taken, but the transition started earlier and focused from the beginning on aggression against children. For the same reasons Americans were immediately receptive to Freudian theorizing about the sexual development of minors, they were concerned about adult men who had sex with them, a group associated with homosexuals and regarded as "sex perverts."

Based in large part on reports in the popular press, Freedman's timetable does not account for criminal law data. As noted above, the states pioneered novel statutes prohibiting the immoral use of minors, taking indecent liberties with children, and contributing to the delinquency of minors before 1910, and by the end of World War I most of the big-population states had at least one such statute in place. As Appendix A3 attests, California, Illinois, Indiana, Louisiana, Massachusetts, Michigan, Missouri, New Jersey, and Wisconsin had multiple statutes comprehensively regulating adult interference with childhood sexual development. More states adopted such statutes after 1921, and states with child abuse statutes revised them, but the statutory movement to protect childhood sexuality bespeaks continuously mounting interest from 1881 to 1946 rather than a big break after World War I.

The law enforcement data support the hypothesis of overall continuity, with upswings coming before and during World War I and before World War II. After 1900, arrests for aggressive sex crimes against women and minors increased substantially but at varying rates outside the Deep South. Between 1900 and 1915 in St. Louis, rape arrests doubled, sodomy arrests increased tenfold, and men began to be arrested for white slavery and enticing girls into immoral activities, trends that continued after the war (Appendix C4). Chicago and San Francisco saw similar increases, and police departments in both cities in 1909 created a new reporting category of "crimes against children," which immediately generated double-digit arrest figures.[120] From 1881 through 1921, New York City witnessed steadily increasing arrests for the crime against nature, rape of underage females, and seduction of adult females, with an explosion in all categories in the period 1914–1921; a new reporting category of "impairing the morals of minors" was added in 1931.[121] As in St. Louis (Appendix C4), arrests of women for prostitution dwarfed the arrests of men for sexual aggression throughout the period and into World War II.

Freedman's thesis that the sex panic of 1936–1937 generated greater regulatory enforcement of crimes against children, especially men against boys, is supported by the data. In New York City, arraignments for crimes against nature, rape of underage females, degeneracy, and impairing the morals of minors sharply and significantly increased between 1935 and 1938.[122] Appendix C1 shows that sodomy arrests went up substantially from 1936 to 1940 for most of the cities where temporal comparisons can be made, namely, Baltimore, Cleveland, Washington, D.C., Miami, New York, and St. Louis. It is probable that the same trend would apply to most other large northern cities. Who was being arrested for sodomy? Appendix C2, analyzing reported sodomy decisions by state appellate courts, suggests that the 1930s witnessed a significant shift in sodomy enforcement—away from sodomy with animals and between consenting males (11 percent and 28 percent of the decisions between 1911 and 1925, but only 2 percent and 11 percent of the decisions between 1926 and 1940) and toward forcible sodomy with adult females and sodomy with underage males (7 percent and 29 percent of the decisions between 1911 and 1925, but 17 percent and 48 percent of the decisions between 1926 and 1940). A report to the mayor of New York City said that 91 percent of the crime against nature arrests during the 1930s involved sex between adults and underage males.[123] The period during and after World War II reflects a similar shift. Most tantalizing but hardest to generalize are data for sex offenders committed to Michigan prisons. After steady increases in absolute numbers as percentages of all inmates, the incarcerations for rape, statutory rape, indecent liberties, and sodomy almost doubled between 1936 and 1937 and jumped from 9.8 percent of all commitments to 14.9 percent.[124]

The increasingly aggressive policing of sexual degenerates and psychopaths starting in the early decades of the century generated this problem: What should be done with the sex offender once he is apprehended? Putting him in prison would contribute to prison corruption, especially by homosexuals, and releasing him would endanger future victims, including children. The authorities never solved this problem during the period in question, but various solutions were floated, and drastic solutions were set in place on the eve of World War II. In 1911 Massachusetts adopted a law allowing the state to incarcerate mentally disabled lawbreakers for indefinite periods of time in therapeutic institutions; the law was specifically aimed at controlling degenerates and other "mental defectives."[125] Although other states followed Massachusetts' indefinite incarceration approach, a more popular response was laws sterilizing specific categories of criminals, typically including "moral degenerates and sexual perverts." Such laws were challenged on grounds that they unfairly augmented criminal punishments and violated precepts of due process, but the Supreme Court rebuffed the constitutional objections, and the laws flourished.[126] One judge took the next logical step. Between 1933 and 1947, California Judge Frank Collier allowed forty-seven sex offenders, most homosexual, to be relieved of long prison sentences by agreeing to castration, which the judge thought "completely cured their unnatural sex desires."[127] California in 1941 established procedures for "asexualization" (castration) of "moral or sexual degenerate or pervert" prisoners who were repeat offenders.[128] Enthusiasm for castration was limited among health professionals, however. Hospitals were more likely to rely on prefrontal lobotomies (2,000 performed on sex offenders between 1938 and 1946), massive injections of male hormones, electrical shock, and other aversion therapy to treat sex offenders.

Expanding on the old "mental defectives" measures, new "sexual psychopath" laws were enacted in Michigan (1935), Illinois (1938), California (1939), and Minnesota (1939) before World War II. The pioneering Michigan law created special procedures for identifying people convicted of sex offenses who "appear to be psychopathic, or a sex degenerate" or a "sex pervert." Once identified, the "sex degenerate or pervert" could be committed for an indeterminate time in a state mental hospital, where under a 1929 statute the inmate might be sterilized as well as rehabilitated.[129] The Illinois law was more specific, allowing incarceration (until permanently recovered from psychopathy) in a mental institution only for defendants shown to have "criminal propensities to the commission of sex offenses."[130] In the first ten years of the law's operation, the only reported case of psychopathic recovery in Illinois involved a hairdresser who had been charged with committing oral sex with a sixteen-year-old boy but served four years under the psychopathy law before facing the sodomy charges.[131]

Note how far the criminal law traveled between 1881 and 1946. During the 1880s female inverts were occasionally arrested for cross-dressing, and male inverts for indecent exposure, but the criminal law did not particularly target either group. As the criminal law in urban jurisdictions focused more aggressively on degeneracy at the turn of the twentieth century, sexual inverts like Mugarietta and Werther were more likely to be harassed or arrested. Some but not many were arrested for sodomy in the period around World War I. On the eve of World War II, however, a homosexual with an active social life had a good chance of spending time in jail, possibly for sodomy but more likely for misdemeanors such as disorderly conduct, lewd vagrancy, indecent exposure, lewd or lascivious conduct, indecent liberties with minors, loitering near a public toilet or schoolyard, or sexual solicitation.[132] In 1940 in New York City 158 men were arrested for sodomy and 638 men and sixty-nine women for disorderly conduct-degeneracy; in Los Angeles nineteen men were arrested for sodomy, twenty men and one woman for oral copulation, 111 men and one woman for indecent exposure, and 116 men and fifty women for lewd vagrancy.[133] Although the aggregate numbers were lower, the pattern was the same in other urban areas. Most important, the consequences of arrest and more certain conviction of crimes associated with homosexuality had often tragic collateral consequences: not only incarceration in a jail or mental institution but also loss of one's job, court-martial or administrative separation from the armed forces, deportation if one were a noncitizen, and continued surveillance and harassment by police officers or detectives. The homosexual was not only a sexual outlaw but one who by World War II had clearly caught the eye of the government.

Suppressing Homosexuality in the Modern Regulatory State

With the growth of gay subcultures, the biggest regulatory concern was to suppress public visibility of homosexuality. George Chauncey's argument that in the 1930s the state conducted a multifaceted assault on "Gay New York," seeking to erase it from public view, has application to other communities. The modern regulatory state cut its teeth on gay people. Government police, censors, medics, and licensors worked, episodically, to suppress homosexuality from public awareness. The hope apparently was that people could be deterred from being homosexual and might seek private cures, paralleling the public cures offered by sexual psychopath laws. Also, to the extent that positive role models and useful information about homosexuality were not available, youths would not be tempted into choosing this orientation.

Suppression of Homosexual Association. There were surprisingly many spaces for same-sex socializing in big and medium-sized cities after World War I— parks, streets, cafes, public toilets, churches, YMCAs, theaters, subways, and diners. Allan Bérubé argues that gay bathhouses and bars, descended from the old brothel-saloons, were critical institutions for gay subculture because they were potentially safe places where folks could let their hair down and meet partners on terms of equality, in contrast to the street trade sought out by fairies such as Werther at the turn of the century.[134] For gays of color and some working-class gays, private parties, including the famous "rent parties" staged to raise money for a tenant's rent, were important venues for association. "Drag balls" in Harlem, Chicago, midtown Manhattan, St. Louis, Washington, D.C., New Orleans, and other cities were occasions for gender spectacle and sexual liaisons even when peopled by straights mingling with gays.

Governmental responses to these various forms of association varied dramatically from city to city and year to year. Prodded and advised by its unusually well-organized antivice societies, New York developed the classic response: police were organized into vice teams whose members observed gay hangouts, posed as decoys to attract solicitations, and raided gay bars, baths, and other spaces.[135] The agenda of early vice enforcement, like that of the private societies, was to control prostitutes, but during and after the war control of homosexuals became an important secondary goal.[136] Similar squads came to be deployed in cities such as San Francisco and Los Angeles, while other cities— such as Chicago, Detroit, and Buffalo—had police departments that were willing to look the other way, typically in return for payoffs.[137]

The most dramatic application of state disorderly conduct laws to homosexual association involved the Society for Human Rights, the first American group formed to protect the rights of "people [with] mental and physical abnormalities." The Chicago-based Society was chartered in December 1924 under the leadership of Henry Gerber, who encountered German homophile groups during his military service in World War I. The Society had a minuscule membership and a modest agenda—to educate citizens of Illinois about homosexuality and to seek repeal of the state sodomy law. The wife of one of the members complained to the police, who without a warrant arrested Gerber and two others on disorderly conduct charges and seized the Society's records and Gerber's personal diary. One of the defendants pleaded guilty to disorderly conduct; Gerber, however, retained lawyers and won a dismissal of his case, but lost his job as a postal worker. The "parting jibe" of the Chicago detective was, "What was the idea of the Society for Human Rights anyway? Was it to give you birds the legal right to rape every boy in the street?"[138]

Scarcely less important than Chicago's suppression of Gerber's society was the episodic suppression of cross-dressing. Drag balls flourished in major cities during the 1920s, and the famous "pansy craze" of female impersonation packed burlesque shows with straight as well as gay customers in the early years of the Depression. Although Chicago's interracial extravaganzas continued unabated, drag came under fire elsewhere. In 1931 New York police raided the Pansy Club and initiated a campaign of harassment against drag balls and streetwalkers; similar antidrag campaigns followed in Los Angeles (1932), Atlantic City (1933), and San Francisco (1933). Police harassment at the 1938 affair impelled Hamilton Lodge in Harlem to cancel its 1939 drag ball, ending an annual tradition dating back to 1869.[139] Because gender deviation was strongly associated with sexual deviation, big cities cracked down on drag as they refocused criminal attention on predatory homosexuality in the 1930s.

Revocation of Gay Bar Licenses. Less dramatic but more effective than raids as a means of controlling gay socialization were licenses. At the turn of the twentieth century, places serving liquor had to be licensed by municipalities, many of which required the license holder to be of "good character" and to prevent the premises from becoming a "resort of disreputable persons."[140] Identifiably gay bars such as Mona's and Finocchio's in San Francisco and the Pansy Club in New York flourished during Prohibition (1920–1933), when all liquor establishments were illegal. The end of Prohibition was the beginning of liquor regulation at the state level and an ongoing struggle for survival by lesbian and gay bars.

Half the states in the 1930s regulated the sale of alcohol through a licensing system.[b] In most of these states, the statute or agency practice required that licensees be of "good moral character" (negated if convicted of a crime of moral turpitude) and that the premises not be "disorderly" or have a bad reputation.[141] Violation of these conditions meant that a liquor license—and the establishment's main source of income—could be suspended or revoked by the state liquor agency. This was a potentially powerful regulatory weapon, but one whose effectiveness was limited by the policy of most states, such as California, to treat liquor licensing as just a way to raise money and by the inability of regulators to identify and prove that an establishment was a gathering place for prostitutes and "sex perverts," the usual demons.

b. Arizona, Arkansas, California, Colorado, Connecticut, Delaware, Florida, Illinois, Indiana, Kentucky, Louisiana, Maryland, Massachusetts, Minnesota, Missouri, Nebraska, Nevada, New Jersey, New Mexico, New York, Rhode Island, South Carolina, South Dakota, Texas, and Wisconsin.

New York was the most vigorous investigating jurisdiction before World War II. New York's law conditioned an establishment's liquor license upon the requirement that it not "suffer or permit such premises to become disorderly."[142] Following the construction of the state disorderly conduct law to apply to "degenerates," the State Liquor Authority (SLA) interpreted "disorderly" to preclude bars from serving prostitutes, homosexuals, and other undesirables. To enforce this rule, the SLA had its own investigatory agents, who gathered evidence of disapproved patronage. An early casualty of New York's policy was Gloria's, a campy bar at the corner of Third Avenue and Fortieth Street. The SLA threatened to revoke the license because the bar allowed its premises "to become disorderly in permitting homosexuals, degenerates, and undesirable people to congregate." This charge was based upon reports by investigators that male patrons had behaved in a "feminine" manner, that a patron had "fondled" one of the investigators, and that two "degenerate" patrons had solicited the investigators. When Gloria's failed to purge itself of all degenerates as demanded, the SLA not only revoked its license but torpedoed the owner's investment by preventing the premises from being licensed to anyone else for a year.[143] Hundreds of bars apparently met the same fate as Gloria's, including some bars that merely tolerated but did not solicit a homosexual clientele.[144]

Defending its revocation against Gloria's unsuccessful judicial challenge, the SLA argued that, even if no lewd acts had occurred, the agency was authorized to close down a bar simply because "lewd and dissolute" people congregated there. Such a rule was adopted by New Jersey in 1934, such that no licensee could allow in the premises "any known criminals, gangsters, . . . prostitutes, female impersonators, or other persons of ill repute."[145] California had a vaguer version of such a rule,[146] and other states adopted anticongregating rules after World War II. None of these states, except New York and possibly New Jersey, devoted significant resources to investigation before the war, however.

Censorship. After Freud and World War I opened the United States to a broader view of sexuality, homosexual themes became more common in Anglo-American literature. Most of these works were arguably obscene by the standards of the day, but the censors only acted episodically to stop them. Allowed into this country were Marcel Proust's *A la Recherche du Temps Perdu* (1913–1926) and Virginia Woolf's *Orlando* (1928), subtle literary treatments of inverts and gender-benders. Also uncensored were works by the sexologists[147] and an increasing number of openly homophobic novels.[148] Clemence Dane's *Regiment of Women* (1917) created a classic description of female "vampirism," as the author termed the effort of lesbian spinster Clare Hartill to "squeeze[]
dry" her younger protegée, Alwynne.[149]

Censored were popular novels depicting homosexual conduct and society as relatively normal, including Charles Henri Ford and Parker Tyler's *The Young and the Evil* (1933), an ultracampy depiction of "gay" life in Greenwich Village; Sir Richard Burton's 1886 edition of *The Arabian Nights,* with its gay-friendly closing essay; and *The Memoirs of Fanny Hill,* a ribald eighteenth-century novel—all were seized by U.S. Customs.[150] The Customs Service also suppressed importation of Radclyffe Hall's lesbian romance, *The Well of Loneliness,* when it was published in 1928 but later relented and allowed its importation.[151] The Service may have been nervous about its policy, for in 1929 it was severely criticized in Congress for excessive zeal. When Congress in January 1930 reauthorized the Service to block "obscene or immoral" materials, it gave the agency discretion to allow entry of literary "classics."[152]

Foreign-published materials that were acceptable to the Customs Service might still be censored by state or local authorities, and this was the fate of *Well of Loneliness.* On January 11, 1929, the New York City police seized 800 copies of the novel at the behest of the Comstock Society. The summons charged that *Well* violated New York's law prohibiting the distribution of obscene literature. City Magistrate Hyman Bushel upheld the censorship in *People v. Friede.* "The book can have no moral value, since it seeks to justify the right of a pervert to prey upon normal members of a community, and to uphold such a relationship as noble and lofty." By "focusing attention upon perverted ideas and unnatural vices," the book was found to be "calculated to corrupt and debase those members of the community who would be susceptible to its immoral influence," particularly minors.[153] This ruling was a double triumph for the sexologists, who inspired both Hall's portrait of the mannish lesbian and Bushel's suppression to "'protect the helpless members of society against the invert'" (quoting Ellis). The ruling, however, was overturned by a three-judge appellate panel.[154]

Bushel's opinion banning *Well* also relied on a 1927 New York statute making it a misdemeanor to present any play or show "depicting or dealing with, the subject of sex degeneracy, or sex perversion."[155] This statute was similar to those in many states and municipalities that banned immoral, indecent, or obscene plays; it was different from analogous laws in that it targeted "degeneracy" and "perversion" by name. The 1927 law was a response to controversy over three plays: *The Captive,* a French play treating lesbian relationships seriously; *Sex,* a campy play written by and starring Mae West; and *The Drag,* another Mae West play and the most provocative of all. It opened with a doctor's denunciation of criminal penalties for same-sex intimacy and ended with a spontaneously performed drag show raided by the police. *Captive* and *Sex* were on Broadway at the beginning of 1927, and *Drag* was on its way. In response to public outrage and a campaign by the Hearst newspapers, the New York police on February 9 raided *Captive* and *Sex,* temporarily closed down the shows, and arrested West and other cast members. Although the producers obtained injunctions, West ultimately went to jail for ten days on "public nuisance" charges and decided not to bring *Drag* to Broadway; producers of *Captive* closed down that show, which was ultimately held obscene by the courts. Within a few months the District Attorney was successful in procuring legislative enactment of the law (quoted above) criminalizing plays like *Captive* and *Drag.*[156]

The effect of controversies over such works as *Well* and *Captive* was to bring intense public attention to same-sex intimacy. Responding to *Well* in particular, novel after novel in the 1930s depicted lesbians as monsters and homosexual men as sex maniacs.[157] Even the most sympathetic novels, such as Mrs. Blair Niles's *Strange Brother* (1931) and Djuna Barnes's *Nightwood* (1937), presented homosexuals as tragic figures who were deranged or dead by the end of the novels. On the other hand, outstanding autobiographical works by gay authors were also published in the 1930s: Gertrude Stein's *Autobiography of Alice B. Toklas* (1933), André Gide's *If It Die* (English translation, 1935), and Diana Frederics's *Diana, A Strange Autobiography* (1939). Only Gide's book was censored by state authorities, a move overturned in the New York courts.[158]

State and municipal censors attacked film depictions of homosexuality with greater success because the Supreme Court had exempted movies from first amendment protection. Once New York in 1921 adopted its film licensing law, banning "obscene, indecent, immoral" and "sacrilegious" movies, a majority of the moviegoing audience lived in jurisdictions regulating movie morality. The New York censors approached gay-themed movies with sharp scissors. For example, Alla Nazimova's *Salome* (1927), filmed with an all-gay cast, was savagely cut by the censors because scenes of same-sex eroticism were considered "[s]acrilegious." The American distribution of *Mädchen in Uniform* (1931) was halted when the New York censors denied the film a license because it sympathetically depicted female boarding school relationships, including a schoolgirl-teacher relationship of the sort condemned in *Regiment of Women.* To satisfy the censors, the distributors agreed to cuts that diluted the lesbian overtones to such an extent that when the film opened in 1932, it was described by one critic as a "simple, clean, wholesome little tale of schoolgirl crushes."[159]

Hoping to head off further regulation and disasters such as Broadway faced in 1927, the film industry adopted the Hollywood Production Code in 1930 and gave it enforcement teeth in 1934.[160] The Code permitted moviemakers to depict vices such as murder, adultery, and prostitution so long as they were depicted negatively, but banned any reference to a few immoral practices. "Sex perversion or any inference to it is forbidden," said Particular Application II.4.

Mention or open depiction of homosexuality all but disappeared from celluloid for a generation, replaced by "sissy" and "tomboy" surrogates.

Lillian Hellman's play *The Children's Hour* was the story of two schoolteachers whose careers were ruined by a schoolgirl's charges of a lesbian relationship. Perhaps because the lesbian relationship was not consummated, and the older teacher committed suicide, the play enjoyed a successful Broadway run in 1934, although it was banned in Boston and Chicago.[161] Even this negative treatment was not enough to satisfy the Production Code, however. The movie version of the play avoided even Hellman's title (*These Three* [1936]) and suppressed any scent of lesbianism; the teachers were ruined by rumors that one of them had premarital sex with her male fiancé.

The Military Exclusion of Homosexuals

During the isolationist decades after World War I, issues of same-sex intimacy were not prominent in the military. The main debate was an internal one within the War Department. Psychiatrists argued that "sodomists" (the department's old-fashioned term) should not be imprisoned as criminals but instead treated for their sickness, while the department's lawyers insisted that sodomists were properly criminals who should be court-martialed rather than coddled in hospitals.[162] Although the top officials held firm to the formal policy of criminalization, it was not vigorously enforced. Between 1904 and 1939 the Navy conducted only 224 court-martial trials for sodomy, including those involving the Newport sailors in 1919–20.[163] Section Eight of the separation regulations ("inaptness or undesirable habits or traits of character") was the mechanism by which most sodomists were usually drummed out of the service, apparently in unimpressive numbers.

In 1940 America reinstituted the draft, and issues of exclusion reemerged. As same-sex eroticism was once more debated within the War Department, a pseudo-Freudian understanding of treatable orientation competed with the degeneracy and sodomy theories that had been official policy since 1921. Psychiatrists Harry Stack Sullivan (himself gay) and Winfred Overholser persuaded the Selective Service to screen inductees for psychiatric as well as physical problems and, then, to include "homosexual proclivities" in the list of disqualifying "deviations."[164] In 1941 Sullivan and Overholser developed materials to train doctors to screen for homosexuality, which was repeatedly decribed in the old-fashioned argot of sexual psychopathy and gender deviance (sissies).[165] Overholser worked a paragraph on "Sexual Perversions" into the 1942 revisions of the Army's mobilization regulations, again emphasizing effeminacy as well as perverted acts as a basis for rejecting men for service.[166]

This decision to medicalize homosexuality combined with the draft to bring thousands of men under scrutiny. For almost all the young men, the induction interview was the first time in their lives they were asked about their sexual preference. Most of the homosexuals lied, and the medical examiners believed them or acquiesced in their lies.[167] At first, lesbians were not even required to lie, as they were asked no questions about their sexual orientation. That changed after July 1944, when the Women's Army Corps (WAC) Selection Conference decided to reject applicants presenting sexual problems. A subsequent War Department medical bulletin warned examining psychiatrists to be on guard against the "homosexual who may see in the WAC an opportunity to indulge her sexual perversity."[168] Nonetheless, of the millions of Americans inducted into the Army during the war, only 4,000 or 5,000 were explicitly rejected for "homosexuality."[169]

As a large number of gay people were not detected by the porous gatekeepers, the armed forces also developed policy documents dealing specifically with homosexuals in service. Under their therapeutic approach, the psychiatrists emphasized instruction as the best way to prevent trouble. Thus, WAC developed, as one of its sex hygiene lectures, a lecture on homosexuality, which acknowledged the possibilities of sexual intimacy between women and urged administrative solutions, with separation from the service reserved for lesbian "addicts."[170] The lawyers and top brass in the War Department, however, continued to emphasize a punitive approach well into the war, in which sodomists were court-martialed and jailed or, by 1943, simply separated from the service. As manpower needs escalated, the punitive approach died, and the doctors prevailed.

In an influential 1943 memorandum, the Army's Surgeon General posited that homosexuality should be dealt with as a medical rather than criminal matter. The homosexual should be reclaimed rather than punished, so long as he did not engage in sex with children or by force.[171] This policy substantially prevailed through War Department Circular No. 3, issued in January 1944. Entitled "Homosexuals," rather than "Sodomists," the memorandum directed separation rather than court-martial, even for the "true or confirmed homosexual not deemed reclaimable." For the "reclaimable" homosexual whose misconduct was not aggravated by independent offenses such as rape, the policy was hospitalization and treatment. The category of reclaimables was expanded to include not just normal men who had been seduced but also the "true or confirmed homosexual[s]" whose "cases reasonably indicate the possibility of reclamation." The circular did not address the increasingly important issue of the serviceman who confessed to "homosexual tendencies" but had done no unlawful acts. In 1945 the Army's policy was that "[t]he mere confession by an individual to a psychiatrist that he possesses homosexual tendencies will not in itself constitute sufficient cause for discharge," but instead required hospitalization and further evaluation.[172]

The effect of the new policy focus on homosexuality was complex. One was to de-emphasize court-martials for sodomy. Where the Army reported fifty-two sodomy prosecutions in September 1943, it reported only eleven in April 1944 as a direct consequence of Circular No. 3.[173] This was good news for gay personnel, but the broader implications of the therapeutic policy were not. Because consensual sodomy was difficult and expensive to prove, the old punitive policy caught fewer homosexuals than the newer policy, which left much discretion with company commanders to summarily ship personnel off to a hospital for treatment. According to Allan Bérubé, more than four thousand sailors and five thousand soldiers were hospitalized and dismissed from service as "homosexuals" between 1941 and 1945,[174] figures that understate the matter because many homosexuals were discharged for other reasons by sympathetic psychiatrists. Even these conservative figures reflect a far bigger haul than the hundreds debarred for sodomy in the four previous decades. Additionally, the new system's focus on desire rather than just acts created new room for regulatory cat-and-mouse games: malingerers could more easily avoid military service, celibate homosexuals were newly at risk, and all personnel—straight and gay and undecided—were under pressure to prove their legal status by daily performances of heterosexuality.

The new medical focus also established a firmer basis for investigating lesbians. Because criminal sodomy, long the military's primary concern, focused on the penis, it was not a crime associated with women. Degeneracy was associated with women, but typically with prostitutes. But once the military shifted its focus from acts to desires, women came under regulatory examination. Indeed, the first major armed forces' witch-hunt since Newport was the War Department's investigation of the WAC training camp at Fort Oglethorpe in the spring of 1944.[175] The investigation was triggered by a letter from an anguished mother, complaining that Fort Oglethorpe "is full of homosexuals and sex maniacs," one of whom had molested her "little [twenty-year-old] girl." The investigators concluded that Fort Oglethorpe was not "full of homosexuals and sex maniacs," but that several female couples were carrying on homosexual affairs. They recommended treatment for five women and separation for only one.

The Fort Oglethorpe investigation reflects the substantial transition that had been made between 1881 and 1945, from a focus on the sodomite to a focus on the homosexual in the state's regulation of same-sex intimacy. The modernization and secularization of state policy involved the following conceptual shifts in emphasis: from Bible-based natural law thinking to medicine-based functional thinking, from unnatural act to sexual orientation, from an exclusively male-centered understanding of sexuality to one that considered women sexual actors. The Fort Oglethorpe investigation also suggests that these shifts were never clear-cut breaks. That is, the sodomite *and* the invert *and* the homosexual were all relevant, and perhaps overlapping, paradigms for the investigators. The "real perverts," the ones who should be discharged in the opinion of WAC psychiatrist Alice Rost, were those who were sexually interested in and pursued just women, had sex with women, and engaged in cross-gender behavior such as dressing in men's clothing.

From Social Stigma and Masquerade to Legal Stigma and the Closet

Social and intellectual developments strongly influenced the law. Consider the converse: legal developments influenced society and the evolution of our thinking about sexuality and gender.[176] As Michel Foucault suggested, legal rules and enforcement mechanisms help create or undermine power relationships, instill or disperse categories of knowledge, and normalize or problematize patterns of discourse.[177] These phenomena had profound consequences for our culture, the most notable of which was the creation of a sexual closet that was suffocating and unstable.

Law and the Mask (Early Twentieth Century). The naming of sexual inverts and then homosexuals, and the shaming of their deviation from gender and sexual norms, constituted a social ideology with a medicalized vocabulary for reexpressing an underlying natural law morality. As the new ideology and the vocabulary became widely known, the person who realized she or he fell into the disfavored category internalized the shame and assumed what Edward Stevenson in 1906 called "the mask," a silence about the "secret of his individuality" that one maintained "each and every instant, resolving to make it his natural face."[178] The masked invert was analogous to the woman passing as a man, and in the nineteenth century precisely that metaphor had been used for passing women.[179] Elvira Mugarietta, who openly cross-dressed as Babe Bean in the 1890s, became Jack Garland, whose sex was masked even to her friends in San Francisco after the turn of the twentieth century. Both the masked invert and the passing woman lived a never-ending masquerade.

Travesty was internalized mainly in response to social pressure. Playing a supporting role, law reinforced social pressure by *normalizing* sex around marital procreation and by *empowering* relatives who sought to control or strangers who victimized the invert. As to normalization, the importance of updated sodomy and new antiprostitution laws for the invert was as much their positive message as their threat of arrest: sex must be at least potentially procreative and within a companionate man-woman marriage, where the husband still held most of the legal entitlements.

As to empowerment, law operated in a gendered way. Law empowered parents and husbands to enforce their desire that the female invert be a wife and mother. If Freda Ward had reciprocated Alice Mitchell's affections, the law stood ready to enforce her parents' control over her social relationships. The law also stood ready to support the future authority of her betrothed husband, who would have been legally immune from charges of raping and beating Ward were she to resist her sexual obligations to him.[180] Against male inverts, law empowered strangers. Werther's autobiography describes threats and beatings at the hands of police, soldiers, and working-class youths, all implicitly authorized by the law. "A fairie is often thus treated by cruel, lecherous adolescents, since they know he is an outlaw and cannot bring them to justice."[181] Stevenson's *Intersexes* made out a detailed case for the proposition that the illegality of same-sex intimacy exposed male inverts to blackmail at the hands of trade and the police.[182] Note the class features of law's empowerment of police, youths, and blackmailers—likely to be working class—against the male invert—often middle class.

The law played a more ambiguous role by its early contributions to discourse, as it publicized and dramatized the idea of inverted gender and sexuality. Legal authorities did not murder Jeanne Bonnet, but they did repeatedly make an example of her by arresting her for wearing male attire. Such examples were a warning to Elvira Mugarietta when she moved to San Francisco in 1901 and began her lifelong masquerade. Alice Mitchell's insanity hearing was a national sensation, reported and speculated upon in the yellow press, and it may have had the effect here that Oscar Wilde's three trials assertedly had in England, which Havelock Ellis felt "contributed to give definiteness and self-consciousness to the manifestations of homosexuality, and to have aroused inverts to take up a definite attitude. I have been assured in several quarters that . . . since that case the manifestations of homosexuality have become more pronounced."[183] In short, law's discourse contributed to people's consciousness of their own inversion or possible inversion, a self-consciousness that the mask insisted be left publicly unexpressed.

Law and the Double Life (World War I). By the time America entered World War I, it was divided between places where the mask was intact—rural areas, small towns, southern cities—and places where the mask had slipped—big and some medium-sized cities of the North, Midwest, and West. The independent variable was the existence of gay subcultures: without them, homosexuals and gender-benders wore the mask;[184] with them, some female and many male homosexuals dropped the mask frequently and lived what Werther described as the "double life," where the gay person wore the mask in normal social intercourse but dropped it with other gay people.[185] When a community had a visible gay subculture, there was greater social concern about inversion and homosexuality, but social pressure had less effect. It was then that the law was called upon to play a greater role in keeping the mask from dropping.

During this period the law began seriously to focus on homosexuals as a regulatory class apart from other gender-benders. Recall the "constitutional psychopathic inferiority" exclusion in the Immigration Act of 1917, the Kent case, the Newport scandals and the Army's Regulation 40-105, New York's vagrancy and disorderly conduct law revisions, the advent of raids targeting gay clubs and baths in New York and San Francisco, California's "vag lewd" law, state code revisions protecting boys as well as girls against adult sexual predation, New York's degenerate play law and the attempt to suppress the novel *Well of Loneliness,* and the legal and industry prohibitions against any mention of "sex perversion" in movies. The goals of these measures were to keep sexual perversion out of the public sphere and to disrupt the aborning institutions of gay subculture. The state was normalizing Freudian heterosexuality and empowering a broader array of officials and doctors in addition to the local police.

Just as Prohibition barely dented America's love affair with liquor but served to drive it underground, so these antihomosexual measures probably dissuaded few from being homosexual or even from committing sodomy, but did help mold the context of the double life. For men in particular, their outlaw status contributed to a sexual culture of risk and furtiveness. First-person accounts in the 1930s are replete with stories of fear and uncertainty about their objects of desire, and the way the law empowered those objects to abuse, rob, and beat the homosexual.[186] For some men, the risk became part of the sexual excitement. Werther, who protested throughout his autobiography against the abuse to which he was subjected, continued to enter dangerous situations and admitted, "The physical suffering and discomfort were extreme, but I was so fascinated by the savagery and the beauty of my tormentors that I experienced a species of mental satisfaction, being willing to suffer death if only I could contribute to their pleasure."[187] In a literal way, the law was creating sexual variety, in this case of a sadomasochistic nature: by teaching thugs that they could have their way with fairies without accountability, the law encouraged their sadism; by teaching fairies that they were subhuman, the law inculcated in some of them a victim mentality of masochism. For most other homosexuals, the law was less brutal, but it still augmented the excitement of same-sex intimacy by rendering it an intrinsically outlaw form of love.

The deepest effect of the law on gay subcultures arose not from criminal prohibitions but from law's contribution to racial apartheid and women's confinement to the home. The most vibrant gay subculture in the period of flourishing after World War I was Harlem, where whites and blacks, men and women, and (to some extent) middle- and working-class gender-benders mixed and matched to the benefit of all.[188] Conceptualizing from the perspective of double outsiders (gay blacks), Langston Hughes and other thinkers of the Harlem Renaissance generated the first deep critique of American (white) middle-class attitudes about the body and sexuality. This kind of synergistic thinking about sexuality/race/gender was not replicated in other cities with mixed-race populations because of either legally (e.g., Washington, D.C.) or culturally (e.g., Chicago) imposed racial segregation. Law's growing inducements to marriage and its continuing empowerment of husbands discouraged many women from acting on their sexual preferences, and the law's gender discriminations and antiprostitution rules discouraged women from entering the workplace, which reinforced their dependence upon men. The creative possibilities of gay subcultures—in the arts, in forming relationships, in thought about social issues—were stifled because homosexual men/women, blacks/whites/Asians, and middle/ working-class people were kept from making more common cause around their shared rejection of gender role.

Law and the Closet (World War II). As Estelle Freedman has argued, the law went after homosexuals more aggressively in the 1930s. Allan Bérubé has shown how World War II yielded an explosion of same-sex intimacy and of state inquiry into sexual orientation that, together, fueled the postwar growth of gay subcultures detailed by John D'Emilio. George Chauncey maintains that New York's post-1935 antihomosexual campaign made possible the "closet." Chauncey's claim is too bold unless closet is understood as something more than secrecy about sexual aberration, for secrecy was the norm for this entire period. The terms gay people still used for that secrecy in the 1930s and 1940s were "wearing the mask" or engaging in "masquerade."[189] The closet did not emerge as a popular term until after the war, and did not overtake the mask as the governing metaphor until the 1960s (Chapter 2).

While it is unclear whether society led law or vice-versa, the modern regulatory state played a role in the construction of a new kind of sexual secrecy later entailed by the closet metaphor. Masquerade and the double life operated under the assumption that homosexuals could usually control the terms upon which they were regarded. By the end of World War II, it was increasingly apparent that the terms of the masquerade were being set by a nosier state: police and FBI decoys and spies who aggressively probed one's most private activities, military medics and investigators who quizzed recruits about their sexuality, and undercover agents who invaded gay bars and tearooms to note and report same-sex intimacies. By 1946 it was apparent, thanks in part to the law, that the mask could be torn off by the sexuality gendarmerie as well as dropped by the homosexual. The postwar idea of the closet captures the intrinsic insecurity of sexual masquerade: the closet door can be opened by either the homophobe or the homosexual, and at any time anywhere.

Additionally, wearing the mask was not consciously all-consuming for gender-benders earlier in the century but became an ongoing performance by 1946. The agents of the totalizing state—police, FBI operatives, military doctors—initiated discussion of sexual deviancy, and when these agents tried to stop discussion they were often thwarted by the judiciary, which was becoming insistent upon first amendment freedom to speak about political and psychological matters.[190] The inability of the state to censor and the ability of the state to question helped generate a gabfest about sexual orientation. A minor effect of state interrogation was to suggest the possibility of deviant sexual feelings to a national audience. A major effect was to force or enable people to self-identify, to take an affirmative position as to their sexual orientation. Where the mask could be silence about one's sexuality, the newly pervasive state questioning precluded silence and put homosexuals on the spot. They could affirmatively lie and commit to a never-ending masquerade, where one lie led to another and often to a life brimming with hypocrisy. Or they could tell the truth and face ruin, including jail or an asylum. Alice Mitchell faced this choice in 1892; Oscar Wilde in 1895; Samuel Kent in 1919; millions faced it in the 1940s and afterwards, thanks to the new regulatory, war-fighting state. Almost all of the people facing this choice chose to lie, as Kent and Wilde did. Their perjuries and society's hypocrisies created tragic masquerades and established the closet as a suffocating situs of sexual secrecy.

2. Kulturkampf and the Threatening Closet, 1946–1961

The sacking of Sumner Welles was a harbinger. A cold, brilliant patrician, Welles was appointed Under-Secretary of State by his school chum, President Franklin Roosevelt, in 1937. In 1941 FBI Director J. Edgar Hoover plied Roosevelt with information pertaining to Welles's interracial homosexual activities. William Bullitt, a friend of Roosevelt's, argued to the president that "the maintenance of Welles in public office was a menace to the country since he was subject to blackmail by foreign powers" and could open the administration to "a terrible public scandal." According to Bullitt, "morale in the Department of State and Foreign Service was being ruined by the knowledge that a man of the character of Welles was in control of all appointments and transfers." Roosevelt felt that these charges were irrelevant to Welles's capacity for public service and refused to believe that any newspaper would publish them. But when the story threatened to break two years later, with a Senate investigation and more press coverage sure to follow, Roosevelt asked Welles for his resignation.[1]

Welles's demise reflected the emergence of homosexuality as an issue of national security, and of the closet as a prison-refuge for homosexuals. Roosevelt—who as Under-Secretary of the Navy in 1919 approved the Newport investigations described in Chapter 1—thought Welles could lead a "double life" so long as he was discreet. By the 1940s such discretion was much harder to assure, in part because homosexuals were tiring of the masquerade, and in part because many heterosexuals were anxious to know who was masquerading. The pervasive state and press were fulfilling Louis Brandeis's prophecy that "what is whispered in the closet shall be proclaimed from the house-tops."[2] Once homosexuality became a topic of widespread public as well as private discourse, the "closet" emerged as an apt metaphor. An early example is John Horne Burns's *Lucifer with a Book* (1949), a novel about budding sexuality in a New England boys' school. The central character, instructor Guy Hudson, is a scarred war hero of intense but ambiguous sexuality, the key to which is a lewd Renaissance print he keeps in his dormitory closet.[3] Other characters pry into his closet to explore that sexuality, and their glimpses contribute to his expulsion from the school. The cultural reference was the idea of deviant sexuality as a "skeleton in the closet," a connection explicitly made to homosexuality no later than the 1950s.[4] The closet then became a metaphor for "the absolute necessity for secrecy from the majority (which, immediately, included your family and the police, but also all other heterosexuals) regarding the truth of your sexuality."[5] At the same time the closet was a secret haven, it was one that an increasing number of homosexuals wanted to escape. Burns in the 1950s described his publication of *Lucifer* as his way to "come out of the cloister."[6] Moreover, fearful heterosexuals increasingly wanted to cast people like Burns out of the closet. To fight against "homosexual recruiting of youth," Florida's Legislative Investigating Committee wrote in 1964 that "the closet door must be thrown open and the light of public understanding cast upon homosexuality."[7]

These references illustrate not only how the vocabulary of the closet was worked out but also how the closet could be either *protective* or *threatening,* or both.[8] For the homosexual, it could be a safe refuge or a scary prison. For the heterosexual, the closet could be a place where skeletons are secluded from view so that they do not disturb household harmony or, more sinister, a place within the home where dangerous monsters hide. These fears must be situated in the context of the explosion of gay subcultures all over the country after World War II, an explosion classically described by John D'Emilio.[9] This chapter discusses how post–World War II American law went much further than prewar law to suppress gay subculture and how antigay Kulturkampf (state war of subcultural suppression) contributed to the closet. A theme of this chapter is how the closet's meaning changed from threatening to protective for heterosexuals at the same time it was changing from protective to threatening for homosexuals.

The postwar antihomosexual campaign sought not only to deny homosexuals any public space (i.e., the prewar philosophy) but also to pry them out of their closets and expose and punish them. This regulatory effort was a notable failure, to which the law also contributed. The law offered multiple points of resistance and protection for hunted homosexuals. Nervous about the antihomosexual Kulturkampf, legal elites posed the mutually protective closet as a compromise: we don't ask about your sexuality, you don't tell us about it. Both witch-hunters and tolerant liberals contributed in the 1950s to an *apartheid of the closet,* whereby homosexuals were segregated from civilized society, not physically, but psychically and morally. So long as they confined their expressions and actions to a mutually protective closet, homosexuals were promised a regime of "separate but equal" safety from the witch-hunters.

But the apartheid of the closet was an unstable regime. From a homophobic perspective, the closet protected enemies of the people who threatened America's youth and national security. From a homophile perspective, the closet was a prison-refuge purchased at the price of both freedom and integrity. Jim Willard, the protagonist of Gore Vidal's *The City and the Pillar,* grew "annoyed at the never-ending masquerade. He was bored by his own necessary lies. How he longed to tell them exactly what he was!"[10] The masquerade yielded a self-fulfilling prophecy whereby homosexuals were persecuted, in part, because they were untrustworthy and susceptible to blackmail, traits made possible because of their illegal status. Law contributed to the failure of the mutually protective closet by its vacillation between protecting homosexual privacy and permitting antihomosexual manias and witch-hunts. The emerging first amendment tradition empowered homophile expression in ways that facilitated discursive resistance to the closet.

Kulturkampf: The Straight-Threatening Closet

The election of 1946 marked a shift to the right in American politics and was followed by a national antihomosexual Kulturkampf.[11] By offering unprecedented opportunities to women and by throwing men and women into homosocial settings, World War II had relaxed gender and sex roles and fueled the postwar expansion of homosexual urban subcultures described by D'Emilio. While the state tolerated widespread gender and sexual deviance during the war, both society and the state renormalized with a vengeance after the war. The country not only sought to reaffirm the dad-works/mom-raises-children family but stigmatized criticism of or deviation from that heterosexual norm. The postwar baby boom was a tribute to the comeback of the traditional family and obliterated memory of wartime deviations. It also precipitated the revival of social concern about sexual predation against children, and in 1947 the popular press teemed with articles on the danger "sexual perverts" posed to children and the family.[12]

Most homosexuals sought cover in what would come to be termed the closet, but the state destabilized the potential equilibrium whereby homosexuals could hide in the closet in exchange for society's promise not to open the door. Many antihomosexual Americans viewed the closet as a Trojan horse whose secluded occupants were a fifth column threatening the United States morally and politically. Like the Communists, homosexuals were viewed as dangerous "pod people" out of the popular movie *The Invasion of the Body Snatchers*—weird aliens mingling with normal Americans and seeking to turn them into pod people as well. As Florida's Legislative Investigating Committee wrote in 1964, "if we don't stand up and start fighting, we are going to lose these battles in a very real war of morality."[13] The antihomosexuals mobilized the forces of state power in the 1950s to "throw open" the "closet door" and destroy homosexuality before it destroyed the country, as the committee put it. Hence, the state invested unprecedented resources not only in suppressing sexual and gender deviation from the public sphere but also in flushing such deviants out of their hiding places in various criminal, military, and civil witch-hunts. In the extended panic that followed, the homosexuals' closet became their prison, a place where they were forced to be but that could be invaded at any time by state officers.

Hunting the Homosexual (Criminal Law)

Responding to a wave of well-publicized sexual assaults on children, FBI Director Hoover in July 1947 announced that the "most rapidly increasing type of crime is that perpetrated by degenerate sex offenders" and complained that "depraved human beings, more savage than beasts, are permitted to rove America almost at will."[14] The press fanned the flames of this alarm, which caught the mood of the country: not only did the prewar anxiety about child-molesting psychopaths reemerge in 1947, it reemerged with a vengeance and triggered unprecedented police attention to homosexuals, who were tagged with responsibility for molesting minors as well as adults, girls as well as boys.[15] Unlike the period before World War II, however, the postwar mania was nationwide, including much of the South. The state between 1946 and 1961 imposed criminal punishments on as many as a million lesbians and gay men engaged in consensual adult intercourse, dancing, kissing, or holding hands.

New Laws Targeting Sexual Perversion. Exercising its jurisdiction over the District of Columbia, Congress adopted after the war a series of measures that reflected an emerging national consensus that children's sexuality was at risk and homosexuals were the biggest threat. The Miller Act of 1948 created the District's first sodomy law. Reflecting heightened concerns about child molestation, the law carried a higher maximum penalty (twenty rather than ten years) if the victim of the sodomy were under sixteen years old. In addition, the statute created new crimes of indecent exposure to children of either sex under age sixteen and indecent liberties with such children.[16] Urbanized states such as California, Illinois, Michigan, and New York already had statutes making lewdness with children a crime (Chapter 1), but their legislatures returned to the issue after the war, revising their laws to impose harsher penalties on people who committed sodomy or other homosexual conduct, especially with minors (Appendix A3). California was the most dramatic example because its response was most clearly antihomosexual. In the wake of a series of child murder-assaults, Governor Earl Warren called a special session of the legislature in December 1949 to deal with the sex offender problem and in January 1950 signed legislation increasing the penalties for sodomy, creating a new crime for loitering around a public toilet, and requiring registration of toilet loiterers and lewd vagrants. Subsequently, the legislature increased penalties for child molestation (1950, 1951) and increased the maximum penalties for oral copulation with a minor and sodomy to life in prison (1952).[17] Taking a milder approach, New York in 1950 reduced sodomy between consenting adults to a misdemeanor while creating heightened penalties for sodomy by force or with a minor, and Illinois in 1945 increased the penalties for taking indecent liberties with minors.[18] During the 1940s and 1950s, southern and western states, most for the first time, adopted statutes crimnalizing the taking of indecent liberties or engaging in lewd behavior with children under specified ages.[19]

Title II of the Miller Act included a "sexual psychopath" law for the District.[20] Although a few states had adopted laws providing indeterminate sentences and psychiatric treatment for sex offenders before 1945 (Chapter 1), such statutes became a national craze after World War II. Between 1946 and 1957 twenty-nine states, including all the urbanized jurisdictions of the East and West Coasts and the Midwest, either enacted new sexual psychopath laws or revised existing laws, or both (Appendix B1).[21] No fewer than eleven states established legislative study commissions to evaluate existing laws applicable to sex offenders and to suggest statutory changes.[22] The most thoughtful reports (California, Illinois, Michigan, New Jersey, New York) were pessimistic that such statutes contributed much to the war against child molesters, and the craze subsided after 1955. Although these sexual psychopath laws were inspired by the child molestation panic, only Florida, Oregon, and South Dakota limited their statutes to sex crimes involving children. The most common jurisdictional basis was conviction of sodomy, including sodomy between consenting adults. In California, the District, Florida, Illinois, Indiana, Iowa, Michigan, Minnesota, Missouri, Nebraska, New Hampshire, and Washington—almost half the jurisdictions with such statutes—simply a *charge* of sodomy or another sex crime or even just a *petition* to the court could trigger the statutory procedures.

The first sexual psychopath cases adjudicated in one jurisdiction involved such crimes as public masturbation, the following of a white woman by a person of color, the passing of bad checks by a suspected homosexual, and so on. In most states homosexuals were the primary focus of regulatory action. Almost half of the first one-hundred sexual psychopaths adjudicated in New Jersey were convicted of lewdness (homosexual overtures), sodomy, and fellatio.[23] Few of the jurisdictions had the facilities required to treat people committed as sexual psychopaths, and where they did the experience could be hellish. The most famous institution was California's Atascadero State Hospital, opened in 1954 and soon known as "Dachau for Queers." There and elsewhere, people convicted of consensual sodomy as well as child molestation were subjected to lobotomies, electrical and pharmacological shock therapy, and "asexualization," or castration, authorized by a 1941 law.[24] As Jonathan Katz has documented, such treatments were not unique to California.[25]

Another widely deployed strategy for regulating homosexuals was registration. Like many other municipalities, Los Angeles required "convicted persons" in the city to register with the police. In 1950 Los Angeles amended its law to specify registration of all sex criminals, including those convicted of sodomy, oral copulation, and lewd vagrancy. As thousands of people were charged each year with being lewd vagrants, the 1950 amendment greatly expanded the ambit of registration. California in 1947 enacted a statewide registration for sex offenders and expanded the law in 1950 to include lewd vagrancy, loitering around public toilets, and other minor sex crimes.[26] Bills requiring national registration of sex offenders were proposed in 1951 and 1952.[27] Although nationwide registration fell short, its adoption in California and various other jurisdictions heightened the consequences of being caught soliciting sex from a consenting adult: public notoriety, probable loss of employment, and perpetual police wardship.

Under the Miller Act, the District's laws effectively regulated only public and not private same-sex intimacy. In a move that reflected a more fearful understanding of the closet, Congress in 1953 rewrote the District's indecent exposure law to make it unlawful to commit any "obscene or indecent" exposure, sexual proposal, or act anywhere in the District.[28] Congress intended to ensure criminal prosecution of private homosexual acts or solicitation by removing the common law public place requirement for indecency, lewdness, or lewd solicitation. Again, other jurisdictions followed Congress's lead, so that by 1961 twenty-one states (including Florida, Massachusetts, Michigan, New Jersey, North Carolina, and Ohio) had removed public place requirements from their lewdness or indecency statutes.[29] Other states went after private lewdness by applying vaguely worded laws, such as California's lewd vagrancy statute and New York's disorderly conduct statute, illustrated below. As a result, in most of the United States it became a crime not only for same-sex couples to engage in private consensual sodomy but even to propose such conduct at any time or place.

Flushing Out the Homosexual. As the foregoing survey suggests, the criminal law targeted "homosexuals and sex perverts" for an increasing variety of conduct and with escalating penalties. The corollary question was how to identify perpetrators. Where same-sex intimacy did not involve force or a minor, the state was essentially the complainant and had to flush out the homosexual from the shadows. The mechanisms for such aggressive enforcement had been developed in New York and other cities before World War II: *police stakeouts* of homosexual hangouts, which was the best way to obtain evidence of oral sex and indecent exposure; *decoy operations,* whereby homosexuals could be caught in sexual solicitation of an undercover officer; and *police raids,* which netted large numbers of socializing homosexuals and charged them with disorderly conduct, cross-dressing, and other minor offenses (Chapter 1). The period after World War II, therefore, did not innovate aggressive police tactics but did much to regularize, popularize, and modernize them.[30]

Regularization came to most cities through the creation or reconfiguration of police department vice or morals squads, which boomed in cities with large gay subcultures during the period of heightened child molestation anxiety. Vice squads consisted of officers wholly devoted to ferreting out sex crimes, and (judging from annual police reports) their productivity was measured by the number of prostitutes, sexual perverts, and drug dealers they arrested. Their attention increasingly focused on homosexuals after 1946. For an extreme example, sodomy or solicitation of sodomy generated almost 60 percent of the arrests by Philadelphia's morals squad in 1949, its first year of operation, and in 1950 the squad was hauling 200 homosexuals to court each month.[31] In New York City, a longtime center of antihomosexual police attention, between 117 and 487 people were arrested for sodomy and between 1,054 and 3,289 for disorderly conduct-degeneracy each year between 1947 and 1957 (Appendix C1 and C3); arrests for loitering around a public toilet were usually even higher. Los Angeles's police department had a morals division as early as the 1920s, and after World War II arrested gay people by the thousands.[32] New York, Philadelphia, and Los Angeles had been centers for antihomosexual police harassment before the war and continued in that role after the war. Baltimore, Boston, and St. Louis continued as secondary centers of harassment. San Francisco moved up from secondary to primary status no later than 1959, when the key issue in a vicious mayoral campaign was whether "Sex Deviates Make S.F. Headquarters," as one newspaper put it. That charge galvanized a two-year campaign by the smeared Mayor George Christopher to purge San Francisco of homosexuals.[33]

For most other cities with visible homosexual subcultures, the postwar era saw the first (quasi)systematic police efforts to seek out and arrest homosexuals in larger numbers. Spurred by congressional interest, Washington, D.C., emerged overnight as a center for arrests. Lieutenant Roy Blick and his vice squad arrested hundreds of men for sodomy, indecent assault, and lewdness, all crimes Congress created or updated between 1948 and 1953.[34] Cities as different as Cincinnati, Cleveland, Denver, Minneapolis, Kansas City, Oklahoma City, Pittsburgh, Providence, Salt Lake City, Santa Monica, and Sioux City saw concerted antihomosexual vice campaigns in the 1950s.[35] Smaller university towns such as Palo Alto, Gainesville, and Ann Arbor deployed their police forces in organized restroom stakeouts.[36] Nowhere were these campaigns more pronounced than in southern cities, most of which, like Washington, D.C., had not arrested homosexuals in great numbers before the war. Police invested unprecedented resources to search out and arrest homosexuals in Atlanta, Charlotte, Dallas, Houston, Memphis, Miami, New Orleans, Richmond, and Tampa during the 1950s.[37] Chicago, famed for its police corruption, may have been exceptional. Though police harassed gay people, especially people of color and cross-dressers, they were happier to take payoffs in return for toleration of Chicago's gay bars, its famed drag balls, and street solicitation.[38]

On the whole, police tactics were much more aggressive and invasive than they had been before the war. Spying on homosexuals often meant spending hours perched above public toilets, peeking into parked cars, and even following homosexuals and peering through doors into bedrooms.[39] Decoy cops allegedly forced themselves on the men they then arrested, as Los Angeles's Dale Jennings claimed in 1952.[40] Most remarkably, raids carried out by police departments in all kinds of cities resulted in wholesale arrests of gender and sexual deviants, including unprecedented numbers of women. For examples reported in the homophile press of the period, a 1955 raid on the Pepper Hill Club in Baltimore resulted in 162 arrests for disorderly conduct based on observations of same-sex hugging and kissing; a 1956 raid on Hazel's Bar near Redwood City, California, yielded ninety arrests (including ten women) on vagrancy charges and one arrest (bar owner Helen Nickola) for permitting lewd dancing without a license; a 1957 raid on Jimmie's Tavern in Tampa, Florida, led to arrests of twelve women for their "mannish" dress; a series of raids by Philadelphia police in 1959 ended in dozens of men and women being hauled off from the Hummoresque Coffeehouse and other cafes; a 1960 raid on the Tay-Bush Cafe in San Francisco resulted in 103 arrests (fourteen women) for same-sex dancing, under the charge of disorderly conduct; and a 1962 raid of the Yuga drag ball in Jefferson County, Louisiana, netted ninety-six arrests.[41]

Arrests often followed a *panic* scenario, where one incident triggered a wave of media and political attention, resulting in a frenzy of antihomosexual arrests, detentions, and harassment by police. During the summer of 1959, for example, Houston whipped itself up into its greatest "sex-fiend hunt" when the body of twelve-year-old Merrill Bodenheimer was found in an icebox. The police arrested seven black youths and obtained confessions that they had raped and killed the white boy. Several of the youths recanted what they claimed were confessions beaten out of them and produced alibi witnesses attesting to their innocence. They were released after the victim's mother publicly denounced the hysteria.[42] The Bodenheimer panic illustrates important themes: explicit attention to sexual perversion in southern cities and deployment of child molestation to target minority racial as well as sexual communities. A panic in Miami was triggered by publicity surrounding the murder of William Simpson, a homosexual man; the 1955 murders of three Chicago boys stimulated police roundups of homosexual men all over the Midwest; Stephen Nash's 1956 confession that he had murdered several homosexuals triggered an antihomosexual cleanup operation in Santa Monica.[43]

Sometimes incidents generated a *mania,* where the state would seek out larger homosexual conspiracies over a longer period of time. Complaints that the city was being overrun by homosexuals triggered a "Miami Hurricane" in 1953–54, which included police sweeps of beaches and bars to arrest "sex degenerates and female impersonators," bar raids and closings, and the enactment of new ordinances against cross-dressing, drag shows, and homosexual congregating. Political echoes reverberated in Miami and Florida long afterward; the hurricane generated much of the wind that powered the Florida Legislative Investigating Committee (Johns Committee) from 1956 to 1964. Other local manias occurred in Boise, Idaho (1955–1957) and Miami (1960–1961) after boy-prostitution rings were uncovered; in Tampa (1957–1961) when authorities became alarmed that the Miami cross-dressers had migrated to their city; and in San Francisco (mid-1950s, 1959–1961) where local police, Army investigators, and liquor regulators achieved an unusual degree of cooperation in warring against an increasing gay visibility.[44]

Unprecedented Numbers of Gay People Arrested for Consensual Behavior. For consensual same-sex intimacy, which was illegal in every state during this period, the state basically determined the crime rate. Typically having no complainant, sodomy and solicitation between consenting adults required the state to search out the crime, which required a calculated investment in police resources for stakeouts, decoy operations, and raids. As there was a huge amount of consensual sodomy going on and homosexual men were ridiculously easy to catch, the state could determine, ex ante, how much sex crime it would have. By investing more in vice squads, it was sure to raise the sex crime rate, to the point of diminishing marginal returns; by investing less, the rate would be lower. The arrest figures in Appendix C1 to C4 show an impressive postwar investment.

Sodomy law arrests reached historic highs in the period from 1946 to 1961, particularly in East Coast cities like New York and Baltimore and in West Coast cities like San Francisco and Los Angeles. Southern cities such as Atlanta and Washington, D.C., showed new highs in sodomy arrests, but figures that would be topped in the 1960s and 1970s. Altogether, an average of 678 people were arrested for sodomy each year from 1946 to 1965 in New York, Los Angeles, Baltimore, Washington, D.C., and San Francisco (Appendix C1). In the country as a whole, I estimate 2,000 to 5,000 arrests per year for this serious crime. Many of the sodomy prosecutions were for sex between an adult male and a male or female child, and some were for male-female sex, usually coerced by the male. Somewhere between 40 and 85 percent of the arrests were for consensual same-sex adult intimacy.[a] Hence, each year between 1946 and 1965, between 800 and 4,250 people, on average, were arrested for consensual sodomy. These were the most serious encounters with the law, and some sodomy defendants went to jail or a mental hospital for decades. (Most, however, plea-bargained to a lesser offense.)

Police also arrested people who cross-dressed, danced or flirted with someone of the same sex, loitered in public restrooms, and solicited sodomy; these mutually consenting activities could be the basis of arrests for solicitation, vagrancy, public indecency, loitering, and disorderly conduct, depending on the jurisdiction. Because these crimes were easier for the state to prove than sodomy, they yielded potentially many more arrests, albeit also less jail time. The ratio between sodomy arrests and arrests for lesser crimes varied enormously. In New York City 112 men were arrested in 1949 for sodomy, 3,227 people for disorderly conduct-degeneracy, and 2,213 men for loitering around public toilets.[45] In Los Angeles eighty-six men were arrested in 1948 for sodomy, 386 men and eleven women for oral copulation, 133 men and four women for indecent exposure, and 1,413 men and 142 women for lewd vagrancy.[46]

---

a. A lower limit (25 percent) would reflect the percentage of consensual sodomy cases that were reported for the category "sodomy" in the West National Reporter System for the years 1941–1955 and 1956–1970 (Appendix C2). This greatly understates the number of consensual sodomy arrests, however, because they tended to be plea-bargained to misdemeanors and hence rarely became the source of a reported appeal. Therefore, I examined samples of sodomy complaints in two different jurisdictions over time. The lower limit in the text reflects my survey of sodomy complaints filed with or by the District of Columbia police between 1950 and 1969: there were 999 complaints, 888 of which involved same-sex sodomy, 433 same-sex sodomy between an adult and a male minor, and therefore 455 complaints of same-sex sodomy between two adults. The rate has been discounted from 45 to 40 percent to reflect the fact that not all the adult-adult complaints would have been consensual. The upper limit in the text reflects the percentage of sodomy and oral copulation cases found in the Los Angeles County Superior Court for the years 1962–1964 by the able students participating in research for "Project: The Consenting Adult Homosexual and the Law," 13 *UCLA L. Rev.* 647, 799 (1966), statistically analyzed in Brent McIntosh, "Gaylaw Arrest Projections" (December 1998).

A conservative estimate is that, for the country as a whole, these misde-meanor arrests were ten to fifteen times the number of sodomy arrests in this period; a liberal estimate would be twenty to thirty.[b] Given a multiplier of ten to fifteen, an educated guess is that between 20,800 ([2000 times ten] plus 800) and 79,250 ([5,000 times fifteen] plus 4,250) people, mostly men, were arrested each year for nonconforming gender or sexual behavior that inflicted no tangi-ble harm on other persons. Because of the conservative assumptions, the arrest figures were probably higher, as many as 154,250 ([5,000 times 30] plus 4,250). Additionally, countless more people, especially women, were accosted or threatened with arrest or in some cases coerced to have sex by police bullies.[47] Tens, perhaps even hundreds, of thousands of gay (or suspected gay) people had some kind of harassing encounter with the police each year during the gen-eration after World War II.

Purging Homosexuals from Government Service

Arrests and sometimes just detentions for minor homosexual offenses (cross-dressing, disorderly conduct, loitering, lewdness or indecency, lewd vagrancy) typically had more severe civil than criminal effects, as the culprits often had their identities publicized in the newspaper, suffered social and familial ostracism, and lost their jobs. Consistent with the straight-threatening closet, the federal government, followed sporadically by leading states and cities, affir-matively sought to uncover and purge "homosexuals and other sex perverts" from government, including military service, and some officials sought to expose such people to civil society as well. This policy was implemented in a series of witch-hunts at both the federal and state levels.[48]

Federal Exclusions and Witch-Hunts—the Truman Administration. Testifying before a Senate subcommittee in 1947, Secretary of State George Marshall was

---

b. For New York City yearly arrests for sodomy ranged between 100 and 200; arrests for disor-derly conduct-degeneracy were typically ten to twenty times those figures (compare figures in Appendix C1 and C3); arrests for toilet loitering were also much larger. Los Angeles area prosecu-tions for the early 1960s suggest a multiplier of twenty-five. The UCLA study (cited in note a) found 439 sodomy cases in Los Angeles courts for a three-year period (1962–1964), or 146 cases per year. The study found 2,994 defendants in the courts for a one-year period (May 1964–April 1965), against whom the state alleged misdemeanors for lewd vagrancy, public indecency, and obscenity. Taking into account that the 439 cases involved more than 439 defendants and that the sodomy/oral perversion sample was taken from a larger county-wide jurisdiction, factors that cut in different directions, one is left with about twenty-five charges for homosexual solicitation or expression for every charge of sodomy. See Brent McIntosh, "Gaylaw Arrest Projections" (Decem-ber 1998) (statistical analysis of the L.A. projection). New York and Los Angeles may have been more energetic in seeking out the minor offenses, thus justifying a conservative multiplier, ten to fifteen, for the entire country.

given a memorandum admonishing him about "the extensive employment in highly classified positions, of admitted homosexuals, who are historically known to be security risks," like Sumner Welles.[49] Senator Kenneth Wherry, the Senate minority leader, and other Republicans accused the Truman administration of running a government crawling with sexual as well as political subversives. In response the Truman administration adopted a loyalty security program to weed out Communists and started looking for "homosexuals and other sex perverts" in earnest. Between January 1947 and April 1950, the administration investigated 192 cases of "sex perversion" in civil government, most of which resulted in discharge or resignation.[50] During the same period 3,245 personnel were separated from the military, at triple the discharge rate during World War II. Contrary to the War Department's policy as late as 1946, the discharges were generally less-than-honorable "blue" discharges, thereby depriving these personnel of veterans' benefits promised in the G.I. Bill of Rights and exposing them to discrimination in the private sector when the nature of the discharge was leaked by local boards.[51]

A Defense Department memorandum of October 11, 1949, codified a sterner policy for excluding sexual deviants from the armed forces. The new policy made mandatory the prompt separation of all "known homosexuals." Heterosexuals who fell into homosexual offenses could, implicitly, be retained. Homosexuals fell into three groups: Class I, who engaged in coercive sex or sex with minors, were to be court-martialed; Class II, who engaged in "one or more homosexual acts" or proposals or attempts "to perform an act of homosexuality," were to be court-martialed or allowed to resign under less-than-honorable (blue) conditions; and Class III, who "only exhibit, profess, or admit homosexual tendencies" but had not engaged in forbidden conduct, were to be retained or discharged (honorably or generally) depending upon the recommendation of a personnel board.[52]

When Lieutenant Roy Blick of the Washington, D.C., Vice Squad told the Senate in 1950 that there were 5000 homosexuals working for the government, a figure Blick made up, Senator Wherry called for a full-fledged investigation, and the Republican national chairman charged that "sexual perverts" just as "dangerous as the actual Communists" had "infiltrated the government."[53] The Truman administration stepped up its efforts, investigating 382 civil servants (most of whom resigned) in the next seven months, and the Senate authorized the investigation demanded by Wherry in a subcommittee chaired by North Carolina Senator Clyde Hoey. The Hoey subcommittee's December 1950 report made out the case against having "homosexuals and other sex perverts" in the government. "The social stigma attached to sex perversion is so great that many perverts go to great lengths to conceal their perverted tendencies," making them easy prey for "gangs of blackmailers," the argument made in 1941 against Sumner Welles. Also, "those who engage in overt acts of perversion lack the emotional stability of normal persons," and "indulgence in acts of sex perversion weakens the moral fiber of an individual to a degree that he is not suitable for a position of responsibility." Finally, "perverts will frequently attempt to entice normal individuals to engage in perverted practices. This is particularly true in the case of young and impressionable people who might come under the influence of a pervert . . . One homosexual can pollute an entire offfice."[54]

The subcommittee approvingly reported the progress that had already been made against this menace. It held up the armed forces' large-scale purge of homosexuals as the model, which was being followed by civilian agencies. The Civil Service Commission's regulation barring from federal employment people who engage in "immoral conduct" was interpreted to include "homosexuality and other types of sex perversion" as "sufficient grounds for denying appointment to a Government position or for the removal of a person from the Federal service."[55] To enforce this policy, the Commission began checking fingerprints of job applicants against FBI files of arrests across the country. Between 1947 and 1950 the agency denied government employment to 1,700 applicants because they had "a record of homosexuality or other sex perversion." The subcommittee applauded this energy and criticized the "false premise" that what government employees did on their own time was their private business, when the employees engaged in "sex perversion or any other types of criminal activity or similar misconduct."[56] Agencies were expected to investigate all complaints as aggressively as possible, and the FBI beginning in 1950 correlated morals arrests everywhere in the country against lists of government employees. After the subcommittee report, the investigations and separations continued until the antihomosexual witch-hunt exceeded the anti-Communist witch-hunt in its impact. In 1951 the State Department fired 119 employees for homosexuality, and only 35 as other security risks (Communists); the figures were 134 and 70, respectively, in 1952.[57]

At the same time the Hoey subcommittee was studying ways to purge homosexuals inside the government, a subcommittee of the Senate Judiciary Committee was drafting a law to keep homosexuals out of the country. From 1950 to 1952 the immigration subcommittee headed by Senator Patrick McCarran developed a comprehensive redraft of the immigration law. A major focus of the McCarran bill was the exclusion of Communists, anarchists, and other subversives. Reflecting fears that homosexuals were sexually subversive, the McCarran bill excluded all "persons afflicted with psychopathic personality, or who are homosexuals or sex perverts."[58] Upon the assurance of the Public Health Service that the term "psychopathic personality" was broad enough to "specify such types of pathologic behavior as homosexuality or sexual perversion," the Senate as well as House Judiciary Committees settled for an exclusion simply of "persons afflicted with psychopathic personality," and that was the exclusion finally enacted as section 212(a)(4) of the McCarran-Walter Act of 1952.[59] The Immigration and Naturalization Service read the exclusion as simply reiterating the pre-1952 exclusion of people afflicted with "constitutional psychopathic inferiority" and enforced it against persons with records of consensual homosexual offenses, which also fell under the "crimes of moral turpitude" exclusion that the McCarran Act had similarly carried forward.[60] Ironically, immigration authorities aggressively enforced the antihomosexual exclusions of the Immigration Act of 1917 in the years right after World War II, but debarred fewer noncitizens—and fewer relative to total debarred—after 1952, under the McCarran-Walter version of the exclusions (Appendix C6).

Federal Exclusions and Witch-Hunts—the Eisenhower Administration. The Eisenhower administration was more aggressively antihomosexual than the Truman administration. In April 1953 President Eisenhower issued Executive Order 10,450, which officially added "sexual perversion" as a ground for investigation and dismissal under the federal loyalty-security program.[61] In the next two years more than 800 federal employees resigned or were terminated because they had files indicating "sex perversion," typically charges—but not convictions—of loitering, solicitation, or disorderly conduct. Bruce Scott, for example, was fired from his Labor Department job because of a 1947 arrest for loitering in Lafayette Park, a homosexual cruising spot.[62]

The rate of expulsion abated in the late 1950s, but unabated was the Eisenhower administration's industrial security program, which denied security clearances to private as well as public employees who engaged in "immoral" conduct or "sex perversion."[63] Thus, an employee of a defense contractor as well as the Defense Department itself was subject to Eisenhower's antihomosexual policies. Over two million private sector employees were subject to this program by the 1960s. Another way federal antihomosexual policy spilled over into the private sector was the sharing of police and military records with private employers. For all these reasons, persons discharged from a federal agency as "sex perverts" often found themselves blacklisted by private employers as well. Franklin Kameny, for example, was dismissed from his job with the Army Map Division in 1957, based upon a morals arrest the year before. Because of the 1953 executive order, he was unemployable in any federal agency; because of the security program, he was unemployable by private firms as well, as security clearances were necessary for the scientific work he did. Kameny almost starved to death as he sought to adjust to a life without his chosen career.[64]

The Washington, D.C., of the 1950s was a city that would have horrified

Franklin Roosevelt, as charges of perversion were tossed around like hand grenades.[65] The antihomosexual campaign in Washington was accompanied by a similar nationwide campaign pursued by the armed forces to warn against homosexuality. The Navy's revised indoctrination lectures, for example, went well beyond those developed during World War II by asserting that homosexuals were aggressive psychopaths who preyed upon normal people. Women were warned that association with homosexuals could render them unfit for future marriage or friendships and that "deterioration and destruction of character and integrity are the end results of homosexuality. Even such gross crimes as robbery, suicide, and murder often grow out of homosexuality." Officials told men as well as women that homosexuals used insidious methods to lure them into vice and urged them to monitor their same-sex friendships and report friends they believed to be homosexual.[66]

Military policy directed not only that confirmed homosexuals be separated, but that they be sought out as well. The Army's 1950 regulation said: "It is the duty of every member of the military service to report to his commanding officer any facts which may come to his attention concerning overt acts of homosexuality. Commanding officers receiving information indicating that a person has homosexual tendencies or has engaged in an act of homosexuality shall inquire thoroughly and comprehensively."[67] Personnel were repeatedly questioned for clues to roust them from their closets, and undercover investigators sought out personnel in homosexual bars, known male cruising areas, and women's softball teams. More important, once military investigators had evidence (or just accusations) against one soldier, they often threatened that person with court-martial and unfavorable publicity unless she or he reported other names. Once one person gave names, others often rushed forward, lest they receive the sucker's payoff. An early witch-hunt of this type was conducted at the Kessler Air Force Base in Biloxi, Mississippi. The investigators reportedly promised accused lesbians general discharges if they cooperated by naming sexual partners and suspected homosexuals, but eleven women were dishonorably discharged contrary to the promises, and others resigned. Twenty women at Lackland Air Force Base were similarly kicked out, and two allegedly committed suicide as a result of their disgrace.[68]

The tangible results of this substantial investment were not as impressive as one might have expected. Between 1950 and 1965 the Navy cashiered as Class II and III homosexuals an average of more than 1,000 enlisted personnel per year (Appendix C5), about 40 percent of the Navy's total undesirable discharges for those years. All told, it is estimated that between 2,000 and 3,000 personnel were separated each year for that period, at a rate of one person separated each year for each 1,000 serving in the armed forces and with a significantly higher rate of discharge for women than for men.[69] These figures strongly understate the effect of the policy, as many personnel left the armed forces before investigators got to them or upon the slightest pressure.

State Exclusions and Witch-Hunts. At the same time the armed forces and other federal agencies were initiating witch-hunts, state and local governments were taking similar actions. One of the first significant cases was that of Miriam Van Waters, superintendent of the Massachusetts Reformatory for Women. Starting in 1947, she was criticized for tolerating female relationships among inmates and retaining suspected lesbians as reformatory officers. The State Commissioner of Corrections dismissed her in January 1949. Van Waters' deputy, Margaret O'Keefe, was also targeted, as a leader of a "doll racket" of intimacy among women because of her "mannish" dress and a vice (prostitution) charge against her two decades earlier. Replying candidly that female friendships were a good way to rehabilitate lost women, Van Waters was a sitting duck in the new climate, where toleration of discreet homosexuality was anathema.[70]

What happened to Van Waters could happen to virtually any state employee during the antihomosexual panic. The publicity given the federal antihomosexual witch-hunt beginning in 1947 stimulated analogous witch-hunts at the state level. If New York was the key situs for antidegeneracy campaigns before World War II, California was the key situs for antihomosexual campaigns after the war. Under California law, persons who engaged in "immoral conduct"—explicitly including sodomy, oral copulation, and lewdness with children—stood to lose their state jobs or teachers' certificates or both.[71] Because most homosexuals prosecuted for these crimes by the state were able to plead guilty to lesser crimes, California in 1952 expanded the bases for revoking teaching certificates to include any conviction for lewd vagrancy and loitering at a public toilet, misdemeanor sex crimes enforced almost entirely against homosexuals.[72] California also required applicants for teaching credentials to furnish their fingerprints and the state crime bureau to furnish all records pertaining to the applicants, so that the board of education could screen out people with sex crime records.[73]

Like teachers, other professionals could not ply their trade without state licenses, and most states had prohibitions that enabled regulators to deny or revoke licenses of people exposed as homosexuals. In California, as in almost all other states, "gross immorality" was a statutory basis for professional disciplinary action against doctors, dentists, pharmacists, embalmers, guardians, and a host of other licensed professionals.[74] The most common basis for revoking a professional license in most states, conviction of a "crime involving moral turpitude," reached dozens more occupations in California.[75] It is unclear how many professionals lost their licenses, but California courts construed these laws to allow state professional boards and the state bar association to revoke licenses for such minor crimes as lewd vagrancy and public indecency. Because these crimes were a matter of public record, which the state police supplied to relevant agencies, homosexual professionals did frequently see their licenses challenged or withdrawn.[76] Although California apparently pursued these cases most vigorously, it was not alone in purging the professions of homosexuals, and indeed the most systematic campaign was, surprisingly, in the South.

Beginning in 1956, Florida authorized a series of Legislative Investigating Committees to expose subversion in the state, originally focusing on Communism and integrationism but soon settling on homosexuality as the main target. In 1959 the "Johns Committee" (after its frequent chair, Senator Charley Johns) found that "[s]ome of the State's instructional personnel at the higher educational level have been and are recruiting young people into homosexual practices and these young people have been and are becoming teachers in the public school system of Florida, and some of them are recruiting teen-age students into homosexual practices."[77] In response, the committee engaged in a six-year campaign to purge state schools of homosexuals. The campaign involved identifying suspected homosexuals who were high school teachers, college students, and university professors; confronting them with accusations of homosexuality, often on the record at inquisitorial hearings with no counsel present, and asking them to confirm their homosexuality and that of other suspects; and then pressing for state dismissal if the accused did not resign voluntarily. The committee also pressured the state board of education to revoke teachers' certificates, which the legislature seconded with a 1959 statute authorizing certificate revocation for "moral misconduct" and a 1961 statute setting forth expedited procedures for revocation.[78]

Near the end of its rolling tenure, the Johns Committee announced that the board had revoked seventy-one teachers' certificates (sixty-three more cases pending), fourteen professors had been removed from the state universities (nineteen more cases pending), and thirty-seven federal employees had lost their jobs (fourteen state employees faced removal in pending cases). According to the University of Florida's records, sixteen students were suspended or withdrew from the university, and twenty-five were placed on probation because of the committee's revelations.[79] These figures do not reflect the hundreds of state employees who departed "voluntarily" from their positions, as many of the interrogated employees did after confessing their crimes to state investigators, or the dozens of university students who were scarred when the contents of their closets spilled out during the investigation.

Lawyers, officers of the court, were disbarred for homosexual activities with consenting adults in Florida, California, and other states.[80] Ronald Kay, to take an interesting example from the 1960s, was disbarred in Florida because his violation of an indecent exposure ordinance involved homosexual solicitation. "In addition to [Kay's] homosexual activity," the bar association found dispositive his "lack of candor."[81] Kay probably did prevaricate—to the police who arrested him, the judge who sentenced him, the bar association, his family, and most of his friends. His case reflects the dilemma of the closet, for honesty about homosexuality meant social death and legal disabilities, but lying was dishonest and justified civil penalties. The impressive array of state inquiries into sexual orientation forced homosexuals to talk, and anything they said or did not say could and would be used against them.

Suppression of Homosexual Association and Expression

Straight anxiety about threatening features of the closet simultaneously stimulated much talk about sexual perversion *and* obsessive secrecy about it. Government witch-hunts inspired the formation of homophile organizations, which operated under mysterious names (the Mattachine Society and the Daughters of Bilitis) and whose members knew each other only by pseudonyms. Progay publications spoke in the most cautious of ways about homosexuality, rarely affirming it as a normal condition and mostly begging for the toleration any decent person would afford a sick dog. The most systematic theoretician, Edward Sagarin, wrote under the pen name Donald Webster Cory. Even homoerotica was closeted: men masturbated over physique magazines and Sears Roebuck catalogs, while women fantasized about lesbian characters who met the requisite tragic ends in pulp romances. Consistent with conceptions of the closet as threatening, a deviance gendarmerie sought to flush out, intimidate, and ultimately destroy networks of information and support that might attract new "recruits" to homosexuality by infiltrating the homosexual underground and harassing its denizens.

Surveillance and Harassment. Starting no later than 1937, FBI Director J. Edgar Hoover maintained private files containing reports about the homosexuality of prominent people, including Sumner Welles and Senator David Walsh, the chair of the Naval Investigations Committee.[82] According to the Hoey subcommittee investigations in 1950, the Navy had a file of over 7,000 "known or alleged homosexuals" obtained in the course of its investigations, the Army had a list of over 5,000, and vice squads in the District and elsewhere had their own lists of people, including civil servants and military personnel. The subcommittee charged the FBI to serve as a clearinghouse for all this information and to channel it to the Civil Service Commission. The Bureau expanded its charge to include surveillance of homosexuals and their organizations and their political activity, as well as investigations of people associating with known homosexuals. Once its agents had gathered the information, the FBI used it in various ways, including leaks to local officials and employers and interrogation to pry out the names of other homosexuals.[83]

The FBI was intensely interested in homophile groups. The Mattachine Society was a secret homophile society founded in 1950 by Harry Hay and a tiny circle of friends. In January 1953 the first mass circulation homophile journal, *One, Inc.,* was published by Mattachine members but in a separate organizational form; the Society itself published the *Mattachine Review* starting in 1955. The Daughters of Bilitis was formed for lesbians in the autumn of 1955 by Del Martin and Phyllis Lyon, both operating under assumed names. Beginning in October 1956, the Daughters published *The Ladder,* "with the vague idea that something should be done about the problems of Lesbians, both within their group and with the public."[84]

The FBI initiated an internal security investigation into the Mattachine Society in the spring of 1953, and started a more open-ended file on the Daughters of Bilitis in the summer of 1959. Although Hay and other Mattachine members had been Communist Party members or sympathizers before the war, the FBI by December 1953 recognized that Mattachine was completely "law-abiding," as one agent put it when he closed the internal security file.[85] The Daughters were never suspected of being internal security threats. Nonetheless, FBI agents infiltrated both organizations, archived their declarations and publications, reported their meetings and activities, recruited informants, compiled lists of members whom they could identify, and speculated on the organizations' influence and future activities.

The FBI's internal documents do not reveal how this surveillance information was deployed, but do reveal the details of the Bureau's most direct interaction with homophile organizations. The November 1955 issue of *One, Inc.,* contained an article by David Freeman stating that "Tory" homosexuals, deeply closeted, "occupy key positions with oil companies or the FBI (it's true!)." This allegation came to the attention of FBI Director Hoover and his associate Clyde Tolson in January 1956. According to FBI records, Tolson responded, "I think we should take this crowd on and make them 'put up or shut up.'" Hoover said, "I concur." The Los Angeles office of the FBI was instructed to locate Freeman and interview him to determine precisely what FBI authorities he had in mind. (There were rumors throughout Hoover's career of a sexual liaison between him and Tolson.) Agents visited the offices of *One* and told a staff member that "the FBI would not tolerate any such baseless allegations in this ('One') or any other publication." FBI headquarters instructed the agent in charge to develop derogatory information concerning Freeman and other staff, as well as information that could cause trouble for the magazine as an obscene publication with state authorities, the Department of Justice, or the Post Office. Although the agents never determined Freeman's identity, they visited most members of the *One* staff and notified their employers, with the expectation (apparently unfulfilled) that the homophiles would lose their jobs.[86]

Although less well documented than the national FBI network, police in jurisdictions all over the country, but especially in the sunbelt states, made it their business to monitor, harass, and publicize the names of lesbians and gay men. The Johns Committee created a network of correspondents throughout Florida and parts of the South with whom its investigator shared information, intending to make homosexuals pariahs wherever they worked or traveled. In cities as disparate as Memphis, Philadelphia, Atlanta, Buffalo, Tampa, Miami, and San Francisco, police surveillance had a terrorizing effect, especially on tiny lesbian communities, because it occasionally led to raids on private parties or dinners, arrests for disorderly conduct or cross-dressing, and unwelcome newspaper publicity.[87]

Censorship of Homophile Media. The municipal, state, and federal obscenity laws described in Chapter 1 affected the development of a homophile press in the 1940s. An early journal was *Vice Versa* (1946–1947), a mimeo of short stories, news, and essays produced by "Lisa Ben," an anagram for "Lesbian." Said the author years later: "I had no idea how daring or dangerous this was . . . until somebody said, 'Don't you know you could get into trouble for mailing this?'" *Vice Versa* ceased publication when its author took a new secretarial job that left her with no privacy to turn out the publication in complete secrecy.[88] While some authors in the 1940s openly explored homosexual themes in their writings, John Horne Burns and Tennessee Williams were more typical, especially after 1947, in expressing gender-bending themes indirectly. During the 1950s a homophile press (*One, Mattachine Review, Ladder*) and literature, including erotica, developed, and it came to the attention not only of the censors but of state and federal legislators. In May and June 1955 the Senate Subcommittee on Juvenile Delinquency held hearings to support Senator Estes Kefauver's thesis that "after young people have been exposed to these pornographic pictures and movies showing all types of perversion, they may tend to regard these things as normal. Indeed the influence is to lead them to embrace the abnormal and thus mar youthful lives."[89] This kind of thinking had an extraordinarily uneven application, as censors suppressed such classics as *Fanny Hill* while ignoring the more widely read lesbian romances of Ann Bannon.[90]

Published overseas right after the Kefauver hearings, Allen Ginsberg's poem *Howl* combined themes of homosexuality, gender revolt, and political insubordination—the surest recipe for censorship. Still, *Howl*'s first printing in 1956 got through Customs in New York and was openly sold in Lawrence Ferlinghetti's City Lights bookstore in San Francisco. Its second printing, however, was confiscated at San Francisco's port as obscene. "You wouldn't want your children to come across it," said the Customs censor. (The San Francisco branch is believed to have stopped 700 pieces of private mail a year and one publication in twenty on the basis of obscenity.) Ferlinghetti thereupon printed a domestic edition of the work. In June 1956 Captain William Hanrahan of the Juvenile Division of the San Francisco Police Department seized all copies of *Howl* and arrested Ferlinghetti and his sales clerk, Shigeyoshi Murao, for selling obscene works—*Howl* and William Margolis's *The Miscellaneous Man*, another work of sexual deviance.[91]

The closest thing to published homoerotica in the 1940s and 1950s was the male physique magazine. Pioneer Herman Womack published *MANual, Trim*, and *Grecian Guild Pictorial*, which contained photographs of seminude male models, posed suggestively and sometimes in pairs. The censors were not fooled for long. On May 25, 1960, the Alexandria, Virginia, Postmaster seized 405 copies of the magazines pursuant to the Comstock Act. Finding that the magazines appealed only to the prurient interest of "sexual deviates" and had no literary or other merit, the Judicial Officer of the Post Office opined that the books were not mailable. The Post Office and the Department of Justice also went after gay pen-pal clubs and, in their most bizarre escapade, the exceedingly tame *One*.

In April 1954 Senator Alexander Wiley wrote the Postmaster General protesting the willingness of the Post Office to carry *One*, a magazine "devoted to the achievement of sexual perversion," contrary to the administration's anti-homosexual policies.[92] In response, the Los Angeles Postmaster sent a copy of each issue of *One* to the central Post Office for evaluation under the Comstock Act. The August 1954 issue (homosexual marriage touted on the cover) was held up by the Post Office for several weeks before it was allowed to circulate. The Solicitor of the Post Office determined that the October 1954 issue was obscene and lewd, based upon a poem, an ad, and an article, "Sappho Remembered," whose depiction of a lesbian's affection for a twenty-year-old "girl," who gives up her boyfriend to live with the lesbian, was considered obscene because "lustfully stimulating to the average homosexual reader." Upon these findings, the Post Office determined the issue to be nonmailable and returned 600 copies to the sender. Pursuant to a 1950 statute, the Post Office also had the power to impound mail flowing to any person found to be using the mails to provide information about any "obscene" matter.[93] While this power was not invoked against *One* (as it was against more explicit homosexual mailers), issues after that of October 1954 were held up for months as postal inspectors poured through them, weighing their potential for corruption.[94]

Movies continued to operate under three layers of censorship: federal customs screening of foreign films for "obscenity"; state and local licensing laws such as New York's, which in 1954 was amended to ban movies depicting "sexual immorality, perversion, or lewdness"; and the Motion Pictures Code, forbidding any reference to "[s]ex perversion."[95] To obtain the Code imprimatur necessary for national distribution of a movie, the producers had to satisfy the Code censors that their movie did not refer to sex perversion. This often required a negotiating process, whereby movies were cut or rewritten to satisfy censors, as Warner Brothers in 1950 consented to do with Tennessee Williams' *Streetcar Named Desire,* a pattern replicated with other of Williams' plays adapted to movies, such as *Cat on a Hot Tin Roof* (1958). The Customs Service was no less bashful about impounding sexually oriented foreign films such as *491,* a Swedish movie including explicit scenes of homosexual fantasies and man-boy sex.[96] On the other hand, the cognoscenti could easily recognize the clouded homosexual themes in the movie versions of plays such as *Suddenly, Last Summer* (1959) and *Tea and Sympathy* (1956). Even a big hit like *Ben-Hur* (1959) suggested a galvanizing homosexual relationship between chariot rivals Stephen Boyd and (unsuspecting) Charlton Heston, hatched by mischievous screenwriter Gore Vidal.[97]

Closing Down Homosexual Congregation. New York was the only state that regularly closed gay bars before World War II, but stopped short of a rule explicitly prohibiting homosexuals from congregating together; New Jersey had such a rule but did not aggressively enforce it (Chapter 1). After the war, gay bars boomed all over the country, multiplying in cities that had them before the war (Miami, St. Louis, San Diego, and Washington, D.C., as well as New York, San Francisco, and Los Angeles) and starting up in cities with no permanent subcultural fixtures before the war, including cities like Albuquerque, Atlanta, Cleveland, Columbus, Denver, Hartford, Louisville, Omaha, Pittsburgh, Richmond, Roanoke, Seattle, and Tucson.[98] With the rise of the gay bar, more states and municipalities explicitly (like New Jersey) or effectively (like New York) prohibited licensed premises from serving liquor to homosexuals.[99] Also, New York's aggressive enforcement, including use of undercover investigators, became increasingly common. The most ambitious new regulatory efforts were in California and Florida. Although their regulators had the same power as those in New York, namely, to close down premises that were a threat to "public morals" or "disorderly,"[100] the regulators did not regularly exercise that power against gay bars until the late 1940s (California) or mid-1950s (Florida).

The most celebrated investigations involved Sol Stoumen's Black Cat Bar, a gay mecca near North Beach in the San Francisco Bay area. Its first license revocation case grew out of an undercover investigation in 1949, which yielded evidence that the bar was a homosexual hangout. After the courts overturned the revocation, the California legislature in 1955 amended its liquor licensing law to require license revocation for any premises permitted to become a "resort for illegal possessors or users of narcotics, prostitutes, pimps, panderers, or sexual perverts" and allowing the Alcoholic Beverage Control (ABC) Department to consider as evidence "the general reputation" of the premises as a resort for "sexual perverts."[101] Based upon the new law and evidence of males kissing and caressing other males and of lewd propositions made by patrons to undercover investigators, the ABC Department again revoked the Black Cat's license in 1957. At the same time, the Department was seeking to close dozens of other bars, including Pearl Kershaw's Oakland bar, which lost its license because investigators spotted women dancing with women, two men displaying wedding rings, and same-sex fondling.[102]

The 1955 California statute was merely the most explicit legal notation for a war against homosexual bars all over the country in the mid-1950s, based upon heterosexual fears of the threatening closet. In 1954 Miami adopted an ordinance making it unlawful for a bar to knowingly employ *or* sell alcohol to "a homosexual person, lesbian or pervert, as the same are commonly accepted and understood, or to knowingly allow two or more persons who are homosexuals, lesbians or perverts to congregate or remain in his place of business." Part of the antihomosexual Miami Hurricane, the ordinance was justified "to prevent the congregation at liquor establishments of persons likely to prey upon the public by attempting to recruit other persons for acts which have been declared illegal."[103] Through police harassment as well as liquor board pressure, all of the Miami and Miami Beach gay bars went out of business in the late 1950s. Similarly, the municipal police, the county sheriff, and state liquor regulators worked to close many of the Tampa bars, especially the lesbian bars, in the middle of the decade. As the Tampa experience illustrates, bar closings and raids were a tactic with disproportionate effect upon working-class lesbian "butch-fem" bar cultures that flourished in cities of all sizes and regions (including the South) during this period.[104]

Like Florida, other jurisdictions became more aggressive in policing gay bars in the late 1950s and early 1960s. After 1954, for example, New Jersey's ABC Department stepped up its enforcement activities and proceeded under its Rule 5, as amended in 1950 to require licensees to police their premises against "any lewdness, immoral activity, or foul, filthy or obscene language or conduct." Like the statutes in Miami and California, Rule 5 was invoked against licensees who allowed homosexuals to congregate in their establishments; the Department disciplined them because the assembly of homosexuals in any public space constituted a "threat to the safety and morals of the public."[105]

Liquor regulators all over the country followed this policy of closing down bars simply because they were "havens for deviates," as the New Jersey Department put it. The primary consequence of this regulatory activism was the creation or perpetuation of an extortion racket, by which police and liquor inspectors could extract a price from homosexuals and their bars in return for official silence about the illegal homosexual congregations. Typically, and pervasively in places like Chicago, Detroit, Seattle, and Buffalo, the price was regular monetary payoffs.[106] Another kind of price was the enjoyment some police and liquor inspectors derived from ritual humiliation of homosexuals. In Los Angeles and New York, police sometimes employed snap raids: officers would march into a bar, line up the patrons, taunt them with sexual threats, and arrest or detain people at random. Sometimes those detained would agree to provide oral sex to officers in return for their silence. "Being forced to give some fat cop a blow job in the back of his car is about as degrading an experience as you can imagine," recalled one California man bitterly.[107]

Another consequence of the official policy was that homosexual bars typically had short lives, albeit with possibilities for reincarnation. In 1960 the New York State Liquor Authority (SLA) closed thirty gay bars in New York City, with new ones replacing them almost overnight. In 1961–62 the California ABC Department closed twenty-four bars in San Francisco, but twenty-five remained open, including the Black Cat, still fighting for the last of its nine lives.[108]

Survival: The Mutually Protective Closet

The antihomosexual campaigns in the United States from 1947 to 1961 were an echo of the antihomosexual terror in Nazi Germany from 1933 to 1945. Both were fueled by a pseudo-medical ideology fearful of the homosexual's threat to gender norms, children, and national security and manifested their fears through similar deployments of the law:[109]

- In 1933 Chancellor Adolf Hitler declared "homosexuals" to be an enemy of the state because of their threat to German youth, morals, and reproductivity. In 1950 Congress declared "homosexuals and other sex perverts" to be an enemy of the state because of their threat to American youth, morals, and national security. President Eisenhower made a similar pronouncement in 1953.

- The Prussian Minister of the Interior in 1933 ordered the closing of homosexual bars and banned obscene publications. New York, California, Florida, New Jersey, and other states similarly closed gay bars. Such states and the federal government banned gay-friendly publications and plays from the 1920s onward.
- The Minister in 1934 ordered detention of habitual sex criminals convicted of molesting children. Following Michigan, Illinois, and California, Congress in 1948 ordered detention of sexual psychopaths in the nation's capital, including people not charged with a crime. These and other jurisdictions ordered detention of habitual sex criminals convicted of any kind of deviant conduct, including sex between consenting adults of the same sex.
- In 1935 the German sodomy law was expanded to include any kind of "sex offense" between men, including mutual masturbation; higher penalties were introduced for same-sex intimacy with a minor; women were not included. In 1948 Congress adopted a sodomy law with higher penalties than those adopted by the Nazis, either for ordinary sodomy or sodomy with minors; in 1953 Congress expanded the District of Columbia's public indecency law to include private fondling and solicitation. Similar developments occurred at the state level. Almost all sodomy laws applied to women.
- In 1936 the German Criminal Police established special units for detecting homosexuals; by the late 1930s homosexuals tended to be arrested in groups as a result of raids. The number of prosecutions and severity of sentences rose sharply after 1936. Most American cities established special vice squads for flushing out homosexuals; by the 1950s homosexuals were often arrested in groups as a result of raids. The number of prosecutions and severity of sentences rose sharply after 1946.
- In 1936 the Reich Office for the Combatting of Homosexuality and Abortion was created as a clearinghouse for information about homosexuals. Starting in 1937, the FBI collected information on homosexuals, and after 1950 it systematically shared information with other agencies and employers. California after 1947 required registration of homosexuals and used that information to deny them jobs and certificates.
- In 1937–38, the Prussian Minister of the Interior decreed that loitering for sexual contact was illegal; enforcement was by undercover police. Police surveillance and decoy cop entrapment of homosexuals had been routine in New York since 1900 and became routine elsewhere after World War II. Loitering near public toilets was illegal in New York after 1939 and California after 1950.
- From 1942 to 1944 the Wehrmacht High Command developed guidelines for homosexuality in the armed forces. The regulations distinguished

between offenders engaging in homosexuality because of "predisposition," who were expelled, and those "who basically have healthy sexual feelings" and were therefore allowed to serve in the armed forces. From 1942 to 1944 the United States Defense Department developed similar guidelines; after 1946 the American guidelines were more punitive than those of the Wehrmacht.

- Beginning in 1937, the Reich sentenced a fraction of its homosexual offenders to concentration camps, where they were subjected to experimental medical treatments, such as castration. After 1946 American jurisdictions sentenced a fraction of their homosexual offenders to hospitals or special prison wards, where they were subjected to experimental medical treatments, sometimes castration, but more typically electrical and pharmacological shock treatments and lobotomies.

The main difference between Nazi law and American law was that the Nazis' penalties were harsher in effect—frequently death in concentration camps. This difference justifies different terminologies: the Nazi goal was *Holocaust*, genocide, while the American goal was *Kulturkampf*, erasure.

Still, the points of similarity are striking. In retrospect, the regimes seem distinct mainly because the antihomosexual terror in America was a flop. Whereas the Nazis eradicated the thriving German homosexual subculture, the antihomosexual Americans destroyed thousands of human lives but did little to achieve their stated goal of discouraging and erasing homosexual subcultures.

The Kinsey reports, for example, revealed that laws prohibiting homosexual activity were honored mostly in the breach: for every homosexual arrest there were tens of thousands of unarrested homosexual acts.[110] State study commissions reported that sexual psychopath laws were virtual dead letters in all states but California by 1953.[111] The witch-hunts expelling gay people from military and civil service positions were efficacious only for brief periods. Among active homosexuals, more than 95 percent were able to retain their jobs in either the military or civilian service.[112] Lesbian and gay bars dropped like flies in the face of liquor board or police harassment, but like the hydra every bar that closed was replaced by two more. Notwithstanding censors, homosexual literature flourished like Tuscan wildflowers and yielded distinguished authors such as Tennessee Williams, Carson McCullers, James Baldwin, Willa Cather, William Inge, and an explosion of lesbian pulp romances that made Ann Bannon famous.[113] Notwithstanding censors' efforts, lesbians were electrified and depressed by *Well of Loneliness,* and men masturbated over physique magazines.

Why did the American terror fail? The terror was vulnerable on pragmatic grounds for it would have been grossly expensive to carry out properly, rested upon questionable and sometimes wacky ideas, and—critically—included middle-class white men in its dragnet. Relatedly, the terror generated its own opposition. The fear upon which the terror built not only created a sense of shared identity and anger among gay people but outed many of them. Outed homosexuals had nothing to lose by resisting, and angered or concerned citizens joined them. Ironically, the American antihomosexual terror helped create a homosexual rights movement. Our nation's decentralized and libertarian constitutional structure, moreover, gave the early homophile movement breathing room to weather the most intense public and private suppression.

The foregoing problems with the antihomosexual campaign, in turn, affected the organization and strategies of homosexuals seeking survival. If a problem with the antihomosexual Kulturkampf was the nation's live-and-let-live libertarian bent, the main homophile strategy was a live-and-let-live right to privacy. Thus, Hal Call led a coup in 1953 to take control of the Mattachine Society away from founder, and former Communist, Harry Hay. Openly assimilationist, Mattachine and the Daughters of Bilitis emphasized gay people's legal privacy rights and de-emphasized their legal equality rights. Few writers were willing to say "gay is good"; instead, the defense was "please leave us alone." Privacy became a common ground for homosexuals and moderate homophobes, that is, people who were revolted by homosexuality but advocated tolerance so long as the homosexual did nothing public or assaultive. Privacy also defined the mutually protective closet: homosexuals would reside discreetly in the closet, and heterosexuals would not open the door. The legal working out of this distinctively American compromise revealed its conceptual and practical limitations, however.

Substantive Privacy

Chapter 4 of John Stuart Mill's *On Liberty* (1859) is the inspiration of a substantive understanding of legal privacy: neither the community nor the state has any business telling a person how to live her or his life (private decisions) unless the person's actions harm others or the community at large (public consequences). Under Mill's libertarian philosophy the community cannot forbid one to do something simply because it offends other people. This conception of substantive privacy served as a baseline for criticizing the intrusive antihomosexual campaign, and this critique appealed to many lawyers and doctors. But legislators were less receptive, and the experts diluted the conception of substantive privacy to the point of absurdity.

Substantive privacy had its most powerful articulation in criminal code reform commissions. Paul Tappan's New Jersey report and Francis Allen's

Illinois report, both promulgated in 1953, articulated and defended the "distinction ... between sexual deviates whose conduct in the community offends morals (homosexuals, exhibitionists), and dangerous, aggressive offenders whose behavior is a community threat (aggressive rapist, etc.)."[114] The argument of both reports, as well as those in California and New York, was Millian: the state should focus its scarce enforcement resources on sexuality that invades other people's private spheres—rape, sex with children, peeping Toms—and leave people alone so long as they do no harm to others.

Following the sex offender commissions, the prestigious American Law Institute narrowly voted in May 1955 to decriminalize consensual sodomy in a tentative draft of its proposed Model Penal Code.[115] The ALI reasoned that "[n]o harm to the secular interests of the community is involved in a typical sex practice in private between consenting adults. This area of private morals is the distinctive concern of spiritual authorities." Criminalizing such practices sapped police resources, fueled blackmail rings, and undercut "the protection to which every individual is entitled against state interference in his personal affairs when he is not hurting others."[116] On the other hand, the Model Penal Code recommended that homosexual solicitation, sex with minors, and any kind of public indecency should remain criminal.[117] These reformers were decidedly antihomosexual but willing to set aside a private space—the mutually protective closet—where homosexuals could exist without state harassment. Essentially the same position was taken by the United Kingdom's Wolfenden Report of 1957.[118]

These suggestions stimulated debate but little immediate statutory action. The center for antihomosexual repression in the 1930s, New York in 1950 followed the suggestions of Governor Dewey's study commission and broke sodomy up into three crimes: coercive sodomy and sodomy with a minor, both felonies, and consensual sodomy, reduced to a misdemeanor. In 1961 Illinois took the next step, adopting the Model Penal Code, including its decriminalization of consensual sodomy and its criminalization of sexually deviant solicitation. As Abner Mikva (one of the Code sponsors in the legislature) recalls, the sodomy deregulation provoked heated off-the-record debate, in which pragmatists of both parties prevailed. According to Dr. Charles Bowman, the chair of the lawyers' committee supporting the Code, supporters headed off opposition from the Roman Catholic Church to sodomy reform by narrowing the Code's defenses to abortion.[119]

In the 1950s Millian thinking had a greater meliorative effect on the application of antihomosexual laws. Applying libertarian assumptions of due process and the rule of lenity (ambiguities in criminal statutes should be construed against the state), judges were sometimes willing to narrow sodomy laws, albeit in bizarre ways. In *People v. Randall* (1961), for example, New York's Court of Appeals interpreted its sodomy law to criminalize only active and not passive fellatio, thereby freeing an adult defendant fellated by a minor.[120] On the other hand, decisions like these were exceptional. Most rule of lenity arguments were rejected, even when the state law only prohibited the "infamous crime against nature," because such laws assertedly had an established judicial and popular meaning. In the few cases where the rule of lenity narrowed sodomy statutes, legislatures were willing to override, as New York did to *Randall* in 1962. Also, so many different state criminal laws were applicable to homosexual activity that prosecutors could simply shift from a narrowly construed law to a broader one. The court in *Randall,* for example, reminded the state that the adult fellator could be prosecuted as an abettor of the minor's criminal sodomy.

Most of the narrowing of sodomy laws came through more informal lenity by trial judges and prosecutors. In Los Angeles, a center for homosexual arrests after the war, prosecutors were willing to accept misdemeanor pleas in most cases. A study by law students at UCLA found that 40 percent of the sodomy and oral copulation defendants in the early 1960s were able to plea down to lewd vagrancy or, in the majority of cases, public indecency. Trial judges accepted and often insisted upon public indecency as the maximum penalty because a conviction of oral copulation or lewd vagrancy required registration and revocation of professional licenses, while conviction for public indecency did not.[121]

The completely open-ended language of solicitation, vagrancy, disguise, loitering, and disorderly conduct laws—staples for arrests of ordinary homosexuals—made them candidates for narrowing constructions inspired by due process concerns. In 1947 New York City magistrates complained of the "increasing tendency to employ section 722 [disorderly conduct-degeneracy] whenever it is determined that a person should be arrested." The magistrates rejected prosecutions that did not prove intended or probable breaches of the peace and active solicitation of sodomy.[122] "The statute is not aimed at sex deviation as such—'degeneracy.'... We may not predicate guilt on the basis of personal aversion, revulsion or detestation. Justice under law is objective and impersonal."[123] Although the New York Court of Appeals ultimately rejected this approach, construing the disorderly conduct, loitering, and disguise statutes to apply to gay solicitors, "loitering homosexuals," and drag queens, respectively,[124] the magistrates' lower conviction rates drove down arrests (Appendix C3).

The District of Columbia Court of Appeals was also lenient. After a period of indecision, the court rejected prosecutions under a general assault statute when a homosexual touched a decoy cop who signaled that such touching would be welcome.[125] The court's narrowing construction still left the police free to prosecute the same conduct under a 1953 amendment, making it a crime to make lewd or indecent proposals or perform lewd or indecent acts within the District of Columbia. But in 1960 the court held that the 1953 law "was not designed or intended to apply to an act committed in privacy in the presence of a single and consenting person."[126] Relying on the common law's animus against criminalizing private conduct and against status crimes, the same ideas animating New York's trial judges seeking to trim back its disorderly conduct law, the court substantially nullified Congress's effort in 1953 to make private solicitation illegal.

The idea of lenity was also bruited about in the armed forces. An amazing glimpse into internal debates is provided by the report of a board set up to evaluate Navy policy regarding homosexuals. Captain S. H. Crittenden's 1957 report accepted "the necessity within the naval service to adhere to the policy of general non-acceptance of the homosexual offender," but subjected "fallacies concerning homosexuality"—notions that homosexuals were per se "security risks" or suffered from psychopathic mental diseases—to skeptical analysis.[127] Privacy and pragmatism explain the report's unalarmed recognition that discreet homosexuals could almost always serve without detection and its cautious proposals that Navy psychiatrists be authorized to withhold their patients' homosexual confessions, that personnel separated for homosexual tendencies presumptively be given honorable rather than blue discharges, and that personnel committing homosexual acts be permitted to remain in service if they could persuade a board that they were not "confirmed homosexuals."[128]

The Crittenden Report suggests that the military compromise reached during World War II was the long-term equilibrium policy: homosexuals could serve so long as they did not invade third-party rights and were exceedingly discreet—don't ask, don't tell. Like the Model Penal Code, this understanding of privacy epitomized the mutually protective closet. The homosexual in the Navy could have an active sex life but had to keep quiet about it, so that there would be no public scandal and homophobic sailors would not be fearful. Even more than the Model Penal Code, the Crittenden version of the closet was stacked against the homosexual, who bore the risk of exposure and was expected to lie whenever sexual orientation was a topic.

Procedural Privacy

Where substantive privacy prevented the state from criminalizing nonharmful personal conduct, procedural privacy required the state to follow specified procedures before it could apply the criminal sanction. Almost half of the assurances in the Bill of Rights involve criminal procedure, including rights to be free of unreasonable searches and seizures (fourth amendment); not to incriminate oneself (fifth); to fair bail, counsel, and trial by jury (sixth); and to be free of cruel and unusual punishment (eighth). Most state constitutions contain similar assurances. In addition to these specific procedural protections were those that judges had developed from the due process clause, especially rules against state "entrapment" of defendants and conviction upon insufficient evidence.

The Mattachine Society felt that procedural protections such as these were extremely important. Indeed, the entrapment defense helped establish the Society as the nation's premier homophile group. Responding to member Dale Jennings' arrest for allegedly soliciting an aggressive undercover cop, the Society in 1953 established a Citizens Committee to Outlaw Entrapment to raise money for Jennings' defense and public consciousness about abusive police tactics. Not only did Jennings win a hung jury using the entrapment defense, but the Mattachine Society gained its first press coverage.[129] This success reinforced the Society's legal rights orientation. The January 1954 issue of *One* contained a one-page statement of "Your Rights in Case of Arrest," which was a practical application of the abstract rights in the Constitution. The key advice was to say nothing to the police and repeatedly to ask to consult with an attorney.[130]

Did these procedural rights really matter, as Mattachine thought they did? The main reasons to think so are that additional procedures can provide defendants more opportunities to escape punishment, may raise the costs of implementing antihomosexual policies through criminal laws, and may sometimes shift public attention away from the defendant's terrible conduct to the state's horrible methods. None of these reasons, however, is clearly borne out by gay people's experience during the Kulturkampf. The main problem with the first two reasons is that, out of fear of further exposure, almost everybody pleaded guilty to charges of lewd vagrancy, degeneracy, and sodomy, and they pleaded guilty at higher rates than defendants did for similar crimes such as vagrancy, disorderly conduct, and rape.[131] In a system where everybody pleads guilty, procedural protections not only fail to raise the costs of the criminal sanction but also legitimate criminal justice systems and obscure their corrupt features.[132] When defendants fought the charges against them, the results were rarely those achieved by Mattachine in the Jennings case.

Moreover, the procedural protections actually afforded homosexual defendants depended upon political context and, hence, differed from year to year and defendant to defendant. An Oklahoma court in 1946, before the antihomosexual panic began, showed leniency toward the Reverend Kenneth Cole, accused of sodomizing a fourteen-year-old boy in his congregation *(Cole v. State)*. Because the court found the boy was a consenting accomplice—a questionable inference drawn from the boy's going to church the next day and failing to complain immediately—the judges overturned Cole's conviction for lack of corroboration.[133] Five years later, during the terror, the same court upheld the conviction of Cleveland Woody for committing two unnatural acts upon a fifteen-year-old boy *(Woody v. State)*. Unlike *Cole,* there was no evidence the boy was anything but a delighted participant, yet the court (also unlike *Cole*) refused to apply the accomplice rule. The court observed that "perversion is sufficiently prevalent that the moral forces of our State and Nation should 'view with alarm' and become greatly concerned . . . if a Sodom and Gomorrah is to be forestalled."[134] Also unlike *Cole,* where the defendant was a white minister, *Woody*'s defendant was a black janitor.

The Oklahoma cases suggest the hypothesis that abstract procedural protections did not slow down the antihomosexual juggernaut when defendants lacked resources or social standing to appeal to judges and jurors. Woody, a black man caught with a boy, was doomed, whereas middle-class child molesters like Cole sometimes got second chances, and middle-class white men who were accused only of adult solicitation, like Jennings, could get off entirely if they fought the charges (although they usually did not). The most despised group was drag queens and butch lesbians, cross-dressers outside the middle class who often dated outside their races. Although they were arrested, beaten, and harassed by the police even more than other kinds of gay people,[135] I could not find a single reported decision in the 1940s or 1950s where their procedural rights were contested or even discussed. The most legally silent were surely the least protected.

Even when the defendant was a middle-class white man doing nothing predatory, and the police were engaged in sneaky tactics, procedure usually did little good. Most of the defendant-protective rules were not highly protective. The Jennings case is the only one I have found where the defendant won with an entrapment defense, and the rule itself was full of landmines. The federal rule, followed in most states, allowed entrapment as a defense only if the defendant could establish that he had no "predisposition" to commit the crime.[136] This requirement allowed the prosecution to refocus the case on the defendant's "homosexual tendencies" or prior sex offense convictions.[137]

The U.S. Court of Appeals for the District of Columbia devised an evidentiary rule to regulate the risk of abusive undercover tactics better than the entrapment rule did. In *Kelly v. United States* (1952), Judge E. Barrett Prettyman ruled that the testimony of single witnesses to homosexual solicitations should be received "with great caution"; the defendant ought to be able to introduce evidence of good character; and trial judges ought to "require corroboration of the circumstances surrounding the parties" and their interaction.

The court extended the *Kelly* rule to homosexual assault (fondling) cases in 1956.[138] On the other hand, *Kelly*'s rule was rejected in other jurisdictions and even by the ALI's Model Penal Code. Nor was *Kelly* enthusiastically followed in the District of Columbia, whose judges and juries continued to convict homosexuals based upon nothing more than the decoy's evidence.[139]

The tendency of courts to allow prosecutors to put the defendant's sexual orientation on trial is illustrated by other evidentiary rules as well. In a leading case, *State v. McDaniel* (1956), the Arizona Supreme Court overruled fifth amendment (unlawful confession) objections to police testimony that, in casual conversation after the arrest, sodomy defendant Winston McDaniel admitted seeking medical help to cure "his proclivity or desires for having unnatural sex acts with persons of the same sex as he." The court further sustained the testimony of three youths who said that McDaniel had solicited oral sex with them before the charged incident. The traditional Anglo-American rule is that evidence of prior crimes is inadmissible, on the ground that its relevance to the probability that defendant committed the charged crime is outweighed by its likely prejudice to the defendant as a "bad person." The court defended an exception to this rule in homosexual overture cases, in part on the ground that it was introduced only to show defendant's modus operandi and in part on the ground that past evidence of "unnatural proclivities" has a particularly direct bearing on crimes "stemming from a specific emotional propensity for sexual aberration."[140]

Following *McDaniel,* most state courts held that "any act of the defendant, which . . . tends to show a course of lascivious conduct, degeneracy and sexual perversion is admissible" to show his "character and moral disposition."[141] Judges in the coastal states were more reluctant to allow such evidence.[142] In those states the main debate was whether defendants could bring in expert evidence that they were not homosexual. The Supreme Court of California ruled in *People v. Jones* (1954) that trial judges were required to allow defendants accused of sodomy to present psychiatric evidence to establish that they were not "sexual deviates." New Jersey's Supreme Court rejected such evidence as speculative but required judges to allow spouses and family to attest to defendants' heterosexuality. The leading Pennsylvania case rejected both approaches, on the view that "many admitted sodomists are also given to the more normal and accepted methods of sexual expression."[143] The Court of Military Appeals went so far as to hold that any credible evidence of heterosexual "good character" was enough to raise a reasonable doubt in court-martial sodomy proceedings.[144]

Note how even prohomosexual proof requirements, such as those of *Kelly* and *Jones,* yielded a choreography of the closet, in which a homosexual accused of illegal acts was offered an opportunity to prove he was heterosexual. Kelly's conviction was overturned in part because his coworkers were willing to vouch for his heterosexuality, and he plausibly claimed that he was walking through the park after a date with a young woman. In other cases, girlfriends or wives were useful character witnesses.[145] But once defendant's character was invoked, the prosecution was usually allowed to impeach that character, as by introducing evidence of prior homosexual acts.[146] Even in pure "homosexual act" cases, it was really the defendant's "homosexuality" that was on trial.

Civil Privacy

Before the Kulturkampf began in earnest, it was often possible for accused homosexuals to protect their jobs. Miriam Van Waters, for example, appealed to the governor of Massachusetts to preserve her job as superintendent of the Reformatory for Women, and a panel appointed by the governor recommended in 1949 that she be retained. Estelle Freedman believes that Van Waters was saved, in part, by society's confusion about the existence or nature of lesbianism. Although her lawyer denied any homosexuality at the prison, Van Waters refused to lie and, instead, sidestepped such questions by insisting that her duty was to help rehabilitate the women, not monitor their sex lives. Her unwillingness to save her job and good name by denouncing female bonding at the prison was admirable in 1949 and amazing in light of subsequent events. In 1957, just before Van Waters was to retire, the Boston newspapers rekindled the old charges of perversion ("Girl Inmates 'Wed' in Mock Prison Rites" was one headline). A legislative committee reported that "aggressive homosexuals and troublemakers" engaged in "unnatural acts" and "indoctrinated the new admissions," unchecked by the administration. The inmates were, literally, running the asylum. Margaret O'Keefe, Van Waters' long-standing deputy and her designated successor, resigned under pressure.[147]

If Van Waters survived the antihomosexual witch-hunts in the 1940s, others like O'Keefe did not in the 1950s. Unlike Van Waters, most of the survivors relied on the deep closet, daily performances of heterosexuality, or even hypocrisy—denunciations of homosexuality and accusations against homosexuals—to keep their jobs. It is striking how few relied on the law to protect their jobs or licenses, for the Supreme Court in the 1940s held that government employees enjoyed constitutional assurance of fair treatment and in the 1950s regularly overturned state employment policies aimed at political dissenters.[148] The Warren Court acknowledged a legitimate state interest in "good character" requirements but ruled that "it is equally important that the State not exercise this power in an arbitrary or discriminatory manner nor in such a way as to impinge on the freedom of political expression or association."[149] In 1958 the

Court established that military administrative discharges, like court-martial discharges, were reviewable in the courts.[150] These principles were more vigorously applied to protect political, as opposed to sexual or gender, dissidents in the 1950s.

As a practical matter, few legal protections were available to accused "sex perverts" in government employment because most accused or suspected homosexuals went without a fuss. The procedural guarantees were short-circuited by credible threats of ruinous exposure if the soldier or civil servant objected to her or his treatment. Even if suspects wanted to fight their discharges administratively or in court, there were virtually no lawyers willing to help. In response to an Air Force woman's petition for assistance, for example, the American Civil Liberties Union (ACLU) in 1951 advised her to seek medical treatment so that she could "abandon homosexual relations" that had landed her in trouble. In 1957 the ACLU's national board took the position that "[h]omosexuality is a valid consideration in evaluating the security risk factor in sensitive positions . . . It is not within the province of the Union to evaluate the social validity of the laws aimed at the suppression or elimination of homosexuals."[151]

A handful of accused homosexuals did mount legal challenges to civil exclusions. Air Force Corporal Fannie Mae Clackum was pressured to resign in 1951 upon vague allegations of homosexuality. She demanded a court-martial so she could confront the charges. The Air Force dishonorably discharged her under regulations reserving the power to issue a dishonorable discharge when there was insufficient evidence to support a court-martial. Although Clackum received a hearing on administrative appeal, the tribunal upheld her discharge based upon secret hearsay-ridden affidavits that Clackum never saw. The Court of Claims overturned the discharge on the ground that it was accomplished "without any semblance of an opportunity to know what the evidence against her was, or to face her accusers in a trial or a hearing."[152]

The decision in Clackum's case rested upon the procedural dimension of due process protection. William Lyman Dew, an air traffic controller, pressed the substantive dimension, by which government is not supposed to penalize employees without objective and defensible reasons. The Civil Aeronautics Authority terminated Dew's employment when it discovered prior admissions that he had engaged in four "unnatural sex acts" with men when he was eighteen years old. Dew introduced psychiatric expert evidence that he did not have "homosexual personality disorder" and that he was happily married with two children. Notwithstanding these trophies of heterosexuality, Dew was still let go in 1960. A divided panel of the D.C. Circuit denied his appeal. The majority deferred to the administrative hearing officer, who had found that anybody who has committed acts "repugnant to . . . decency and morality" would undermine "the efficiency of the service," the criterion for federal employment separation. Dissenting Judge J. Skelly Wright countered that "Dew is normal in all respects" and that there was no rational connection between adolescent sexual experimentation and Dew's ability to be an air traffic controller, a "job which he badly needs to support his wife and two children." Although the court upheld Dew's dismissal, the agency reversed itself and restored Dew to his position after the Supreme Court granted review in the case.[153]

These successful due process challenges to federal witch-hunts were themselves evidence of the power of the closet. William Dew presented himself as a wronged heterosexual, and Fannie Mae Clackum secluded her sexuality behind procedural veils. Like the entrapment and corroboration defenses in criminal cases, the due process arguments in employment cases deployed classic libertarian technique: shift focus from the shameful substance (homosexuality) to neutral procedure (state arbitrariness and dirty dealing). The libertarian strategy not only mimicked the mutually protective closet but helped create it, by offering homophile groups and moderate homophobes a common ground in which homosexuals would be let alone so long as they acknowledged the shamefulness of sexual and gender deviation.

Resistance: The Gay-Threatening Closet

By 1961 the mutually protective closet was American public policy. But it was an unstable policy, in part because it was such a rotten deal for gay people. Increasing numbers of them were fed up with a privacy jurisprudence that allowed plenty of room for homophobes to penetrate the closet and attack homosexuals in unpredictable spurts of witch-hunting. An article in the *Village Voice* explained why "so many fairies [have] come out in the open" in the late 1950s, after years of "cring[ing] behind a mask of fear." They were fed up with "this degrading of our personalities" through police harassment, job discrimination, state exclusions, and sham marriages. "Merely to live, we must assert ourselves as homosexuals," and "accept it or not, we will force our way into open society and you will have to acknowledge us."[154] Every bad encounter a gay person had with the law was an opportunity for the sort of epiphany playwright James Barr had when he was run out of the Navy: "For the first time in my life it was not a completely personal issue with me. Whether I wanted to or not, in defending myself I was forced to defend the rights and concepts of a group numbering hundreds of thousands."[155]

The law helped engender a *group identity* among gay people both by persecuting them as gays and by protecting gay public expression. The first feature grew out of the failures of privacy jurisprudence, the second out of the successes of first amendment jurisprudence. A third feature, the insistence by gay people that they were a minority group entitled to the same treatment as everyone else, was encouraged by equal protection jurisprudence.

Freedom of Association (Organizations and Bars)

Just as gay people were becoming politically mobilized, the Warren Court was giving the first amendment teeth, protecting the rights of Communists and African Americans to associate and criticize state policies.[156] The Court was building a first amendment tradition defined by its willingness to protect unpopular groups. As one judge put it, "Even homosexuals and reprobates who prey upon their hapless condition are entitled to find refuge in [constitutional] dictates. Freedom of association is one of them. Freedom of expression is another."[157] This statement, by the way, came in a dissenting opinion. The first amendment was not *that* empowering to homosexuals, but it did assure them some breathing room to socialize and organize.

The Daughters of Bilitis and the Mattachine Society tailored their goals around the first amendment's core protections. Thus, Mattachine described itself as "a group of persons (not necessarily variants), interested in doing research, education and conducting social action for the benefit of the variant minority and, in turn, for the benefit of society as a whole." The Daughters' goals were "to enlighten the public about the Lesbian and to teach them that we aren't the monsters that they depict us to be," and to "offer[] the Lesbian an outlet in meeting others."[158] Even the homophobic FBI acquiesced in these organizations' right to exist, but it was an existence that kowtowed to fifties' orthodoxies. It was not until the late 1950s that members of these organizations dropped their pseudonyms, even with one another. Neither organization argued that public solicitation or even consensual sodomy was acceptable, or that the first amendment protected indiscreet homosexuals from losing their jobs.

During the antihomosexual terror, the most sustained legal resistance involved the revocation of liquor licenses. Owners of profitable gay bars could afford to pay off investigators or, failing that, to retain counsel to challenge regulatory action. In most states they regularly lost. The New York Court of Appeals held in 1952 that the State Liquor Authority (SLA) could close bars that became regular resorts of homosexuals.[159] The only cases that regulators seemed to lose in the 1950s were those where there were insufficiently systematic observations by shocked police officers.[160] The SLA tended to win all the cases where it relied on detailed affidavits by its undercover investigators who returned time and again to an establishment to be solicited and fondled. Most state courts were even more acquiescent, allowing license suspensions simply for "permitting persons who conspicuously displayed by speech, tone of voice, bodily movements, gestures, and other mannerisms the common characteristics of homosexuals *habitually* and *in inordinate numbers* (on one occasion, as many as 45) to *congregate.*"[161]

Only one state's courts offered substantial protection for gay bars. The California Supreme Court in *Stoumen v. Reilly* (1951) overturned the revocation of the Black Cat's liquor license. The Alcoholic Beverage Control (ABC) Department rested its decision on the fact that homosexuals socialized at the Black Cat, with Stoumen's knowledge. The court held that this was legally insufficient. "Members of the public of lawful age have a right to patronize a public restaurant and bar so long as they are not committing illegal or immoral acts." It was not clear whether that right was constitutional, common law, or merely statutory, but (unlike New York and New Jersey courts) the California court relied on the right as the basis for holding that the ABC statute was not violated by proof of "patronage of a public restaurant and bar by homosexuals . . . without proof of the commission of illegal or immoral acts on the premises."[162]

The legislature responded to *Stoumen* in 1955 with the law (quoted above) closing down establishments that were a "resort" for "sexual perverts." Under this broad legislative authorization, the ABC Department was able to close down homosexual bars right and left, including Hazel Nickola's bar and Pearl Kershaw's bar, and of course the Black Cat.[163] In a test case, Mary Azar and Albert Vallerga, owners of the First and Last Chance Bar in Oakland, conceded that their bar was a "resort for homosexuals" and argued that the 1955 amendment was unconstitutional. Their position was supported by an amicus brief prepared by ACLU attorneys Morris and Juliet Lowenthal. In *Vallerga v. Department of Alcoholic Beverage Control* (1959), the California Supreme Court cautiously invalidated the 1955 amendment as inconsistent with the freedom of association recognized in *Stoumen*. The court emphasized that the ABC Department did not rely on investigative reports of lewd conduct and did not rely on its revocation authority under the pre-1955 statutory prohibition of bars' being used as a "disorderly house or place . . . in which people abide or to which resort [is had] for purposes which are injurious to the public morals."[164] The court further recognized that the right of association does not carry with it the right to engage in indecent public displays and suggested that reports of "women dancing with other women and women kissing other women," the conduct sanctioned in the Kershaw litigation, would have sustained a revocation consistent with *Stoumen.*[165]

Although it was the first decision to strike down an antihomosexual statute as unconstitutional, *Vallerga* was a compromise that established a closet on terms unfavorable to homosexuals: they had a theoretical right to congregate but not if they touched or kissed one another, as that would be offensive to the hypothetical heterosexual. The California appellate courts deployed this narrow reasoning to uphold post-*Vallerga* license revocations of the 585 Club, the Paper Doll, and (of course) the Black Cat based upon decoy cop testimony about kissing, dancing, and advances by homosexual patrons.[166]

Freedom of Speech and Press (Homophile Publications)

By the 1950s it was settled that the first amendment protects some sensual publications but not obscene ones. Two California decisions handed down in 1957 illustrated vastly different viewpoints as to what was obscene. *One, Inc.* had sued for an order declaring its October 1954 issue mailable as nonobscene. On appeal from an adverse trial judgment, a federal court of appeals applied the traditional depraves-the-morals test to hold that the three items cited by the Postmaster were "nothing more than cheap pornography calculated to promote lesbianism" (short story "Sappho Remembered") and material that was "dirty, vulgar and offensive to the moral senses" (a poem) and "morally depraving and debasing" (a magazine ad).[167]

The depraves-the-morals approach had been rejected during the 1930s in cases involving *Well of Loneliness, If It Die,* and *Ulysses* (Chapter 1) in favor of an approach that examined the work as a whole to determine whether it had any redeeming artistic or social value, or appealed to nothing but prurience. In *People v. Ferlinghetti* Municipal Judge Clayton Horn applied this newer approach to acquit the defendants for selling Allen Ginsberg's *Howl.* As to the state's charge that *Howl* used "filthy, vulgar, obscene, and disgusting language," Horn's opinion replied that the first amendment protects "novel and unconventional ideas," even when they "disturb the complacent." He continued:

> The People state that it is not necessary to use [vulgar] words and that others would be more palatable to good taste. The answer is that life is not encased in one formula whereby everyone acts the same or conforms to a particular pattern. No two persons think alike; we were all made from the same mold but in different patterns. Would there be any freedom of press or speech if one must reduce his vocabulary to vapid innocuous euphemism?[168]

This remarkable opinion matched Ginsberg's remarkable poem. *Howl* was a raucous, sodomy-saturated, mocking attack on conformity in general and closeted sexuality in particular, and Horn's opinion said this was precisely what the first amendment protects.

Later that year, in *Roth v. United States* (1957), the Supreme Court reaffirmed that obscenity was not speech under the first amendment but limited obscenity to "material which deals with sex in a manner appealing to prurient interest," that is, "material having a tendency to excite lustful thoughts." Justice William Brennan's *Roth* opinion seemed to fall between the broad view of obscenity in *One, Inc.* and the broad view of the first amendment in *Ferlinghetti.* Indeed, he explicitly endorsed the centrist approach expressed by the ALI's draft Model Penal Code. The ALI posited that a work was obscene "if, considered as a whole, its predominant appeal is to prurient interest, i.e., a shameful or morbid interest in nudity, sex, or excretion, and if it goes substantially beyond customary limits of candor in description or representation of such matters."[169] Under such a vague standard, however, reasonable people might differ as to the obscenity of *Howl* or "Sappho Revisited."

In January 1958 the Supreme Court in a one-sentence unsigned opinion reversed the Ninth Circuit's *One, Inc.* disposition, under authority of *Roth.*[170] This suggested that the Court was open to the view that discussion of homosexual intimacy was not in itself an appeal to "prurient" interests. The next year, in *Kingsley International Pictures Corporation v. Regents* (1959), the Court struck down New York's film licensing law on the ground that it targeted movies because of their content ("sexual immorality, perversion, or lewdness"). In *Manual Enterprises, Inc. v. Day* (1962), the Court held that the Post Office could not refuse mail services for male physique magazines because pictures of semi-nude male physiques were not "patently offensive" to community standards.[171]

Although lower federal and state courts did not read *Roth* and its progeny liberally,[172] these obscenity decisions contributed to the growth of lesbian and gay subcultures. The Court's precedents gave nationwide protection against state censorship to homophile informational publications and literature *(One)*, physique magazines *(Manual Enterprises)*, and movies treating issues of sexual expression *(Kingsley).* Freedom to publish meant that a few openly homosexual authors could reach millions of curious readers. The same year that *Roth* was handed down was the year Ann Bannon's *Odd Girl Out* was published. Bannon went on to become the most successful of the lesbian romance authors, and her novels and other "lesbian pulps" were needed supplements to the depressing *Well of Loneliness.* While the girl did not always get the other girl, as occurred in "Sappho Revisited," these novels presented lesbians as worthy, interesting people. Women in the most rural community could share with their sisters in the city the electrifying idea that it was natural and romantic for women to love other women. Male physique magazines revealed to men all over the country that the male body could be a source of erotic attraction. Just as the censors feared, ideas and images could be revolutionary.

Equal Protection (State Employment)

After he lost his federal job in 1957, Franklin Kameny sued. His lawyers followed the safe approach of challenging the procedures and reasons surrounding the discharge, and they lost. Writing his own petition for review by the Supreme Court, Kameny introduced egalitarian arguments similar to those of Donald Webster Cory's *The Homosexual in America* (1951). The civil service's action and allied federal policies reduced homosexuals like himself to second-class citizenship, Kameny argued. Discrimination based upon homosexual orientation was "no less illegal than discrimination based on religious or racial grounds." The Supreme Court denied the petition without comment in 1961, and Kameny founded the Mattachine Society of Washington (MSW) shortly thereafter.[173]

Whereas the West Coast Mattachine groups sought to persuade straight society to tolerate homosexuals who would occupy a mutually protective closet, MSW followed Kameny's Supreme Court petition to insist upon equal rights of the "homosexual minority." The stated goals of the group were "to secure for homosexuals the basic rights and liberties established by the word and spirit of the Constitution of the United States" and "[t]o equalize the status and position of the homosexual with those of the heterosexual by achieving equality under law, equality of opportunity, equality in the society of his fellow men, and by eliminating adverse prejudice, both private and official" and "[t]o secure for the homosexual the right, as a human being, to develop and achieve his full potential and dignity, and the right, as a citizen, to make his maximum contribution to the society in which he lives."[174] This statement of purpose represented an intellectual turning point in the history of gaylaw. The libertarian closet that Mattachine (Los Angeles) and the ALI viewed as mutually protective was considered a threatening closet by Kameny and Mattachine (Washington), a prison and not a refuge for homosexuals. The jurisprudence of privacy was superseded by a jurisprudence of equality.

Kameny explicitly invoked the civil rights movement as a model for gay people. In a letter to Attorney General Robert Kennedy, Kameny argued that MSW was engaged in the same kind of civil rights struggle as the National Association for the Advancement of Colored People, namely, "fighting personal prejudice at all levels. For these reasons, and because we are trying to improve the position of a large group of citizens presently relegated to second-class citizenship in many respects, we should have, if anything, the assistance of the Federal government, and not its opposition."[175] Inspired by the Warren Court's activism against race-based apartheid, MSW initiated a litigation campaign against what I call the apartheid of the closet. This equality-based agenda opened up a new era in the struggle for gay rights, explored in the next chapter.

3. Coming Out and Challenging the Closet, 1961–1981

The homosexual in 1961 was smothered by law. She or he risked arrest and possible police brutalization for dancing with someone of the same sex, cross-dressing, propositioning another adult homosexual, possessing a homophile publication, writing about homosexuality without disapproval, displaying pictures of two people of the same sex in intimate positions, operating a lesbian or gay bar, or actually having oral or anal sex with another adult homosexual. The last was a serious felony in all states but one, and in most jurisdictions also carried with it possible indefinite incarceration as a sexual psychopath. Misdemeanor arrests for sex-related vagrancy or disorderly conduct offenses meant that the homosexual might have her or his name published in the local newspaper, would probably lose her or his job, and in several states would have to register as a sex offender. If the homosexual were not a citizen, she or he would likely be deported. If the homosexual were a professional—teacher, lawyer, doctor, mortician, beautician—she or he could lose the certification needed to practice that profession. If the charged homosexual were a member of the armed forces, she or he might be court-martialed and would likely be dishonorably discharged and lose all veterans' benefits.

This situation was intolerable to a growing number of gay people. The law's role in maintaining a regime of the closet was under light fire before 1961, but that year saw heavier volleys on both coasts: Frank Kameny founded the Mattachine Society of Washington (MSW) as the first group insisting on equal legal rights for gay people, and José Sarria, a well-known waiter at the Black Cat bar, won 6,000 votes as the first openly gay candidate for a seat on San Francisco's Board of Supervisors. Sarria's candidacy inspired the formation of the Society for Individual Rights (SIR) in early 1964. Like MSW, SIR informed gay people of their constitutional rights at the same time it insisted upon equal rights for the homosexual minority. Historian John D'Emilio has documented the efflorescence of homophile organizations during the 1960s and their general embrace of an unapologetic approach epitomized by Kameny's catchphrase, "Gay Is Good."[1]

The invigorated homophile movement confronted authorities in a series of public protests and melees in Washington, Philadelphia, and San Francisco. The grand melee came on the night of June 27–28, 1969, when the New York City police raided a Greenwich Village gay bar, the Stonewall Inn. Rather than going along with the raid and arrests, the drag queens, butch lesbians, and fairies fought back—freeing the prisoners and pelting the police with cans, bottles, and coins. Mild rioting occurred that night and the next two. Among the witnesses was poet Allen Ginsberg, who remarked: "You know the guys there were so beautiful—they've lost that wounded look that fags all had ten years ago."[2] Literally overnight, the Stonewall riots transformed the *homophile reform movement* of several dozen homosexuals into a *gay liberation movement* populated by thousands of lesbians, gay men, and bisexuals who formed hundreds of organizations demanding radical changes in the way gay people were treated by the state.[3]

The overriding political goal was to end the tyranny of the "closet" by assuring gay people space in which to "come out."[4] This, in turn, involved three overlapping legal struggles, all of which had started in the 1950s. Some gays in the 1950s used the term "coming out" to denote one's first sexual experience,[5] and the most basic struggle was to assure *private gay spaces*—the home, the car, the toilet booth—against spying and intrusion of the police. As early as the 1930s, coming out had been used to denote a person's entry into gay subculture, like a debutante's coming out into polite society.[6] Thus, a second struggle for gays was the creation of stable *institutions of gay subculture*—bars and restaurants, social and educational organizations, and literature, including erotica. By the early 1960s, coming out also came to mean sharing one's sexuality with outsiders,[7] and "coming out of the closet" translated into public openness about one's minority sexual orientation. A third struggle, therefore, was for *equal gay citizenship*. Like African Americans before them, openly gay people insisted on equal treatment as employees, soldiers, immigrants, and parents.

Like the civil rights movement, the gay rights movement necessarily turned to the law, which had recently targeted them for erasure. By the 1960s, gay rights advocates seized upon new constitutional rights to pursue each of the foregoing struggles: the right to privacy (due process and the fourth amendment) was the rallying call for protecting private gay spaces; rights of assocation, speech, and press (first amendment) protected the territory of gay subculture; and equality rights (due process, then equal protection) pressed the agenda of full gay citizenship. Litigation accompanied and sometimes preceded political efforts. In each arena, gay-friendly attorneys and groups appropriated doctrines developed by the U.S. Supreme Court in other contexts—involving Communists, African Americans, and women—and pressed them in progay directions.

The remainder of this chapter will trace the main legal developments and the ways in which gay people benefited from the civil rights movement and its nationalization of rights. The criminal, first amendment, and equality rights the Warren Court created at the behest of the civil rights movement and the American Civil Liberties Union (ACLU) were directly applicable to gay people. The image of a neutral law provided just about the only way gays could appeal to an antigay judiciary to protect private gay spaces and the territory of gay subculture, even if episodically. Contrary to its critics, rights discourse with all its fuzzy edges tangibly worked to the benefit of the most despised minority in America, at least by empowering gays in their interactions with antigay police, censors, and state employers. Indeed, rights created for the benefit of blacks and the poor may have benefited white middle-class gay people more than they actually helped blacks and poor people.

On the other hand, gay citizenship did not make much progress until gay people came out of their closets in substantial numbers. Gay equality was impossible before gay people mobilized politically. This is a phenomenon women as well as people of color have understood: judges did them little good until they had proven themselves to be a robust interest group that must be accommodated in a viable pluralism. This suggests a broader point: law changes as the balance of social power changes, and changes in the law provoke new social movements. Thus, the antihomosexual Kulturkampf in the 1950s triggered the gay rights movement, which in turn contributed to the crystallization of the religious right as a political movement in the 1970s.

The law itself enjoyed this triumph: by 1981 discourse about homosexuality had, to some extent, shifted from moral and medical discourses to rights discourse. Not only did gay people come to see their demands in terms of legal rights but so did their opponents. Without abandoning religion-based (homosexuality is immoral) or medical-based (and sick) rhetoric, antigay campaigns countered gays' right to come out of the closet with the right of children, parents, and homophobes to keep gays in the closet, at least in some fora. Although progress toward gay rights was made across the board by 1981, antigay discourse preserved military service and marriage as compulsorily heterosexual. In both cases, opponents capitalized on deep-seated prejudice and fear of gay people, but under the banner of often unprejudiced rights rhetoric: gays in the military would invade the privacy rights of straights, and same-sex marriage would undermine the marriage rights of different-sex couples. In these areas alone, the apartheid of the closet held firm: gay people could serve in the military and get married only so long as the state could look the other way.

Private Gay Spaces (Due Process, Fourth Amendment)

Although the due process clause is often taken to be the traditionalist anchor of the Constitution, the Warren Court interpreted it in light of the general policy it embodied: individual liberty should not be at the mercy of arbitrary state intrusion. Thus, the Court in the 1960s nationalized the criminal procedure protections in the Bill of Rights to apply to state police harassment of people of color and ethnic minorities; created a substantive right of privacy to protect women's reproductive freedom through contraception and abortion; and gave teeth to the doctrine that vague criminal laws were unenforceable, applying this doctrine to strike down vagrancy laws and other relics of the past that were used to control the lives and movement of poor people. None of the Court's due process decisions involved openly gay litigants, but gay-friendly lawyers deployed the precedents to protect private gay spaces against police intrusion and harassment. Unlike the 1950s, when due process rights had little utility, now due process arguments often had bite for gay people, in large part because they contributed to gay political empowerment, which in turn affected police practices on a large scale. During the period 1961 to 1981, enforcement of criminal laws in most major American cities shifted from a focus on incidents of cross-dressing, consensual oral sex and solicitation, and same-sex fondling and dancing to a focus on incidents of homosexual and transgendered prostitution, sex with minors, and pornography.

The Criminal Procedure Revolution

Between 1961 and 1969 the Warren Court nationalized the rights of criminal defendants by "incorporating" most of the Bill of Rights into the due process clause, which rendered them directly applicable to the states. Among the rights of criminal defendants that were nationalized were the fourth amendment right to be free of unreasonable searches and seizures, expanded to exclude evidence illegally obtained; the fifth amendment right not to incriminate oneself, expanded to require police to warn the accused that anything he said might be used against him; the sixth amendment rights to speedy trials, confrontation of witnesses, and state-provided counsel, expanded to require police to tell suspects they had a right to counsel; and the eighth amendment right to be free of cruel and unusual punishment, including the right not to be arrested for a status crime.[8]

Homophile organizations were alert to these legal rights and helped gay people to make use of them. Elaborating on *One, Inc.*'s 1954 list, MSW and SIR in the mid-1960s distributed to their gay communities a detailed instructions sheet on what to do "if you are arrested."[9] The main advice was to say nothing to the police and to demand an attorney. Homophile organizations and the ACLU also helped gay people escape punishment by suppressing illegally obtained evidence in individual cases. When Philadelphia police in March 1968 arrested twelve customers at a lesbian bar and extracted admissions from them, the Daughters of Bilitis retained a lawyer who persuaded the district attorney to drop the charges because the interrogations violated *Miranda*.[10] By the early 1970s gay defendants were not only able to resist the criminal justice system by suppressing evidence but occasionally sued the state for damages to compensate for rights violations.[11]

The vigorous new criminal procedure rights worked for gay people in various ways: ex post, by providing a basis for reversing their convictions or persuading the state not to prosecute and, ex ante, by raising the costs of antigay prosecutions generally and by assuring defendants of attorneys who put the state to its proof, which was typically shaky. These rights had more utility for gay people than in the 1950s because middle-class defendants were less willing to plea-bargain charges. Emboldened not only by their new rights, but also by coaching from the requisite counsel, gay people increasingly fought the charges, often won, and in state courts were sometimes able to create new procedural rights particularly relevant to gay defendants. In *Bielicki v. Superior Court* (1962), the California Supreme Court overturned Robert Bielicki's conviction for oral sex in a public toilet. The court suppressed the testimony of police toilet spies, under both the California and U.S. Constitutions, because spying invaded the "personal right of privacy of the person occupying the stall" and represented an abusive police practice. By extending the protective closet to include water closets, the court was extending unprecedented legal rights to homosexual male cruisers.[12]

The Warren Court endorsed *Bielicki*'s privacy-based understanding of the fourth amendment in *Katz v. United States* (1967). The Court held that use of a public telephone booth is constitutionally protected against warrantless searches because the user has a "reasonable expectation of privacy."[13] After *Katz* ratified its analytical framework, the *Bielicki* holding that (closed) toilet stalls are a zone of privacy was adopted in states as diverse as Texas, Maryland, and Michigan.[14] California's Supreme Court extended *Bielicki*'s rule against police surveillance to open toilet stalls in *People v. Triggs* (1973), finding that the "expectation of privacy a person has when he enters a rest room is reasonable and is not diminished or destroyed because the toilet stall being used lacks a door."[15] Some courts expanded *Bielicki* and *Katz* to review sodomy convictions for men having sex in automobiles and adult theater booths.[16]

The translation of "rights" into acceptable police practices was a political rather than purely legal process, as illustrated by the experience in San Francisco between 1961 and 1981. A benefit ball hosted by the Council on Religion and the Homosexual (CRH) was raided by the police on New Year's Day 1965, in violation of an agreement with the city and of the fourth amendment's warrant requirement. The raid triggered a firestorm of press attention and outrage, less because of its constitutional improprieties and more because respectable ministers and other straight people felt the harassment usually reserved for gays.[17] The controversy cowed police harassment for several years and impelled the department to establish a liaison with the gay community, which in turn formed a "Citizens Alert" answering service where people could report police misbehavior. When the police again stepped up harassment in 1970–71, gay groups not only protested but went to the ballot box to elect a progay sheriff, Richard Hongisto. Electoral muscle proved to be the turning point: after 1971, police harassment immediately shifted from sex in restrooms and parks to commercial sex, pornography, and public solicitation. Gay political power increased with the election of Harvey Milk as Supervisor and George Moscone as Mayor in 1978 (both were later assassinated), and with it police receptiveness to gay interests. By 1981, San Francisco sported openly gay police officers and prosecuted straight youth for gay-bashing incidents.[18]

Progress was more uneven in New York City. Although elected with gay support, Mayor John Lindsay in 1966 announced a campaign to rid Times Square of undesirable elements, including people the *New York Times* referred to as "promenading perverts." The New York Mattachine Society and the ACLU protested the crackdown; their main talking points were the violation of rights by police when decoy cops entrapped gay people and illegally interrogated them. In response, the police promised to avoid entrapment and to reduce the number of officers assigned to gay vice; arrests, naturally, fell off, only to revive in 1969 (when Lindsay was reelected), culminating in the Stonewall riots of June.[19] A turning point was a 1970 raid of The Snake Pit, resulting in the arrest of 167 patrons and the death of one frightened arrestee who was impaled on a spike iron fence. Gay organizations conducted a vigil for the dying "criminal," and mainstream politicians, including Congressman Ed Koch, savaged the police. After 1970, police beatings of gay people triggered detailed documenta-tion, press coverage, and often protests, followed by meetings with the mayor's office, police officials, and the human rights office. By 1973, gay groups gained regular access to police chiefs, who proved increasingly responsive to gay demands. When Koch became mayor in 1978, one of his first acts was a direc-tive prohibiting sexual orientation discrimination by all municipal agencies, including the police department, which established an Office of Equal Employ-ment Opportunity to investigate discrimination complaints within the depart-ment. By 1980, "serious police harassment of gay people had become uncommon in New York City. When it did occur the reaction was swift and strong."[20]

A similar story of harassment/protest/abatement/renewed harassment/ political turning point can be told for most big cities in this period. In Washing-ton, D.C., the turning point was home rule in 1975: the Gay Activists Alliance (GAA) persuaded the city council to eliminate funding for the District's morals squad in 1975, and enacted a Human Rights Act in 1977, which formally assured gays of city employment nondiscrimination. In Los Angeles, it was the election of Burt Pines as district attorney in 1973: Pines was able to halve the number of lewd vagrancy arrests by 1974 and eat away at the vice squad's bud-get, so that Los Angeles's notorious antigay vice enforcement had been largely defanged by 1981. And so on.[21] The details of these stories in individual cities are less important than the general lesson: rights for gay people accused of con-sensual sex crimes did not affect arrest rates until gay political power forced police departments to consider their interests. In turn, however, gay politics deployed rights discourse to put the police on the defensive and, gradually, to leverage concessions from the political system. Once an electorate could iden-tify progay candidates such as Hongisto, Pines, and Koch with "law and order," such candidates were electable in big cities.

The Substantive Right of Privacy

The Model Penal Code reflected a modest conception of sexual privacy. Until 1969, however, the Code's decriminalization of private sodomy between con-senting adults was adopted in Illinois alone and was specifically rejected by reform-minded commissions or legislatures in Florida, Minnesota, New York, and Maryland.[22] Such a gay-averse understanding of privacy was reflected in *Griswold v. Connecticut* (1965), where the Supreme Court recognized a consti-tutional "right to privacy" as the basis for invalidating anticontraception laws. Because the plaintiffs were married, Justice Douglas's opinion for the Court emphasized the marital features of the new right. Concurring Justices Harlan,

Goldberg, Brennan, and Warren explicitly distanced the right to marital privacy from "[a]dultery and homosexuality," two foci of apparently legitimate state regulation.[23] With two dissenters from the judgment and at least four Justices explicitly denouncing "homosexuality" and the opinion for the Court stressing the marital context of the contraception, *Griswold* did not appear to protect private gay spaces.

Yet *Griswold* opened the courts to a new constitutional ground for challenging state sodomy laws and was the occasion for a new ally to join the homophile cause: the national ACLU, which not only reversed its antigay 1957 policy after *Griswold* but agreed with gay rights groups that the new constitutional right to privacy was inconsistent with the criminalization of consensual adult sodomy.[24] Subsequent Supreme Court articulations of the right to privacy encouraged this interpretation. Justice William Brennan's opinion for the Court in *Eisenstadt v. Baird* (1972) held that *Griswold* was not limited to the marital relationship. "If the right of privacy means anything, it is the right of the *individual,* married or single, to be free from unwarranted government intrusion into matters so fundamentally affecting a person as the decision whether to bear or beget a child." For that proposition, Brennan cited *Stanley v. Georgia* (1969), where the Court had ruled unconstitutional the invasion of a person's home to arrest a man for possessing illegal pornography.[25]

Encouraged by these precedents, the ACLU brought a class action lawsuit challenging Virginia's sodomy law in 1973. The majority of the three-judge court rejected the ACLU arguments, reading *Griswold* in light of the antihomosexual rhetoric of its concurring opinions. Dissenting Judge Robert Mehrige interpreted *Griswold* and *Eisenstadt* as implementing the ALI's position that consensual adult sexual intimacy conducted in private cannot be criminalized. The Supreme Court summarily affirmed the panel in *Doe v. Commonwealth's Attorney* (1976).[26] Although summary affirmances have unclear precedential value, the Burger Court was unmistakably signaling its disinclination to expand its procreation-oriented privacy jurisprudence to protect homosexually oriented sodomy.

Still, sodomy law challenges continued at the state level, where the right of privacy was pressed under state as well as federal constitutional law. Consistent with *Doe,* the large majority of judges—and every state judge to address the issue in the South—rejected such challenges (Appendix A1). Illustrative was the case of Eugene Enslin, the manager of a massage parlor in Jacksonville, North Carolina. As part of a campaign to close down Enslin's massage parlor, the police enlisted the services of a seventeen-year-old marine, who offered the massage parlor thirty dollars for acts of heterosexual prostitution. When Enslin refused, the marine expressed interest in sex with Enslin himself, which was mutually acceptable without payment. Although the police staking out the massage parlor could not view the encounter, the marine testified that he and Enslin engaged in consensual oral sex. Enslin was sentenced to a year in jail for violating North Carolina's "crime against nature" statute. (The marine was not prosecuted but did transfer to another unit outside North Carolina.) The ACLU's new Privacy Project, founded in 1973 by Marilyn Haft, litigated and lost Enslin's case in North Carolina courts; only Justices Brennan and Marshall of the Supreme Court were willing to review the case.[27]

By the time Enslin's privacy arguments were conclusively rejected in 1976, similar arguments had prevailed in nineteen other states, usually in their legislatures rather than their courts.[a] Most of the states repealed their consensual sodomy laws as part of a general recodification of their criminal codes along the lines suggested by the Model Penal Code. Many state legislators did not focus on the revisions' allowance of consensual sodomy. Indeed, two states (Arkansas [1977] and Idaho [1972]) reinstated their sodomy laws after it came to legislators' attention that their enactment of the Model Penal Code protected the privacy of "homosexuals"! Reflecting similar sentiments, six states decriminalized different-sex sodomy and left same-sex sodomy a crime, albeit a misdemeanor (Kansas [1969], Texas [1973], Kentucky [1974], Arkansas [1977], Missouri [1977], Nevada [1977]). Tennessee followed in 1989. Montana's revised code maintained same-sex sodomy as a felony when it decriminalized different-sex sodomy; Oklahoma and Maryland reached the same results after 1981 by judicial decision. The evidence from these states suggests that in the Baptist South and the Mormon West moralist opposition to homosexuality was a substantial barrier to decriminalization of homosexual conduct, even when equally sinful heterosexual conduct was decriminalized.

Even in less traditionalist states, the privacy-moralism debate was fierce. California's Committee for Sexual Law Reform conducted a constitutional guerrilla war against the state sodomy and oral copulation laws in the early 1970s, regularly winning dismissals of criminal prosecutions from trial judges and simultaneously pressing for state adoption of Representative Willie Brown's sex law reform bill in Sacramento. Originally introduced in 1969, Brown's bill was the first state legislative initiative that focused on reforming sodomy law in particular. Its enactment over determined opposition in May 1975 was a water-

---

a. The states were Illinois (1961), Connecticut (1969), Colorado (1971), Idaho (1971, sodomy law reinstated 1972), Oregon (1971), Delaware (1972), Hawaii (1972), Ohio (1972), North Dakota (1973), New Hampshire (1973), Arkansas (1975, sodomy law reinstated 1977), California (1975), Maine (1975), New Mexico (1975), Washington (1975), Indiana (1976), Iowa (1976), South Dakota (1976), and West Virginia (1976). The years in parentheses reflect dates of enactment; most of the statutory repeals did not take effect for a year or two later. For citations, see Appendix A1.

shed. The debate saw two previously unorganized groups coalesce: a gay rights lobby versus an evangelical Christian lobby. Each contended for the votes of the middle, and when the evangelicals in California lost they, significantly, formed a "Coalition of Christian Ministers" to seek a state referendum to repeal the law. Although the coalition drew too few signatures to trigger a referendum, their effort foreshadowed twenty years of antigay referenda. Moreover, the California debate revealed sharp new lines of intellectual debate over the meaning of privacy. Progay legislators like Brown argued for privacy as a right to be let alone by the government in matters of personhood, fundamentally including sexual expression. Antigay legislators like H. L. Richardson went beyond—but did not ignore—traditionalist arguments ("homosexuality is a sin" and gay people "molest children") by denying that the Brown bill's allowance of homosexuality could be confined to the private sphere: homosexuals spread venereal disease and therefore were a public health menace; courts would extend the bill's protections to "the beaches, the bushes, and the restrooms" (as California's high court had already done); and impressionable children would receive the message that "homosexuality is okay."[28]

Because it uncloseted the relationship between privacy and homosexuality and revealed the intensity of political opposition, the California debate marked the end of the period where sodomy repeal could free ride on general criminal code revision along Model Penal Code lines. In 1976 (the year California's reform took effect), four states repealed their consensual sodomy laws as part of a general criminal code revision; three states did so in 1977; two did so in 1978; none have done so since 1978 (see Appendix A1). After 1978, sodomy repeal efforts had to stand on their own, and for that reason the successes were usually tied to judicial more than legislative campaigns. For example, the New Jersey Supreme Court's expansive view of the right to privacy pushed that state's legislature toward sodomy repeal in 1978. After New Jersey's repeal, decriminalization came by judicial decree in New York (1980), Pennsylvania (1980), Kentucky (1992), Tennessee (1996), Montana (1997), and Georgia (1998), and by targeted legislative repeal in Wisconsin (1983), Nevada (1993), the District of Columbia (1994), and Rhode Island (1998).

The New York Court of Appeals' decision in *People v. Onofre* (1980) was potentially the most significant, as it adopted the vision of privacy pressed in amicus briefs by the Bar of the City of New York, the ACLU, and the Lambda Legal Defense and Education Fund. According to the court, the right to privacy is not limited to marriage and procreation-based activities and is "a right of independence in making certain kinds of important decisions, with a concomitant right to conduct oneself in accordance with those decisions, undeterred by governmental restraint."[29] Three years later, the court of appeals extended that reasoning to invalidate New York's lewd solicitation law; Pennsylvania courts followed a similar approach to strike down that state's sodomy and lewd solicitation laws as well.[30] This radical view of privacy enjoyed wide support. By 1983 twenty-five states, representing almost 60 percent of the American population, had decriminalized consensual sodomy;[b] eleven states representing about 15 percent of the population had reduced consensual sodomy to a misdemeanor or to misdemeanor-level sentence;[c] fourteen states and the District of Columbia, representing more than a quarter of the population, prohibited consensual sodomy as a felony.[d] Even in states that continued to criminalize sodomy, moreover, the law was almost never applied in situations where two adults were engaged in secluded, consensual sexual intercourse (Appendix C2). Sodomy laws were in these states overwhelmingly deployed in nonconsensual cases of rape and sex with a minor, cases usually involving heterosexual intercourse. As applied in consensual situations, sodomy laws were used as the legal basis to monitor gay cruising areas (like public restrooms) and to investigate or raid quasi-public fora—adult bookstores, sex clubs, gay baths, and massage parlors (the situation in *Enslin*). The only reported case I have seen in the last twenty-five years where a sodomy law was applied to criminalize consensual sex in a private home was the case where the Supreme Court rejected the view of privacy adopted in *Onofre* and the Model Penal Code: *Bowers v. Hardwick* (1986), which Chapter 4 will examine in detail.

Vagueness and Statutory Obsolescence

Long before *Griswold,* the Supreme Court held that statutes providing insufficient notice for citizens and police to know precisely what conduct is criminal are too "vague" to satisfy the demands of due process.[31] In addition to the obvious policy of fair notice, the vagueness doctrine implements constitutional policies against arbitrary enforcement of broad criminal laws and against obsolescent crimes. All of these values were implicated in *Papachristou v. Florida*

    b. Alaska, California, Colorado, Connecticut, Delaware, Hawaii, Illinois, Indiana, Iowa (judicial invalidation followed by legislative repeal), Maine, Nebraska, New Hampshire, New Jersey (judicial invalidation followed by legislative repeal), New Mexico, New York (judicial invalidation), North Dakota, Ohio, Oregon, Pennsylvania (judicial invalidation), South Dakota, Vermont, Washington, West Virginia, Wisconsin, and Wyoming. See Appendix A1.

    c. Alabama, Arizona, Arkansas (criminalizing only same-sex sodomy but at the misdemeanor level), Florida (sodomy law invalidated but misdemeanor for "unnatural and lascivious conduct" left in place), Kansas (same-sex only), Kentucky (same-sex only), Minnesota (misdemeanor-level penalty of one year maximum), Missouri (same-sex only), Nevada (same-sex only), Texas (same-sex only), and Utah. See Appendix A1.

    d. Georgia, Idaho, Louisiana, Maryland, Massachusetts, Michigan, Mississippi, Montana, North Carolina, Oklahoma, Rhode Island, South Carolina, Tennessee, and Virginia. See Appendix A1.

(1972), which invalidated a Jacksonville, Florida, ordinance making it a crime for people to be "vagabonds" or "lewd, wanton, and lascivious persons." Invalidating the ordinance in a case where two white women and two black men riding together in an automobile had been arrested, the Supreme Court found that the vagrancy law was not intelligible to "[t]he poor among us, the minorities, the average householder," criminalized ordinary conduct considered an amenity of normal life, and seemed to be enforced mainly against "nonconformists."[32] Invoking these principles, gay litigants argued that laws criminalizing "crimes against nature," "lewd vagrancy," and "disguise" were analogous to the vagrancy ordinance in *Papachristou*. Their antiobsolescence pitch was surprisingly successful in deregulating same-sex intimacy even beyond the traditional ALI-type privacy position.

Sodomy Laws. "Crime against nature" laws would appear vulnerable under the Court's vagueness precedents for they were adopted in the nineteenth century, deployed a term understood in 1800 but not in the 1970s, and were enforced in arbitrary and resource-wasting ways. State courts in Alaska (1969) and Florida (1971) invalidated crime against nature laws on those grounds but left standing prohibitions against "sodomy" and "lascivious acts," respectively; Massachusetts (1974) narrowed its "unnatural and lascivious acts" law to avoid vagueness problems but left its "crime against nature" law untouched.[33] Nonetheless, the Supreme Court in *Wainwright v. Stone* (1973) rejected this line of attack under the federal due process clause. The Court held that "crime against nature" has been judicially and socially construed often enough to give the average person an idea what is prohibited.[34] If *Doe v. Commonwealth's Attorney* confirmed that sodomy is a love that dare not speak its name, *Stone* held that the state need not speak its name in making it a crime.

Lewdness and Sexual Solicitation Laws. States that substantially adopted the Model Penal Code continued to criminalize loitering in order to solicit "deviate sexual intercourse," and many municipal ordinances also made such solicitation illegal. Defendants and their ACLU allies challenged these laws, with mixed results. Ohio courts, for example, struck down ordinances prohibiting sexual solicitation and narrowly interpreted the state homosexual solicitation prohibition to ameliorate vagueness problems. The District of Columbia Court of Appeals invalidated its lewd or indecent act law used to prosecute homosexual solicitors on vagueness grounds, but upheld the remainder of the law one year later. Most other high courts rejected such challenges altogether.[35]

Even when legal challenges prevailed, the police often continued to enforce invalid laws. In 1971 Colorado adopted the Model Penal Code, thereby repealing its consensual sodomy law but retaining an offense for "loitering for the purpose of engaging or soliciting another person to engage in prostitution or

deviate sexual intercourse." Denver Judge Irving Ettenberg declared the loitering law unconstitutionally vague in 1972, yet the police continued to arrest gay
cruisers under authority of Denver ordinances against loitering for lewd purposes. Predictably, Ettenberg declared the municipal loitering law unconstitutional as well, but the police remained undeterred; arrests soared from sixty per
month in 1971 to 125 in Feburary 1973. A newly formed gay coalition protested
the discriminatory enforcement and sued to enjoin it. Only after further defeats
in court did Denver promise to change its enforcement policy.[36]

The same process of grassroots politics and aggressive litigation characterized gay challenges to California's broad array of sexual regulations. In 1962 the
California Supreme Court held that municipal laws regulating sex and lewdness were preempted by the state's comprehensive regulation of these issues,[37]
thereby eliminating the detailed sex codes adopted in most California municipalities (see Appendix A2). As the California Supreme Court and legislature
proceeded substantially to deregulate consensual same-sex intimacy, there were
no fallback local laws as there had been in Colorado. A lower court invalidated
California's "public indecency" statute as unconstitutionally vague in 1966, the
legislature repealed the state sodomy and oral copulation laws in 1975, and the
California Supreme Court in *Pryor v. Municipal Court* (1979) held that the state
lewd vagrancy law violated due process guarantees because it was vague and
arbitrarily enforced only against "male homosexuals."[38] *Pryor* was particularly
important, as it capped a long litigation campaign by the ACLU, Gay Rights
Advocates (a gay law firm), and the National Committee for Sexual Civil Liberties against the statute. This victory not only reduced police discretion but
empowered local gay rights coalitions in their negotiations with police departments all over the state.

The California Supreme Court in *Pryor* ruled, further, that the criminal law
could be applied to truly public solicitation of sexual conduct or to unwelcome
or offensive sexual touching. This privacy-based understanding of permissible
criminal law, more gay-friendly than the Model Penal Code, was adopted in
other urbanized states. In most jurisdictions the legislature took the lead,
repealing broadly phrased vagrancy and disorderly conduct laws and replacing
them with statutes criminalizing specified acts of public disorder. Although
New York's highest court had by 1960 upheld the targeting of gay people pursuant to the state's general disorderly conduct and vagrancy laws (Chapter 2),
the legislature repealed those laws and replaced them with more narrowly tailored statutes in the mid-1960s. The only remaining gay-specific law, a prohibition of public loitering to solicit "deviate sexual intercourse," was invalidated by
the court of appeals under *Onofre's* privacy rationale.[39]

Cross-Dressing Ordinances. Transvestites—the great heroes of Stonewall—grew bolder in the 1970s, and *Papachristou* gave butch lesbians, drag queens, and their ACLU allies winning arguments against police harassment for improper attire. Representative was the Ohio Supreme Court's decision in *City of Columbus v. Rogers* (1975). Columbus was one of the first cities to make cross-dressing a crime (1848). The Ohio Supreme Court ruled the old ordinance too vague to be applied to present-day drag queens. The court took lavish judicial notice of recent changes in social mores as to obligatory male-female attire. In light of of such developments, "the terms of the ordinance, 'dress not belonging to his or her sex,' when considered in the light of contemporary dress habits, make it 'so vague that men of common intelligence must necessarily guess at its meaning and differ as to its application.'"[40]

Rogers-style reasoning was invoked by judges to strike down cross-dressing ordinances in Chicago, Cincinnati, Detroit, Fort Worth, Miami Beach, St. Louis, and other cities.[41] Defendants were almost always gay or transgendered people, and at least one invalidated law (Toledo's) prohibited only the "homosexual, lesbian, or other perverted person" from cross-dressing.[42] At least one reported case rejected due process challenges to cross-dressing laws. Richard Mayes, a transsexual (later Rachell Mayes), was arrested a dozen times in Houston for cross-dressing. Mayes's vagueness challenge to the law was rejected by the Harris County, Texas, court, and the Supreme Court declined to hear an appeal.[43] Subsequently, eight transsexuals challenged the same law on the ground that cross-dressing was needed therapy for them. After a federal judge accepted their arguments, Houston repealed the ordinance.[44]

Like the sodomy and sexual solicitation cases, the cross-dressing cases illustrate the way in which state and federal constitutional law reflect changing social power. It was only after lesbians and gay men came out of the closet in great numbers that most sodomy laws were repealed or nullified, and it was only after transvestites and transsexuals were similarly emboldened that cross-dressing laws bit the constitutional dust. The vagueness doctrine was a vehicle for these groups to translate their social message and power into legal liberties.

Institutions of Gay Subculture (First Amendment)

The public cross-dressing cases illustrate how due process could provide some protection for gay subcultural space, but the main legal protections were the first amendment's rights to associate, publish, and speak. The first amendment litigation was relatively successful,[45] in part because the litigants (bars and publishers) were institutions able to devote substantial resources in litigation and in part because gay people fit well into the emerging first amendment tradition and were able to attract respectable allies, such as the ACLU. If sexual as well as political dissidents could find protection in the first amendment, then its principles were truly universal and robust against popular sentiment.

Rights of gay people to come out of the closet, to publish homophile or homoerotic literature, and to form gay-supportive groups were pretty much established by 1969, when Stonewall triggered a genuine explosion of coming out, publication, and group formation. Thus, the first amendment helped both to create Stonewall as the formative metaphor for gay baby boomers and to channel gay liberation in peacefully expressive directions. The latter was encouraged by the legal backlash of the 1970s, when gay rights came under cultural fire and hostile Supreme Court scrutiny. Ultimately the first amendment was both profoundly radical—facilitating the formation of a gay *nomos,* a community of sex-positive and gender-bending idealists, and requiring a sex-negative America to give gays a hearing—and profoundly conservative—empowering white middle-class gays in the internal debates over the soul of that *nomos.*

Rights of Association

Gay Bars. The most intense crackdown on gay bars in American history occurred between 1959 and 1962 (Chapter 2). Invoking the 1954 ordinance making it illegal for bars to allow gays to congregate, Miami police and those of surrounding jurisdictions harassed all of Miami's gay and lesbian bars out of existence, albeit briefly, in 1960. The bars resurfaced, of course, and challenged the ordinance as inconsistent with the right to association recognized in *National Association for the Advancement of Colored People (NAACP) v. Alabama* (1958). Ignoring *NAACP,* a state appeals court ruled that the city policy was justified "to prevent the congregation at liquor establishments of persons likely to prey upon the public by attempting to recruit other persons for acts which have been deemed illegal." Harassment and closures continued—until Miami's bars formed a Bar Owners Association in 1971. The Association won a judicial ruling that the "congregating homosexuals" ordinance was constitutionally invalid.[46] After that, official harassment abated.

The Miami experience was characteristic of cities with large gay populations: in the 1950s and 1960s municipal police terrorized gay bars and baths with periodic raids and name-taking, while state alcoholic beverage control boards closed down premises that violated their anticongregation rules; in the 1960s and 1970s law reform coalitions or bar associations, supported by the ACLU, resisted those policies by challenging them legally and by bargaining with the police politically; by 1981 regulation in most jurisdictions had shifted from a focus on cross-gender dress and behavior to nude dancing and prostitution, and gay bars and baths proliferated like mushrooms after a spring rain.[47] The right of association recognized by the Supreme Court played a role in empowering bar associations to discredit "congregating homosexuals" policies such as Miami's.

The most dramatic litigation was in New Jersey, whose supreme court in *One Eleven Wines & Liquors, Inc. v. Division of Alcoholic Beverage Control* (1967) held that bars could not be disciplined simply because gay people congregated in them and engaged in gender-crossing behavior and dress. Adopting the position advanced by a Mattachine Society amicus brief, Justice Jacobs' opinion held that homosexuals have "the equal right to congregate within licensed establishments such as taverns, restaurants and the like."[48] Relying on the Supreme Court's privacy and association decisions, Jacobs required the state to show strong reason to invade "rights of homosexuals to assemble" and the bar's corresponding right to serve them. After this remarkable introduction, the court dismissed the usual third-party effects—straight patrons who wander in will be shocked by effeminate behavior, homophobes might attack patrons, the public will lose confidence in the liquor industry—as insufficiently established in the record. Less restrictive regulations could deal with the third-party effects without sacrificing patrons' rights. *One Eleven Wines* and similar decisions elsewhere made it administratively and politically costlier to revoke gay bars' liquor licenses, even in southern states.[49]

With the demise of anticongregation rules, regulatory attention shifted to a focus on lewd fondling, nudity, and prostitution. These regulations, too, were challenged but were generally upheld. The Supreme Court ruled in *California v. LaRue* (1972) that states were empowered to regulate lewdness and nudity in licensed bars more extensively than other associational activities, pursuant to extra authority granted states to regulate the sale of liquor by the twenty-first amendment.[50] This ruling came too late to save anticongregation policies and did little to stanch the post-Stonewall boom in gay bars. Chicago, which had about a dozen gay bars in the mid-1960s, sported between sixty and seventy-five ten years later; San Francisco and Los Angeles had 130 and 300 gay bars, respectively; New York's bar culture doubled in that period; multiple bars opened in cities previously without places for lesbian and gay socializing. It was estimated in 1976 that there were 2,500 gay bars in America, as well as 150 gay bathhouses.[51] These numbers would not have been possible without an emerging regulatory consensus that gay people were entitled to associate and dance with, as well as have private sex with, one another at institutions of their own creation.

Gay Organizations and Churches. A lesson from *One Eleven Wines* is that the right to associate was an appealing normative argument in both the political and judicial arenas. Thus, by the time Stonewall unleashed the energy to form thousands of new gay groups, alarmed local authorities were legally powerless to suppress them directly. Big cities that had local chapters of the Daughters and Mattachine in 1969 had dozens of gay-supportive organizations by 1981. Many of them were religious groups: more than 100 gay congregations associated with the Metropolitan Community Church (MCC) were formed in the 1970s, and gay groups formed within the Roman Catholic, Methodist, Presbyterian, Quaker, Episcopalian, Reformed Jewish, and Unitarian faiths. These religious groups provided counseling, places for socializing, and gay-friendly programs all over the country.[52]

What the state could not do directly it tried to do indirectly, against gay resistance. Thus, police continued to harass and spy on gay organizations into the 1970s, but, assisted by lawyers, the gay groups were usually able to obtain injunctions and generate publicity embarrassing to the state.[53] (An exception was the North American Man-Boy Love Association [NAMBLA], formed in 1977 and successfully harassed by the police.) Also, as they had done with gay bars, officials tried to deny routine benefits or licenses as a mechanism of suppression. The earliest example of this also illustrates how gays resisted from the beginning. In 1962 the Mattachine Society of Washington (MSW) registered as an educational organization under District of Columbia law, so that it could solicit funds. Representative John Dowdy introduced a bill in Congress to revoke MSW's license, on the ground that the state could not sanction association by people whose acts were banned under the laws of God, nature, and the District. At congressional hearings, MSW's Frank Kameny defied Dowdy and was backed up by the District's own lawyers and the local chapter of the ACLU, who insisted that even gay people had associational rights that could not be indirectly suppressed in this way.[54] Although the Dowdy bill passed the House, it died in the Senate and had as its main effect the generation of valuable publicity for MSW.

Would a judge have agreed with the lawyers testifying in 1963? In most places, yes, but not everywhere. Even in the early 1970s, judges were sometimes unwilling to intervene when administrators interfered with gay people's efforts to organize. The Ohio Supreme Court upheld the decision of its secretary of state to disallow the Greater Cincinnati Gay Society's articles of incorporation because "the promotion of homosexuality as a valid life style is contrary to the public policy of the state."[55] On the other hand, the New York Court of Appeals overrode public policy objections to order its secretary of state to incorporate the Gay Activists Alliance and its lower courts to approve the Lambda Legal Defense and Education Fund as a legal assistance corporation.[56] States like New

York were more likely to accommodate the post-Stonewall rush to organize because the political equilibrium in those jurisdictions had already shifted toward recognizing gay power. States like Ohio were still shocked by the post-Stonewall visibility of gay people. This was even more true in southern, border, and western states, where gay groups typically did not even petition for state recognition or incorporation until the 1980s, at which point it was clear that the state had no legal basis to deny gay groups regular rights associated with incorporation.[57] On the other hand, the first amendment did not stop at the Mason-Dixon Line. The Florida Supreme Court in 1971 overturned a 1969 state law to revoke charters of corporations whose officers were involved in the overthrow of the government, "organized homosexuality," or prostitution.[58]

A particularly waffling strategy was adopted by the Internal Revenue Service (IRS), which in the early 1970s granted tax-exempt status to organizations not having "gay" in their names (such as MCC) and was willing to give "gay" groups exemptions if they stipulated that they did not "promote" homosexuality or if they accepted homosexuality as a "diseased pathology." In 1973–1974, the IRS exempted Gay Community Services Center of Los Angeles and Lambda Legal Defense but then denied exempt status to the Pride Foundation, a progay educational and legal organization. The IRS found that Pride's "efforts toward the elimination of unjustified and improper discrimination . . . are insignificant when compared to the possible detriment to society," specifically, "advancing the unqualified and unrestricted promotion of the alleged normalcy of homosexuality." Once this justification was out in the open, gaylegal representatives plied the IRS with arguments and information undermining its premises. Lawyers for the Fund for Human Dignity in New York worked for two years to persuade the IRS formally to assure exempt status to gay educational groups, without any disclaimer, in a September 1977 ruling. As constitutional icing on the cake, the D.C. Circuit held in 1980 that the IRS's old rule violated due process antivagueness requirements as applied to a feminist journal that favorably discussed lesbianism.[59]

Gay religious, educational, and legal organizations were not nearly so numerous as gay bars and baths by the end of the 1970s, but they were ultimately more significant because they reached women as well as men, straight feminists as well as gay people, and because they contributed to mainstream culture as well as the gay subculture. As the IRS struggle suggests, the first amendment not only protected such organizations from direct suppression but also helped frame the discourse of indirect suppression. Briefly stated, antihomosexual discourse shifted from "let's harass gay organizations and expose the names of members" (the Dowdy approach) to "no promo homo" (no promotion of homosexuality). The first amendment not only contributed to this shift, as the former was clearly in violation, and the latter an open question, but provided gay groups with persuasive responses to the new line of defense.

Gay School Clubs. Before Stonewall, few homosexual college students were out of the closet. The earliest homophile student group was formed by Rita Mae Brown and others at Columbia University in 1966. After Stonewall, lesbian and gay college groups grew like wild flowers. The main goal of such groups was to create a gay-friendly community within the university that would be a center for social as well as educational exchanges. There was little college administrations could do to stop this, except deny college or university recognition and funding to those groups. Like other gay organizations denied such equal rights, the student groups found homophile and ACLU attorneys eager to litigate their cases under the first amendment's right of association.

The Supreme Court in 1972 held that students have a first amendment associational right to form a Students for a Democratic Society (SDS) chapter at public universities.[60] Although the Court cautioned that a university can safeguard the traditional academic atmosphere, the gay-friendly implications of the decision were confirmed by Judge Frank Coffin, who required the University of New Hampshire to recognize a gay student group. His opinion in *Gay Students Organization v. Bonner* (1974) rejected the argument that gay student groups could be prohibited on the ground that straight students and taxpayers were offended, and insisted that public colleges not discriminate against gay association unless they could demonstrate actual illegality. Coffin's opinion was followed in even the most conservative federal courts.[61] By 1981 four-fifths of all public colleges and universities had recognized gay student groups, with a quarter of the private institutions following suit.[62]

The battle lines shifted in the 1980s from public colleges to high schools, where the Supreme Court insisted upon deference to school administrators, and private colleges, where the first amendment was inapplicable. In these fora, the law only occasionally required toleration of gay student association.[63] More important was the shift in antigay action from outright suppression of gay expression, clearly illegal under the first amendment, to expression of the state's antihomosexual viewpoint through educational funding, library book-buying decisions, and curricular requirements, whose legality was at least debatable.[64]

Freedom of the Press (Media)

Just as the privacy debate started a dialogue that put gay-bashing police on the defensive, the obscenity debate started a dialogue that put sex-negative censors on the defensive. The biggest effect the law had on gay subculture was to discourage censorship, a move that critically paved the way for homoerotica to be accessible nationwide, for gay subcultures to develop local as well as national publications, and for gay people, or their stereotypes, to gain access to national print and electronic fora. What is most remarkable is that the first amendment proved most liberating to the gay press and media at precisely the point—the 1970s—when the Supreme Court was handing down a series of unrelentingly antigay decisions.

Literature and Newspapers. The Warren Court decisions in *Roth* and *One, Inc.* (Chapter 2) assured homophile literature and information sheets constitutional protection but did not say how much. The Court started to say how much in the famous *Fanny Hill* case (*Memoirs v. Massachusetts,* 1966), which overturned state censorship of that polymorphously sexual eighteenth-century fantasy. Justice Brennan's plurality opinion refined the *Roth* test to allow censorship only when (a) the dominant theme of the material taken as a whole appeals to a prurient interest in sex; (b) the material is patently offensive to contemporary standards for sex; and (c) the material is utterly without redeeming social value. Six Justices rejected the dissenters' argument that material can be suppressed because of "exaggerated and morbid emphasis on sex, particularly abnormal and perverted practices."[65] If *Fanny Hill* could not be censored because of its depiction of female masturbation and lesbian relations, the tame lesbian romances and other gay literature were safe, too. On the other hand, because *Fanny Hill* was a literary classic and described same-sex intimacy with more color than specificity, the decision did not forbid censorship of grubbier literature with more explicit sexuality.

On the same day it decided the *Fanny Hill* case, the Court (also in opinions by Brennan) decided two other cases that confirmed censors' continuing authority. At issue in *Mishkin v. New York* (1966) were fifty different paperback pulps, some depicting "normal heterosexual relations, but more depict such deviations as sado-masochism, fetishism, and homosexuality," and many depicting "scenes in which women were making love to women." Most of the pulps, especially those depicting "flagellation, fetishism, and lesbianism," had little apparent prurient interest to the average person, yet the Court held that the prurient appeal prong of the *Memoirs* decision was satisfied. "Where the material is designed for and primarily disseminated to a clearly defined deviant sexual group, rather than the public at large, the prurient-appeal requirement of the *Roth* test is satisfied if the dominant theme of the material taken as a whole appeals to the prurient interest in sex of the members of that group," the Court held. In *Ginzburg v. United States* (1966), the Court upheld the censorship of nonobscene material that "pandered" to adolescent sexual prurience.[66]

After the *Memoirs* decision, even as limited by *Mishkin,* courts could reverse censorship for general depictions of same-sex intimacy.[67] More important, the

Supreme Court in the 1960s took away censors' procedural advantages. Before 1961, censors could and often did seize publications without notice; the publisher would have to sue for return of the materials, which gave the state advantages of inertia. In *Marcus v. Search Warrant* (1961), the Court held that seizure of allegedly obscene materials (including the book *Sexual Deviation*) based upon an ex parte petitition to a magistrate was unconstitutional because it was a prior restraint presumptively illegal under the first amendment. The Court subsequently extended this ruling to prohibit informal restraints and restraints against allegedly obscene movies.[68]

The Warren Court's scrutiny of censorship suggested that anything without pictures of actual intercourse was protected by the first amendment. The censors' defeats allowed openly progay publications such as San Francisco's *Vector,* Philadelphia's *Drum,* and Los Angeles's *The Advocate* to flourish in the 1960s and to advocate prosex as well as progay values. Although *Drum* ran into legal trouble when it printed frontal male nudity,[69] *Vector* and *The Advocate* got away with such nudity. The dozens of new journals and community-centered newspapers established after Stonewall tended to be radical, supporting lesbian separatism, free love, and political militancy. Local newspapers became a forum for debates within lesbian and gay communities, publicized social events, conducted dating services, and carried advertisements for openly gay and gay-friendly businesses. The newspapers expanded gay subculture well beyond bars and restrooms. By 1975 there were 300 identifiably gay publications, with a combined circulation estimated at 200,000 to 350,000 readers.[70]

Serious gay literature flourished like azaleas in April. The collapse of censorship after *One, Inc.* rendered publishers more willing to publish classics such as James Baldwin's *Another Country* (1962), Christopher Isherwood's *A Single Man* (1964), and Audre Lorde's increasingly lesbian-erotic poetry. Some works, such as John Rechy's stark *City of Night* (1963), would probably not have been publishable at all in the 1950s. Writing after the *Fanny Hill* case, gay authors—Adrienne Rich, Rita Mae Brown, Edmund White—not only contributed to the deepening of gay intellectual culture but also addressed a larger national audience in their nonfiction essays as well as their novels and poetry.[71] Lesbian intellectuals such as Rich criticized the ideology of "compulsory heterosexuality," institutions such as marriage, and the persistence of gender stereotypes. Gay male intellectuals such as White focused more on individual sexual experience and evolution.

The demand for gay-friendly work sustained feminist and gay publishing houses, including Feminist Press (New York, founded 1970), Naiad Press (Tallahassee, 1973), Gay Sunshine Press (San Francisco, 1977), Spinsters, Ink. (Duluth, 1978), Alyson Press (Boston, 1980), and Firebrand Books (Ithaca, 1984). The literature produced by these and less literary writers was read by gay adolescents as well as adults trying to come to terms with their sexuality. A sociological study of gay men found that 15 percent had developed an understanding of their sexual orientation through reading.[72]

Homoerotica. Gay men in 1961 were more interested in physique magazines than in literature. When the Court held such magazines nonobscene in *Manual Enterprises* (Chapter 2), new forms of homoerotica arose to test the limits of first amendment tolerance. After the *Memoirs/Mishkin/Ginzburg* trilogy of 1966, the Supreme Court decided cases by ad hoc memoranda affirming or reversing lower court determinations of obscenity vel non. Those decisions often focused on homoerotica. In Maryland, for example, most of the published obscenity opinions in the late 1960s involved homoerotic materials. Maryland courts refused to censor movies and photographs of nude men or even boys (following *Manual Enterprises*) but censored depictions of homosexual fellatio, masturbation, bondage and discipline, and nudity accompanied by "hard core" commentary (following *Mishkin*). In an agonized decision, the Maryland Court of Appeals held that the publication *The Boy Lovers* was not obscene because the nude males did not carry erect penises and the commentary was a serious discussion of homosexuality.[73] The Supreme Court vacated that judgment in light of five obscenity decisions handed down at the end of the 1972–73 term, all authored by Chief Justice Warren Burger in opinions decided by votes of five to four.

In two decisions the Court broadly sustained Congress's power to prevent importation of and commerce in obscene materials.[74] The other three, all involving gay erotica, sustained state regulatory power. *Paris Adult Theatre I v. Slaton* (1973) upheld a civil injunction against an adult theater, on the basis of state interest in morality. *Kaplan v. California* (1973) held criminally obscene a book describing "[a]lmost every conceivable variety of sexual contact, homosexual and heterosexual." This was the first post-*Roth* case to affirm an obscenity conviction against a book without pictures. Upholding obscenity convictions for material described in the briefs as "depictions of cunnilingus, sodomy, buggery," *Miller v. California* (1973) redefined the *Roth/Memoirs* test by applying the "community standards" prong with reference to local rather than national standards, and by eliminating "utterly" from the "utterly without redeeming social value" prong.[75]

Reflecting the Nixon-era reaction to Kennedy-era sexual freedom, the *Miller* trilogy triggered a flurry of local suppression of gay erotica and, in some locales, even informational journals such as *The Advocate*.[76] The Supreme Court itself leaned heavily on antihomosexual animus in applying its revised standards. For example, the Court sustained the convictions of publishers of a homoerotic brochure publicizing an "Illustrated" version of the Report of the President's Commission on Obscenity and Pornography on the same day that it unanimously overturned the conviction of a defendant who exhibited *Carnal Knowledge,* a sexually explicit movie about promiscuous heterosexuals.[77] In *Ward v. Illinois* (1977), the same five-Justice majority upheld the application of Illinois' obscenity law to two books about sadomasochism. To refute the charge that the publisher had insufficient notice that such books were criminally obscene, Justice Byron White's opinion relied on three Illinois state court opinions that defined obscenity in Illinois as anything "abnormal," lumping consensual sadomasochism with both rape and with "homosexual necking" or intercourse.[78]

The Burger Court majority seemed at once fascinated and repelled by homo-erotica and sought to construct a legal regime that would turn the tide against it, especially in rural and southern locales. Prosecutors and judges in some jurisdictions followed the Court's lead. Under *Miller* prosecutors could play on juror revulsion against or ignorance of homoerotic materials to prove violation of community standards and insufficient redeeming social value, but under *Mishkin* defense counsel could not rely on the materials' strangeness to defuse prurient appeal. Texas courts, which produced more reported decisions on homosexual erotica than any other state, interpreted *Mishkin-Miller* to allow judges to preserve juror ignorance by excluding expert testimony on issues of sexual deviation. "[I]t is not necessary for jurors to have an understanding of deviant group interests; the pornography speaks for itself."[79]

Although the *Miller* trilogy enabled southern jurisdictions to go after homo-erotica, these cases probably had little overall influence on its actual availability. By 1976 national mail-order homoerotic films and magazines were well estab-lished; the Colt and Falcon studios made forty films a year, while magazines such as *Blueboy* and *Mandate* sold tens of thousands of issues.[80] Thus, Texas cit-izens could obtain forbidden erotica by ordering it through the mail, which the federal government no longer policed. The continuously expanding porn mar-ket did run up against a political limit: child pornography, which Congress and virtually every state prohibited after 1977, and which some states prohibited even if nonobscene, a position congenial to the Burger Court. Because some child pornography was homoerotic and the best organized adult-minor associ-ation was the North American Man-Boy Love Association, these developments represented a new, and more robust, focus in the censorship of homoerotica.[81]

Broadcast Media. Gay people had been discreetly depicted in movies under the Motion Picture Code of 1930, and occasionally surfaced in radio during the 1950s, but they did not fully come out in the broadcast media until 1961–62. The Motion Picture Association of America announced in October 1961 that it was dropping the Code's prohibition against any cinematic reference to "sex perversion"; in September, public television network KQED in San Francisco aired *The Rejected,* a program presenting interviews with gay-friendly scientists and members of the Mattachine Society, which was rebroadcast by forty other stations; and in July 1962 the Pacifica radio group's New York affiliate WBAI broadcast *Live and Let Live,* a discussion of homosexuality by gay activist Randy Wicker and seven other openly gay men. The law played a different role in each of these media.

The major reasons the Motion Picture Code was revised were market pressure and the unworkability of the prior prohibition.[82] A facilitating reason was the Supreme Court's insistence in 1959 in *Kingsley International Pictures* (Chapter 2) that states could not censor films based upon their nonobscene depiction of sexual nonconformity. The revised Code followed the law but only partly, as it insisted that "sexual aberration could be suggested but not actually spelled out." And the censors vigorously discriminated, giving immediate Code approval to *The Children's Hour* (1961) and *Advise and Consent* (1962), where guilt-ridden gay characters committed suicide, while denying approval to Basil Dearden's *Victim* (1961), a sympathetic view of a married man who came out as gay in order to avoid blackmail. Hollywood preferred its gay characters to conform to lurid stereotypes—the vampire lesbian, the sexual psychopath—and to die by movie's end.[83] Public censors also sometimes discriminated. *The Killing of Sister George* (1968), a sexually tame movie with a serrating message about the silencing of lesbians, was found to be in violation of Massachusetts' and Connecticut's obscenity and film licensing laws, requiring cuts of any lesbian sexuality.[84] California's intermediate court allowed censorship of Jean Genet's film *Un Chant d'Amour* (1947) for its depiction of homosexual masturbation, sodomy, oral copulation, sadism and masochism, and voyeurism, all within a prison context. Because the film went "far beyond the customary limits of candor in offensively depicting certain unorthodox sexual practices and relationships," the court found it went well beyond *Manual Enterprises* and was similar to the material censored in *Mishkin;* the Supreme Court agreed.[85]

After Stonewall, a more balanced cinematic depiction of gays began to develop, relatively unimpeded by state censorship. Although foreign movies such as *Sunday, Bloody Sunday* (1971) continued to be more gender-bending and gay-friendly than American movies, Hollywood attended to the growing gay-interested audience with such fare as the film adaptation of Mart Crowley's play, *The Boys in the Band* (1970). In 1973 gay groups developed "Some General Principles for Motion Picture and Television Treatment of Homosexuality" insisting upon less stereotypical depiction of gay characters. Principle three: "Use the same rules you have for other minorities. If bigots don't get away with it if they hate Catholics, they can't get away with it if they hate gays."[86] The remainder of the 1970s saw a fair number of movies reflecting a gay sensibility as well as gay characters.[87] Grotesque depictions of gay people in William Friedkin's *Cruising* (1980) and Gordon Willis's *Windows* (1980) provoked angry protests from gay organizations and individuals fed up with Hollywooden stereotypes. Finally sensitive to these kinds of criticisms, American films in the 1980s included gay-friendly as well as homophobic depictions.[88]

In contrast to film, television and radio are regulated by the Federal Communications Commission (FCC). Thus, the discourse about the acceptability of sexual references and characters was relatively centralized within one federal agency, not the state courts and private associations.[89] The pioneer in feminist and gay programming was the Pacifica Foundation, created in 1946 as an alternative source of information to that provided by corporate radio. Its station in Berkeley, KPFA, made radio history when in the 1950s it broadcast readings of *Howl* by author Allen Ginsberg. KPFA got into regulatory trouble, however, when its 1963 rebroadcast of *Live and Let Live* triggered a petition to the FCC for license revocation on grounds of "indecent" programming. Although the FCC ruled that it had authority to regulate indecent as well as obscene programming (notwithstanding *Roth*), it further ruled that the first amendment assured Pacifica's right to broadcast gay-themed programs—otherwise, "only the wholly inoffensive, the bland, could gain access to the radio microphone or TV camera."[90] Thus affirmed, KPFA and Pacifica's other affiliated networks in Los Angeles (KPFK), Houston (KPFT), New York City (WBAI), and Washington (WPFW) ran gay-informative programs through the 1960s and instituted regular gay programming in the 1970s, none of which was censored. Pacifica's main regulatory problems grew out of its broadcast of George Carlin's "Seven Dirty Words" monologue, not its gay programming.[91] Television, as a big business, was slow to schedule gay-informative programs allowed by the Pacifica decision. The most-watched television program about gays before Stonewall was CBS's documentary on *The Homosexuals* (1967), a mishmash of sweeping antigay statements and pathetic images.[92]

The feminist movement stimulated the creation of lesbian-friendly radio, but again not television, programming. The FCC initiated proceedings against a Seattle radio station for playing the song "Every Woman Can Be a Lesbian" over and over on its show *Make No Mistake About It—It's the Faggot and the Dyke,* which prompted the station to drop the show.[93] So long as feminist programs steered away from vulgar language, lesbian themes were tolerated. Frieda Werden and Katherine Davenport produced what may have been the first syndicated multipart series on homosexuality, *What's Normal,* in 1975. Werden also founded the Women's International News Gathering Service. Washington,

D.C.'s Media Collective produced *Sophie's Parlor* beginning in 1972; after 1977 this show was broadcast over the Pacifica affiliate, WPFW. Another Pacifica affiliate, Los Angeles's KPFK, ran *Lesbian Sisters*. Producer Helen Rosenbluth recalls many listeners calling the station to say how the program helped them deal with their sexuality. "They didn't feel crazy anymore, like they were the only ones. The power of radio is amazing."[94]

After Stonewall, gay efforts focused on television and were more aggressive in obtaining accurate media treatment. Mark Segal and the "Gay Raiders" disrupted national and local programming to demand attention to gay issues. Loretta Lotman's Gay Media Action group, founded in 1973, monitored television programs and organized grassroots protests against antigay stereotyping in programs such as *Marcus Welby, M.D.*[95] In 1974 her group and the National Gay Task Force (NGTF) petitioned the National Association of Broadcasters to revise its radio and television codes to discourage antigay slurs and defamations; the Association responded that existing code provisions protected against homophobic remarks and invited gay people to file complaints with the respective boards.[96] Gays also pressed the FCC to require its radio licensees to be more sensitive to the needs of gay groups. After the agency adopted a "community ascertainment" checklist of groups that licensees were supposed to consult, the NGTF and 143 local organizations in forty-nine states petitioned the FCC to include gay groups.[97] The Media Access Project in 1980–81 persuaded the agency to apply its fairness doctrine to sustain a complaint by the Dallas Gay Political Caucus to require a local television station to provide equal time for gays to respond to antigay remarks in a show featuring an evangelist.[98] Although television in particular remained essentially a vast wasteland for gay characters and issues in the 1970s, this pressure on the networks and the FCC's openness were necessary conditions to the more gay-friendly programs of the 1980s.[99]

Freedom of Speech (The Right to Come Out)

The easiest first amendment issue for this period was the right of gay people to express themselves through public speech without fear of criminal penalty. Conversely, the most difficult first amendment issue was the right of a public servant to speak about issues of sexual orientation or to come out of the closet at work. These were hard cases because American law's libertarian baselines make it much harder for the state to deprive citizens of liberty than to condition state benefits, such as employment, on citizen restraint. In the gay speech cases, this distinction linked up with the idea of the closet: even if the state cannot imprison sexual or gender minorities, it can discourage them from being open about their sexuality, such as by denying them employment if they are too far "out."

The first amendment applies to any state actor, including the state as employer, and so it goes without saying that public employees do enjoy some protection for their public speech. In *Pickering v. Board of Education* (1968), the Supreme Court held that a high school teacher could not be dismissed simply because he made erroneous statements when criticizing the school board's handling of a local bond issue. As there was no showing that the statements undermined the teacher's effectiveness or the operation of the schools generally, Justice Thurgood Marshall's opinion found no legitimate state interest that could justify penalizing the teacher for speaking on issues of public concern. Read with *Robinson v. California* (1962), where the Court held that the state could not criminalize the status of being an alcoholic, *Pickering* created an analytical basis for a personal right not to be penalized by the state for coming out of the closet.[100] Lower courts did not read the cases this way, however.

The Eighth Circuit held that the University of Minnesota could withdraw an offer of employment to an openly gay librarian, James McConnell, because he was seeking "the right to pursue an activist role in *implementing* his unconventional ideas concerning the societal status to be accorded homosexuals and, thereby, to foist tacit approval of his socially repugnant concept upon his employer."[101] Analytically, the court transformed McConnell's identity *speech* into activist *conduct,* unprotected by *Pickering.* The Fourth Circuit followed *Pickering* in *Acanfora v. Board of Education, Montgomery County* (1974) to hold that a school system cannot discipline an employee, Joseph Acanfora, simply because of his public comments after he had been "outed" as gay, but distinguished *Pickering* on the ground that Acanfora had wrongfully withheld material information (his homosexuality) from his original teaching application.[102] This holding was in tension with *Shelton v. Tucker* (1960), where the Supreme Court held that teachers could not be required to disclose their organizational activities.[103] McConnell's and Acanfora's cases illustrate the mixed progress for gay people by 1981. Although they were free to form organizations, publish newspapers, and speak publicly, openly gay people were not welcome as schoolteachers or other public servants. This represented progress for gays from a *Dred Scott* regime where the homosexual was presumptively an outlaw to a *Plessy v. Ferguson* regime of separate but unequal rights. This apartheid, however, was friendlier than that in *Plessy,* as gay people could choose their form of segregation—physical segregation for openly gay people versus emotional segregation for those who remained in the closet. Nonetheless, by 1981 some states were beginning to acquiesce in a post-closet regime, where openly gay people could participate in the public culture.

This transition is best reflected in *Gay Law Students Association v. Pacific Telephone & Telegraph Co.* (1979), where the California Supreme Court held that the state labor code's prohibition of workplace discrimination on the basis of "political activities or affiliations" entailed sexual orientation discrimination. The court found that "the struggle of the homosexual community for equal rights, particularly in the field of employment, must be recognized as a political activity." Because a "principal barrier to homosexual equality is the common feeling that homosexuality is an affliction which the homosexual worker must conceal from his employer and his fellow workers," a key feature in "the struggle for equal rights is to induce homosexual individuals to 'come out of the closet,' acknowledge their sexual preferences, and to associate with others in working for equal rights."[104] This reasoning linked identity speech with political activism and illustrates how and why privacy was yielding to equality as the chief aspiration for gay rights.

Equal Gay Citizenship (Due Process, Then Equal Protection)

In June 1962 Frank Kameny wrote Attorney General Robert Kennedy, introducing himself and the Mattachine Society of Washington (MSW). Analogizing his group's struggle to that of the civil rights movement, Kameny petitioned Kennedy to end the federal government's "official prejudice and discriminatory policy and practice" and to support MSW in its efforts "to improve the position of a large group of citizens presently relegated to second-class citizenship." Kennedy ignored the plea, which MSW constantly repeated to public officials and the press.[105] The First National Planning Conference of Homophile Organizations adopted a resolution in 1966 insisting upon "social and economic equality of opportunity" for gays, including the right to nondiscrimination in public employment and military service.[106] This was a pipe dream in 1966, but part of the dream was achieved by 1981 through legislation, executive orders, and judicial decisions based upon due process (nonarbitrariness) as well as equal protection arguments.

Government Employment Exclusions

Equal gay citizenship required assurances that homosexuality would not be the basis for losing one's job. The first target for equality claims was therefore government employment discrimination. Outside of the armed forces and southern state governments, that goal was substantially achieved by 1981. Surprisingly, many urban jurisdictions adopted laws protecting against discrimination in the private sector as well.

Federal Civil Service: Collapse of the Exclusion. In 1962 the Civil Service Commission (CSC) refused either to meet with MSW or to provide a justification for its exclusionary policy. Kameny's ragtag band of activists and lawyers mounted a full-court press against the policy. Kameny's strategy was a synthesis of privacy and equality: individual passive resistance to job-related interrogations and publicized group protests of the exclusionary policy. As to the former, MSW developed a mimeo sheet on "How to Handle a Federal Interrogation" by FBI, military, and civil service investigators. As to questions about homosexuality, the only admissible answer was "These are matters which are of no proper concern to the Government."[107] As to the exclusionary policy, MSW mobilized in 1965. In April ten well-dressed homophiles, seven men and three women, picketed the White House. Twenty-five picketed CSC in June, twelve picketers marched in front of the State Department in August, and thirty-five returned to the White House in October. At the last, Kameny presented a letter to the president, signed by various Mattachine groups, objecting to official federal discrimination against gay people. The message was summed up by the placards, "Private Sexual Conduct Is Irrelevant to Federal Employment," and "U.S. Claims no second class citizens—What about homosexuals?" The FBI and the print media wrote up the demonstration and took pictures.[108]

Complementing the advice sheet and the public protests were lawsuits against the government. MSW secretary Bruce Scott and his ACLU-allied lawyer won a landmark victory against the CSC's firing him in 1962 because of "immoral conduct," namely, disorderly conduct arrests. In *Scott v. Macy* (1965) Chief Judge David Bazelon of the D.C. Circuit voted to remand his case to the Commission because it had not given a sufficiently precise reason for the action. "The Commission must at least specify the conduct it finds 'immoral' and state why that conduct related to 'occupational competence or fitness'."[109] The Commission responded that it dismissed Scott because of his "failure to respond to the question as to whether or not [he had] ever engaged in homosexual acts," but in a second appeal Bazelon rejected this ground because the Commission had not given Scott sufficient notice of it.[110]

After the first *Scott* decision, the Commission finally met with MSW. In a February 1966 letter to MSW, the Commission explained, for the first time in public, its policy. CSC Chair John Macy claimed that the Commission did not exclude "homosexuals" per se, only people who engaged in "overt" homosexual "conduct" that became public through an arrest or general knowledge. So long as the homosexual does not "publicly proclaim that he engages in homosexual conduct" or "prefers such relationships," Macy suggested he could serve and the Commission would not pry. But once the word is out, the Commission must consider the "revulsion" of coworkers and "offense to members of the public."[111]

What Macy was offering was "don't ask, don't tell," the mutually protective closet. This was unacceptable to the new homophile leaders like Kameny. Surprisingly, it was no longer acceptable to some judges. On the eve of Stonewall, Bazelon rejected the Commission's policy in *Norton v. Macy* (1969). The Commission fired a NASA budget analyst caught cruising another man in Lafayette Park. Bazelon found no evidence that Clifford Norton's midnight incident undermined his ability to do his technical, number-crunching job; no coworkers or citizens had complained. In light of Kinsey's findings that 95 percent of American men have violated state sex laws, the Commission's abstract vision of morality was too broad, potentially disqualifying everyone, and beyond the agency's competence or statutory mandate, the "efficiency of the service." Particularly in light of *Griswold* and gay people's privacy rights, Bazelon held that the Commission could not dismiss a gay employee without showing a "nexus" between his sexual orientation and job performance.[112]

A wedding of the Supreme Court's privacy jurisprudence and MSW's equality jurisprudence, *Norton* stimulated reconsideration of gay-exclusionary policies within the federal government. The Post Office and Government Printing Office allowed openly gay employees to retain their jobs in 1972.[113] Although the D.C. Circuit initially failed to apply *Norton*'s nexus requirement to police the federal government's job-destroying revocations of security clearances to known homosexuals, later cases applied *Norton* to require a neutral justification for denying or revoking security clearances.[114] In early 1973 the Society for Individual Rights brought a class action lawsuit against the Commission. Following *Norton*, a federal trial judge enjoined the CSC from excluding or discharging employees because of their homosexuality or their private activities.[115] The court's injunction came amidst the agency's own internal deliberations about how (not whether) to revise its policy.

On December 21, 1973, CSC notified federal agencies that they could "not find a person unsuitable for Federal employment merely because that person is a homosexual or has engaged in homosexual acts," and could only dismiss such an employee where his "homosexual conduct affects job fitness— excluding from such consideration, however, unsubstantiated conclusions concerning possible embarrassment to the Federal service." In 1975 this instruction was formally codified in the Commission's rules for disqualification, which also dropped "immoral conduct" from the list of disqualifying conditions.[116] Guidelines for "Infamous or Notoriously Disgraceful Conduct" were revised to the same effect, and the civil service statute was amended in 1978 to prohibit discrimination "on the basis of conduct which does not adversely affect the performance of the employee or applicant or the performance of others."[117]

Before the new rules took effect, John Singer was dismissed from his clerical job at the EEOC—the agency enforcing federal workplace discrimination law. The Ninth Circuit upheld the dismissal against *Pickering* attack, on the ground that Singer was engaged in offensive conduct that undermined his effectiveness as an employee: wearing gay pride buttons, applying for a license to marry his partner Paul Barwick, and kissing another man twice in public. Although it would have been unthinkable to discharge a man for wearing a "straight pride" badge, applying for a license to marry a woman, and kissing a (consenting) woman in public, the court upheld the penalty. Singer appealed, and the Supreme Court, surprisingly, granted certiorari. The government promptly agreed to apply the new civil service policy to Singer.[118]

Military Exclusion: Standing Firm. Military personnel expelled in the 1960s and early 1970s for alleged same-sex intimacies denied that they were homosexual and relied on due process arguments to put the state to its proof.[119] Only well after Stonewall did gay service personnel openly announce their sexual orientation and challenge the military exclusion more broadly, albeit still in the argot of due process. In an early case, two women discharged under honorable conditions publicly admitted that they were lesbians and argued that their exclusion was irrational. After the Navy insisted that dismissal of lesbians was not mandatory, the appeals court dismissed the women's case so that they could exhaust their administrative remedies.[120] The nonmandatory-dismissal policy backfired in the D.C. Circuit, however, in *Matlovich v. Secretary of Air Force* and *Berg v. Claytor* (1978). Upholding the claims of openly gay Sergeant Leonard Matlovich and Ensign Vernon Berg, the court held that if the Air Force and Navy, respectively, followed a discretionary-dismissal approach, due process required them to give reasons for separating some gay personnel while not separating others.[121] Implicitly, the court followed *Norton,* requiring that there be a nexus between the disapproved conduct and legitimate state needs in the military discharge cases.

In the wake of these decisions, more service personnel came out of their closets and successfully challenged their exclusion. Yet the Carter administration snatched substantial victory from the jaws of apparent defeat. The government's morale argument, resting upon the hostility of straight personnel to gays, was repeatedly rejected in the lower courts but was finally accepted by the Ninth Circuit in *Beller v. Middendorf* (1980). Just after *Beller,* the Department of Defense addressed the *Matlovich* problem by promulgating new regulations that removed official discretion to allow openly gay personnel to serve in the armed forces.[122]

Beller and the new regulations slammed the door of the military closet. Why were gay rights efforts so unsuccessful here, in contrast to their success against the civil service exclusion? Doctrinally, the key distinction was the deference courts pay to military judgments, a deference the Supreme Court in 1981 deployed to justify discriminating on the basis of sex in draft registration.[123] That the top brass in the armed forces strongly opposed allowing openly gay people to serve not only carried weight in the courts but, more important, blocked the kind of internal rethinking that undermined the civil service and security clearance exclusions. Rhetorically, the armed forces de-emphasized the old arguments that gay people are unstable and subject to blackmail, and recentered the exclusion around the third-party effects of allowing openly gay people to serve: given the close quarters of military life, the privacy of heterosexual soldiers would be invaded; as a consequence, morale and unit cohesion would suffer. Cultural reasons for the military exclusion will be explored in Chapter 5.

State and Local Government Policies: From Exclusion to Protection. Constitutional challenges to state and local antigay exclusions were rarely successful in the 1960s, but a new receptiveness was signaled by the Calfornia Supreme Court in *Morrison v. State Board of Education* (1969). Justice Mathew Tobriner's opinion overturned the discharge of a teacher for once engaging in same-sex intimacy with another man, and restricted the statutory "immoral conduct" disqualification to activities impairing a teacher's pedagogical effectiveness. This narrowing interpretation avoided three "serious constitutional problems" with a broad construction: it would be too vague to give teachers notice of conduct they should avoid; would threaten teachers' *Griswold* rights by tempting states to pry into their private lives; and would violate the *Shelton-Pickering* principle that "[n]o person can be denied government employment because of factors unconnected with the responsibilities of that employment." Following the philosophy of *Norton,* Tobriner ruled that "[t]he private conduct of a man, who is also a teacher, is a proper concern to those who employ him only to the extent it mars him as a teacher."[124]

Applying the *Norton* nexus requirement to teacher qualfications, *Morrison* was distinguished more often than it was followed in the lower courts. Still, the California Supreme Court expanded *Morrison* to overturn the dismissal of a teacher arrested for sexual solicitation in *Board of Education v. Jack M* (1977). Although the alleged homosexual conduct was not as private as it had been in *Morrison,* the court affirmed the trial court's findings that the teacher's conduct did not come to public attention nor did it impair his effectiveness as a teacher.[125] *Jack M* was not widely followed in other jurisdictions, whose courts applied *Morrison's* nexus requirement with deference to school board determinations that homosexuality alone was sufficient to undermine a teacher's effectiveness.[126] Even when courts found that a school board had acted unconstitutionally, as in *Acanfora,* they usually found some way to deny relief or reinstatement.[127] On the other hand, courts did invalidate state policies penalizing teachers because they publicly advocated progay views.[128]

The public school remained a charged setting for openly gay teachers because of parents' concerns about sexual predation or progay role models who might influence their children's sexualities, a topic revisited in Chapter 5. Similar concerns defeated challenges to antigay exclusions from police departments unless the exclusion went to *Pickering*-like public stances.[129] Cleveland Mayor Ralph Perk justified police exclusion of anyone who engaged in sex that was not "normal," memorably dubbing gay people "pornomaniacs."[130] Other state antigay discriminations were more successfully challenged. States as different as New York and Florida rejected sexual orientation as a criterion for membership in the legal bar.[131] An ABA survey in 1976 found no state bar asked applicants about their sexual orientation, and all but a handful reported that they would not ordinarily consider such information.[132]

Ironically, the principles of *Jack M* and *Norton* were more readily followed by city councils and state legislators than by judges. In February 1972 New York Mayor John Lindsay issued an executive order banning sexual orientation discrimination in city employment. More than forty cities, including almost all the nation's largest, adopted similar policies between 1971 and 1984. (See Appendix B2 for cities and years.) Pennsylvania was the first state to bar sexual orientation discrimination in state employment in April 1975, when Governor Milton Shapp issued a controversial executive order to that effect. Similar antidiscrimination directives were issued by the governors of California (1979), New York (1983), and Ohio (1983)[133] and were legislatively enacted in Wisconsin (1982).[134]

In parallel fashion, most of these foregoing jurisdictions considered broader measures to prohibit sexual orientation discrimination by private employers as well. The first jurisdictions to do so were university towns in Michigan (Ann Arbor and East Lansing, both in 1972), but the first significant law was adopted by Washington, D.C. In 1973 gay and feminist activists persuaded Councilmember Marjorie Parker to include sexual orientation as a prohibited classification in her human rights measure, which barred discrimination in employment, housing, public accommodations, real estate, and credit practices.[135] Other important jurisdictions prohibiting private workplace discrimination included Minneapolis (1975), San Francisco (1978), Detroit (1979), Los Angeles (1979), and Philadelphia (1982). Wisconsin adopted the first state statute barring such discrimination in 1982. Recall that the California Supreme Court had construed the state labor code to the same effect in 1979 in *Pacific Tel. & Tel.* (See Appendix B2 for a list of state and municipal laws.)

Contrast the success of local gay activists in the District with their failure to persuade Congress to adopt a similar law nationwide. On May 14, 1974, Representative Bella Abzug introduced a federal gay rights bill that would have protected against sexual orientation discrimination in public and private workplaces, public accommodations, and housing. Although similar bills were introduced in every Congress after 1974, none even received a congressional hearing until the 1990s. Also sobering was the limited efficacy of the measures that were adopted. Until the 1980s most cities that officially or informally stopped discriminating against gay people still had police departments that did.[136] Also, measures that were adopted were sometimes, in the words of reporter Randy Shilts, "toothless paper tigers." Most of the laws provided only an administrative mechanism and no damages relief for grievants. Because of their fear of publicity, gay employees were less likely than others to risk a lengthy process for so little payoff, and virtually no one filed charges in most cities, San Francisco, typically, being an exception.[137]

An ironic consequence of gay rights laws was their contribution to a new politics of traditional values. One of the first jurisdictions to adopt a job nondiscrimination measure, Boulder, Colorado, was also the first the see it repealed by a popular referendum in May 1974. Seasoned by success there and failure in California (1976), a new form of antigay politics made its national debut in Dade County, Florida, in 1977, where Anita Bryant's "Save Our Children" campaign repealed the county gay rights law by popular referendum. Bryant argued not only that "homosexuality is immoral and against God's wishes," but also charged that the gay rights law would encourage people to cross-dress, molest children, and rape animals. Her campaign maintained that gay rights infringed the rights of third parties, namely, parents and their children. "Miami's law infringed upon my rights," Bryant said, "or rather discriminates against me as a citizen and a mother to teach my children and set examples of God's moral code as stated in the holy scriptures."[138]

Wichita, Kansas, St. Paul, Minnesota, and Eugene, Oregon, immediately followed Dade County in repealing their gay rights ordinances by referenda. California in 1978 faced a statewide initiative sponsored by state Senator John Briggs that would have overridden *Jack M* and disqualified from public school employment anyone engaged in the "advocating, soliciting, imposing or encouraging or promoting of private or public homosexual activity directed at, or likely to come to the attention of, schoolchildren and/or other employees."[139] The Briggs initiative directly implicated first amendment concerns and placed gay-friendly heterosexuals at risk as well. Former Governor Ronald Reagan joined Governor Jerry Brown in opposing the initiative, and it was soundly defeated. Although the Briggs initiative dampened the impact of the Bryant initiative, antigay initiatives continued to be introduced for the next twenty years and enjoyed an unparalleled 79 percent success rate.[140]

Immigration and Naturalization Exclusions

As interpreted by the Immigration and Naturalization Service (INS), the requirement by the Immigration and Nationality Act (1940) of "good moral character" excluded foreign homosexuals from becoming U.S. citizens. To the INS and the Public Health Service (PHS), the exclusion by the Immigration and Naturalization Act (1952) of persons "afflicted with . . . psychopathic personality" warranted preventing homosexuals from entering the country and deporting them if they got through (Chapter 2). During the 1960s, challenges to these exclusions by people who admitted to almost any kind of same-sex intimacy were unsuccessful. In 1968, for example, a state judge denied naturalization to Olga Schmidt on grounds of immoral conduct because she had engaged in intimate relations with a female friend in her home. "'Few behavioral deviations are more offensive to American *mores* than is homosexuality.'"[141]

The only successful challenge was short-lived. The Ninth Circuit in *Fleuti v. Rosenberg* (1962) held that the term "psychopathic personality" was too vague to be constitutionally applied to homosexuals generally. The court relied on medical studies and experts skeptical of the precision or usefulness of the old term.[142] At the urging of the PHS and INS, Congress promptly amended section 212(a)(4) in 1965 to override *Fleuti,* rewriting that part of the statute to exclude aliens "afflicted with pschopathic personality, or sexual deviation, or a mental defect."[143] In *Boutilier v. INS* (1967), the Supreme Court not only interpreted "psychopathic personality" to be a code word for "homosexual," but also extended the exclusion to an apparent bisexual who was undisputedly functional. The Court brushed aside *Fleuti*'s concern with vagueness and failed even to mention equal protection problems with reading a broad sexual orientation classification into an ambiguous statute. Three Justices followed *Fleuti. Boutilier* was read to support the mere admission of homosexuality as a basis for exclusion.[144] Lower federal courts held that committing minor homosexual acts, such as disorderly conduct (degeneracy) and lewd vagrancy, constituted a crime of moral turpitude, which independently justified exclusion.[145]

After Stonewall, both exclusions bled to death. Judge Walter Mansfield ruled in *In re Labady* (1971) that private homosexual conduct is no bar to a finding of good moral character because "the likelihood of harm to others is minimal and any effort to regulate or penalize the conduct may lead to invasion of the individual's constitutional rights."[146] He recognized that there was some tension between his construction of the 1940 naturalization law and *Boutilier*'s construction of the 1952 immigration law but reconciled the two by noting that one of Boutilier's morals offenses had been sexual activity in a public park. Bowing to Mansfield's *Griswold*-like arguments, the INS in 1976 announced that a "sexual deviate" would not be denied citizenship unless she or he had a criminal conviction, engaged in fraud or sex with minors, took money for sex, or solicited for sex in a public place.[147] It is not clear how many gay people were affected by this change in policy, but the INS after 1976 continued to quiz gay applicants intensely about their sex lives and continued to deport gay noncitizens under *Boutilier*.

After the American Psychiatric Association (APA) dropped homosexuality as a mental disease in the APA's diagnostic manual in 1973–74, APA President John Spiegel urged the INS to "use your statutory powers of discretion to refrain from the exclusion, deportation or refusal of citizenship to homosexual aliens."[148] The INS General Counsel responded that *Boutilier* and the 1965 statute precluded such a change in the immigration exclusion and that the medical evidence did not speak to the good character issue involved in the citizenship exclusion. In 1977 executive department officials met with ACLU and National Gay Task Force leaders to discuss the latter's petition for the INS to abandon the immigration exclusion. The Public Health Service (PHS) in November notified the INS that it could no longer participate in the exclusion of gay people as "psychopathic personalities." The INS, however, not only refused to abandon this policy but took the position that *Boutilier* required PHS participation as well.[149] The PHS stewed in this legal soup until the summer of 1979, when gay Canadian Carl Hill obtained an injunction against his exclusion as a "psychopath" when that term had no medical meaning. Responding to the Hill injunction, the Surgeon General in August publicly announced that the PHS could no longer participate in the statutory scheme, consistent with "current and generally accepted canons of medical practice with respect to homosexuality."[150]

Because a PHS certificate was statutorily required for the INS to exclude an immigrant for one of the seven medical exclusions,[151] the PHS's announcement threw the statutory scheme into turmoil. The Office of Legal Counsel advised the INS that it was required to enforce *Boutilier* even without the PHS's cooperation.[152] The INS in 1980 devised an ingenious policy: a noncitizen entering the country would be asked nothing about "sexual preference" but should be examined "as to homosexuality" only if she or he "makes an unsolicited, unambiguous oral or written admission of homosexuality." In that event, the noncitizen could be debarred.[153] The INS applied this new policy anemically in the 1980s but still suffered the indignity of having it invalidated when Carl Hill returned to the United States and won an injunction from the Ninth Circuit against enforcement of the psychopathic personality exclusion without a PHS certificate.[154]

In an end game that Kafka could have designed, the INS, after declining to seek Supreme Court review of the decision, refused to follow the Ninth Circuit's opinion in any other circuit. The PHS agreed to issue a certificate for "self-proclaimed homosexual aliens presented by the [INS]," but only in the Ninth Circuit. Elsewhere, the PHS continued its prior policy of noncooperation. The INS, in turn, adopted the policy of telling "self-proclaimed homosexual aliens" that they could apply for a "waiver of excludability" that would defer action excluding them for the duration of their stay in the United States. Moreover, the alien could apply for the waiver before the alien came to the United States, the suggestion being that such waivers would be routinely granted.[155] Congress finally repealed the immigration exclusion in 1990.[156]

Family Law Discriminations

Outside the bedroom, the most intimate private space is the family. For gay people, this also became the most contested public space, as most states proved reluctant to recognize gay families. Chapter 8 suggests cultural reasons for this resistance. Doctrinally, the law rejected all efforts to recognize same-sex unions as marriages but recognized contract-based unions and ties with one's biological children.

Same-Sex Marriage. Stonewall stimulated great interest in gay marriage, much of it critical. Critics such as the Radicalesbians and the Gay Liberation Front charged that marriage suppressed women's equal dignity and sexual liberty, two of the chief goals of gay liberation. Other gay activists did not subscribe to the ideas and rhetoric of the radicals.[157] The National Coalition of Gay Organizations drew up a comprehensive list of demands for law reform in February 1972 and closed with "Repeal of all legislative provisions that restrict the sex or number of persons entering into a marriage unit and extension of legal benefits of marriage to all persons who cohabit regardless of sex or numbers." More important, lesbian and gay couples were voting with their feet, as they marched into clerks' offices to demand marriage licenses, which were usually denied by shocked clerks.[158]

Jack Baker and Mike McConnell were the first gay couple to file a lawsuit seeking recognition of their marriage. McConnell lost his job and the plaintiffs lost their lawsuit in *Baker v. Nelson* (1971), but they were followed by a steady stream of lesbian and gay couples seeking legal recognition for their unions. Drawing from the Supreme Court's invalidation of state prohibition of different-race marriages in *Loving v. Virginia* (1967), attorneys for same-sex couples invoked two different kinds of arguments. Most invoked the fundamental "right to marry" that *Loving* had found in the due process clause. In the Baker-McConnell case, the Minnesota Supreme Court held that the right to marry was inapplicable to same-sex unions because marriage by definition required a man and a woman, not two men.[159] Even though the Supreme Court strengthened the right to marry in 1978 and 1987 (Chapter 8), no appellate judge, as of 1999, has held that the fundamental right to marry includes gay couples.

Another line of argument built on *Loving*'s first ground for decision, that the state prohibition of different-race marriage is race discrimination. Attorneys for John Singer and Paul Barwick argued that state prohibition of marriage for same-sex couples is sex discrimination, in violation of the state of Washington's equal rights amendment. Just as the ban of different-race marriages is a classification on the basis of race (the white-white couple can get married, while the white-black couple cannot), which is presumptively unconstitutional, so the ban of same-sex marriages is a classification on the basis of sex (the woman-man couple can get married, while the woman-woman couple cannot), and presumptively unconstitutional, too. In *Singer v. Hara* (1974), the state court rejected this argument, holding that the equal rights amendment could be construed only to protect women and not homosexuals.[160] Although the sex discrimination argument saw a revival in the 1990s (Chapter 6), it saw little further action in the 1970s.

The only arguable victory was a New Jersey decision recognizing the marriage of a post-operative male-to-female transsexual and a biological male, but the judges reached this result only because they were able to persuade themselves that the partners were different sexes.[161] Otherwise, legal agitation for gay marriage in the 1970s was a complete flop. One reason was that allowing gay people to marry seemed like a recognition of complete equality, when virtual equality was all society was willing to accept. Other reasons will be explored in Chapter 8.

Legal Relationships Short of Marriage. Some of the rights of spousehood can be created by private contracting. Thus, lesbian and gay couples have long been able to purchase property in joint tenancy, establish joint checking accounts, grant one another powers of attorney, and name one another primary beneficiaries in their wills.[162] Many of these mechanisms were not available for working-class gays, and even the well-to-do found that the law did not always enforce agreements. Blood family sometimes challenged wills bequeathing estates to same-sex partners, on the ground that the heir exercised "undue influence" on the testator. After Gertrude Stein's death in 1946, for example, the Stein family stripped her forty-year life partner, Alice Toklas, of virtually all inheritance.[163] Gay testators in the 1960s and 1970s ran some risk of similar dispositions. The

New York courts refused to honor the will that left the Kay Jewelry fortune to the decedent's lawyer-lover. A letter declaring the decedent's love for his attorney was interpreted by the court as reflecting not sincere love, but "gratitude utterly unreal, highly exaggerated and pitched to a state of fervor and ecstasy." A dissenting judge accused the majority of reasoning from "surmise, suspicion, conjecture and moral indignation and resentment."[164]

A mechanism for imposing spousal *obligations,* as opposed to *rights,* arose out of *Marvin v. Marvin* (1976), where the California Supreme Court held that unmarried partners could sue for enforcement of explicit or implicit promises of support or financial sharing.[165] *Marvin* rights were not available in all states, and even California courts sometimes refused to apply *Marvin* to gay couples. In other cases all over the country, courts were willing to enforce contract rights notwithstanding the sexual orientation of the participants, often by just ignoring evidence of the parties' homosexual relationship. Another strategy for gay couples to obtain spousal rights or their equivalents was to fit themselves into other existing legal categories. Gay couples sometimes were able to form legal relationships through the adoption of one partner by the other. This strategy was limited by state age, relationship, and other restrictions; states as disparate as Florida and New York blocked adoption as a way to establish legal rights for gay couples.[166]

A final strategy was to create a new institution, namely, domestic partnership, where government would extend symbolic recognition of the unions to registered couples and attach a few rights for the benefit of the partners. The first major domestic partnership bill was passed by the San Francisco Board of Supervisors in 1982, but Mayor Diane Feinstein vetoed it on the ground that it unacceptably "mimics a marriage license." Two years later, Berkeley adopted the first operative domestic partnership policy, and more than fifty other cities followed in the late 1980s and the 1990s.[167] Although many local officials took the Feinstein position that domestic partnership was too close to gay marriage for their comfort, the analogy was far-fetched: domestic partnership imposed none of the obligations of marriage and at most one or two of its tangible benefits.

Custody of Children. Many of the people who came out of the closet after Stonewall were married with children. It was exceptional for the state to try to take away a gay parent's children, in part because the Supreme Court had recognized people's fundamental right to the companionship and care of their children.[168] Where one parent's coming out ended the marriage, however, there was often a contest between the two parents over custody or visitation. The large majority of the early cases yielded little usable law because judges sealed the records of trials, refused to report decisions on appeal, and referred only obliquely in published decisions to the sexual orientation issue. Once judges started to address custody issues publicly, they created a variety of discriminations against lesbian and gay parents.[169]

One discrimination was a per se rule that homosexuality disqualified a parent from custody. Early cases rested the per se rule on the "immorality" of the gay parent's "lifestyle,"[170] a proposition that eroded in the 1970s. A key case was *Schuster v. Schuster* (1978), where Sandy Schuster and Madeleine Isaacson presented expert evidence that parental orientation is irrelevant to a child's development and that their children were healthy and normal. The courts left custody with the mothers, but with conditions. The trial court admonished the mothers not to "use" the children as a showcase for "homosexuality," and the appeals court refused to allow the mothers to live together. This was not an unusual condition. The first open lesbian to win custody of her children, Camille Mitchell, was burdened with severe constraints on same-sex socializing by a Santa Clara County court.[171]

During the 1970s, antigay discourse shifted from the per se rule to a rule requiring judges to consider the best interests of the child, including homophobic third-party reactions. In *S. v. S.* (1980), the Kentucky Court of Appeals required that child custody be shifted from mother to father when the mother came out as a lesbian. The court accepted as a fact that "the lesbianism of the mother, because of the failure of the community to accept and support such a condition, forces on the child a need for secrecy and the isolation imposed by such a secret, thus separating the child from his or her peers."[172] The leading case insisting upon a more gay-friendly best interests of the child inquiry was *Bezio v. Patenaude* (1980), where the Massachusetts Supreme Court held that there had to be a specific showing of harm to the child, exclusive of general societal prejudice, to justify depriving a gay parent of custody.[173]

Another discrimination was a rule against unsupervised visitation by the gay parent. In *In re J.S. & C.* (1974), New Jersey's Superior Court ruled that a gay father's constitutional interest in the companionship of his children militated against a per se rule prohibiting any visitation or contact with the children. Nonetheless, the court held that the welfare of the children justified restrictions on that visitation. The court relied on the father's advocacy of gay rights (he was a member of the Gay Activists Alliance) and the "speculative" possibility that, according to the mother's expert, the children "would be subject to either overt or covert homosexual seduction which would detrimentally influence their sexual development." Accordingly, the court limited the gay father's visitation time and conditioned any visitation on the father's agreement that he "not involve the children in any homosexual related activities or publicity" or have his lover present at any time. Such discriminatory conditions on visitation by gay parents were commonly imposed and approved by state trial and appellate judges.[174]

part two

REMNANTS OF THE CLOSET
(DON'T ASK, DON'T TELL)

The gay rights movement had won many successes by 1981—judicial nullification or legislative repeal of laws criminalizing consensual sodomy in most jurisdictions, of almost all state criminal laws targeting same-sex intimacy and municipal cross-dressing ordinances, of the immigration and citizenship exclusions, of all censorship laws targeting same-sex eroticism, of almost all laws or regulations prohibiting bars from becoming congregating places for gay people, and of exclusions of gay people from public employment in most jurisdictions. These changes partially dismantled the apartheid of the closet, whereby gay people were formally excluded from citizenship and left to a sociopolitical state of nature. Since 1981, an increasing number of states and cities have adopted laws affirmatively protecting gay people against private discrimination and violence, recognizing gay families as domestic partnerships, and allowing second-parent adoption by a parent's same-sex partner.[1]

Nonetheless, gay people remain second-class citizens in the United States, a state of the law documented in Appendix B3 to this book. As I write in January 1999, government policy still pervasively discriminates against people based on their sexual or gender orientation:

- *Marriage.* All states exclude same-sex couples from receiving civil marriage licenses routinely given to different-sex couples. Legal efforts to obtain such rights have met with strong opposition in Hawaii, Vermont, and Alaska and have triggered anticipatory responses elsewhere. Thirty states have adopted statutes refusing to recognize other states' same-sex marriages in their jurisdictions. The Defense of Marriage Act (DOMA) exempts these statutes from challenge under the full faith and credit clause and directs that 1,049 federal statutes adverting to spousehood or marriage never include same-sex couples.[2]

- *Crime.* Nineteen states still criminalize sodomy between consenting adults, six of them only same-sex sodomy (Appendix A1). Emphasizing that it was only addressing "homosexual sodomy," the Supreme Court rejected a right to privacy challenge to such laws in *Bowers v. Hardwick* (1986).[3] Some states that have decriminalized sodomy still make it illegal to solicit for "deviate sexual intercourse."

- *Children.* Several states have created express presumptions against child custody for lesbian or gay male parents when former spouses desire custody, and other states have effectively the same approach because they consider social prejudice when determining the "best interests of the child."[4] Similar presumptions have been imposed against transsexual parents, and at least one state allows their parenthood rights to be terminated.[5] Three states officially prohibit gay people from adopting.[6]

- *Employment.* The United States armed forces exclude gay people, as well as anyone who commits same-sex sodomy and cannot persuade the military that she or he is straight.[7] Some state and local governments formally or informally exclude openly gay people from employment as teachers, police officers, or even firefighters.

- *No Promo Homo.* Several states require or recommend that their schools teach that homosexuality or same-sex intimacy is not acceptable in their states.[8] Similar "no promo homo" (no promotion of homosexuality) provisions are regularly proposed for federal legislation. AIDS education and funding for the arts programs are supposed to consider "offensiveness," a code for editing out materials that are gay-friendly.[9]

- *Antidiscrimination Rules.* Federal law prohibits discrimination because of sex in private as well as public schools and workplaces. These policies protect females and males discriminated against because they do not conform to gender stereotypes, except nonconforming transsexuals, transvestites, lesbians, bisexuals, and gay men. These policies have been interpreted to protect women harassed by men, men harassed by women, straight men harassed by straight or gay men, but not gay employees harassed by homophobic straight employees.[10] All but eleven states and the District of Columbia have similar gaps (Appendix B3).

The foregoing list is just the tip of the iceberg, as it reflects only the official discrimination against gay people; a great deal more informal discrimination occurs that no one acknowledges.

The tension between gay demands for equal rights and continuing antigay discrimination has made issues of gaylaw central to American public law at the turn of the millennium. Whether the state can criminalize same-sex intimacy between consenting adults remains a central issue of privacy law, notwithstanding *Hardwick* (Chapter 4). The don't ask, don't tell policy of the armed forces and some state employers fundamentally challenges the nation's commitment to the free expression ideal of the first amendment (Chapter 5). And among the cutting-edge issues of equal protection are those raised by *Romer v. Evans* (1996), where the Supreme Court struck down a Colorado initiative that amended the state constitution to override local ordinances prohibiting sexual orientation discrimination. The Court majority held that the initiative's narrow goal of conserving scarce enforcement resources was not reasonably related to its language and probable effect, and that its apparent purpose (gaybashing) was illegitimate.[11] Because the initiative was bizarrely drafted and the Court's opinion more broadly reasoned than needed to decide the case, *Evans* raises more questions than it answers. Can *Hardwick* stand? Don't ask, don't tell? Bars to same-sex marriage? DOMA? The object of Part Two is to exploit the opportunity offered by *Evans* to rethink public law's continuing antigay discriminations. Any rethinking should account for three things: current constitutional doctrine, public law norms that might inform the application of *Evans,* and the lessons of history, including the history examined in the first part of this book. Its account of the gaylegal experience between 1881 and 1981 is brimming with implications for larger themes of American public law and jurisprudence, as well as for gaylaw's continuing challenges to what remains of the legal regime of the closet.

Thesis number one is that evolution in public law is driven, but not predetermined, by changes in society and culture generally, and changing social and political power in particular.[12] When gender-benders and homosexuals were powerless individuals so anathematized by social consensus that they crouched in the closet, the law suppressed and persecuted them. Once gender-benders and gay people came out of their closets in great numbers and organized themselves as a minority group, they graduated from social anathema to social distaste—and the law changed immediately. Over time, law moved from suppression to mild toleration to occasional support. That movement, in turn, contributed to the congealing of the religious right as a political force seeking to preserve state policies reflecting traditionalist values.

This thesis has critical consequences for understanding legal reasoning in public law. In the larger time frame of Part One (1881–1981), public law was never just the application of neutral principles, but was a struggle to determine what "neutral" application of agreed-upon principles and criteria might be. A lot of public law issues that were settled in 1981 were settled in the opposite way in 1881, or even in 1961, including the validity of making cross-dressing a crime, the opportunity of people of the same sex to dance and congregate in bars, the admissibility of gender-deviant noncitizens into this country or as citizens, and the suitability of such folks for parenthood and public employment. The changes were, on the whole, not driven by legal logic so much as by new social facts about gay people and their existence as a group the pluralist system felt it had to accommodate.

The first thesis can be illustrated horizontally (divergent law occurring at the same time) as well as vertically (divergent law over time). Different jurisdictions today adopt strikingly different resolutions of the same gaylegal issues, such as the legality of same-sex intimacy and the legal recognition afforded gay families of choice. Generally, nonsouthern jurisdictions with big cities have resolved these issues in gay-friendly ways, while jurisdictions dominated by rural and small-town populations have resolved these issues in favor of traditional values. The former have long had organized gay populations centered in big cities, and the political community realized it had to accommodate that constituency. The latter have had smaller and less organized openly gay populations and more powerful groups who made it their business to oppose gay rights. A related variable continues to be religion: states dominated by the Southern Baptist Convention and the Church of Jesus Christ of the Latter Day Saints have been more likely to deny gay people rights than states dominated by Roman Catholic, mainstream Protestant, and Jewish faiths.

A corollary of the first thesis is that the particular sources of public law make less difference than the evolving political equilibrium. Thus, I am skeptical about Cass Sunstein's argument that the due process clause is intrinsically less useful for gays because it is *backward-looking,* while the equal protection clause is more useful because it is *forward-looking.*[13] Sunstein's thesis is a way to reconcile *Evans* and *Hardwick*—the latter due process decision defers to traditionalist sodomy laws, while the former equal protection decision looks ahead to equal gay citizenship—but is belied by gaylegal history (Chapter 3). In the 1970s the vagueness and criminal procedure cases, all traveling under the due process umbrella, were more dynamic and forward-looking for gay people than equal protection cases were. As the cross-dressing cases illustrate, due process tradition is not static, especially if the clause is read in light of the general principles confirmed by tradition (for example, the criminal law must give fair notice of its commands) and the application of those principles in light of ever-evolving social conventions (for example, the dress of one's sex is unclear today in ways it would not have been in 1864). Relatedly, equal protection and due process are interconnected rights. The due process right to nonarbitrary treatment by the state is related to the equal protection right to similar treatment of similarly situated people: the former demands a reasoned basis for the state's action that hurts me; the latter demands a reasoned basis for the state's hurting me but not you. Thus, the Mattachine Society and other gay rights organizations saw their due process challenges to civil service exclusions of gay people as forward-looking and as an important step toward equal citizenship. Decisions like *Norton, One Eleven Wines,* and *Morrison* (Chapter 3) advanced gay equality by overturning unreasonable discriminations aganst gay people but were based on the due process requirement of nonarbitrariness.[14]

Due process and equal protection are particularly intertwined in the consensual sodomy law challenges because existing laws not only threaten privacy rights but also discriminate on the basis of sexual orientation, either on their face or in practice. The argument of Chapter 4, opening this part of the book, is that *Hardwick* must be narrowed in light of *Evans* and cannot be read to allow state regulation only of homosexual, and not heterosexual, sodomy. Stripped of its antihomosexual rhetoric, *Hardwick* can no longer be applied to deny other rights to gay people and should be narrowed or overruled outright. The only reasoned argument for not overruling *Hardwick* would be judicial reluctance to extend the right to privacy, which has ambiguous mooring in the U.S. Constitution. In that event, however, two other arguments can be made for overruling *Hardwick:* state criminalization of private sodomy between consenting adults restricts free expression in violation of the first amendment (Chapter 5), and the six states prohibiting only same-sex sodomy also violate the equal protection clause (Chapter 6).

I do not maintain that law is irrelevant. *Thesis number two,* indeed, is that law has played an increasing role in national discourse about same-sex intimacy and gender-bending. Discourse about same-sex intimacy has shifted from an exclusive emphasis on religious natural law rhetoric, to a correlative focus on medical rhetoric, to a concentration on legal rights rhetoric. The shifting discourse has generally been to the advantage of gay people and gender-benders, who had few arguments for their behavior under natural law, some arguments under medical premises, and many rights-based arguments. Contrariwise, anti-gay rhetoric has shifted from religious tropes about immoral sodomites, to medical ones of degeneracy and inversion and psychopathy, to legal metaphors invoking the rights of parents, children, and heterosexuals. The rhetorical shift has been cumulative, as new arguments augment rather than displace old arguments. For example, antigay policies were justified in the 1960s by arguments that homosexuals are immoral and disgusting, medically sick and gender-deviant, and predatory against children. Gays and their allies responded in the late 1960s and early 1970s with feminist and Marxist critiques of natural law as a paradigm for policy, medical evidence against the sickness and child molestation myths, and positive arguments grounded upon privacy, civil rights, and free expression. Although traditionalists still made the most discredited arguments, their discourse shifted in the mid-1970s to emphasize a more modern argument: even if homosexuals should not be put in jail, homosexuality should not be promoted by the state, and in many contexts homosexual presence would be an invasion of heterosexuals' privacy.

This shift in antigay rhetoric illustrates what Reva Siegel calls the *modernization of justification.*[15] From women's experience, Siegel argues that opposition to minority rights can often be strengthened by rejustifying old policies under modernized rhetoric. Consistent with Siegel's thesis, the military exclusion and the bar to same-sex marriage emerged from the post-Stonewall period as strong as ever. Their continued robustness today may be due in part to modernized rhetorical justifications, but the more likely explanation is that these antigay policies are mythically too central to heterosexual culture to abandon easily. Contrary to Siegel's hypothesis, other antigay policies—laws criminalizing sodomy, public lewdness, and cross-dressing; rules against gays congregating in bars, student clubs, and the workplace; censorship of homoerotica; employment discrimination against gay people, especially in education and police forces; and bars to lesbian and gay parenting—decisively lost ground in the 1970s and 1980s even though there were plenty of defenders and the defenses refocused on no promo homo and heteroprivacy arguments. The dynamic of evolving justification that Siegel excavates is genuine, but it has no general consequences for gay rights.

The chapters of Part Two maintain that the internal dynamics of legal discourse support expansion of gay rights in still-contested arenas. Chapter 4 questions a decision *(Hardwick)* that few academics defend anymore; even a narrowly defined privacy right undermines the gays-are-presumptive-criminals rationale for other discriminations against gay people. Chapter 5 criticizes the military exclusion on the ground that it constitutes multiple suppressions of expression protected by the first amendment. The military exclusion can survive court challenges only if judges strongly defer to the military, and to a degree that would be harmful to the judiciary and to the country. Chapter 5 further maintains that the state normally cannot, consistent with first amendment principles, censor the identity speech of state employees. The most significant antigay policies today, of course, are those that openly discriminate against gay people, such as laws that criminalize only same-sex but not different-sex sodomy. Chapter 6 makes three different kinds of equal protection arguments against such laws: they rest upon no rational basis and therefore fall under *Evans;* their discrimination on the basis of sexual orientation requires something more than a rational basis, which such laws do not have; and their discrimination is also a sex-based discrimination, which must be justified by a strong state interest.

Can the recognition of legal rights make more than a rhetorical difference? *Thesis number three* is that public law is an independent variable affecting minority group experiences and, for gay people, has both contributed to the construction and maintenance of the closet (Chapters 1 and 2) *and* even more dramatically to its instability (Chapters 2 and 3). Although most of the Warren Court Justices were homoignorant or phobic, that Court facilitated the process by which the Stonewall riots—which occurred the year Chief Justice Earl Warren retired from the Court (1969)—became the great turning point in gay political and legal history. The Court's contribution was to establish a public law consensus around certain premises that protected unpopular groups from state erasure: censors could not obtain ex parte prior restraints *(Marcus)* and could not suppress informational or nonprurient publications *(Roth* and *One, Inc.);*[16] the state could not prohibit unpopular people from forming political and social groups *(NAACP)* or discipline public employees for addressing issues of public concern *(Pickering);*[17] public schools and universities could not censor students' expression *(Bonner);*[18] the police could not entrap defendants *(Sherman),* invade their private spaces *(Griswold, Katz,* and *Stanley),* or arrest people without informing them of their right to counsel *(Miranda).*[19]

This complex web of constitutional expectations, many of which were well ahead of American public opinion, not only protected the fledgling gay rights movement that began in earnest before Stonewall but also facilitated the explosion of coming out stories, gay rights organizations, and political and social activism immediately following Stonewall. Without the Warren Court rights in place, gay people would have been more fearful about coming out, and the police and the censors would have been a lot more bold about suppressing gay groups. Just as legislative and administrative organs of the state had created a suffocating closet during the McCarthy era (1947–1956), so judicial organs laid the foundation for its partial collapse during the Warren Court era (1953–1969). Indeed, the two phenomena worked together: the McCarthy era pushed people like Frank Kameny out of the closet by witch-hunting them, and the Warren era gave Kameny and like people enough legally protected room to organize gay liberatory organizations, publications, and churches that flowered after 1969. The role of law was symbolic and hortatory as well as space-creating. The Warren Court's race discrimination decisions inspired closeted gay people to think that they, too, might be entitled to human dignity, and the Court's criminal procedure and privacy decisions empowered allies of gay liberation such as the ACLU and shackled its enemies, especially homophobic police.

This facilitative process changed during the antigay Supreme Court of Chief Justice Warren Burger. The Burger Court not only denied rights in almost every decided case involving openly gay litigants or materials but narrowed Warren Court decisions that potentially empowered gay people against homophobes. Thus, *Hardwick* ruled it facetious for gays to claim the privacy right established for heterosexual intercourse in *Griswold; Miller* changed the *Roth* test for obscenity in ways that made it easier to suppress homoerotica, and *Hamling* and *Ward* applied the new test in an explicitly antihomosexual manner;[20] *Rose v. Locke* (1975) held that *Papachristou* should not be applied to sodomy laws, and the denial of certiorari in *Mayes* refused to apply *Papachristou* to cross-dressing laws either;[21] the *NAACP* right of association, extended to congregating in gay bars in some states, was trumped in *LaRue* by the twenty-first amendment;[22] exceptions to equality and free speech guarantees were created by the Court for military, high school, and prison contexts, which were the basis for denying gay claims in those fora *(Beller)*;[23] and so on. By treating sex as dirty conduct rather than expression and "homosexuals" as presumptive sodomites rather than as citizens, the Burger Court did what it could to preserve the remnants of the closet. *Don't ask, don't tell* sums up the Burger Court philosophy, itself derived from the approach still taken in rural and small-town America: gay people should be unseen but not heard.

The Burger Court did not require antigay policies, however; it only permitted a local option to choose such policies. During that period (1969–1986), the California Supreme Court, the state legislature, and the city of San Francisco opted for a gay-friendly understanding of public law at odds with that allowed by the Burger Court vision. Due process in California meant that vague, turn-of-the-century criminal laws were unenforceable against private sexual expression (*Bielicki, Pryor,* sodomy repeal).[24] First amendment freedoms meant that gay publications and erotica were available anywhere in the state, and thousands of gay bars, social organizations, and political groups flourished *(Vallerga)*.[25] Equality meant not only that the state would not discriminate on the basis of sexual orientation in its own employment and law enforcement policies (*Morrison* and *Jack M*), but also that the state protected gay people against private discrimination (*Pacific Tel. & Tel.,* local ordinances).[26] The upshot of these developments was to adopt as state policy the idea that there are several acceptable sexual variations and to give gay people space to come out of their closets.

Contrast California's approach, followed in urbanized jurisdictions of the Northeast, Midwest, and West Coast, with that of the Burger Court, followed in less urban jurisdictions of the South, the Great Plains, and the West. The animating principle of the updated traditionalist approach is *tolerable if closeted sexual variation:* gay people should not be penalized for their sexual orientation (and we won't ask), as long as they are discreet about it (so don't you tell). The animating principle of the more progressive approach is *benign sexual variation:* one's variation from gender and sexual norms should not ordinarily be any more legally stigmatizing than one's variation from religious or racial norms. The transsexual, the lesbian, the gay men, and the bisexual should have all the rights now accorded the Mormon, the Jew, and the African American— all of whom were previously and similarly stigmatized and even sexualized by our legal culture. The central and recurring normative argument of Part Two is that there is nothing about gender and sexual variation that justifies legal discrimination and that the public culture ought to implement the principle of benign sexual variation by recognizing equal rights for gay people. "Homo equality" would entail state nondiscrimination as to gay people, state neutrality as to these sexual variations, and state insistence on nondiscrimination in the marketplace. Once the state endorses gay equality, sexual orientation will begin a long process of melting away as a stigma.

This view is an optimistic one. Looking at the integration and criminal procedure cases important in the struggle for racial equality, Michael Seidman says that legal victories such as *Brown* and *Miranda* did their beneficiaries little good and actually may have impeded social pressure for racial equality.[27] This perverse result came about because the legal victories were empty without follow-up, induced smugness in civil rights groups that impeded such follow-up, and stimulated racist reactions that undermined the whole enterprise. Seidman's analysis and his characteristic despair about the efficacy of legal rights have sharp relevance for gaylaw. For example, criminal procedure rights did gay defendants little good—just as Seidman would suspect—until gay political power persuaded cities to call off their decoy cops, vice patrols, and urinal spies. Contrary to Seidmanian pessimism, however, gay organizations in San Francisco, Denver, New York, and elsewhere were able to deploy police violations of neutral rights as a means to pressure the police by generating publicity and some public sympathy. What undermines the Seidman hypothesis for gay people is the importance that legal rights assumed in gay/police negotiations, substantiated by the firsthand accounts of such negotiations.[28]

Consider, too, the ordinances protecting gay people against job discrimination in the public and private sector. On paper, these laws look like great legal victories, but reporter Randy Shilts complained that they were "just toothless paper tigers": few government resources are invested in enforcement of antidiscrimination guarantees, few employees file complaints, and often neither employees nor management is even aware of such laws or their precise protections.[29] Moreover, such ordinances have invigorated antigay political coalitions and triggered antigay initiatives, 79 percent of which have been successful at the polls, including the Colorado initiative invalidated in *Evans*. On the other hand, there have been tangible short-term benefits from these laws. San Francisco's ordinance prohibiting sexual orientation discrimination in the private sector and the California Supreme Court's decision in *Pacific Tel. & Tel.* were key reasons for a radical change in policy by one of the state's largest employers, Pacific Telephone & Telegraph Company. The company became one of the best employers in the state for gay people, and the legal prods over several years were a decisive reason for that volte-face. A recent long-term study of gay rights ordinances concludes that, notwithstanding the modest enforcement and the antigay backlash, these ordinances have had substantial effects—empowering gay employees to come out of the closet and serving as focal points for companies to treat gay employees with dignity equal to that accorded their straight employees.[30]

4. *Hardwick* and Historiography

Michael Bowers, adulterer, and Michael Hardwick, sodomite, are forever coupled in the legal imagination. For in 1986 Bowers, then Attorney General of Georgia in the midst of a long-term adulterous affair, successfully defended Georgia's sodomy law against Hardwick's claim that the constitutional right to privacy prohibited its application to oral sex between him and a consenting adult man in the bedroom of his home. Although the Georgia sodomy law prohibited oral and anal intercourse between two people of either sex, Justice Byron White's opinion for a five-Justice majority in *Bowers v. Hardwick* (1986) insisted that the "only claim properly before the Court . . . is Hardwick's challenge to the Georgia statute as applied to consensual homosexual activity."[1] As narrowed in this way, Hardwick's claim struck the Supreme Court as unlike those in earlier right to privacy cases, which had arisen in the context of heterosexual intimacy. Key to the Court's analysis was its belief that the due process right of privacy could only be applied to protect those fundamental liberties "'deeply rooted in this Nation's history and tradition.'" Because "homosexual sodomy" had long been criminal in Anglo-American law, the Court held that there was no "'deeply rooted'" liberty Hardwick could claim. In the light of history, the Court majority found Hardwick's fundamental rights claim "at best, facetious."[2] The Court then ruled that Georgia's sodomy law rationally reflected the "presumed belief of a majority of the electorate in Georgia that homosexual sodomy is immoral and unacceptable."[3]

The Court's decision in *Hardwick* has become infamous, partly because White went out of his way to focus on "homosexual sodomy" and to disrespect "homosexuality," a feature more pronounced in Chief Justice Warren Burger's concurring opinion, which invoked "Judeo-Christian moral standards" and "millennia of moral teachings" against "homosexual sodomy."[4] The association of sodomy with homosexuality resonated in the popular mind in 1986; seven states had reformed their sodomy laws to decriminalize consensual sodomy for different-sex but not for same-sex partners, and three others followed this course shortly after *Hardwick.*[a] Nonetheless, this kind of rhetoric turned the *Hardwick* decision into an exemplar of legal homophobia. Contributing to the belief that the decision was an expression of prejudice were reports that Justice Lewis Powell, the critical fifth vote for the majority, switched his vote after hysterical lobbying from the Chief Justice; Powell himself fueled *Hardwick*'s bad odor when he publicly proclaimed it the vote he most regretted.[5] Although gay people are predictably critical of the decision, commentators of all sexualities and genders have criticized *Hardwick* as manipulative, ignorant, inefficient, violent, historically inaccurate, misogynistic, authoritarian, and contrary to precedent.[6] If some of the Justices aimed to disrespect homosexuality, they ended by wounding the Court.

The Court sought to atone for *Hardwick* in *Romer v. Evans* (1996), which invalidated a Colorado initiative preventing state and local government units from carrying out laws or policies whereby "homosexual orientation" could be the basis for any positive legal claim. The Court emphasized two features of the initiative, either fatal to its constitutionality. On the one hand, the initiative sought to accomplish something the state could not do, namely, "singling out a certain class of citizens for disfavored legal status or general hardships." On the other hand, the initiative raised an "inevitable inference that the disadvantage imposed is born of animosity toward the class of persons affected."[7] Although Justice Anthony Kennedy's opinion for the Court declined to discuss the earlier decision, the logic of *Evans* calls *Hardwick* into question.

To focus sodomy prohibitions on "homosexual sodomy" alone, as *Hardwick* suggested and as ten states have expressly done, is to "singl[e] out a certain class of citizens for disfavored legal status" because of popular "animosity toward the class of persons affected," contrary to *Evans*. Reconceiving Georgia's sodomy law more narrowly than the statute was written, *Hardwick* found a rational basis for Georgia's sodomy law in the "presumed belief of a majority of the electorate in

a. Arkansas (1977), Kansas (1969), Kentucky (1974), Missouri (1977), Montana (1973), Nevada (1977), Texas (1973). Soon to join this array were Oklahoma (juducial decision, 1986), Tennessee (1989), and Maryland (judicial decision, 1990). Nevada repealed its same-sex sodomy misdemeanor in 1993. Appendix A1 provides references for each state.

Georgia that homosexual sodomy is immoral and unacceptable," but *Evans* struck down a law that rested upon the actual, voted-upon belief of a majority of the electorate in Colorado that gay people are immoral and equal rights for them unacceptable. To satisfy *Evans,* an antigay law requires something more than popular animosity; the state must show that the disfavored class of people is committing harm, which was never charged in Hardwick's case. Although *Evans* does not overrule—or even mention—*Hardwick,* the two decisions do not rest easily together in the same logic set. Justice Antonin Scalia recognized this in his *Evans* dissent. "If it is constitutionally permissible for a State to make homosexual conduct criminal [*Hardwick*], surely it is constitutionally permissible for a State to enact other laws merely *disfavoring* homosexual conduct [*Evans*]."[8] The majority opinion failed to deny this assertion. Now that *Evans* has been decided, the assertion can be reversed: If it is constitutionally impermissible for the state to enact laws disfavoring people who engage in "homosexual conduct," then is it not impermissible to penalize the conduct itself?

Once *Hardwick*'s rationalization of sodomy laws as antihomosexual measures falters, the states prohibiting only same-sex sodomy can no longer defend their laws; indeed, four of the ten states with such discriminations have already repealed (Nevada) or judicially invalidated (Kentucky, Tennessee, Montana) their same-sex-only sodomy laws (Appendix A1). Additionally, states that criminalize all sodomy must defend their laws by reference to heterosexual as well as homosexual sodomy. At least three-quarters of the straight population engage in oral sex, and almost a fourth have engaged in anal sex.[9] It would be absurd to brand all these people criminal, yet that is what a neutral regime criminalizing consensual sodomy would have to do.

The foregoing is one argument for limiting or overruling *Hardwick.* The remainder of this chapter exploits *Hardwick*'s vulnerability by exploring other problems with the decision: its inconsistency with the Court's precedents, its misleading use of history, and its incoherence with productive state policy in the postindustrial world. This chapter also considers normative issues underlying the *Hardwick* debate. Supreme Court precedent both before and after *Hardwick* suggests that the right of privacy precludes the state from commandeering people's bodies and directing private sexual exploration by consenting adults into state-approved channels. Courts in other Western countries and traditionalist states in this country have recognized that this principle protects same-sex intimacy just as much as different-sex intimacy. The Supreme Court in *Hardwick* sought to avoid the gay rights implications of this principle by invoking the historical pedigree of laws against "homosexual sodomy" at the time of the framing of the fourteenth amendment (1868). This chapter will demonstrate the multifaceted failure of this project: the oral sex Michael Hardwick was

engaging in was not "sodomy" under the common law and was not legally regulated anywhere in this country until 1879; for evidentiary and normative reasons, sodomy laws were not regularly applied to consensual private intimacy
until the twentieth century; the framers of the fourteenth amendment would
not have justified sodomy laws as antihomosexual measures but instead would
have viewed them as measures to assure that sex be procreative and gendered, a
regime inconsistent with the Supreme Court's privacy and equal protection
jurisprudence. Augmenting the inconsistency with *Evans*, this chapter makes
out a case for overruling *Hardwick* based on privacy principles, precedents, and
even history. Jurisprudentially, my argument is that the Court cannot avoid
normative issues by mechanical reliance on original intent and historical arguments.

Critique of *Hardwick*'s Analysis of Precedent

Although privacy is not named as a protected right in the U.S. Constitution,
American judges since the nineteenth century have read constitutional assurances of due process of law to have a substantive libertarian component. In *Union
Pacific Railroad v. Botsford* (1891), the Supreme Court held that the state could
not require people to submit to required physical examinations.[10] The right to
bodily integrity formed the core of the early right to privacy, but the Court
understood the right to include intimate associations as well. In 1923 the Court
explained that due process liberty includes "not merely freedom from bodily
restraint [*Botsford*] but also the right of the individual to contract, to engage in
any of the common occupations of life, to acquire useful knowledge, to marry,
to establish a home and bring up children."[11] Significant in this catalog was the
omission of sexual liberty. This omission was underscored by Justice Oliver
Wendell Holmes's opinion in *Buck v. Bell* (1927), which treated as a routine
matter Virginia's forced sterilization of mentally disabled people.[12] Reflecting
the ideology of American degeneracy theorists as well as the progressives' disinclination to allow judges to tinker with legislated social engineering, Holmes
was pretty satisfied with himself for writing a dismissive opinion. But the next
generation of judges, reflecting the views of Margaret Sanger and Sigmund
Freud, were more likely to believe that sexuality is a key feature of one's personal development and, therefore, a liberty as fundamental as family and more
fundamental than economic freedom.

Thus, the New Deal Court struck down a sterilization scheme applicable to
certain classes of habitual criminals (such as thieves) and not others (such as
embezzlers). Justice William Douglas's opinion in *Skinner v. Oklahoma* (1942)
ruled that sterilization involves "one of the basic civil rights of man. Marriage

and procreation are fundamental to the very existence and survival of the race." The person sterilized "is forever deprived of a basic liberty."[13] At the moment Douglas recognized a constitutional right to procreate, Sanger and her allies in the planned parenthood movement insisted that ordered liberty also included the obverse of *Skinner:* the right to engage in sex without fear of pregnancy.[14]

The Supreme Court twice dismissed on procedural grounds planned parenthood lawsuits against Connecticut's law criminalizing the sale or use of contraceptives. In the second challenge, *Poe v. Ullman* (1961), dissenting Justice John Harlan argued that Connecticut's ban violated the due process clause, which protects rights "'which are *fundamental;* which belong . . . to the citizens of all free governments.'" Citing *Skinner,* Harlan argued that the privacy involved in lovemaking by a married couple in their home involves the "most fundamental aspect of 'liberty'" and requires strict judicial scrutiny. Harlan immediately qualified his argument: "The right of privacy most manifestly is not an absolute. Thus, I would not suggest that adultery, homosexuality, fornication and incest are immune from criminal enquiry, however privately practiced."[15]

In *Griswold v. Connecticut* (1965), the Court struck down Connecticut's anti-contraception law as inconsistent with a right of privacy Justice Douglas cobbled together from the "penumbras" of the Bill of Rights.[16] *Griswold* confirmed and expanded *Skinner*'s holding that an individual has a fundamental liberty interest in her or his sexuality. Whereas *Skinner* emphasized the traditional goal of procreation, *Griswold* delinked constitutional protection of private sexuality from procreation. Whereas *Skinner* struck down a eugenics-based statute that was a relative innovation in American law, *Griswold* struck down an 1879 anti-contraception law that was preceded by anticontraception laws at the national, state, and local levels. Not only had Americans not traditionally enjoyed free access to contraceptives, but the due process clause was adopted (in 1868) against the backdrop of anticontraceptive sentiment. *Griswold* was a dynamic interpretation of the liberty assured by the due process clause.

In other ways, however, *Griswold* offered a traditionalist understanding of the right of sexual privacy. Douglas's opinion for the Court emphasized the marital features of the new right of privacy, the "bilateral loyalty" and intimacy involved in plaintiffs' marriage. Concurring Justices Harlan, Goldberg, Brennan, and Warren quoted from Harlan's *Poe* dissent to distance the right to marital privacy from "[a]dultery and homosexuality,"[17] ironically, the two crimes committed by Bowers and Hardwick two decades later. Nonetheless, the Court expanded *Griswold* beyond marital sexuality after Harlan's retirement. In *Eisenstadt v. Baird* (1972), a divided Court struck down a statute preventing unmarried couples from receiving contraceptives. Justice William Brennan's opinion for the Court emphasized the right of *"the individual,* married or single to be free from unwarranted governmental intrusion into matters so fundamentally affecting a person as the decision to bear or beget a child."[18] The individual's right to sexual privacy was dramatically underscored when the Court in *Roe v. Wade* (1973) held that an unmarried woman has a fundamental liberty interest in the decision whether to obtain an abortion.[19]

Brennan later said that *Griswold* protected "individual decisions in matters of childbearing"[20] but said nothing about the further ambit of the right. Relevant to this question was *Stanley v. Georgia* (1969), which overturned defendant's conviction for possessing obscene materials in his home. Justice Thurgood Marshall's opinion for the Court rested upon first amendment protection for the dissemination of ideas, *Griswold*'s right of privacy, and the fourth amendment "'right to be left alone'" to one's own "'thoughts . . . emotions and . . . sensations,'" at least in the "privacy of his own home." Marshall essentially suggested that private masturbatory fantasies, with pictorial aids, were beyond state interference, especially when they occurred at home.[21] A plurality of the Court in *Moore v. City of East Cleveland* (1976) applied the right of privacy to invalidate a law limiting cohabitation to married and closely related persons.[22]

Although the Burger Court refused to override state sodomy laws throughout the 1970s (Chapter 3), it did not write a full-scale decision addressing the privacy issues. Commentators read the precedents to create broad constitutional protection for personal freedom in matters of sexual behavior between consenting adults,[23] and state judges outside the South began to follow suit in the late 1970s (Appendix A1). In *People v. Onofre* (1980), the New York Court of Appeals invalidated the state consensual sodomy law on privacy grounds. The court read *Eisenstadt* and *Stanley* to require that the right of privacy be extended to prevent "government interference with the practice of personal choice in matters of intimate sexual behavior out of view of the public and with no commercial component."[24]

What were the limits of the sexual privacy right in 1982, when Michael Hardwick challenged Georgia's sodomy law? Consider the following array of cases:

1. procreative marital intercourse (nineteenth-century cases);
2. nonprocreative marital intercourse *(Griswold)*;
3. nonprocreative vaginal intercourse outside of marriage *(Eisenstadt)*;
4. abortion *(Roe,* applying *Botsford)*;
5. masturbation in one's bedroom *(Stanley)*;
6. nonnuclear family living arrangements *(Moore)*;
7. vaginal intercourse in a secluded automobile *(Onofre)*;
8. adultery (distinguished in the *Poe* dissent);
9. incest (same);

10. commercial sex (distinguished in *Onofre*);

11. intergenerational sex (same);

12. forcible sex (same).

Where did consensual oral sex within the home—the conduct for which Hardwick was charged—fit?

To answer that question, one needs to determine what principle undergirds the cases. The most apparent principle is the Millian idea that people should be left alone by the state unless their conduct has third-party effects unrelated to "nosy preferences" (my preference to make you just like me).[25] Under that principle, Hardwick's behavior would seem protected because he was doing no one any harm. His conduct fell closest to categories 3–5, as it involved his chosen deployment of his own body *(Botsford)* within the privacy of his own home *(Stanley)*, even if outside the context of procreative marriage *(Eisenstadt)*. This was the view of privacy taken in the Model Penal Code and *Onofre*, as well as the court of appeals in Hardwick's case. In *Poe* and *Griswold*, Justice Harlan had indicated that "adultery, homosexuality, fornication and incest" might be outside the right to privacy, but his views (expressed in dicta) never commanded a majority of the Court. Under the libertarian principle articulated in *Eisenstadt*, private sexual intimacy between consenting adults, including fornication and sodomy, could fall within the right to privacy. Contrast Hardwick's conduct, which harmed no one, with that left unprotected in *Onofre* (categories 8–12), which had clearer third-party effects: adultery's violation of marriage vows to a partner, disruption of the family implicated in adultery and incest, the association of commercial sex with drug and venereal disease problems, and the consent problems in intergenerational and forcible sex.

Other principles might be invoked to explain the Court's array. *Botsford,* the leading case, suggests an anticommandeering reading of privacy: the state cannot commandeer our bodies for its rather than our uses, absent a compelling public interest. *Griswold* and *Moore* would extend this idea to our feelings and our relationships. Under this theory, a defense of *Griswold* and *Roe* (categories 2–4) is that the state presumptively has no sufficient reason to impose a *condition* (pregnancy) upon women's bodies and a totalizing *identity* (motherhood) upon women's lives. As Jed Rubenfeld argues, such a principle equally applies to Hardwick's case, for the state's regulation of "homosexual sodomy" commandeers gay peoples' bodies and channels gay people into a network of social roles (compulsory heterosexuality) that will occupy, even dominate, their lives, and without good justification.[26]

Hardwick limited the Court's precedents to a narrower principle—a "fundamental individual right to decide whether or not to beget or bear a child" (categories 1–4).[27] This was an incomplete reading of the precedents, for it provided no account of *Botsford* and other cases assuring a right of bodily integrity outside of pregnancy. Moreover, the Court had extended the right of sexual privacy beyond this limit in *Stanley* (category 5). *Hardwick* dismissed *Stanley* as just a first amendment decision, but the earlier decision presented itself in privacy terms and relied critically on *Griswold* and fourth amendment privacy cases. The Court's characterization also failed to account for *Moore* (category 6). Ultimately, the Court had no robust positive theory rendering its privacy precedents a coherent body of law and relied upon a defensive theory instead: the nontextual right of privacy should not be readily extended to new activities, and certainly not to "homosexual sodomy," which has traditionally been regulated in Anglo-American law and not left to individual decisionmaking, just like adultery and incest (categories 8–9). As White's opinion maintained, what Hardwick did—oral sex with a consenting adult in his bedroom—was an offense at common law and in all thirteen states at the founding, was illegal in thirty-two of the thirty-seven states when the fourteenth amendment was ratified (1868), was illegal in all fifty states until 1961, and remained criminal in twenty-four states and the District of Columbia as of 1986.[28] Given this pervasive history of state concern, White concluded that it was "at best, facetious" for Hardwick to claim a right to engage in such conduct.

The Court's response, and ultimately the entire opinion, rested upon a principle of history: only activities unregulated in 1868 could be considered liberties protected by the due process clause. Yet such a principle had been rejected in the abortion cases. In *Roe,* the Court protected a woman's right to control her pregnancy through an abortion, even though states prohibited women from obtaining abortions in the nineteenth century; in 1868 thirty-six states or territories made this a crime, twenty-one of which statutes were still in effect in 1970.[29] Neither *Griswold* nor *Eisenstadt* had considered nineteenth-century regulation of contraception relevant. Hence, *Hardwick*'s key analytical move, emphasizing historically protected rights with a focus on 1868, was in as much tension with precedent as its neglect of the libertarian and anticommandeering principles that best explain the Court's privacy precedents.

Critique of *Hardwick*'s Historiography

To the extent *Hardwick* rested upon Justice White's history of "homosexual sodomy," it should be tested against historical and historiographical materials.[30] There are several ways to examine White's historiography: Is it accurate as a matter of positive fact? Does it reflect a sophisticated appreciation of law's evolution? Does it pose its inquiry in a neutral manner? At all levels, *Hardwick*'s

historiography disappoints. It is beclouded with white lies, ahistorical generalizations, and contestable value choices masquerading as historical analysis. This
section will present a more sophisticated history of sodomy regulation in this
country and then will explore the implications of such a history for *Hardwick*'s
analysis. Ironically, an historiographically sophisticated treatment of the original understanding of sodomy at the time of the framing of the fourteenth
amendment undermines the Supreme Court's equation of sodomy with oral
sex, consensual intercourse, or homosexuality.

Historical "Facts" and "White Lies"

At the behest of Henry VIII, the Reformation Parliament of 1533 criminalized,
under pain of death, "the detestable and abominable vice of buggery committed with mankind or beast."[31] This and subsequent statutes secularized offenses
that had traditionally been regulated by the Roman Catholic Church, which
Henry was renouncing. As subsequently interpreted by the English courts, buggery was understood to include anal intercourse between two men or between a
man and a woman ("sodomy") and any sexual intercourse between a human
and an animal ("bestiality"), but not oral intercourse between humans.[32] Sexual intercourse between women was unregulated by the Act of 1533.

The English crime of buggery was generally applicable in the American
colonies, either as a matter of common law or by statutory decree.[33] Invoking
Biblical admonitions, the New England colonies sought to expand upon the Act
of 1533. The Massachusetts Bay Colony debated but rejected Reverend John
Cotton's 1636 proposal that woman-woman intercourse be included as
sodomy, but the New Haven Colony in 1656 prohibited men lying with men,
women lying with women, masturbation (if aggravating circumstances), and
any other "carnall knowledge."[34] Masturbation and women lying with women
were dropped as offenses when the Connecticut Colony was formed in 1665.
Altogether there are records for as many as twenty sodomy prosecutions and
four executions during the colonial period.[35] The most remarkable case was
that of William Plaine of Guilford in the New Haven Colony, a married man
who was executed for committing "sodomy" with two persons in England,
engaging in "masturbations" with the "youth" of Guilford, and planting "seeds
of atheism."[36] Moreover, colonial authorities were sometimes willing to prosecute men and on at least one occasion a woman for "lewdness," or unspecified
sensual activity with someone of the same or opposite sex.

Between independence and 1830 the original thirteen states all adopted laws
making buggery or sodomy a serious offense (Appendix A1), but the large
majority eliminated the death penalty imposed by the Act of 1533. None of the

statutes defined the crime, for it remained "a detestable and abominable sin, amongst Christians not to be named," as Sir Edward Coke put it in 1644.[37] Most of the early statutes were revised by the middle of the century to criminalize what Coke and Blackstone had termed "the infamous crime against nature," and that terminology dominated the laws adopted by new states and territories.[38] Judges and commentators in the nineteenth century read the sodomy, buggery, carnal knowledge, and crime against nature laws—hereinafter collectively described as "sodomy" laws—to criminalize "unnatural" intercourse between men and women and men and men, but not between women and women.[39] Although there were only a handful of reported cases, sodomy prosecutions occurred episodically throughout the century. In 1880 there were sixty-three persons imprisoned for the crime, two-thirds of them people of color and foreign immigrants.[40]

The introduction of public sentiment anxious about gender inversion and then homosexuality, a process that occurred between 1880 and 1921, drove a revolution in Anglo-American sodomy law, the legal centerpiece of which was the redefinition of sodomy to include oral sex (Chapter 1). Before 1879, every Anglo-American authority accepted the fact that the common law excluded oral sex from buggery, sodomy, and the crime against nature. Pennsylvania's 1879 statute defining "sodomy and buggery" (quoted in Chapter 1) was the first official American authority to include oral sex as sodomy. The British Parliament responded with the Labouchere Amendment to the Criminal Law Amendments Act of 1885, which made it illegal for a man to commit or attempt "any act of gross indecency with another male person," namely oral sex.[41] After 1885, thirty-one states and the District of Columbia followed either Pennsylvania to amend their sodomy laws to include oral sex, or England to create a new statutory crime (usually a misdemeanor) targeted at oral sex.[b]

Even without legislative authorization, police sought to expand sodomy laws to include oral sex. At first, they were unsuccessful. Texas judges in the leading case, *Prindle v. State* (1893), expressed anguish that abominable oral sex was not included in the crime against nature statute, but announced themselves powerless to change the common law understanding of the term, which was

---

b. Following the Pennsylvania approach of specifying the crime against nature more precisely within state sodomy laws were New York (1886), Ohio (1889), Wyoming (1890), Louisiana (1896), Wisconsin (1898), Iowa (1902), Washington (1909), Missouri (1911), Nebraska (1913), North Dakota (1913), Oregon (1913), Alaska (1915), Virginia (1916, 1924), Minnesota (1921), Utah (1923), West Virginia (1923), and seven states after the Depression, including Texas (1943). Following the English approach of creating a separate crime for oral sex were Massachusetts (1887), New Hampshire (1899), Michigan (1903, 1939), New Jersey (1906), California (1915, 1921), Maryland (1916), Arizona (1917), and Florida (1917). Appendix A1 provides references for each state.

limited to anal sex. *Prindle* was followed in California (1897), Virginia (1923), and five other states.[42] In all of these states, the judicial interpretation was overridden by legislation broadening the definition of sodomy or, in the case of California, creating a new crime. Rejecting *Prindle*'s rule, the Illinois Supreme Court in *Honselman v. People* (1897) held that oral sex was a crime against nature, as it "is as much against nature . . . as sodomy or any bestial or unnatural copulation as can be conceived." *Honselman* was followed by the courts of ten states in the West and South before 1921, and after 1921 by six more state courts.[c]

The reconfiguration of sodomy laws to include oral sex was an essential move in the expansion of arrests after 1880. Because oral sex was more widespread than anal sex and could be accomplished more quickly and in compact spaces, such as a public restroom, its criminalization was a necessary prelude to heightened police enforcement and the creation of sodomy stakeouts in big cities. Oral sex could also be perpetrated by women with other women, and for the first time in Anglo-American history lesbian relationships could be made illegal (although few states did so before World War I). For all these reasons, sodomy arrests shot up in most large American cities in the period around World War I (Appendix C1). Seventy percent of the reported sodomy cases for this period involved sodomy between people of the same sex—what was coming to be known as "homosexual sodomy"—but only 25 percent of the reported cases involved consenting adults of the same sex (Appendix C2).

The generation after World War II saw equally significant increases in sodomy arrests, mainly because sodomy had become a crime that southern and middle-sized cities were keen on enforcing. The pattern of enforcement was the same as before: 62 percent of the reported cases involved "homosexual sodomy," with 24 percent between consenting adults (Appendix C2). Nonetheless, as Chapter 2 documents, it was precisely during that period that penologists, doctors, and legal experts formed a tentative consensus that, as the American Law Institute (ALI) put it in 1955, "[n]o harm to the secular interests of the community is involved in a typical sex practice in private between consenting adults. This area of private morals is the distinctive concern of spiritual authorities." Criminalizing such practices undercut "the protection to which every individual is entitled against state interference in his personal affairs when he is not hurting others."[43] The ALI's consent-based rules on sodomy were a point of resistance in most of the states that considered adopting the Model Penal Code, and the reason for resistance was animus against homosexuals.[44]

---

c. *Honselman*, 48 N.E. 304 (Ill. 1897), was followed by courts in Georgia (1904), South Dakota (1910), Indiana (1913), North Carolina (1914), Nevada (1914), Delaware (1915), Kansas (1915), Montana (1915), Idaho (1916), Oklahoma (1917), and by six other states after World War I. Appendix A1 provides references for each state.

The next revolution occurred after Stonewall, which released political energy against consensual sodomy laws. By 1986, when *Hardwick* was decided, twenty-five states had repealed or nullified the application of sodomy laws to consenting adults, and twelve other states had reduced consensual sodomy from a felony to a misdemeanor or circumscribed the penalty to misdemeanor level (Chapter 3). In less than a generation more than four-fifths of the states—most states outside the South—declassified consensual homosexual sodomy as a felony. Enforcement of sodomy laws changed just as dramatically. Between 1971 and 1985, 30 percent of the reported cases involved homosexual sodomy, and just 6 percent, virtually all in the South, homosexual sodomy between consenting adults (Appendix C2). Most of the cases involved unconsented sex between a man and a woman (52 percent) or a man and a girl (17 percent).

The legal regime described in *Hardwick*—"homosexual sodomy," where sodomy meant oral sex between consenting adults in the home—bore little resemblance to the actual regime in place in 1868, when the fourteenth amendment was adopted. Although most states had sodomy laws, as White said, few if any of them applied to same-sex activities between women, and none of them was enforced against women having sex with women. Indeed, sodomy laws were rarely enforced against anyone before the 1880s, and it is not clear they were much applied to consensual male intercourse. Not a single sodomy opinion or police report before the twentieth century mentioned the words "homosexual" or "homosexuality," terms that did not enter the English language until 1892.[45] The "homosexual sodomy" demonized by the *Hardwick* majority was a creation of the twentieth century, and not exactly the crime condemned by "millennia of moral teachings."

White's historical generalizations were particularly inappropriate in Hardwick's case. As Anne Goldstein first said, the oral sex for which Hardwick was arrested was not known as "sodomy" or the "crime against nature" in any American jurisdiction in 1868. Oral sex would probably have been proscribed by the New Haven statute of 1656 and conceivably (but never explicitly) by a few other colonial sodomy laws, but it was not formally proscribed after the Revolution or the Civil War. Even as late as 1879, there was no authoritative American statute or judicial decision disagreeing with the common law rule that oral sex was not a crime against nature. When the legal equilibrium changed after 1880, a large majority of the states—and almost all the states with big cities—accomplished the transition by statute, creating a *new* crime that was prospective in operation. Admittedly, a minority of states updated sodomy through retroactive judicial construction. Georgia's 1904 decision declaring oral sex to be a crime against nature purported to declare preexisting natural law. As Janet Halley argues, such decisions reflected the always protean nature of sodomy, but (contrary to Halley) they are scant evidence that oral sex had been a crime against nature "all along."[46] Indeed, Georgia was the only big-population state to follow Illinois' *Honselman* decision, and Georgia's judges were themselves ambivalent about their innovation: the Georgia Supreme Court found fellatio to be a crime against nature in 1904, extended that idea to cunnilingus in 1917, found cunnilingus between two women not to be such a crime in 1939, and overruled the application of the law to any kind of cunnilingus in 1963.[47] The Georgia cases reveal how slowly and unevenly states assimilated oral sex into sodomy laws, and how marginal "homosexual sodomy" was to the precise statutory scheme the Court evaluated in *Hardwick.*

Historical Norms Underlying Sodomy Laws

Criminal laws operate both negatively and positively. They act negatively by *stigmatizing* certain conduct; they act positively by *normalizing* the conduct not prohibited. White's ahistorical misreading of the prohibitory regime of sodomy laws helped obscure a deeper problem with his analysis, namely, his ahistorical misreading of the normative regime of sodomy laws. Sodomy laws have at different points in time reflected no fewer than three different normalizing regimes: sexual acts must be procreative and marital, must be mutual and consensual, and/or must be gendered or heterosexual. Focusing only on the third option, White imposed his own normalizing regime and ignored the norms that would have justified sodomy regulation in 1868 and before.

As Burger's concurring opinion appreciated, the primary historical justification for penalizing sodomy was the Judeo-Christian valorization of sex within the context of procreative marriage.[48] Under Roman Catholic natural law and Protestant (Puritan) fundamentalism, fornication, adultery, and same-sex sodomy are sins because they by definition occur outside the context of marriage; contraception, abortion, masturbation, and all kinds of sodomy are sins because they are by definition nonprocreative. From this religious perspective, sodomy is doubly sinful, both undermining marriage and denying the procreative imperative. When American states codified their criminal laws in the middle third of the nineteenth century, most of them followed this Judeo-Christian tradition and included sodomy prohibitions in close proximity with abortion, fornication, adultery, and incest—all termed "crimes against public morals and decency."[49] Although the framers of the fourteenth amendment would have rationalized sodomy laws as requiring that sex occur within procreative marriage, White ignored this rationale because it was foreclosed by the Court's precedents. *Griswold* recognized as fundamental people's right not to procreate when they have penile-vaginal intercourse. *Roe* and *Eisenstadt* expanded

Griswold to nonmarital contexts. These precedents rejected the teachings of either natural law or the Bible as the basis for privacy doctrine and emphasized an evolving idea of liberty suitable for an industrial society.

Thus, *Hardwick's* originalist approach to the fourteenth amendment stands in contrast not only to the Court's previous refusal to follow an originalist approach to that amendment *(Griswold* and *Roe)*, but also to the Court's non-originalist approach to the state sodomy laws it charged the framers with know-ing and approving. At the level of *specific intent,* there is no evidence that a single framer would have thought sodomy involved consensual oral sex in 1868. At the level of *general intent,* every framer would have thought the pur-pose of sodomy laws to be insurance that sex occurred only within the context of procreative marriage, an unconstitutional goal under the Court's post-1960 privacy jurisprudence.

It can be objected that, if the framers had "thought about" oral sex, they would have been so appalled that they would have considered it a crime against nature. They probably would have been appalled, but not every appalling thing was sodomy, as the common law firmly held.[50] Moreover, the framers might have been reluctant to categorize consensual oral sex as sodomy, as their second-best rationale for sodomy laws was protection of vulnerable people and animals against predatory rape-like conduct. At common law, sodomy and rape were sibling crimes: both were considered carnal knowledge entailing violent assaults upon the person of the victim; the law originally required penetration and emission in both crimes but abandoned the emission requirement in the nineteenth century.[51] Many and perhaps most state codes between indepen-dence and the Civil War formally linked sodomy and rape.[52] Moreover, like rape, sodomy prosecutions were generally against aggressive men deriving sexual pleasure from a weaker person, usually a boy, girl, woman, animal, or ward.[53] Indeed, common law proof requirements made such prosecutions unlikely. Where the victim of sodomy consented to the act, she or he was deemed an accomplice (unless she or he was a minor), and the perpetrator could not be convicted without independent corroborating evidence of anal penetration.[54] A consequence of the accomplice-corroboration rule was that sodomy prose-cution was practically impossible where it involved consensual adult sex in a private place.[55]

The third rationale for sodomy laws was their reinforcement of traditional gender roles in sexual intercourse—a thrusting male penetrating a receptive female with his penis. (This would have been a more comprehensible rationale for the framers of the fourteenth amendment [1868] than for those of the fifth [1791], because the Civil War period was one where gender role was emerging as self-consciously important.) Under this normalizing regime, Michael Hardwick might have been characterized as a gender "invert," because he had another man's penis in his mouth. But this option too was unavailable to Justice White because of the Court's sex discrimination precedents, which precluded the state from forcing men or women into traditional gender roles.[56]

Instead, White faulted Hardwick for engaging in "homosexual" sodomy. *Hardwick*'s rationalization for sodomy laws, compulsory heterosexuality, would have been literally incomprehensible to the framers of the fourteenth amendment, who would not have recognized the words "homosexual" or "heterosexual." It cannot even be shown that the framers focused on same-sex consensual sodomy because female-female sex was unregulated and the regulation of male-male sex did not focus on sex between consenting adults. Excluding the large number of decisions that did not reveal the sex or even the species of the parties involved,[57] the reported cases from the nineteenth century fell into three roughly equal groups: bestiality with barnyard animals,[58] sex between an adult man and a boy or "youth,"[59] and man-man and man-woman cases.[60] One would read the pre-1900 cases in vain to find any mention of homosexuality, a condition that did not even exist. To be sure, nineteenth-century America was appalled that a man would be anally penetrated, but it was appalled because that penetration was sinfully nonprocreative, was probably without meaningful consent, and violated the gender role of the victim.

At bottom, Byron White's choice of a normalizing regime for sodomy laws had nothing to do with the expectations of the nineteenth-century legislatures that adopted such laws or of the framers of the fourteenth amendment. His choice was *his choice*, alone. His choice was rooted in twentieth-century law's creation of the "homosexual" as the object of criminalization, persecution, and erasure. Understood in this way, *Hardwick* upheld proscriptions that had neither "ancient roots" nor sanctification by "millennia of moral teaching." The "roots" of the Court's focus on homosexuality were, instead, the antifeminist movement and the eugenic sexologists before World War I (Chapter 1). The "moral teaching" of antihomosexual animus was that of modernized natural law and theories of sexual psychopathy, the same "moral teachings" preached by the Nazis (Chapter 2).

Mark this irony. Implicitly, *Hardwick* contrasted abortion and contraception, which were not crimes at common law and hence might merit due process protection, with sodomy, which was a crime at common law and therefore not within the tradition of ordered liberty guaranteed by the due process clause. But the sodomy that was the crime at common law was male-female as well as male-male rape-like anal sex, not consent-like oral sex or female-female intercourse or even "homosexual sodomy" as such. Oral sex was not a crime until the period 1879–1921; female-female oral sex was not a crime in most jurisdictions until the twentieth century; and "homosexual sodomy" was not a concept until the turn of the twentieth century, and not a key regulatory concept before World War I. In contrast, a mother's abortion before quickening became a crime in many jurisdictions before the Civil War, and distributing contraceptives was criminalized during Reconstruction—in both instances *before* private oral sex was a crime in a single American state. This turns Justice White's syllogism on its head: if the reference point is what pre-1868 law protected or did not prohibit, Michael Hardwick's conduct made out a better case for originalist protection than either Estelle Griswold's or Jane Roe's conduct.

Hardwick *and Historiography*

Hardwick said that the Court should be chary of creating new constitutional rights unless supported by the original intent of those who framed the fourteenth amendment. The main problems with originalism are well illustrated by the foregoing critique of *Hardwick*.[61] The defenders of originalism claim that it is more objective than other methods of interpretation and therefore better constrains interpreters, but *Hardwick* illustrates holes in that defense. As the *Hardwick* dissenters charged, White's arguments depended upon arbitrary characterization: the case was about "homosexual sodomy" and not "intimacy." That biased characterization affected every other feature of the case, including the historical inquiry and the determination of the law's current rational basis.

Additionally, *Hardwick* classically illustrates the indeterminate nature of an originalist application of an old text to unforeseen circumstances. Although most states had sodomy laws in 1868, when the fourteenth amendment was adopted, and about half still had them in 1986, when *Hardwick* was decided, that similarity masked changes that affected every other feature of the constitutional question:

- What did sodomy laws prohibit? In 1868 the common law refused to say much about what was a "crime against nature"—except that it did not include oral sex. In 1986 oral sex was synonymous with sodomy.
- What goal(s) did sodomy laws subserve? In 1868 the main goal was state insistence that sex be within the institution of procreative marriage. By 1986 that goal was not one the state could constitutionally pursue.
- What was the relationship between sodomy and homosexuality? In 1868 there was no term for same-sex attraction. By 1986 homosexuality had become a culturally totalizing term.

Because the issue before the Court in *Hardwick* was so different from the issues debated in the Reconstruction era, there was no neutral way to frame the interpretive question.

There are some ways of framing the question that are more simplistic than others, and White's inquiry exemplifies distorting simplicity: "Would the framers have considered homosexual sodomy a protected activity?" A less ahistorical inquiry would be something closer to the following: "If the framers had been asked about oral sex between two men in a private home, would they have understood that activity to be free from state police intrusion?" People in the 1860s might have answered "yes" to that question, but they would probably have answered "no" to an equally historicist variation: "If the framers had been asked about oral sex between two men in a private home, would they have understood such conduct to receive affirmative protection from the constitutional amendment they were drafting?" To be truer to a reconstructive inquiry, however, the question would have to be more complex, such as the following: "If the framers could have foreseen that laws prohibiting contraception and abortion would be held to violate the amendment they drafted, because the amendment was construed to encode a right to sexual privacy, would the framers have felt that oral sex between consenting adults in the privacy of their home was distinguishable?" And so on.

The argument for originalism is neither its objectivity nor its constraint—for originalism has neither quality—but instead its conservatism. If the burden of persuasion rests with the party asserting a constitutional right, originalism makes it harder to recognize new rights or expand recognized rights to new situations. Indeed, that is surely what White had in mind when he warned that the Court's legitimacy is most in peril when it expands nontextual constitutional rights, like privacy, without support in the framers' original expectations. Yet it was White's originalist opinion that landed the Court in legitimacy trouble. The reason has to do with another problem with originalism: its insistence that law is just a matter of vertical coherence (this interpretation is consistent with all that came before) with no theoretical room for horizontal coherence (this interpretation is consistent with other rights and rules today).

Buck v. Bell—Holmes's opinion accepting the constitutionality of forced sterilization—was an opinion perfectly supportable by a vertical understanding of constitutional law: "Show me where there is a right to reproduction in the Constitution or its contemporary understanding, and I'll recognize your right to be free from state interference." Holmes's position could not long have survived the knowledge that Nazi Germany deployed the same eugenic philosophy to commandeer human bodies for sexual experimentation, or that Carrie Buck, the woman Virginia sterilized, was not mentally disabled as the state thought.

Constitutional law has a learning curve, and it must include horizontal as well as vertical considerations if it is to contribute to government's overall legitimacy. If the Constitution's protection of "life, liberty, and property" does not assure protection for the body itself, what meaning can due process possibly have for proper governance? This was the question that sunk Judge Robert Bork. Will it sink *Hardwick*?

Should *Hardwick* Be Overruled?

Hardwick's antihomosexual rhetoric and questionable reasoning denude it of the authority that derives from a court's exercise of reasoned judgment, and lawyers and judges ought to give *Hardwick* a cautious reading (Chapter 6). Should the Supreme Court overrule *Hardwick*? Stare decisis, the rule that even questionable precedents should be followed, is not so strong a rule in constitutional cases as in common law and statutory cases. In *Planned Parenthood v. Casey* (1992), where the Court reaffirmed a diluted version of *Roe,* the plurality opinion expressed doubt about the reasoning and analytical framework of *Roe* but insisted upon further inquiry before deciding whether to overrule. The *Casey* inquiries are relevant to *Hardwick,* especially whether its central rule "could be removed without serious inequity to those who have relied upon it or significant damage to the stability of the society governed by the rule in question; whether the law's growth in the intervening years has left [*Hardwick*'s] central rule a doctrinal anachronism discounted by society; and whether [*Hardwick*'s] premises of fact have so far changed in the ensuing [time period] as to render its central holding somehow irrelevant or unjustifiable in dealing with the issue it addressed."[62]

Faulty Premise: The Public Irrationality of Homophobia

Hardwick's reasoning is faulty in (1) characterizing the precedents, (2) setting the terms of the inquiry, and (3) representing the history of state regulation of oral sex. The existence of so many errors, together with White's and Burger's gratuitous antihomosexual rhetoric, suggest that deep emotions rather than neutral reason drove the decision.[63] John Jeffries' sympathetic biography of Powell demonstrates that the critical fifth vote came from a man who considered same-sex intimacy repulsive and who was wary that any constitutional protection for "homosexual sodomy" would empower homosexuals to seek other rights.[64]

Such homophobia is understandable for men of Powell's generation but is treacherous as a basis for constitutional policy. It is irrational, in part because it rests upon gross misperceptions. Dispassionate studies by the leading experts in anthropology,[65] biology,[66] and psychology[67] indicate—without any reputable rebuttal—that there is nothing intrinsically dysfunctional about same-sex intimacy, including "homosexual sodomy." As Part One of this book shows, antihomosexual policies have been unproductive in American history: they have not only wasted state resources that could be devoted to genuine problems but have empowered the most hateful of our society to go after some of the most gentle.

It was comforting to Powell that the state could send a symbolic antigay message without sending Hardwick to prison. This would have been a humane policy in the 1950s, but not after Stonewall and *Eisenstadt*. The Supreme Court's privacy jurisprudence assures all of us sexual breathing room—to be disgusting in our bedroom without being penalized for it in the courtroom. *Hardwick* denied that dignity to lesbians, bisexuals, and gay men. This discrimination is defensible only if its objects are closeted; Powell, incredibly, maintained that he had never met a homosexual. When gay people are not out and in one's company, a person can casually condemn their "homosexual conduct," but that stance is problematic once one learns that there are functional gay people in her or his family, fraternity, and office—or judicial chambers! Can one look an open lesbian straight in the eye and tell her, "You are a second-class citizen because what you do with other women disgusts me." Can one in good conscience say that to the lesbian if one is engaging in oral sex just like she does? If that is not rank hypocrisy, it at least seems inconsistent with *Evans*.

Evans opened with language from the dissent in *Plessy v. Ferguson* (1896): "there is in this country no superior, dominant, ruling class of citizens . . . In respect of civil rights, all citizens are equal before the law."[68] The Court majority in *Plessy* rejected this idea for African Americans, and they could do so with impunity so long as people of color were politically marginal. No Justice would dare defend racial apartheid today—not because the Justices are more morally advanced but because people of color are part of American political culture, and many are legal insiders. *Hardwick* is the gay *Plessy*, the ratification of an apartheid of the closet that becomes logically as well as politically indefensible once its denizens come out. Is *Evans* the gay *Brown*?

Doctrinal Anachronism: Emerging International Consensus

Hardwick angered gay people with its disrespect and with its unembarrassed ignorance about homosexuals and their history. In defiance of what was considered open bigotry, many gay lawyers came out of the closet, and gaylegal activism was reenergized overnight. American culture itself—from movies and television to newspapers and magazines to the new electronic media—seemed gay-crazy all of a sudden. A decision intended to stop discussion about sodomy fueled unrelenting chatter about it. As openly gay people seized upon *Hardwick* as a symbol of hetero-ignorance, Burger and White's homophobia of disrespect became an object of denunciation or ridicule for half the nation, while Powell's homophobia of denial became an object of nostalgia for the other half. The more gay people came out of the closet, the more *Hardwick* has been pushed into a constitutional closet.

After *Hardwick,* gaylegal challenges to sodomy laws shifted from the U.S. Constitution to state constitutions. Although most state courts have continued to duck challenges on the ground that the challengers were not arrested for private sodomy between consenting adults,[69] the courts in Kentucky (1992), Tennessee (1996), and Montana (1997) have invalidated their consensual sodomy laws on state constitutional privacy grounds, showing *Hardwick* the disrespect that *Hardwick* showed to gay people (Appendix A1). No reported decision since *Hardwick* has applied a state sodomy law to private consensual intimacy between two adults of the same sex. Even the Supreme Court has been wary of the decision. The joint opinion in *Casey* ignored *Hardwick* and rejected its originalist methodology for figuring the contours of the liberty protected by the due process clause. "Neither the Bill of Rights nor the specific practices of States at the time of the adoption of the Fourteenth Amendment mark the outer limits of the substantive sphere of liberty which the Fourteenth Amendment protects."[70] Chief Justice William Rehnquist's opinion in *Washington v. Glucksberg* (1997), which rejected a general due process right to die, failed even to cite *Hardwick,* even though the opinion sought to revive *Hardwick*'s methodology of declining to recognize a substantive due process right not specifically established in the common law tradition.[71] Although the Court in *Glucksberg* unanimously rejected a general right to die, five Justices were open to a "constitutionally cognizable interest in controlling the circumstances of [one's] imminent death," especially to avoid pain.[72] If due process protects a person's decision to die without pain, why does it not protect the gay person's decision to love without shame?

International experience supports the proposition that laws criminalizing same-sex intimacy are anachronistic for modern urbanized societies and cannot be defended before policymakers and jurists who are not hysterical about homosexuality. Most of the major industrial countries of Europe, Asia, and Latin America leave consensual sodomy unregulated.[73] Straggler countries or provinces have been subjected to legal as well as political pressure to abandon such laws. In *Dudgeon v. United Kingdom* (1981), the European Court of Human Rights ruled that Northern Ireland's consensual sodomy prohibition contravened the right to privacy set forth in Article 8 of the European Convention on Human Rights. The Court applied *Dudgeon* to declare the sodomy laws of Ireland and Cyprus similarly in derogation of the convention, thereby completing a clean sweep of such regulations in the European Community.[74] The Constitutional Court of South Africa invalidated that country's sodomy and unnatural acts laws in *National Coalition for Gay and Lesbian Equality v. Minister of Justice* (1998). The unanimous court relied on both equality and privacy grounds. As to the latter, the court recognized "a right to a sphere of private intimacy and autonomy which allows us to establish and nurture human relationships without interference from the outside community."[75]

The United Nations Human Rights Committee ruled in *In re Toonen* (1994) that Tasmania's consensual sodomy law violates article 17(1) of the International Covenant on Civil and Political Rights (ICCPR), which protects against "arbitrary or unlawful interference with [a person's] privacy, family, home or correspondence."[76] Tasmania complied by repealing its consensual sodomy law in 1997. *Toonen* is of special significance because the United States has also signed and ratified the ICCPR.[77] Thus, the United States has accepted international obligations under the covenant. Although it has not agreed to amenability to international adjudication of grievances before the Human Rights Committee, the United States expressed a readiness to take such "measures as may be necessary to ensure that the States of the Union implement the rights guaranteed by the Covenant" when the Committee expressed specific concern "at the serious infringement of private life in some states which classify as a criminal offence sexual relations between consenting adult partners of the same sex carried out in private."[78] The ICCPR would not alone justify the Supreme Court's overruling *Hardwick,* but the international obligation created in the wake of *Toonen* ought to be considered by the Court when it interprets domestic law, including constitutional law.[79] Additionally, *Toonen, National Coalition, Dudgeon,* and the post-*Dudgeon* EC decisions are subsequent developments that support a reconsideration of precedent and, more pointedly, that highlight the anachronistic or nonneutral quality of *Hardwick*'s rule and its reasoning.

Unproductive Public Reliance on Hardwick

Although *Hardwick* is a recent precedent, the sodomy laws it ratified existed long before and had been slanted by a *Hardwick*-like homophobia for decades. Most of the openly antihomosexual policies have been rescinded, but certain policies might be unsettled if *Hardwick* were to be overruled. Police policies in some jurisdictions, mostly in the South, would have to be rethought. Could local vice squads arrest people for having sex in public toilets, automobiles, erotic nightclubs, or adult bookstores? For soliciting decoy cops for private sex? In all these situations, right of privacy challenges have been successful in some state courts,[80] but of course they need not be protected by a federal right of privacy as defined by the Supreme Court.

The most important policy that might be unsettled by overruling *Hardwick* is the armed forces' exclusion of lesbian, gay, and bisexual personnel. The exclusion is defended in part as a corollary to the military's criminal prohibition of sodomy. Gay soldiers can be excluded either because they commit sodomy, or because they have a "propensity" to commit sodomy.[81] If *Hardwick* were overruled, the consensual sodomy prohibition in the Uniform Code of Military Justice would be more vulnerable to constitutional attack. Because the Supreme Court often defers to military statutes and regulations that would be invalid if adopted in a civilian context or by the states, this is not a foregone conclusion. (One possible resolution would be for the Court to allow the armed forces to prohibit sodomy on military premises but not in soldiers' homes or off-base.) Still, the sodomy prohibition would be more vulnerable without *Hardwick,* and if the sodomy prohibition fell there would be fewer arguments for the military exclusion of gay people. On the other hand, the military's propensity argument is problematic even if the armed forces could criminalize consensual sodomy (Chapter 5).

Although overruling *Hardwick* could unsettle some policies, many of the issues identified above could be settled by a cautious approach to an overruling. Moreover, the policies that would be most unsettled are among the least defensible. Toilet stakeouts and decoy operations, for example, are a lavish deployment of scarce police resources in cities with high rates of violent crime. Most important, overruling *Hardwick* would have potentially powerful affirmative effects on public policy discourse. Consider a few.

Mutuality as the Prerequisite to Sexual Intimacy. A criticism of *Hardwick,* offered above, is that it aligns the symbolic power of law with the wrong normative regime. When *Hardwick* emphasized an antihomosexual policy for sodomy laws, it not only chose an unproductive policy but missed an opportunity to stress a productive policy. The norm for sexual intimacy that has been advanced by feminist and gaylegal theory is mutuality: sex is good and normal when the participants welcome it, when the sex is truly a joint enterprise meeting the needs of the partners (Chapter 7).[82] A danger posed by *Hardwick* is the suggestion to men that their intercourse with women is validated, in part, by the mere fact of its heterosexuality. This partial validation threatens to deflect attention from the mutuality goal.

This criticism of *Hardwick* should be tempered by the realization that sodomy law has long been moving toward a regime of mutuality. All the states now regulate "forcible" sodomy, and "ordinary" sodomy prosecutions since 1969 have usually involved situations where the sex is alleged to be unwelcome (Appendix C2). For example, in *Schochet v. State* (1990), the defendant was accused of raping and sodomizing a woman he met at a bar; he admitted to oral and vaginal sex with her but claimed it was consensual. The jury acquitted Schochet of all rape and forcible sodomy charges but convicted him of consensual sodomy. The Maryland Court of Appeals overturned that conviction by interpreting its sodomy law to exclude consensual heterosexual sodomy.[83] On the one hand, prosecutors use sodomy laws in rape cases to enhance the odds that the defendant will be convicted of something even if the jury disbelieves the complaining witness's testimony that she was coerced. Given the difficulty of winning convictions in cases of "real rape," this may not seem unjust. On the other hand, this strategy might make it too easy for juries to escape the difficult issues of consent and settle on sodomy as an acceptable compromise, and might make it too easy for a jury to imprison a person who in fact was falsely accused of rape.

Preventing the Spread of HIV. David Robinson, a law professor, filed an amicus brief in *Hardwick* arguing that sodomy laws are justified as a way to prevent the spread of HIV, the virus that causes AIDS. The Supreme Court correctly ignored the argument. Anal sex can transmit HIV, just as vaginal sex and probably oral sex can, but prohibiting sodomy contributes little or nothing to slowing AIDS. The mode of intercourse is not so important in transmission as the failure to use safety precautions. By focusing attention on the sexual act rather than on the safety of the sex, sodomy laws divert attention from the most productive way to fight the disease, education about the risks of all kinds of sex and about safer sex. Sodomy laws are counterproductive when they are invoked, as they sometimes are, to oppose public school sex and AIDS education as well as condom-distribution programs. Public health experts believe that such measures are the best way to fight AIDS, and there is thus far no empirical evidence that such measures actually increase disapproved sexual activity.[84]

Even if sodomy rather than unsafe sex contributed decisively to the spread of HIV, laws prohibiting sodomy would not help fight the disease. Ever since Kinsey reported that 95 percent of American men had violated one or more of the popular sex laws, including sodomy laws, there has been doubt that sex laws necessarily deter the conduct they forbid. Not only is the risk of detection miniscule (and therefore the deterrence nil), but the forbidden zone created by sex laws helps create lines that make the forbidden fruit all that much sweeter.

The primary deterrent effect of sodomy laws is to keep sex in the closet, hidden and underground, precisely the terrain that bred and spread HIV in the late 1970s and early 1980s. Many public health professionals believe that sodomy laws modestly impede AIDS programs by discouraging people from being tested for the virus or treated for the disease, and by pushing prohibited sex into dark corners unilluminated by education and safer sex guidelines.[85]

Eroding the Act-Status Argument. As Janet Halley has said, sodomy is the metonym for the homosexual. Homosexual identity is defined by presumptions about homosexual conduct. Because *Hardwick* ratifies state prohibition of homosexual conduct, it is regularly invoked as a basis for denying gay people equal treatment. As the Virginia Supreme Court put it in 1995, "[c]onduct inherent in lesbianism is punishable as a . . . felony," and that is an "important consideration in determining custody" of a woman's biological child.[86] The state court debate in child custody and adoption cases has spilled over into the federal cases evaluating the mililtary exclusion of gays. Judicial rulings discriminating against gay litigants regularly deny they are discriminating based on sexual orientation; citing *Hardwick,* they can plausibly say they are merely regulating problematic conduct.[87] At a more abstract level, opponents of gay rights reject analogies to race or sex or even religion discrimination on the ground that antigay discrimination is based on *conduct* rather than *status.*

A recent occasion for revisiting the status-conduct debate was afforded by Michael Bowers in 1991. Still attorney general of Georgia, Bowers invoked *Hardwick* as the basis for revoking an offer of employment in the attorney general's office to lawyer Robin Shahar because she planned to marry another woman. Bowers's view was that his employment of Shahar, a presumptive sodomite, would undermine public confidence in the office's ability to enforce the laws of Georgia. Several years later, Bowers admitted to a long-term adulterous affair, also a crime in Georgia. The hypocrisy of Bowers' position did Shahar no good in *Shahar v. Bowers* (1997).[88] Invoking *Hardwick,* the court of appeals, sitting en banc, accepted Bowers's argument. Invoking *Evans,* dissenting judges argued that Bowers's action was pure status discrimination inconsistent with *Evans.*

Shahar reflects the current legal debate. Judges are no longer constrained by *Hardwick* in equal protection cases and can follow *Evans*'s lead if they choose to do so. But judges desiring to reject challenges to antigay policies can follow *Hardwick* and limit *Evans* to its unusual facts. This lack of authoritative guidance is probably what the Supreme Court expected after *Evans:* state courts and lower federal courts would struggle with issues of sexual orientation discrimination on a case-by-case basis, less constrained by Supreme Court precedent because of the *Hardwick* versus *Evans* choice now available. At some point, however, the Supreme Court will have to choose: *Hardwick* or *Evans?* Other courts are already making this choice. In a final irony, the Georgia Supreme Court in 1998 construed its state constitutional right of privacy to invalidate the sodomy law that *Hardwick* had upheld against federal constitutional attack.[89] The U.S. Supreme Court should follow Georgia's lead and should overrule *Hardwick* for it violates the central lessons of the Court's privacy jurisprudence: the state has no business in the bedrooms of consenting adults, and in a Freudian culture we are permitted to do disgusting things with other consenting adults behind closed doors without incurring legal disabilities. If *Hardwick*'s error is not palpable enough under the Court's privacy jurisprudence, the Court has other doctrinal options—the first amendment, as I shall argue in Chapter 5, and sex or sexual orientation discrimination prohibited by the equal protection clause, an argument in Chapter 6.

5. The Sexualized First Amendment

Marjorie Rowland, a guidance counselor in the Mad River Local School District, Ohio, and Dirk Selland, a Navy lieutenant, both lost their jobs because they said who they were. After President William Clinton announced his intention to end the exclusion of gays from the military in January 1993, Selland told his commanding officer he was gay. He should have waited. The president abandoned his pledge and, instead, supported a statute codifying a policy of "don't ask, don't tell."[1] Under the statute, Selland was discharged: the government didn't ask, but he had told. In the fall of 1974 Rowland confided in her secretary and the assistant principal that she was bisexual and lived with another woman. After gossip about her sexuality spread through the school, the principal summarily dismissed her. Like Selland, Rowland was ruined because she disclosed her sexual orientation to an unwelcoming and chatty bureaucracy.

Rowland and Selland sued to get their jobs back. Both invoked the equal protection clause assurance against discriminatory treatment (Chapter 6) and the first amendment's assurance of free expression (this chapter). To dismiss a public employee because she or he says "I am gay (or bisexual)" is state censorship that requires justification. In both cases the government claimed that open identity as a bisexual woman or a gay man sexualized fragile workplaces. The school district also argued that Rowland's private confessions were not about matters of sufficient "public concern" to trigger first amendment attention and, further, that Rowland had compromised the privacy of two students, whom she identified to her secretary as gay. The Navy also argued that Selland's confession was evidence of a propensity to commit sodomy, illegal under the Code of Military Justice. After losing the initial rounds to Selland (who got a preliminary injunction) and Rowland (who was awarded damages by a federal magistrate), the government ultimately won both cases.[2]

The first amendment lost. Any policy where the state penalizes persons for saying who they are ought to be strenuously cross-examined under a constitutional provision maintaining that the state can make "no law . . . abridging the freedom of speech." Can a school board cashier a teacher who says she is a Jew, on the ground that it wants the students protected from Jewish culture? Can the military expel a soldier who says he is a KKK member, on the ground that this offends people of color in the barracks? The first amendment would seem to preclude such government action; even the elbow room courts have carved out for institutional needs in the public employment context is not commodious enough to allow state suppression of identity speech.[3] If the first amendment protects one's right to come out as a Jew or a KKK member, one has the same right to come out as gay or bisexual.

As David Cole and I have argued, don't ask, don't tell policies—state codifications of the mutually protective closet—implicate the first amendment and its long-standing rule against content-based censorship.[4] In the military context, the Defense Department responds that it is not censoring speech but is merely using speech as evidence of criminal conduct, sodomy.[5] Cole and I also maintained that first amendment principles and jurisprudence support the further, surprising, conclusion that laws prohibiting sodomy also implicate free expression values. This chapter, therefore, outlines a first amendment path for reconsidering *Bowers v. Hardwick* (1986), criticized in Chapter 4.

That Selland and Rowland were being disciplined for the content of their expression does not inevitably mean that the first amendment was violated, however. Under the Court's current jurisprudence, the state can inhibit the speech of its employees when the speech does not involve matters of "public concern" or when the state interest in the "efficiency of the public services it performs" outweighs the speech interest.[6] Moreover, the Court, especially in the military context, defers to institutional efficiency judgments. Sexualized first amendment claims mobilize these conceptual tropes—institutional deference and efficiency—but also expose their tension with other first amendment concerns—the chilling effect and heckler's vetoes—when expression occurs within the state itself. In the public employee cases, resistance to a sexualized first amendment reflects fear of a sexualized state. A further argument of this chapter is that the state is already sexualized, and the Court risks its own unique position when it sacrifices first amendment principle to prop up the collapsing sexual closet.

The most intellectually serious objections to giving genuine first amendment protection to sexual speech are slippery slope ones. Most things sexual would then implicate the first amendment, and its core principle of freedom of political expression might thereby be diluted. A sexualized first amendment would, in fact, expose problems with the Court's unpersuasive distinction between political and sexual expression—and ultimately the distinction between public and private expression—but this process has long been afoot. Even the conservative Rehnquist Court is already sexualizing the first amendment. A salutary effect of a sexualized first amendment would be to bring analytical order to the Supreme Court's chaotic jumble of cases involving obscenity, indecency, and child pornography.

Sexual Expression and First Amendment Values

The free speech clause of the first amendment is implicated only by efforts to communicate. If one engages in conduct without any intent to communicate, or if nobody would understand one's action as communicating anything, there is nothing for the first amendment to protect. Thus, the threshold inquiry in any free speech case is whether the plaintiff's conduct was intended to communicate a message and would be understood by others as communicative.[7] An admission of sexual identity is expressive in the strictest sense of the word. If I say "I am a vegetarian," I am engaged in speech about myself that is at the core of the first amendment. Rowland's statement "I am bisexual" and Selland's statement "I am gay" are also pure speech. What about hand-holding? Kissing? Marrying someone of the same sex? These activities, all of which can trigger the military exclusion, are not pure speech but are "expressive conduct" protected by the first amendment. The Supreme Court has held that flag-burning, destroying draft cards, and wearing swastikas are all expressive conduct that can be prohibited only to serve a substantial government interest unrelated to the suppression of expression.[8] If these activities expressing hostility are entitled to first amendment protection, isn't a lesbian marriage ceremony expressing love entitled to protection as well?

The government's response in the military cases is that the statement "I am gay" is not being penalized but is merely being used as evidence that the soldier has a *propensity* to engage in oral or anal sex, the military crime of sodomy. It is true that "the First Amendment does not prohibit the evidentiary use of speech to establish the elements of a crime," such as intent.[9] It is also true that a gay person is likely to have engaged in sodomy—as has a straight person. More than 70 percent of Americans have reportedly engaged in oral sex, and more than 20 percent in anal sex.[10] Because military law makes heterosexual sodomy just as illegal as homosexual sodomy, the statement "I am gay" is not much better evidence of propensity to commit sodomy than the statement "I am straight," and for women it is no better evidence.[a] This difference in treatment suggests that the expression is penalized primarily as evidence of status (homosexual orientation), not conduct (sodomy). It is hard to imagine a robust first amendment that does not prohibit censorship of pure identity speech such as this. During the Cold War, for example, the Supreme Court refused to permit the state to penalize self-identification as a Communist, even though the Communist Party and its conduct were themselves illegal.[11]

There is a deeper problem with the government's syllogism that statements about homosexual orientation are just evidence of prohibited homosexual conduct. The conduct that is allegedly the target of the statute, sodomy between consenting adults, can itself be "expressive conduct" because of its typically communicative intent and nature. In *Barnes v. Glen Theatre, Inc.* (1991), eight Justices agreed that erotic dancing is "expressive conduct" for this kind of reason.[12] The ninth, Justice Antonin Scalia, found erotic dancing indistinguishable from recreational dancing, which has not been considered expressive conduct. Scalia wrote that expressive conduct is limited to activity "that is normally engaged in for the purpose of communicating an idea, or perhaps an emotion, to someone else."[13] Sexual conduct—from hand-holding to kissing to intercourse—is expressive in precisely this way. While also engaged in for pleasure and procreative purposes, sex is for most of us communicative and may express a wide range of emotions—love, desire, power, dependency, even rage or hatred.[14] Indeed, sex is uniquely communicative. To say "I love you" is one thing; to hold a lover's hand can express something more powerfully intimate; and to make love is often a still more profound expression of what one feels and thinks. All of these acts are, to use Scalia's terms, "normally engaged in for the purpose of communicating an idea, or perhaps an emotion, to someone else."

This argument will be jarring to readers who assume that sexual intercourse is just a matter of calisthenics or scratching a sexual itch, and perhaps it is just that for some people. This is at best a partial view of sex, traditionally the view expressed by male pornography and much religious literature, but one not held by most women and many straight as well as gay men.[15] For most of us, the acts of intercourse communicate love, appreciation, joy, and passion to one's partner. These ideas are no less—and sometimes a great deal more—communicative

---

a. Gay women are more likely to have engaged in oral sex than straight women but less likely to have engaged in anal sex.

than erotic dancing, flag-burning, and wearing hate symbols. Consider, too, how this sexualized first amendment fits the core policies of that amendment: liberty and personal autonomy, pluralist tolerance, and neutrality or equality.

Libertarian and Autonomy Values

The first amendment protects the individual's freedom to explore and develop her or his identity. In this way, the Constitution assures that the state may not seek to control a person's thoughts or beliefs, those intellectual characteristics that are central to our evolving personhood.[16] This is on the whole a nonutilitarian justification: the first amendment values individual autonomy per se and assures each individual she or he will have opportunities to explore and express an identity. Thus, the first amendment protects people's rights to express anger and even profanity, as when the Supreme Court overturned the conviction of a young man for displaying the message "Fuck the Draft" on his bomber jacket in *Cohen v. California* (1971).[17]

Psychologists and some philosophers consider expression of the sexual side of ourselves to be more identity-generative than expression of our verbal, intellectual side. They posit that a goal of flourishing human beings is "self-expansion," which seeks "anything experienced as rapidly expanding the self, such as bursts of creative insights, religious conversions, discoveries . . . and, notably, falling in love and intense sexual experiences."[18] In our Freudian culture, sexual orientation is a critical feature of one's identity. Talking about and engaging in sex are useful and perhaps necessary ways for a person to explore, discover, announce, or renounce her or his orientation,[19] and this is particularly important for the person who has a minority sexual orientation. For the gay person more than the straight, developing an integrated stable personality depends upon exploring and sharing with others similarly situated. The sharing includes sex as well as talk about sex.[20] Recall from Chapter 2 that the term "coming out" was originally understood by gay people to mean one's first sexual experience with someone of the same sex, then also came to mean associating with others in gay subculture, and finally came to mean identifying one's sexuality to outsiders. All of these forms of coming out were communicative as well as sexual, where gay people expressed gender and sexual variance by their statements and their expressive activities, including actual intercourse.

A unanimous Supreme Court in *Hurley v. Irish-American Gay, Lesbian and Bisexual Group of Boston* (1995) held that the state could not, consistent with the first amendment, require a St. Patrick's Day parade to include a gay marching group. The Court agreed that the gay group wanted to "bear witness to the fact that some Irish are gay, lesbian, or bisexual, and the presence of the organized marchers would suggest their view that people of their sexual orientation have as much claim to unqualified social acceptance as heterosexuals." The Court considered this an expressive interest—but one that the state could not force into someone else's parade. The "principle of autonomy to control one's speech" allowed the parade organizers to edit their message in any way they saw fit.[21] If this principle allows people to express a message of compulsory heterosexuality, the same principle should allow Rowland and Selland to deny the same without punishment from the state.

Don't ask, don't tell policies are contrary to these libertarian values. Not only do they directly suppress desired expression but they indirectly compel undesired expression. A condition of being a guidance counselor in Mad River was being able to pass, to engage in a never-ending masquerade, as heterosexual. Anyone who dropped the mask, even for a minute, was subject to swift discipline (Rowland was kicked out of her office the day the principal confronted her with the rumor) and unrelenting pursuit (after Rowland fled town, she was still harassed by private vandals and the police).[22] The compelled masquerade is constitutionally problematic if it "forces an individual, as part of his daily life ... to be an instrument for fostering public adherence to an ideological point of view he finds unacceptable."[23] That the state policy in *Rowland* was unofficial and uncodified makes it even more questionable, for such fuzzy policies have a *chilling effect* not only on the speech and expressive conduct of people who are gay but also on the speech and expressive conduct of people who are potentially gay. Because the ultimate audience for Mad River's policy of sexual conformity were the adolescents struggling with their own issues of sexual identity, the policy sought to establish a chain of masquerades.

Sodomy statutes similarly implicate developmental and communicative interests of the individual. Although most people in the United States engage in sodomy at some point in their lives, only a minority do so on a regular basis. It appears that most people do not enjoy sodomy as much as other means of sexual expression or find that it does not work for particular relationships. Oral sex is meaningful and expressive for some people and not for others, but you don't know until you've tried it. Sodomy laws are classic censorship, seeking to close off sources of information and communication that are potentially useful for individual flourishing. The vagueness of many sodomy laws and the plasticity of all of them under *Hardwick* amplify their chilling effect on speech and expressive conduct. The characterization game played in *Hardwick* was one that can be turned on nonconforming straights just as on nonconforming gays.

Pluralism Values

The first amendment also has a strong political component. Its protection of individual autonomy is thought to engender collective benefits in the body politic by fostering a diverse citizenry and assuring that "debate on public issues should be uninhibited, robust, and wide-open."[24] When Rowland's sexual preference became the talk of Mad River, her bisexual identity challenged the political ideologies of compulsory heterosexuality (everyone must be straight) and orientation binariness (everyone is either gay or straight). According to traditional first amendment thinking, this alone is valuable. Rowland may be aberrational, but her identity stood as a conceptual challenge to Mad River orthodoxy. By disciplining Rowland, Mad River was seeking to silence and close off debate about proper sexuality—the antithesis of the first amendment's aspiration toward "uninhibited, robust, wide-open" debate on public issues.

Expression to others of minority sexual orientation is uniquely useful speech. Because gay people have traditionally passed for straight, many Americans are not aware that they know people whose lives refute stereotypes about homosexuality. By coming out, openly gay people make a contribution to the education of straight America. Gay people believe, with good justification, that their fair treatment by the legal system depends upon officials knowing and talking with openly gay people. As the California Supreme Court put it when it held identification as gay to be political speech, "one important aspect of the struggle for equal rights is to induce homosexual individuals to 'come out of the closet,' acknowledge their sexual preferences, and to associate with others in working for equal rights."[25] The legal as well as political importance of coming out was illustrated in the deliberations surrounding *Hardwick.* The key fifth vote to uphold laws criminalizing consensual "homosexual sodomy" was cast by a Justice who claimed, in deliberation with his closeted gay law clerk regarding *Hardwick,* that he had never met a homosexual.[26]

Homosexual conduct, from public hand-holding by same-sex couples to private sexual conduct, likewise contributes to the diverse and robust polity that the first amendment envisions. Public expressions of same-sex affection are as important a critique of gender assumptions and roles as any published treatise.[27] That gestures like hand-holding are symbolic of ideas and attitudes rather than literal statements of position in a debate does not diminish their importance. Public debate has never been limited to books, speeches, and signs; it has always included symbolic gestures such as dancing, visual art, advertising imagery, public demonstrations, clothing, and physical conduct. If a "Fuck the Draft" jacket contributed to the exchange of ideas, as the Court held in *Cohen,* a man's holding the hand of another man surely qualifies as well.

Even private same-sex intimacy plays an important role in shaping public debate. Because gay people and other gender-benders explore and develop their identity through private sexual conduct, that conduct is critical to their ability to take part as lesbians, gay men, transgendered people, and bisexuals in public life. Sodomy laws and employment exclusions are two of many mechanisms by which society has sought to discourage such personal exploration and development. The repression is political as much as personal for it reflects a social effort to keep sexual and gender variation in the closet, not only hidden from the public but incapable of contributing to public discourse and politics. The first part of this book documents the extensive state efforts, climaxing in the 1950s, to obliterate gay visibility in the public sphere. All such efforts focused on silencing gay people, not only by keeping their sexuality in the closet but by discouraging even private expression of that sexuality. The state's discipline of Rowland and Selland is a faint echo of the policies of the 1950s, but it can be traced directly to that terror.

Since Stonewall, large numbers of gay people have defied the tyranny of the closet, and only that defiance has made it possible for their voices to be heard in American politics. So long as gays kept their orientation a secret, they could pass in American society. The ease of passing exacted incalculable personal costs to individuals but also exacted what the first amendment considers a social cost, discouraging the formation of an openly gay subculture and gay, lesbian, and transgendered political activism. Once people started defying that suppression, they formed political as well as cultural communities. Those communities could not exist without expression, including hand-holding, cross-dressing, and oral sex. For gays, as much as for feminists, the personal is the political.

The first amendment serves a pedagogical function in reflecting our pluralist commitment to tolerance.[28] Insisting that society restrain its impulse to persecute unpopular minorities, the first amendment sets a public example that might inspire cooperative rather than exclusionary conduct throughout society. In the past, the first amendment has protected the Amish, Jehovah's Witnesses, the NAACP, Communists, and various ethnic groups—all despised in their day by popular majorities. The first amendment's willingness to insulate groups against suppression has contributed to its strength over time. By their sexual conduct, gay people are creating or searching for their own identities and voices, and the first amendment insists that this group be given the same public space as previous groups have been afforded.

Both the military policy and sodomy laws strike at the pluralism and toleration values implicit in the first amendment. Kenneth Karst has shown how military service in American history has been a badge of citizenship, and that exclusions from military service reflect exclusions from citizenship. In fact, he argues, the exclusion and later segregation of people of color, the exclusion and later segregation of women, and the exclusion of gay people can be attributed to an ideology of "manhood," where one race, one gender, and one sexual orientation are held up as the only acceptable template for people who ought to run and defend our country.[29] For the same pluralist reasons that racial segregation was terminated and exclusions of women are on the wane, a pluralist country ought to rethink its exclusion of gays and lesbians—as Canada recently did (without any repercussions) and as most other industrialized countries did long ago. Sodomy statutes similarly offend the values of toleration. To prescribe by criminal law the forms of nonharmful sexual intimacy that consenting adults may engage in is the very definition of intolerance. A truly pluralist society would tolerate forms of same-sex intimacy that do not directly harm another person, the stance taken by virtually all other industrial countries (Chapter 4).

Equality Values

A central theme of first amendment jurisprudence is that the state cannot selectively discriminate against expressive conduct simply because of what it communicates. For example, in *Police Department of Chicago v. Mosley* (1972), the Court invalidated an ordinance prohibiting picketing because it exempted labor picketing, thus violating the principle of neutral treatment of similarly situated speakers. "Because picketing plainly involves expressive conduct within the protections of the first amendment, discriminations among pickets must be tailored to serve a substantial governmental interest." Had the ban applied neutrally to all picketing, it would have been upheld, but the Court was unwilling to tolerate regimes "selectively suppressing some points of view."[30]

The first amendment demands viewpoint neutrality to ensure that there is "'equality of status in the field of ideas.'"[31] This feature of the first amendment is both individualistic and social. Viewpoint neutrality assures the citizen that she or he will not be censored under circumstances when more acceptable citizens would be allowed to speak. It also prevents the political majority from achieving a regulatory goal at the expense of the expressive interests of an unpopular or less powerful minority. The most dramatic application of the first amendment's requirement of viewpoint neutrality came in a case where a defendant was prosecuted under a municipal hate crime law for burning a cross in front of a home owned by a family of color. Cross-burning is expressive conduct that bristles with violence. The Supreme Court in *R.A.V. v. City of St. Paul* (1992) evaluated a hate crime ordinance that had been construed to ban only cross-burning as constituted "fighting words" outside the first amendment's protection.[32] Nonetheless, the Court invalidated the ordinance because it did not treat all symbolic "fighting words" equally but selectively prohibited only those based on race, color, creed, religion, or gender. "The First Amendment generally prevents government from proscribing speech or even expressive conduct because of disapproval of the ideas expressed."[33]

The equality value of viewpoint neutrality was directly implicated in Rowland's case. She would not have been disciplined if she had told her secretary that she was living with a man. Indeed, the assistant principal initially considered her bisexuality acceptable in Mad River because he thought bisexuals were people who preferred to have sex in pairs.[34] Rowland was disciplined because of the horrified reaction of others in the school and their disapproval of what her bisexuality represented. In short, the school was "proscribing speech" about her sexual orientation "because of disapproval of the ideas expressed," that women do not need to have sex only with men and that human beings do not have to be heterosexual. Surely public employees' expressions of sexual orientation should be extended at least as much protection from viewpoint regulation as hate speech, as some courts have held.[35] The same defect applies to the military's policy because it singles out homosexual conduct for different treatment than heterosexual conduct. Like the hate speech ordinance in *R.A.V.* and the selective picketing prohibition in *Mosley,* don't ask, don't tell must therefore be subjected to the first amendment drill.

Federal military and most state prohibitions of sodomy are not so vulnerable on their face because the prohibitions apply to both heterosexual and homosexual conduct. But the equality value underlying the requirement of viewpoint neutrality is implicated because sodomy regulation is not evenhanded in practice or effect. The Code of Military Justice does not treat all sexual conduct equally for it permits penile-vaginal intercourse while prohibiting oral and anal sex. Thus, it selectively singles out some sexual conduct for prohibition, just as the ordinance in *R.A.V.* singled out some symbolic fighting words. Moreover, the provision, like all sodomy statutes, reflects an official message that the only form of acceptable sex is penile-vaginal intercourse. Straight people subject to sodomy laws at least have the option of engaging in the state-sanctioned activity; gay people do not realistically have that option. Hence, even "neutral" sodomy laws have nonneutral effects on lesbians and gay men.

Regulatory Justifications for Don't Ask, Don't Tell Policies

Because so much conduct is expressive, the critical first amendment inquiry is why the government has regulated the particular conduct. If those reasons are unrelated to the expressive elements of the conduct, the regulation is subject to relaxed scrutiny and generally upheld.[36] Rape laws, for example, regulate sexual conduct that is expressive (anger or misogyny), but the state regulation can be justified by reference to rape's tangible third-party effects, violence against another person. If, on the other hand, the regulation is animated by what the conduct communicates to others, the law must be treated as if it were a regulation of speech itself and subjected to strict scrutiny.[37] As Justice Scalia once put it, "freedom of expression makes the communicative nature of conduct an inadequate *basis* for singling out that conduct for proscription. A law *directed at* the communicative nature of conduct must, like a law directed at speech itself, be justified by the substantial showing of need that the first amendment requires."[38]

For example, when Texas and then the United States outlawed flag-burning, the Court subjected the laws to stringent scrutiny because the governmental interest was in suppressing the messages associated with flag-burning. By contrast, when protesters who sought to dramatize the plight of the homeless by sleeping in Lafayette Park challenged the National Park Service's ban on sleeping in parks, the Court upheld the ban under minimal scrutiny.[39] It found that the governmental interest in prohibiting sleeping in parks had nothing to do with the message a would-be sleeper might communicate but instead was predicated on safety and upkeep of the parks. The Lafayette Park case illustrates this general precept. All expression can be seen as comprised of both physical and superficial characteristics (time, place, and manner) and strictly communicative elements (content). Just as regulation motivated by the communicative content of expressive conduct triggers stringent scrutiny, so too does a content-based regulation of speech. Similarly, regulation of conduct "unrelated to the supression of expression" is analogous to regulation of the time, place, and manner of speech.

Thus, the critical question in reviewing any regulation of expressive conduct is whether the government's interest in banning the conduct is related to the suppression of expression. The very terminology for the policies that excluded Rowland and Selland predetermines this inquiry: "don't ask, don't tell" is concerned only with what homosexual identity or expressive conduct communicates to others. General Colin Powell testified in 1992 that gay men and lesbians have always served with honor in the military. Responding to inquiry whether there is any evidence of behavior problems as a result of the long-standing presence of gays in the military, Powell said, "No, because as a matter of fact they have kept, so-called, in the closet. It is quite a different thing when it is openly practiced or openly known throughout the force and within the units. I think it makes very difficult management problems."[40] Powell's view is now the official

Defense Department line.[41] Desert Storm's General Norman Schwarzkopf testified to the same effect: a statement of one's homosexual orientation was "conduct" that could not be tolerated because it "would polarize the organization."[42] In other words, it is not homosexual identity that is the problem—just its expression to others.

A don't ask, don't tell policy makes sense only if homosexual conduct and identity are not in themselves problematic; if they were, there would be no basis for directing military officers *not* to ask about or investigate the possibility of *private* homosexuality. The policy is triggered only by *public* declarations of homosexuality, whether through making statements or symbolic gestures or being outed by someone else. Thus, same-sex hand-holding or marriage, two public statements of sexual identity, are presumptive grounds for discharge. By contrast, hand-holding in private or a private commitment to a lifelong homosexual relationship does not trigger investigation. When government selectively regulates public conduct in this way, first amendment concerns are heightened. By singling out public conduct, the regulations imply that the government's interest does not have to do with the physical aspects of the conduct but with what the conduct communicates to others. Similarly, the fact that the military's new policy singles out admissions of homosexuality, but does not inquire into whether an individual is homosexual absent such an admission, underscores the military's concern for what is communicated rather than for the underlying reality of homosexual orientation.

The military's stated rationales for its policy also reflect a concern for what homosexual conduct communicates to others. The military strenuously argues that "morale" and "unit cohesion" will be threatened by the presence of openly gay personnel.[43] But the "don't ask" half of its policy concedes that morale and unit cohesion are not unduly threatened by the presence of *closeted* gay personnel. Thus, the problem has less to do with identity or conduct itself than with the expression of that identity or conduct to others. The military's interests are threatened only by the communication of gay members' sexual identities to other, presumably homophobic, members of a military unit.

For these reasons, the new policy ought to be more vulnerable to a broad first amendment attack than the old policy.[44] The old policy maintained that the military was penalizing service members only for their identity and not for their speech. Current Defense Department regulations, however, concede that homosexuality itself is not incompatible with military service and focus instead on the communication of one's homosexuality to others. For this reason, don't ask, don't tell is a legally unstable policy. It seeks to avoid the unsupported stereotypes about gay people that underlay the old policy[45] but at the price of hypocrisy and more explicit tension with first amendment values.

The state's prohibition of sodomy also requires stringent first amendment scrutiny under the foregoing analysis. Because sodomy is potentially expressive, stringent first amendment scrutiny applies unless the government's interest in regulating sodomy is unrelated to the suppression of expression. The rationale consistently advanced for the regulation of sodomy is community morality. Sodomy is said to be immoral, and society condemns it for that reason, as the Supreme Court held in *Hardwick*. Such an answer begs the question. One might equally claim that burning a flag or cross is immoral. To say that conduct is immoral is to say little more than that the majority disapproves of it. The question is *why* does society condemn sodomy as immoral? If it is immoral because it causes harm in a noncommunicative manner, as rape or sexual assault does, the first amendment's stringent review would not be appropriate. But if the moral harm it causes results from what it communicates, its regulation should trigger strict scrutiny. How does consensual homosexual conduct harm the military community, except by virtue of what it expresses to that community? A consensual act of same-sex intimacy has no physical effect on the community and causes no harm to the individuals involved. It can affect the broader community only if the fact that it occurred is communicated to the community, thereby offending or demoralizing its homophobic members. Because the military's interests can be undermined only if the fact of the proscribed conduct is in some way communicated, the government's interest in regulating sodomy is necessarily related to sodomy's expressive character.

To summarize up to this point: the realities of modern sexuality and the Supreme Court's aggressive expansion of the first amendment to cover nonpolitical expression logically suggest that key remnants of the apartheid of the closet—don't ask, don't tell policies and sodomy laws—implicate first amendment freedom of expression. That the first amendment is implicated does not, however, end the constitutional inquiry. If the state's rationales are compelling, and if the means it has chosen are narrowly tailored to further those ends, the challenged policy may withstand strict or heightened scrutiny.[46]

The Rowland and Selland cases have in common this structure of justification: courts should defer to expert decisionmakers who run important government institutions, and the experts think that openly gay personnel would undermine the efficiency of their institutions. Consider the tensions within free speech jurisprudence that these justifications expose. The first amendment is considered one of the few principled areas of constitutional law and has protected the most unpopular litigants against the "chilling effect" of state censorship (Chapter 2), but deference is an elastic loophole allowing courts to tack to political winds when a group is subject to popular scorn. Freedom of expression jurisprudence has generally disfavored the "heckler's veto," whereby speech can be suppressed because of the reaction it triggers in others, but institutional efficiency or morale is an elastic loophole allowing courts to consider intensely felt third-party reactions. Both contrasts reflect a fundamental tension between first amendment values and the practicalities of the complex political and institutional system within which the courts implement those values. For don't ask, don't tell policies, however, the deeper state justification is the fear of sexualizing the institution. This is a self-defeating justification, however, because a regime of challenge-and-suppression is just as likely to sexualize the institution as a regime of free expression.

What kind of limits should the first amendment set in sexual expression cases? Where the state is regulating sexual expression as sovereign (*Hardwick*), the first amendment should presumptively, and perhaps flatly, rule out prohibitions that either discriminate against homosexual expression or that regulate private sexually expressive conduct simply because it offends homophobes. Where the state is regulating sexual expression as employer (*Rowland*), the first amendment should allow reasonable regulation of expressive conduct and job-related speech in the workplace but should not permit censorship of identity speech, especially when the censorship is viewpoint-based discrimination. Where the state is regulating sexual expression in the armed forces (*Selland*), the first amendment should allow regulations of general application as they apply to soldiers on military property or during working hours but ought not allow either regulation of off-duty activities in private homes or regulations that discriminate against homosexual expression.

Deference and the "Chilling Effect"

In defending don't ask, don't tell policies in court, the government's initial argument tends to be that judges should defer to the expert judgment of educators (*Rowland*), civil service commissions (Chapter 3), or generals and admirals (*Selland*). Deference arguments are invitations for courts to bend principle to accommodate practice and politics. That courts are political as well as legal institutions creates a dilemma in their continual struggle to maintain their authority. If judges blur first amendment bright lines, they risk chilling of protected speech of citizens cowed by the threat of censorship, a big sacrifice of first amendment principle. If judges sacrifice principle too often or too openly, they lose their unique role as the enforcers of constitutional rules of law. On the other hand, if judges apply principle at too great an expense or in the face of overwhelming popular heat, they are rebuked by an angry political system. If judges are found to have disrupted the operation of another branch of government, they lose face within our system of federalism (*Rowland*) and separation of powers *(Selland)*. That deference demands a delicate balancing act does not mean that it is not susceptible to analysis, even principled analysis perhaps. Recall the national furor over the Court's decision to protect flag-burning in *Texas v. Johnson* (1989). Overall, the Court emerged from the controversy with its prestige not only intact but enhanced. Contrast *Bowers v. Hardwick* (1986), where judicial deference to popular prejudice diminished the Court.[47]

The Court routinely defers to military judgments about the need for "discipline" and "good order."[48] *Goldman v. Weinberger* (1986), for example, allowed the Air Force to prohibit an orthodox Jewish chaplain from wearing a yarmulke, pursuant to a regulation generally barring the wearing of headgear indoors. *Goldman* was viewed as a questionable deference, as there was no evidence that anyone was bothered by Rabbi Goldman's yarmulke, except the headgear gendarmerie.[49] In retrospect, however, the *Goldman* regulation was defensible as it was a regulation of general application that only had an incidental effect on religious free exercise, which the Court subsequently held not to violate the first amendment.[50] For a closer parallel to Selland's case, the Court in *Rostker v. Goldberg* (1981) deferred to the judgment of the armed forces, the president, and the legislature to exclude women from draft registration, even though the government's administrative convenience arguments would not ordinarily have justified the sex discrimination embedded in the statutory policy.[51] Under *Rostker,* should the exclusion of gay people be exempt from meaningful review?

There are limits to deference even in the military setting, however. Neither *Goldman* nor *Rostker* held that the state can target the expression of a specific group for discrimination or can make private conformity a condition of military service. *Goldman*, for example, would have been a different case if the Air Force had forbidden Jews and Jews alone from wearing headgear or had forbidden personnel from wearing headgear off duty; instead, its regulation was limited to military functions indoors. Likewise, Selland's would be a different case if the armed forces merely excluded people who commit sodomy on military facilities. For another example, *Greer v. Spock* (1976) upheld a policy excluding all political candidates from a military base, noting that the base's purpose was to train soldiers, not to serve as a public forum, and that the military had a strong interest in avoiding partisan politics. In dictum, the Court suggested that the first amendment would be violated if a military commander selectively sought to bar political candidates of one party from speaking on base.[52] The D.C. Circuit held that military academies cannot compel attendance at chapel, deference notwithstanding.[53]

The Supreme Court has followed a mild version of this approach in public employment cases, where the Court usually defers to employer regulation of speech about purely institutional matters but not to its efforts to censor discourse about larger public issues. "The government cannot restrict the speech of the public at large just in the name of efficiency," the Court ruled in *Waters v. Churchill* (1994). "But where the government is employing someone for the very purpose of effectively achieving its goals, such restrictions may well be appropriate."[54] The Court required, however, that the state response be *reasonable*. Under first amendment premises, it is not reasonable to discharge a bisexual employee for identifying her partner to coworkers, when a straight employee would not be discharged, nor is it reasonable to penalize the bisexual for being outed by the state itself. The only legitimate justification available to the state in Marjorie Rowland's case was its claim that she violated confidences of two students whom she was counseling, but the trier of fact found that justification to have been pretextual.

Selland and Rowland were susceptible to the deference argument because their speech was on the job, not in the world. If Rowland had been cashiered for a radio interview in favor of equal rights for bisexuals, deference would have been less appropriate because the school district would have been asserting expertise well beyond its jurisdiction. Schoolyard conversations are within its jurisdiction; public speeches, not.[55] If the armed forces had discharged Selland based on photographs of him holding hands with another man at an off-base gay club, deference would have been less appropriate, because the military could be seen as looking to create trouble in its own ranks. Hand-holding in the barracks is within its jurisdiction; in an off-base club, less so.

Another limiting precept is this: the more targeted the assault on principle and the less reasonable the government's reaction, the less inclined the Court will be to defer. For example, the Supreme Court in *Rankin v. McPherson* (1987) ruled that a law enforcement employee could not be summarily fired for expressing disappointment that an assassination attempt against the president had failed. Because the admittedly distasteful comment obviously implicated matters of public concern, the Court refused to defer to the constable's judgment that the comment's disrespectful content would undermine the law enforcement work of the constable's office.[56] Similarly, if the regulation in *Goldman* had focused on yarmulkes alone and not headgear generally, the Court would probably not have deferred, as this would have been a direct sacrifice of core first amendment principle.[57] If Congress determined that women could never serve in the armed forces, that would be a very different case from *Rostker* for the exclusion would be a broad affront to women's equal citizenship.

Consider a more pointed analogue. Until 1948 the armed forces insisted upon the segregation of African Americans from whites in military service. Would the Supreme Court defer to this expert judgment? In the 1940s the Court might have deferred—and such deference would have been to the

Court's lasting discredit, as we would recognize today. What has changed is not the quality of the argument or the principle that racial segregation violates, but the political equilibrium. It is no longer publicly acceptable to deny people of color the formal trappings of citizenship. Is it still acceptable to deny them to gay people? This remains to be seen, but *Romer v. Evans* (1996) suggests the Supreme Court is reconsidering this issue for gays, as it did for Communists a generation ago. In 1967, after the perceived Communist threat had receded, the Court struck down a statutory ban against employing Communist Party members in defense facilities. The Court rejected the argument that it defer to the political process in the interest of national defense. "It would indeed be ironic if, in the name of national defense, we would sanction the subversion of one of those liberties—the freedom of association—which makes the defense of the Nation worthwhile."[58]

Relatedly, the Supreme Court is aware that yesterday's demonized group (Jews, Catholics) or politically marginalized group (women) may be part of tomorrow's pluralist mainstream—and even tomorrow's Court. If the same process of pluralist accommodation seems to be occurring for gay people, it is risky today for the Court to disrespect them as it did in *Hardwick*. Kicking sand in the face of a 98-pound weakling is mean, but such meanness is risky if the weakling later bulks up into Charles Atlas or even into Richard Simmons. The institutional risks posed by shortsighted deference are illustrated in *Korematsu v. United States* (1944). Deferring to military judgment that Japanese Americans posed a security threat, the Court upheld their internment in detention camps during World War II.[59] That decision is notorious in its sacrifice of principle to politics and institutionally embarrassing because it is associated with the kind of racist prejudice that is no longer acceptable in our polity. As antigay prejudice becomes less acceptable in our polity, it becomes increasingly difficult for the Court to write an opinion deferring to military judgment that openly gay people will destabilize the armed forces.

Finally, any argument that the courts should defer to the government's expert judgment in matters of military discipline needs to consider that the government's own experts have often been skeptical of the exclusion. The Crittenden Report written for the Department of Defense in 1957 was critical of the military's justification for excluding gays and lesbians in the 1950s, namely, the argument that such soldiers would be subject to blackmail (Chapter 2). The Department suppressed that report. The Defense Personnel Security Research and Education Center (PERSEREC) reports written in 1988 and 1989, and also suppressed, concluded that the exclusion of gay people rests upon no demonstrated harm to military efficacy.[60] Outside experts from the Government Accounting Office and the Rand Corporation were underwhelmed by the military's current justifications for excluding gay personnel.[61] If the best-informed experts advising the government are skeptical of the need for exclusion, one ought to hesitate before deferring to the expertise of other government officials inspired more by politics or simple prejudice than by the nation's defense needs.

Internal Efficiency and the Heckler's Veto

During the 1993 congressional hearings on the gay exclusion, Colonel William Henderson made the government's case for the proposition that the presence of openly gay soldiers will undermine "discipline, good order, and morale." Citing studies of the Wehrmacht and the U.S. Army during World War II, he posited that the cohesion of the unit is the "central factor" in the success of a military unit.[62] Henderson then argued that unit cohesion is impossible without basic agreement among unit members about cultural values, an agreement that is shattered if one of the unit members reveals himself or herself to be gay or lesbian. The testimony of General Powell, Secretary of Defense Les Aspin, and other top brass echoed Colonel Henderson's analysis.

The unit cohesion argument is a stronger version of administrative efficiency arguments typically raised as bases for disciplining disruptive government employees. The Supreme Court has held that state and federal employers who disrupt efficient office operations can be disciplined.[63] It would stretch this doctrine to extend it to Rowland, whose only disruption was a consequence of identifying who she was, but most judges have been sympathetic to this argument in the military context, and not just for deference reasons. Because the well-functioning armed forces need complete cohesion in the chain of command and at each level for a complex operation to succeed, and because the cost of failure is potentially extraordinary, even small risks of breakdown assume greater importance than they would in a civilian setting. If the presence of an openly gay soldier like Selland would throw the unit into turmoil, the unit might perform badly, and its performance might affect an entire assault, whose failure could ruin a campaign, which in turn might result in losing the war. Too much is at stake to stand on principle.

Even put this way, the unit cohesion argument still echoes the "heckler's veto," where the speaker is silenced by hecklers in the audience. The first amendment tradition is antithetical to the heckler's veto, and courts have repeatedly held it impermissible to silence speech because of the reaction of a hostile audience.[64] The impermissibility of the heckler's veto is a core first amendment principle that should protect state employees such as Rowland, and there is no Supreme Court decision that suggests otherwise. Should the principle protect soldiers as well? Consider this. The study of American troops during World War II relied on by Henderson found that religion was the main cohering force for our soldiers.[65] Almost all of the soldiers were Christians, mostly Protestant, and their faith afforded a strong mutual bond. Many American soldiers were devoutly anti-Semitic. Under the unit cohesion rationale, the presence of an openly Jewish soldier would undermine cohesion in a unit containing anti-Semites. Would it have been justifiable in the 1940s for the armed forces to have excluded Jews because of anti-Semitic animosity?

The reader might find this hypothetical far-fetched, but the military's pre-1948 policy of racial segregation was defended on precisely those grounds. The Army defended segregation by reference to polls taken in 1942 showing 90 percent of the white soldiers supported segregated units, as did 30 to 40 percent of the black soldiers. "The soldier on the battlefield deserves to have, and must have, utmost confidence in his fellow soldiers," reasoned the Army. "They must eat together, sleep together, and all too frequently die together. There can be no friction in their every-day living that might bring on failure in battle. A chain is as strong as its weakest link, and this is true of the Army unit on the battlefield."[66] Ironically, when the Army actually deployed a few racially integrated units near the end of World War II, the perceptions of soldiers changed radically, according to the Army's surveys: while only a third of the white soldiers in the integrated units were comfortable having blacks in their units before the experiment, afterward 77 percent said they found the arrangement more favorable after having served with blacks, and virtually none found it less favorable.[67] Although the Army suppressed these reports and continued a policy of segregation, President Truman overrode the experts in 1948. Once the Army actually integrated its units during the Korean War, its own as well as outside experts found that the new policy worked "without undue friction and with better utilization of manpower," notwithstanding overwhelmingly racist feelings on the part of white soldiers before integration. Combat commanders "almost unanimously favor integration," the Army concluded, after the fact.[68]

American experience with desegregation of the armed forces suggests some tentative lessons for the current exclusion of gays. One is that courts should be cautious about deferring to military judgments about citizenship and community. The Joint Chiefs of Staff cried wolf when they supported the internment of Japanese Americans during World War II *(Korematsu),* and they cried wolf again when they insisted that racial desegregation would destroy morale and unit cohesion. They now cry wolf and make the same argument in support of the exclusion of gay people. Not only is superdeference uncalled for under these circumstances, but there are strong reasons to believe that the morale argument is just as questionable for the military's gay exclusion as it was for its racial segregation. Gays have long served in our armed forces and have often served openly—all without disruption of morale. Historically, the gay exclusion has been relaxed during times of war,[69] precisely when unit cohesion should presumably be most important. The government's own internal studies provide no evidence that openly gay service personnel actually disrupt unit cohesion,[70] and considerable anecdotal evidence demonstrates that thousands of servicemembers have been known by their colleagues to be lesbian or gay, with no negative repercussions for morale and unit cohesion during wartime.[71] The United States is virtually alone among Western nations in excluding gays; their inclusion in other armies has had no documented ill effect on morale.[72] A final consideration is the following: unit cohesion may be undermined rather than inculcated by policies that impel soldiers to lie about themselves. This is a standard lesson of both the first amendment and market economics—more complete information is presumptively better for all concerned.

Fear of Sexualizing Institutions

A variation of the morale argument is that allowing gays to serve would invade the privacy of straight soldiers. Marine Corps Commandant Carl Mundy asked, "How would you (or most American families) react if your son called and informed you that his roommates for the next few years were homosexuals. Would you not be concerned?"[73] This appeals to fears that the homosexual secretly lusts after and will attack the heterosexual. Such fears are irrational; gay attacks against straights are as rare as straight attacks on gays are commonplace.[74] A better expression of the privacy concern is the shower-room argument: straight male servicemembers are said to be nervous about being seen naked in the shower room by someone who might find them sexually attractive. While there is no evidence that shower-room observations ever lead to sexual assaults, the straight soldier hates the gay gaze because it sexualizes his body in unwelcome ways.[75]

At first blush, the shower-room argument seems an odd support for don't ask, don't tell. As the Defense Department claims to enforce it, the policy only bars the open lesbian or gay man. The closeted homosexual would still be able to serve and to gaze lustfully but discreetly at shower-room colleagues. How is the gay gaze less threatening? Closeted soldiers would theoretically pose a greater threat to straight privacy than openly gay ones for the fearful straight soldier would have no way of identifying who might pose this threat. This response misconceives the shower-room objection, however. The anxiety it taps is the homophobe's uncertainty about her or his heterosexuality, a fear that the gay gaze is responding to queer features of her or his own sexuality.[76] Heterosexual insecurity is reduced if the gay gaze must remain anonymous, but confronted with the gaze of a specific gay person the straight person may become unhinged.

The shower-room argument relates directly to the unit cohesion argument. Military training is a leveling process that strips away the soldier's previous status. Boot campers are to be judged based only upon their skill, cleverness, and ability to fit into the team dynamics of the military. Hence, one's race or one's social background is supposed to be irrelevant after boot camp, but sexual orientation is less benign in this setting because it exposes boot camp's homosocial bonding to suspicions that it is "latently" homosexual. The study of morale in the Wehrmacht relied on by Colonel Henderson found that "primary group solidarity in the Wehrmacht was based in part on latent homosexual tendencies" among the soldiers.[77] Perversely, homosexual attraction may be useful to the unit cohesion of same-sex units, but only so long as the existence of a sexual feature to this bonding can be plausibly denied. Don't ask, don't tell, therefore, works as a way to maintain the public appearance of the army as a heterosexual institution, while allowing a liberal amount of homosexual bonding to go on beneath the surface. Relatedly, the government fears that openly gay personnel will sexualize the armed forces. For many of the same reasons the military insists on sex segregation, it insists on sexual orientation exclusion: the introduction of sexual "others" into the barracks will be destabilizing because it will introduce unpredictable emotional tensions and loyalties at odds with the chain of command.[78] Many in the armed forces remain resentful that women now serve in this traditionally male preserve and believe that women have introduced all sorts of trouble for the military—sexual harassment scandals, sex-inspired rivalries between men, and antidiscrimination rules. The political culture insists that women serve, however, and the frustration traditionalists bear between gritted teeth about women in the military makes them all the more resistant to open gays as well.

Mad River School District was probably acting out similar fears when it disciplined Marjorie Rowland. That she was helping two gay teenagers work through their sexual uncertainties invoked the traditional antigay stereotype of the vampire lesbian who preys on youngsters, but the main reason she was expelled was that her words sexualized the school. By making apparent that the people in charge had undomesticated sexual feelings, and that women in charge did not need men for their sexual needs, Rowland was tossing timebombs into the impressionable minds of Mad River students. The open bisexual whose identity challenges compulsory heterosexuality puts everybody's sexuality on the spot. It is for this reason that many homosexual soldiers would prefer that activists not challenge the gay exclusion, for the lawsuits themselves sexualize the military environment.[79] Some of the Mad River school personnel felt this way about Rowland and her attorneys.

That open homosexuality may sexualize the workplace is a Pyrrhic defense of don't ask, don't tell, however. Both Selland and Rowland were discreet, considerate gender-benders, confiding only in trusted colleagues and friends. Their sexuality only became a public phenomenon because the persecutocracy outed them, and that might not have happened if the state did not essentially make it an offense to be gay or bisexual. In this sense, the antigay policy itself created a scene of public sexuality on nervous display. By making homosexuality a matter of high state concern and question-asking, the armed forces and the Mad River School District were rousing as well as discouraging discourse about sexuality within their institutions. Indeed, they were thrusting a particularly negative kind of sexual discourse—an intolerant, hysterical sex negativity—upon soldiers and high school students. Negativity about such a natural function as sexual attraction is more likely to generate neurosis and rebellion than the sex conformity that its boosters seek.

Michel Foucault theorized that the effect of a prohibitory regime is to stimulate discourse about the prohibited object.[80] A regime of the closet cannot suppress once the door cracks, and will generate more discourse, which in turn will be productive in perverse and unexpected ways. The one way to assure that Pandora will open the box is for the state to admonish her that the box contains unspeakable evils. By taking the state out of sexual censorship, a sexualized first amendment could lower the stakes of sexual discourse, which might advance the state's ultimate interest—educated and adjusted high school graduates—better than a prohibitory policy of the closet. Under Mad River's version of don't ask, don't tell, the explosive chain reaction triggered by Rowland's revelation to her secretary and assistant principal was a product, in part, of the state censorship. The gaylegal history of Part One suggests that the publicity and disruption implicated in Rowland's abrupt firing would have been received in complicated ways by the Mad River students: some would have been confused, others turned on, still others would have regarded Rowland as a martyr. Consider an alternative scenario, where the Supreme Court had made it clear that public employees could not be disciplined for identity speech. In homophobic Mad River, Rowland would decidedly not have been an out-of-the-closet activist, but she would have felt free to confide in her secretary and assistant principal, probably without the witch-hunting hysteria that accompanied Rowland's actual confidence. Sexual discourse without hysteria might actually yield more sexual peace and less sexual neurosis.

Sexuality as a Test of the First Amendment

The don't ask, don't tell cases are a test of the limits for gay rights in this country, but they are more significant as a test of the first amendment itself. The first amendment has been tested before, and its unique constitutional strength has derived from its ability to respond successfully to hard challenges. Before 1961, most of the tests involved efforts to suppress the political association and expression of sociopolitical radicals—abolitionists, anarchists, unionists, Communists, and the like. Before the New Deal, judges construing the first amendment usually found ways to accommodate this suppression,[81] with the result that the first amendment had little constitutional bite until the Warren Court. The next great test involved racial radicals who engaged in expressive conduct—freedom marchers, cross-burners, sit-in protesters, and nazis displaying swastikas. The first amendment, as construed by the Supreme Court, passed this test after some hesitation.[82] This assured the first amendment its current primacy as the only constitutional right relatively immune from current political fashions.

Issues of sexuality, especially sexual variation, present a third arena of challenge for the first amendment. Thus far, the first amendment, as construed, has performed unevenly. It has protected gender-bending literature such as *Well of Loneliness* and magazines such as *One, Inc.,* assured gay people rights to associate in clubs and college campuses, and protected the right to come out of the closet—but not when the person coming out is a state employee or military person, when the association involves the sale of liquor, or the gender-bending literature is explicitly homoerotic (Chapter 3). Indeed, the Supreme Court has in the last twenty years inverted the first amendment in cases involving homosexuality: not only have its guarantees not been applied to allow the "Gay Olympics" to use the 2,000-year-old "Olympics" symbol routinely appropriated by nongay groups, to allow gay soldiers or bisexual educators to self-identify, to treat homoerotica the same as heterosexual male erotica, or to require viewpoint neutrality when government funds the arts,[83] but the first amendment has been an excuse for the Court to invalidate nondiscrimination laws when applied to homophobes but not to misogynists or racists (*Hurley,* discussed more fully in Chapter 9). This array of cases ought to concern the Court for they bespeak an orthodoxy of compulsory heterosexuality signaled not only by the policies the Court has left in place but also thus far by the Court's discriminatory treatment of homosexual speech. In short, the Supreme Court itself has engaged in both content and viewpoint discrimination by its negative treatment of sexual speech and its yet more negative treatment of gay identity speech.

The Supreme Court has justified suppression of sexual, and especially homosexual, speech on grounds that it has minimal social value that is outweighed by its great social disutility, is (evidence of) conduct and not speech, or has third-party effects, especially for minors and eighteen-year-old army recruits. These are similar to the rationales the Court deployed in early cases to suppress the political speech of socialists and syndicalists and the race speech of white supremacists and civil rights protesters—all in decisions that were short-sighted and have been subsequently repudiated by the Court.[84] Just as these earlier decisions did not prevent the Court from later protecting politically and racially divisive speech, so the early sexual speech decisions do not prevent the Court from later recognizing the first amendment value of sexual speech, a process the Court has initiated with its recognition in *Barnes* that sexually expressive conduct is protected by the first amendment, in *Hurley* that sexual identity speech is also protected, and in *R.A.V.* that the government cannot engage in pure viewpoint discrimination even when it regulates the most objectionable forms of expressive conduct, namely, cross-burning.

The argument of this chapter, that gay identity speech and even sexual intimacy itself implicate core first amendment values, presses this process further than the Court has gone and insists that the process cannot legitimately be anti-gay, as it thus far has been. Drawing from the materials in the previous chapters, the further argument is that the sexualized first amendment does present challenges to some traditional first amendment ideas, and so applying the first amendment to sexual speech would have broader ramifications. I start with ramifications the sexualized first amendment will *not* have, and those are the parade of horribles Lord Devlin posed to any legal regime of sexual liberty, a parade now led by Justice Scalia. The Devlin-Scalia parade of horribles is a lavender herring, but the sexualized first amendment would press the Court to reconsider other constitutional sacred cows: the role played by the public-private distinction and the exclusion of obscene speech from the first amendment entirely. Ultimately, the emergence of a sexualized first amendment depends upon the further erosion of America's hysterical ambivalence about sex. A culture that regards sex as both disgusting and fascinating, that remains both puritanical and prurient, will resist the implications of the sexualized first amendment. The paradox is that as the first amendment itself is sexualized, and even homosexualized, the sexual will lose some of its power to shock and perhaps even to titillate.

Sliding Down the Slippery Slope?

Justice Scalia has already registered his objection to the consequences of the argument advanced here. Writing alone in *Barnes,* he warned that the Court's willingness to treat nude dancing as expressive conduct was an invitation to subject "sadomasochism, cockfighting, bestiality, suicide, drug use, prostitution, and sodomy" to first amendment scrutiny.[85] Scalia's list, adapted from Lord Patrick Devlin's *reductio* argument against sexual libertarianism in *The Enforcement of Morals* (1959), might be pruned to eliminate consensual sadomasochism and cockfighting, which are little regulated in the United States, and possibly suicide as well, which (unlike *assisted* suicide) has been largely decriminalized. As to consensual sodomy, Scalia is right that it cannot be regulated under *Barnes*'s philosophy, as this chapter argues. Edit his parade of horribles, therefore, to "bestiality, drug use, prostitution." This is a slippery slope argument but one susceptible to the response that slopes slip both ways. Scalia worries that if erotic dancing cannot be suppressed because of what it communicates to people, then bestiality might be protected, too. I worry that if erotic dancing and sodomy can be censored because of what they express to other people, then why not flag-burning, which is much more revolting than erotic dancing.

A related concern is that the first amendment may be diluted for all when its protection of expressive conduct is extended to new, unforeseen areas like sodomy. By sexualizing the first amendment, the Court might undermine the heavy lifting free speech jurisprudence is most needed to accomplish when political speech—real speech—is regulated. If that is the concern, the Court crossed the Rubicon long ago when it extended the first amendment to protect commercial speech, corporate speech, and expressive conduct. Scalia himself wrote *R.A.V.*, which extended the no-viewpoint-discrimination dimension of the first amendment to hate speech. The cross-burning in *R.A.V.* is as despicable as anything the Court has ever protected, but the decision exemplifies the first amendment's great aspiration as an unusually principled jurisprudence. The same principle that provides some protection for hate ideas in *R.A.V.* must apply to love ideas in *Rowland* and *Selland*.

Scalia also overstates the ambit of a sexualized first amendment. Even as to the edited list, conventional first amendment doctrine makes it easy to draw some of the lines Scalia suggests would dissolve. Rules against bestiality can be neutrally justified to prevent unconsented intercourse or cruelty to animals; the latter justification would apply to cockfighting. Engaged in to satisfy a bodily craving, and often done alone, drug use is typically no more expressive conduct than drinking a cup of coffee. Thus, drug use is not expressive conduct in the way that erotic dancing is, and seems less expressive than recreational dancing, which has been held not to be protected under the first amendment.[86] Even if drug use were expressive activity entitled to first amendment attention, the state has available to it justifications unrelated to what drug use communicates to others, including criminal activities on the part of drug users, such as robbery and theft to support drug use; rape and disease and accidents facilitated by the state of mind created by drugs; and default in responsibilities to children and family occasioned by expense and state of mind.[87]

The last Devlin-Scalia horrible, prostitution, is the most complicated. What separates sex-for-pay from other consensual sex or from nude dancing in a bar is that it is not as clearly expressive. To the extent it is expressive, sex-for-pay is, presumably, commercial speech, which the Court has traditionally allowed the state to regulate more freely than other forms of expression.[88] Even under a lenient regime, however, some state justifications for regulating prostitution would be problematic. Debra Satz's moral argument that prostitution is a "theatre of inequality—it displays for us a practice in which women are subordinated to men"[89]—not only fails to justify regulation of male prostitution but is a problematic constitutional justification because it purports to suppress sexual expression on account of what it communicates. A better justification is the externalities associated with prostitution, such as disease and crime, but it is not clear that criminalization, rather than regulation, rationally serves such health and safety goals.[90] The best justification is Margaret Radin's and Carole Pateman's objection that prostitution commercializes personhood and undermines people's capacity for human flourishing.[91] There is a fine line between this objection and Satz's theatre-of-inequality objection, but it is a line worth pursuing. It might suffice for the legislature to find that prostitution contributes to a social dynamic whereby people lose the capacity for intimacy.

Mark this irony. The Devlin-Scalia list of crimes reflects a republican vision of the state as exemplar of public values. This is an attractive vision of the state in the abstract, but the public values it instantiates (no sodomy anywhere! bestiality prohibited!) are the values of the nineteenth rather than the twenty-first century. The Court's recent first amendment decisions have diluted public values that have greater intrinsic moral appeal: hate crime laws *(R.A.V.)* and antidiscrimination statutes *(Hurley)*. The Court was right to invoke the first amendment in those cases because first amendment principle protects us all even when cross-burners are protected. What is that principle? "The First Amendment generally prevents government from proscribing speech or even expressive conduct because of disapproval of the ideas expressed," wrote Scalia in *R.A.V.*[92] "The very idea that a noncommercial speech restriction be used to produce thoughts and statements acceptable to some groups or, indeed, all people, grates on the First Amendment, for it amounts to nothing less than a proposal to limit speech in the service of orthodox expression. The Speech Clause has no more certain antithesis," wrote Souter in *Hurley*.[93] A neutral application of these ideas would provide gay people with space to come out of their closets and to engage in intimate expression on the same terms as straight people.

The Public-Private Distinction

The sexualized first amendment highlights an anomaly in free expression jurisprudence. Normally, first amendment concerns are greatest when a person engages in expressive activity in public. Classic images capture this thought: the soapbox speaker, the dissident burning a flag on the steps of the Capitol, protest marchers. The same images in a private setting—standing in one's living room making a speech, burning a flag in one's basement, marching around the house—would appear to raise less urgent first amendment issues. This is so in part because of the first amendment's concern with protecting public debate and dialogue, but it may also be attributable to the fact that such conduct is rarely if ever prosecuted. Both practical difficulties of detection and other constitutional protections, such as the fourth amendment and the right to privacy, limit the state's ability to intrude upon these private realms independently of the first amendment (Chapters 3 and 4).

On the other hand, the first amendment may provide greater protection to private than to public conduct in matters sexual. For example, the Supreme Court has frequently upheld state regulation of the public sale or display of obscene or even indecent materials,[94] but the Court in *Stanley v. Georgia* (1969) overturned a conviction for possessing obscenity in the home. "If the First Amendment means anything," the Court said, "it means that the State has no business telling a man, sitting in his house, what books he may read or what films he may watch." In other words, Stanley's sexual fantasies were his business—and not the state's. *Stanley's* reasoning, predicated on an amalgam of first amendment and privacy concerns, is fully applicable to sodomy laws and provides a first amendment-based, as opposed to privacy-based, rationale for protecting the same-sex intimacy left unprotected in *Hardwick*. "[The makers of our Constitution] 'sought to protect Americans in their beliefs, their thoughts, their emotions and their sensations. They conferred, as against the government, the right to be let alone—the most comprehensive of rights most valued by civilized man.'"[95]

Stanley suggests that the erotic dancing examined in *Barnes* could not constitutionally be regulated by the state if it occurred in the home, at least in part for first amendment reasons. A narrow Court majority in *Barnes* allowed regulation, but not prohibition, of erotic dancing in a bar, a semiprivate place. It would probably be consistent with both *Stanley* and *Barnes* for the state to regulate, and perhaps prohibit, erotic dancing in a public park. This reveals a paradox in the Court's first amendment jurisprudence: the first amendment is currently most vigilant in protecting political expression in a public setting, while most vigilant in protecting sexual expression in a private setting. The paradox is probably inspired more by culture and practice than by logic. Politics is considered intrinsically public, and sex intrinsically private (notwithstanding *Hardwick*). Indeed, sex in America has traditionally been a matter for secrecy and taboo. Even public displays of heterosexual intimacy are regulated, sometimes severely, while private expressions of consensual intimacy are substantially unregulated.

A partial explanation of this phenomenon is that the state has a plausible interest in regulating public sexuality: concern for children. Although nonobscene but dirty speech is entitled to first amendment protection normally, the Supreme Court has held that sexually explicit words and indecent but not obscene pictures can be regulated by the state if they involve children, either as participants or as likely audience.[96] If Stanley's dirty magazines had been kiddy porn, the Supreme Court might not have protected him. The concern-for-children rationale does not deny the first amendment values involved in sexual expression, so much as it establishes an important state justification for regulation of expression. Hence, the court of appeals in *Rowland v. Mad River Local School District* was wrong when it denied that Marjorie Rowland's expressions of bisexuality implicated first amendment values, but it could have reformulated its conclusion by reference to a state interest in shielding adolescents from exposure to overtly sexual topics. The problem with this response would have been that it was not viewpoint-neutral: Mad River disciplined a woman for living with another woman but, according to Rowland, tolerated women living with men.

The more fundamental basis for the paradox is the traditional nervousness of a sex-negative culture in talking about a topic that secretly obsesses most of us. Enthusiasm for the right of sexual privacy is broad in middle America because it is supported both by people who are sex positive and by many who are not. Realizing that any regulation leads to endless discourse about a topic with which they are uncomfortable, many sex-negative people would prefer not to know what goes on in other people's bedrooms but for the same reason would be appalled to run into any kind of public sexuality. Thus, the cloistered obscenity in *Stanley* and the bedroom sex in *Hardwick* and maybe even the erotic dancing in *Barnes* would be acceptable to this group of citizens, but public obscenity, erotic dancing, and sodomy would not. Indeed, public hand-holding and kissing are strongly objectionable to this group if it is by people of the same sex.

The sexualized first amendment can live with the public-private distinction but would contribute to its erosion. The court of appeals denied that Rowland had engaged in *any* protected expression because her statements about sexual orientation were matters of private, rather than public, concern and hence did not even trigger the Supreme Court's balancing approach in state employee speech cases. The court was both right and wrong: Rowland's statements were uttered in private and dealt with matters she did not want widely publicized, but once she was outed the statements became matters of public concern, as the state's reaction testified. Rowland's experience epitomized a generation of gender-bending the public/private dichotomy. Following the feminist lesson that the private is public, post-Stonewall gay activism teaches that revelation of personal sexual identity not only has political effects, but that tolerance of gay people does not happen without people coming out of their closets (Chapter 3).[97] What had once been private, and secret, has become public, and political. Dissenting from the Supreme Court's denial of certiorari in *Rowland,* Justice William Brennan put it well: "The fact of petitioner's bisexuality, once spoken, necessarily and ineluctably, involved her in that [public] debate" about sexual variation in southern Ohio.[98]

In the military context, Selland's statement of sexual identity also defied the public-private distinction, as did the armed forces' defense of their policy in the ensuing congressional hearings. For example, their unit cohesion argument is both the corollary and the flip side of coming out: the personal becomes the political, but from the perspective of homophobes it is oppressive rather than liberatory, and from the perspective of the chain of command it is disruptive rather than diversifying. Ironically but perceptively, the military proponents of the exclusion make the same move this chapter makes—arguing that sexual expression has public dimensions—but with the opposite twist—the public dimensions are potentially catastrophic. This was a brilliant strategy on Capitol Hill but ought to be problematic in court because it penalizes conduct simply for what it expresses and asks judges to accept the heckler's veto on faith that the top brass are not crying wolf a third time.

Rethinking Obscenity

The sexualized first amendment potentially provides a way to (re)organize the Court's chaotic line of obscenity decisions. *Roth v. United States* (1957) held that obscene speech, narrowly defined, is not protected by the first amendment. The *Roth* framework has become obsolete. It rests upon the sectarian idea that sexuality is shameful; although such sex negativity remains a part of our culture, it is a receding part. As our culture has changed, so has the definition of obscenity and what materials fall under the shifting definition. In the 1920s, before *Roth,* romance between two women or even female cross-dressing was definitional of obscenity because such ideas might corrupt vulnerable minds; after *Roth,* obscenity included open depictions of oral or anal sex; after *Miller v. California* (1973), some communities banned lesbian or gay romances as well as oral and anal sex—all of which would be considered nonobscene today. Maybe. Not only has the Court never successfully defined exactly or stably what is the difference between unprotected obscenity and protected indecency, but the current formulation of *Miller*—work appealing to "the prurient interest in sex," adjudged "patently offensive" to local community standards, and having no redeeming social value—is so vague that it might cover virtually anything, or nothing, depending upon local context. Hence, *Miller*'s framework has encouraged censorship of harmless gay pornography while allowing violently misogynistic straight pornography. Even its lax standard was partly abandoned in *New York v. Ferber* (1982), which allowed regulation of indecent as well as obscene kiddy porn. The *Roth* experiment in defining proscribable obscenity has not been a success.[99]

The least defensible feature of *Roth* was its premise that patently offensive sexual speech is not first amendment "speech." This idea is oxymoronic, a point the Court conceded in *R.A.V.* when it said that fighting words and obscenity are covered by the first amendment, of course, but at a minimal level allowing content but not viewpoint discrimination.[100] As it did with commercial speech, which was also not "speech" when *Roth* was decided, the Court ought to take the next step and recognize that obscene speech is entitled to some kind of first amendment protection for the same reasons that indecent speech is. In this context, homoerotica, long the most vulnerable under the first amendment, ought to impel a judicial reconsideration of obscenity's status because depictions or descriptions of same-sex intimacy meet the autonomy, political, and equality values of the first amendment as well as the classic speaker on a soapbox.[101] Just as two generations of women learned much about their feelings for other women from reading *Well of Loneliness,* so two generations of gay men and some lesbians have learned much from graphic gay pornography. The value of gay porn is not limited to information but also includes affirmation that others in the country share one's sexual tastes and that men as well as women can be subject to domination dramas in pornographic theater. Because gay people have been sexualized in highly negative ways, gay erotica, including such tame works as *Well of Loneliness,* has been much more likely to be considered obscene than straight pornography. This is evidence that even neutrally written obscenity laws will usually be applied disproportionately against homoerotic materials.

If obscene speech and press were viewed as falling within the first amendment orbit, they would hardly be immune from regulation. Indeed, Supreme Court decisions in the last generation point the way for the proper analysis of obscenity regulation, away from the *Roth-Miller* regime. Most of the decisions pertain to inconvenient zoning of adult entertainment, which can in most instances be defended under traditional first amendment doctrine as time, place, and manner restrictions. To the extent that zoning is intended to protect against premature exposure of children to sexually explicit materials, such restrictive zoning of indecent materials has been properly given a wide berth. *Ferber* is defensible for a different reason: a compelling state interest, unrelated to the ideas communicated, in protecting children from having their bodies memorialized in erotic materials. *Ferber* was written as an exception to *Miller* but is best read as a displacement of the earlier decision: rather than regulating sexy materials because they appeal to prurient interests and are offensive, the state can adopt viewpoint-neutral regulations for materials that have harmful third-party effects. Those effects might include unconsented degradation of those performing in the pornography *or* unconsented harm to third parties triggered by the pornography, both emphasized by the Court in *Ferber.*

The *Ferber* justifications for regulating child pornography are precisely the ones posed by Catharine MacKinnon for regulating adult heterosexual pornography: such pornography routinely degrades female performers without their consent and triggers violence against women.[102] The normal first amendment, unencumbered by the sex-negative obscenity exception, requires the judiciary to subject MacKinnon's proposals to serious scrutiny, but with equally serious attention to the state's recognized compelling interest not only in preventing violence against women but also in ameliorating women's social and economic inequality. Although I cannot agree with MacKinnon that pornography's communication of subordinating stereotypes exempts it from first amendment scrutiny, I equally reject the unwillingness of many of her critics to explore and debate the tangible evidence of third-party effects.[103]

Litigation challenging the antipornography ordinance MacKinnon drafted for Indianapolis generated a moment of irony under the sexualized first amendment. The Seventh Circuit, whose opinion was summarily affirmed by the Supreme Court, accepted the factual premises of the ordinance, that misogynistic male porn directly causes violence against women, but still struck down the law on the ground that it suppressed speech because of what it communicated, namely, misogyny. Quoting a famous flag-saluting case, the court ruled: "'If there is any fixed star in our constitutional constellation, it is that no official, high or petty, can prescribe what is orthodox in politics, nationalism, religion, or other matters of opinion . . .' Under the first amendment the government must leave to the people the evaluation of ideas."[104] This nice rhetoric is hypocritical in a case involving sexuality, where there is a prescribed *orthodoxy*, compulsory heterosexuality, that courts have upheld in cases like Rowland's, Selland's, and Hardwick's—all cases that much more deeply implicate core first amendment values than the heteroporn case does.

6. Multivocal Prejudices and Homo Equality

There are today more antigay laws than ever before; they are collected in Appendix B3. Antigay laws take three different forms. Some, such as the federal military exclusion and presumptions against custody or adoption by gay parents, explicitly discriminate on the basis of sexual orientation. Others, such as bans against same-sex marriage and sodomy laws applying only to same-sex partners, discriminate on the basis of sex, but their overwhelming effect is against gay people, and homophobia is what keeps these laws on the books. Still other laws without sex or sexual orientation classifications have discriminatory effects on gay people, especially consensual sodomy laws and statutes prohibiting race and sex, but not sexual orientation, discrimination in the private as well as public sector. These laws deprive gay people of privacy and nondiscrimination protections taken for granted by other Americans.

All of these laws might be said to violate the core principle of the equal protection clause, that similarly situated people must be treated similarly by the state. Thus, gay people can argue from *Romer v. Evans* (1996), the Supreme Court's decision striking down Colorado's antigay initiative, that gay soldiers are not treated the same as straight soldiers and gay parents not the same as straight parents, and that the different treatment is grounded upon antigay animus, an impermissible state goal. *Evans* also might be read to caution against a discriminatory construction excluding gay people from protection under federal antidiscrimination statutes. As for sex-based classifications harming them, gay people can argue that the Supreme Court's precedents support the Hawaii

Supreme Court's determination in *Baehr v. Lewin* (1993) that exclusion of same-sex couples from civil marriage is constitutionally problematic sex discrimination.[1]

These are all logical but not inevitable readings of the equal protection clause and the precedents. Neither *Evans* nor the sex discrimination cases commit the Court to full "homo equality," a position that would draw the ire of the many Americans who not only feel antigay animus but consider it constitutive of their own identities. Indeed, the Court might not adopt a reading of equal protection that invalidates all the above discriminations until a majority of the Justices accept the idea of *benign sexual and gender variation* and believe there is enough political cover for them to enforce the idea under the equal protection clause, as they have done for sex equality. For now, however, *Evans* and the sex discrimination cases can be read to commit the current Court to the idea of *tolerable sexual and gender variation,* that most variations in sexuality and gender ought to be tolerated by the state, even if not encouraged. This reading is morally and politically desirable as well as doctrinally supportable. There is no credible evidence that gay people pose a threat to others, and state demonization of gay people creates unproductive political channels of persecution and hiding. The first part of this chapter will explore the implications of *Evans* for current antigay policies, and the second part will address the harder issue of same-sex marriage, which can rigorously be presented as a question of sex as well as sexual orientation discrimination. The chapter will conclude with arguments for including sexual orientation in general antidiscrimination laws.

Gaylaw, again, reveals the strong connection between changing social attitudes and statutory as well as constitutional law. The account that follows also exposes particular themes of equal protection jurisprudence, especially the decline of the traditional equal protection focus on *class-based* policies that reflect prejudice against discrete and insular minorities, and a refocus on suspicious *classifications* and illegitimate state goals; the interconnection of prejudices, with sexism and compulsory heterosexuality enjoying the strongest connection; and the movement of discrimination law from constitutional to statutory protection and a corresponding institutionalization of discourse. Most important, gaylaw illustrates law's complex relationships to prejudice itself. Homophobia is at once a pervasive prejudice, one held by most Americans, and a disabling one, as it is an amalgram of several prejudices (anti-Semitism, racism, and sexism). Its unpredictable combination of animus and morality renders homophobia the testing ground for equality jurisprudence and poses dilemmas for the judiciary in particular.

Antigay Policies and Equal Protection of the Law

The Constitution's equal protection guarantee is too broad to be applied literally, as all laws make distinctions and government could not operate if all its distinctions were continually in question. Any realistic theory of equal protection must find a principle that identifies those situations where serious scrutiny is justified. The framers of the clause and the early Supreme Court decisions focused equal protection attention on laws that subjected classes of citizens to special disabilities unjustified by natural differences.[2] The original expectations and early cases reflected a *class-based* approach. Especially when the Justices found that the class burdened by a state rule was a racial minority, mainly African American, they subjected it to serious scrutiny. But the Court cautioned in *Plessy v. Ferguson* (1896), the decision instantiating the separate-but-equal formula, that the state was not responsible for private attitudes or actions that were class-based.[3] The *Plessy* policy proved unstable in the face of the National Association for the Advancement of Colored People's litigation campaign showing that separate-but-equal was simply a way that African Americans were subordinated as a class. The New Deal Court viewed apartheid as a national embarrassment, a racist regime for which the state was responsible.[4]

It was in this context that the Court in *United States v. Carolene Products* (1938) refined equal protection doctrine to justify serious scrutiny toward class-based legislation reflecting "prejudice" against a "discrete and insular minority," not just African Americans but also Asian Americans and Jews. Judicial activism was best justified when the political process had failed, and the Court considered a process infected with prejudice a failed process. *Carolene*'s refinement was important background for *Brown v. Board of Education* (1954), which invalidated school segregation policies because of their class-based consequences.[5] *Brown* substantially overruled *Plessy* because the Justices insisted on state responsibility for private prejudice underlying and flowing from apartheid.

Brown swept away hundreds of laws requiring racial segregation, culminating in *Loving v. Virginia* (1967), which invalidated a statute criminalizing different-race marriages. *Loving* reflected another doctrinal adjustment. Chief Justice Earl Warren's analysis of the miscegenation law ignored its effect on discrete and insular minorities (blacks) and focused instead on the law's *irrational classification* (race) and *illegitimate purpose* (white supremacy).[6] Analytically, *Loving* replaced *Brown* as the key race case. The Court has ruled that policies hurting blacks as a class but not invoking race as a classification are constitutional unless plaintiffs can show a racist purpose[7] and that policies invoking race as a classification but benefiting racial minorities are nonetheless constitutionally suspect—turning *Carolene Products* on its head.[8] On the other hand, *Loving* confirmed *Carolene*'s "double standard": most discriminating laws only have to reveal a "rational basis," a test hard to fail; only those laws using disapproved classifications, such as the race classification in *Loving*, are subjected to "strict scrutiny" and usually invalidated.

The women's rights movement followed the *Loving* approach to assert that sex, like race, is a suspect classification and that state policies seeking to confine men and women to traditional gender roles are illegitimate. In *Craig v. Boren* (1976), the Court concluded that sex-based classifications are quasi-suspect, mainly because they tend to reflect irrational stereotypes about women and men. Secondarily, the Court noted that such classifications have had a class-based effect upon women, but this class-based reasoning was subordinate to the classification-based reasoning; many of the aggrieved plaintiffs, such as the eighteen- to twenty-one-year-old men who could not buy beer in *Craig*, were men.[9] *Craig* emphasized the relationship between suspect classification and illegitimate state goal: just as the Court would not tolerate race-based classifications motivated by a policy of white supremacy or race stereotypes *(Loving)*, so the Court would not tolerate sex-based classifications motivated by a policy of gender stereotypes or male supremacy *(Craig)*. The sex discrimination cases were argued under the Court's double standard but immediately destabilized it. Some sex discriminations were invalidated under the rational basis test,[10] while others were struck down under heightened-but-not-strict scrutiny *(Craig)*, and yet others were upheld under standards the Court left unclear.[11]

The sexual orientation discrimination cases have followed the pattern of the sex discrimination cases: gay rights lawyers have argued that sexual orientation is a suspect classification, like race, or a quasi-suspect one, like sex, *and* that morality-based defenses of antigay laws amount to the same kind of inadmissible prejudice or stereotyping as racism and sexism. It remains to be seen how these arguments will fit into equal protection jurisprudence, but the Supreme Court's first serious effort, *Romer v. Evans*, is analytically fascinating in its synthesis of that jurisprudence. Justice Anthony Kennedy's opinion opened with a quotation from the *Plessy* dissent's objection to class legislation, where one group is excluded from ordinary legal protection.[12] Like *Brown* and unlike *Loving*, *Evans* emphasized the class-based effects of the Colorado initiative, which not only overrode ordinances prohibiting sexual orientation discrimination but also foreclosed gay people, alone, from seeking a broad range of relief from the state. Keeping the Court's options open, *Evans* said nothing about whether sexual orientation is a suspect classification but still struck down the law under the rational basis test, as there was no legitimate state goal for the initiative. Like

Loving and unlike *Brown, Evans* emphasized the initiative's impermissible purpose, "animus" against gay people.

Some features of the opinion justify deeper exploration: the Court's assertion that animus rather than morality was the state goal, its belief that the initiative was class-based in the old-fashioned sense, and its sidestepping the level-of-scrutiny issue but giving the rational basis test sharper teeth. *Evans* commits the Court to no particular posture in future sexual orientation discrimination cases and might be viewed as the Court's offer to judges and commentators to provide the Justices with further information about the history, politics, and possible prejudices underlying antigay laws. At a minimum, *Evans* should be read to problematize antigay measures that are both underinclusive (focusing penalties only on gay people when broader penalties would better serve the statutory goals) and overinclusive (gay people are penalized more than the statutory goal would warrant). Such measures should be found invalid if the circumstances of their adoption suggest antigay prejudice. *Evans* found such evidence in the novelty and unprecedented breadth of the Colorado initiative but did not articulate a theory of antigay prejudice. This section will pose such a theory: such prejudice is discourse resting upon traditional antigay tropes that are not supported by experience or empirical evidence. Those tropes include hysterical demonization of gay people as dirty sexualized subhumans, obsessional fears of gay people as conspiratorial and sexually predatory, and narcissistic desires to reinforce stable heterosexual identity and gender roles by bashing gay people.

Prejudice and Sodomy Laws

Although not the first time the Court had given rational basis review greater bite,[13] *Evans* was remarkable in the strictness of the Court's examination. Colorado's Amendment 2 prohibited or preempted any law or policy "whereby homosexual, lesbian or bisexual orientation, conduct, practices or relationships shall constitute or otherwise be the basis of or entitle any person or class of persons to have or claim any minority status, quota preferences, protected status or claim of discrimination." The state asserted that this discrimination was needed to conserve scarce resources for enforcing civil rights laws; to protect the rights of landlords and employers not to associate with gay people; and to send a message that homosexuality was disapproved by the state. All of these policies seem more rational than the antihomosexual sentiment held to be a rational basis for sodomy laws in *Bowers v. Hardwick* (1986), but *Evans* ruled the Colorado initiative invalid because "its sheer breadth is so discontinuous with the reasons offered for it that the amendment seems inexplicable by anything but animus toward the class that it affects." The Court characterized the initiative as a "status-based" law aimed at a class of citizens; such laws violate the core equal protection command that "'a bare . . . desire to harm a politically unpopular group cannot constitute a legitimate government interest.'"[14] This reasoning has implications for *Hardwick* and other antigay policies.

To begin with, *Evans* places *Hardwick* in equal protection limbo. *Hardwick* did not address equal protection problems with sodomy laws. Also, it is factually distinguishable from *Evans,* for the Georgia sodomy law had a long Anglo-American pedigree and created a class defined by conduct rather than status. But *Hardwick*'s suggestion that "homosexual" but perhaps not "heterosexual" sodomy can be criminalized is problematic after *Evans.*[15] The distinction is a novelty, not showing up in state sodomy law until 1969 (Appendix A1), and stigmatizes gay people with a particularly severe disability, potential criminal liability for consensual conduct. Laws criminalizing same-sex sodomy are way overinclusive; indeed, they might have no relationship to a passable state objective. The most apparent reasons for making oral sex between two women, but not between a woman and a man, criminal would be insistence upon rigid gender roles or social prejudice against gay people. The first reason is inadmissible under *Craig,* and the second reason illegitimate under *Evans.* A third reason, that same-sex sodomy is more likely to spread venereal disease than different-sex sodomy, is sometimes advanced[16] but is unsupported by empirical evidence and has been rejected by medical health professionals, who maintain that sodomy laws impede the medical campaign against AIDS.[17] To the extent that same-sex sodomy laws are justified as expressions of public disapproval of sodomy itself, they are way underinclusive. Most sodomy in America is committed by different-sex rather than same-sex couples (Chapter 5).

Evans, therefore, supports an equal protection challenge to state laws criminalizing only same-sex sodomy and should be read as a rejection of *Hardwick*'s focus on homosexual sodomy alone. But once *Hardwick*'s focus on homosexual sodomy is jettisoned, then its purported rational basis—antihomosexual sentiment—also falls away, and the Georgia statute might be stranded in the same way the Colorado initiative was, without a legitimate state goal supporting it. The deep inconsistency between *Evans* and *Hardwick* also creates the following puzzle: sexual orientation discriminations will, potentially, be both defensible as expressions of public antihomosexual *morality (Hardwick)* and vulnerable as expressions of antigay *animus (Evans).*[18] Because responses to sexual or gender variation can usually be categorized as driven by either morality (homosexuality is an abomination) or animus (I hate queers), *Evans* potentially expands lower court discretion in deciding sexual orientation discrimination cases. An argument of this chapter is that the foregoing puzzle needs to be resolved in favor of general skepticism about antigay measures. The historical materials in this book suggest that *Hardwick* ought to be overruled or, at least, narrowly construed (Chapter 4) and that *Evans* correctly identified antigay feelings as questionable animus rather than worthy morality.

Justice Kennedy's use of the term "animus" borrows from the race cases and suggests a linkage explicitly made by philosopher Elisabeth Young-Bruehl, also in 1996.[19] She maintains that homophobia often resembles racial prejudice in its *hysterical qualities:* like the racist, many homophobes view objects of their hatred as dirty people whose fantasized disgusting conduct justifies imagined or acted-out violence against them. Antigay sentiment can also resemble anti-Semitism in its *obsessional qualities:* like Jews, gay people are viewed as an advantaged conspiratorial group preying on the homophobe and her or his kin. Finally, homophobia resembles sexism in its *narcissistic qualities:* like people of the opposite sex, gay people are viewed as "the Other," a group whose different-ness helps the homophobe define her or his own sexual identity. Homophobia is, in short, an all-purpose prejudice. The campaign yielding the *Evans* initiative, spearheaded by Colorado for Family Values, made arguments closely tracking the hysterical and obsessional arguments previously deployed against African Americans and Jews: gay people were defined as AIDS-diseased because of their "voracious," "high-risk" (anal sex), and promiscuous sexual lives, and as a wealthy group seeking "special rights" so they could be free to "attack" the family and the church and to "indoctrinate" and recruit the state's young people.[20] The overall thrust of the campaign was narcissistic, as it emphasized traditional gender roles that were threatened by gay people. The Colorado campaign might be taken as exemplary of irrationality, whereby factually erroneous and emotional assertions were made that strongly resembled those that have been the bases for racism, anti-Semitism, and sexism, as well as homophobia. Chapter 4 argues in detail that *Hardwick*'s reasoning was even more factually inaccurate, and the opinion's unnecessary focus on "homosexual sodomy" both hysterical and obsessional, making its inconsistency with *Evans* all the more striking. On the other hand, *Evans* might be distinguishable from cases where the links to prejudiced discourse are less strong.

History and Baselines: Custody and Adoption

Evans was handed down on (almost) the 100th anniversary of *Plessy* and opened with the *Plessy* dissent's admonition that the Constitution "neither knows nor tolerates classes among citizens."[21] Justice John Harlan's *Plessy* dissent maintained that once slavery was abolished, apartheid was the racists' strategy to deny African Americans equality; this suppression by law had bad consequences for the polity, as it fostered racial animus and class hatred. Part One of this book makes a similar showing for gay people: once the state Kulturkampf against homosexuals abated, an apartheid of the closet was the homophobes' strategy to deny gay people equality; this suppression by forced silence has had bad consequences for the polity, as it has fostered antigay animus and class hatred. Harlan's *Plessy* dissent and the Court's sex discrimination opinions suggest that antigay policies challenged after *Evans* should be evaluated in light of their history and evolution. An historical approach helps differentiate between admissible *morality* and inadmissible *animus*. A policy represents the latter if it can be traced to traditional antigay stereotypes and discourses rather than traditionally public-regarding policies.

Consider this reading of *Evans* as applied to rules against adoption by gay people and presumptions against child custody by gay parents. These rules are of recent vintage but are neither as unprecedented nor so broadly sweeping as Colorado's initiative was; hence, *Evans* might be distinguished. On the other hand, the antigay adoption and custody rules have become increasingly isolated; no fewer than three states (Arizona, Florida, Utah) explicitly forbid gay people from adopting, and a larger but shrinking number of states presume, in varying degrees of clarity, against child custody for gay parents (Appendix B3). States with such antigay policies typically fail to apply the same policies against heterosexual fornicators, adulterers, sodomites, and other outlaws.[22] A Florida court recently took a child away from its mother and placed the child with the father, a convicted murderer just released from prison; the court based its decision on the "sexual conduct," with consenting adults, of the mother and de-emphasized the conduct of the father, murder of an unconsenting adult.[23] Florida's open discrimination against adoption or custody by gay parents, in particular, is more historically connected with class legislation than was the Colorado initiative because Florida was one of the epicenters of antigay Kulturkampf in the 1950s (Chapter 2), and Florida's antigay policies create a class of people denied family-oriented protections even more basic than those denied by the Colorado initiative. Most important, the fit between antigay custody policy and legitimate state rationales is so wobbly as to suggest antigay animus as the policy's goal, a goal that would make *Evans* squarely applicable.

Traditionally, judges reasoned from the existence of sodomy laws that gay people—presumptive "sodomites" in hysterical discourse—are per se so immoral that they should be disfavored when the state is involved in child placement.[24] This argument has lost most of its force in jurisdictions without sodomy laws and would lose more force if *Hardwick* were overruled. Additionally, because the large majority of heterosexuals engage in sodomy, there is scant reason to invoke sodomy laws to discriminate against gay people—unless the state sodomy law discriminates, which is itself inconsistent with *Evans*. Finally, the state goal in the areas of adoption and custody is the "best interests of the child." Any effort by the state to use children to make a symbolic statement of animus against gay people is more vicious than the *Evans* initiative, unless a parent's sodomy can be cogently tied to the child's best interests by a nonhysterical, nonnarcissistic, nonobsessional chain of factual reasoning. If it cannot, the antigay policy is not only greatly underinclusive (it allows most sodomites and other lawbreakers to have custody), but greatly overinclusive too (it excludes parents who will be the "best" for many children)—precisely the problem that *Evans* found unconstitutionally irrational in the Colorado initiative.[25]

The foregoing reasons have pressed almost all states away from per se rules against gay parental custody, but a number of states still have discriminatory presumptions (Appendix B3). The modernized justification for these presumptions is that gay people are not good parents or are not as good at parenting as straight people.[26] Several features of these presumptions suggest that they are driven by antigay animus, questionable under *Evans*, and not the best interests of the child. That they are lineal descendants of the discredited per se rules suggests that the presumptions are modern pretexts for older, more obvious class legislation aimed at gay people. The pretextual nature of these presumptions is supported by the substantial gap between their antigay policy and the best interests of the child, which suggests that hysteria about or obsession with fantasized gay predation still underlies the policies.

Dozens of empirical studies have compared the development of children raised by gay parents or households with those reared by straight parents or households.[27] No study that I have seen endorses broad presumptions against gay custody or adoption, and the large majority of the studies specifically support a gay-neutral rule consistent with *Evans*. Although most of the studies state at the outset that they offer only provisional conclusions given their small and necessarily nonrandom samples,[28] a recent meta-analysis correcting for small sample size (but not for nonrandomness) found that the data "indicate no difference between homosexual and heterosexual parents," and support rules that do not take sexual orientation into account when making custody and visitation decisions.[29] On developmental criteria such as self-esteem, adjustment to new circumstances, and emotional disorder, the children raised in same-sex parental households are not significantly distinguishable from children raised in different-sex parental households. The few studies that have compared two-mother households with single-mother households have found that children raised in the former are better adjusted than children raised in the latter, whether the single parent is straight or lesbian.[30] These studies support the *Evans*-like finding that antigay childrearing presumptions are weakly connected with children's interests.

Lawyers who defend antigay presumptions do so on grounds that can be directly linked to antigay prejudice of the sort that *Evans* faulted. Lynn Wardle, the main academic defender, argues that children will be harmed by same-sex parents because (1) such parents engage in immoral extramarital conduct, (2) the children of such households tend to depart from and to be confused about traditional gender roles, and (3) the children will tend to become homosexual themselves and may even be molested by their gay parents.[31] Responding to Wardle, Carlos Ball and Janice Pea argue in detail that there are no factual bases for Wardle's claims that these children tend to be confused, grow up to be gay, or are molested. Child development experts overwhelmingly agree with Ball and Pea. In trial court proceedings for the Hawaii same-sex marriage case (*Baehr*), the state made Wardle-like arguments and presented evidence that mom-dad families are best for children. But even the state's expert witnesses rejected Wardle's arguments that children in same-sex households will be confused about gender identity or will be molested; the state's experts agreed with the plaintiffs that "in general, lesbian and gay parents are as fit and loving parents as non-gay persons and couples."[32] The trial judge accepted this proposition as a matter of fact and found no credible scientific evidence to the contrary.

The defenses of antigay presumptions are not only factually slipshod but can be directly linked to antigay prejudice of the sort that *Evans* faulted. Wardle's molestation assertion is particularly striking, as the social science evidence shows that molestation is overwhelmingly a male activity, with straight men more prone to it than gay men, and lesbian as well as straight women the least prone.[33] Illuminating his factual misstatements is the striking way Wardle's argumentation rhetorically tracks prejudice-based antihomosexual rhetoric in this century, namely, (1) the hysterical focus on "dirty" sexual activities such as sodomy and extramarital sex, (2) the narcissistic insistence on rigid gender identities, and (3) the obsessional focus on the predatory homosexual seeking to recruit new homosexuals. As in *Evans* itself, the weak connection between antigay rules and their ostensible policy goals and the strong connection between antigay rules and traditional prejudice are mutually reinforcing.

Another lesson of the custody and adoption cases is that *Evans* concerns ought to inform judicial interpretations of common law and statutory authorities. It is a standard rule of statutory interpretation that laws should be construed to avoid severe constitutional problems,[34] and the common law should be applied with similar sensitivity to constitutional boundaries. With *Evans* in mind, courts ought to construe adoption statutes and child custody precedents to avoid imposing special disabilities on lesbian, gay, bisexual, and transgendered parents. Because interpretations imposing such disabilities are questionable on equal protection grounds, while interpretations creating gay-neutral rules are constitutionally unimpeachable, courts should systematically prefer the latter, as they have tended to do in Minnesota and New York.[35] Some state courts have vigorously applied such a precept to construe adoption statutes not only to allow gay people to adopt but to allow "second-parent adoptions" of the children of their partners.[36]

Don't Ask, Don't Tell and No Promo Homo Policies

Evans poses problems for some of the don't ask, don't tell policies. Equal protection arguments against policies that ended the educational career of Marjorie Rowland and the military career of Dirk Selland complement the first amendment arguments in Chapter 5. Where a gay person is disciplined under circumstances where a similarly situated straight person is not, she or he is denied equal protection of the laws unless the state can show a non-animus basis for such policies. But the standard arguments for such policies—the gay person is a disgusting sodomite, violates gender norms, and by her or his status threatens vulnerable heterosexuals—are not legitimate bases for discriminating against gay people. As a bisexual, Rowland, for example, was no more likely to violate sodomy laws or molest students than straight women and much less likely to do those things than straight men. Although Mad River may have been penalizing Rowland for upsetting gender roles, that is an invalid state policy after *Craig.* Relatedly, arguments to exclude gay people from educational and military institutions closely track the hysterical, narcissistic, and obsessional features of classic American race, sex, and ethno-religious prejudices. Exclusions of blacks, women, and gays from service in the nation's armed forces have historically been justified for the same reasons: the excluded persons have been faulted for sexualizing military units and therefore potentially disrupting morale, and their exclusion has served the ideological goal of reaffirming the "manhood" of those allowed to serve.[37] Just as the equal protection guarantee of the fifth amendment should counsel against excluding racial minorities or women from military service, so it should counsel against the exclusion of openly gay people.

On the other hand, judges are reluctant to interfere with state employment and, especially, federal military policies (Chapter 5). Although the Supreme Court never ruled on the military's exclusion of black people and women, it strongly deferred to the president and Congress when they excluded women from draft registration.[38] If courts insist on deferring to the political process as to matters of military policy, however, *Evans* requires clear statements of exclusion. Thus, federal courts should construe ambiguous laws to minimize the extent of antigay exclusion. For example, federal courts of appeals have properly rejected arguments that the 1993 statute excluding openly gay people from the armed forces also excludes gay people who neither self-identify nor engage in detectable sodomy.[39] Although the statutory text and legislative history lend some support to the more exclusionary interpretation, the equality principle of *Evans* suggests that judges have properly rejected it. In a nation struggling toward norms of homo equality, institutional deference impels judges to avoid unreasonable or draconian constructions of antigay policies.

Evans is also just a starting point for thinking about state rules prohibiting classroom or other state discussion that either "promotes" homosexuality or depicts it as a "positive alternative life-style."[40] Like Colorado's Amendment 2, such policies are an unusual and recent innovation, targeting gay people as a class and having a potentially vicious effect on gay adolescents in particular.[41] Such statutes might pass *Evans* muster if they are viewed as not depriving gay people of important protections and as, instead, directing state expression in the field of education, where the state is usually allowed to "inculcate" its vision of the good life.[42]

A hard case is presented by the federal Defense of Marriage Act (DOMA), which provides that 1,049 federal statutes involving marriage or spousehood can never be construed to include same-sex couples.[43] DOMA might be vulnerable to *Evans* attack if it denies same-sex married couples an extraordinary range of rights and obligations normally accorded other married couples, involves the federal government in micromanaging family formation issues that traditionally have been left to the states, and can be characterized, as it was by congressional opponents, as premature and unnecessary legislation seeking to scapegoat gay people.[44] On the other hand, the arguments made by DOMA supporters generally lacked the hysterical and obsessional flavor of the arguments made by the proponents of the Colorado initiative and of presumptions against gay parental rights. While some supporters spoke of same-sex marriage in apocalyptic terms,[45] the key supporters made arguments such as this: "Should the law express its neutrality between homosexual and heterosexual relationships? . . . Should Congress tell the children of America that it is a matter of indifference whether they establish families with a partner of the opposite sex or cohabit with someone of the same sex?"[46] The gap between the opponents' perceptions and the supporters' arguments exposes deep issues of equal protection law.

The no promo homo rationale of DOMA and other policies is that, even if the state does not consider gay people criminals and is willing to employ openly gay people, the state should be free to express its own republican vision of a happily and heterosexually married society. Rather than *compulsory heterosexuality*, the intolerant stick-like *Hardwick* policy, or even the closet-based policy of don't ask, don't tell, the state ought to be free to adopt a policy of *preferred heterosexuality*, a more tolerant, carrot-like policy. Senator Daniel Coats made this precise distinction in the DOMA debates: "[W]hen we prefer traditional marriage and family in our law, it is not intolerance. Tolerance does not require us to say that all lifestyles are morally equal."[47] As Scalia's *Evans* dissent emphasized, one of Colorado's justifications for the initiative was its signal of the community's belief that heterosexuality is better, more normal, than homosexuality as an orientation. Although the Court did not accept this justification as a rational basis for the initiative, it did not dispute or even recognize it either. Thus, another way that *Evans* could be narrowed is that the state cannot penalize gay people for being out of the closet, and perhaps cannot take away local protections either, but is free to encourage people—especially the proverbial wavering adolescent—to be straight. But surely the state cannot encourage people to feel attraction only for those of their own race. If not, why can the state encourage people to feel attraction only for those of the opposite sex?

This analysis of DOMA presents one issue *Evans* ducked and an equally important issue not presented in *Evans*. As to the first: Should sexual orientation, like race and sex, be viewed as a (quasi)suspect classification requiring heightened scrutiny, whereby an antigay rule must narrowly serve a compelling or substantial state interest? The main justification for heightened scrutiny is that sexual orientation categories rarely serve rational state goals *(Evans)* and reinforce mutually destructive divisions within the country (*Plessy* dissent). For the reasons advanced by Judge William Norris a decade ago, the Supreme Court's precedents, especially the sex discrimination cases, could justify treating sexual orientation as a suspect or quasi-suspect classification.[48] Sex is a questionable classification because it so frequently bears no relation to ability to perform or contribute to society, is typically motivated by stereotypical rather than fact-based thinking, and pervasively affects a class of citizens traditionally subjected to legal disabilities.[49] Sexual orientation is just as irrelevant as sex or even race to an individual's intelligence, psychological stability, and cooperativeness.[50] Furthermore, laws focusing on homosexuality or gay people have usually been motivated by hysterical, obsessional, or narcissistic and not public-regarding, fact-based reasoning; have repeatedly proven to be socially unproductive laws that either wreak policy havoc or waste state resources or (if unenforced) simply serve as symbolic spite measures; and focus on a class of people subject to unjustified social scorn and violence, whose unfair plight has typically been worsened by state brutalization and stigma. Reread Chapter 2 for examples of these points.

Although sexual orientation fits the traditional criteria for heightened scrutiny, the Court is not eager to add a new category to the list. As prejudice has expanded to include animus against the disabled, ageism, accent discrimination, and so forth, the concept has become not only multivocal but pervasive. Because the Court cannot monitor all state expressions of prejudice, it must choose which prejudices to police. Sexual orientation classifications merit such special monitoring. Antigay discriminations remain pervasive (Appendix B3), yet notwithstanding their documented injustice and lack of utility, they are hard to remove through the ordinary political process because of the kind of prejudice recognized in *Evans,* a prejudice for which the state bears some responsibility. Moreover, homophobia is a prejudice intimately linked to those already recognized in equal protection law. Indeed, the case for heightened scrutiny is strengthened by the fact that many of the antigay laws, such as DOMA, are logically vulnerable under the Court's sex discrimination precedents. The link to sex discrimination not only contributes to the argument that sexual orientation discrimination is problematic, but also represents an independent basis for heightened scrutiny of antigay measures.

Sex Discrimination Arguments for Homo Equality

Formally, some of the discriminations that most affect gay people are those that classify by *sex* rather than *sexual orientation.* Thus, gay people can marry in all states, so long as they marry someone of the opposite sex; people of the same sex generally cannot marry. Similarly, six states prohibit consensual sodomy only when the partner is of the same sex. Some of the people harmed by these laws have Homer Plessy's problem: just as Plessy, seven-eighths European, objected to being categorized as "colored" by the state, so male-to-female transsexuals object to being categorized as "male" by the state. Transgendered people disagree with the category that the state forces upon them, especially for marriage purposes. Women as a group are harmed by these laws for reasons explored below. But the most obvious class of people affected by these sex-based exclusions are lesbians, gay men, and bisexuals.

In the early 1970s a challenge to these sex discriminations took shape from arguments posed by lesbian feminists and male antifeminists, otherwise working at cross-purposes. Feminists argued that patriarchy is the common enemy of both liberated women and gays because heterosexuality is a practice that instantiates women's dependence upon men. Adrienne Rich declared that "compulsory heterosexuality," society's insistence that everyone be heterosexual, is a "profound falseness," a lie that distorts the lives of all women.[51] At the same time, opponents of the proposed equal rights amendment (ERA) were articulating a "miscegenation analogy" for same-sex marriage. In congressional testimony, Professor Paul Freund said that "if the law must be as undiscriminating toward sex as it is toward race, it would follow that laws outlawing wedlock between members of the same sex would be as invalid as laws forbidding miscegenation."[52] Freund's position was based upon *Loving*'s holding that denying a black-white couple a marriage license is race discrimination because the classification, the regulatory variable, is the race of one partner. Analogously, denying a female-female couple a marriage license is sex discrimination because the classification, the regulatory variable, is the sex of one partner. Echoing Freund, ERA opponents in Congress and in state ratification debates argued that the ERA would invalidate state sodomy laws and require states to recognize "homosexual marriages," a charge disputed by one ERA sponsor, Senator Birch Bayh.[53]

Freund's prediction and feminist hopes did not materialize. About a third of the states have adopted equal rights amendments, and the Supreme Court has interpreted the equal protection clause to subject sex-based classifications to intermediate scrutiny. But the argument that denying same-sex couples marriage licenses is sex discrimination was decisively rejected in *Singer v. Hara* (1974).[54] In at least one leading case, the miscegenation analogy was deployed to challenge a sodomy law. Missouri's law only criminalizes same-sex sodomy. The defendant in *State v. Walsh* (1986) argued that his solicitation of oral sex was illegal only because he had solicited it from a man, not from a woman, and therefore application of the statute to him was sex discrimination. Echoing Bayh and *Singer*, the Missouri Supreme Court held that the statute "applied equally to men and women because it prohibits both classes from engaging in sexual activity with members of their own sex."[55]

Given the law's uniform rejection of sex discrimination arguments for gay rights, academics and litigators gave up on them—until 1988, when Sylvia Law and Andrew Koppelman revived this line of argument.[56] Law linked homosexuality's social stigma to rigid gender roles that maintain women in traditional roles as wife, mother, and man's helper. Koppelman revived Freund's miscegenation analogy but in support of gay rights rather than in opposition to women's rights. The sex discrimination argument for gay rights assumed new relevance with the Hawaii Supreme Court's decision in *Baehr v. Lewin* (1993) that the state's refusal to issue a marriage license to Ninia Baehr and Genora Dancel is sex discrimination that requires compelling state justification to survive the state's ERA.[57] Responding to *Baehr*, thirty states have enacted laws preventing same-sex marriages from being recognized by their courts (Appendix B3), and Congress adopted DOMA to ratify those sex-based discriminations and write them into federal statutory law as well. In light of these important developments, the miscegenation analogy deserves a fresh look.

Doctrinal Analysis of the Sex Discrimination Argument for Homo Equality

The miscegenation analogy has a transvestic quality, dressing up gay rights in sex equality garb. The immediate reaction of lawyers is: this is a trick argument—and has got to be wrong! Consider one way equal protection theory can reject the miscegenation analogy. *Loving* emphasized that Virginia's rule against different-race marriages subserved a regime of "White Supremacy," which was antithetical to the core purpose of the fourteenth amendment. *Singer* avoided the miscegenation analogy by limiting *Loving* to cases where an invidious classification is used to suppress a group whose identity is defined by that classification. *Baehr* may not be a sex discrimination case in the same way *Loving* is a race discrimination case. The classification in *Baehr* is sex, but the class being disadvantaged is defined by sexual orientation (gay people) and not by sex (women). The philosophy that justifies their disadvantage is compulsory heterosexuality, not simple sexism. Table 6.1 maps the differences among the cases as one might read them.

Note, initially, how the middle column is misleading. In *Loving*, the disadvantaged class was actually "miscegenosexuals," Sam Marcosson's term for people who fall in love with someone of another race. Because most African Americans were not inclined toward different-race marriage, they were disadvantaged by the classification only by reasoning from the underlying ideology, white supremacy. Hence, the middle column in *Loving* reflects an indirect reasoning process rather than direct harm. The *Craig* line must be qualified in the same way. In *Craig*, the disadvantaged group was college-age males who were denied the right to buy low-alcohol beer that college-age females enjoyed. Subjecting the law to heightened scrutiny, the Supreme Court emphasized that sex-based classifications ostensibly benefiting women are just as objectionable as those ostensibly benefiting men when they reflect "outdated misconceptions concerning the role of females in the home rather than in the 'marketplace and

Table 6.1 The miscegenation analogy

	Classification	Disadvantaged class	Philosophical motivation
Loving	Race	Racial minorities	White supremacy
Craig	Sex	Women	Sexism
Baehr	Sex	Sexual orientation minorities	Compulsory heterosexuality

world of ideas.'"[58] When traditional gender stereotypes animate a sex-based classification, women as a group suffer, at least indirectly. Again, the second column only reflects indirect harm, deriving from the underlying philosophy (sexism) and not from the classification in a particular case (women can buy drinks earlier than men).

To complete the miscegenation analogy, however, one still might have to show something like the following: denying a same-sex couple a marriage license subserves a regime of sexism that is antithetical to the core purpose of a state ERA or of the fourteenth amendment as interpreted in *Craig*. This is the task Sylvia Law started, and which Andrew Koppelman has expanded. They argue that homophobia historically depends upon *and* contributes to sexism, including the maintenance of sex hierarchy where men dominate women.[59] Revised Table 6.1 suggests the outlines of the foregoing analysis. Parentheses are used for the middle column in order to suggest that the disadvantaged class is based upon inference from the underlying philosophy. Under Revised Table 6.1, *Baehr* is the same as *Craig* and analytically indistinguishable from *Loving*.

Koppelman makes the same kind of argument against state sodomy laws. Following *Singer*, *Walsh* held that, so long as male-male and female-female sodomy are treated the same, there is no sex discrimination. The miscegenation analogy is again telling. The Supreme Court had accepted precisely that logic in *Pace v. Alabama* (1883) to uphold a law criminalizing different-race sex; each race was treated the same, the Court reasoned, in a case that anticipated *Plessy*. But *Pace* was overruled in *McLaughlin v. Florida* (1964), where the Court struck down a statute prohibiting cohabitation between different-race couples.[60] The defendants, a black-white couple, would not have violated the law if they had been a cohabiting white-white couple. The Supreme Court held this was race discrimination because the classification, the regulatory variable, was the race of one of the partners. Under the reasoning of *McLaughlin*, *Walsh* is as incorrect as *Singer*.

Revised Table 6.1   The miscegenation analogy

	Classification	Disadvantaged class	Philosophical motivation
Loving	Race	Miscegenosexuals (racial minorities)	Racism
Craig	Sex	18-to-21-year-old males (women)	Sexism
Baehr	Sex	Gay couples (women)	Sexism

Antigay Sex Discriminations and Rigid Gender Roles

A majority of the Supreme Court is committed to the proposition that any classification based on sex that insists on rigid gender roles requires an exceedingly persuasive state justification under the equal protection clause. When the state controls "gates to opportunity," it "may not exclude qualified individuals based on 'fixed notions concerning the roles and abilities of males and females.'"[61] Discrimination that is "merely the accidental byproduct of a traditional way of thinking about females" is unacceptable.[62] The Court's skepticism about sex-based classifications subserving traditional gender roles extends to almost all state judiciaries.

American law regulating sexuality and sexual unions has historically been gendered to the core: women cannot have sex outside of procreative penile-vaginal intercourse in marriage to a man, and men cannot have sex outside of procreative penile-vaginal intercourse in marriage to a woman. State law in the colonial era[63] and in the nineteenth century[64] made it a serious crime for unmarried men and women to have penile-vaginal sex (fornication) or anal sex (sodomy); marriage rendered any kind of penile-vaginal sex legal and indeed rendered forcible sex immune from rape laws; the sexual crimes a married man could commit were penile-vaginal sex with a woman (adultery) or girl (seduction) not his wife, or anal sex (sodomy) with his wife, another woman or girl, or a male. Once contraception, abortion, and oral sex came to be more commonly practiced as means of facilitating sexual pleasure without the risk of pregnancy, states adopted new laws making those practices illegal as well.[65] This regime of criminal laws was completely gendered, directly reflecting a religious natural law philosophy: sex is bad unless practiced in a procreative way within the institution of male-female marriage; the role of a woman is to receive the sperm of a man, become impregnated, and bear and raise the child; the role of the man is to impregnate the woman and rule over the household formed as children are born.

This century has seen a relaxation of the natural law regime. Many of its gendered features have been repealed or invalidated, including the complete exemption for rapes within marriage, the wife's lack of independent legal rights, and prohibitions of abortion and the distribution of contraceptives. Some of the antisex features have been repealed in many but not all states, including the crimes of fornication, adultery, and sodomy.[66] Although state law no longer makes procreation the linchpin of marriage, it does continue to refuse to recognize marriages between two women or two men, a discrimination based on the sex of one of the partners that "exclude[s] qualified individuals based on 'fixed notions concerning the roles and abilities of males and females'" and is, historically, a "byproduct of a traditional way of thinking about females." Sodomy laws indirectly reflect the same regime, as they center sexual expression around pregnancy-based penile-vaginal intercourse; laws prohibiting only same-sex sodomy directly instantiate a gendered regime whereby women can only have sex with men. In short, these sex-based classifications strongly originated in and continue to serve the kind of rigid gender stereotyping that the Supreme Court has rejected. Indeed, the policy against allowing two women to marry is driven by a more obvious insistence upon traditional gender roles than the policy of allowing eighteen-year-old women but not men to buy beer that was invalidated in *Craig*. The requirements of Revised Table 6.1 would appear to be satisfied.

The thoughtful reader might well believe that the syllogism is still too strict a reading of the Court's precedents to bring sex-based marriage and sodomy rules within sex discrimination law. A central doctrinal objection might be grounded upon the Court's recognition that "inherent differences" between men and women can justify sex-based rules.[67] Indeed, the argument that has usually prevailed in the same-sex marriage challenges is that marriage naturally and inevitably involves a man and a woman because their biological differences make them congenial opposites that nonetheless attract. The Minnesota Supreme Court in *Baker v. Nelson* (1971), the first reported decision rejecting a legal challenge to the same-sex marriage bar, began its constitutional discussion with the premise that "[t]he institution of marriage as a union of man and woman, uniquely involving the procreation and rearing of children, is as old as the book of Genesis."[68] *Baker* was followed by every appellate court to address the issue until *Baehr*. Yet its factual assertions are not only gendered but factually erroneous as well.[69]

The natural law conception of marriage that *Baker* adopted is itself sexist, as it practically and by some accounts necessarily relegates women to traditional roles stereotypically assigned to women: wife, mother, homemaker. These gendered roles are precisely the ones reflected in the law's traditional persecution of lesbians, where the standard reproach has been that women should stay in their place—in the home, at the side of a man. Allowing two women to get married would undermine the gendered nature of marriage because at least one of the women (and sometimes both) would assume the traditional male role of breadwinner. When the Court has invoked the inherent differences doctrine to acquiesce in a sex-based classification, it has generally been a classification that opens up new opportunities for or benefits women; the doctrine is *not* applicable to rules that were adopted "for denigration of the members of either sex or for artificial constraints on an individual's opportunity."[70]

A deeper, yet perhaps more obvious, objection is that sexuality and gender are simply different. Why should gay men benefit from a jurisprudence designed to put women on an equal plane with men? As the theory of prejudices suggests, however, homophobia and sexism share common roots in narcissistic impulses. Empirical studies have found correlations between antigay feelings and "a belief in the traditional family ideology, i.e., dominant father, submissive mother, and obedient children," as well as "traditional beliefs about women."[71] A few studies claim a causal link: "a major determinant of negative attitudes toward homosexuality is the need to keep males masculine and females feminine, that is, to avoid sex-role confusion."[72] The Kinsey Institute's 1989 survey of Americans' attitudes about sex and sexuality found that one variable significantly linked to antigay feelings is the respondents' own fears and anxieties about the opposite sex. The researchers believe that people who feel threatened by the opposite sex will be hostile to homosexuality as a defense mechanism, displacing an identity-shattering fear onto a socially safe object (gender-bending queers). "'Accordingly, we may condemn the homosexual in order to reduce sex role confusion.'"[73]

The narcissistic roots of homophobia are supported not only by current social science but also by the history of gender and sexuality (Chapter 1).[74] Responding to the challenge posed by the "New Women" of the late nineteenth century, middle-class male culture reacted, directly, by suppressing women's economic opportunities and controlling women's bodies and, indirectly, by creating "the homosexual" as an object of special scorn. Setting up the effeminate man as a degeneration of masculinity, men were reassured of their own manhood. Setting up the lesbian as an object to be feared, men asserted their central role in women's lives. The creation of homosexuals as a despised class reinforced the gender norms of male superiority and control. In short, there is a historical as well as logical connection between *compulsory gender binarism,* the idea that men must be masculine and women must be feminine, and *compulsory heterosexuality,* the idea that sexuality must consist of a man having sex with a woman.

Indeed, the idea of rigid gender lines historically preceded the idea of compulsory heterosexuality. Recall from Chapter 1 that laws against cross-dressing and prostitution focused regulatory concern about sexuality first on proper gender role, at the same time regulators were enacting abortion and contraception laws—all designed to shore up procreative marriage. Gender role then became the fulcrum by which homosexuality was attacked. Women and men who departed from their biological gender roles (passive/nurturing and aggressive/entrepreneurial, respectively) were deemed "inverts" by the sexologists and then by regulators. Havelock Ellis said outright what others dimly perceived: the gender-inverting lesbian was the natural consequence of feminism's encouraging women to go out in the world.[75] Reflecting a stronger ongoing influence of natural law thinking, American doctors were even more dogmatic about the connection between gender-bending and sexual inversion.[76]

After World War I, as oral sex was booming among married couples, it was more heavily policed than ever before among same-sex couples. Compulsory heterosexuality, the new policy, completed the sexist shift from disgusting acts to departure from gender role as law's focus. As *Hardwick* later suggested, oral sex between husband and wife waned as a regulatory concern just as oral sex between two men waxed. The cultural impulse to affirm rigid gender lines is only a fragment of the story, however. Fear of uncontrolled (male) sexuality also played an important role in the law's harsher focus on same-sex intimacy, as suggested by the shift in regulatory emphasis from the gender-bending "invert" to the predatory "homo*sexual*" whose freudian id was out of control (Chapter 1). An early expression of this ideology, by an Ohio judge, described "sexual perverts" as "wild ferocious animals," many of whom prey on "little boys or little girls."[77] Policemen arresting and assaulting homosexuals, legislators enacting sexual psychopath laws, judges requiring castration or long prison sentences for "sexual perverts," and bureaucrats chasing gays out of the civil service and the school system—all acted out hysterical and obsessional fears that gay people were dangerous aliens, like the pod people from *Invasion of the Body Snatchers* (Chapter 2).

Consequently, antihomosexual policies developed during and after World War II were responsive to multiple anxieties. This complexity is reflected in the War Department Inspector General's investigation of the Women's Army Corps training camp at Fort Oglethorpe in 1944. The investigators were unwilling to refer women to treatment as lesbians unless they were persuaded that the women were homosexual in orientation *and* had engaged in "unnatural acts" with one another *and* exhibited cross-gender characteristics, especially dressing or passing as a man.[78] Military training lectures in the early 1950s warned female recruits to beware of predatory lesbians and instructed them that "[t]he Creator has endowed the bodies of women with the noble mission of motherhood and the bringing of human life into the world. Any woman who violates this great trust by participating in homosexuality not only degrades herself socially but also destroys the purpose for which God created her."[79] The dual themes of gender inversion and sexual predation were also apparent in the state manias and panics described in Chapter 2. For example, when Miami began its purge of "sex perverts and degenerates" in 1953, local police officials specifically invoked images of "men who affect female mannerisms" and molest children.[80] During the antihomosexual campaign, Miami adopted new ordinances making it a crime for "female impersonators" to perform in the city (1952), "lesbians and homosexuals" to congregate (1954), or for any person to cross-dress or engage in lewd behavior (1956).[81]

After 1961, the antihomosexual terror melted into thermidor, during which gay people were able to claim some rights against state persecution (Chapter 3). The effect of women's liberation on gay liberation was complicated. On the one hand, the acceptance, even if partial, of equal rights for women contributed to homo equality as well. Discriminated against first because they were women and then because they were gay women, lesbians benefited directly from any policy protecting against sex discrimination. Laws against cross-dressing were undermined by cultural acceptance of women's freedom to wear comfortable men's clothing. The women's movement also facilitated a dramatic post-1969 reconfiguration of sodomy laws: at the same time gays were protesting state harassment of same-sex intimacy, women were insisting upon more vigorous state attention to female child molestation and rape; the result was a revolution in sodomy law enforcement from an emphasis on same-sex male intimacy to an emphasis on male-female rape or child molestation (Appendix C2). Most of the connections were less direct. Cities and states with populations favoring equality for women were not only more likely to decriminalize same-sex intimacy after 1961 but also much more likely to adopt laws prohibiting sexual orientation discrimination.[82]

On the other hand, antigay arguments continued to be made, albeit with new rhetorical emphases (Chapter 3). Feminism discredited explicitly sexist appeals and pressed antigay rhetoric toward alleged homosexual predation. For example, Anita Bryant's 1977 campaign to repeal Dade County's law prohibiting antigay discrimination operated under the moniker "Save Our Children." Rhetoric supporting the armed forces' exclusion made a similar shift: the privacy and morale of straight soldiers would be threatened by the shower-room gaze of openly gay comrades. The shower-room argument reflects the continuing power of American fears about sexuality. It also reflects the gendered nature of those fears, as men are much more hysterical about being sexualized by the homosexual gaze than women are. The operation of the exclusion is also gendered, as female service personnel have long been and continue to be discharged at significantly higher rates than male personnel. This might reflect a greater incidence of lesbians than gay men in the armed forces, but it also reflects sexist assumptions about military service (man's work) and women's place (if not in the home, in a man's bed).[83] Even though they have substantially vanished from public antigay rhetoric, the prevalence of sexist assumptions is revealed by continuing folk discourse about gay people, especially popular and even academic obsession with the "sissy" or effeminate gay man and the "mannish" lesbian.[84]

The history of American regulation of gender and sexual variation described in Chapters 1 through 3 provides qualified support for the sex discrimination argument for homo equality. The account supports Adrienne Rich's view that the law's operation against lesbians has been and remains directly inspired by cultural resistance to women's deviation from traditional gender norms. The bargaining position for all women within the military, in marriage, and in child custody disputes is undermined by social and legal disapproval of women having sex with or partnering with other women. That women as well as men disapprove of lesbian relationships can be attributed largely to narcissistic emotional needs to create a stable identity in opposition to the lesbian Other, a process the law has supported. The obsessional and hysterical features of homophobia are much less prominent in antilesbian prejudice. Although early disapproval of male sexual inverts focused on narcissistic anxieties, the hysterical and obsessional features of homophobia since World War I have more strongly contributed to social disapproval of and even violence against gay and bisexual men. The predatory homosexual (man) has been a more powerful rallying point for homophobia than the vampire lesbian. Even today, in debates over same-sex marriage, the natural law opponents often claim that homosexuals convey venereal disease (AIDS) and prey on children, even though the data make clear that it is men generally (and not gay men alone) who do these things and that lesbians seem to have the lowest rates of AIDS and child molestation of any of the groupings.

If the sex discrimination argument for homo equality falters in any way with respect to bisexual and gay men, it loses little or none of its power with respect to gay and bisexual women. For example, sodomy laws, including laws regulating only same-sex sodomy, reflect a sex negativity directed primarily at the most sexualized group in our society, gay and bisexual men. Although men are the only gay people arrested under these laws—they are ridiculously easy to catch—the laws are deployed against lesbians in custody and other legal proceedings and hence reinforce their sexist effect. The sex discrimination argument outlined in Revised Table 6.1 is fully applicable to laws that make intercourse between two women, but not a woman and a man, illegal: the law classifies based on the sex of one of the partners, which is sex discrimination in the same way that the law in *McLaughlin* was race discrimination; the sex-based classification on its face confines women to the traditional gender role of availability for sex with men; the anxieties underlying the prohibition are the narcissistic anxieties that sexism and homophobia most intimately share. The sex discrimination argument outlined in Revised Table 6.1 is substantially applicable to laws that make intercourse between two men, but not a woman and a man, illegal: the law classifies based on the sex of one of the partners, which is

sex discrimination; the sex-based classification on its face confines men to traditional gender role of man-penetrates-woman; the anxieties underlying the
prohibition are narcissistic anxieties that sexism and homophobia most intimately share, as well as hysterical and obsessional anxieties that are not directly
sexist but that are gendered (many people do not find oral sex between a man
and a woman disgusting in the way they do oral sex between two men).

The narcissistic feature of homophobia seems to be the dominant reason for
state refusal to recognize same-sex marriages for men as well as women. The
most popular arguments against same-sex marriage are that marriage is defini-
tionally male-female and, relatedly, that same-sex marriage would undermine
the institution by obliterating that important requirement of sex differentiation. These are openly gendered, narcissistic arguments, although others are
not. Some opponents make the hysterical argument that recognizing same-sex
marriage would place a state stamp of approval on unions that are by nature
promiscuous or unclean.[a] This argument is undercut by the Court's insistence
that the right to marry cannot constitutionally be premised on the morality of
the partners.[85] Moreover, the hysterical argument has no factual basis as regards
lesbians, who appear to be nonpromiscuous as a group. Although more factually based, the asserted promiscuity of gay and bisexual men supports the idea
of gay marriage and its requirement of fidelity. The hypersexual person in our
society is seen as needing the civilizing features of marriage even more than the
ordinary person because the institution civilizes the male and productively
channels his sexual energy. Society does not entertain this belief for two men
who want to marry, in part because of gender stereotypes about men and the
assumed absence of children. If same-sex marriage holds out no hope for tam-
ing the wild beast, it can once more be traced to the strong hold that traditional
gender attitudes exercise in our culture—and offers another reason why the sex
discrimination argument for homo equality works so well in the context of
same-sex marriage.

Pragmatic Objections to Same-Sex Marriage

Because there are strong privacy and first amendment arguments for overruling *Hardwick* (Chapters 4 and 5), the sex discrimination argument may not be
as important for attacking sodomy laws as for the bar to same-sex marriage,
where the argument fits like a glove. Conceding that point, Judge Richard

---

a. Opponents also make an obsessional argument that the state stamp of approval would induce
the wavering adolescent to "go gay." This argument rests upon the fanciful premise that the state can
do anything at that late age to affect sexual preference.

Posner says the killer argument against a right to same-sex marriage is the same one that defeats a right of gay people to serve in the military, that is, naked pragmatism: same-sex marriage is too unpopular for the Supreme Court to force upon an unwilling nation.[86] Posner's criticism has deep implications for equal protection theory yet is an incomplete stance for the same-sex marriage and gays-in-the-military issues.

Philip Frickey and I anticipated Posner's point as part of a political theory of the Court's equal protection jurisprudence. Contrary to *Carolene Products*, the Court's practice in equal protection cases rarely protects completely powerless minorities; instead, the Court tends to protect previously powerless groups once it has become clear that the group is politically mobilized and potentially a partner in the pluralist system.[87] Thus, the Court did not strike at apartheid until it had become a national embarrassment *(Brown)*, did not invalidate miscegenation laws until they had been repealed everywhere outside the South *(Loving)*, did not seriously review state and federal sex discriminations until the ERA was passed by Congress *(Craig)*, and did not nullify state sodomy laws when half the states still had them *(Hardwick)*, but pounced on a squirrelly antigay initiative adopted by narrow margins in an outlier state *(Evans)*.

Thus, Posner may be right—but only half right. What needs to be added is that a pragmatic Court ought not reject the foregoing argument either, unless it can write a more persuasive opinion than the one in *Hardwick*. An analytically or factually flawed opinion would open the Court to harsh criticism and fresh charges of antigay bias, especially if public opinion shifted on the issue.[b] Even pragmatic theories cannot ignore principle in a period of shifting equilibrium. Worse for the Court, an unpersuasive opinion would further expose the Court's activism in cases where racial classifications seek to remedy the continuing legacy of apartheid. Consider an analogy to affirmative action.

In *Adarand Constructors v. Pena* (1995), the Court applied a nontextual (not in the fifth amendment) equal protection right to hold that federal affirmative action must be subjected to strict scrutiny. Unlike *Loving*, where the race-based classification was motivated by precepts of white supremacy, *Adarand* made the race-based classification the sole basis for strict scrutiny of a policy that was intended as a remedy for the very white supremacist philosophy that undergirded apartheid. (Four justices vigorously dissented from the Court's ironic use of equal protection law.) Equally striking is the analytical similarity between *Adarand* and *Baehr*, diagrammed in Table 6.2.

---

b. This is a risk even if it takes decades for public opinion to shift, as it did between *Plessy* and *Brown*. Who on the Court wants to go down in history as the author of an antigay version of *Plessy*?

Analytically, *Adarand* and *Baehr* are similar in that the suspect classification itself triggered heightened scrutiny without any necessary link to traditional equal protection considerations, namely, a pervasively disadvantaged class and invidious, prejudice-based motivations. If *Baehr* is a radical extension of sex discrimination law, it is merely following the example of *Adarand* in race discrimination law. (Indeed, if homophobia is related to sexism, as in Revised Table 6.1, *Baehr* is not radical at all.) Conversely, a Court claiming to subject remedial preferences to strict scrutiny on grounds of consistency with other equal protection race precedents, as the Court claimed in *Adarand,*[88] should be subject to strong criticism for abandoning consistency with equal protection sex precedents. For the Court to be exposed to serious charges of unprincipled constitutional reasoning is bad enough; that the apparent motivation for the inconsistency would be pandering to public opposition to basic rights for gay people and remedies for people of color might strongly undermine the Court's perceived neutrality.

If Posner and I are both right, the Court is in a bind. But there are ways of negotiating the bind, what Alexander Bickel called "techniques of 'not doing,' devices for disposing of a case while avoiding judgment on the constitutional issue it raises."[89] For the foreseeable future, the Court should leave state courts alone to develop the sex discrimination argument for same-sex marriage. Presumably, such courts will rely on state constitutional grounds, over which the Supreme Court has no review authority anyway. If a state appeals court were bold enough to rely on the U.S. Constitution to strike down a state constitutional amendment barring same-sex marriage, the Supreme Court should avoid the case, either by denying review or finding the case prudentially or constitutionally nonjusticiable, courses of action that would have saved the Court

Table 6.2 The affirmative action analogy

	Classification	Disadvantaged class	Philosophical motivation
Loving	Race	Miscegenosexuals (racial minorities)	Racism
Adarand	Race	Racial majority	Remediation for Jim Crow/slavery
Craig	Sex	Young men (women)	Sexism
Baehr	Sex	Sexual orientation minorities (women)	Compulsory heterosexuality (sexism)

embarrassment in *Hardwick*. More important, such a course of action could allow for the state experimentation that the Court has praised in its federalism cases. If one state out of fifty recognizes same-sex marriage, that state's experience would be invaluable for testing antigay arguments in other states and at the national level. My firm prediction is that the hysterical and obsessional arguments against gay marriage will prove groundless: same-sex marriage will marginally strengthen rather than undermine the institution and contribute to public health campaigns against AIDS and other sexually transmitted diseases. The narcissistic fears will be marginally realized, however: gay marriage will show how productive unions can exist with men doing housework and women working outside the home.

Protection against Private Antigay Discrimination

In *Evans*, Colorado defended its initiative on the ground that it only sought to preempt local ordinances prohibiting sexual orientation discrimination, which constituted "special rights" unacceptable to most Coloradans. The Court found "nothing special in the protections Amendment 2 withholds. These are protections taken for granted by most people either because they already have them or do not need them." *Evans* can be read as the Court's recognition that the state contribution to the closet carries with it today a modest state responsibility not to reinforce the closet, as the Colorado initiative sought to do and for reasons that resonated with traditional tropes of prejudice.[91] Indeed, the Canadian Supreme Court adopted such a stance in *Vriend v. Alberta* (1998), which held a provincial human rights act inconsistent with the Canadian Charter on the ground that its comprehensive bases for nondiscrimination did not include sexual orientation. As its constitutional remedy, the Court ruled that the law be expanded to include sexual orientation discrimination.[92] (*Vriend*'s reasons that discrimination because of sexual orientation is indivious would similarly justify heightened scrutiny under U.S. equal protection law.)

For pragmatic reasons, the U.S. Supreme Court might decline to follow *Vriend* to require state or federal antidiscrimination law to include sexual orientation. Such a move might be considered a retreat from principle and the reasoning of precedent. But, as before, the Court has available to it techniques for avoiding the constitutional issue. Samuel Marcosson, for example, argues that the federal prohibition of sex discrimination in the workplace (title VII of the 1964 Civil Rights Act) protects gay employees.[93] Firing a male employee because he has a male lover is sex discrimination because the employer would not have reacted negatively but for the sex of the employee (a female employee with a male lover would not have been fired). Again, the miscegenation analogy is applicable: firing a black employee because he has a white lover would be race discrimination because the employer would not have reacted negatively but for the race of the employee (a white employee would not have been fired). In *Bob Jones University v. United States* (1983), the Supreme Court held that a fundamentalist university was not entitled to federal tax exemption because it forbade different-race dating and marriage, which the Court treated as simple race discrimination.[94]

Federal circuit courts have generally not construed title VII in this way. In *DeSantis v. Pacific Telephone & Telegraph Co.* (1979), for example, the Ninth Circuit ruled that an assertedly effeminate man, a gay man, and a lesbian couple had no title VII sex discrimination claims.[95] Neither *DeSantis* nor the other early decisions discussed the miscegenation analogy, which is much strengthened by the Supreme Court's subsequent decisions in *Bob Jones* and *Price Waterhouse v. Hopkins* (1989).[96] Ann Hopkins was denied partnership at Price Waterhouse, in part because she was considered too "mannish." Consistent with *Craig,* the Court ruled that discriminating against Hopkins because she violated traditional gender roles (women must be feminine) is sex discrimination. If Price Waterhouse violates title VII in discriminating against masculine women, so too must discrimination against an effeminate man violate title VII, contrary to *DeSantis.* If discrimination against effeminate men and masculine women violates title VII, why does it not follow that the statute also bars discrimination against male employees who date other men and female employees who date other women? Plug *Bob Jones* (for *Loving*), title VII (for *Craig*), and *DeSantis* (for *Baehr*) into Revised Table 6.1 and you have the miscegenation analogy for title VII.

Lower courts have extended *DeSantis* to preclude gay employees from complaining of workplace harassment. Judges have reasoned that gay employees are harassed "because of sexual orientation," not "because of sex," as required by the statute.[97] This is the same kind of argument deployed to deny title VII relief to the early sexual harassment plaintiffs, women whose abuse was deemed to be discrimination because of "an inharmonious personal relationship" and not because of "plaintiff's sex."[98] The Supreme Court's decision in *Oncale v. Sundowner Offshore Services* (1998), allowing claims for harassment by someone of the same sex, may reopen the issue for some lower federal courts. In an analogous context, the Department of Education and the Seventh Circuit have found that an educational institution's failure to provide relief to gay students harassed by homophobic classmates can be sex discrimination.[99]

The policy of title VII as it has been applied by the Equal Employment Opportunity Commission and the courts is to make gender stereotypes irrelevant to job decisions and to protect workers against the sexualized heckler's veto.[100] This policy is as fully applicable to discrimination against gay people as to discrimination against women. Under *Hopkins,* employer discrimination against effeminate men and mannish women is actionable, and employers ought not be able to argue that they were acting on the basis of homophobia, for the narcissistic connections with sexism are particularly clear. Under *Oncale,* gay or bisexual men ought to have a claim for relief if similar harassment would not have been tolerated by an employer if its victim had been female. There is no analytic reason for the Supreme Court not to construe title VII to eliminate these inconsistent treatments, especially in light of the *Evans* point that these antidiscrimination protections are baselines for modern citizenship.

The fairness and analytical problems with title VII's current protection for gender-bending women and harassed straights but not gender-bending or harassed gays also offer a substantial reason for Congress to follow the District of Columbia and eleven states (Appendix B2) in creating a cause of action against employers who discriminate because of sexual orientation, such as that in the proposed Employment Non-Discrimination Act (ENDA).[101] This legislation would clear up the logical inconsistencies or tensions between the lower court decisions denying gay people protection of any sort and the Supreme Court decisions in *Hopkins* and *Oncale.* There is no persuasive reason, as a matter of title VII policy or abstract justice, why an employer ought to be able to fire a female employee because she is lesbian but not because she is mannish, or ought be liable to a male employee for workplace harassment if a gay supervisor assaults him but not if a straight supervisor does.

Moreover, the title VII policies support statutory protection. Like sex and gender discrimination, already illegal, sexual orientation discrimination is typically irrational. It is no more rational for employers to hire or promote only people who are of a specified sex or whose gender matches her or his sex than to hire or promote only people of a particular sexual orientation. The details of some of the cases provide anecdotal evidence of the vicious nature of workplace discrimination against gay people, and this lesson of the cases has been backed up by empirical evidence. As many as two dozen surveys have asked gay people to report whether they have experienced some form of significant discrimination in obtaining or retaining jobs; between 16 and 46 percent of the respondents have reported significant discrimination.[102] This is comparable to recent surveys of African Americans' workplace experiences with discrimination. Although the early surveys were insufficiently randomized to assure critics that antigay discrimination is anything but episodic, economist Lee Badgett has documented the apparent effects of this discrimination in a more systematic way. Analyzing pooled data from a national random sample, the General Social Survey, Badgett found the annual average earnings of employees by sex and sexual orientation were as follows:[103]

Heterosexual men	$28,312
Homosexual/bisexual men	$26,321
Heterosexual women	$18,341
Homosexual/bisexual women	$15,056

Badgett's data reflect the previously documented wage gap between women and men and demonstrate that a similar wage gap exists between gay/bisexual and straight employees for each sex. Badgett also subjected the data to regression analysis, which considers whether other factors, such as education, explain the large income differences, or whether sexual orientation alone explains the difference. She found that no other factor could explain gay/bisexual men's income differential, which was 11 to 27 percent less than straight male incomes after accounting for other variables. Badgett found lower income for gay/bisexual women, but the differential for lesbians was not measured at a statistically significant level. This may indicate that lesbian employees are mainly penalized for their sex and only secondarily for their sexual orientation.

Finally, the cases illustrate the many ways that the state itself has contributed to private antigay discrimination. A generation ago, the state actively encouraged gay-bashing by setting a bad example for private employers, "outing" gay people to their employers, and denying gays security clearances needed for many high tech jobs (Chapter 2). The state's complicity in past and continuing antigay discrimination provides a moral and perhaps political justification for ENDA: it is an opportunity for the federal government to serve as a focal point for nondiscrimination and to redeem its earlier witch-hunting of its own gay employees.

Three different kinds of arguments have been made against ENDA and might be made against an interpretation of title VII to protect gay employees in some instances. None of the arguments is analytically robust, but each argument suggests subtle problems with relying on statutory protections to instantiate homo equality.

Enforcement Issues. The biggest concern of employers is that expanded antidiscrimination protections will open a floodgate of frivolous but costly lawsuits. No jurisdiction that protects against sexual orientation discrimination has found this to be a problem, however. Illustrative is the experience in the District of Columbia, a liberal jurisdiction whose Human Rights Act (1977) prohibits employment discrimination on the basis of race, sex, sexual orientation, disability, age, personal appearance, religion, family responsibilities, and marital status. About 4 percent of the complaints each year concern sexual orientation, well below the annual figures for complaints dealing with race, sex, national origin, age, disability, and even personal appearance.[104] The District's Department of Human Rights reports the data shown in Table 6.3 concerning the disposition of sexual orientation claims between 1990 and 1995.[105] These data confirm that private employers are not flooded with complaints of sexual orientation discrimination, and that the large majority of the complaints are handled administratively. Human Rights Commissioner Cornelius Alexander reported to me that only two cases reached formal administrative adjudication between 1986 and 1996. Finally, there are only six reported decisions on sexual orientation discrimination in the twenty years the act has been in effect,[106] in contrast to thirty-six decisions involving sex discrimination.

The District's experience is representative of the experience in other cities and states that directly prohibit sexual orientation discrimination in employment. The in-depth survey by James Button and his colleagues of enforcement in Philadelphia, Santa Cruz, and Iowa City found exactly the same pattern as in the District and reported no significant burden on businesses, which have generally come to support such legislation. A 1993 survey found that sexual orientation claims make up less than 5 percent of the discrimination claims filed in states

Table 6.3   Disposition of D.C. sexual orientation claims, 1990–1995

Type of complaint	Fiscal year					
	1990	1991	1992	1993	1994	1995
Discrimination complaints filed	608	371	290	412	419	435
Sexual orientation complaints filed	19	14	16	20	11	20
Private sector employment complaints	14	13	16	17	11	17
Disposition:						
No probable cause	5	5	7	8	3	1
Settlement	4	5	0	2	2	2
Withdrawn	4	1	6	4	4	3
No jurisdiction	1	1	1	1	0	1
Still open (1996)	0	0	2	1	2	10
Other	0	1	0	1	0	0

including this as a prohibited category.[107] These enforcement figures then pose the question Randy Shilts asked two decades ago: Are antidiscrimination laws "toothless paper tigers," providing few benefits for gay employees?[108] The answer is still not clear. Theoretically, a national antidiscrimination law ought to signal all businesses in all regions of the country that they must follow the gay-friendly policies of employers such as AT&T and would empower some gay employees in their dealings with antigay supervisors or coworkers within the corporate structure. Empirically, it is too early to tell what independent effect antidiscrimination laws have. In a preliminary sounding, Button's national survey found that more than a quarter of the gay respondents believed such laws actually reduced discrimination; most respondents believed they have had beneficial effects as focal points signaling supervisors and coworkers that antigay prejudice was no longer an acceptable workplace norm; and about a third believed that such laws galvanized opposition to gay rights or had no effect at all.[109]

The underlying phenomenon is the employment closet. The main reason antidiscrimination laws generate so few complaints is that most gay employees are not "out" in the workplace. Over time, employment discrimination laws might encourage more employees to feel safe about coming out in the workplace. That process, in turn, makes even moderate homophobes nervous. Proponents of the *Evans* initiative portrayed antidiscrimination ordinances as direct threats to workplace integrity, the church, and even the family, in part because they empowered gay people to make their presence known in public spaces. The problem faced by proponents of antidiscrimination laws is to sell them to straight people as measures that would yield minimal workplace disruption, but to gay people as measures that would protect them for being out at work.

Behavior versus Status Issues. For the foregoing reasons, corporate America has not opposed ENDA, and opposition has come from cultural conservatives. They maintain that gay people are not "like" other groups the state has protected against private discrimination. Opponents of ENDA totalize gay people around lewd behavior that gays are all supposed to engage in.[110] During the 1994 ENDA hearings, Senator Nancy Kassebaum wondered why sexual orientation, a behavior, should be a protected characteristic, when civil rights laws have traditionally protected only status-based characteristics such as race, sex, age, and disability. Witnesses pointed out that civil rights laws also protect against discrimination based on religion, which, like sexual orientation, involves behavior. Kassebaum was incredulous. While there are "certain behavioral characteristics that one could associate" with religion, it was not a characteristic based *wholly* on behavior, as sexual orientation is.[111] Such remarks misconstrue sexual orientation, which is based upon a mix of cognition and conduct similar to religion. Religion involves both thought and action: a Presbyterian believes in God's omnipotence and mercy, and engages in activities such as churchgoing, prayer, charitable work, and so forth. Sexual orientation similarly involves both thought and action: a typical lesbian feels erotic attraction or emotional bonds to other women and engages in sexual and social activities with other women.

Kassebaum's widely shared incredulity stems from the cultural phenomenon whereby homosexuality (the status) is considered equivalent to sodomy (the conduct). From her point of view, the conduct part of homosexuality dominates, if not obliterates, the cognition part, just as the Supreme Court had done in *Hardwick*.[112] This is hysterical discourse at its most unproductive. Consider a thought experiment. When Senator Kassebaum sees an open lesbian, she must think "here is someone who performs perverse sexual acts," not "here is a woman who loves and appreciates women and their beauty in a way I do not." When she sees an openly straight woman, she does not think "here is someone who performs perverse sexual acts," even though that woman is much more likely to have engaged in anal sex than the gay woman and just about as likely to have engaged in oral sex.[113] Such a cognitive process is sexist as well as hysterical. What distinguishes the straight from the gay woman is not behavior so much as desire and status: the lesbian's desire for other women challenges the orthodoxy of compulsory heterosexuality.

Perform the thought experiment from another angle. In the 1950s in rural Appalachia where I grew up, some Protestants could meet an openly Roman Catholic person and think "cannibalism" or "Pope worshipper,"[c] not "here is a sister who loves and appreciates God in ways I was not taught." Catholics saw the matter differently, and so do almost all the rest of us today. When Kassebaum sees a self-identifying Roman Catholic today, she thinks "here is a brother who loves God, etc.," not "cannibalism." This is good. What she focuses on is the cognition she shares with the religious person, not the conduct she does not share. A goal of antidiscrimination laws is to change our focus from hysterical, narcissistic, or obsessional stereotypes to more positive appreciation of connections in the face of cognitive differences. ENDA would encourage such a focus.

A final variation in my thought experiment reveals a problem with ENDA itself. Transsexual and transvestite orientations are excluded from ENDA's coverage just as they have been construed to be outside title VII, even though they

---

c. Roman Catholics believe in transubstantiation, that during Communion the bread and wine actually become the flesh and blood of Christ. Because the communicants and the priest then ingest the bread and wine, thinking this is so, the practice was labeled cannibalistic in some fundamentalist quarters. Catholics, in turn, could look at an openly Jewish person and think "Christ killer" or "food fetishist."

are either sexual orientation (ENDA) or gender (title VII) categories or both, and even though discrimination against transsexuals and transvestites seems to operate even more viciously than that against lesbians and gay men. One rhetorical justification for not protecting transsexuals/transvestites is that they are discriminated against because of their conduct (their cross-dressing), not their orientation. This is questionable for the same reason Kassebaum is wrong that lesbians and gay men should not be protected because the discrimination is because of their conduct: in both cases the discriminatory classification, like religion, involves both cognition and conduct. Is there a principled reason to exclude transsexual and transvestite orientations from ENDA or from existing title VII? I am dubious for discrimination against them rests upon hysterical and narcissistic sentiments associated with antigay prejudice.

Dilution of Existing Protections. Similar to the proponents of the *Evans* initiative, opponents of ENDA also argue that gay people are an advantaged minority seeking "special rights" that will undermine the existing civil rights of racial minorities.[114] They conceptualize antidiscrimination law as a zero-sum game, in which every new protection detracts from existing ones. More plausible, however, is the traditional Martin Luther King vision of antidiscrimination law as synergistic: every new protection strengthens preexisting ones by reaffirming the nation's commitment to civil rights and by expanding the range of people who believe their own careers and lives are invested in antidiscrimination protection. Also, the enforcement data such as that in Table 6.3 strongly support the notion that race discrimination and sex discrimination remain the overwhelming focus of antidiscrimination laws long after sexual orientation is added as a new category.

The deeper, and unanswerable, question posed by this oppositionist argument returns to our culture's evolving understanding of prejudice. It is not just multivocal and universal but commonplace. In a world where weight discrimination and affirmative action are increasingly conceptualized as prejudices just like old-fashioned racism, the prejudiced person is no longer just the Nazi or the Klan member but middle-class you and me. This popularization has cost prejudice some of its ability to appall, and theorists like Young-Bruehl consider prejudice psychologically functional.[115] For many Americans, antigay prejudice may help them form stable identities (narcissistic prejudice), cope with economic marginality (obsessional prejudice), and even feel good about themselves (hysterical prejudice). Query: Will disrespecting Americans' favorite prejudice, namely, homophobia, undermine their respect for civil rights protections generally? Or can the law signal that the workplace and public accommodations, as well as the state itself, are inappropriate fora for homophobes to act out these private prejudices?

part three

AFTER THE CLOSET: QUEER THEORY AND THE SEXUAL STATE

T he sexual closet is a space in transition. Many gay people are now out of their closets, and the law is less inclined to discipline them for it. Now that gays contribute to American culture and are active in American politics, gaylaw might contribute to American public law. Part Two illustrates how the right to sexual privacy, freedom of sexual expression, and equal protection of the law are being reconfigured in response to the challenges presented by gaylaw and feminism. In a polity such as ours, where identity is both gendered and sexualized, the state ought not make either gender role or sexual orientation compulsory without a strong justification, and there is a decent case to be made for imposing a weaker obligation of gender and sexual diversity on private workplaces as well.

Part Three maintains that gay experiences and queer theory[1] can make broader contributions to jurisprudence. While not unique, gay experience offers a different point of view for thinking about gender role, the relationship between sex and reproduction, and the risks of sex; gay experiences also offer affirmative models of human interaction. Starting with Gayle Rubin's idea of *benign sexual variation,* queer theory promises to unsettle preexisting understandings of liberty, equality, and citizenship.

Gender role, for example, should be more a matter for individual and social play rather than for serious social and political stakes. As a society, we need to recognize that sex is not binary (woman, man), that sex can be changed (transsexuals), that clothing does not have to match up with sex in the traditional way (woman wears dresses), that gender does not have to match up with sex in the traditional way (woman = feminine), that social role does not have to match up with sex and gender in the traditional way (woman = feminine = wife), and that sexual role does not have to match up with sex and gender in the traditional way (active man has sex with passive woman). Gaylaw asks to take the hysteria out of sexuality and gender. Relatedly, same-sex intimacy, since it is between sex equals, offers possibilities for the feminist aspiration of mutuality. Mutuality means more than consent, the traditional legal paradigm. It means informed consent; it means negotiated consent where each person wants to know what will please the other; *no* and *stop* are taken seriously.

In gay experience, sex is decoupled from procreation and linked instead to its social function of deepening human relationships. This separation of sex and procreation has long been natural law's reproach to gay people, but gaylaw counters that this separation is its positive contribution to the larger society. Gay families are *families of choice:* children are chosen, not accidentally conceived, and parental or partnership roles are chosen, not dictated by traditional husband-wife rules. More important, gaylaw views sex as good and not shameful, public as well as private. That does not mean that sex is not special, or even hazardous. Gay experience, especially with AIDS, offers this caution: sex can be risky, especially if it becomes a superhighway for viruses to leap from body to body in epidemic fashion.[2] Gaylaw in this way would press the law toward a new normative model of sex, but it is not clear which one. Should the focus be safety and hygiene? Relationship-building? Marriage?

So long as the main threats to gay people were the police and the censor, gaylaw was strongly liberal: the state must justify its interference with personal autonomy. As the police and the censor have receded in importance for gay people, a post-liberal queer theory has emerged. Like feminism, gaylaw realizes that freedom from state interference is not liberty when private discrimination and violence are pervasive. On the other hand, gaylaw cautions that state action against private discrimination and violence may be not only inefficacious but may engender discourses that deepen the problem—the flip side of antigay state policies, which not only failed to stamp out sexual deviancy but instead created politicized sexual minorities.

Gay experience and queer theory offer important insights in contemporary debates within the sexual regulatory state and within feminist theory. Unfortunately, queer theory in particular offers none of the pat answers that natural law theory and liberal feminism have offered. Issues of sexual interaction, family, and identity politics resist firm resolution given our rudimentary knowledge of factual material and the nation's underlying intellectual diversity on these matters. Nonetheless, gaylaw can try to illuminate the underlying cultural divisions and can offer some normative suggestions for regulatory as well as feminist thought. Chapter 7, for example, explores issues of sexual consent. Although many feminists and gay people support this liberal concept as the lodestar for sexual intercourse,[3] their aspiration has been frustrated, first, by the persistence of status-based rules for regulating intercourse; second, by ambiguities in the liberal concept of consent; and, finally, by the state's tendency to produce sexuality, often of a brutish sort, when it does intervene. On some issues, such as informed consent and consensual sadomasochism, gaylaw offers affirmative insights. On other issues, most prominently incest and intergenerational sex, gaylaw offers only paradoxes.

A second important feminist idea is its emphasis on human connection and relationship rather than individual autonomy—the locus of liberalism.[4] Chapter 8 takes up this theme, arguing that the focus of regulatory interest should not simply be the sexual actor, but her or his relationships, family, and children. This, surprisingly, is a general approach feminism and gaylaw share with traditionalism and natural law, and is as generative of ideas as it is surprising. Chapter 8 conducts an intellectual archaeology of the same-sex marriage debate. Under purely liberal premises, arguments against same-sex marriage and related arguments against gay adoption and child custody are vacuous. Yet they remain persuasive to most because they relate to underlying cultural anxieties. These anxieties can and should be addressed by considering the positive good of gay relationships and family.

Finally, many feminists reject the win-lose all-or-nothing conception of legal rights characteristic of both liberalism and traditional moralism.[5] One species of feminist methodology, albeit one hardly unique to feminism, is an accommodative pragmatism that seeks to reconcile apparently colliding norms or interests rather than just to choose one and reject the other.[6] This methodology is put to a pragmatic test in Chapter 9, which examines the hard issues arising when nondiscrimination norms supporting sexual and gender equality are pressed at the expense of first amendment ones protecting religious liberty.

7. Sexual Consent Paradoxes

Pat Califia's short story, "Jessie," recounts a night of passion between Liz, lover of "butch-looking women," and the leathered, electric Jessie, the bass guitarist for a band called "The Bitch." During the drive to Jessie's apartment, Liz recounts her initiation, years earlier, into lesbian bondage and discipline. At the apartment, Jessie slaps Liz hard enough to redden her face, caresses her back and thighs, binds her hands together, and forces Liz's mouth onto her genitals. "I am going to possess you utterly for my own pleasure, make you completely and totally mine. Are you willing?" asks Jessie. "I've never wanted anything more," is the response. Jessie binds Liz to her poster bed and tortures her with hot wax. "Oh! No, no, no!" cries the narrator. "The first rain of fire fell upon my skin. I struggled and cried for mercy. 'I can't stand this,' I wept." Liz begs Jessie to beat her, and the scene ends when Liz passes out in ecstasy.[1]

The story of Jessie and Liz challenges our thinking about a concept as mystical as it is critical to the regulation of sexuality: consent. Legal as well as popular discourse about sexual intercourse focuses on whether both parties have consented, consistent with the old claim that modern law is a movement from status to contract, from a status-based, collectivist understanding of human relations to a choice-based, liberal one. But even today, Anglo-American law ties individual consent in sexual interaction to familiar status categories, such as married persons. Thus, the liberal-traditionalist debate about when sex is proper is one that has never been resolved, and current law shows traces of both liberal and traditionalist influences. In most states of the United States and in England, Liz and Jessie could be jailed for their "consensual" activities.

The big movement in the jurisprudence of sexual intercourse has not been liberal, that is, making consent the lodestar for sexual intercourse, so much as it has been feminist, that is, rethinking both status and consent from women's points of view. Debates within feminism have partly displaced the old liberalism-moralism debates. "Regulatory feminists" have refocused state attention on patriarchy and the ways in which sexual interaction is a mechanism by which men dominate women. The liberal's regulatory device, consent, must be applied within the feminist understanding of context, where apparent consent often should not be credited. Regulatory feminists advocate a positive goal of mutuality and usually advocate prohibitory state regulation to achieve that goal. This agenda has been challenged by "prosex feminists," who maintain that regulatory feminists misread sexuality as gender domination and share with traditionalists an insufficient appreciation for sexual diversity. The regulatory-prosex feminist debate is illustrated in connection with the issues of sadomasochism and intergenerational sex, especially sex between adults and minors.

Gaylaw is poised to deepen this debate. Gay experience sharply reveals the persistence of, and in some areas a resurgence of, status-based rules of sexual intercourse in a supposedly liberal and increasingly feminist polity. Queer theory accepts the feminist thesis that status and choice are related but challenges the productivity of state sex regulation, not because it deprives people of liberty, but because it creates new sexual closets and discourses that not only undermine state objectives but threaten to perpetuate sexuality as a predominantly negative rather than positive experience. Although gaylaw is strongly skeptical about legal regulation of consensual sadomasochism and sex between minors, it offers fewer clear lessons for the regulation of sex between adults and minors, or intergenerational sex.

This examination will reveal the inevitably paradoxical nature of state regulation of sex. The liberal's paradox arises from the inseparability of status and choice. Choice makes a difference, as the law increasingly recognizes the right of women to say no to unwelcome activities and the right of sexual minorities to say yes to the forms of pleasure they prefer. But the legal interpretation of an apparent yes or no is filtered through norms that are typically expressed in the form of status-based rules. The norm of encouraging marriage is enforced through special rules for husbands and wives, for example. Preservation of social institutions of trust and protection of vulnerable people against coerced consent inspires other special rules, such as those applicable to employees and supervisors, fathers and daughters, and doctors and patients.

Many of the newer status-based rules are responsive to feminist objections to the ways formal consent can be deployed to keep women in subordinate roles. The feminist's paradox involves the relationship between sexuality and gender. Viewing sexual interaction as an instrument of patriarchy, regulatory feminist theory has urged vigorous, status-based regulation but at the risk of undermining women's sexual agency. This is the liberal's paradox at work again but is something more, too. Feminist theory leaves us unsure about the relationship between sexuality and gender. There is no swift basis for resolving this uncertainty, and choosing the wrong path might destroy feminism as a serious force.

Gaylegal history, set forth in Part One, suggests general reasons to fear state regulation of sexuality. State regulation too often falls into an unproductive sex negativity, tends to focus on scapegoats rather than those who are causing the most harm, and, even when morally justified, alternates between excessive and neglectful correctional measures. Gaylaw's own deeper paradox is inspired by social constructionism. Many of the problems of sexual exploitation are too compelling for the sexual state to ignore yet too complex for the sexual state to solve. As a result, regulation of outlaw sexuality today remains what it was in the 1950s: ultimately tragic. Even acting with perfect moral justification, state intervention frequently—and theory would suggest typically—results in harm for all involved.

The Liberal's Paradox: The Inseparability of Status and Choice

Liberal theory assumes autonomous decisionmakers who choose rational strategies to satisfy their preexisting preferences. The main limitation liberal theory places on sexual intercourse is that it be consensual: parties ought to be able to engage in sex if they both agree to it.[2] Party one says *yes* and party two says *yes:* legal intercourse. Party one says *no* or party two says *no:* illegal intercourse. Unfortunately, such a simple scenario falls far short of capturing the law of sexual consent, even in our ostensibly liberal polity.

The Many Faces of Sexual Consent

Think about sex in Virginia. Although the state advertises that "Virginia is for lovers," it (like other states) criminalizes most of what lovers actually do.[3] Whether sex is legal depends less on whether both parties say yes, and more on the identity of the parties, their relationship, and what form their intercourse takes. Consider the following circumstances where apparent consent is either negated or rendered irrelevant under Virginia law.

1. Consent Negated Only by Serious Physical Injury (Marital Rape). Traditionally, the law did not recognize rape if the sexual partners were married. As of

1997, this "marital rape exemption" has been narrowed in twenty-nine states and abolished in twenty-one states[a] and the District of Columbia. Virginia is one of the former group. Penile-vaginal sex between cohabiting husband and wife is not rape in Virginia, so long as there is no "serious injury," an unusually broad marital rape allowance.[4] If Liz and Jessie were cohabiting wife and husband, the bondage and punishment described by Califia would be immune from state rape law, even if Liz's protests constituted a withdrawal of her consent to sexual intercourse. Of course, the marital rape allowance is not available to Liz and Jessie, but it would allow a male husband to do some things to Liz that Jessie could not.

2. Consent Negated Only by Physical Coercion or Threat (Rape). Sex is illegal rape in Virginia where one party resists the intercourse and is coerced into sex by "force, threat or intimidation."[5] Rape law is popularly considered an example of consent-based rulemaking, but as of 1997 only eight states define consent and only fifteen states make nonconsensual sexual contact or penetration a crime without also requiring force.[6] Did Jessie "rape" Liz? While sex was forced upon Liz over her verbal objections, it can be argued that Liz had earlier consented to a scenario where no meant yes.

3. Consent Negated by Economic Inducement (Workplace Harassment, Prostitution). Rape law has traditionally held that economic threats or inducements are not coercion that would override apparent consent.[7] Other kinds of statutes, however, have made economically induced sex illegal. As a matter of federal law, sex between an employer and employee is not consensual if it occurs over the employee's objections, or if the employee is coerced into sex by physical force, or is induced into sex by economic threats or promises.[8] Every state except Nevada makes it a crime to exchange sex for money.[9] Thus, if either Jessie or Liz were a prostitute, their sex for pay would be illegal. If Jessie were Liz's workplace supervisor, their intercourse would be illegal if Jessie made it a condition of job security or advancement.

4. Consent Irrelevant because of the Identity of One of the Participants (Minors, Animals, Disabled People). The first three scenarios are ones where consent is negated by certain pressures or inducements. In this and the next two scenarios, consent is legally irrelevant. Agreement is irrelevant when a competent adult has sex with someone the law deems legally incapable of consenting to sex. Thus, sex between two parties in Virginia is a serious felony if one party is under the age of fifteen,[10] or is an animal,[11] or was led into intercourse by

---

a. Alabama, Colorado, Delaware, Florida, Georgia, Hawaii, Indiana, Kansas, Maine, Massachusetts, Minnesota, Mississippi, Missouri, Montana, Nebraska, New Jersey, New Mexico, North Dakota, Oregon, Utah, and Vermont. Richard A. Posner and Katharine B. Silbaugh, *A Guide to America's Sex Laws,* 35–43 (1997).

reason of her or his mental incapacity or physical helplessness.[12] Although few states make it a crime to have sex with an animal, almost all follow Virginia in criminalizing sex with a person incapable of consent because she or he is under age or is disabled.[13] The ages of consent range from fourteen to eighteen. Jessie's sexual assault on Liz while the latter was tied up might be rape in Virginia because of the victim's physical helplessness. If Jessie had taken advantage of Liz sexually after getting her inebriated, there is a clearer case of rape. If Jessie were HIV-positive and transmitted the virus to Liz without informing Liz of her status, she would have committed a statutory crime in twenty-five states.[b] Virginia has no such statute but would probably follow the jurisdictions whose courts have held that knowing or reckless transmission of the virus is a tortious or criminal assault.[14]

5. Consent Irrelevant because of the Relationship of the Participants (Adultery, Fornication, Incest). Consent can also be rendered irrelevant by the relationship between the participants. Consent is no defense to sex between closely related persons; this is incest, a crime in Virginia and every other state but Rhode Island.[15] Nor is consent a defense to sex between two parties not married to one another; this is the crime of either adultery, where one of the participants is married but not to the other participant, or fornication, namely, sex outside of marriage.[16] (Only fifteen states[c] and the District of Columbia criminalize fornication. Twenty-four states[d] and the District criminalize adultery.) This category is not as easy to score: as unmarried sex partners, Liz and Jessie might have committed the crime of fornication, but this is a crime virtually unenforced in Virginia and is probably applicable only when the participants have engaged in penile-vaginal sex.

6. Consent Irrelevant because of the Form of the Activity (Sodomy, Sadomasochism). In Virginia and twelve other states (Appendix A1) sex between two parties of any sex is illegal if it involves the "crime against nature," that is, oral, anal, or oral-anal sex.[17] In the neighboring state of Maryland and five other states (Appendix A1), sodomy is illegal only between two people of the same sex.

b. Arkansas, California, Colorado, Florida, Georgia, Idaho, Illinois, Indiana, Kentucky, Louisiana, Maryland, Michigan, Mississippi, Missouri, Montana, Nevada, New Jersey, New York, North Dakota, Oklahoma, Rhode Island, South Carolina, Tennessee, Washington, and West Virginia. Some states criminalize the transmission of other sexually transmitted diseases but have not yet included HIV. Posner and Silbaugh, *Sex Laws,* 72–82.

c. Arizona, Florida, Georgia, Idaho, Illinois, Massachusetts, Michigan, Minnesota, Mississippi, North Carolina, North Dakota, South Carolina, Utah, Virginia, and West Virginia. Posner and Silbaugh, *Sex Laws,* 98–103.

d. Alabama, Arizona, Colorado, Florida, Georgia, Idaho, Illinois, Kansas, Maryland, Massachusetts, Michigan, Minnesota, Mississippi, New Hampshire, New York, North Carolina, North Dakota, Oklahoma, Rhode Island, South Carolina, Utah, Virginia, West Virginia, and Wisconsin. Posner and Silbaugh, *Sex Laws,* 103–110.

The easiest-to-spot illegality in the Califia short story is oral sex. More ambiguous is whether Jessie's role-playing physical assault against Liz is illegal notwithstanding Liz's apparent consent. In 1993 the United Kingdom's House of Lords ruled that consent is not a defense to assault in cases where physical harm results from "homosexual sadomasochism," even if both parties have said yes and have enjoyed the experience.[18] It is possible that Virginia would follow that rule, as the state takes a broad view of assault[19] and a dim view of homosexual relations of any kind. Most other states would probably not follow the House of Lords.

From a liberal point of view, the foregoing legal array is incoherent. Sex is often illegal when both parties say yes, because of the status of the conduct—prostitution, sodomy, sadomasochism—or of at least one party—sex with a prepubescent minor (pedophilia), adolescent (hebephilia), animal (bestiality), person having a disability, inebriated person, married person (adultery), person not one's spouse (fornication), close relative (incest). Conversely, in Virginia and many other states, it is legal for a man to have sex with a woman if she says no, so long as the man does not use or threaten significant force. It may also be legal in Virginia for a man to forcibly rape a woman if she says no and resists only after penetration has occurred.[20]

The Liberal's Incomplete Explanations

Although this catalog suggests that the liberal idea of consent is not the governing variable for determining when sexual intercourse is within the law, the liberal is not left speechless. For example, consent is negated under liberal theory if one of the parties has insufficient capacity to make autonomous decisions. But this argument is limited to the fourth category above, where it remains a fuzzy justification. Virginia law suggests that it is illegal to have sex with a mentally disabled person, but given the wide range of mental disabilities, it is hard for a liberal to accept this exception across the board. The rule risks treating people with mental disabilities as less than full humans, when in fact they have sexual desires and need for intimacy just like everyone else. The irrelevance of consent might be easier to accept in regard to fifteen-year-old minors. But many people of that age have engaged in sexual intercourse, some regularly. An adolescent woman has a constitutional right to use contraceptives and, in most states, is considered a decisionmaker competent to make medical decisions for children she bears.[21] If she has capacity to make those decisions, why does she not have capacity to decide to have sex? This idea is reflected in state statutory rape laws. Most states now make it legal for two adolescents of about the same age to have sex but not legal for an adult and an adolescent to have sex.[22] Such a regime cannot be defended on the liberal ground that the adolescent has no capacity for consent, for two adolescents can consent to have sex with one another; the defense must be the difference in social power or maturity presumed between the adolescent and the adult, a status-based rather than purely liberal reason.

The first and third categories might be rationalized through liberalism's public-private distinction: the state should be most reluctant to interfere in private zones like marriage and most willing to interfere in public zones like the workplace. But this argument does nothing to justify the regulation of Liz and Jessie (categories four through six) and is an illiberal way to distinguish between categories one and two. Why should the victim of marital rape receive less protection than the victim of date rape? The liberal also has trouble distinguishing date rape from prostitution, as both involve action in the sexual marketplace.

The liberal's last resort is to suggest that consent is only gradually displacing status and conduct as the basis for regulation. Thus, category two, an arguably liberal regime, is the focus of current regulation; categories one and four through six are increasingly irrelevant holdovers from the olden days. It is true that the marital rape exemption has swiftly eroded in recent years, and the criminal prohibitions in categories five (consensual fornication and adultery) and six (consensual sodomy) are not regularly enforced today.[23] On the other hand, category three (prostitution) is vigorously enforced and indeed has been expanded to include workplace harassment. Also, Virginia and other states have done virtually nothing to ameliorate the incoherences created by categories one, four, five, and six. Even the states that have fully regulated marital rape and deregulated fornication and adultery have left sex with minors, disabled people, and relatives criminally regulated. Moreover, these prohibitions continue to have legal consequences even when only episodically enforced. The Virginia Supreme Court has held that the fornication prohibition bars a lawsuit by a partner infected with herpes simplex from suing her unmarried lover, and that the sodomy law justifies a presumption against child custody by lesbian mothers.[24]

The Connection of Status and Consent

American law regulating sexuality is as much concerned with status as with consent. Person A asks Person B to have intercourse, and B declines. The next day A offers B a diamond ring if B will have intercourse with A, and B accepts the ring and has sex with A. This may sound like quintessential, and legal, consensual sex, but legality is not clear without further information about the context of this exchange:

- The intercourse between A and B is *legal* if A and B are dating or are married (categories one and two). Indeed, this is the classic scenario by which the couple segues from dating to marriage.
- The intercourse between A and B is *legally problematic* if A is B's employer and is *illegal* if B earns a living by trading sex for valuables (both category three). In the first variation, A the employer might be sued for sexual harassment, and in the second, B (and possibly A) might be arrested for prostitution.
- The intercourse between A and B is *illegal* if A and B engage in sodomy or harmful sadomasochism (category six) or B is married to C (category five). The intercourse is *illegal* if B is related to A (category five) or is a minor or is mentally disabled (category four).

The same actions by A and B will have strikingly different legal meanings depending upon B's status as a spouse, employee, or sex worker, or as a homosexual, relative, child, or mentally disabled person.

Not only is legality still tied to status but so is consent. What is recognized as a consensual choice is not, even in our liberal society, separable from recognized statuses. This connection is not a historical accident, for both consent and status are conceptions serving a larger regulatory regime. The key policy remains the traditional one: sex is presumed guilty unless absolved by the immunity conferred by (potentially) procreative marriage.[25] Under this policy, an important role of the state is to protect the sanctity of marriage by lenient regulation of sex within the union (category one) and by policing sex outside of marriage, namely, fornication and adultery (category five). Sexual activities not contributing to the procreative project—bestiality (category four) and sodomy (category six)—are symbolically disapproved. For reasons of the sanctity of the family unit and scientifically questionable eugenics, marriage is not available to closely related people (category five) or to minors and the mentally disabled (category four). Once procreative marriage is seen as the organizing principle, Virginia's law of sexual consent is more explicable, a thesis strikingly supported by the state's oddest sex rule: a fourteen-year-old girl can "retroactively" consent to sex with an adult man if he later marries the girl.[26] That is, marriage by the adult and the child is not only legally sanctioned hebephilia but also absolves the adult from the prior crime of statutory rape.

Although most states follow Virginia in centering much of their formal regulation of sex around procreative marriage, the model is in relative decline. The state rarely arrests adults for nonforcible sodomy, adultery, or fornication. But the decline of the traditionalist link between consent and status has not paved the way for a wholly liberal regime because consent is linked to status in another way. People of low status sometimes agree to sex with people of higher status because the former internalize the preferences of the latter. They say yes partly because they want to please their higher-status partners. Women are socially conditioned to form their sexual preferences relationally vis-à-vis men, employees may do so out of self-interest or even loyalty to the boss, and minors out of a sense of obedience to or trust in a beloved adult.[27] The law has responded to this phenomenon by creating prophylactic rules against sex between some kinds of people in unequal power relationships, particularly parents and children, supervisors and employees, and doctors and patients.

The Feminist's Paradox: Patriarchy and Sex Negativity

Another way to conceptualize Virginia's array of sex laws is through the lens of feminism. Virginia's sex code reflects a traditional male viewpoint: rape is hard to prove (especially within marriage), and the images that have long been threatening to middle-class heterosexual males—the sodomite, the child molester, the homewrecker—are placed cleanly beyond the realm of sexual consent. The politics of sex has changed in Virginia as elsewhere, and the law is changing with it. Although women have not achieved equal opportunities, they are nonetheless a political and legal force to be reckoned with. Legal debates about sexual regulation have changed in important ways in response to women's voices. Reflecting but deepening the liberal's paradox, those changes have not been in a uniformly, or even generally, liberal direction. More important, feminist theory has confronted its own paradox in the uncertain relationship between patriarchy and sexuality. If they are interrelated, much stronger status rules are needed. If they are not, such status rules will undermine women's own sexual agency.

Formal Changes in the Law of Sexual Consent

The law of rape has seen the greatest transformation, in large part as a consequence of women's voices in the post–World War II period. Prewar rape law required the prosecution to establish the victim's "utmost resistance" and to corroborate the victim's testimony with independent evidence before the finder of fact could conclude that she had been raped. By the 1960s, most states had modified the corroboration requirement and had abandoned the utmost resistance requirement in favor of something like a "reasonable resistance" requirement.[28] Since 1970, most states have eliminated corroboration as a formal requirement for conviction of rape; virtually all states have abandoned the requirement of reasonable resistance and permit rape convictions upon proof of physical force and coercion that overbear the victim's will; most states have recodified their rape laws as "sexual assault" laws that are gender neutral; and numerous states have created new laws criminalizing unconsented "sexual contact" (sexual touching without penetration).[29] Finally, every state has either abolished the common law's complete exemption of marital rape or has replaced the exemption with a more narrowly formulated marital sex allowance, which most states will ultimately eliminate.[30] There are notable limitations of the law of sexual assault as thus reformulated. Because of the requirement of force or threat, in most states it is still not illegal for a man to have sex with a woman who does not want it and tells the man no. Even this limitation is eroding, as an increasing number of states have not only abandoned the force requirement but are redefining sexual consent to mean a "positively displayed willingness to join in the sexual act rather than mere submissiveness."[31]

Only slightly less dramatic have been changes in the law of statutory rape or seduction. Like rape, these crimes are now usually gender neutral. The age of consent in most jurisdictions has fallen from sixteen to eighteen years in the 1950s to fifteen and sixteen years as the norm today. Perhaps most important, criminal law generally treats adult-adolescent sex differently from adolescent-adolescent sex. In Virginia, for instance, it is a serious felony for an adult to have sex with a child under age thirteen, a lesser felony for an adult to have sex with an adolescent between thirteen and fifteen, and a misdemeanor for an older adolescent to have sex with someone between thirteen and fifteen.[32] Most states now follow a similarly nuanced approach to sex with minors, reserving serious criminal sanction for cases when one party is significantly older than the other.[33]

Third, women's perspective has influenced the law's regulation of sexual exploitation of a position of authority. This influence is best evidenced in the prohibitions against sexual harassment on the job. Although women have long complained of sexual harassment in the workplace, their complaints were rarely successful under either the common law or title VII of the Civil Rights Act of 1964, which protects against job discrimination "because of sex."[34] Not until the mid-1970s did women's voices start to register with the interpreters of title VII; in 1980 the Equal Employment Opportunity Commission (EEOC) followed feminist writers and recognized sexual harassment as a claim for relief under title VII.[35] Under the EEOC's guidelines, unwelcome sex, sexual contact, or sexual overtures by a supervisor are illegal. Also reflecting feminist perspectives, most states have adopted laws making it criminal for specified persons of authority (most often, a guardian, health care worker, educator, or doctor) to have sex with persons under their supervision.[36]

Consistent with the liberal's paradox, feminist-inspired changes in the law have made the law more consent-based in some respects and status-based in others. Most of the changes in the law of rape have sought to facilitate prosecution of unconsented sex by men against women—eliminating or restricting the marital rape exemption, rendering irrelevant the prior sexual history of the victim, and reducing the importance of the relationship of the victim and the accused. On the other hand, much feminist theory insists upon the relationship between status and consent. Because women are socialized to value men's preferences and men are socialized to slight women's, feminism has emphasized the ways in which formal consent is problematic if induced by a power imbalance or even different social conditioning. The crime of incest has been revivified by this insight, and new rules have been created to discourage various forms of child abuse, sexual harassment, and sex between people in some unequal power relationships.

Operational Changes in the Law of Sexual Consent

Women's increased prominence in the public arena has had harder-to-assess consequences for the operation of the criminal law of sexual consent. Again, the focus has been rape law. Because women have laid out the unfairness of past practice and prosecutors and police are now sometimes women themselves, it appears that more resources are devoted to rape cases, the police are a bit more responsive to rape complaints, the victim's sexual history is usually disallowed, and juries and judges are better educated about the meaning of no. FBI data indicate that slightly more than 100,000 rapes—which the FBI defines as "carnal knowledge of a female forcibly and against her will"—are reported to the police each year. This number amounts to approximately ninety-five reported rapes per 100,000 women twelve years of age and over. This reflects progress, but incomplete progress, as a large majority of rapes are not reported.[37] Empirical studies tentatively suggest that rape reform has slightly increased the likelihood that victims will report their sexual assaults to the police and has (except in acquaintance rape cases) significantly increased the likelihood that arrested rapists will go to prison.[38]

Partly in response to women's perspectives, rape and child abuse have emerged as the paradigmatic sex crimes. Prosecutions for sodomy included sex between consenting adults for most of this century, but forcible sodomy and sodomy between an adult and a minor are virtually the only forms of sodomy now found in the reported opinions (see Appendix C2). This change reflects an alliance between gay rights and feminist interests to refocus sodomy law around issues of consent (forcible sodomy) and adult-minor rather than homosexual status (child abuse). Relatedly, prostitution is still prosecuted but less severely than in the past and more often against male clients and pimps as well as female sex workers. This reflects feminism's ambivalence about prostitution: criminalizing it narrows women's economic choices, but allowing it tempts women to sell what some consider an inalienable part of themselves.[39]

The language of incest law has changed little, but the women's movement has affected its enforcement. Unlike fornication and adultery, incest is still enforced, sometimes vigorously. Its prominence in American criminal law is indebted to consciousness-raising and feminist literature depicting the severe trauma and psychological injury that can occur for female children who have sex with male relatives, especially their fathers.[40] As with rape, incest and child molestation complaints are taken more seriously by the legal system, and law enforcers have worked to make it easier for girls to testify against their fathers without fear of retaliation. The Supreme Court has allowed relaxation of some criminal procedure rules in child molestation and incest cases.[41] On the other hand, child sexual abuse within the family is still largely unreported and unevenly prosecuted.[42]

The Debate within Feminism about Regulating Sex

As late as *Bowers v. Hardwick* (1986), legal debate about criminalizing sex followed the liberal-traditionalist axis, illustrated by the exchange between liberal H. L. A. Hart and traditionalist Patrick Devlin over the 1957 Wolfenden Report recommendation that sodomy between consenting adults be decriminalized.[43] Even though Devlin's pro-regulatory position retained popular support, most intellectuals agreed with Hart's position that people ought to be allowed to engage in private consensual forms of sexual intimacy. Today, the liberal-traditionalist debate is intellectually overshadowed by the debate within feminist theory.

Andrea Dworkin and Catharine MacKinnon represent one perspective in the debate, regulatory feminism.[44] In their view, sexuality is a social process by which the gendered system controls women and ensures their subordination. The gender stereotypes of woman as vulnerable, passive, and domestic parallel women's supposed sexual availability, receptiveness, and desire to bear and raise children. Sexual traditions define a gendered politics where man is on top and woman is on the bottom. Thus, rape is men's reminder that any woman is always potentially available to any man, and the marital rape allowance is the legal assurance that the wife is the husband's sexual slave; incest is the father's appropriation of the daughter from her mother's world into his world, where she is subordinate to men; employer or coworker harassment is men's insistence that the workplace be sexualized on terms that ensure their supremacy; prostitution is the symbol of all women as part of a harem that can be called upon for service as token of man's superior purchasing power; and so on.

An implication of regulatory feminism is that status (maleness, and what men want) is the linchpin to traditional rules of sexuality and that status (femaleness, and what women need) is the linchpin to meaningful reform. Consent, liberalism's normative criterion, is meaningless and misleading in male-dominated contexts. That a wife agrees to have sex with a husband who demands it is not necessarily more consensual than her agreeing to have sex with a boss who demands it, or even a burglar who demands it. Regulatory feminists, moreover, have little use for a liberalism that liberates men from the few restrictions traditionally imposed upon them. Liberalism's private sphere is one of male tyranny, and so regulatory feminists turn to the state to re-regulate sexuality in ways that better assure women's equality. The regulatory principle should be jointly defined mutuality rather than male-defined consent.[45]

Many of the reforms demanded by regulatory feminists, such as abolition of the marital rape allowance, are broadly supported. Other reforms are more controversial, notably their proposed ban on pornography and their ambivalence or silence about deregulating prostitution, sodomy, fornication, adultery, and intergenerational sex. Their counterpoints on these issues are prosex feminists such as Gayle Rubin and Pat Califia.[46] These writers dispute the claim that sexuality is simply the mechanism by which gender oppression is instantiated and enforced. Erotic desire is not the same thing as gender differentiation, and to brand sexuality as the chief tool of gender oppression is little more than a cross-dressed version of that old American bogeyman, sex negativity. Rubin and Califia are critical of the nation's punitive attitude toward sexuality, whereby sex is presumed guilty unless proven innocent, usually by showing that it was private, nonpromiscuous, vanilla intercourse between two opposite-sex adults. Sex-negative pogroms have in the past hurt women as much as men, and sex-negative attitudes deny women sexual agency. For women as well as men, sex ought to be considered normal and joyful rather than exceptional and shameful. Because everyone enjoys sex in different ways, we ought not be horrified at deviations from the norm. Our society tolerates the tail ends of bell curves in matters as disparate as hair color, religion, and diet; sex should be no different.

This general debate is illustrated by the specific debate about sadomasochism (SM). "Consensual" SM has only occasionally been prosecuted in the United States,[47] but an entire SM club was brought to the bar of justice in the United Kingdom. In *Regina v. Brown* (1995), known as the "Spanner" case from Scotland Yard's code name for the investigation, the House of Lords held that consent is no defense to a charge of sexual assault or battery, even in a regimented SM scene.[48] The expensive police sting operation, the lurid prosecution, and the Law Lords' split (three to two) decision produced a sensation in the United Kingdom. Liberals assailed the decision as a wasteful display of moralism at the expense of the liberty of freely consenting adults. Moralists defended the appropriateness of prosecuting conduct that trial Judge Rant termed "degrading" and Law Lord Templeman called an "evil thing."

Feminist essays *Against Sadomasochism* (1982) sound a feminist case in favor of the Lords' approach.[49] Recognizing that consensual SM, especially in a club setting, is quintessentially liberal sex, these regulatory feminists argue that it is bad and hurtful sex. SM is a pastiche of patriarchal sex: not only are the top-bottom roles more rigid, but the violence and power games historically implicit in penile-vaginal sex are eroticized explicitly by SM. According to anti-SM feminists, even when two women, such as Liz and Jessie, are engaged in SM, they are not only reenacting patriarchy's top-bottom script, but they are poisoning it further with the eroticization of violence. SM in this way is like the worst pornography: by objectifying the bodies of the bottoms, usually women, it is a ritual that hurts all women. Consent is a weak defense under such circumstances, either because it is giving up an integrity that is inalienable, or because it is given under conditions of structural, systematic inequality, or because it reinforces our culture's tendency to eroticize powerlessness. When powerlessness is eroticized, women lose.

Califia has responded to these arguments.[50] Sadomasochism is what many people enjoy, and feminists have no business imposing their romantic preferences on Liz and Jessie. If mutuality, and not just consent, is the criterion for good sex, as most feminists argue, then SM is just as valid as vanilla sex. The good top is one who will stimulate the bottom more ways than Sunday; the sex in "Jessie" creates an intimacy that many women do not find in less intense sex. Califia scolds regulatory feminists for mistaking sexual fantasy for life, when it is more like professional wrestling or drama, something that removes us from life. Good drama does not confirm our preexisting notions; it shakes them up. Good sex does not parrot social categories; it rattles them as it deploys them for nasty variations. Sex is not politically correct.

A similar feminist debate has addressed intergenerational sex. Many liberal feminists supported lowering the age of consent, but regulatory feminists have cautioned against this move on the ground that it is harmful to girls.[51] Because boys and men are acculturated toward aggressive conquest of girls and because rape laws only criminalize forcible coercion, minor females, many of whom lack confidence needed to resist unwanted pressures, need the rule of strict liability afforded by statutory rape laws. Statutory rape laws usefully reverse the balance of power from the hyperaggressive male to the deliberating female. Prosex feminists dispute this analysis as itself too accepting of traditional stereotypes. Girls as well as boys are sexually active in their teens, and this is not to be lamented.[52]

SM and intergenerational sex forcefully present both the liberal's and the feminist's paradoxes. From a liberal point of view, it is not only debatable whether the SM bottom or the adolescent is a victim, but there is no neutral way to arbitrate the various claims about consent in these situations. From a feminist point of view, it is not only debatable whether sex that eroticizes power differentials is patriarchal or potentially fulfilling for women, but it is not clear which is the greater risk for women—perpetuating patriarchal mores or reducing women's sexual agency. In 1987 Robin West opined that only by women's own consciousness-raising could this impasse be broken,[53] but more than a decade of women's stories has failed to do so.

Gaylaw's Paradox: The Tragic Dynamics of Sex Regulation

Gay experiences have been systematically different from straight experiences, and those differences can contribute to debates about the regulation of sex. To begin with, for gay people, sexual intimacy is disconnected from procreation and marriage. Without an anchor in procreation, same-sex intimacy is openly committed to other values, such as self-expression, bonding with another person, and pleasure. Having no current connection with marriage, same-sex intimacy is grounded in an ongoing process of negotiation and agreement. These features of gay experience press arguments in a liberal direction. Gaylaw, therefore, starts off skeptical not only of consensual sodomy laws but also of the marital rape exemption and of laws prohibiting prostitution, fornication, and incest between consenting adults.

Socially constructionist queer theory may lend some support to the liberal program, albeit for illiberal reasons.[54] State regulation of sexual choice is particularly ineffective, as illustrated in Part One of this book. For example, rules barring gay people from military service during World War II had little effect in keeping such people out of the armed forces or in preventing them from having sex with one another, but great effect in stimulating a curiosity and a discourse about soldiers' feelings for people of the same sex. Theory suggests why. As parents in each generation learn anew, sexuality is hard to dictate from the top down. Prohibitory rules often have a perversely productive effect by stimulating spirals of discourse and interaction. Thus, rules defining and disapproving of sexual deviance may provoke feelings of self-awareness, neurosis, and fear about the taboo topic. Those feelings may or may not produce conformity to the regulatory program.

A second feature of gay experience relates to the metaphors of the closet and coming out.[55] These have pressed queer theory in decidedly antiliberal directions. The main effect of state sex regulation is initially to push sex deeper into the closet and then to yield to counterpressures if people start coming out of their closets. The phenomenon of the closet involves state-imposed hypocrisy that globally problematizes consent. To avoid an undesirable status, a lesbian may marry a man, but the relationship is ambiguously consensual in light of the alternatives. Marital sex for that lesbian is only qualitatively different than sex between a woman and a man holding a gun to her head: in both cases, the woman consents because she rationally fears the alternative, but it is a corrupt consent because she only agrees in order to avoid social or biological death. When the closet is fully mobilized, as it was in the 1950s, one can never be sure that yes ever means yes. A further irony of the closet is that *private* sexuality, the liberal's haven, is not possible until *public* sexuality, many people coming out of their closets, occurs.

Liberals could say that their philosophy opposes the closet, as it stifles individual self-expression, but the matter is not that simple. The closet is also dynamic. Once people start coming out of one discredited closet, new closets emerge like heads of a hydra. The first generation of coming out stories by literary pioneers such as Edmund White were stories of homosexual deviation, but the second generation of stories by writers such as Paul Monette and Pat Califia involve coming out as a person with AIDS or as a sadist.[56] There are yet very few coming out stories by open pedophiles, however. And that points to intractable difficulties. Some sexual conduct might be shameful, and people should closet their feelings. But how can society tell the truly unproductive activities from the marginal but productive-for-some activities? And if an activity is really bad, does state prohibition protect against it, if its inevitable effect is to drive the activity into a deeper closet? Is lesbian SM an expression of women's sexual agency, or is it destructively patriarchal or violent? If the latter, would making it illegal undermine the violence or worsen it?

Like social constructionism, therefore, theories of the closet pose challenges for traditional sex rules and for the additional ones advocated by regulatory feminism. The closet is the pannicked construction of a society that alternates between fascination and horror at sexual variation and whose sex negativity insists that lines be drawn. The significance vested in sex raises the stakes too much: society draws overly broad lines without considering hard evidence of costs and benefits; people on the wrong side of the lines risk being consumed by suicidal guilt or bitter rage; and the supposed victims are destroyed by the process that is supposed to help them. The lesson of the closet is not that the state should deregulate sex but rather that the state needs to realize that the regulatory effort is bound to yield a costly dynamic and will contribute to the ongoing tradition of sex negativity in America.

A third distinctive feature, felt primarily and recently by the bisexual and gay male community, is generated by the AIDS epidemic. If gay sex sidesteps the creation of life, it now waltzes in the shadow of death.[57] For most of human history, sex has posed health risks. For a fleeting historic moment, these risks were substantially lowered by treatments and vaccines. With AIDS, the risks are back. AIDS provides new rationales for state regulation and has made sex education mandatory. Most important, the disease introduces another status category into the law, sex with a person who is HIV-positive (category four). Most states would not absolve an HIV-positive person for transmitting the virus to an uninfected person simply because the latter had consented to unsafe sex. The regulatory key in such cases is *informed* consent, and not just consent. In this important way, the idea of sexual fraud is seeping into American law.

AIDS discourse has been dominated by the debate between moralists who see it as the cost of promiscuity versus liberals who see it as a new factor to consider in one's sexual education and calculus. Although queer theory has, understandably, focused on the ways in which AIDS is a new chapter in America's ongoing sexual politics of puritan prurience and homophobia,[58] theorists have an obligation to face this hard fact: like penile-vaginal sex that potentially results in pregnancy, unsafe sex that potentially results in death reintroduces serious collective stakes in individual sex acts. Thus, not only does status reenter the bedroom but so do society and the state. As that has happened, social values have clashed with hedonic ones, and new closets have formed.

The foregoing features of gay experience and queer theory—sexuality as an unregulable discourse, the dynamic and unstable closet, and AIDS as a new collectivizing focus—ultimately deepen the paradoxes of regulating sex. Not only are status and consent interrelated, but both are part of a larger sexual discourse that reflects and refracts power dynamics and collective action problems. Patriarchy is no isolated source of oppression but is connected with compulsory heterosexuality and other points of pressure and resistance. Most important, gaylaw teaches that the regulation of sex is tragic: some choices and statuses call out for state intervention, which proves inefficacious and, frequently, disastrous for all concerned.

"Consensual" SM?

Anglo-American law allows bodily assaults and batteries when they are consented to: surgery, abortion, roughhousing, and football are examples. What goes on in ordinary sex—fondling, nibbling, penetration by a tongue, finger, or penis—is assault and battery but for the consent involved. On the other hand, the same legal system does not allow consent as a defense to brawling, severe maiming, and suicide. Dissenting in the Spanner case, Lord Mustill argued that consent is presumptively a defense to assault, that the circumstances of the case were insufficiently like brawling to rebut the presumption, and that it was up to Parliament and not the courts to expand the criminal law. Under liberal assumptions, Lord Mustill's argument would appear cogent, yet three of the five Law Lords rejected it based upon their own constructions of the club.

Lord Templeman, who wrote the lead opinion, called the SM club a "cult of violence." Yet sociological studies of SM subcultures suggest that violence is no more a part of those subcultures than it is a part of mainstream heteroculture.[59] Carol Truscott explains how. She defines SM as "behaviours between consenting adults that are sexually pleasurable, that involve a short- or long-term exchange of power and responsibility, and that may involve activities not traditionally associated with sexual behavior, such as bondage, flagellation, cutting, branding, and the adoption of roles in which one partner is 'dominant' and the other 'submissive.'"[60] Most SM is premised upon the ability of two or more people to match their fantasy roles. Thus, the person who fantasizes about being a sadistic prison guard is a poor match for someone with the same fantasy role but a potentially good match for someone who fantasizes about being a helpless prisoner. Once a match has been made, there is typically a process of discussion and negotiation, where each partner shares her or his erotic turn-ons and turn-offs and optimal expectations for the fantasy.

SM games usually involve pain, but only when the pain and its precise form are desired by both of the partners. For reasons not fully understood, pain and pleasure have intimate connections. Like fitness gurus Jane Fonda and Arnold Schwarzenegger, SM practitioners believe in the maxim "no pain no gain" and report the same sort of ecstasy that runners report when they break the pain barrier. In SM, pain is customized: the participant who is stimulated by body piercing is pierced, she who loves to be spanked is spanked, the bondage enthusiast is tied up rather tightly—all with the option of ending or ameliorating the pain with a safe word. In short, SM theory distinguishes pain from violence. As Truscott says, "Consensual sadomasochism has nothing to do with violence. Consensual sadomasochism is about *safely* enacting sexual fantasies with a *consenting* partner. Violence is the epitome of nonconsensuality, an act perpetrated by a predator on a victim."[61]

A recurring theme in the SM literature is that giving one's body entirely over to the bonds and whips of another person represents sex at its most deeply consensual because the surrender of one's body to the control of another is an act of extraordinary trust that requires an equally extraordinary responsibility. The literature suggests both procedural and substantive methods by which to achieve the feminist goal of mutual benefit from sex in a society of diverse sexual preferences. Procedurally, the SM encounter is supposed to be prefaced by a discussion of what is enjoyable and what is unwelcome for each party. The participants agree upon a "safe word" that stops the action when it has gone too far for either one. Substantively, the play of bondage and discipline is supposed to be limited to the scene and not reflected in daily life. Leathersex seeks to liberate its participants from sexual hang-ups and to defuse social aggression and violence.

Taken from accounts by participants, apologists, and perhaps friendly scientists, is the foregoing an idealized understanding of SM? This is not clear. On the one hand, social science has tentatively established a connection between sexual aggression against women and men's exposure to sexually aggressive images and fantasies.[62] This research has been applied to same-sex sexual aggression in at least one empirical study, which found sadomasochists had significantly more fantasies about being forced, or forcing someone else, to do something sexually and were significantly more likely to engage in such activity. That study, however, neglected to pose the "double consent" question: Would you be willing to force someone to do something who had not consented to participate in an SM or forced-sex "scene"?[63] Also, there are celebrated anecdotal accounts of SM practitioners whose aggression allegedly led to rape and murder. Art dealer Andrew Crispo and spree-killer Andrew Cunanan are two recent examples. Although neither committed their alleged crimes in the context of consensual SM, frothy press accounts insinuated that their alleged crimes were an outgrowth of their SM activities.[64]

On the other hand, policy ought not be driven by anecdotes and magazine innuendo. While there has been no rigorous empirical test of the effect of consensual SM on its practitioners over time, the histories of SM clubs (notably the Catacombs in San Francisco) lend tentative support to Truscott's account,[65] as does the Spanner case—the biggest SM prosecution in Anglo-American history. The SM club had been operating for a decade when Scotland Yard busted it, yet there was not a single person who claimed that he had been abused or mistreated by the participants. There was no evidence that any member of the SM club was sociopathic or had evidenced any violent tendencies outside the controlled context of the club; so far as can be determined, the members were model citizens, outlaws only after the House of Lords made them so. If you took a random sample of liaisons among twenty heterosexuals over the same period, you would not get such a good record. If there is a "cult of violence" in our culture, it is the male-female dating game, where as many as one female in three is raped or sexually assaulted.[66] No SM club or subculture has such a rotten record, in large part because no such club would tolerate such behavior.

Gaylaw insists that consensual SM raises serious and unresolved regulatory issues, but also that *Brown* was a most misguided application of the criminal law. From a legal perspective, the Law Lords' main crime was their violation of the Anglo-American tradition of lenity in criminal cases.[67] It is inconsistent with our rule of law to sentence people to prison for private conduct not clearly prohibited by a criminal statute; retroactive criminality is unfair and, in the United States, unconstitutional. From a gaylegal perspective, the prosecution was a misapplication of scarce prosecutorial resources in state campaigns against sexual violence. The Law Lords voting to affirm the convictions all mentioned the possibility that even consensual SM activities could "get out of hand," resulting in severe injury or HIV transmission, but there was no evidence that anyone had been injured or infected during club activities (two members died of AIDS, but their sources of infection were unknown). If society is concerned about sexual violence, it should be devoting more resources to rape cases, including sadistic rape, where a man abuses and rapes a woman or a man because he claims that she or he "enjoys" it. These cases are common enough and demand more resources from a society that claims to abhor sexual violence.[68] Crispo, for example, was prosecuted for sadistically raping an allegedly unconsenting partner, but he was acquitted when the outmatched prosecution left the jury uneducated as to the rules of consent within SM interactions.[69] If society is concerned about HIV transmission, it should be engaging in serious sex education programs way beyond the tepid and sex-negative programs in effect for most jurisdictions.

From the perspective of queer theory, the oddest feature of the Spanner prosecution is that it threatens to drive SM further into a closet and to isolate its practitioners, which would be much worse for society than for SM. The SM club offers an attractive social arrangement: its members can satisfy their sexual appetites with matching partners, and in a context where the desire for repeat playing with the same partner or other members of the club provides strong incentives for participants to play safely and with mutual satisfaction. The gay experience with state regulation in the United States indicates that the most effective, and perhaps only effective, enforcement of sexual mores comes in the subcultural context. People will have their sexual fun whatever their parents or the state says, but not if they cannot find willing sexual partners; those partners will not be available if such people are known to violate the rules of decency and consent settled on by their subculture. A lesson of gaylaw is that, in matters sexual, positive subcultural incentives work better than criminal or cultural prohibitions.

Lord Lowry gave the only coherent reason uttered by the Law Lords for regulating the sex club in the Spanner case: "Sado-masochistic homosexual activity cannot be regarded as conducive to the enhancement or enjoyment of family life," namely, man-woman marriage with children. The statement links the suppression of homosexual SM to compulsory heterosexuality. Earlier portions of this book have argued against compulsory heterosexuality as a worthy or attainable goal for society. The only thing to add is that breaking up a gay SM club is not going to induce its members to marry women, nor induce astonished adolescents to go straight. It is more likely to be a signal of state hate that adolescents would view with despair or scorn. The despairing adolescents often commit suicide, surely one of the least useful consequences of state homophobia.[70] The scornful adolescents are capable of almost anything. Some SM enthusiasts testify that they turn to SM and other deviant activities as a rebellion against nosy authority figures.[71]

The Law Lords' action in the Spanner case was itself a drama of puritanical violence and prurient closetry. Echoing Lord Lane's more detailed account in his opinion for the court of appeals, Lord Templeman obsessively laid out the precise perversions each defendant engaged in, mainly to disgust readers but also to titillate them.[e] After teasing the readers thus, the Law Lords then submitted the law of assault, which has generally included a consent defense, to the inquisitor's rack, until it coughed up the gloss forced on it by Judge Rant. The point of the Law Lords' tortured reading of the statute was to insist upon the drawing of lines to protect society, lest its citizenry feel that they were unconstrained in their pursuit of sexual pleasure. The consequence of the Lords' legal whipping was that the appealing defendants went to prison for several years apiece, where it is likely that, especially as they are notorious sex criminals, they would be subject to unconsented rape. An indirect consequence is that Scotland Yard can terrorize other citizens at its pleasure. This exercise illustrates the distinction between consensual SM (the defendants' activities, retroactively criminalized) and unconsented, violent sadism (the Law Lords' disposition).

Intergenerational Sex

Felice Picano's *Ambidextrous: The Secret Lives of Children* (1985), a "memoir in the form of a novel," reminisces lustfully about the eleven-year-old author's

e. The activities carefully described by Lord Lane included branding a man's buttocks, lightly scorching a man's nipples, striking a man's penis with a ruler and holding his testicles with a spiked glove, applying stinging nettles to the genitals and buttocks of a man, inserting map pins into the buttocks of a man, caning a man's thighs and whipping his buttocks with a cat-o'-nine-tails or a studded belt, biting a man's nipples and buttocks, shaving a man of his body hair and then hitting him with stinging nettles, prolonged beating of a man with a strap and cane and bare hands, dripping hot wax on a man's penis, nailing a man's penis to a bench and slightly cutting him in several places, sandpapering a man's testicles, rubbing thistles into a man's testicles, and pushing a wire into a man's penis and then piercing it with fishhooks.

sexual initiation by the skilled hands of Susan Flaherty in a suburban basement. At age fourteen he had his first love affair, with Ricky Hersh, who introduced him to blow jobs, public masturbation, and other violations of fifties' legal norms. Ricky himself had learned of gay sex from the "bj buddy" of his father, killed during the Korean War. Tony Warner had brought Ricky his father's foot-locker, whose contents included pictures of his father and Tony engaged in oral sex. Ricky and the author spent langorous afternoons masturbating over these images and developed fantasies of their own. Ricky considered the author his "bj buddy" but admitted that "someone older" had been his own sexual initia-tion. An echo of that admission occurs a few pages later in the novel. The two fourteen-year-olds have habitually engaged in shower-room sex after swimming practice. One afternoon, a nineteen-year-old male catches them in the act but tells them not to stop. "I was about to say no, but the guy was already at the doorway, so Ricky immediately knelt in front of me to continue. As the man watched he masturbated, coming all over Ricky's shoulder."[72]

What is the law to make of these scenarios? The law's deepest closet involves the sex lives of children and the ways in which adults interact with their bud-ding sexuality. During the 1950s, at least one episode in the author's dalliance with Susan Flaherty and her sisters would have been statutory rape, and his oral sex with Ricky Hersh was definitely illegal. Today, the law in most states sensibly leaves alone the basement games between the author and the sisters, the author's mutual masturbation with Ricky, and the oral sex between the two boys. But the law today specifically regulates activity substantially unregulated in the 1950s, namely, Tony Warner's supplying "pornography" to young Ricky and the nineteen-year-old's ejaculation onto fourteen-year-old Ricky. Tradi-tionalists deplore the adults' sexualizing youth and spoiling them for marriage. Liberals worry that the adolescent is too immature to consent to sex with more experienced adults. Feminists caution that the adult man might exploit the youth, deploying his superior status to pressure the youth into premature sexual activity. The American gayocracy has feverishly distanced itself from man-boy love. In short, everyone assumes that adult-minor sex is normally predatory on the part of the adult and harmful to the minor.

There is danger in this assumption. Gaylegal history is replete with criminal-izations based on unrepresentative stereotypes and with sex-regulatory manias responding disproportionately to exaggerated claims of predation (Chapter 2). Adults who have sex with children are demonized as maniacs who cannot control their oversexed libidos, mentally pathological, and predatory. Precisely the same generalizations were earlier invoked as a basis for demonizing homo-sexuals, who were thought to be about the same as child molesters. Generaliza-tions like these might be true, but the gay intellectual should insist upon a factual basis for them. Some experts in child sexual development claim that all three generalizations are backwards: adults desiring sex with children tend to have underdeveloped sex drives, are mentally indistinguishable from the rest of the population, and are approached by curious children more often than vice versa. The "sex" they have with children consists mostly of fondling, kissing, and foreplay.[73]

Even more prominently absent in American policy and regulation of adult sex with children has been fact-based theorizing about children's sexual development and the effects of sex with older people on that development. On the one hand, the evidence is strong that children are sexual beings for whom experimentation is both natural and healthy. The medical literature debunks long-held notions that prepubescent children are not sexual, that masturbation is either unnatural or unhealthy for children, and that children do not have orgasms. The doctors tell us that children are sexual even before puberty, and that repression and ignorance about that sexuality do the child no good.[74] Coming out literature such as *Ambidextrous,* the most popular form of gay autobiography, supports the medical literature. These stories typically contain examples of nontraumatic and indeed joyous sexual experimentation by adolescents under the age of fifteen, Virginia's age of consent.[75]

Queer theory would suggest that anxiety about adult-child sex derives from the joint legacy of our culture's traditional sex negativity and modern sexualization of children. Historians report that early modern families treated children's sexuality more casually, tolerating without mishap sex play by adults with children.[76] Anthropologists report that different cultures have different customs for sex play or even sex rituals between adults and children or adolescents; what is considered child abuse in the United States is considered normal or even valuable in other cultures. The Melanesian manhood ritual is but one of many examples: the adolescent boy receives an older man's sperm anally as the key moment in his maturation ritual.[77]

On the other hand, whatever the nature of human sexual response in history and in other cultures, American law is concerned with its response in contemporary American culture. Stories from our society and the medical literature agree that childhood sexuality is a source of anxiety and is closeted from parents whatever the legal rules; that is, both masturbation (not illegal) and oral sex (illegal in some states) are secret affairs. Concomitant with such closetry, the child is both embarrassed and excited by the possibility of orgasm and is prone to fantastic and uninformed beliefs, for example, that masturbation is sinful or unusual. Consistent with this account is the well-reported phenomenon that a child is typically troubled and often traumatized by sexual experience with an adult. Minor females suffer both particularly and intensely from premature sexual experiences with male adults, especially family members.[78] But also consistent with this account is the view of some developmental psychologists that "the greatest damage to the child's personality is caused by society and the victim's parents, as the result of (1) the need to use the victim to prosecute the offender, and (2) the need of parents to prove to themselves, family, neighborhood and society that the [child] was free of voluntary participation and that they were not failures as parents."[79]

Note the reappearance of law. The availability of law as a mechanism for a parent to exact retribution on the offending adult, often in the context of a family breakup, can have highly negative effects on the child. This poses an irresolvable dilemma for the law. If it intervenes, it may exacerbate harm to the child by focusing more attention on the sexual conduct. If the law seeks to minimize harm to the child, as by video testimony by the child without adversarial confrontation, it risks sacrificing the rights of accused adults and fostering false accusations planted by a parent with an ax to grind. The whole process risks sexualizing the family, the antithesis of the law against child molestation and incest. If the state intervenes more proactively, as through sting operations, the risk is strong that the regulation itself will help create a culture of child love. This was the Supreme Court's fear in *Jacobson v. United States* (1992). In that case, the United States set itself up as marketer, publicist, and then punisher of a child porn distribution ring. The Court held that the defendant was entrapped into committing a criminal act by the state's own lascivious campaign.[80]

Gay experience suggests another complexity, namely AIDS. The HIV virus has infected the adolescent population through sex with older infected people who play upon teens' immaturity to induce unsafe practices.[81] It is likely, though, that most adolescent transmission of the HIV virus, a transmission apparently on the upswing, is through sex or drug use with other teens. The frequently immature decisionmaking skills of teenagers, which has traditionally been the justification for deeming adolescents incapable of forming a legal consent to engage in intercourse, is now a reason to establish elaborate sex and AIDS education programs. Traditionalists fear that such programs will create a dialectic of sexuality that will encourage earlier sex, but the problem is that early initiation is occurring without sex education and therefore in a way that breeds HIV infections. The only effective AIDS education is one that teaches more than the facts of transmission and the consequences of infection, and facilitates adolescent culture to embrace mores of safer sex, *no* means *stop*, and full disclosure.[82] Note the similarity between effective AIDS education and the negotiated-sex philosophy of SM communities.

Gay experience and queer theory support current statutory rape reforms that deregulate sex between teenagers. The state can no longer afford to ignore the reality of teen sex and must instead address adolescent sexual issues as matters of public health and education rather than criminal law. Gaylaw has no hard-and-fast suggestions for regulating intergenerational sex, however, beyond a skepticism that most instances of it, as in *Ambidextrous,* are substantially more benign than a legal storm would be. Gay and feminist experience suggests a tentative hierarchy of harm from most risk of harm to least risk of harm:

1. Prepubescent child has sex with a related adult.
2. Prepubescent child has sex with an adult outside the family.
3. Adolescent girl has sex with a related male adult.
4. Adolescent girl has sex with a male adult outside the family.
5. Adolescent boy has sex with a related adult.
6. Adolescent boy has sex with an adult outside the family.

All six scenarios are currently criminal, as are the relatively rare instances of sex between female adult and child. The evidence supports the illegality of scenarios one and two: prepubescent children are unlikely to be capable decisionmakers, and the possibility for harm to their development seems to be great. Sexual intercourse, certainly, and sexual fondling, probably, ought to be illegal. Unfortunately, scenarios one and two are also the scenarios where hysterical legal or parental intervention is likely to be most harmful as well. This is the chief situs of the tragedy described above.

Although it is constitutional for the state to choose illegality for scenarios three through six (adolescent-adult sex), the policy case is ambiguous: most adolescents are ready for sex and have had sex by age fifteen but are still not mature decisionmakers; intergenerational sex within a family can be extremely disruptive, but legal intervention may deepen rather than alleviate the disruption; the power imbalance between an adolescent and an adult, especially a family member, is often significant, although it does not always favor the adult. Feminist theory and the stories of harm to girls who have had sex with male family members, especially fathers, justify making scenario three illegal, consistent with current law. Actually enforcing the law in such cases would also appear less threatening to the minor's sexual development because she is older; in many cases enforcement would be empowering for her. On the other hand, the most detailed feminist examinations of this issue recommend therapeutic rather than criminal solutions to the victim's plight.[83] There is little evidence that criminalization actually deters this conduct.

The hardest issue for gaylaw is what to do with scenarios four through six. Writing from a feminist perspective, Heidi Kitrosser argues that sex between adolescents and adults should be presumptively, rather than conclusively, criminal. That is, the accused adult should have an opportunity to rebut the presumption of nonconsent by showing that the sex was mutually desired.[84] Kitrosser does not address differences between sex with family members and sex with other adults nor does she consider the gender asymmetry in harm,[f] but her proposal is a useful starting point for discussion.

General Theory for Regulating Sex

The Model Penal Code was considered gay-friendly because it decriminalized consensual sodomy, and some states decriminalized sodomy mainly because they adopted the Code (Chapter 3). But the Code was a mishmash of liberal and traditionalist provisions, including one criminalizing solicitation for deviate sexual intercourse. The Code has become increasingly irrelevant as states deal with feminist-inspired rape law reform, the AIDS epidemic, and renewed interest in child molestation and pornography. Gaylaw's perspective should escape from the Code's liberalism-traditionalism debate and focus on the feminist discourse, which emphasizes sexual mutuality.

Feminists such as Martha Chamallas have developed the substantive contours of mutuality theory, which would expand regulation by eliminating the marital rape exemption or allowance (category one), ameliorating or deleting the force requirement in rape cases (category two), and further criminalizing sex between people in authority and those under them (category three).[85] Mutuality theory would probably diminish regulation based upon the relationship of the participants, especially fornication (category five), and the form of the activity, especially sodomy (category six). Gay experience and queer theory generally support the impulses of those feminists who favor the criminal deregulation of prostitution (category three), sex with mentally disabled people

---

f. Although the balance of productive sexual experience versus possibility of harm would support greater criminality for scenarios three and four (girls) than for scenarios five and six (boys), this would introduce both a sex and a sexual orientation discrimination into the law: sex with a female minor would be illegal, but with a male minor only presumptively so; because most adults having sex with adolescents are males, heterosexual sex with minors would be illegal, homosexual sex only presumptively so. Although the Supreme Court upheld this kind of discrimination in a California case where statutory rape only applied to sex with girls, *Michael M. v. Superior Court,* 450 U.S. 464 (1981), the state had other statutes criminalizing intergenerational sodomy with adolescents, and the Court rested its decision upon the shaky rationale that the state has a special interest in preventing female pregnancy. The better rationale for any such discrimination derives from patriarchy: minor females are more systematically exploited and harmed by adult males than minor males are by adult males or females. But any such distinction would be politically unsustainable because it would treat male heterosexual acts more harshly than homosexual acts and would play into popular fear of gay people preying on adolescents and children.

(category four), adult incest and adultery (category five), and consensual sado-masochism (category six).

More important, gay experience would urge a procedural component to mutuality theory. As SM experience suggests, mutual respect entails a conversation about what one enjoys and what one does not enjoy, and it entails stopping when one's partner says so. (The cliche that men "just can't stop" in the midst of passionate intercourse is a canard. When status equals—two women or two men—have sex and one says "stop" or a safe word, the action generally stops or shifts to another activity that is mutually satisfying.) As HIV experience suggests, mutual respect entails an informative conversation where each party reveals any health risks she or he may pose. Sexual fraud may be just as harmful as sexual assault.

Unfortunately, queer theory questions the utility of making violations of the foregoing rules criminal offenses. The criminal law could be useful if it deterred men from assaulting women and minors, empowered women in their dealings with men and minors in their dealings with adults, or served as an impetus for therapeutic intervention. But there is no uncontroverted evidence that the criminal law deters men from sexually assaulting women, minors, or family members. Even though rape and sex with children are somewhat more likely to be reported today and perpetrators are much more likely to go to jail, these phenomena continue unabated and perhaps at higher levels than before. Michel Foucault argued that heightened regulatory attention to incest and sex with minors instantiates the family as a "hotbed of constant sexual incitement."[86] By drawing lines, the law reinforces social taboos. By publicizing these taboos, providing courtroom dramas based on them, and interrogating people about them, the law creates or intensifies a discourse about the taboos. This sexualizes the taboos for a portion of the population.

Nor is it clear that the law generally empowers the victims of incest, rape, or intergenerational sex. The law does empower, but it mainly empowers its own officials—police officers, prosecutors, state doctors, and jurors. Those officials can themselves be fearsome. The criminology literature suggests that the biggest reason child abuse is not reported is the child's, and often the mother's, fear that the family will be destroyed if the state is mobilized against the father.[87] This is not a wholly irrational fear. State intervention not only threatens the father's liberty but initiates a process that can be destructive to the victims. The most harmful features of that process are those guaranteed to the defendant by the Constitution. The same rules of criminal procedure that ultimately helped slow down state prosecution of gender-benders in the 1960s (Chapter 3) now impede state prosecution of rapists, child molesters, and sadists. Some of those rights, such as the requirement that the state prove both illegal acts and mental intent beyond a reasonable doubt, make it hard for the state to win convictions of guilty people. Other rights, such as the right to avoid self-incrimination and to have counsel paid for by the state, diminish the odds that the defendant will confess and initiate a healing process for himself and the victim. Yet other rights, such as the right to confront witnesses against the defendant, require the victim's extended cooperation and subject the victim to defense counsel's typically painful cross-examination. To be sure, few criminal prosecutions actually mobilize these rights because the large majority of cases are plea-bargained. But any involvement by the legal system poses at least some of these possibilities, making the criminal law as risky a proposition for the victim as for the perpetrator.

Criminalization might be defended on symbolic grounds: it expresses society's revulsion and disapproval of morally objectionable conduct. What good is that if it does not also change people's behavior or attitudes? Gay people are still subject to symbolic state disapproval through the criminal law in states like Virginia and through their exclusion from institutions like marriage and the armed forces in other states and at the federal level. Yet the antigay symbolism is toothless, especially when combined with robust public discussion of homosexuality that is guaranteed by the first amendment. There is scant reason to believe that symbolic state disapproval of incest and intergenerational sex is any more efficacious. Indeed, symbolic disapproval through criminalization might be counterproductive because it may deflect attention from approaches that would be more helpful. By making incest and intergenerational sex serious felonies and occasionally staging publicized prosecutions, the state can claim that it has *done something* about the problem, when in fact the state has done next to nothing. Criminalization allows sex-negative groups to oppose spending state money on sex education and victim-centered therapies without admitting that they are beggaring a solution.

Liberal, feminist, and gaylegal theories all contribute insights into a global paradox in the law of sex crimes. In drawing the line between lawful and unlawful sex, the polity is balancing consent-based values of sexual agency against status-based concerns with coerced or false choices. Wherever the line is drawn, we shall be uncertain whether the right balance has been struck. My further fear is that law's enforcement of that balance will alternate, on the whole, between the neglectful and the destructive. The crushing paradox of the law of sexual consent is that every case is potentially like the Spanner prosecution—exquisite legal torture, wringing sex until it is bled dry and everyone is victimized.

8. Beyond Families We Choose

Nowhere has modern law's shift from status to contract been more apparent than in family law. State regulation of family and children has moved from rules centered around the status of marriage or blood relationship toward an emphasis on the self-imposed duties created by contract. This shift reflects widespread adoption in the family law context of the liberal conception of the self as an autonomous actor constrained only to the extent the actor so agrees (contract) or harms others (tort and crimes). Gay people have been the avant-garde of this shift, for their typical families have not been the conventional husband-wife-kids but instead "families we choose"—circles of consent-based rather than kinship-based intimacy. Families of choice increasingly include children. The lesbian baby boom of the 1980s came about through articifial insemination; gay men fathering children with surrogate mothers have followed with a boomlet. Lesbians, gay men, and transsexuals may in the future take advantage of technology allowing them to clone their genetic material or to splice the genes of partners. In the future, a lesbian couple may be able to have children who are genetic hybrids of the two women: that is, procreation without sex, sperm, or men.[1]

With increased visibility, the concept of gay families we choose has stimulated status-based points of social resistance. As a practical matter, gay persons lack many of the options enjoyed by straight persons: the right to marry and, in some jurisdictions, the right to adopt children and the right to presumptive custody of their biological children (Appendix B3). The gay response to these denials is to argue that they are outdated in light of modern law's embrace of the liberal self and its freedom to negotiate the terms of intimate relationships. In brief, gays should be able to do what they want, subject to standard limits imposed by contract (follow your promises) and tort (do not harm others). The first part of this chapter shows how the liberal premises of constitutional law support equal access of gay people to families of choice, including same-sex marriage.

Even though the precedent-based liberal arguments for same-sex marriage are strong,[2] few Americans, and fewer judges, agree. Simple prejudice is not the only reason, for Americans who favor equal job opportunities for gay people gag on gay marriage. The same-sex marriage debate suggests deeper cultural reasons for opposition, reasons that are historical, relational, collectivist—decidedly illiberal. The middle part of this chapter reconsiders the Supreme Court's jurisprudence of the family from this perspective and sets forth a deeper basis for thinking about same-sex families—a conceptualization that reaches beyond families we choose. A consequence of families we choose may be a fracturing of self, and conceiving of gay families in libertarian terms risks sacrificing the advantages of relational features that constitute self.

While contract-based libertarian arguments for gay families are incomplete, status-based egalitarian arguments can also be raised to challenge law's discriminations. By denying gay people encouragement for human interconnection routinely afforded other people, the law denies gay people opportunities for the formation of the relational self. If arguments about the relational self are the proper background for debate, what would be next? Polygamy? Maybe, but the stronger implications are "polyparenting" and new possibilities for a lesbian nation.

Constitutionalizing Families We Choose

American family law has been reconceived in the last generation, apparently accepting the liberal view of the self as autonomous and self-regarding, constructing patterns of intimacy on its own terms rather than the terms dictated by traditional institutions and roles. Same-sex couples have been the shock troops of the liberalized family described by commentators such as Jana Singer and Milton Regan.[3] Anthropologist Kath Weston associates *families we choose* with the coming out process itself.[4] As traditionally conceived, coming out is a liberal move, as the self asserts its acontextual identity as gay in defiance of social norms. For the "out" gay person, family is much less likely to be defined by either blood or marriage than is the case for the closeted gay or the straight person because some members of the blood family will not accept the gay person's identity, and the gay person does not have the formal option of getting married to the person she or he loves. Hence, gay persons are left to construct and reconstruct their own families—to choose and make new choices—more or less outside the law.

Sharon Lynne Bottoms illustrates the promise, the difficulties, and the legal limits of families we choose.[5] Bottoms married Dennis Doustou in 1989 and became pregnant the next year. In 1991, before her child, Tyler Doustou, was born, she left her husband and began to date women. In 1992 Bottoms began living with April Wade, her life partner. Her relationship with Wade has precipitated a rupture in her blood relationship with her mother, Kay Bottoms, who opposes her daughter's "homosexual life style."

Under liberal assumptions, Sharon Bottoms ought to be able to construct a family on terms acceptable to her and her consensual partner, notwithstanding social and familial disapproval. If Bottoms were cohabiting with a man of a different race, the odds are that both blood families and society would throw up obstacles, but the law would protect the couple in their relationship. Although Virginia long made different-race marriage a crime, the Supreme Court in *Loving v. Virginia* (1967) invalidated that policy and now stands ready to require Virginia to grant a marriage license to any different-race couple. The marriage license would protect the couple against family prejudice and would offer other tangible benefits, such as employer health coverage for the entire family, social security benefits, and decisionmaking and inheritance rules favoring the chosen spouse over the blood family. The law would also protect Bottoms's relationship with Tyler if her blood family or her former husband tried to take Tyler away from her because they did not want him raised in an interracial household, as the Court held in *Palmore v. Sidoti* (1984).[6] Bottoms and her hypothetical husband would also have the law's protection if they tried to adopt a child and encountered opposition because of their relationship. All of these protections reflect a liberal regime of legal rules, for they protect the individual's choice, so long as she or he is not breaking promises or harming others.

This liberal regime of rules was not available to Sharon Bottoms, for her social fault lay not in loving a man of a different race but in loving a woman. Under Virginia law, she could not marry April Wade. Although many of the advantages of marriage can be achieved by contract, Bottoms and Wade were not rich enough to afford an attorney needed to draft documents such as a will, a power of attorney, or a joint property agreement. Other advantages of marriages cannot be achieved by contract in any event. A married couple would be able to adopt in Virginia; a lesbian couple cannot. Although some jurisdictions allow a lesbian partner to adopt her lover's biological child, Virginia does not permit this option either. Indeed, a Virginia trial judge took Tyler from his mother and awarded him to his grandmother, largely because the trial judge disapproved of Bottoms's lesbian relationship. The Virginia Supreme Court affirmed that order and, in the process, painted Bottoms as a bad parent. Desperate to see her son, who had been withheld from her for two years, Bottoms in 1996 abandoned further challenges to the court's termination of her custodial rights. Virginia's treatment of Bottoms illustrates how families we choose are treated differently by the law than other socially disapproved relationships and are sometimes destroyed by the law. This phenomenon is inconsistent with liberal constitutional premises of family law.

The Right to Marry

The exclusion of same-sex couples from state-recognized marriage is suspect under liberal premises, which are reflected in the Supreme Court's right-to-marry precedents. Part I of the Court's opinion in *Loving* focused on the law's race-based classification and provides an analytical basis for the sex discrimination argument for same-sex marriage, discussed in Chapter 6. Part II of *Loving* briefly presented an independent ground for striking down the different-race marriage law. "The freedom to marry has long been recognized as one of the vital personal rights essential to the orderly pursuit of happiness by free men," said the Court. "To deny this fundamental freedom on so unsupportable a basis as the racial classifications embodied in these statutes . . . is surely to deprive all the State's citizens of liberty without due process of law."[7]

Loving was unclear whether its due process right to marry had constitutional bite outside the race context. The Court clarified matters in *Zablocki v. Redhail* (1978), which invalidated a law prohibiting remarriage by persons owing support obligations from a prior marriage. Justice Thurgood Marshall's opinion for the Court held that no state restriction of the "'freedom of personal choice in matters of marriage and family life'" can be sustained unless the state can show that its restriction is narrowly drawn to serve an important public purpose. Because there was no suspicious classification in *Zablocki* comparable to the race-based classification in *Loving,* the stricter judicial scrutiny was justified solely from the law's restriction of the right to marry. Marshall ruled that the "right to marry" be "placed on the same level of importance as decisions relating to procreation, childbirth, child rearing, and family relationships." *Zablocki* established a doctrinal structure logically applicable to other cases: a state law or practice that places a "direct legal obstacle in the path of persons desiring to get married" denies those persons the equal protection of the laws unless the state policy is "supported by sufficiently important state interests and is closely tailored to effectuate only those interests."[8] Doctrinally, the burden of persuasion as to same-sex marriage lies with the opponents. The issue is not "Why gay marriage?" but instead "Why *not* gay marriage?" This was precisely why Justice Lewis Powell refused to join the majority opinion.[9] Although the majority rejected Powell's position, it left open the question whether the right to marry existed when there was no possibility of procreation, the traditional linchpin of marriage.

The issue in *Turner v. Safley* (1987) was whether the state could limit marriages of prison inmates to cases approved by the warden. Justice Sandra Day O'Connor's opinion for a unanimous Court discreetly conceded the right of prisons to impose "substantial restrictions" on inmate marriages, probably referring to connubial visits, but insisted that *Zablocki* and *Loving* remained relevant. "Many important attributes of marriage remain, however, after taking into account the limitations imposed by prison life," including "expressions of emotional support and public commitment"; "spiritual significance"; sexual "consummat[ion]"; and "government benefits (e.g., Social Security benefits), property rights (e.g., tenancy by the entirety, inheritance rights), and other, less tangible benefits (e.g., legitimation of children born out of wedlock)."[10]

Turner adds nothing to the analytical structure created by *Loving* (due process) and *Zablocki* (equal protection). *Turner* is important, however, as the clearest articulation of the reasons marriage is a fundamental interest, and at no point did O'Connor mention childbearing as a necessary basis for marriage. The shift in emphasis from *Loving* (procreation) to *Turner* (commitment) reflects the evolution of America from a procreative farm-based society to a hedonic urbanized one. This point is both descriptive and normative. American law has shifted from a *procreative* to a *unitive* understanding of marriage, and this has been a good shift. Procreation is a lesser goal in the modern world. Baby production has narrowed women's personal choices, and a unitive understanding of marriage reflects greater equality between the marital partners. Finally, children enrich a family whether or not they are the result of the parents' intercourse.

In light of the foregoing precedents, the state's refusal to recognize same-sex marriages is both the denial of a fundamental liberty *(Loving)* and discrimination in the allocation of a fundamental right *(Zablocki)*. In light of our society's emphasis on the unitive goal of marriage, the constitutional requirement that the state not discriminate against same-sex marriages is a good requirement. Policy-makers and judges should eagerly embrace it. As of 1999, however, no appellate judge or attorney general in the United States has ever applied the foregoing jurisprudence to hold that same-sex couples have a fundamental right to marry.[11]

Parents' Right to Raise Their Children

More remarkable than Virginia's refusal to recognize the Bottoms-Wade relationship was its transfer of Bottoms's child to his grandmother and severance of the mother's visitation rights. This is in conflict with the constitutional precept that "the custody, care and nurture of the child reside first in the parents, whose primary function and freedom include preparation for obligations the state can neither supply nor hinder."[12] While such early statements came in cases where a husband-wife family was asserting authority over their children's education or health, the Supreme Court has applied this "cardinal principle" in two dozen or more cases involving rights and interests of nonmarital children and their parents.[13] Although the Court has sometimes deferred to state regulation, it has regularly rejected the traditionalist philosophy that children born out of wedlock can be treated differently as a way to express society's "condemnation of irresponsible liaisons beyond the bonds of marriage."[14]

In *Stanley v. Illinois* (1972), the Court invalidated an Illinois law allowing the state to take a nonmarital child upon the death of his custodial parent. The Court held that the interest of a parent in the "companionship, care, custody and management of his or her" biological but nonmarital children "undeniably warrants deference and, absent a powerful countervailing interest, protection."[15] *Stanley* should, in a liberal state, be read to protect the rights of gay parents to raise their children in households of their choice, as millions of children are being raised today.[16] Some of these children were born to lesbians as a result of artificial insemination; a smaller number were born to gay or bisexual men through surrogacy arrangements; some were adopted; like Tyler Doustou, most were conceived in prior marriages. In the future some children may be clones of gay people or gene-spliced hybrids of gay or transgendered couples. However the children are conceived by their lesbian mothers or gay fathers, the parents have constitutionally robust interests in rearing their children.

Stanley does not recognize this as an absolute right, however. For example, the parent's interest is reduced when she or he has taken no interest in the upbringing of the child because "the importance of the familial relationship . . . stems from the emotional attachments that derive from the intimacy of daily association, and from the role it plays in 'promoting a way of life' through the instruction of children . . . as well as from the fact of blood relationship."[17] This exception typically has little or no application to gay parents denied custody of or visitation with their children. Indeed, Virginia inverts the liberal rights recognized by the *Stanley* line of cases by presuming against child custody for lesbian or gay parents when the other biological parent seeks custody, however little connection the straight parent has had with the child. And in *Bottoms v. Bottoms* (1995), Virginia took away a child from his custodial mother and awarded him to a nonparent relative.[18]

The Virginia Supreme Court deferred to the trial court's findings of fact, which the court believed supported the conclusion that the "best interests of the child" required the transfer. The majority of reported decisions from other states reject Virginia's presumption against custody with the gay parent when the straight parent objects, but many state courts have reached substantially the same result under the best interests of the child standard.[19] Their reasoning is that the child will suffer psychologically if she or he is exposed to gay relationships and third-party teasing and the shame they entail. A normative problem with the third-party prejudice argument, in particular, is that it is exactly the same argument used to deny custody to parents involved in different-race relationships, an argument rejected in *Palmore:* "The Constitution cannot control prejudices but neither can it tolerate them. Private biases may be outside the reach of the law, but the law cannot, directly, give them effect." After *Romer v. Evans* (1996), and for many judges before *Evans,* this reasoning is applicable in sexual orientation as well as race discrimination contexts.[20]

Both the trial court and the state supreme court in *Bottoms* emphasized that the lesbian partners had hugged and kissed in Tyler's presence. This has been a justification for denying custody to lesbian mothers in other states as well, and courts often condition visitation rights of gay or lesbian parents on their not displaying affection for or even living with same-sex partners.[21] Such state-imposed conditions burden gay parents' *Stanley* rights without good justification. There is no impartial study showing that exposure of children to hand-holding and kissing by lesbian partners has any detrimental effect on the children, or has any effect different from hand-holding and kissing by heterosexual partners.

Nondiscrimination in Adoption

In at least seven jurisdictions, April Wade could have adopted Tyler Doustou as a means of sealing the mother/mother/child family unit.[22] Such a "second-parent adoption" is not possible in Virginia, and, because of their sexual orientation, it is doubtful that Bottoms or Wade would be able to adopt any child. Although only Florida has a statute prohibiting adoptions by gay applicants, other states presume against such adoptions as a matter of administrative practice or judicial case law.[23] The right to adopt has not been recognized as fundamental like the right to raise one's biological children, but the difference is a matter of degree, as parenting is such a unique opportunity in our culture. However fundamental the interest, the liberal state is obligated to treat adoption issues rationally and neutrally. Thus, the state cannot create irrebuttable presumptions that do not have a factual basis, nor may the state draw distinctions between individuals based only on differences that are irrelevant to legitimate government objectives.[24] *Evans* suggests that the state may not sweepingly penalize gay citizens out of animus. The statutory prohibition in

Florida, which prohibits any homosexual from adopting or being a foster parent, rests upon no fact-based record regarding the best interests of the child goal that the legislature endorsed (Chapter 6). In a liberal polity the presumption ought to be against the constitutionality of such policies.

Status-Based Arguments for Families We Choose: Commitment and Childrearing

Logic suggests that the Supreme Court's liberal precedents require the state to recognize gay families of choice, yet no state does so completely, most states refuse any kind of recognition, and some states persecute such families. Why is that? It might be because the liberal state is hypocritical, holding itself out as libertarian while selectively denying the liberty of despised status groups. It might be because liberalism is an evasive aspiration in a heterogeneous polity and status categories are inevitable in the law. It might be both. If so, arguments for gay families must rest on something more profound than choice, and they in fact do: gay families are good for gay people and good for America because they provide fora in which people form mutual commitments and children are reared. Any effort by the state to discourage gay families is perverse because it discourages commitment and harms children.

The Persistence of Status-Based Arguments against Gay Families

Opposition to gay families, particularly to same-sex marriage, has traditionally been, and to some extent still is, articulated in status terms. Under liberal premises, the objections are analytically vacuous. Liberal arguments, however, have usually been unable to defeat them because the status-based arguments are responsive to underlying cultural anxieties that cannot be ignored.

Natural Law Arguments and the Endowment Effect. Antigay family law discriminations have traditionally been justified by natural law. Thus, early court decisions denied gay couples the right to marry because "[m]arriage has always been considered as the union of a man and a woman."[25] Similarly, the traditional rule against custody by gay parents rested upon their status as "sodomites," presumptive criminals. This was the reason the trial judge took Tyler Doustou away from his mother, for example.[26] Yet these natural law arguments overstate the strength of the tradition they invoke. Many human cultures have recognized same-sex marriages or their equivalents, and Western culture has often allowed same-sex couples to marry notwithstanding its formal bars.[27] Moreover, the intercourse between two women scorned by the Virginia judge in *Bottoms* was not considered "sodomy" until this century (Chapter 4). From a liberal point of view, traditionalist arguments are not only inaccurate but are circular and beg the question: Is a state denial of individual claims justified by a neutral state goal? *Zablocki* and *Turner* demand that the state justify the lines it has drawn for excluding people from civil marriage. *Loving* and *Palmore* refute the proposition that definitional arguments alone can justify an invidious discrimination.

Although analytically anemic, definitional or natural law arguments remain culturally potent. For one thing, such arguments are a matter of religious faith for many Americans, and the main opponents of gay family rights remain natural law-inspired religious groups.[28] But the appeal of natural law arguments is not limited to the religious fundamentalist. The longer a discrimination has been in place the more "natural" it appears to people. In economic transactions people are subject to an "endowment effect"—they ask a higher price for something they have than they would be willing to offer for the same thing were it not theirs.[29] Thus, if the state endows you with a property right in a beautiful book of Henri Matisse's paintings, you will not part with the book for less than $150, even though you would only pay me $125 for the same book had the state said that it belonged to me. You would also much rather forgo the gain of a book marketed at $125 than lose your book having a market value of $125; the longer the period of possession the greater the disparity. The same idea can be applied to the less tangible rights entailed in status.[30] If the state endows you with a right to a favored status, whereby your relationships are rewarded in ways that other relationships are not, you may not part with that right for less than $150, even though you would only pay the state $125 for the same right if the state accorded it to other people but not to you.

Thus, in the same way people have internalized the idea that the Matisse book belongs to someone, people internalize the criteria establishing relational endowments—legal markers of status that set them above other people in society. For the same kinds of reasons people object to the state's taking their property entitlements without generous compensation, people object to the state's fiddling with their relational entitlements, especially long-standing ones. Once relational endowments have been internalized, they will become naturalized or socially invisible. Relational endowments in this way are background norms that strongly influence social interaction and can influence those disadvantaged as well as those advantaged by them. The endowment effect is probably one reason women continue to experience unequal burdens and rights within companionate marriage: women as well as men have internalized notions of women's work and unequal pay, and normal interaction naturalizes this state of affairs as unproblematic.[31] Similarly, opponents of same-sex marriage do not see the exclusion of gay couples as any kind of discrimination. Even people who have come to believe that gays should not be put in jail will not go along with giving them the "special rights" entailed in changing a long-standing status endowment like marriage. Nor will their attitudes change overnight.

The Defense of Marriage/Family Argument and the Slippery Slope. The most irritating argument against gay families is that their recognition would undermine families generally. When President William Clinton, Senate Majority Leader Robert Dole, and House Speaker Newt Gingrich secured the enactment of the Defense of Marriage Act (DOMA) in 1996,[32] the hypocrisy of the nation's highest ranking adulterers "defending" marriage was lost on a populace uneasy about gay marriage. Marriage and family values are, in fact, under siege. But, as Representative Harry Johnston said during the DOMA debate, "[e]veryone knows that the only true threat to marriage comes from within," and gays were being flogged as the "demon de jour."[33] Representative Barney Frank wondered: "How does the fact that I love another man and live in a committed relationship with him threaten your marriage?" Representative Steve Largent, one of DOMA's sponsors, responded that *his* healthy heterosexual marriage was not threatened, but the institution of marriage *was*.[34] This is analytically lame. While straight people's problems and infidelities have undermined the institution, it is gays who suffer the consequences of straights' marriage anxiety.

While the foregoing stance is unfair, it is altogether human. Because people are risk averse as well as invested in their relational entitlements, the endowment effect has a double force when the challenged status or institution is in decline, such as marriage. The decline of marriage, moreover, is perceived by many as a consequence of the shift in family law from a traditionalist focus on obligation of each spouse to the family to a liberal focus on autonomy of each spouse within the family. The same liberal shift that brought the country no-fault divorce and high rates of marital breakups now brings gay people to the altar. For those Americans who already think marriage law is already too liberal, gay marriage is not only a continuation of a bad trend but the apotheosis of it. (This is especially troubling for those who stereotype gay people as narcissistic and selfish.)

The double threat of losing a favored status and weakening a beloved institution also inspires slippery slope arguments against same-sex marriage. If the most central, long-standing man-woman requirement of marriage were relaxed, then other requirements would fall away too, and there would be no special status left to being in the institution. Such reasoning underlies the famous polygamy argument. If the requirement of a *male-female* couple were relaxed, then why not relax the *couple* requirement as the logical next step?[35] This argument could be avoided by invoking sex discrimination, rather than a generalized fundamental right to marry, as the basis for problematizing the same-sex marriage bar (Chapter 6). Denying a woman-woman couple a marriage license is discrimination because of *sex,* a quasi-suspect classification. Denying a man-woman-woman trio a marriage license is discrimination because of *numerosity* or *marital status* (if the first two are already married and want to add the third), neither being a suspect classification invoking the kind of heightened scrutiny the Hawaii Supreme Court demanded in *Baehr v. Lewin* (1993).[36]

Although logically vulnerable, the polygamy argument persuasively plays on people's stereotypes about gays and their romantic views about marriage. Marriage in our culture is a balance between sex and romance: marriage without sex is boring, but marriage without romance is arid. The metafear is that if the most sexualized of our citizens, gay people, are allowed to marry, the balance between sex and romance will be decisively altered, opening up marriage to oversexed and unfaithful unions, culminating in polygamy. (Polygamy is stereotyped, also unfairly, as oversexed and unfaithful.) That this is happening to heterosexual marriage already—no-fault divorce has led to serial marriages, which are the next step toward polygamy—just deepens the fear; homosexual marriage would be a concession that fidelity is a lost cause and romance, as opposed to sexual lust, is dead.

The polygamy argument against same-sex marriage suggests a deeper reason for opposition to gay custody and adoption—a fear that children run a higher risk of sexual molestation in gay than in straight households.[37] Factually, this may be backwards. Some surveys have found that children are more at risk in straight households than in gay ones, and all the surveys find that the significant variable is sex (men molest children) and not sexual orientation (lesbians do not).[38] Nonetheless, this heterofear seems to consider any kind of same-sex affection as posing a danger of sexualizing the child or, perhaps more accurately, sexualizing the child in the wrong direction. This leads to the final, and deepest, argument against gay families.

The Stamp of Approval (Role Model) Argument and the Wavering Adolescent. The main argument made by respected intellectuals against state recognition of gay families is that it would constitute a "stamp of approval" for relationships that are inferior to those of heterosexuals.[39] This is a kinder, gentler version of antigay discourse: for practical reasons, the state should not lock gay people in jail or mental hospitals but neither should the state give them one ounce of encouragement. It is not entirely clear how the state is giving a stamp of approval to homosexuality were it to give same-sex couples marriage licenses and rights to adopt. When the state gives different-sex couples marriage licenses, it makes no evaluation of their worth as a couple; consistent with *Turner,* every state allows convicted sex criminals to marry, but no one accuses the state of "approving" sex crimes. The policy the state is enforcing is that marriage is a good institution of commitment that the state wants to encourage. Why is such an institution not good for gay people just as it is for straights?

Like the definitional and defense of marriage arguments against equal rights for gay families, stamp of approval arguments depend heavily on hidden normative baselines. The state is not perceived as approving sex crimes or "rapist marriages" when it gives marriage licenses to convicted rapists because the state has traditionally recognized these marriages. The stamp of approval issue only arises when the state is empowering new groups. This ties in with a deeper inspiration for stamp of approval arguments, namely, parental fears that their own children might be converted to homosexuality once the state ceases to signal its strong disapproval. As one DOMA supporter put the question: "Should this Congress tell the children of America that it is a matter of indifference whether they establish families with a partner of the opposite sex or cohabit with someone of the same sex?"[40] This stamp of approval argument against same-sex marriage is similar to the role model argument against gay child custody and adoption. Indeed, such an argument makes more sense in the latter context, for the state there is supposed to be making a normative evaluation, grounded in the "best interests of the child." As a rule, are children's best interests served by denying their bonds with gay parents and relocating them in heterosexual households? To be concrete, was Tyler Doustou acquiring better role models when the state took him from his mother and her female lover and handed him over to his grandmother and her unmarried male lover?

Limitations of the Liberal Conception of Self

Without understanding their underlying force, liberal responses, including my own, have typically talked past the foregoing deep cultural objections, namely, attachment to the status quo, fear of oversexualizing the family, and concern that adolescents might "go gay." It may not be enough for the liberal to insist that neutral principles (*Zablocki*'s right to marry, *Stanley*'s right to raise children) require state recognition of gay families of choice. It may not be enough for the liberal to recall that these same kinds of arguments have been rejected in the race context (*Loving* and *Palmore*). It may not be enough for the liberal to invoke *Evans*'s warning against state caste systems segregating the homosexual. Liberals must confront the limitations of their own pro-choice philosophy.

As Chapter 7 suggested, arguments of status cannot easily be separated from arguments of choice. One's status is defined in the context of one's relationship to other people, and the liberal admits that her or his freedom is limited by the freedom of other persons. Hence, the status duties owed other persons must be valued by the liberal, especially when those duties are known to and assumed by the actor. Family law poses this connection more sharply than other areas of law. The lodestar for child custody determinations is the best interests of the child, an ideologically loaded term that seeks to assess the consequences of different custody arrangments upon the most vulnerable party. When the Virginia Supreme Court created a presumption against custody to gay parents, it cited the "intolerable burden upon [the child] by reason of the social condemnation attached to [the gay parent], which will inevitably afflict her relationships with her peers and with the community at large," an argument accepted by many other judges and legislators.[41] The interrelation of status and choice is fainter but still discernible in the context of marriage. For some heterosexuals, to give state sanction to gay marriages would be to diminish their own, which is a third-party effect of such recognition and an effect that sometimes assumes striking proportions. The context in which one's choice is assessed is infinitely elastic, and there is nothing inherent in a liberal philosophy that compels one context (what I want) over another (the effect on my prejudiced neighbor). Most liberal philosophies, to be sure, devalue "nosy preferences," but it is not clear how they can justify that move normatively.[42]

Not only have status arguments remained a part of family law, but few believe they should disappear. Consider surrogacy contracts, in which a woman needing money agrees to bear a stranger's child and to relinquish her parental rights. Such contracts and other forms of "baby selling" are a logical consequence of liberal thinking, subject to the objection that the third-party effects upon the child must be considered. Notwithstanding the libertarian appeal of surrogacy arrangments, they are prohibited in more than a dozen states and heavily regulated in other jurisdictions.[43] Opponents of such laws rely upon the liberal conception of families we choose, against which the supporters respond with the status-based argument that surrogacy laws express society's valorization of the parent-child connection as inalienable.[44] But the status-based argument can be expressed in liberal terms: the woman's choice is really not a free one because she will systematically undervalue the connection she will feel with the child as the pregnancy progresses and after the child is born. This liberal argument justifies a revocation period even in states that allow surrogacy arrangements. And the liberal arguments can be expressed in status-based terms: depriving a woman of the choice to use her body to have another's child is sexist for it rests upon old-fashioned stereotypes about the woman as nurturing.

An insight of the status-based objections to liberal gay marriage and parenting is that the acontextual self of liberalism is incomplete.[45] Human beings are not autonomous bundles of exogenously defined preferences seeking satisfaction. Instead, we are social beings struggling to make connections with one another. That the self is formed in relation to other people is most obvious in family contexts. The most important people in children's lives are their day-to-day caretakers, usually their parents. Who a child becomes will be influenced by the child's interaction with those caretakers. The parent-child connection receives and ought to receive special legal protection because it is critical to the formation of the "relational self."[46] The Virginia Supreme Court justified its decision in *Bottoms* by reference to evidence that Sharon Bottoms was a neglectful mother and that she and April Wade could not provide as stable a home as Kay Bottoms could. Straights-only adoption can be justified as a way to allocate willing parents to needy children along lines that the state thinks will be most productive for the children.

The relational self also forms by one's connection with larger society. This is the role model argument: if the adolescents, or even adults, see the state endorsing same-sex unions or lesbian families, they will internalize that approval, and that will influence their own life choices. The continuing appeal of status groups derives from both their symbolic and their practical value. By excluding gay people from marriage and family, the state sends a message of compulsory heterosexuality to young people in particular. That message, the majority hopes, will help mold adolescent preferences in the desired direction and thereby contribute to a healthy society. Is the majority's hope realistic?

An immediate problem with these arguments is that the liberal conception of predefined self may be realistic as regards sexual orientation. There is strong evidence that one's sexual orientation is more acontextual than other features of one's personality. Thus, identical twins separated at birth will usually have the same sexual orientation upon maturity.[47] The high correlation may be genetic, hormonal, or physiological, depending upon the school of medical thought one accepts.[48] The reason is not important. Whatever the cause, sexual orientation may not be relational in any meaningful way. In that event, the liberal arguments retain almost full strength. If homosexuality is hardwired, compulsory heterosexuality cruelly stigmatizes and penalizes gay people for traits they cannot control, and hurts nongay people who enter into unfulfilling relationships with closeted gays.

This new gay science is controversial, especially among gay people. Although it is likely that there is a substantial amount of hardwiring from early in life, enough to make liberal premises freshly relevant for sexual orientation, I am willing to assume—way beyond what appears plausible—that there is no genetic, hormonal, or morphological dimension to sexual orientation and that one's orientation is purely relational. Even under this heroic assumption, status-based arguments do not support state discrimination against gay families of choice.

Status-Based Arguments for Gay Families

The surrogacy issue suggests status-based arguments for overturning antigay family law rules. The mother-child connection is close to inalienable because of the mother's relational interest, which is in turn related to the best interests of the child. While a loving adoptive parent will often do just as well for the child's development, the birth mother values that particular child for its biological, emotional, and perhaps genetic connection with her own personhood. In short, from the child's perspective almost any mother will do, but from the mother's perspective her birth child is unique. This latter point, of course, can then have an effect on the former. The birth mother will sacrifice her own interests, sometimes even her own life, for the benefit of her child because she internalizes the child's interests. This process is no different for the lesbian mother than it is for the straight mother, and the love for her children is no different for either. Presumptively depriving mothers such as Sharon Bottoms of their children, as Virginia does, not only harms the mother irreparably but probably does the child no good either.

Social scientists have repeatedly found that children raised in lesbian households are as well socialized, psychologically adjusted, and capable of peer relationships as children raised in different-sex or single-parent households.[49] (Indeed, studies have thus far found no higher incidence of homosexuality in this group of children.) This is still a new area of inquiry; lengthy time series have not been reported yet, and the samples have generally been small and nonrandom.[50] Still, the consistency of the studies' findings is remarkable; no reported empirical study has conclusively found that the homosexuality of the parent has any bearing on the child's mental, psychological, or even sexual development. As to the feared third-party effects, the evidence cuts in different directions. On the one hand, when adults are not hysterical about the matter, children can readily assimilate alternative households and still relate well to conventional households. On the other hand, because so much of the social environment is antigay, some children of mother/mother households do experience stress because of the teasing.[51] But, factually, there is no evidence this is a problem mothers cannot handle, just as parents handle it in the race context.

The same application of theory and experience provides a status-based argument for gay adoption and marriage. Many people and couples cannot have biological children but feel that their lives would be incomplete without raising children. The relational self helps us understand that impulse, as the interaction with children we raise is one of the deepest forms of personal giving and growth that humans can know. The other deep form of giving and growing is through intimate unions with partners. Empirical studies of gay couples have repeatedly shown that they bond in the same way as straight couples and enjoy the same emotional benefits of partnering, including the raising of children.[52]

Consider this thought experiment. You are seated in an airplane plummeting to oblivion. What goes through your mind in the last minutes of life? For most of us, it would not be the great sex we have had, the property we have acquired, or the awards we have won. It would, instead, be the parents who nurtured us, the romances we have enjoyed, and the children we have raised. The magic moments are relational, and the memories of those we have touched and who touched us will form an indefinite chain of being between our parents and those who survive us. Straights have no monopoly on such a desire for connection. Human relationship knows no sexual orientation. For the state to single out gay people and to try to discourage their relational fulfillments epitomizes prejudice and discrimination. Antigay family law policies cannot be tolerated unless they are supported by neutral state interests.

Arguments drawing upon the idea "homosexuals are outlaws" should not survive *Evans,* for the reasons explored in Part Two of this book. In particular, arguments drawing upon stereotypes of gay people as promiscuous or predatory are derived from historical prejudice (Chapter 6) and should be discredited in public discourse. As to the role model and stamp of approval arguments, the initial inquiry is: What is the state really producing when it stigmatizes gay families? Is it producing *heterosexuals,* or is it producing *broken families*? The antigay Kulturkampf of the 1940s and 1950s produced closeted homosexuals but not genuine heterosexuals; even today, it is common for gay people to grow up in the most homophobic contexts. The closeted homosexual may indeed enter into a different-sex marriage, but such marriages have tended to be unfulfilling for both partners and painfully unfair if the straight partner is deceived.[53] Consider the race parallel. State laws against different-race relationships have never been shown to have dampened people's ardor for having them, and the outlaw sexuality inscribed in those laws could just as well have contributed to the sexiness of different-race love. (Outlaw love is definitional of erotic excitement. Recall Romeo and Juliet, Oedipus and Jocasta, Zeus and Ganymede.) What is *sexy* is not determined by fiat from above but by longing from below. The only predictable effects of state sexual stigmas are a series of boundaries that will themselves become foci of sexual speculation, adventure, and appetite.[54]

One answer to these status-based arguments is that gay people are good role models and gay couples ought to receive state stamps of approval.[55] Stories to that effect abound. Everyone knows gay people in their own lives who illustrate this precept. The social science evidence is to the same effect. Lawrence Kurdek's 1997 study of the ongoing relationships of 239 heterosexual couples, seventy-nine gay male couples, and fifty-one lesbian couples is the most thorough statistically comparative analysis of couples to date. Controlling for the other major variables, Kurdek found that the quality of the relationships over time was comparable for the gay male and straight couples, but that the lesbian couples showed a significantly higher quality of relationship after five years.[56] This particular finding suggests that same-sex marriage will provide new models from which different-sex families might learn. If woman/woman partnerships can produce unusually bonded arrangements that yield high satisfaction to women, different-sex partnerships might learn something. In short, same-sex couples are not only acceptable role models; they might be better role models than many out there now.

Kurdek also found that gay male and lesbian couples had a significantly higher separation rate than the straight couples, all of whom were married. While it is notable that most of the lesbian and gay male partnerships endured, Kurdek speculated that the lower endurance rate was due to the lack of social and legal supports for same-sex unions. It is reasonable to believe that legal recognition of same-sex marriages would improve the ability of gay partners to assess one another's level of commitment and, once committed in a legal way, enhance the durability of the relationship. In short, the state's stigmatization of gay unions undermines gay interpersonal commitment, albeit to an indeterminable extent.

It also hurts children in gay families. A few studies have found that children raised in a two-parent lesbian household are better adjusted than children raised in a single-parent household, whether the single parent is straight or lesbian. For example, Susan Golombok and her colleagues compared twenty-seven families headed by lesbians (most of them with partners) with twenty-seven families headed by single (heterosexual) mothers.[57] The researchers found no differences between the children in the two groups along most dimensions, including sex role behavior, gender security, and the ability to form and maintain peer relationships. They did find a significantly higher percentage of children with psychiatric problems in the heterosexual-mother group than in the lesbian-mother group. The hypothesis was that children raised by two adult women were better off than children raised by one adult woman. This hypothesis has been supported by a few other studies.[58] If borne out, these studies suggest the cruel irony that an illiberal state is going out of its way to hurt the children it purports to be protecting. That is, by denying lesbians and other gay people the right to marry, the state is forgoing an opportunity to reinforce the stability of the two-parent household for the children of those relationships.

Because of the double endowment effect, the evidence such as that surveyed here and in Chapter 6 will not immediately overcome society's strong presumption against same-sex marriage. The presumption will be overcome, if at all, only over decades of practical experience by extended families that integrate lesbian and gay couples, companies and municipalities that adopt domestic partnership policies, attention by the media and the Internet to marriage ceremonies and stories of same-sex couples, and accounts of same-sex unions that have been legally recognized in the Scandinavian countries and may soon be recognized in France and Germany as well. In this country, one or a few states need to recognize same-sex unions as marriage or a reasonable substitute so that the rest of the country can adapt to the social facts that same-sex marriage is definitionlly possible, does not undermine the institution of marriage, and does not elevate gay people to any special status.

Way Beyond Families We Choose: Polygamy, Partnership, and Polyparenting

The same-sex marriage debate within the gay community has also raised status-based concerns but from feminist perspectives. Paula Ettelbrick, the leading critic, maintains that gays should reject marriage and its patriarchy, and should instead seek to form their own families.[59] Most responses to Ettelbrick have been simply liberal (gays ought to have the same choices straights do), but Nan Hunter responds, more deeply, that same-sex marriage would destabilize gender-based status arrangements in traditional marriages.[60] Hunter's response enriches our thinking about the defense of marriage argument: traditionalists might be right that same-sex marriage would undermine the institution because it would undermine the patriarchal features of marriage (man works/ woman keeps house). From most feminist perspectives, those are features of marriage that *ought* to be undermined.

Another status-based argument appeals to a different feature of the institution of marriage: commitment. A decision to marry is a decision to foreclose one's future choices, a commitment to consider the interests of another person in the future. The promise and expectation of partnership and commitment are valuable for reasons of both personal security and the fulfillment of self. We are all products of our own parent-child relationships, and the healthiest such relationships were ones where the child felt secure about the parent's commitment to the child. The mutual love between parent and child is usually in part a consequence of the mutual expectation that the relationship will be a lasting one. An analogous point can be made about partnership relations: they will have deeper meaning and significance for the relational self if they are conducted within a mutual understanding of lasting commitment. As Milton Regan has argued, status—including the status of spousehood—protects people's capacity for intimacy and thereby fosters a stable sense of self over time. The stable sense of self is at risk in a society of nothing but choice because such a world fractures self. (Buridan's ass, the animal that found itself equidistant from two haystacks and starved because it could not choose between them, may be an early example of the fractured personality, torn apart by too many choices.)

The commitment and antipatriarchy arguments for same-sex marriage provide a basis for evaluating "domestic partnership" laws that have been adopted in many American jurisdictions. Virtually all of the domestic partnership laws provide only one or two tangible benefits for the domestic partners, typically hospital visitation and spousal benefits if one of the partners is a municipal employee.[61] The main problem with these laws, however, is not their ridiculously skimpy array of *benefits* but their failure to insist on partnership *obligations*. Dissolving domestic partnerships is as easy as filling out a form, and therefore such arrangements do little to cement the interpersonal commitment of the domestic partners. Without some attention to reciprocal obligations, the domestic partnership movement is an empty liberalism. Similar problems inhere in efforts to litigate statutory benefits for same-sex couples on a benefit-by-benefit basis. Without insisting on the responsibilities and obligations of marriage along with the benefits, liberals are missing the main functional point of marriage.

Short of marriage itself, a better model is the "registered partnership" statutes adopted in Denmark and several other northern European countries.[62] These laws provide all the obligations as well as almost all the benefits of marriage but not the name. Even diluted versions of registered partnership laws could be useful for the United States so long as they include obligations as well as benefits. Such laws could be a social experiment along the lines suggested by Hunter. Same-sex couples would be able to marry in the eyes of religions and social communities that recognize their unions as marriages, and the state would back up their interpersonal commitments with tangible obligations making the unions harder to dissolve. Whatever the legal name of the institution thus created, it could stand as a less gendered counterexample to patriarchal marriage. Indeed, I would urge that such partnerships be open to transgendered people and different-sex couples as well as to lesbian and gay couples.

Would this social experiment be subject to the slippery slope? The arguments of Hunter and Regan for same-sex marriage or registered partnerships could be applied to polygamy. From a liberal, choice-based perspective, it is hard to argue against polygamy. If a man and two women desire to become a family unit, and all three consent to the arrangement, why should the state not recognize it and accord it legal benefits and obligations of marriage? The liberal who believes that "rarely is a person better off by having an option removed" is hard-pressed to deny this recognition.[63] The main liberal reservation would be that polygamy undermines women's equal enjoyment of marital benefits in ways not appreciated when women consent to the arrangement. Women's bargaining position within the male-female marriage is bad enough due to traditional role expectations and women's lower earning power.[64] It could be worse under polygamy because competition among the wives would give the husband a unique bargaining position that would often be exploited. From a status-based perspective, the question would be: Does polygamy undermine the mutuality of commitment, the greater security of self that marriage offers? The concern of both liberal (choice) and feminist (status) theory is that polygamy as it would typically be practiced in the United States, with one man taking on plural wives, would tend to diminish the wives' security over time and, with it, the mutuality of the relationships.

On the other hand, some plural wives in fundamentalist Mormon communities today testify that this does not occur; polygamy may even enhance commitment by encouraging mutually loving sisterhood as well as spousehood within a family unit that frees wives from many of the unequal burdens of monogamous marriages.[65] This is an attractive proposition, but can it be generalized? Carol Rose invokes game theory and the history of Mormon polygamy to that effect.[66] Assuming that women are, or are perceived to be, more cooperative than men, Rose maintains that in a system of monogamous different-sex marriage a certain number of cooperative women will be stuck with "loutish," noncooperative men. Once that occurs, women will steadily lose ground during the marriage because their loutish husbands will hold out for advantages and the wives will give in over and over. Rose suggests polygamy as a solution: cooperative men will attract most of the cooperative women, leaving the louts with what they deserve (being alone in their loutishness) and giving the next generation of men incentives not to be as loutish. She refers to examples of happy plural marriages among Mormons, past and present, where the wives testified to the advantages of sisterhood and division of labor.

Rose's game theory has several holes. Choice is made with ridiculously incomplete information. Women often end up with louts because the prospective husband conceals his loutishness during courtship, or because the husband grows increasingly loutish during marriage. Moreover, escape options are limited. Although women can bail out of marriages to louts, many choose not to because of sunk costs (children) or wasting assets (the aging woman thinks she cannot attract a new mate of good quality). Most important, Rose's game theory provides no basis for believing that the parties to the game will, over time, internalize the relational preferences that are necessary for the "commitment" needed by the relational self. The history of plural marriage among Mormons in the nineteenth century is not uniformly encouraging.[67] Mormon leaders Joseph Smith and Orson Pratt, leading theologians of polygamy, took plural wives, to the dismay of their first spouses, Emma Smith and Sarah Pratt. The latter suffered through Orson's inattention to their thirteen children and his obsession with marrying younger women. Sarah ended their marriage in 1868 and condemned polygamy because it "completely demoralizes good men, and makes bad men correspondingly worse. As for the women—well, God help them! First wives it renders desperate, or else heart-broken, mean-spirited creatures."[68] Other plural wives spoke in opposition to Sarah Pratt's unkind words, and it is impossible to tell how widely shared her views were. Mormon historians have found 20 to 25 percent breakup rates for plural marriages; friendship rather than romantic relationships as the norm for husbands and wives; and distant or nonexistent relationships between children and the fathers in polygamous marriages.[69] Accounts of plural marriages in polygamist communities in today's West are similarly inconclusive. Some polygamous families are apparently situses of flourishing, while others have been situses for uxorial loneliness and child abuse.[70]

The evidence from Mormon history is at best suggestive. It suggests *both* that the "men are louts" argument sees polygamy through Rose-colored glasses *and* that neither liberal nor feminist opponents of polygamy can decisively show that recognizing it would hurt marriage or women's interests. The "men are louts" argument should be explored further. One avenue for exploration is that suggested by Hunter's defense of same-sex marriage: if men are louts and women are relationship-building, same-sex marriage is the best idea of all. Unless a woman is strongly committed to having regular heterosexual intercourse—an exercise many women enjoy less than their male partners—same-sex unions or marriages offer her more advantages than polygamy, as she will be cooperating with other on-the-whole cooperative women. With the possibility of cloning and gene-splicing on the horizon, female couples can have their own genetic children without men's help at all. Whatever their orientations, women committed to raising children should, under Rose's logic, consider having them in female-female rather than male-female-female unions. Why isn't polygamy without the lout the best option of all?

This lesbian nation twist on Rose's theory provides another reason the same-sex marriage experiment needs to be tried in at least one state. Consider another gaylegal experiment: "polyparenting." Our legal system separates legal obligations to partners from those owed to children. If persons one and two are married, they owe marital obligations to one another; either or both owe separate obligations to children they might have. Person one might have other independent obligations to her or his child outside of marriage with person three. In second-parent adoptions, the female partner of a child's biological mother can adopt the child and be its "second mother."[71] For the relational reasons suggested earlier, second-parent adoption is a good institution—good for the two women and good for the children. Should it be extended to the biological father of the child?

Courts interpreting their states' adoption statutes to allow two women or two men (the biological parent and her or his partner) to be legal parents rely on the gender neutrality of the adoption statutes.[72] A child can have two legal mommies. At least some adoption statutes are ambiguous as to the number of parents a child can have. Why might a child not have two legal mommies and a legal daddy? Problems with such a proposal include the possibilities of diluted commitment by each parent or, more likely, greater conflicts among committed parents.[73] Like Rose's polygamy argument, these problems cannot be evaluated without more experience and evidence. To obtain that experience and evidence, one jurisdiction should openly allow "third-parent" adoptions, where the mother's partner adopts the child with explicit preservation of both the biological mother's and the biological father's parental rights. The proposal is animated by the relational opportunities that are lost to the father/sperm donor and to the child if the biological father loses all parental rights upon a second-parent adoption. Correlatively, surrogate mothers ought to be able, at least in some cases, to maintain their parental rights even though the biological father's female or male partner adopts the child.

The following chart roughly maps the new kinds of rules that families of choice challenge the law to accept:

	No binariness assumptions	No gendered assumptions
Reform for marriage	Polygamy	Same-sex Marriage
	Not yet, open in future	Not yet, yes for future
Reform for childrearing	Polyparents	Second-parent adoption
	Unclear, open in future	On the way to yes

Strong liberalism should endorse all four of the moves in the chart. The post-liberal idea of a relational self also supports same-sex marriage and second-parent adoption, urges experimentation with polyparenting, and is less negative about polygamy than might be expected. My own thinking about polyparenting makes me more open to Rose-type arguments for polygamy. If issues of ego, jealousy, and coordination problems can be resolved in polyparenting, I would be more inclined to believe that they could be managed in polygamy.

9. Religion and Homosexuality: Equality Practice

Conflicts among religious and ethnic groups have pervaded American history. Some conflicts have involved campaigns of suppression against minority religious and ethnic groups by the mainstream. There is now, however, a public law consensus to protect the autonomy of religious and ethnic subcultures as well as the ability of their members to self-identify without penalty. Such a public law consensus ought to extend to sexual orientation minorities as well.

Like religion, sexual orientation marks both personal identity and social divisions. In this century, sexual orientation has replaced religion as a key element of personal identity that situates that person within society. In 1900 one's identity was defined by one's ethnicity, social class, sex, and religion. The norm was Anglo-Saxon, middle-class, male, Protestant. The Jew, Catholic immigrant, or rural black was considered deviant and was subject to social, economic, and political discrimination. In 2000 one's identity is defined by one's race, income, sex, and sexual orientation. The norm is white, middle-income, male, heterosexual. The lesbian, gay man, or transgendered person is considered deviant and is subject to social, economic, and political discrimination. Although America has internalized the idea of *benign religious variation* and is moving toward benign gender variation, it rejects the idea of *benign sexual variation*. Just as most Americans in 1900 viewed significant religious deviation as strange, shameful, or wicked, so most in 2000 view significant sexual deviation as strange, shameful, or wicked.

The connection of religion and sexuality has another dimension. Religious precepts are invoked as a reason for rejecting the idea of benign sexual variation. Although the rhetoric of family values and sexual abstinence is increasingly secular, it resonates with and is often inspired by religious doctrine. Along with abortion and school prayer, gay rights issues have helped galvanize religious activism in the political arena.[1] Gay rights rhetoric, in turn, seeks to relocate policy away from the sex negativity integral to many American religions. A goal of this chapter is to explore common ground between religious and sexual communities and to suggest some rules for a neutral state to follow that accommodate their differences.[2]

Religious and sexual subcultures have value-laden visions for the lives of their members and for the larger society as well. They tend to be, in Robert Cover's language, *nomic* communities, people bonded by associations that preserve and develop a common normative heritage.[3] Nomic communities have a vision of what is morally good. That evolving vision constitutes an internal law that guides the lives of their members. Cover saw religious groups as the classic law-creating, or *jurisgenerative*, communities. For all but the most insular religious groups, their visions of value and law compete with those of other communities, which today would include gay communities.[4] In the case of nomic communities competing to persuade the polity of their different values, Cover said, the judiciary stood available as a *jurispathic*, or law-killing, institution. The very office of judging arises out of the need "to suppress law, to choose between two or more laws, to impose upon laws a hierarchy."[5]

Cover's understanding of contending visions of law, only one of which will survive the lethal eye of the judge, was echoed and contested by Justice Antonin Scalia's dissenting opinion in *Romer v. Evans* (1996), the Colorado initiative case. Echoing Cover, Scalia charged the Court with mistaking a "Kulturkampf," which he probably meant as a culture clash between fundamentalist and progay *nomoi*, with a vicious "fit of spite."[6] Contesting Cover, Scalia denied that courts must play a jurispathic role and maintained that courts should remain neutral in such culture clashes. Ironically, the term chosen by Scalia supports Cover's view that it is hard for the judiciary to be neutral. Historically, "Kulturkampf" means a state war to assimilate a threatening minority or to force it into a state-directed conformity. The first Kulturkampf, the campaign that gave rise to the term, was German Chancellor Otto von Bismarck's effort between 1871 and 1887 to yoke the Roman Catholic Church to the ideal of German nationalism through state control over Catholic education, priests, and institutions.[7]

Scalia's dissent relied on two precedents of the Court as exemplars of law's neutrality that instead revealed unusually assaultive jurispathy. Two prominent examples of Kulturkampf in the United States during the last 100 years were the campaign in the 1880s to discipline the Church of Jesus Christ of Latter Day Saints and the campaign in the 1950s to suppress homosexuality. The anti-Mormon Kulturkampf was ratified by the Supreme Court's decision in *Davis v. Beason* (1890) (among other cases), which Scalia invoked for the proposition that a community can be excluded from privileges of citizenship if there is popular moral disapproval of its members' consensual practices. The antihomosexual Kulturkampf was ratified by the Court's decision in *Bowers v. Hardwick* (1986) (among other cases), which Scalia invoked for the proposition that gay people can be excluded from at least some privileges of citizenship if there is popular moral disapproval of their consensual practices.[8] Both decisions relied on mainstream religious traditions to place sexualized groups (Mormons and homosexuals) outside of the law because of their deviant consensual conduct (polygamy and sodomy).

Starting with the Kulturkampf connection, this chapter argues that religion and sexual orientation have much in common as identity categories, that antireligious prejudice is systematically similar to antigay prejudice, and that the religion clauses of the first amendment as they have been interpreted are a model for the state's treatment of sexuality. The first amendment's protections of free speech, association, and press are the leading constitutional assurances against Kulturkampf. The religion clauses embody a more particularized vision of nomic diversity along lines of religious belief. The free exercise clause of the first amendment, as the Court has read it, prevents the state from censoring or discriminating against deviant religious belief. The establishment clause prevents the state from enforcing religious orthodoxy. Similar rules against censorship, discrimination, and orthodoxy are being developed by courts and legislatures to protect sexual orientation minorities as well. The religion clauses illustrate a more general public law insight: the state must allow individual nomic communities to flourish or wither as they may, and the state cannot as a normal matter become the means for the triumph of one community over all others. This is a constitutionalism that is inspired by the positive value of diversity and by the negative experiences of Kulturkampf, exemplified historically by both gay and religious experience.

Gay and religious experience should join in opposing state Kulturkampf, but they often part company when the state guarantees homo equality. With the advent of laws prohibiting sexual orientation discrimination (Appendix B2), religious liberty and sexual equality norms collide, and their collision entails a clash of constitutional commitments—between the liberty of one group to exclude and the desire of an excluded group for equal treatment. Cover is right to tell us that in situations of direct clash the state typically cannot remain neutral, but he provides few insights as to how the state ought to resolve the clash.

Among the most interesting and important cases are those involving direct or indirect clashes between religious and gay communities. Emblematic is the controversy between Georgetown University and the Gay Rights Coalition, an early gay, lesbian, and bisexual student group.[9] The Georgetown case provides a rich context within which to discuss different ways of treating the equality and liberty interests of gay and religious interests. The judicial resolution of the controversy was jurisgenerative in a way that respected the Roman Catholic *nomos* without unduly compromising public commitments to equal gay citizenship.

Indeed, the phenomenology of "coming out of the closet" suggests principles that illuminate the Georgetown case, especially the value of identity speech and its relevance for both sides of the controversy, and that lend support to the court's Georgetown opinion, especially its accommodation of each side's identity needs and the encouragement of nomic dialogue. Most generally, the jurisprudence of coming out contributes to the public law project of understanding and constructively resolving identity clashes, a project initiated by Kenneth Karst and others.[10] The last portions of this chapter apply these ideas to other clashes involving the constitutionality of applying antidiscrimination statutes to require religious groups to accommodate people they view as sexual sinners.

Identity in America: Connections between Religion and Sexuality

While often at loggerheads, religion and sexual orientation have much in common as identity categories. Similarly, antireligious prejudice has manifested itself in American history in ways not unlike antihomosexual prejudice. The two great American Kulturkämpfe of the last century involved groups defined by their religion (Mormons in the 1880s) and sexual orientation (homosexuals in the 1950s). The first amendment has been read to prohibit censorship of, discrimination against, and orthodoxy of religion. The normative reasons for protecting religious belief and *nomos* apply just as well to censorship of, discrimination against, and orthodoxy in matters of sexual orientation.

Religion and Sexuality as Categories of Identity and Prejudice

Chapter 6 argued that sexual orientation operates much like race, ethnicity, religion, and sex as a dividing characteristic that can blind decisionmakers to the objective merits of individuals. Specifically refuted was the argument that sexual orientation discrimination is different from religious discrimination because it is conduct- rather than status-based. In addition to their mix of cognition and conduct, religion and sexual orientation are identity categories that have other common features.

One's sex, race, and ethnicity are usually apparent upon casual observation, unless the person makes an effort to cloak these characteristics. In contrast, one's religion and sexual orientation are not apparent, unless one is making an effort to self-identify. We reveal our religious or sexual identities only by what we say and what religious- or sexual-specific conduct we engage in. Thus, a religious or sexual orientation minority can almost always "pass" for mainstream, simply by expressing the religious or sexual views associated with the majority and keeping secret the conduct characteristic of one's minority group.[a] More important, religious and sexual identity is dependent upon the ability and willingness both to express the identity and to engage in activities characteristic of the identity.[b]

One's sex, race, and ethnicity are popularly seen as biologically determined in a straightforward way: they are invariably derived from the sex, race, and ethnicity of one's parents. Although one's religion and sexual orientation are usually the same as those of one's parents, they need not be and often are not. That the impulse behind religion and sexual orientation is not predetermined creates room for speculation, conversion, and nosy intervention. There is a human tendency to view one's own religion and sexual orientation as *given*, impelled by inner needs or external forces, but to view a "deviant" religion or sexual orientation as *chosen* for some perverse reason. Although religion may be easier to change than sexual orientation (the conversion experience), that attitude is wrong in both cases. One rarely "shops" for a religion or sexual orientation; the impulse comes from feelings we do not consciously process.

Finally, religion and sexual orientation tend to be more nomic than the other identity categories. Both are emotional and are characterized by bonding with a cohort of people linked by similar emotions and beliefs, moments of ritual ecstasy and fantasy, and fascination with sumptuary pomp. Religious and

a. Ethnicity is particularly porous. See Eve Kosofsky Sedgwick, *The Epistemology of the Closet* 75–81 (1990), discussing the story of Queen Esther, who "comes out" as a Jew. Women have passed for men throughout Western history, and some people can pass for one of a different race. The point in the text is that these cases are exceptional, while religious and sexual minorities routinely pass.

b. Hence the famous Kinsey scale of sexual orientation considers the person's self-identification, erotic fantasies, and actual sexual activities. A Kinsey *six* is someone who identifies as a homosexual, is only attracted sexually to people of the same sex, and has had primarily same-sex experiences. Alfred Kinsey et al., *Sexual Behavior in the Human Male,* 638–641 (1948). A similar exercise can be conducted for religion. A devout Catholic (a John Paul *six)* is someone who identifies as a Catholic, believes most Catholic theology, and regularly takes Communion, goes to confession, and so forth.

sexual orientation communities are institutionalized, albeit in different ways. Religious community is focused around the local church or congregation, which is usually the lowest rung in a larger hierarchy; sexual community is more loosely focused around a larger variety of subcultural institutions, including churches, newspapers, professional associations and social clubs, and gay ghettos.

Given these striking similarities between religion and sexual orienation, it is not surprising that antireligious prejudice in American history strongly resembles more recent antihomosexual prejudice. Most religious groups that are considered mainstream today have been the objects of intolerance and state-imposed disabilities in the past, including Jews, Roman Catholics, and Baptists.[11] Like disabilities placed upon homosexuality, those placed on certain religions stem from people's firm belief that their religion is universally true *and* that the existence of other religions is harmful. When the orthodoxy is premature and the paranoia unjustified by demonstrable harm, apart from the anxiety created in the fearful mind, we call it *animus* or *prejudice*. Persecution and Kulturkampf flow from prejudice when majority culture feels insecure in general and threatened by a minority gaining in social power or public visibility.

Nativist and racist hysteria was the characteristic reaction in the United States to periods of intense social tension until World War I; the objects of nativist hysteria were ethnic and, especially, religious minorities. Ideological and sexual (as well as racist) hysteria has been the characteristic reaction in the United States to periods of intense social tension since World War I. The scholarship describing antireligious prejudice in the United States and other Western societies discovers the same pattern as that found in antigay prejudice: disempowered segments of the majority demonize or scapegoat "deviants" as social threats and invoke their supposed predation as a justification for violence against deviants.[12] Specific tropes include warnings that the polity faces irrevocable decline because of corrosive forces within the polity; depiction of the despised group as dirty, immoral, lecherous, subversive, disloyal, and militant, based upon unrepresentative examples or simple fabrications; and fixation on the ways in which the despised group is bent on "recruiting" other Americans, particularly the young. Antireligious discourse is characterized by the same rhetoric as the antihomosexual discourse discussed in Chapters 2 and 6: *hysterical* attribution of dirty sexual features to a dehumanized minority, *obsession* with asserted predation by its members, and *narcissistic* deployment of the minority's otherness to bond the majority into its own group identity.

Once mobilized, social prejudice against a religious or sexual minority aims at erasure of the minority and its *nomos*. The extreme goal is elimination— from outright genocide to expulsion and exile to forced conversion. The moderate goal is assimilation, where the minority renounces its most distinctive nomic values. Whatever the ultimate goal, the processes for achieving it are expensive, requiring great mobilization of state apparatus to hunt down deviants and reprogram, expel, or imprison them. Because such a campaign is so costly, it usually does not last long and is succeeded by an accommodation of some sort. Sometimes the accommodation is a truce premised on the view that the deviant group has survived.[13] More often, it is premised on the view that the deviant *nomos* has been crushed and can be assimilated into the mainstream culture.[14] In the latter instance, a remnant of the deviant minority goes underground, typically with the understanding that the state will not seriously look for them. This regime, where members of the minority accept their shameful status and keep their identity secret in exchange for survival, is the closet.

Anti-Mormon and Antihomosexual Kulturkämpfe in the United States

The process described in the last paragraph is Kulturkampf. The classic Kulturkämpfe in western history have been religious ones, such as the Spanish pogroms between 1391 and 1482, which produced the Marranos (Jews who converted to Catholicism); the religious purges and wars of the late sixteenth and early seventeenth centuries; and secular campaigns against the Roman Catholic Church and Judaism in Europe as well as the United States in the mid- and late nineteenth century.[15] The most ambitious Kulturkämpfe undertaken by the United States in the last century further illustrate conceptual and tangible connections between religious and sexual deviance.

After the 1840s, the Church of Jesus Christ of Latter Day Saints (LDS) encouraged its members to engage in plural marriage. Polygamy generated considerable anti-Mormon sentiment that pressed the community to relocate in the Utah Territory, where the federal government became the Mormons' chief foe. In 1874 Mormon elder George Reynolds was convicted of the federal crime of bigamy; the Supreme Court rejected his free exercise claim in *Reynolds v. United States* (1878), holding that Reynolds' admittedly sincere religious beliefs could not redeem his crime. Polygamy, the Court ruled, was "odious" conduct that undermined not just marriage but the stability of the polity as well.[16] The antibigamy law that Reynolds was convicted of violating was the precursor of a broader campaign to destroy the LDS so long as its members adhered to polygamy.[17] The Edmunds Act of 1882 made "unlawful cohabitation" (easier to prove than polygamy) a federal crime, deprived polygamists of their right to vote and to serve on juries or in public office, and offered amnesty to polygamists who renounced their religious practice. Although Apostle John Henry Smith testified that the legislators "were filled with venom" and acted out of an "evil design," the Supreme Court did not consider the design evil enough to be unconstitutional.[18]

All three branches of the federal government united against the Mormon *nomos,* and a Kulturkampf followed. More than 1,000 Mormon polygamists, or "cohabs," were hunted down by federal marshals, convicted by juries packed with non-Mormons, and sent to jail. Yet Mormon resistance continued. The federal government responded with the Edmunds-Tucker Act of 1887, which disenfranchised not only polygamists but also any person advocating polygamy, confiscated the property of the LDS Church, made it easier to prove guilt in polygamy cases, declared children of plural marriages illegitimate and prohibited inheritance from their parents, and abolished all elective offices and female suffrage in Utah. The Supreme Court upheld these various invasions of civil and religious liberties in *Beason* and a companion case.[19]

Those decisions confirmed the constitutional sanction for an anti-Mormon Kulturkampf. The campaign was successful in that the LDS leadership officially abandoned polygamy in this life as a religious principle after *Beason.* The campaign was less successful in that it drove polygamy underground. Leading Mormons continued to practice plural marriage for years after the church's capitulation, and after the LDS hierarchy actually abandoned plural marriages many faithful continued to embrace them. Today there are communities of fundamentalist Mormons who preach and practice polygamy in this life as religious principle.[20]

There are striking parallels between the anti-Mormon Kulturkampf of the 1880s and the antihomosexual Kulturkampf of the 1950s, described in Chapter 2. Just as the long-standing crime of bigamy was mobilized as a mechanism for regulating Mormon plural marriage, so the long-standing crimes of sodomy, indecency, and cross-dressing were deployed as a mechanism for regulating homosexual intimacy and excluding gay people from working for the government, entering the country, or holding professional licenses. Just as the judiciary upheld novel and heightened penalties against Mormon polygamists, the judiciary upheld novel and heightened penalties against homosexual sodomites.[21] *Hardwick* is a modern echo of *Reynolds,* for in both cases sexual activities were criminalized and defendants demonized because their behavior was inconsistent with traditional religious morality.

Constitutional Protections against Kulturkampf

Reynolds, Beason, and other decisions ratifying the anti-Mormon Kulturkampf are in tension with the first amendment, discussed in Chapters 3 and 5. The right of association the Supreme Court has found in the amendment assures nomic communities the right to band together without state suppression or harassment. The community and its members have explicit first amendment rights to speak freely, to assemble peaceably, to lobby the government, and to publish their views. The religion clauses, preventing the state from burdening religious free exercise and from establishing a state religion, reflect more general constitutional principles of anticensorship, nondiscrimination, and rejection of orthodoxy: the state must allow nomic communities to flourish or wither as they may, and the state cannot as a normal matter become the means for the triumph of one community over all others.

The anti-Mormon decisions are inconsistent with developments in American public law, albeit developments only possible because the political culture has internalized the idea of benign religious variation. *Reynolds* is at odds with the Supreme Court's privacy precedents, which provide some assurance that people can make their own cohabitation decisions, and is inconsistent with the Court's free exercise jurisprudence, which holds that the state cannot target a particular religion under the aegis of neutrally regulating conduct.[22] Even if *Reynolds* were good law, *Beason* would not be. The Court's free speech jurisprudence is inconsistent with *Beason*'s holding that the state can criminally punish mere advocacy of polygamy; the cases recognizing a fundamental right to vote would probably require a different result; and the free exercise clause prohibits the state from destroying an entire religion simply because popular majorities consider its practices immoral.[23]

The religion clauses disable the state from imposing religious orthodoxy, from discriminating against disfavored religions, and, generally, from conducting an antireligious Kulturkampf such as the anti-Mormon campaign and Bismarck's campaign against the Catholic Church. The religion clauses teach that forced conformity in matters of faith is not a goal justifying the human suffering, anger, and cruelty imposed by such campaigns. The underlying principle is *benign religious variation:* it is both acceptable and good that we are a nation of diverse religious communities. It is acceptable because there is no one religious truth and the practice of forced conversion is inconsistent with fundamental freedom. Religious diversity is good because it offers spiritual and emotional satisfaction to a broad range of people, including gay people, many of whom worship in mainstream denominations or in gay-oriented Metropolitan Community Churches all around the country.[24]

Given the similarities between religion and sexual orientation, religious and sexual *nomoi,* and antireligious and antihomosexual prejudice, similar precepts should govern the American public law of sexuality: the state is presumed to have no authority to engage in a Kulturkampf against sexual minorities; the state has a presumptive duty not to censor people's sexual expression or discriminate on that ground; the underlying principle is one of *benign sexual variation,* which recognizes that it is both acceptable and good that we are a nation of diverse sexualities. There are no "sexuality clauses" in the Constitution analogous to the religion clauses, but all three precepts can inform judges' reading of the due process and equal protection obligations of the Constitution. As Justice Scalia complained in his dissenting opinion, *Evans* opens up the due process and equal protection clauses to such a reading.

A Jurisprudence of Coming Out: Gaylegal Precepts for Reconciling Colliding Liberty and Equality Norms

The precepts of benign religious and sexual variation support affirmative as well as negative obligations for the state. Just as the state is constitutionally prohibited from engaging in public antireligious or antigay censorship or discrimination, so it should be encouraged to prohibit private censorship or discrimination on the basis of religion or sexual orientation. Just as the Civil Rights Act of 1964 prohibits discrimination because of religion in employment and public accommodation, the laws of eleven states and more than 150 cities and counties prohibit discrimination because of sexual orientation in employment; many of these jurisdictions also prohibit sexual orientation discrimination in public accommodations, education, housing, or credit (Appendix B2). Because these antidiscrimination laws necessarily restrict economic liberties of employers, landlords, banks, and public accommodations, they have presented fresh constitutional problems. Among the most difficult problems involve collisions of the norms of religious liberty and sexual orientation equality. Consider the case of *Gay Rights Coalition of Georgetown University Law Center v. Georgetown University* (1987).[25]

Georgetown University in Washington, D.C., is affiliated with the Roman Catholic Church. While there are no religious tests for admission or employment at the university, most trustees are typically officers of the Church, and its president has since 1825 always been a member of the Society of Jesus (the Jesuits). In 1977 two groups of gay students organized at the university's main campus and law center. Their stated goals were nomic, to foster "an atmosphere in which gay people can develop a sense of pride, self-worth, awareness and community" (main campus group) and to provide information to lesbian and gay students about the area's gay community (law center group). Beginning in academic year 1978–79, the main campus group sought university "recognition" that would give it access to services and benefits, such as an office, routinely available to other student groups. Reasoning that university recognition would imply approval of gay activities, contrary to Catholic religious doctrine,

Georgetown denied the students' first application in 1979 and every other application after that.

The student groups sued Georgetown, arguing that its refusal to recognize them and make available services and benefits accorded other student groups violated the District's Human Rights Act (1977), which makes it "an unlawful discriminatory practice . . . for an educational institution . . . to deny, restrict or to abridge or condition the use of, or access to, any of its facilities and services to any person otherwise qualified, wholly or partially, for a discriminatory reason, based upon . . . sexual orientation."[26] Georgetown argued that any state requirement that it recognize or support a gay group would be compelled speech and a burden on the free exercise of religion, both invalid under the first amendment. These arguments prevailed at trial, and the students appealed.

The seven judges who heard the appeal wrote seven different opinions. The judgment of the court was delivered by Judge Julia Cooper Mack, who interpreted the Human Rights Act to require Georgetown to provide the student groups with equal access and benefits but not to require it to grant official recognition to the groups. Mack narrowed the broad language of the statute to avoid constitutional problems but ruled that the statute's core demand, that the students receive equal access, was a strong state interest justifying less direct burdens on Georgetown's religious mission.[27] Dissenting opinions argued that Mack's resolution was unprincipled. Judge John Ferren criticized her acceptance of a regime that treated gay groups differently from other groups. Ferren maintained that university recognition would not have been tantamount to endorsement and that remediation of discrimination is a compelling state interest justifying any abridgment of Georgetown's first amendment rights.[28] Conversely, Judge James Belson took the court to task for forcing Georgetown "to subsidize activities by those groups that offend the religious beliefs to which the university adheres," and Judge Frank Nebeker added that there could be no compelling state interest in such forced speech because of the "felonious" nature of the "conduct inherent in homosexual 'life-style.' "[29]

Gay Rights Coalition illustrates our normative heterogeneity, and a strength of Mack's opinion is that it values the claims of both *nomoi*. The Roman Catholic community in which the court situated Georgetown is a world-creating *nomos*, for it draws upon a common tradition in which its members are educated and which provides the community with "a sense of direction of growth that is constituted as the individual and his community work out the implications of their law"; it is a "strong community of common obligations" and common "initiatory, celebratory, expressive, and performative" discourse.[30] The Catholic *nomos*, including Georgetown University, offers "homosexuals" compassion and inclusion so long as they renounce "homosexual behavior" as a sin.[31] Mack's starting point was the principle that the human rights law be interpreted in light of free exercise principles, but her opinion also recognized the birthing of a new *nomos,* the gay community. Though different from the Catholic Church, the gay community shares some of its nomic characteristics, including similar experiences that have engendered a common framework of thinking about a wide range of issues; formal organizations for reporting and comparing those experiences, expressing group identity, and developing group positions; and a collective commitment to implementing shared values in people's lives. The human rights law represented the District's devotion to ameliorating antigay discrimination, to which the state had contributed after World War II, and Mack's opinion invoked that value to justify the statute's requirement that even religiously affiliated schools have to provide facilities and services to gay students.

The objections to Mack's resolution are serious. Ferren charged that her interpretation of the statute "permits a 'separate but equal' access to university facilities reminiscent of the justification that once permitted blacks on public buses, but only in the back."[32] Ferren's argument is supported by the Supreme Court's decision in *Bob Jones University v. United States* (1983), which interpreted the Internal Revenue Code to strip Bob Jones of its exemption as a charitable institution because it discriminated on the basis of race. Bob Jones argued that its policy, prohibition of interracial dating and marriage among students, was mandated by its fundamentalist religious beliefs. The Court rejected the constitutional defense because the burden served the "fundamental, overriding interest in eradicating racial discrimination in education—discrimination that prevailed, with official approval, for the first 165 years of this Nation's constitutional history."[33] (A majority of the judges in *Gay Rights Coalition* ruled that fighting sexual orientation discrimination has been just as much a priority for the District as fighting race discrimination.)

Belson, on the other hand, charged that Mack's interpretation forced a Catholic institution to support students in sacrilegious advocacy and pornography. This was not just a burden on free expression and the exercise of faith; it was state direction to church officials to violate their faith.[34] His argument is supported by the Supreme Court's decision in *Wooley v. Maynard* (1977), which held that the first amendment prevented New Hampshire from requiring a Jehovah's Witness couple to display the state motto, "Live Free or Die," on the license plate of their car. Because the state measure "forces an individual as part of his daily life ... to be an instrument for fostering public adherence to an ideological point of view he finds unacceptable," it implicated core first amendment interests, whose sacrifice was hardly justified by the administrative (traffic control) and ideological (state pride) reasons advanced by the government.[35]

Common ground for Mack, Ferren, and Belson was that antidiscrimination and free exercise/speech norms collided, and their collision reflected two nomic communities in conflict. Where the judges differed was how to resolve disputes among colliding norms and how to calibrate the legal entitlements of the clashing groups. Only Mack recognized, properly, that the precedents did not cleanly resolve the case. Authorities like *Wooley* demonstrated that Georgetown's free speech and free expression were implicated, but authorities like *Bob Jones* demonstrated that reducing historical discrimination was a compelling state interest that could justify some burdens on first amendment interests. Both *Wooley* (where the state interests were so weak) and *Bob Jones* (where the state interest was the exceptionally important one of reducing race discrimination) were easier cases than Georgetown's case, however.

The most striking distinction of Mack's opinion is its avoidance of traditional rights discourse and its focus on community needs and nomic interests. Rather than speaking accusatorily of the "violation" of Georgetown's free exercise "rights," or of Georgetown's violation of the students' rights of "full citizenship" in the university community, as her dissenting brethren did, Mack discussed the "burden . . . on Georgetown's religious exercise," and the "interest" of the larger community in eliminating discrimination based on sexual orientation.[36] In her treatment of the colliding liberty and equality norms, Mack's opinion was even more distinctive, for she was open to long-submerged voices and sought reasonable accommodation of their needs, but not at the expense of core values of religious autonomy.

Mack's accommodationist approach is subject to the charge that she was just splitting the difference for political rather than principled reasons; the approach can be defended from a pragmatist viewpoint as Solomonic. Elsewhere I have admired Mack's approach to colliding norms by appealing to feminist and republican theories of law.[37] Here I appreciate her approach and her resolution from the perspective of a gaylegal jurisprudence. Reading my account of the debate within the court, the reader might be surprised that the Gay Rights Coalition argued for the Mack position, not for the Ferren position. There were strategic considerations involved in the students' arguments, but they also reflected the best jurisprudential insights of the gay experience and the phenomenology of coming out of the closet.

The students' desire to form a campus group was an effort to oppose the sexual closet at all levels: students would find a supportive group as they struggled with issues of their sexuality; a gay *nomos* would be established at Georgetown, one that was linked to the District's subculture; and gay political power would be asserted against the shame of the closet. There is a jurisprudence suggested by the coming out experience[38] that can generate ideas relevant to the collision of the first amendment and equality norms in cases like *Gay Rights Coalition.* Although the ideas suggested by the coming out phenomenology are not unique to gaylaw, they are distinctive to it, and to the extent they are consonant with precepts drawn from other sources (such as feminism) their value is enhanced.

The Value of Identity Speech. Once a culture has elevated one personal trait to the level of an identity characteristic, that characteristic becomes socially relevant. Where the characteristic is not apparent from appearance or a social signal, others will assume the person is like the majority, and people who actually are like the majority need say nothing. For religious and sexual minorities, it is both more important and harder to self-identify. It is more important to self-identify because the assumption of "normalcy" will materially mislead others or because revealing identity will help correct misimpressions some have about her or his minority or because self-identification offers the chance to create connections with others similarly situated. It is harder because the minority person fears disapproval or ostracism. This, therefore, is the dilemma of the closet suggested in Chapter 2: it is a safe hiding place, but it forecloses individual, social, and political opportunities. The closet diminishes not only the integrity of its denizens but also their mental health. Those bearing socially disapproved identity traits tend to internalize society's disapproval. Psychologists have found that internalized homophobia, in particular, obstructs the development of an emotionally healthy life, and that the best-adjusted gay individuals have gone through a process of acceptance and appreciation of their sexual identity.[39] Virtually every coming out story is one of relief, that its teller can feel honest about herself or himself and free to pursue more productive life opportunities.

Self-identification as gay is also important for the formation of a *nomos,* consisting of a discernibly gay history, institutions, and mores, and is essential to political power. The gay experience reinforces the feminist idea that the personal is political. Coming out of the closet as a gay person is an act of self-identification that is also an explicitly political act.[40] The anonymity of closeted homosexuals in the 1950s was key to their political marginalization and contributed to antihomosexual stereotypes; because folks did not realize that their friends and relatives were gay, they were more likely to believe that homosexuals were lonely, psychopathic, and dysfunctional. Closetry disabled gay people from forming social and political groups and thereby enabled homophobes to persecute gay people virtually at will. Only after a significant number of gay people came out—or were cast out—of the closet did the polity let up on persecuting gays generally, a claim supported in Chapter 3.

Consider this final twist. Once minorities become more salient through identity speech, the majority has an incentive to speak as well. Minority speech destabilizes the norm, which loses its social invisibility. At that point, individuals or groups in the majority will speak out to assert or reassert their identity. Typically, there will still be an asymmetry, as the majority will tend to self-identify in negative rather than positive ways. Rather than saying "I'm a good old-fashioned heterosexual," the majority will say things like "I'm no pansy" or "Those queers are sick" or "Gays are a threat to family values." Note the irony. In a regime of the closet, the "deviant" views herself or himself in a negative way, as "not normal." Once the closet door flies open and former "deviants" proclaim themselves normal, many in the mainstream initially find themselves in a state of denial, and many deniers will root their identity more firmly in what they are not.

Social Costs of Suppressing Identity Speech. Suppression of identity speech is harmful at three distinct levels, for it undermines the flourishing of individuals, their nomic communities, and the polity itself. At the first level, identity speech suppression has all the disadvantages of ordinary censorship—including an inability to suppress the impulses or activities censored—plus this additional one: it discourages citizens of minority sexual orientations from accepting their sexualities. A generation of social scientists have confirmed Erving Goffman's argument that the conformity options available to stigmatized people (passing as normal, minimizing or obliterating the trait) are self-destructive and that the healthiest strategy is usually to recognize their sexual difference and seek out others similarly situated.[41] Among the worst costs of the sexual closet is the self-recognition of lying about something important. Living a lie by outwardly conforming to compulsory heterosexuality undermines the authenticity of one's life, disrupts relationships with others, and hurts those whom one marries or otherwise implicates in the lie. The suffocating effects of the closet are illustrated by exceedingly high suicide rates for bisexual and gay teenagers and by the loneliness and anomie depicted in autobiographical or even fictional accounts of unfulfilled lives.[42] The worst effects of the closet occur when accused individuals triumph by becoming accusers, stimulating a chain reaction of suspicions and disclaimers. Recall the Reverend Samuel Kent's successful deployment of this strategy (Chapter 1). Joe McCarthy, J. Edgar Hoover, and Roy Cohn were subsequent demons of the closet.[43]

Suppression of identity speech may have social consequences, as it potentially inhibits or distorts the flourishing of *nomos*. A *nomos* is a chain of interlocking identities, linked to the past as well as in the present by stories of struggle and identification. The gay *nomos* is one marked by recognition within each new generation that certain members feel attraction to persons of the same sex, and that these new personal narratives relate to those of the previous generation as well as those of the new generation. In this century, the American state has traditionally sought to disrupt the gay *nomos* as "perverted," but the gay experience has been that it is censorship that perverts. When a state seeks to destroy a *nomos*, its legacy is a *nomos* of fear and hiding. Consider this parallel. Between 1391 and 1478 powerful popular and political forces in Spain sought to destroy Judaism in an early example of Kulturkampf. Although attacks on the Jews impelled many to convert to Christianity, these forced conversions perverted Spain as well as its Christianity. The "Old Christians" never trusted the "New Christians." The Inquisition—a national calamity—was invited to Spain in order to root out Jewish practices among the *conversos*. Although Judaic *nomos* was diminished, it was not publicly erased until the Jews' expulsion from Spain in 1492. After 1492, Judaic tradition survived among the "secret Jews" who passed as Catholic but continued to practice their religion notwithstanding the Inquisition. Even today, centuries after the Inquisition and after their families fled Spain, some Marranos remain "closeted," ostensible Catholics who practice their Jewish faith in private.[44]

Admittedly, society would be better off without some nomic communities, but how do nomic censors make the right choices? The bad *nomoi* on my list (antigay coalitions) are not on yours (liberal academia). Another quandary is that identity suppression may have the effect of reinforcing the identity it is trying to suppress. The early Christian Church, persecuted by the Romans, exemplifies this phenomenon, as does the gay subculture created out of the interrogations and witch-hunts described in Chapters 1 and 2. Even when a society is better justified in suppressing a *nomos* than America was in persecuting polygamists and homosexuals, it needs to consider the harms generated by the process of suppression. By investing so much social effort in hunting and hiding, the state is wasting valuable human resources that could be expended in producing and problem-solving. At the elementary level of two-person cooperation, when one person feels the need to be guarded and secretive about herself or himself, the whole enterprise of cooperation will be compromised, maybe a little, sometimes completely. Multiplied by many breakdowns in cooperation, the social loss quickly becomes significant.[45]

Identity suppression also creates big risks for a society, especially the possibility of a malignant dynamic of anger, as it raises the stakes of clashing nomic communities. When the state makes it a crime to express oneself as a person of color or as gay, the state is likely to embitter the objects of the suppression and to empower its own worst bigots. (The person who is most likely to enforce rules of suppression is a person who feels the most intense animosity toward the targeted class.) By demonizing a vibrant nomic community, the state may initiate a spiral of vicious acts and retaliations, definitional of social turmoil. In short, Kulturkampf is politically dangerous as well as morally questionable.

Private Discrimination and Public Censorship. Gay experience suggests the many ways identity expression can be silenced—by direct prohibition or by indirect threat of losing promised benefits, by pain of criminal sanction or of civil penalties, and by private as well as public sources of power. A jurisprudence of coming out reinforces the interconnection between anticensorship and nondiscrimination principles suggested by the religion cases. Specifically, identity is just as easily closeted by private discrimination as it is by public censorship. Consider how they relate in the Georgetown case.

The case involved two different kinds of identity speech claims. Georgetown argued that it was discriminating, if at all, only on the basis of the students' expression and not their sexual orientation. Because only the latter was forbidden by the Human Rights Act, the former was legal, the university maintained. Mack properly rejected this argument. The main way gay people are discriminated against is by forcing them into a closet; hence, claims of private discrimination and censorship merged in the Georgetown case. Indeed, antidiscrimination cases usually involve this kind of relationship because discrimination on the basis of identity is a way of undermining a *nomos* and because prohibiting such discrimination limits the ability of institutions to censor its members' expression through their politics of presence.

Georgetown also argued that requiring it to recognize the student groups would be censorship of its identity. By refusing to recognize the gay groups, Georgetown was expressing its identity as an institution supporting Roman Catholic values and that faith's intellectual tradition. This claim is admissible. If the gay students wanted to express their identity and connection with larger lesbian and gay culture, Georgetown wanted to express its identity as a Roman Catholic institution. Forcing Georgetown to recognize the gay student groups could create the same sort of masquerade—a phony identity—that compulsory heterosexuality forces upon lesbian, gay, and bisexual people.[46]

Identity speech values therefore cut both ways in the Georgetown case. How should a judge resolve the cross-cutting claims? A facile answer would be that, because the Constitution just regulates state action, only the District's censorship of Georgetown's identity implicates the constitutional commitment to anticensorship. Gay experience resists making so much of the public-private distinction in this way. The closet that obstructed gay *nomos* was enforced by institutions of private (corporate) as well as public (state) authority. Tangible fear of losing one's job was and remains, next to family shame, the most powerful motivator for gay people to remain closeted. When gays came out in great numbers and asserted political power, their second agenda, after easing police harassment, was to end state employment discrimination on the basis of sexual orientation (Chapter 3). At the same time, gay activists called for laws prohibiting sexual orientation discrimination in private workplaces and public accommodations as well.

Antidiscrimination statutes such as the District's Human Rights Act are therefore important for ending the regime of the closet and assuring gay people equal citizenship. As Mack held, remedying private censorship can be the sort of compelling state interest that would justify some public censorship. In addition to *Bob Jones,* discussed above, the Supreme Court has recognized the same idea in cases involving sex discrimination. In *Roberts v. U.S. Jaycees* (1984), the Court upheld the application of Minnesota's Human Rights Act to require the Jaycees, a young men's community service organization, to admit women. Justice William Brennan's opinion conceded that the antidiscrimination law burdened the Jaycees' first amendment associational rights but ruled that the law served a compelling state interest that was unrelated to any expressive purpose of the Jaycees as an association.[47] Like Mack in the Georgetown case, Brennan in the Jaycees case found censorship on both sides of the controversy. When state censorship is invoked to protect against and even remedy private censorship or discrimination, the anticensorship principle should not be dispositive, as the Court ruled in *Roberts* and *Bob Jones.*

The Value of Accommodation. How should the legal system resolve colliding norms such as those in the Georgetown case? Scholars from a variety of perspectives maintain that decisionmakers ought to reconcile or accommodate colliding norms rather than just choose one as a winner over the others as "losers."[48] This theme is prominent in Judge Mack's opinion in the Georgetown case. The other judges posed the issues in starkly dichotomous win-lose terms: either Georgetown was required to recognize the gay student groups, with all the attendant benefits, or it was not. This way of posing the issue sharpened the normative conflict in the case. Over the objection of most of her colleagues, Mack bifurcated the issue into a recognition-endorsement feature, which reflected Georgetown's core objection, and an access-to-benefits feature, which reflected the students' main demands. Analytically, this permitted Mack to save the Human Rights Act from serious constitutional difficulty while preserving its core policy. Practically, the move enabled her to show both sides that she had attended to their key interests and to offer a result that accommodated the most significant nomic needs of both groups.

Is this approach unprincipled? Mack's dissenting brethren charged that she violated the nondiscrimination principle by not requiring recognition (Ferren) or that she violated the anticensorship principle by forcing Georgetown to allow an openly gay presence (Belson). A jurisprudence informed by the coming out experience provides support for Mack's approach. Coming out of the closet to one's friends and family has in the last two generations been the defining moment or cluster of moments for most gay people. As discussed above, coming out is an expression of identity and an association of the individual with the gay community, but it is also an invitation to equal treatment: you have been my parent/friend/coworker, and I want you to continue to be my parent/friend/coworker now that you know more about me. This is an invitation sometimes declined and sometimes accepted unconditionally. Most often, however, the invitation is accepted with conditions, such as a tacit insistence that gay persons be discreet in discussions of their sexuality.[49] The conditions themselves may change over time, as the parent/friend/coworker becomes accustomed to the gay person's identity and as the issues her or his coming out raises are discussed. Is it unprincipled for uncloseted gay persons to trim their openness in order to accommodate the needs of other persons?

Philip Bockman's story, "Fishing Practice," recounts the shock his disclosure yielded for his parents. His father implored Bockman to soften the blow of disclosure to his ill mother by agreeing to see a psychiatrist. This Bockman agreed to do (the psychiatrist turned out to be a "friend of Dorothy"). The knowledge that he was seeking professional help made it easier for his parents to deal with this new knowledge, and each parent privately expressed continued love but not yet comfortableness in talking about the subject. "Once, I expressed my frustration to my father about 'the silent treatment.' 'We're trying,' he explained. 'Please give us time.' He smiled, and I was reminded of an incident from my childhood, at about the age of six. He had taken me fishing. He hauled in one fish after the other, while I caught none. At the end of the day, I burst out crying. Kneeling beside me, he told me gently, 'Don't be too sad. Remember, it takes a long time to get good at something. Be patient. Don't think of today as fishing, just think of it as fishing practice.'"[50] After several years, Bockman brought his lover home to meet his parents, who welcomed the friend but still did not feel comfortable talking about homosexuality. Still later, after his mother's death, the author found his father positively affirming and finally willing to talk. Bockman's coming out of the closet with his family occurred over a period of discursive time, not in an instant road-to-Damascus revelation. Mack's judgment gave Georgetown the same discursive breathing room Bockman gave his parents. The question then becomes: How much "equality practice" is required before the gay person, or the state, asks for more?

Principles of Accommodation: Comparative Need and Dialogue. The circumstances of Bockman's and other stories are familiar: a gay person (group) expresses sexual identity to a shocked loved one (institution) with which the gay person (group) desires an ongoing relationship. To preserve the relationship in the face of knowledge that creates a normative rupture, each side has to make accommodations, respectful of the other's different views about sexuality. What principles should guide this process? The substantive principle of accommodation is comparative need: each side should accommodate the central need of the other, unless that accommodation would sacrifice that side's central need. The procedural principle is dialogue: each side should remain open to information about the other and to the common interests that are still shared.

These principles of accommodation are well illustrated in Mack's judgment. The university and the student groups by necessity would have an ongoing relationship. There was ample ground for mutual respect, as the students had chosen to attend Georgetown, which in turn was happy to admit openly gay students. As a Catholic school, Georgetown's greatest need was an official distance from the gay groups, to assure that outsiders or the Vatican would not think that the university was "approving" the student advocacies. The student groups' greatest need was access to the services and benefits afforded other student groups, so that they could have a stable presence within the university. Through the semantic distinction between recognition and equal access, Mack's opinion treated each party with respect and gave each what it most needed: the lesbian and gay students got access to facilities and services on an equal basis with other students, and the university was relieved of the formal association it feared would be inferred from official recognition of the gay student groups.

The Value of Subcultural Diversity: A Nomic Autonomy Exception. Suppose Bockman's family had expelled him because of his sexual orientation. A gay perspective would lament that reaction as an unproductive discrimination, but gaylaw also rejects the notion that the state can force a family to take back its gay relative. Why is it that we are generally unwilling to regulate the family in this way? It is decidedly not because the family is immune from state regulation; if the father assaulted the gay son, the police could justifiably intervene. The key reason is as old as Aristotle: the family is a building block of the polity, as it is a situs of social foundation, inculcation, and diversity. The state should presumptively leave the family alone, should presumptively not censor normative interaction within the family, and should not apply nondiscrimination rules within a family.

Nowhere is the closet more stifling than within the family, as most coming out stories indicate. While the tellers of some such stories lament, deeply, their families' silence or negativity, almost all would agree that this problem is not one for the state to handle through censorship. The best solution is mutual accommodation according to the principles of comparative need and dialogue described above. It is increasingly rare for accommodation not to work, but if it does not, the alternative is for the gay child to separate from the family as early as practicable. Today, that evolution can be informed or assisted by gay subcultures, *nomoi* of like-feeling and potentially supportive individuals, supplemental families of choice. Religious subcultures have long served the useful purpose of supplementing blood families, and in today's society gay subcultures work alongside religious ones. Some of the most poignant coming out stories are those involving gay people who are emerging from a religious cloister.[51]

While society's contribution to closeted sexuality must end as a matter of law, the church's, like the family's, contribution is not susceptible to legal intervention. Like the family, the church can be support or torture for the gay person. When it is the latter, accommodation usually does not work but neither would state intervention. Just as the heterogeneity of families is good for America, so is the heterogeneity of subcultural *nomoi,* so long as their members have the option of separating. Unless one leaves the country, on the other hand, the individual cannot easily separate from non-nomic society, and this exception for nomic autonomy applicable to families and churches should not apply to institutions in the world.

This kind of thinking has direct relevance to liberty-equality clashes. Concurring in the *Roberts* judgment, Justice Sandra Day O'Connor relied on the fact that the Jaycees were a garden-variety commercial organization and therefore not entitled to the strong first amendment protection that intimate or ideological associations receive.[52] The closer an institution is to the center of a *nomos,* the greater freedom should be allowed it by the state. The purpose of a *nomos* is to inculcate values linking its members together. Such values inevitably create discriminations and closets, but those members objecting to the discriminations have the option of leaving, and those refusing to be closeted can be kicked out. Religions are the classic *nomoi,* but so too are gay communities. Georgetown University, in contrast, is an institution with a foot in each arena—the Roman Catholic *nomos* and the secular world. Georgetown, therefore, did not present a good case for invoking a nomic autonomy exception to the nondiscrimination or anticensorship principle.

Other Examples of Equality Practice

The gaylegal principles identified as relevant to the Georgetown case and supportive of Mack's approach to the case can be elaborated by reference to subsequent liberty-equality clashes. A jurisprudence of coming out accepts that there are no pat answers to the following cases, and insists upon a more complex analysis than that adopted by the court in each case.

The Boston Parade Case

Since 1947, the South Boston Allied War Veterans Council has organized and sponsored a parade on March 17 to commemorate both Evacuation Day and

St. Patrick's Day. This is the major civic event of the year in Boston, and the city government lends its seal, some money, and the city streets for the celebration. In 1992 the Irish-American Gay, Lesbian & Bisexual Group (GLIB) was formed and obtained a state court order to march in the parade, over the Council's objections; GLIB's members were among the 10,000 marchers that year, and they marched without incident. In litigation the next year, GLIB won a trial court order that the parade was a "public accommodation," which Massachusetts law barred from excluding GLIB because of its members' sexual orientation. The trial court rejected GLIB's claim that the parade was a governmental event subject to the first amendment but ordered the Council to admit GLIB on the same terms as other groups. The Massachusetts Supreme Judicial Court affirmed that order. The U.S. Supreme Court unanimously reversed in *Hurley v. Irish-American Gay, Lesbian and Bisexual Group of Boston* (1995).[53]

Justice David Souter's opinion started with the proposition that parades are expressive conduct entitled to first amendment protection. GLIB's own participation was likewise expressive—"to celebrate its members' identity as openly gay, lesbian, and bisexual descendants of the Irish immigrants, to show that there are such individuals in the community"—but the first amendment did not protect them because the Council was not considered a state actor. In response to the statutory nondiscrimination claim, the Council maintained that it only wanted to exclude progay messages, not gay people, who were free to march in other contingents. Souter ruled that the state court order requiring the Council to include GLIB as a group "violates the fundamental rule of protection of the First Amendment, that a speaker has the autonomy to choose the content of his own message."[54] The Council's message was one of compulsory Irish heterosexuality, a message that would be disrupted by an openly gay contingent.

The gaylegal principles outlined above are friendly to the result in *Hurley* in the way Souter presented the case. The anticensorship principle is key to the result and reasoning in *Hurley,* which in turn is now the leading precedent for the proposition that the state presumptively cannot censor identity speech. If gays have a right to express their homosexuality, straights have a right to express their commitment to compulsory heterosexuality. The nomic autonomy exception to the nondiscrimination principle also lends support to the result. For Souter, the Council represented the nomic community of Irish Bostonians and, as such, ought to have maximal freedom to express its orthodoxy on issues of sexual orientation. Hence, the nondiscrimination principle ought not counterbalance the general rule against censorship.

There is more to *Hurley* than Souter's opinion reveals, however. Doctrinally, the queerest feature of the opinion is the way the Court's governing precedent, *Roberts,* disappeared into a legal closet. Souter may have felt the state courts were wrong to treat the parade as a public accommodation, like the Jaycees in *Roberts*. Truly, the lower courts stretched the meaning of public accommodation to reach parades,[c] and *Hurley* should be read to cast doubt on the constitutionality of such heroic statutory interpretations. Unfortunately, Souter was stuck with the state determination of the issue. The same jurisdictional constraint—unreviewable disposition in the state court—that took the state action issue out of the case hardwired the public accommodations determination into the case. If the parade were a public accommodation complaining that application to it of a state antidiscrimination law violated the first amendment, *Roberts* must govern. The state courts followed *Roberts'* framework; the Supreme Court scarcely bothered to cite it.

If governed by *Roberts* and the trial court's findings of fact, *Hurley* is not such an easy case. While the parade was not a commercial association in the way that the Jaycees were, neither did the parade have an expressive agenda beyond "Irish are great" and "veterans are wonderful." The Council cited only three instances where it had, in four decades, excluded a group (the KKK, an antibusing group, and a prolife group) from the parade. Souter analogized the Council to a composer orchestrating the theme for a symphony, but the Council's symphony had no theme and everybody was allowed into the orchestra, except identifiable homosexuals. Allowed to participate in the 1993 parade were radio stations, candidates for public office, McGruff the crime dog, a nursing home, a smoke shop, beauty queens, the AFL-CIO, marching bands, Budweiser beer, a water pollution association, a Baptist "Bible trolley," Northern Ireland AID, and Pepsi Cola. The trial court found as a matter of fact a "lack of genuine selectivity in choosing participants" and rejected as a matter of fact the Council's argument that its exclusion of "groups with sexual themes merely formalized that the Parade expresses traditional religious and social values."[55] The factual context of the Boston parade contrasts with that of New York's St. Patrick's Day parade, which gays had tried to crash as well. The trial court in the New York case found that the Ancient Order of Hibernians who ran the parade had always viewed their parade as expressing a particular viewpoint, had been selective in whom they would allow to march, and had rules restricting expression in the parade.[56] The New York findings justified first amendment concern much more than the Boston findings did.

---

c. The Massachusetts statute defined public accommodation as "any place . . . which is open to and accepts or solicits the patronage of the general public," including but not limited to "a boardwalk or other public highway" and "a place of public amusement, recreation, sport, exercise or entertainment." Mass. General Laws §272:92A. The trial court found that the parade was "an open recreational event," but the state public accommodations law applies only to *places*, not *events*.

At best, the Council came to its ideological message, compulsory heterosexuality, only after GLIB sought to participate. Realistically, the Council never had a specific message and was probably excluding GLIB because of antigay animus, again unlike the New York case. The trial judge found that the asserted message was a pretext for discrimination. In 1992 the president of the Council, John "Wacko" Hurley, told GLIB it was excluded because of "safety reasons and insufficient information regarding [the] club." In 1993 Hurley told GLIB it was excluded because its "sexual themes" clashed with a policy "that the Parade expresses traditional religious and social values." At trial, Hurley testified that GLIB was excluded because its members were also members of ACT-UP and could therefore be expected to disrupt the parade. Hurley's final justification for excluding GLIB was, according to the trial judge, "because of its values and its messages, i.e., its members' sexual orientation."[57] Given this record, it was Souter and not Hurley who created a coherent message for the parade. Contrast the Court's blindness to the more obvious expressive idea in *Roberts,* the Jaycees case: business is for guys. A disturbing implication of this contrast is that the Court reflexively considered the message in *Roberts* so off-limits that it overlooked the possibility of a message, while it considered the message in *Hurley* so acceptable that it overrode findings of fact to insist that it must have been the message all along.

Relatedly, *Roberts* held that nondiscrimination is a compelling state interest justifying restrictions on the Jaycees' right of association. An implication of *Roberts* is that, if a parade is a public accommodation, parade organizers cannot exclude women or people of color or (to make the analogy to *Hurley* closer) cannot require women marching in the parade to "pass" as men. Under this reading of *Roberts,* the state's requirement of nondiscrimination would trump any post-hoc rationalization for such exclusions. If such a parade cannot exclude women generally, why can it exclude lesbians? Of course, *Roberts* might be limited to sex and race nondiscrimination, both of which enjoy special constitutional status, but Judge Mack's opinion in the Georgetown case developed a detailed case for the proposition that sexual orientation discrimination ought to be constitutionally problematic as well.[58] (As Chapter 6 argues, *Evans* might be a first Supreme Court step in that direction.) *Roberts* might better be limited to cases where the nondiscrimination principle imposes only incidental burdens on rights of association and expression, and not expanded to cases where nondiscrimination undercuts the expression of a nomic community. For this reason, *Roberts* ought not require New York's Hibernians to allow the gay marchers but might be applied to Boston's Council, where the evidence of nomic expression or an ideological message was mighty thin and rejected by the finder of fact.

Even without reference to *Roberts,* the *Hurley* opinion raised more questions than it answered. At oral argument, Justice O'Connor asked whether the state could require a circus parade to include protesters who objected to circus treatment of animals.[59] Because the hypothetical was so far off point—viewpoint discrimination rather than status discrimination—this question sheds some light on Souter's opinion. Both Justices treated the exclusion as one resting on the basis of GLIB's expression and not on the basis of its members' identity, an assumption rejected by the finder of fact. Only Justices John Paul Stevens and Stephen Breyer showed any curiosity as to the relationship between the identity of GLIB's members and GLIB's message. Stevens wondered whether a cogent parallel might be an exclusion of Jews who wanted to wear yarmulkes. Breyer asked Chester Darling, lawyer for the Council, whether GLIB's signs were "self-identifications" or were they a "message"? Darling beamed: "It's a message, it's an identification, it's a proclamation."[60] Breyer gave him a weary look.

The reason Darling was confused was that he assumed, as his clients did, that GLIB's identity was its message. This was the dilemma in both *Hurley* and *Roberts.* The Jaycees' ideology, determined long before women were knocking at their door, was that business is for guys. Women's mere presence in the Jaycees undermined that message. Sex discrimination was always integral to the association. The Council's ideology, determined only after GLIB came knocking, was that Irish must be heterosexual. The presence of openly gay marchers would have undermined that message. Sexual orientation discrimination was found, after the fact, integral to the association. The main difference between *Hurley* and *Roberts* is that the message would not have been undermined if gay people were dispersed throughout Wacko Hurley's crowd because their sexual orientation would have been invisible to the audience. In contrast, women such as Kathryn Roberts would have been apparent in the Jaycees even without badges and signs. Thus, I need to amend my intuition about the Council's always ambiguous message: it was not compulsory heterosexuality so much as it was the apartheid of the closet.

Like the Jaycees and the Georgetown cases, the Boston parade case was one where identity speech was implicated on both sides of the controversy. Viewed in its factual context, *Hurley* did not implicate the anticensorship principle as strongly as the Court suggested and did squarely implicate the nondiscrimination principle. As to the former, because there was never a theme for the parade it is not clear why Hurley excluded GLIB, nor is it clear whether his views reflected the sense of other paraders. And the nondiscrimination principle suggests that GLIB should have been allowed to participate in the parade. Like the Georgetown case, the Boston parade case was one where the courts should have been open to accommodation. The principle of comparative need would suggest that GLIB be allowed to march (as it did in 1992, without incident) and that other marching groups could choose to distance themselves from GLIB, either physically (their place in the queue) or expressionally (with signs proclaiming family values). Or the Council itself could have issued disclaimers in the media, in programs for the march, or with its own banners. The dialogue principle would suggest that the courts could have required GLIB's inclusion but directed the parties to work out an arrangement subject to judicial supervision.

The Case of the Presbyterian Landlord

Evelyn Smith owned four rental units in Chico, California. A member of the Bidwell Presbyterian Church, Smith believed that sexual cohabitation outside of marriage is sinful. That was why she refused to lease a unit to Gail Randall and Kenneth Phillips, an unmarried cohabiting couple. California's Fair Employment and Housing Commission (FEHC) ruled that her refusal was discrimination on the basis of marital status, in violation of the state's fair housing law. Rejecting Smith's defense that the orders violated her rights under the first amendment and the Religious Freedom Restoration Act (RFRA), the California Supreme Court in *Smith v. FEHC* (1996) substantially affirmed the agency rulings.[61]

The court was unanimous that the agency action did not violate Smith's free exercise rights. In *Employment Division v. Smith* (1990), the Supreme Court narrowed the free exercise clause to allow laws of general application to be applied in ways that incidentally, but not intentionally, burden people's free exercise of religion. This ruling has been criticized as inconsistent with the original intent of the first amendment's framers and with the needs of religious communities.[62] Congress overrode the decision in RFRA, which prohibited state laws substantially burdening religious free exercise absent a compelling state interest. Justice Kathryn Werdegar's plurality opinion in *Smith v. FEHC* held that RFRA did not apply because Smith's free exercise of religion was not substantially burdened by the requirement that she rent to unmarried couples. Werdegar maintained that Smith could have sold her rental units and invested her money in other activities that did not confront her with a choice between obeying the law and following her religious beliefs.

Although the application of the housing law to Evelyn Smith was nothing approaching a Kulturkampf, the principles explored in this chapter are skeptical of Werdegar's approach. For the same reasons the state ought not, without strong justification, censor or discriminate against gay people for coming out of the closet, the state ought not, without strong justification, penalize religious expression, either through direct censorship or indirect discrimination. Forcing Smith to choose between religious principle and the use of her apartments is just as much censorship as forcing a gay person to choose between escaping the closet and keeping her or his government job. The question, properly put, is whether the state had a compelling interest in eradicating marital status discrimination. Dissenting Justice Joyce Kennard argued that the prohibition against marital status discrimination, added to the housing statute in 1975, reflected legislative concern only with single or divorced tenants and not cohabiting ones. There was no evidence that unmarried couples suffered from unusual amounts of discrimination or had trouble finding suitable housing; the importance of nondiscrimination against unmarried couples was undercut by the many other discriminations the legislature had made in favor of married couples.[63] Although California courts have recognized that the right to privacy includes the right to cohabitation, including sexual cohabitation,[64] it is not clear that cohabiting couples are pushed into a closet because of substantial discrimination against them in the housing market.

Concurring only in the court's judgment, Justice Stanley Mosk refused to apply RFRA because he thought it unconstitutional. Indeed, the Supreme Court has subsequently invalidated RFRA as beyond Congress's authority to implement free exercise rights against the states pursuant to its fourteenth amendment powers.[65] The states, of course, remain free to implement the principles of RFRA by statute or by state constitutional rule, and gaylaw as articulated in this book would be friendly to such a move. Absent such action, is the Werdegar-Mosk result foreordained? Perhaps not. Dissenting Justice Marvin Baxter urged that the matter be remanded to the state housing commission to develop a factual record to determine whether exempting landlords like Smith from the housing act's nondiscrimination rule would materially undermine that rule.[66] I would go one step further. All seven justices agreed that the 1975 amendment (adding nondiscrimination on the basis of marital status) protected unmarried cohabiting couples. This was a dynamic interpretation of the statute, beyond the legislature's goal of protecting single men and women. The court justified the dynamic interpretation on the basis of deference to the agency, but when dynamic interpretation runs up against considerations of constitutional principle, as in the case of the Presbyterian landlord, it is inappropriate for courts to defer to agencies.[67]

Courts in such cases should follow Judge Mack's approach in the Georgetown case, where she construed a broad statute more narrowly than the agency and the plaintiffs did, so as to accommodate the constitutional concerns raised by religious dissenters. This is also what the Massachusetts courts should have done in *Hurley:* construe the antidiscrimination law to be inapplicable to a public parade. If the legislature overrides the narrowing construction and broadens the statute, then the constitutional issues are sharpened and the court has a better idea what policies might justify the constitutional abridgments. If Baxter's remand idea had prevailed, the agency should have alerted the legislature that it was narrowing the statute's reach and perhaps reversing its earlier view that the law protected unmarried cohabiting tenants as well as single tenants.

Legislative Equality Practice in Employment, the Armed Forces, and Family Law

Equality comes on little cat's feet, not in a single leap. Like the young Philip Bockman whose initial foray into angling was just fishing practice, recent sexual orientation antidiscrimination laws are equality practice. The ultimate goal of gaylaw is full equality for gay people, but that is not possible in the near term. In some instances, full gay equality would be a fundamental affront to religious groups in ways that full sex or race equality no longer is. For example, few organized religions now oppose legalized marriages of different-race couples (as many did a generation ago), but the large majority are strongly opposed to legalized marriages of same-sex couples. Religion-based opposition is the most important reason few state judiciaries or legislatures will even consider the possibility of same-sex marriages.

The jurisprudence reflected in Judge Mack's opinion suggests a principled legislative resolution to this impasse: separate the recognition issue from the equal benefits (and obligations) issue. Following the Scandinavian countries, states can adopt registered partnership statutes that provide most of the statutory benefits and obligations of spousehood but without recognizing same-sex marriages. This would accommodate the most important needs of gay people who desire equality of rights and of religious people who desire preservation of the special status of marriage. This kind of resolution might be relevant to court cases, for judges uncertain about striking down same-sex marriage bars can signal to legislatures that the invalidity of those bars can be cured by registered partnership laws. In 1995 the Hungarian Supreme Court did something like that: the court upheld the exclusion of gay couples from state-sanctioned marriage but ruled that they could not be excluded from statutes granting marital benefits and obligations to nonmarital partnerships.[68] The Canadian Supreme Court imposed a similar nondiscrimination requirement on Ontario in 1999.

Another illustration of equality practice is the proposed Employment Non-Discrimination Act (ENDA), which would create a federal cause of action for employment discrimination on the basis of sexual orientation.[69] The bill exemplifies equality practice, for its sexual orientation cause of action is weaker than the race or sex cause of action in title VII: ENDA denies gay claimants "disparate impact" claims, makes affirmative action for gay people illegal, and exempts the armed forces. Most striking is ENDA's exemption for "religious organizations," defined to include educational institutions that are managed or controlled by an organized religion.[70]

ENDA can be criticized for making sexual orientation a second-class category of antidiscrimination law, but there are good reasons for these compromises. Disparate impact liability for sexual orientation would be unworkable so long as this is a blurry and easily closeted characteristic. Gay people are themselves ambivalent about affirmative action, a concept under seige in the race and sex contexts. The armed forces exception would preserve the military exclusion of gay people. Chapters 5 and 6 argued that the military exclusion is inconsistent with both free speech and equality principles. Does a jurisprudence of accommodation redeem the 1993 "don't ask, don't tell" compromise? I fear not. The statutory policy met few if any of the needs of gay service personnel, and its application has been the occasion for soaring discharges (Appendix C5). Discharges have increased because obsessional officers have been asking and disgruntled personnel have been telling. The 1993 policy has not yet been a successful example of equality practice, and it is only political necessity that justifies an armed forces exception to ENDA.

In contrast, ENDA's exception for religious organizations is not only analytically defensible but desirable. It may even be required by RFRA, which provides that "government" may not "substantially burden" a person's exercise of religion without narrowly serving a compelling state interest.[71] Although invalidated as applied to the states, RFRA may still apply (and I think ought to apply) to federal policies such as ENDA. Were RFRA inapplicable, the free exercise clause would in some cases require an exemption. *Employment Division v. Smith* held that statutes of general applicability, such as ENDA, could be constitutionally applied to burden religious free exercise, but the Court distinguished cases where a policy burdened both a religious free exercise and another first amendment freedom, such as speech or association.[72] Application of ENDA to require a seminary to admit openly gay applicants contrary to a religion's doctrine would burden both free exercise and the right of association, which includes the right of a *nomos* to exclude persons whose identity or conduct violates its nomic values. From a gaylegal perspective, *Smith* and the Court's other free exercise precedents should be read to protect the core activities of a nomic community. If a religion denies membership or leadership to openly gay people in its association or its societies, the free exercise clause ought to back up that nomic policy.

Note the tension between ENDA, the Boston parade case, and RFRA on one side, and the Georgetown case on the other. As a Roman Catholic-controlled institution, Georgetown could refuse to hire openly gay faculty, consistent with ENDA. Georgetown does not to my knowledge follow any such policy, but if it can exclude gay teachers, why not a right to exclude gay student groups? Indeed, Congress legislated that idea after the Georgetown decision by amending the District's Human Rights Act to allow religiously affiliated educational institutions to discriminate on the basis of sexual orientation.[73] *Hurley* lends some support to Georgetown's argument that it cannot be forced to include groups whose message is discordant with that of the religious university. If RFRA applies to the District because it is under Congress's plenary authority, it would require a compelling state interest to justify the burden *Gay Rights Coalition* imposed on Georgetown. Has Judge Mack's resolution been discredited by subsequent developments in public law?

I think not. The subsequent developments are evidence that Ferren's position was insufficiently attentive to Georgetown's religious concerns, and that Mack's accommodation was the most that the gay students could have hoped for. But Belson's position, rejecting the students' claims entirely, is not required by either *Hurley* or RFRA. *Roberts* and *Bob Jones* remain doctrinal support for the proposition that a narrowly drawn antidiscrimination policy, such as the one Mack constructed, is the sort of compelling state interest justifying burdens on free exercise and association. Most interestingly, Mack's equality practice worked productively at Georgetown for it created a structure friendly to dialogue between the parties over time. I joined the Georgetown University Law Center's faculty soon after the court of appeals' decision and became the sponsor of the law center's bisexual, lesbian, and gay student group. The law center was supportive of student efforts to create a healthy gay community and to provide informative programs; Father Alexei Michalencko, the law center's Catholic chaplain, has been a counselor for students of all orientations and has generously supported gay scholarship as well as gay community at the law center. The main campus was also supportive, and, in my view, the priests who run the university have been respectful of gay identity and issues. The apparatus Mack set in motion has impelled the students and the priests into a productive dialogue, where agreement and mutual respect have dominated disagreement. My impression is that equality practice worked well at Georgetown for all concerned—devout Catholics, devout gays, devout gay Catholics, and the rest of the community.

What of the charge that such accommodationist strategies preserve remnants of the closet? Bockman acquiesced in precisely that when he agreed to go slow with his parents. Rather than viewing this as an unjust concession to prejudice, this can be viewed as a gesture of respect and an open door to further progress. Gay experience is that coming out of the closet is not an all-or-nothing matter. It works best as a process of mutually respectful education, dialogue, and accommodation of respective needs. Ironically, too, the closet is not unalloyedly bad. Good manners and decency require that we closet our feelings much of the time. The closet is a mediation between my desire to express and your desire not to hear. Equality practice is the mechanism for working out the details of the evolving sexual closet. The neutral state provides a forum by which dialogue and accommodation change not only the terms of gay citizenship but also affect the evolution of America and its religious traditions as well.

Appendixes: Regulating Sexual and Gender Variation in the United States

appendix a

Early Municipal and State Regulation
of Sexual and Gender Variation

Appendix A1 State consensual sodomy laws, 1610–1998

State	First law (crime)	First application to oral sex	Constitutional challenges	Recent legislative action
Alabama	Ala. Code §3235 (1852) ("crime against nature")	1977 Ala. Acts No. 607, §§2315–18 ("deviate sexual intercourse")	Challenge rejected, *Horn v. State*, 273 So. 2d 249 (Ala. Crim. App. 1973)	Reduced to misdemeanor, 1977 Ala. Acts No. 607, §2318
Alaska	Alaska (Terr.) Code ch. 7, §130 (1900) ("sodomy")	1915 Alaska Laws ch. 22	Crime against nature clause invalidated (vagueness). *Harris v. State*, 457 P.2d 638 (Alaska 1969)	Decriminalized, 1978 Alaska Laws ch. 166, §121
Arizona	Ariz. (Terr.) Code ch. 10, §48 (1865) ("crime against nature")	1917 Ariz. Laws ch. 2 (new crime: "unnatural sexual relations")	Challenge rejected, *State v. Bateman*, 547 P.2d 6 (Ariz. 1976)	Reduced to misdemeanor, 1977 Ariz. Laws ch. 142, §67
Arkansas	Ark. Penit. Act, Dec. 17, 1838, §4 ("sodomy, or buggery")	*Havens v. State*, 228 S.W.2d 1003 (Ark. 1950)	Challenges rejected, *Connor v. State*, 490 S.W.2d 114 (Ark. 1973); *Carter v. State*, 500 S.W.2d 368 (Ark. 1973)	Decriminalized, 1975 Ark. Acts No. 280; recriminalized as misdemeanor for same-sex couples, 1977 Ark. Acts No. 828
California	1850 Cal. Stat. ch. 99 ("crime against nature")	1915 Cal. Stat. ch. 586 (invalidated); 1921 Cal. Stat. ch. 848 (new crime: "oral copulation")	Challenge rejected, *People v. Hurd*, 85 Cal. Rptr. 718 (App. 1970)	Decriminalized, 1975 Cal. Stat. ch. 71, §7
Colorado	1861 Colo. Laws p.297, §46 ("crime against nature")	1939 Colo. Laws ch. 97 ("carnal copulation per os")	Challenge rejected, *Gilmore v. People*, 467 P.2d 828 (Colo. 1970)	Decriminalized, 1971 Colo. Laws ch. 121

State	First law (crime)	First application to oral sex	Constitutional challenges	Recent legislative action
Connecticut	Act of Dec. 1, 1642, §7 ("man lying with man"); 1672 Conn. Gen. Laws p.9	None reported	None reported	Decriminalized, 1969 Conn. Acts No. 828, §214
Delaware	Act for Advancement of Justice etc., ch. XXII, §5 (1719) ("sodomy, buggery")	State v. Maida, 96 A. 207 (Del. 1915)	None reported	Decriminalized, 58 Del. Laws ch. 497 (1972)
District of Columbia	Act of June 9, 1948, §104, 62 Stat. 347 (placing or taking "into his or her mouth or anus the sexual organ")	Ibid.	Challenges rejected, Riley v. U.S., 298 A.2d 228 (D.C. 1972); Stewart v. U.S., 364 A.2d 1205 (D.C. 1976)	Decriminalized 1981, but U.S. House vetoed; decriminalized, Act of Dec. 28, 1994, §501(b), 42 D.C. Reg. 62
Florida	Act of Mar. 5, 1842, §1, pamph. 20 ("buggery or sodomy"); 1868 Fla. Laws ch. 1637(8), §17 ("crime against nature")	1917 Fla. Laws ch. 7361 (new crime: "unnatural and lascivious acts")	Crime against nature law invalidated, Franklin v. State, 257 So. 2d 21 (Fla. 1971). Unnatural acts law survives, Thomas v. State, 326 So. 2d 413 (Fla. 1975)	Crime against nature decriminalized, 1974 Fla. Laws ch. 74-121
Georgia	Charter of June 20, 1732 (common law in force, including "buggery"); Ga. Penal Code §61 (1816) ("sodomy")	Herring v. State, 46 S.E.2d 876 (Ga. 1904). But see Riley v. Garrett, 138 S.E.2d 367 (Ga. 1963) (sodomy does not include cunnilingus)	Challenges rejected, Bowers v. Hardwick, 478 U.S. 186 (1986); Christenson v. State, 468 S.E.2d 188 (Ga. 1996). Invalidated (privacy), Powell v. State, 510 S.E.2d 18 (Ga. 1998)	Expanded to include oral sex on a woman, 1968 Ga. Laws No. 1157

Appendix A1   *(continued)*

State	First law (crime)	First application to oral sex	Constitutional challenges	Recent legislative action
Hawaii	Haw. (Terr.) Penal Code ch. 13, §11 (1869) ("sodomy, crime against nature")	*Territory v. Wilson*, 26 Haw. 360 (1922)	None reported	Decriminalized, 1972 Haw. Laws No. 9, §1300
Idaho	1864 Idaho (Terr.) Laws ch. III, §45 ("crime against nature")	*State v. Altwatter*, 157 P. 256 (Idaho 1916)	Challenge rejected, *State v. Carringer*, 523 P.2d 532 (Idaho 1974)	Decriminalized, 1971 Idaho Laws ch. 143; recriminalized, 1972 Idaho Laws ch. 336, reenacting §18-6605
Illinois	1819 Ill. Laws p.220, §20 ("crime against nature")	*Honselman v. People*, 48 N.E. 304 (Ill. 1897)	None reported	Decriminalized, 1961 Ill. Laws 2044, §35-1
Indiana	1881 Ind. Acts ch. XXXVII, §100 ("crime against nature")	*Glover v. State*, 101 N.E. 629 (Ind. 1913)	Challenge rejected, *Estes v. State*, 195 N.E.2d 471 (Ind. 1964)	Decriminalized, 1976 Ind. Acts No. 148, §24
Iowa	1892 Iowa Acts ch. 39 ("carnal copulation")	1902 Iowa Acts ch. 148, confirmed, *State v. Gage*, 116 N.W. 596 (Iowa 1908)	Invalidated for different-sex copulation (privacy), *State v. Pilcher*, 242 N.W.2d 348 (Iowa 1976)	Decriminalized, 1976 Iowa Acts No. 1245, ch. 4, §526
Kansas	Kan. (Terr.) Stat. ch. 53, §7 (1855); Kan. Gen. Stat. ch. 31, §231 (1868) ("crime against nature")	*State v. Hurlbert*, 234 P. 945 (Kan. 1915)	Challenge sidestepped, *State v. Thompson*, 558 P.2d 1079 (Kan. 1976)	Decriminalized for different-sex, misdemeanor for same-sex, 1969 Kan. Laws ch. 180, §21-3505

State	First law (crime)	First application to oral sex	Constitutional challenges	Recent legislative action
Kentucky	Ky. Rev. Stat. ch. 28, art. IV, §11 (1860) ("sodomy or buggery")	1974 Ky. Acts ch. 406, §90 ("deviate sexual intercourse")	Invalidated (privacy, equal protection), *Commonwealth v. Wasson*, 842 S.W.2d 487 (Ky. 1992)	Decriminalized for different-sex, misdemeanor for same-sex, 1974 Ky. Acts ch. 406, §90
Louisiana	1805 La. Acts ch. L, §2 ("crime against nature")	1896 La. Acts No. 69, confirmed, *State v. Vicknair*, 28 So. 273 (La. 1900)	Challenges rejected, *State v. McCoy*, 337 So. 2d 192 (La. 1976); *State v. Baxley*, 656 So. 2d 973 (La. 1995)	None
Maine	1821 Me. Laws ch. V ("crime against nature")	*State v. Cyr*, 198 A. 743 (Me. 1938)	Challenge rejected, *State v. White*, 217 A.2d 212 (Me. 1966)	Decriminalized, 1975 Me. Laws ch. 499, §5
Maryland	1632 Charter (common law in force, including "buggery"); 1793 Md. Laws ch. LVII, §10 ("sodomy")	1916 Md. Laws ch. 616 (new crime: "unnatural or perverted sexual practices")	Challenge rejected, *Neville v. State*, 430 A.2d 570 (Md. 1981). Unnatural practices law inapplicable to different-sex, *Schochet v. State*, 580 A.2d 176 (Md. 1990)	None
Massachusetts	Capitall Lawes of New England [Mass. Bay] §8 (1641–42) ("man lyeth with mankind"); 1697 Mass. Acts No. 74 ("buggery"); Act Against Sodomy, 1785	1887 Mass. Acts ch. 436 (new crime: "unnatural and lascivious acts"), confirmed, *Commonwealth v. Dill*, 36 N.E. 472 (Mass. 1894)	Challenge rejected, *Jaquith v. Commonwealth*, 120 N.E.2d 189 (Mass. 1954). Unnatural acts law narrowly construed, *Commonwealth v. Balthazar*, 318 N.E.2d 478 (Mass. 1974)	None

Appendix A1   *(continued)*

State	First law (crime)	First application to oral sex	Constitutional challenges	Recent legislative action
Michigan	Act of May 17, 1820, §4 ("sodomy"); Mich. Rev. Stat. pt. 4th, tit. 1, ch. 8, §14 (1838) ("buggery"); Mich. Rev. Stat. tit. 30, ch. 158, §16 (1846) ("crime against nature")	1903 Mich. Acts No. 198 ("gross indecency" between males); 1939 Mich. Acts No. 148 ("gross indecency" with a female)	Vagueness challenge rejected, *People v. Dexter*, 148 N.W.2d 915 (Mich. App. 1967). Privacy challenge invited, *People v. Howell*, 238 N.W.2d 148 (Mich. 1976)	None
Minnesota	Minn. (Terr.) Rev. Stat. ch. 108, §13 (1851) ("crime against nature")	1921 Minn. Laws ch. 224 ("carnally knows by the mouth")	Privacy challenge sidestepped, *State v. Gray*, 413 N.W.2d 107 (Minn. 1987)	Maximum sentence reduced to one year, 1977 Minn. Laws ch. 130, §4
Mississippi	1839 Miss. Laws p.162, §20 ("crime against nature")	*State v. Davis*, 79 So. 2d 432 (Miss. 1955)	Challenge rejected, *Miller v. State*, 636 So. 2d 391 (Miss. 1994)	None
Missouri	Mo. Rev. Stat. art. 7 §7 (1835) ("crime against nature"); Act of Mar. 27, 1845, art. VIII, §7	1911 Mo. Laws p.198, confirmed, *State v. Katz*, 181 S.W. 425 (Mo. 1916)	Challenges rejected, *State v. Crawford*, 478 S.W.2d 314 (Mo. 1972); *State v. Walsh*, 713 S.W.2d 508 (Mo. 1986)	Decriminalized for different-sex, misdemeanor for same-sex, 1977 Mo. Laws p.687
Montana	1864–68 Mont. (Terr.) 1st Legisl. Ass., Crim. Prac. Acts ch. IV, §44 ("crime against nature")	*State v. Guerin*, 152 P. 747 (Mont. 1915)	Invalidated (privacy), *Gryczan v. State*, 942 P.2d 112 (Mont. 1997)	Decriminalized for different-sex, felony for same-sex, 1973 Mont. Laws ch. 513 (§§45-2-101[20], 45-5-505)

State	First law (crime)	First application to oral sex	Constitutional challenges	Recent legislative action
Nebraska	Neb. (Terr.) Crim. Code ch. 4, §47 (1866) ("crime against nature")	1913 Neb. Laws ch. 69 ("carnal copulation")	Challenge rejected, *State v. Temple*, 222 N.W.2d 356 (Neb. 1974)	Decriminalized, 1977 Neb. Laws L.B. 38, §328
Nevada	1861 Nev. (Terr.) Laws ch. 28, §45 ("crime against nature"); 1912 Nev. Rev. Laws §6459	*Ex parte Benites*, 140 P. 436 (Nev. 1914)	Challenge rejected, *Jones v. State*, 456 P.2d 429 (Nev. 1969)	Decriminalized for different-sex, misdemeanor for same-sex, 1977 Nev. Stat. ch. 598, §17; decriminalized, 1993 Nev. Stats. ch. 236
New Hampshire	Act of Mar. 16, 1679 ("man lye with mankind"); Acts for the Punishment of Certain Crimes, 1791	1899 N.H. Laws ch. 33 (new crime: "unnatural or lascivious act"), confirmed, *State v. Vredenburg*, 19 A.2d 414 (N.H. 1941)	None	Decriminalized, 1973 N.H. Laws ch. 532, §26
New Jersey	Act of May 30, 1668 ("buggery," "sodomy"); Act of Mar. 18, 1796, ch. DC, §7	1906 N.J. Laws ch. 71 (new crime: "private lewdness or carnal indecency")	Sodomy law invalidated (privacy), *State v. Ciuffini*, 395 A.2d 904 (N.J. App. 1978). Private lewdness law limited, *State v. Dorsey*, 316 A.2d 689 (N.J. 1974)	Decriminalized, 1978 N.J. Laws, ch. 95, §2C:98-2

Appendix A1 *(continued)*

State	First law (crime)	First application to oral sex	Constitutional challenges	Recent legislative action
New Mexico	1876 N.M. (Terr.) Laws ch. 34 ("sodomy")	1963 N.M. Laws ch. 303, §9-6	Privacy challenge rejected, *State v. Elliott*, 551 P.2d 1352 (N.M. 1976)	Decriminalized, 1975 N.M. Laws ch. 109, §8
New York	Duke of York's Law, Mar. 1, 1665 ("sodomy"); 1787 N.Y. Laws ch. 21 ("buggery")	1886 N.Y. Laws ch. 31, §303	Invalidated (privacy), *People v. Onofre*, 415 N.E.2d 936 (N.Y. 1980)	Reduced to misdemeanor, 1950 N.Y. Laws ch. 525, §15
North Carolina	Act for the Punishment of the Vice of Buggery (1792)	*State v. Fenner*, 80 S.E. 970 (N.C. 1914)	Challenges rejected, *State v. Enslin*, 214 S.E.2d 318 (N.C. App. 1975); *State v. Poe*, 252 S.E.2d 843 (N.C. App. 1979)	None
North Dakota	1877 Dakota (Terr.) Penal Code §346 ("crime against nature")	1913 N.D. Comp. Laws §9615 ("carnally knows with the mouth")	None reported	Decriminalized, 1973 N.D. Laws ch. 117
Ohio	82 Ohio Laws p.241, S.B. 508 (1885) ("sodomy")	86 Ohio Laws p.251, H.B. 779 (1889)	None reported	Decriminalized, 1972 Ohio Laws pp.1906–11, H.B. 511
Oklahoma	1890 Okla. (Terr.) Stat. ch. 25, art. 31, §6 ("crime against nature")	*Ex parte DeFord*, 168 P. 58 (Okla. Crim. App. 1917)	Challenge rejected, *Canfield v. State*, 506 P.2d 987 (Okla. Crim. App. 1973). Invalidated for different-sex, *Post v. State*, 715 P.2d 1105 (Okla. Crim. App. 1986)	None

State	First law (crime)	First application to oral sex	Constitutional challenges	Recent legislative action
Oregon	Act of Dec. 22, 1853, ch. XI, §12 ("sodomy or the crime against nature")	1913 Or. Laws ch. 21 ("sexual perversity"), confirmed, *State v. Start*, 132 P. 512 (Or. 1913)	Invalidated (vagueness), *Jellum v. Cupp*, 475 F.2d 829 (9th Cir. 1973)	Decriminalized, 1971 Or. Laws ch. 743, §432
Pennsylvania	Penn's Great Law of Dec. 7, 1682 ("sodomy"); Pa. 14th Gen. Ass. ch. CLIV (1790)	1879 Pa. P.L. No. 156	Invalidated (privacy and equal protection), *Commonwealth v. Bonadio*, 415 A.2d 47 (Pa. 1980)	Reduced to misdemeanor, 1972 Pa. P.L. No. 334
Rhode Island	Providence Plant. Code, 1647 ("sodomy, buggery"); Act of 1663, 1647–1719 R.I. Acts p.6 (similar)	*State v. Milne*, 187 A.2d 136 (R.I. 1962)	Challenges rejected, *Milne*, or sidestepped, *State v. Lopes*, 660 A.2d 707 (R.I. 1995)	Decriminalized, 1998 R.I. Laws ch. 98-24
South Carolina	Act for the Punishment of the Vice of Buggery, 1712 S.C. Laws p.49	None reported	None reported	None
South Dakota	1877 Dakota (Terr.) Penal Code §346 ("crime against nature")	*State v. Whitmarsh*, 128 N.W. 580 (S.D. 1910)	None reported	Decriminalized, 1976 S.D. Laws ch. 158, §22-8
Tennessee	1829 Tenn. Acts ch. 23, §17 ("crime against nature")	*Fisher v. State*, 277 S.W.2d 340 (Tenn. 1955)	Vagueness challenge rejected, *Rose v. Locke*, 423 U.S. 48 (1975). Invalidated (privacy), *Campbell v. Sundquist*, 926 S.W.2d 250 (Tenn. App. 1996) (appeal denied)	Decriminalized for different-sex, misdemeanor for same-sex, 1989 Tenn. Acts ch. 591

Appendix A1   *(continued)*

State	First law (crime)	First application to oral sex	Constitutional challenges	Recent legislative action
Texas	1859 Tex. Gen. Laws ch. 74 ("crime against nature")	1943 Tex. Laws ch. 112 ("carnal copulation . . . in an opening of the body, except the sexual parts")	Challenges rejected, *Wade v. Buchanan*, 401 U.S. 989 (1971), or sidestepped, *State v. Morales*, 869 S.W.2d 941 (Tex. 1994)	Decriminalized for different-sex, misdemeanor for same-sex, 1973 Tex. Laws ch. 399, §21.06
Utah	1876 Utah (Terr.) Penal Code tit. XXI, §144 ("crime against nature")	1923 Utah Laws ch. 13 ("with the mouth")	None reported	Reduced to misdemeanor, 1973 Utah Laws ch. 196, §76-5-403
Vermont	Acts and Laws, 1779 (common law in force, including "buggery"); see *State v. LaForrest*, 45 A. 225 (Vt. 1899)	1937 Vt. Acts No. 211 ("copulating the mouth of one person with the sexual organ of another")	None reported	Decriminalized, 1977 Vt. Acts No. 51, §2
Virginia	Code of 1610, §9 ("Sodomie"); English law in force, 1661 ("buggery"); 1792 Va. Acts ch. 100	1916 Va. Acts ch. 295 (same-sex "carnal copulation"); 1924 Va. Acts ch. 358 (different-sex "carnal copulation")	Privacy challenge rejected, *Doe v. Commonwealth's Attorney*, 415 U.S. 901 (1976)	None
Washington	1893 Wash. Laws ch. CXXXIX	1909 Wash. Laws ch. 249, §204	Challenge rejected, *State v. Rhinehart*, 424 P.2d 906 (Wash. 1967)	Decriminalized, 1975 Wash. Laws ch. 260, §9A.92.010

State	First law (crime)	First application to oral sex	Constitutional challenges	Recent legislative action
West Virginia	W.V. Code ch. 149, §12 (1860) ("buggery")	W.V. Code ch. 149, §12 (1931)	None reported	Decriminalized, 1976 W.V. Acts ch. 43
Wisconsin	Wis. (Terr.) Stat. §14 (1839) ("sodomy, or the crime against nature"); Wis. Rev. Stat. ch. 139, §15 (1849)	1898 Wis. Stat. §4591 ("penetration of the mouth . . . by the organ of any male person")	Challenges rejected, *Jones v. State*, 200 N.W.2d 587 (Wis. 1972); *Gossett v. State*, 242 N.W.2d 899 (Wis. 1976)	Reduced to misdemeanor, 1977 Wis. Laws ch. 173, §92; decriminalized, 1983 Wis. Laws ch. 17, §5
Wyoming	1890 Wyo. Laws ch. 73, §87 ("crime against nature")	Ibid.	None reported	Decriminalized, 1977 Wyo. Laws ch. 70, §3

Note: This table does not report constitutional challenges that have been successful in state trial and intermediate appellate courts, unless (as was the case in Tennessee) the state's highest court signaled its agreement with the lower court's invalidation. The Louisiana intermediate appellate court found that state's consensual sodomy law in violation of the state constitution's privacy protections. *State v. Smith*, 729 So. 2d 648 (La. App. 1999). State trial judges in both Maryland and Michigan have found their consensual sodomy laws unconstitutional, in unreported opinions that were not appealed by state attorneys general. See *Williams v. Maryland*, No. 9803603I/CC-1059 (Balt. City Cir. Ct. 1999); *Michigan Org. for Human Rights v. Kelly*, No. 88-815820 (CZ) (Wayne Cty. Cir. Ct. July 9, 1990). As of July 1, 1999, there are constitutional challenges to consensual sodomy laws pending in Arkansas and Texas.

Appendix A2　　Municipal sex offense ordinances, 1850–1950

Location	Cross-dressing	Indecent behavior	Lewd solicitation	Obscene publications	Immoral plays	Indecent films
Alabama						
Birmingham	(1917c)	1917c		1917c	1917c	1917c
Arizona						
Phoenix		1914o		1914o	1914o	
Tuscon	1883o	1883o		1883o	1883o	
Arkansas						
Little Rock		1868o		1891o	1868o	
California						
Los Angeles	(1898o)	1885o	1883o	1936c	1905o	1908o
Oakland	1879o			1899o		1899o
San Diego		1895o	1896o	1926o		
San Francisco	1866o	1866o	1874o	1874o	1866o	
	1903o	1903o	1903o		1909o	1909o
San José	1882o	1882o	1882o	1882o		
Santa Barbara	189?o	189?o			189?o	
Colorado						
Denver	1886c	1886c		1886c	1886c	
Delaware						
Wilmington	1856o	1865o		1896o		
Florida						
Miami	1952o	1945c	1955o		1952o	
	1956o					
Miami Beach	192?o	192?o		193?o	192?o	
Orlando	1907c	1907c	1952c	1907c	1907c	
Pensacola	1920c	1920c		1920c	1920c	
Sarasota	1919o	1919o			1919o	
Tampa	((1908c))	1908c	1908c	1926c		
West Palm Beach	1926c	1926c		1926c	1926c	
Georgia						
Atlanta	((1873o))	1873o		1873o	1873o	1942c
Columbus	1914c	1914c				
Savannah		1918c				
Idaho						
Boise		1922c				1922c
Illinois						
Chicago	1851o	1851o	1911c	1851o	1851o	1907o
Cicero	1897c	1897c		1897c		
Peoria	1884c	1884c		1884c	1884c	

Appendix A2 (*continued*)

Location	Cross-dressing	Indecent behavior	Lewd solicitation	Obscene publications	Immoral plays	Indecent films
Springfield	1856o	1856o		1856o	1856o	1921c
Indiana						
Indianapolis	((1951c))	1869o	1892c	1869o	1951c	1951c
Iowa						
Cedar Falls	1899o	1899o		1899o	1899o	
Cedar Rapids	1906c	1929c	1929c	1906c	1906c	
Sioux City	((1882o))	1882o	1943c	1882o	1882o	
Kansas						
Topeka		1935o		1915o	1915o	
Wichita		1899o	1936o	1899o	1926o	1923o
Kentucky						
Louisville		1853o				
		1898o				
Louisiana						
New Orleans	(1856o)	1856o		1856o		
	((1891o))	1891o	1956c	1889o		
Maryland						
Baltimore					1879c	
Massachusetts						
Boston				1915s	1915s	1915s
Michigan						
Battle Creek		1883o		1883o	1883o	
Detroit	195?o	1870o	1924o	1870o	1906o	1907o
				1892o		
Grand Rapids		1873o		1873o	1920o	1920o
Minnesota						
Minneapolis	1877o	1877o	1919o	1877o	1877o	
Missouri						
Columbia	1883o	1883o	1883o	1883o		
Kansas City	1860o	1860o		1860o	1860o	1928c
	1889o	1889o		1889o	1890o	
St. Louis	1864o	1864o		1864o	1864o	
Montana						
Butte	1885o	1885o		1885o	1885o	
Nebraska						
Lincoln	1889c	1870o		1889c	1889c	
Omaha	1890c	1890c		1890c	1890c	1941c

Appendix A2   (*continued*)

Location	Cross-dressing	Indecent behavior	Lewd solicitation	Obscene publications	Immoral plays	Indecent films
Nevada						
Reno						
New Jersey						
Newark	1858o	1858o		1858o	1858o	
New York						
Buffalo		1878c	1939c	1878c		
New York City	1845s	1881c	1900s	1856s	1927s	1921s
	1876s		1923s			
North Carolina						
Charlotte	((1915c))	1915c	1915c	1915c	1915c	
Raleigh						
Wilmington	1913c	1913c		1913c	1913c	
Ohio						
Akron		1921c	1921c	1921c		
Cincinnati	1974o	1819o		1856o	1849o	
Cleveland	1924c	1854o	1924c	1890c	1890c	
Columbus	1848o	1848o	1919c	1919c	1919c	
Dayton		1842o		1849o		
Toledo	1862o	1858o	1917o	1858o		
Oklahoma						
Oklahoma City		1913c	1913c	1913c	1913c	
Tulsa	((1917c))	1917c	1917c	1917c	1917c	
Oregon						
Portland		1868o	1883o			
		1883o				
Pennsylvania						
Philadelphia						
Pittsburgh			1915o	1927o	1911o	
South Carolina						
Charleston	1858o	1858o		1858o		
Columbia					1917o	1917o
South Dakota						
Sioux Falls	((1882o))	1882o	1901o	1882o	1882o	1908o
	((1901o))			1901o	1901o	
Tennessee						
Memphis	1863o	1857c	1931c	1857c	1931c	1931c
Nashville	1881c	1881c		1917c	1881c	

Appendix A2 (*continued*)

Location	Cross-dressing	Indecent behavior	Lewd solicitation	Obscene publications	Immoral plays	Indecent films
Texas						
Dallas	1880o	1880o		1880o	1911c	
El Paso	(1903c)	1903c		1903c	1903c	
Houston	1861o	1861o	1942c	1922c	1922c	1922c
San Antonio				1942o	1899o	
Utah						
Salt Lake City	((1880o))	1872o		1872o	1888o	
Virginia						
Norfolk		1916o	1944c		1944c	1944c
Richmond		1885c		1885c		1913c
Roanoke		1939c	1939c	1909c	1910o	1910o
Washington						
Seattle	((1907o))	1907o	1907o	1907o	1907o	1907o
West Virginia						
Charleston	1913c	1886c		1883c	1913c	
Wisconsin						
Green Bay	((1911c))	1911c				
Madison		1904c		1904c		
Milwaukee		1906c			1906c	
Wyoming						
Cheyenne	1892o	1892o		1892o	1892o	

Note: The dates are the earliest for which I found laws regulating the noted category of gender-bending or "deviant" sexual conduct—either ordinances ("o") or codes of ordinances ("c") or, for Boston and New York City, state laws ("s"). I have included under *Cross-dressing* ordinances that prohibit disguises (in parentheses) or lewd or indecent dress ((in double parentheses)) as well as those specifically targeting dress of the opposite sex. I have included under *Lewd solicitation* only those ordinances targeted at, or clearly applicable to, same-sex solicitation, and not just different-sex prostitution. A blank space signifies that I was unable to find an ordinance regulating this conduct for the city in question. A blank line indicates that I was unable to find any ordinances regulating this conduct for that city.

Appendix A3   State criminal laws protecting the sexuality of male as well as female minors, 1870–1970

State	Indecent liberties or molestation	Enticement or solicitation	Contributing to sexual delinquency	Exposure to indecency	Immoral use or exhibition	Schoolyard loitering	Sentence enhancement
Alabama	1955 Ala. Acts No. 397		1923 Ala. Acts 296, §12				
Alaska			1929 Alaska Laws ch. 103	1955 Alaska Laws ch. 190 (comics)			
Arizona	1939 Ariz. Laws ch. 13; 1965 Ariz. Laws ch. 20		1933 Ariz. Laws ch. 91	1951 Ariz.	1939 Ariz. Laws ch. 13; Laws ch. 111	1951 Ariz. Laws ch. 110	
Arkansas	1953 Ark. Acts Nos. 48 & 94	1875 Ark. Acts No. 12; 1953 Ark. Acts No. 94		1953 Ark. Acts No. 94	1909 Ark. Acts No. 170	1953 Ark. Acts No. 48	
California	1901 Cal. Stat. ch. 201 (lewd act); 1929 Cal. Stat. 697 (molestation)		1915 Cal. Stat. ch. 631; 1937 Cal. Stat. ch. 369	1907 Cal. Stat. 756 ("degrading practices")	1905 Cal. Stat. 74	1929 Cal. Stat. 697; 1947 Cal. Stat., Extr. Sess. ch. 730	1950 Cal. Stat., 1st Extr. Sess. ch. 28 (habitual criminal); 1952 Cal. Stat., 1st Extr. Sess. ch. 23, §3 (oral copulation)
Colorado	1905 Colo. Laws 181	Ibid.	1909 Colo. Laws 336				

State	Indecent liberties or molestation	Enticement or solicitation	Contributing to sexual delinquency	Exposure to indecency	Immoral use or exhibition	Schoolyard loitering	Sentence enhancement
Connecticut			1907 Conn. Laws ch. 69; 1925 Conn. Laws ch. 66	1925 Conn. Laws ch. 66			
Delaware	1947 Del. Laws ch. 81				1918 Del. Laws ch. 686; 1920 Del. Laws ch. 127		
District of Columbia	Miller Act of 1948, §103(a), 62 Stat. 347	Id. §103(b)		Id. §101(b), 62 Stat. 346			Id. §104(a), 62 Stat. 347
Florida	1951 Fla. Laws ch. 26, 580		1915 Fla. Laws ch. 6906; 1927 Fla. Laws ch. 11,874; 1943 Fla. Laws ch. 21,978	1951 Fla. Laws ch. 26,580 (lewd act)			
Georgia	1950 Ga. Laws 387	Ibid.	1950 Ga. Laws 387–388				1949 Ga. Laws 275 (sodomy)
Hawaii			1925 Haw. Laws ch. 167; 1945 Haw. Laws ch. 187				
Idaho	1949 Idaho Laws ch. 214						

Appendix A3   (*continued*)

State	Indecent liberties or molestation	Enticement or solicitation	Contributing to sexual delinquency	Exposure to indecency	Immoral use or exhibition	Schoolyard loitering	Sentence enhancement
Illinois	1907 Ill. Laws 266	Ibid.	1915 Ill. Laws 369	1889 Ill. Laws 114; 1915 Ill. Laws 368 (lewd acts)	1877 Ill. Laws 90		1961 Ill. Laws 2044 (MPC)
Indiana	1881 Ind. Acts 195-196, §100 (masturbation)	Ibid.; 1975 P.L. No. 325, §11	1945 Ind. Acts ch. 218		1889 Ind. Acts ch. 201		
Iowa	32 Acts Iowa Gen. Ass. ch. 173 (1907)		Iowa Code, 1924, §3658	Iowa Code, 1897, §4955			
Kansas	1955 Kan. Laws ch. 195; 1957 Kan. Laws ch. 258; 1959 Kan. Laws ch. 198	Ibid.	1957 Kan. Laws ch. 256; 1959 Kan. Laws ch. 201				
Kentucky	1948 Ky. Acts ch. 36		1952 Ky. Acts ch. 161	1956 Ky. Acts ch. 244 (comics)		1968 Ky. Acts ch. 105, §8(1)(c)	
Louisiana	1912 La. Acts No. 202; 1942 La. Acts No. 43		1918 La. Acts No. 169; 1942 La. Acts No. 43 (invalidated); 1948 La. Acts No. 388	1942 La. Acts No. 43	1916 La. Acts No. 139		1962 La. Acts No. 60 (crime against nature)

State	Indecent liberties or molestation	Enticement or solicitation	Contributing to sexual delinquency	Exposure to indecency	Immoral use or exhibition	Schoolyard loitering	Sentence enhancement
Maine	1913 Me. Laws ch. 62; 1961 Me. Laws ch. 60 (procuring another)		1955 Me. Laws ch. 414	1885 Me. Laws ch. 348; 1957 Me. Laws ch. 321	1905 Me. Laws ch. 123, §9		
Maryland				1894 Md. Laws ch. 271, §220A; 1955 Md. Laws ch. 720 (comics); 1959 Md. Laws ch. 830 (film); 1961 Md. Laws ch. 473			
Massachusetts	1955 Mass. Laws ch. 763, §4	1886 Mass. Laws ch. 329; 1898 Mass. Laws ch. 444	1906 Mass. Laws ch. 413; 1916 Mass. Laws ch. 243; 1932 Mass. Laws ch. 95	1885 Mass. Laws ch. 305; 1945 Mass. Laws ch. 278; 1956 Mass. Laws ch. 724			

Appendix A3 (*continued*)

State	Indecent liberties or molestation	Enticement or solicitation	Contributing to sexual delinquency	Exposure to indecency	Immoral use or exhibition	Schoolyard loitering	Sentence enhancement
Michigan	1952 Mich. Pub. Acts No. 73	1935 Mich. Pub. Acts No. 174	1927 Mich. Pub. Acts No. 319	1881 Mich. Pub. Acts No. 260; 1893 Mich. Pub. Acts No. 193	1881 Mich. Pub. Acts No. 260; 1893 Mich. Pub. Acts No. 156		1897 Mich. Pub. Acts No. 95 (crime against nature)
Minnesota	1927 Minn. Laws ch. 394; 1929 Minn. Laws ch. 27; 1967 Minn. Laws ch. 507, §7		1917 Minn. Laws ch. 242; 1927 Minn. Laws ch. 192, §7	1917 Minn. Laws ch. 242; 1969 Minn. Laws ch. 1071		1929 Minn. Laws ch. 181; 1939 Minn. Laws ch. 155	1921 Minn. Laws ch. 455 (habitual offender); 1967 Minn. Laws ch. 507, §4 (sodomy)
Mississippi				1968 Miss. Laws ch. 349 (materials, shows, movies)			
Missouri	1949 Mo. Laws 249	Ibid.	1907 Mo. Laws 231; 1959 Mo. Laws S.B.3	1895 Mo. Laws 146; 1949 Mo. Laws 249 (body)	1895 Mo. Laws 205		

State	Indecent liberties or molestation	Enticement or solicitation	Contributing to sexual delinquency	Exposure to indecency	Immoral use or exhibition	Schoolyard loitering	Sentence enhancement
Montana	1913 Mont. Laws ch. 59; 1939 Mont. Laws ch. 70; 1959 Mont. Laws ch. 57			1891 Mont. Laws 255; 1955 Mont. Laws ch. 214; 1967 Mont. Laws ch. 276			
Nebraska	1951 Neb. Laws ch. 82		1937 Neb. Laws ch. 97; 1957 Neb. Laws ch. 93; 1961 Neb. Laws ch. 118	1951 Neb. Laws ch. 82 (body)			
Nevada	1925 Nev. Laws ch. 24; 1947 Nev. Laws ch. 24; 1961 Nev. Laws ch. 92		1909 Nev. Laws ch. 165; 1911 Nev. Laws ch. 328; 1921 Nev Laws ch. 21; 1955 Nev. Laws ch. 152	1911 Nev. Penal Code §196	Ibid.		1951 Nev. Laws ch. 524 (crime against nature)
New Hampshire					1885 N.H. Laws ch. 10 (obscene literature)		
New Jersey	1945 N.J. Laws ch. 242	Ibid.	1912 N.J. Laws ch. 163		1898 N.J. Laws ch. 235, §56		1926 N.J. Laws ch. 172 (sodomy)
New Mexico	1949 N.M. Laws ch. 140; 1963 N.M. Laws ch. 303, §9-9	1963 N.M. Laws ch. 303, §9-10	1963 N.M. Laws ch. 303, §6-3	1949 N.M. Laws ch. 140 (body); 1963 N.M. Laws ch. 303, §9-9			1963 N.M. Laws ch. 303, §9-7 (sodomy)

Appendix A3 (*continued*)

State	Indecent liberties or molestation	Enticement or solicitation	Contributing to sexual delinquency	Exposure to indecency	Immoral use or exhibition	Schoolyard loitering	Sentence enhancement
New York	1927 N.Y. Laws ch. 383; 1929 N.Y. Laws ch. 684; 1933 N.Y. Laws ch. 423; 1937 N.Y. Laws ch. 691; 1950 N.Y. Laws ch. 525, §§11–12		1910 N.Y. Laws ch. 699	1955 N.Y. Laws ch. 836 (comics); 1965 N.Y. Laws ch. 327 (materials, movies) and ch. 372 (porn)	1876 N.Y. Laws ch. 122	1954 N.Y. Laws ch. 519	1950 N.Y. Laws ch. 525, §15 (sodomy)
North Carolina	1955 N.C. Stat. ch. 764			1955 N.C. Stat. ch. 1204 (comics)			
North Dakota	1923 N.D. Laws ch. 167; 1951 N.D. Laws ch. 117; 1953 N.D. Laws ch. 118			1895 N.D. Rev. Code §7213–14			
Ohio	121 Ohio Laws 557 (1953); 126 Ohio Laws 114 (1955)	130 Ohio Laws 659 (1963)		130 Ohio Laws 659 (1963); 133 Ohio Laws HB.84 (1970)			

State	Indecent liberties or molestation	Enticement or solicitation	Contributing to sexual delinquency	Exposure to indecency	Immoral use or exhibition	Schoolyard loitering	Sentence enhancement
Oklahoma	1951 Okla. Laws 60; 1955 Okla. Laws 186	Ibid.	1939 Okla. Laws 15; 1945 Okla. Laws 27		1961 Okla. Laws 230		
Oregon		1953 Or. Laws ch. 641; 1955 Or. Laws ch. 636	1907 Or. Laws ch. 69; 1935 Or. Laws ch. 315	1895 Or. Laws 122–123 (brothel)			1955 Or. Laws ch. 636 (sodomy)
Pennsylvania			1953 Pa. P.L. No. 277; 1961 Pa. P.L. No. 848	1879 Pa. P.L. No. 142 (brothel)	Ibid.		1953 Pa. P.L. No. 276 (sodomy)
Rhode Island			1908 R.I. Laws ch. 1544	1956 R.I. Laws ch. 3686; 1966 R.I. Laws ch. 268	1878 R.I. Laws ch. 683		
South Carolina	1953 S.C. Laws ch. 48; 1964 S.C. Laws ch. 53		1957 S.C. Laws ch. 50	1965 S.C. Laws ch. 54	Ibid.		
South Dakota	1950 S.D. Laws ch. 3; 1955 S.D. Laws ch. 27		1909 S.D. Laws ch. 275	ch. 88	1903 S.D. Laws		
Tennessee			1911 Tenn. Acts ch. 58	1969 Tenn. Acts ch. 278		1949 Tenn. Acts ch. 63	

Appendix A3 (*continued*)

State	Indecent liberties or molestation	Enticement or solicitation	Contributing to sexual delinquency	Exposure to indecency	Immoral use or exhibition	Schoolyard loitering	Sentence enhancement
Texas	1943 Tex. Acts ch. 112; 1950 Tex. Acts ch. 12; 1955 Tex. Acts ch. 112	1950 Tex. Acts ch. 8; 1955 Tex. Acts ch. 110	1907 Tex. Acts 209; 1918 Tex. Acts 125	1950 Tex. Acts ch. 9 (genitals); 1969 Tex. Acts ch. 284 (materials)		1907 Tex. Acts 452	
Utah							
Vermont	1937 Vt. Acts No. 211			1957 Vt. Acts No. 271; 1967 Vt. Acts No. 340 (Adj. Sess.) (publications, movies)			
Virginia	1958 Va. Laws ch. 163; 1960 Va. Laws ch. 358	Ibid.	1914 Va. Laws 394; 1920 Va. Laws 269	1958 Va. Laws ch. 163; 1960 Va. Laws ch. 358 (genitals)	1960 Va. Laws ch. 233		
Washington	1955 Wash. Laws ch. 127	1961 Wash. Laws ch. 65	1917 Wash. Laws ch. 160, §17	1955 Wash. Laws ch. 127 (genitals)		1965 Wash. Laws, 1st Extr. Sess. ch. 112	

State	Indecent liberties or molestation	Enticement or solicitation	Contributing to sexual delinquency	Exposure to indecency	Immoral use or exhibition	Schoolyard loitering	Sentence enhancement
West Virginia			1936 W. Va. Acts, 1st Extr. Sess. ch. 1; 1941 W. Va. Acts ch. 73	1974 W. Va. Acts ch. 35		1973 W. Va. Acts ch. 43	
Wisconsin	1897 Wis. Stat. ch. 198; 1915 Wis. Stat. ch. 199; 1925 Wis. Stat. ch. 4	1887 Wis. Stat. ch. 353; 1889 Wis. Stat. ch. 200			1880 Wis. Stat. ch. 239		
Wyoming	1890 Wyo. Laws ch. 73, §87 (masturbation); 1957 Wyo. Laws ch. 220, §8	1957 Wyo. Laws ch. 220, §5	1927 Wyo. Laws ch. 93; 1957 Wyo. Laws ch. 220, §3	Ibid.	1890–1891 Wyo. Laws ch. 20; 1957 Wyo. Laws ch. 220, §4		

Note: This appendix includes only statutes that criminalize *adult* conduct that endangered the sexuality of *children* of both sexes. (Nineteenth-century seduction, chastity, and abduction laws protected the sexuality of girls alone.) Most of the noted statutes have been repealed or superseded by the state's version of the Model Penal Code.

Modern State and Municipal Regulation of Sexual and Gender Variation

Appendix B1   State sexual psychopath laws, 1935–1961

State Code Reference	Date enacted (amendments)	Jurisidictional basis
Alabama Code tit. 15, §§434–442	1951	Conviction of sex offense
California Welfare & Inst. Code §§5500–5522, 5600–5607	1939 (1945, 1949, 1950, 1951, 1952)	Conviction of any criminal offense with minor *or* petition to court
Colorado Rev. Stat. §§39-19-1 to -10	1953	Conviction of specified sex offenses (including unnatural acts)
District of Columbia Code §§22-3501 to -3511	1948	Petition to court
Florida Stat. §917.12	1951 (1953, 1955, 1957)	Charge or conviction of specified crimes (including sodomy, lewdness, attempts) if they involve minors
Illinois Stat. ch. 38, §§820–825g	1938 (1941, 1955)	Criminal charge (narrowed to crimes against children, 1955)
Indiana Code §§9-3401 to -3412	1949	Charge *or* conviction of any but a few specified crimes
Iowa Code §§225A.1–.15	1955 (1959)	Charge of public offense
Kansas Stat. §§62-1534 to -1537	1953	Conviction of a crime against public morals, including crimes of perversion
Maryland Laws, 1957, ch. 476, §5	1951 (1957)	Criminal charge
Massachusetts Gen. Laws ch. 123A, §§1–11	1947 (1954, 1958)	Conviction of specified sex offenses (including sodomy, unnatural acts, indecent exposure)
Michigan Stat. §28.967(1)-(9)	1935 (1937, 1939, 1950, 1952)	Charge or conviction of criminal offense
Minnesota Stat. §526.09-.11	1939 (1945, 1953)	Petition to court
Missouri Rev. Stat. §202.700-.770	1949	Criminal charge
Nebraska Rev. Stat. §29.2901-.2907	1949 (1951)	Petition to court
New Hampshire Stat. §173:1 to :16	1949 (1953)	Petition to court *or* charge of specified sex offenses (including sodomy, unnatural acts, attempts)
New Jersey Rev. Stat. §2:192-1.13 to -1.23	1949 (1950, 1951)	Conviction of specified offenses and sex crimes (including sodomy, lewdness, indecent exposure, attempts to commit those crimes)

Appendix B1   (*continued*)

State Code Reference	Date enacted (amendments)	Jurisidictional basis
New York Penal Law §§243, 483-a, 483-b, 1944-a, 2010	1950[a]	Conviction of specified sex crimes (including forcible sodomy and sodomy with a child)
Ohio Rev. Code §2947.24-.29	1947 (1950, 1953, 1954)	Conviction of specified felonies (including sodomy) *or* misdemeanors involving sex offenses or "abnormal tendencies"
Oregon Rev. Stat. §137.111-.117	1953 (1955, 1961)	Conviction of sex offense involving a child
Pennsylvania Stat. tit. 19, §§1166–1174	1951	Conviction of specified sex offenses (including sodomy and assault)
Rhode Island Gen. Laws §11-45.1	1961	Charged with being lewd, lascivious, obscene, or indecent and convicted of a crime
South Dakota Codified Laws §13.1727	1950	Conviction of molesting a minor
Tennessee Code §§33-1301 to -1305	1957	Conviction of any sex crime
Utah Code §§77-49-1 to -8	1951 (1953)	Conviction of sex crime
Vermont Stat. tit. 18, §§2811–2816	1943 (1945, 1951)	Conviction of any felony *or* third conviction of a misdemeanor
Virginia Code §§53-278.2–.4	1950	Conviction of a crime indicating sexual abnormality
Washington Rev. Code §§71.06.010 to .260	1947 (1951)	Charged with *or* convicted of a specified sex offense (including sodomy, indecent liberty with child, lewd vagrancy)
Wisconsin Stat. §959.15	1947 (1951)	Conviction of a crime
Wyoming Stat. §§7-348 to -362	1951	Conviction of specified sex crimes (including sodomy, liberties with child, indecent exposure [third offense])

Note: This appendix includes statutes that create a procedure to identify sex offenders likely to pose a recurring danger to others in society, especially children. Such offenders were usually called "sexual psychopaths." The statutes then provided special medical treatment, usually in addition to criminal penalties otherwise applicable.

a. Governor Thomas Dewey vetoed a broad sexual psychopath bill in 1947. The 1950 bill reflected input from the governor's study commission.

Appendix B2　State and municipal laws against sexual orientation discrimination, 1972–1998

Location	Public employment	Public accommodations	Private employment	Education	Housing	Credit
Alaska						
Anchorage	1993					
Arizona						
Phoenix	1992		1992			
Tucson	1997		1997			
California[a]	1979eo	1951	1979	1992		
Alameda	1978					
Alameda Cty.	1990					
Berkeley	1978		1978	1978	1978	1978
Cathedral City	1987	1987	1987	1987	1987	1987
Cupertino	1975					
Daly City	1978					
Davis	1986	1986	1986		1986	1986
Hayward	1994	1994	1994	1994	1994	1994
Laguna Beach	1984	1984	1984	1984	1984	1984
Long Beach	1987		1987			
Los Angeles	1977	1979	1979	1979	1979	1979
Mountain View	1975	1975	1975	1975	1975	1975
Oakland	1984	1984	1984	1984	1984	1984
Pacifica	1992					
Riverside	1990	1990	1990	1990	1990	1990
Sacramento	1983	1986	1986	1986	1986	1986
San Diego	1972	1990	1990	1990	1990	1990
San Francisco	1978	1978	1978	1978	1978	1978
San Jose	1985					
San Mateo Cty.	1992		1992		1992	
Santa Barbara	1993			1993		
Santa Barbara Cty.	1979			1979		
Santa Cruz Cty.	1981					
Santa Monica	1984	1984	1984	1984	1984	1984
West Hollywood	1984	1984	1984	1984	1984	1984
Colorado[b]	1990eo					
Aspen	1977	1977	1977		1977	
Boulder[c]	1988	1988	1988		1988	
Boulder Cty.	1987					
Colorado Springs	1997					
Crested Butte	1993	1993	1993		1993	
Denver	1990	1990	1990	1990	1990	
Fort Collins	1998	1998	1998		1998	
Jefferson Cty.				1997		
Telluride	1993	1993	1993		1993	

Appendix B2 (*continued*)

Location	Public employment	Public accommodations	Private employment	Education	Housing	Credit
Connecticut	1991	1991	1991	1991	1991	1991
Hartford	1977	1977	1977	1977	1977	1977
New Haven	1991	1991	1991	1991	1991	1991
Stamford	1991	1991	1991	1991	1991	1991
District of Columbia	1973	1973	1973	1973	1973	1973
	1977	1977	1977	1977	1977	1977
Florida						
Alachua Cty.	1993	1993	1993		1993	
Broward Cty.	1995	1995	1995	1995	1995	1995
Dade Cty.[d]	1999		1999			
Key West	1991	1991	1991	1991	1991	1991
Miami Beach	1992	1992	1992	1992	1992	1992
Palm Beach Cty.	1990	1990	1990	1990	1990	1990
Tampa[e]						
West Palm Beach	1990	1990	1990	1990	1990	1990
Georgia						
Atlanta	1986					
Fulton Cty.	1992					
Lythia Springs	1997					
Tybee Island	1996					
Hawaii	1991		1991			
Honolulu	1988					
Honolulu Cty.	1988					
Idaho						
Troy	1994					
Illinois	1996eo					
Champaign	1977	1977	1977	1977	1977	1977
Chicago[f]	1982eo	1988	1988	1988	1988	1988
Cook Cty.	1993	1993	1993	1993	1993	1993
Evanston	1980				1980	1980
La Grange					1993	
Oak Park	1989	1989			1989	
Urbana	1979	1979	1979	1979	1979	
Indiana						
Bloomington	1993	1993	1993	1993	1993	
Lafayette	1993	1993	1993	1993	1993	
West Lafayette	1993	1993	1993	1993	1993	

Appendix B2 (*continued*)

Location	Public employment	Public accommodations	Private employment	Education	Housing	Credit
Iowa						
Ames	1991	1991	1991	1991	1991	1991
Iowa City	1977	1977	1977			1977
Kansas						
Lawrence	1988	1988	1988		1988	
Wichita[g]						
Kentucky						
Henderson	1994					
Louisville	1991		1999			
Louisiana[h]						
New Orleans	1985eo	1991	1991		1991	
Maine[i]						
Lewiston[j]						
Portland	1992	1992	1992	1992	1992	1992
Maryland	1993eo					
Baltimore	1988	1988	1988	1988	1988	
Howard Cty.	1976	1976	1976	1976	1976	1976
Montgomery Cty.	1984	1984	1984		1984	1984
Prince George's Cty.	1991					
Rockville	1990	1990	1990	1990	1990	1990
Takoma Park	1993					
Massachusetts	1989	1989	1989	1989	1989	1989
Amherst	1976	1976	1976	1976	1976	1976
Boston[k]	1982eo	1984	1984	1984		1984
Cambridge	1984	1984	1984	1984	1984	1984
Malden	1984	1984	1984	1984	1984	1984
Springfield[l]						
Worcester	1986	1986	1986	1986	1986	1986
Michigan						
Ann Arbor	1972	1978	1972		1978	1978
Birmingham		1992			1992	1992
Detroit	1979	1979	1979	1979	1979	1979
East Lansing	1972	1986	1972		1986	1986
Flint	1990	1990	1990	1990	1990	
Ingham Cty.	1987					
Saginaw	1984			1984	1984	
Ypsilanti	1997		1997		1997	
Minnesota	1986eo	1993	1993	1993	1993	1993
Hennepin Cty.	1974					
Minneapolis	1975	1975	1975	1975	1975	1975
St. Paul[m]	1990	1990	1990	1990	1990	1990

Appendix B2   (continued)

Location	Public employment	Public accommodations	Private employment	Education	Housing	Credit
Missouri						
Columbia	1992					
Kansas City	1993		1993		1993	
St. Louis	1992	1992	1992	1992	1992	1992
Nevada	1999		1999			
New Hampshire Portsmouth[n]	1997	1997	1997		1997	
New Jersey	1991	1991	1991	1991	1991	
Essex Cty.	1990					
Newark	1990					
Vineland	1990					
New Mexico						
Albuquerque	1994					
New York	1983eo					
Albany	1992	1992	1992		1992	
Alfred	1974	1992	1992	1992	1992	1992
Brighton	1992					
Buffalo	1984					
East Hampton	1985					
Ithaca	1994	1994	1994		1994	
New York City[o]	1972eo	1986	1986	1986	1986	
Plattsburgh	1992					
Rochester	1983					
Southampton	1995					
Suffolk Cty.	1988					
Syracuse	1990	1990	1990	1990	1990	
Tompkins Cty.	1991	1991	1991	1991	1991	1991
Troy	1979					
Watertown	1988	1988	1988	1988	1988	1988
North Carolina						
Asheville	1994					
Carborro	1990					
Chapel Hill	1975					
Durham	1986					
Raleigh	1988					
Ohio	1983eo					
Athens	1997	1997		1997		
Cincinnati[p]						
Cleveland	1994	1994	1994	1994	1994	
Columbus	1984	1992	1992	1992	1992	1992
Cuyahoga Cty.	1981		1986			
Yellow Springs	1979	1979	1979		1979	1979

Appendix B2   *(continued)*

Location	Public employment	Public accommodations	Private employment	Education	Housing	Credit
Oregon	1987eo[q]					
Ashland	1993	1993	1993		1993	
Corvallis	1992	1992	1992		1992	
Eugene[r]	1994	1994	1994		1994	
Portland	1974	1987	1987		1987	
Pennsylvania	1975eo					
Harrisburg	1983	1983	1983		1983	1983
Lancaster	1991	1991	1991		1991	1991
Northhampton Cty.	1996					
Philadelphia[s]	1980eo	1982	1982		1982	1982
Pittsburgh	1989	1990	1990		1990	1990
State College					1993	
York	1993	1993	1993		1993	
Rhode Island	1985eo	1995	1995	1995	1995	1995
Providence	1995	1995	1995	1995	1995	1995
South Carolina						
Columbia	1985					
South Dakota						
Minnehaha Cty.	1979					
Texas						
Austin	1975	1975	1975		1975	1975
Dallas	1995					
Houston[t]	1998					
Utah						
Salt Lake City[u]						
Salt Lake Cty.	1992					
Vermont	1991	1991	1991	1991	1991	1991
Burlington	1992		1992			
Virginia						
Alexandria	1990	1990	1990	1990	1990	1990
Arlington	1992		1992			
Charlottesville	1994					
Virginia Beach	1995					
Washington	1985eo					
Clallam Cty.	1976					
King Cty.					1988	1988
Olympia	1986					
Pullman	1981				1981	1981
Seattle	1984		1984		1984	1984
Tumwater	1997				1993	
Vancouver	1993					

Appendix B2   (continued)

Location	Public employment	Public accommodations	Private employment	Education	Housing	Credit
West Virginia						
Morgantown	1977					
Wisconsin	1982	1982	1982	1982	1982	1982
Dane Cty.	1987					
Madison	1979	1979	1979		1979	1979
Milwaukee	1987					

Note: The nonexhaustive list in this appendix is largely taken from one compiled by the National Gay and Lesbian Task Force (August 1998). The dates reflect the earliest known legal prohibition against sexual orientation discrimination, either by executive order (especially for municipal employment) or statute or ordinance. An executive order is indicated by "eo." Footnotes will note instances where popular referenda have repealed previous executive orders or ordinances.

a. California prohibited public employment discrimination by executive order in 1979 and private employment discrimination by court decision in 1979. Both were codified by statute in 1990.

b. A 1992 referendum repealed the 1990 executive order and municipal ordinances, but the U.S. Supreme Court invalidated the referendum. The executive order will expire in 1999 unless reissued by the new governor, however.

c. A 1974 referendum repealed a 1974 antidiscrimination ordinance.

d. A 1977 referendum repealed a 1977 antidiscrimination ordinance.

e. A 1992 referendum repealed a 1991 antidiscrimination ordinance.

f. Chicago's 1982 executive order prohibiting public employment discrimination was superseded by the 1988 ordinance.

g. A 1978 referendum repealed a 1977 antidiscrimination ordinance.

h. Between 1992 and 1998 Louisiana operated under an executive order prohibiting public employment discrimination. The order lapsed when a new governor took office.

i. A 1998 referendum repealed a 1997 state antidiscrimination law.

j. A 1994 referendum repealed a 1993 antidiscrimination ordinance.

k. Boston's 1982 executive order prohibiting public employment discrimination was superseded by the 1984 ordinance.

l. A 1994 referendum repealed an antidiscrimination ordinance.

m. A 1978 referendum repealed the original antidiscrimination ordinance; a 1991 referendum failed to repeal the 1990 ordinance.

n. A 1993 referendum repealed an earlier antidiscrimination ordinance.

o. A 1978 executive order barring private discrimination was overturned in court in 1985. The 1972 executive order prohibiting public employment discrimination was superseded by the 1986 ordinance.

p. A 1993 referendum repealed a 1992 antidiscrimination ordinance; the city council revoked the ordinance during a court challenge to the referendum.

q. A 1988 referendum repealed an executive order but the order was reinstated by courts and by the governor in 1993.

r. A 1978 referendum repealed an earlier antidiscrimination ordinance.

s. The 1980 executive order prohibiting public employment discrimination was superseded by the 1982 ordinance.

t. A 1985 referendum repealed a 1984 antidiscrimination ordinance.

u. A December 1997 antidiscrimination ordinance was repealed in January 1998.

Appendix B3 State and federal policies discriminating on the basis of sexual or gender variation, 1998

State	Same-sex marriage ban (year adopted)	Nonrecognition of same-sex marriages (year adopted)	Consensual sodomy prohibition (year adopted)	Antigay child custody or adoption rule	No promotion of homosexuality (year adopted)	Sexual orientation included in anti-discrimination laws?
Alabama	190 Op. Ala. Atty. Gen. 30 (1983); 1998 Ala. Acts No. 98-500, §2(c)	1998 Ala. Acts No. 98-500, §2(d)	Ala. Stat. §§13A-6-60, 13A-6-65(a)(3), (misdemeanor, 1977)	*In re J.M.F.*, 730 So. 2d 1190 (Ala. 1998) (custody)	Ala. Stat. §16-40A-2(c)(8) (1992) (sex education)	
Alaska	Alaska Stat. §25.05.013 (1996)	Ibid.				
Arizona	Ariz. Rev. Stat. §25-101(c) (1996)	Ariz. Rev. Stat. §25-112 (1996)	Ariz. Rev. Stat. §13-1411 to -1412 (misdemeanor, 1977)	*In re Appeal in Pima Cty. Juvenile Action*, 727 P.2d 830 (Ariz. App. 1986) (adoption)	Ariz. Rev. Stat. §15-716(c) (1991) (AIDS education)	Hate crime data collection law
Arkansas	Ark. Code §§9-11-109, -208(a) (1997)	Ark. Code §9-11-107 (1997)	Ark. Code §5-14-122 (same-sex sodomy only, misdemeanor, 1977)	*Larson v. Larson*, 902 S.W.2d 254 (Ark. 1995) (custody)		
California	Cal. Civ. Code §§4100, 4101(a) (1977)					Hate crime, employment, public accommodations laws

State	Same-sex marriage ban (year adopted)	Nonrecognition of same-sex marriages (year adopted)	Consensual sodomy prohibition (year adopted)	Antigay child custody or adoption rule	No promotion of homosexuality (year adopted)	Sexual orientation included in anti-discrimination laws?
Colorado	Op. Colo. Atty. Gen., Apr. 24, 1975					
Connecticut	Conn. Gen. Stat. §46a-81r(4) (1991)			Conn. Gen. Stat. §45a-726a (1991) (adoption)	Conn. Gen. Stat. §46a-81r(2)-(3) (1991) (education; no quotas)	All major anti-discrimination laws
Delaware	Del. Code tit. 13, §101(a) (1996)	Del. Code tit. 13, §101(b) (1996)				Hate crime laws
District of Columbia	*Dean v. D.C.,* 653 A.2d 307 (D.C. 1995)					All major antidiscrimination laws, but religious educational institutions authorized to discriminate on basis of sexual orientation
Florida	Fla. Stat. §741.04 (1983); id. §741.212(3) (1997)	Fla. Stat. §741.212(1)-(2) (1997)	Fla. Stat. §800.02 (misdemeanor, 1917)	Fla. Stat. §63.042(3) (1977) (adoption)		Hate crime laws

Appendix B3   (*continued*)

State	Same-sex marriage ban (year adopted)	Nonrecognition of same-sex marriages (year adopted)	Consensual sodomy prohibition (year adopted)	Antigay child custody or adoption rule	No promotion of homosexuality (year adopted)	Sexual orientation included in anti-discrimination laws?
Georgia	Ga. Code §§19-3-3.1(a), -30(b)(1) (1996).	Ga. Code §19-3-3.1(b) (1996)		*Buck v. Buck*, 233 S.E. 2d 792 (Ga. 1977) (custody)		Official public employment discrimination. *See Shahar v. Bowers*, 114 F.3d 1097 (11th Cir. 1997)
Hawaii	Haw. Rev. Stat. §572-1 (1994)					Public and private employment laws
Idaho	1993 Op. Idaho Atty. Gen. 119	Idaho Code §32-209 (1996)	Idaho Code §18-6605 (felony, 1972)			
Illinois	750 Ill. Comp. Stat. 5/212 and 5/213.1 (1996)	750 Ill. Comp. Stat. 5/213.1 (1996) (ambiguous)				Hate crime, public employment laws
Indiana	Ind. Code §31-11-1-1(a) (1977, 1997)	Ind. Code §31-11-1-1(b)				
Iowa	Iowa Code §595.2(1) (1998)	Iowa Code §595.20 (1998)				Hate crime law

State	Same-sex marriage ban (year adopted)	Nonrecognition of same-sex marriages (year adopted)	Consensual sodomy prohibition (year adopted)	Antigay child custody or adoption rule	No promotion of homosexuality (year adopted)	Sexual orientation included in anti-discrimination laws?
Kansas	Kan. Stat. §23-101 (1996)	Kan. Stat. §23-115 (1996)	Kan. Stat. §§21-3501, -3505 (same-sex sodomy only, misdemeanor, 1969)			
Kentucky	Jones v. Hallahan, 501 S.W.2d 588 (Ky. 1973); Ky. Rev. Stat. §402.020(1)(d) (1998)	Ky. Rev. Stat. §402.045 (1998)		S. v. S., 608 S.W.2d 760 (Ky. App. 1980) (custody)		Hate crime law
Louisiana	La. Civil Code arts. 89, 96 (1987)	La. House Conc. Res. No. 124, 1996 Sess.	La. Rev. Stat. §14-89 (felony, 1805)	Rowan v. Scott, 665 So. 2d 760 (La. App. 1995) (custody)	La. Rev. Stat. §281A(3) (1987) (sex education)	Hate crime law
Maine	Me. Rev. Stat. tit. 19-A, §§650, 701(5) (1997)	Me. Rev. Stat. tit. 19-A, §701(1-A) (1997)				Hate crime law
Maryland	Md. Code Family Law §2-201 (1984)		Md. Code art. 27, §§553–554 (felony, 1793; misdemeanor, 1916); see Schochet v. State, 580 A.2d 176 (Md. 1990) (voiding law for different-sex intimacy)			Public employment and hate crime laws

Appendix B3 (*continued*)

State	Same-sex marriage ban (year adopted)	Nonrecognition of same-sex marriages (year adopted)	Consensual sodomy prohibition (year adopted)	Antigay child custody or adoption rule	No promotion of homosexuality (year adopted)	Sexual orientation included in anti-discrimination laws?
Massachusetts	Mass. Gen. Laws ch. 207, §6 (1895) (ambiguous); id. ch. 151B, §4 notes (1991)		Mass. Gen. Laws ch. 272, §34 (felony, 1785)			All major anti-discrimination laws
Michigan	Mich. Comp. Laws §§551.1, 551.3-.4 (1996)	Mich. Comp. Laws §551.271-.272 (1996)	Mich. Comp. Laws §750.158 (felony, 1820)	*Hall v. Hall*, 291 N.W.2d 143 (Mich. App. 1980) (custody)		
Minnesota	Minn. Stat. §363.021(4) (1993); id. §517.01, .03(a)(4) (1997)	Minn. Stat. §517.03(a)(4) (1997)	Minn. Stat. §609.293 (misdemeanor, 1977)		Minn. Stat. §363.021(2)-(3) (1993) (education; no quotas)	All major anti-discrimination laws (transgendered people also protected)
Mississippi	Miss. Code §93-1-1(2) (1997)	Ibid.	Miss. Code §97-29-59 (felony, 1839)	*Bowen v. Bowen*, 688 So. 2d 1374 (Miss. 1997) (custody)		
Missouri	Mo. Rev. Stat. §451.022(3) (1996)	Mo. Rev. Stat. §451.022(1)-(2) (1996)	Mo. Rev. Stat. §566.010, .090 (same-sex sodomy only, misdemeanor, 1977)	*G.A. v. D.A.*, 745 S.W.2d 726 (Mo. App. 1987) (custody)		

State	Same-sex marriage ban (year adopted)	Nonrecognition of same-sex marriages (year adopted)	Consensual sodomy prohibition (year adopted)	Antigay child custody or adoption rule	No promotion of homosexuality (year adopted)	Sexual orientation included in anti-discrimination laws?
Montana	Mont. Code §40-1-401(1)(d) (1997)	Mont. Code. §40-1-401(4) (1997)				
Nebraska	1996 Op. Neb. Atty. Gen. No. 25					Hate crime law
Nevada	Nev. Rev. Stat. §122.020 (1861)			*Daly v. Daly*, 715 P.2d 56 (Nev. 1986) (transsexual parental custody)		Employment discrimination and hate crime laws
New Hampshire	N.H. Rev. Stat. §457:1-2 (1987)					Almost all anti-discrimination laws
New Jersey	N.J. Stat. §37:1-3 (1921) (ambiguous)					All major anti-discrimination laws
New Mexico	N.M. Stat. §40-2-1 (1907) (ambiguous)					
New York	*Anonymous v. Anonymous*, 325 N.Y.S.2d 499 (Sup. Ct. 1971) (statute ambiguous)					Public employment

Appendix B3 *(continued)*

State	Same-sex marriage ban (year adopted)	Nonrecognition of same-sex marriages (year adopted)	Consensual sodomy prohibition (year adopted)	Antigay child custody or adoption rule	No promotion of homosexuality (year adopted)	Sexual orientation included in anti-discrimination laws?
North Carolina	N.C. Gen. Stat. §51-1.2 (1995)	Ibid.	N.C. Gen. Stat. §14-177 (felony, 1792)	*Pulliam v. Smith*, 501 S.E.2d 898 (N.C. 1998) (custody)	N.C. Gen. Stat. §115C-81 (e1)(3)-(4) (1995) (AIDS education)	
North Dakota	N.D. Cent. Code §14-03-01 (1997)	N.D. Cent. Code §14-03-08 (1997)		*Jacobson v. Jacobson*, 314 N.W.2d 78 (N.D. 1981) (custody)		
Ohio	Ohio Rev. Code §3101.01 (1885)					
Oklahoma	Okla. Stat. tit. 43, §3 (1975)	Okla. Stat. tit. 43, §3.1 (1996)	Okla. Stat. tit. 21, §886 (felony, 1890); *Post v. State*, 715 P.2d 1105 (Okla. Crim. App. 1986) (limiting law to same-sex sodomy)	*M.J.P. v. J.G.P.*, 640 P.2d 966 (Okla. 1982) (custody)		
Oregon	Or. Rev. Stat. §106.010 (1862)					Hate crime law

State	Same-sex marriage ban (year adopted)	Nonrecognition of same-sex marriages (year adopted)	Consensual sodomy prohibition (year adopted)	Antigay child custody or adoption rule	No promotion of homosexuality (year adopted)	Sexual orientation included in anti-discrimination laws?
Pennsylvania	23 Pa. Cons. Stat. §1704 (1996)	Ibid.				Public employment law
Rhode Island	R.I. Gen. Laws §15-2-1 (1896) (ambiguous)					All major anti-discrimination laws
South Carolina	S.C. Code §20-1-15 (1996)	Ibid. (ambiguous)	S.C. Code §16-15-120 (felony, 1712)			
South Dakota	S.D. Cod. Laws §25-1-1 (1996)	Ibid. (ambiguous)				
Tennessee	Tenn. Code §36-3-113 (1996)	Tenn. Code §36-3-113(d) (1996)				
Texas	Tex. Fam. Code §2.001 (1997)		Tex. Penal Code §21.06 (same-sex sodomy only, misdemeanor, 1977)		Tex. Health & Safety Code §85.007(b)(2) (1991) (AIDS education)	

Appendix B3 (*continued*)

State	Same-sex marriage ban (year adopted)	Nonrecognition of same-sex marriages (year adopted)	Consensual sodomy prohibition (year adopted)	Antigay child custody or adoption rule	No promotion of homosexuality (year adopted)	Sexual orientation included in anti-discrimination laws?
United States	1 U.S.C. §7 (1996) (statutory and administrative use of marriage and spouse can only mean different-sex unions)	28 U.S.C. §1738C (1996) (states do not have to recognize same-sex marriages)	10 U.S.C. §925, art. 125 (military personnel, felony, 1920); 18 U.S.C. §2421 (transportation of person into state for illegal sodomy, felony, 1986; *Bowers v. Hardwick*, 478 U.S. 186 (1986)		Hate Crimes Statistics Act §2(b), 104 Stat. 140 (1990)	Only hate crime data collection law, id. §2(a). Cf. 10 U.S.C. §654(b) (1993) (exclusion from armed forces); 42 U.S.C. §§12208, 12211(a) (1990) (exclusion from ADA)
Utah	Utah Code §30-1-2-(5) (1993)	Utah Code §30-1-4(1) (1995)	Utah Code §76-5-403 (misdemeanor, 1972)	*Tucker v. Tucker*, 910 P.2d 1209 (Utah 1996) (custody)		Hate crime data collection law
Vermont	*Baker v. State* No. 98-32 (Vt. Sup. Ct.) (litigation pending)					All major anti-discrimination laws
Virginia	Va. Code §20-45.2 (1975)	Ibid. (1997 amendment)	Va. Code §18.2-361 (felony, 1792)	*Roe v. Roe*, 324 S.E.2d 691 (Va. 1985) (custody); *Bottoms v. Bottoms*, 457 S.E.2d 102 (Va. 1995) (same)		

State	Same-sex marriage ban (year adopted)	Nonrecognition of same-sex marriages (year adopted)	Consensual sodomy prohibition (year adopted)	Antigay child custody or adoption rule	No promotion of homosexuality (year adopted)	Sexual orientation included in anti-discrimination laws?
Washington	Singer v. Hara, 522 P.2d 1187 (Wash. App. 1974); Wash. Code §26.04.020(1)(c) (1998)	Wash. Code §26.04.020(3) (1998)				Public employment and hate crime laws
West Virginia	W.Va. Code §48-1-1 (1860)					
Wisconsin	Wis. Stat. §765.001 (1959)					All major anti-discrimination laws
Wyoming	Wyo. Stat. §20-1-101 (1876)			Hertzler v. Hertzler, 908 P.2d 946 (Wyo. 1995) (custody)		

appendix c

Statistics

Appendix C1 Sodomy arrests, twelve American cities, 1875–1965

Average arrests per year	Baltimore	Boston	Chicago	Cleveland	District of Columbia	Los Angeles	Miami (Dade County)	New York City	Philadelphia	Richmond	San Francisco	St. Louis
1875–1880	NA	1	2	0	0	NA	NA	NA	2	0	2	1
1881–1885	0	2	3	NA	2	NA	NA	6	13	0	2	0
1886–1890	1	7	4	NA	2	0	NA	15	15	0	4	1
1891–1895	NA	11	11	NA	2	1	NA	22	28	0	6	1
1896–1900	NA	10	18	2	2	1	NA	21	41	0	7	4
1901–1905	NA	10	20	3	3	2	NA	65	22	0	12	4
1906–1910	5	17	34	3	2	2	NA	69	16	0	12	10
1911–1915	7	24	30	4	0	7	NA	81	50	1	23	17
1916–1920	30	28	21	NA	0	14	NA	101	47	1	NA	17
1921–1925	29	50	51	6	1	123	NA	111	49	2	NA	29
1926–1930	36	43	39	9	3	NA	0	119	NA	5	NA	25
1931–1935	38	29	NA	NA	1	NA	6	120	NA	7	NA	27
1936–1940	46	NA	NA	25	6	35	9	169	NA	5	NA	42
1941–1945	53	NA	NA	24	5	NA	13	145	NA	NA	24	NA
1946–1950	62	NA	NA	23	78	242	12	126	NA	NA	23	NA
1951–1955	101	NA	NA	NA	61	NA	NA	187	NA	NA	NA	NA
1956–1960	135	NA	NA	NA	36	NA	NA	349	NA	NA	33	NA
1961–1965	86	NA	NA	NA	63	NA	NA	NA	NA	NA	102	NA

Note: The data in this appendix are taken from the annual reports of the police departments for the listed cities, with the exception of Miami; that city's data are taken from the Florida Attorney General's reports for Dade County. Each entry reflects the yearly average arrests for *sodomy, crimes against nature, sexual perversion,* and (for Boston) *lewd and unnatural conduct,* as well as attempts or assaults to commit such acts, during a five-year period. Some of the entries reflect yearly averages for fewer than five years because one or more years were missing from that city's police archives.

Appendix C2 Reported "sodomy" cases, 1880–1995

	Animals	Same-sex adults			Different-sex adults			Adults and minors			Totals
	Total	Total	Consensual	Forcible	Total	Consensual	Forcible	Total	Girls	Boys	Totals
1880–1895	4	4	3	1	0	0	0	3	0	3	11
	36%	36%	27%	9%	0%	0%	0%	27%	0%	27%	
1896–1910	4	7	6	1	1	0	1	10	0	10	22
	18%	32%	27%	5%	5%	0%	5%	45%	0%	45%	
1911–1925	6	18	16	2	8	4	4	24	8	16	56
	11%	32%	28%	4%	14%	7%	7%	43%	14%	29%	
1926–1940	1	8	6	2	13	4	9	31	5	26	53
	2%	15%	11%	4%	25%	8%	17%	58%	10%	48%	
1941–1955	6	36	35	1	42	10	32	97	36	61	181
	3%	20%	20%	0%	23%	6%	17%	55%	20%	35%	
1956–1970	1	80	64	16	54	5	49	124	40	84	259
	0%	31%	25%	6%	21%	2%	19%	47%	15%	32%	
1971–1985	0	123	60	63	492	19	473	324	163	161	939
	0%	13%	6%	7%	52%	2%	50%	34%	17%	17%	
1986–1995	0	28	13	15	356	6	350	474	306	168	858
	0%	3%	1%	2%	41%	1%	40%	55%	35%	20%	

Note: The data in this appendix are derived from the cases reported in the West Reporting System and in official state reporters and categorized by one or both as "sodomy" cases. Because of rounding, the horizontal rows do not always add up to 100 percent.

Appendix C3 "Degenerates" arraigned in New York City's Magistrates' Courts, 1915–1962

Year	Arraignments (females)	% Convictions (overall %)	% Workhouse (overall %)	Sentences > 2 months (overall %)
1915	>96 (0)	NA	86%	NA
1916	>92 (0)	NA	54%	NA
1917	>127 (0)	NA	NA	NA
1918	>238 (0)	NA	NA	NA
1919	>559 (0)	NA	NA	NA
1920	>756 (0)	NA	NA	NA
1921	>519 (0)	NA	NA	NA
1922	416 (1)	83% (81%)	39% (2%)	26% (34%)
1923	217 (0)	88% (79%)	39% (3%)	32% (34%)
1924	469 (0)	87% (83%)	34% (3%)	26% (34%)
1925	607 (0)	78% (85%)	33% (3%)	20% (35%)
1926	630 (3)	89% (83%)	37% (3%)	27% (32%)
1927	513 (0)	92% (86%)	23% (3%)	40% (37%)
1928	609 (1)	92% (85%)	22% (4%)	20% (37%)
1929	1,070 (0)	90% (80%)	24% (4%)	24% (33%)
1930	1,212 (4)	85% (86%)	33% (4%)	17% (30%)
1931	437 (0)	80% (84%)	26% (2%)	10% (26%)
1932	465 (4)	79% (83%)	24% (2%)	17% (29%)
1933	1,042 (NA)	NA	NA	NA
1934	456 (NA)	NA	NA	NA
1935	554 (82)	70% (83%)	28% (1%)	24% (30%)
1936	543 (100)	80% (85%)	34% (1%)	28% (21%)
1937	610 (39)	83% (86%)	33% (1%)	33% (22%)
1938	726 (67)	79% (87%)	39% (2%)	34% (17%)
1939	647 (41)	86% (90%)	44% (2%)	35% (17%)
1940	707 (69)	85% (88%)	44% (2%)	33% (15%)
1941	735 (61)	80% (81%)	36% (2%)	23% (13%)
1942	717 (NA)	79% (86%)	29% (3%)	27% (14%)
1943	855 (NA)	81% (82%)	32% (2%)	30% (11%)
1944	1,072 (NA)	74% (84%)	30% (1%)	20% (13%)

Appendix C3   (continued)

Year	Arraignments (females)	% Convictions (overall %)	% Workhouse (overall %)	Sentences > 2 months (overall %)
1945	2,146 (NA)	89% (84%)	28% (2%)	9% (10%)
1946	2,473 (NA)	86% (89%)	27% (1%)	11% (12%)
1947	3,105 (NA)	90% (81%)	20% (1%)	11% (10%)
1948	3,289 (NA)	91% (80%)	20% (1%)	10% (9%)
1949	3,227 (NA)	90% (91%)	18% (2%)	NA
1950	2,285 (NA)	85% (90%)	30% (2%)	NA
1951	1,632 (NA)	63% (89%)	87% (1%)	NA
1952	1,330 (NA)	79% (92%)	33% (1%)	NA
1953	1,054 (NA)	80% (92%)	33% (1%)	NA
1954	1,307 (NA)	80% (92%)	33% (1%)	NA
1955	2,148 (NA)	78% (92%)	32% (1%)	10% (7%)
1956	1,887 (NA)	75% (92%)	39% (1%)	11% (6%)
1957	1,862 (NA)	77% (91%)	33% (1%)	10% (7%)
1958	1,197 (NA)	68% (89%)	32% (1%)	NA
1959	1,000 (NA)	63% (89%)	33% (1%)	9% (3%)
1960	787 (NA)	67% (90%)	36% (1%)	10% (3%)
1961	839 (NA)	69% (91%)	32% (1%)	13% (3%)
1962	565 (NA)	68% (90%)	38% (1%)	15% (4%)

Note: The data in this appendix are derived from the annual reports of the New York City Magistrates' Courts. (These may be found in the New York Public Library's microfilm collection, call number *ZAN-10223.) The Fingerprint Bureau (which was established for the Magistrates' Courts in 1913) began keeping separate records for "degenerates" in 1915, but the magistrates did not create a separate category for "degenerates" until 1922. (Before 1922, "degenerates" were included with others arraigned for "disorderly conduct.") Because defendants were typically not fingerprinted until after a disposition (usually a guilty plea or summary conviction), the number of defendants fingerprinted were less than the number arraigned. Hence, the arraignment figures for the years 1915–1921, inclusive, would be *greater than* the fingerprint figures; my use of the greater than sign (>) is intended to signify this idea.

Appendix C4 Sex offense arrests in Saint Louis, 1874–1946

Fiscal year	Prostitution (men)	Sodomy	Lewdness (women)	Cross-dressing (men)	Indecent exposure (women)	Rape
1874	0	0	0	0	224 (39)	24
1875	327 (24)	1	0	0	227 (58)	20
1876	972 (126)	3	0	0	241 (52)	19
1877	1,229 (98)	1	0	0	110 (26)	15
(Gap)						
1884	1,045 (87)	0	0	0	172 (23)	26
1885	1,347 (94)	1	20 (8)	0	182 (27)	19
1886	1,078 (55)	2	30 (15)	0	150 (23)	29
1887	1,398 (29)	0	4 (2)	0	161 (29)	43
1888	1,180 (40)	1	2 (0)	4 (0)	104 (13)	39
1889	1,112 (11)	2	0	0	150 (9)	146
1890	1,232 (9)	2	3 (0)	0	144 (9)	21
1891	1,477 (9)	1	0	3 (2)	183 (14)	38
1892	1,606 (25)	1	4 (0)	0	193 (10)	28
1893	2,105 (153)	0	5 (0)	10 (10)	222 (14)	60
1894	2,861 (284)	0	12 (12)	0	179 (23)	61
1895	3,126 (1)	0	8 (8)	0	119 (21)	34
1896	4,313 (14)	5	8 (6)	8 (2)	138 (17)	42
1897	3,502 (138)	3	41 (5)	2 (1)	67 (6)	29
1898	3,423 (215)	2	50 (7)	0	78 (2)	32
1899	3,562 (224)	4	24 (5)	4 (2)	62 (8)	24
1900	3,311 (163)	4	27 (5)	2 (1)	57 (4)	16
1901	2,941 (119)	3	17 (3)	0	57 (2)	20
1902	3,408 (127)	3	17 (7)	3 (0)	62 (8)	34
1903	3,538 (97)	0	34 (6)	5 (3)	97 (5)	39
1904	2,856 (145)	6	41 (10)	1 (0)	72 (0)	32
1905	3,375 (63)	10	49 (7)	6 (3)	NA	80
1906	2,418 (116)	12	52 (3)	2 (1)	55 (0)	46
1907	2,068 (194)	10	86 (17)	6 (1)	83 (3)	73
1908	2,132 (308)	19	101 (21)	9 (5)	78 (0)	59

Appendix C4   (continued)

Fiscal year	Prostitution (men)	Sodomy	Lewdness (women)	Cross-dressing (men)	Indecent exposure (women)	Rape
1909	1,378 (139)	5	96 (17)	2 (1)	61 (0)	58
1910	1,328 (167)	3	116 (16)	3 (0)	95 (0)	59
1911	925 (68)	5	142 (18)	0	58 (2)	80
1912	846 (86)	5	88 (17)	5 (0)	56 (1)	53
1913	1,068 (118)	15	69 (14)	1 (0)	63 (3)	64
1914	1,333 (203)	23	47 (10)	8 (7)	59 (1)	125
1915	1,858 (234)	32	54 (12)	5 (4)	60 (0)	118
1916	1,578 (273)	12	35 (7)	4 (1)	49 (0)	87
1917	3,915 (1,449)	14	20 (1)	3 (1)	42 (1)	138
1918	5,191 (2,105)	27	40 (11)	10 (3)	55 (0)	126
1919	3,187 (1,535)	18	55 (13)	5 (0)	34 (1)	135
1920	1,641 (535)	12	40 (10)	7 (0)	24 (0)	124
1921	1,641 (425)	23	26 (5)	0	49 (0)	186
1922	947 (368)	40	36 (2)	2 (0)	36 (1)	205
1923	603 (223)	25	39 (10)	0	20 (0)	199
1924	568 (206)	25	41 (18)	0	37 (0)	98
1925	356 (156)	28	17 (4)	0	39 (2)	238
1926	601 (239)	19	35 (11)	0	90 (4)	247
1927	442 (170)	34	68 (15)	0	77 (3)	300
1928	3,114 (2,172)[a]	19	53 (12)	0	69 (1)	244
1929	2,611 (150)	16	44 (17)	0	88 (2)	232
1930	1,929 (100)	34	9 (6)	0	79 (3)	231
1931	1,312 (90)	22	11 (3)	0	79 (0)	189
1932	2,084 (97)	32	16 (5)	0	83 (6)	149
1933	7,913 (419)	15	21 (10)	0	70 (1)	224
1934	7,491 (313)	30	25 (1)	0	120 (18)	309
1935	7,565 (206)	36	23 (1)	0	86 (6)	160
1936	7,997 (167)	23	107 (6)	0	61 (43)	180
1937	NA	32	NA	0	77 (1)	198
1938	5,765 (107)	48	52 (22)	0	78 (3)	224

Appendix C4   (continued)

Fiscal year	Prostitution (men)	Sodomy	Lewdness (women)	Cross-dressing (men)	Indecent exposure (women)	Rape
1939	4,392 (67)	34	45 (7)	0	116 (2)	202
1940	2,909 (47)	64	55 (7)	0	92 (2)	212
1941	1,833 (115)	46[b]	37 (2)	0	86 (3)	182
1942	441 (78)	42	79 (43)	0	99 (2)	157
1943	389 (112)	34	19 (0)	0	100 (10)	160
1944	447 (121)	31	29 (5)	0	77 (1)	162
1945	60 (39)	30	44 (9)	0	79 (0)	157
1946	53 (22)	40	36 (5)	0	89 (2)	180

Note: The data are taken from the "Statistical Reports of Arrests" found in the annual reports of the St. Louis Police Commissioners for the listed fiscal years. These reports are on file at the St. Louis Municipal Library. Like some other cities, St. Louis broke down the arrests by sex, and I do the same in this appendix: for *Prostitution* and *Cross-Dressing,* crimes mostly committed by women, I put the number of men in parentheses; for *Indecency* and *Lewdness,* crimes mostly committed by men, I put the number of women in parentheses. *Sodomy* and *Rape* were always committed by men until 1941, when St. Louis had its first recorded arrests of women for sodomy.

This appendix combines and recharacterizes categories in the following manner: *Prostitution* includes St. Louis's categories "Frequenting Bawdy House" (males), "Inhabiting Bawdy House" (females), "Keeping Bawdy House" (females), "Keeping Disorderly House" (usually females), "Prostitutes Wandering about the Streets" (females), "Prostitutes Plying Their Avocation" (females), "Roping" (probably solicitation, females). These were municipal crimes. After 1910, the authorities began enforcing federal and state categories: "White Slavery" and "Mann Act" (federal) and "Enticing Minor Females for Immoral Purposes" (state). *Sodomy* includes both "Sodomy" and "Crime against Nature" arrests, as well as arrests for attempts or assaults (all serious state crimes). *Lewdness* includes "Lewd and Indecent Act" (municipal crime) and "Lewd and Lascivious Conduct" (state crime). *Cross-Dressing* is usually called "Wearing Unlawful Apparel" or "Wearing Unlawful Male or Female Attire" in the reports (municipal crimes). *Indecency* includes "Exposing the Person" (a municipal crime). *Rape* includes attempts to commit rape as well as rape itself (serious state crimes).

a. In 1928 St. Louis commenced large-scale enforcement of the crime of "Vagrancy," with 281 arrests of men and 1,681 arrests of women for that crime. Most of the women were probably suspected prostitutes; at least some (but surely not most) of the arrests of men were for homosexual cruising. Because I do not include vagrancy arrests in my prostitution figures, the figures greatly understate the matter beginning in 1928.

b. Two women were arrested for sodomy in 1941, the first reported arrests of women for that crime in St. Louis records. Four women were arrested in 1945.

Appendix C5   U.S. military personnel discharged on grounds of homosexuality, 1947–1998

Fiscal Year	Class II/III discharges (homosexual)	Branches included	Total forces for included branches	Discharges as % total forces
1947–50	4,380	All	NA	NA
1950	483	Navy	331,860	.141
1951	533	Navy	661,639	.080
1952	1,352	Navy	735,753	.184
1953	1,335	Navy	706,375	.189
1954	1,020	Navy	642,048	.159
1955	833	Navy	579,864	.143
1956	933	Navy	591,996	.158
1957	1,307	Navy	599,859	.216
1958	1,244	Navy	563,906	.220
1959	1,223	Navy	552,221	.222
1960	958	Navy	554,040	.173
1961	1,148	Navy	551,603	.213
1962	1,664	Navy/AF	1,330,256	.125
1963	1,669	Navy/AF	1,316,222	.127
1964	1,781	Navy/AF	1,305,122	.136
1965	1,857	Navy/AF	1,277,360	.145
(Gap)				
1975	937	All	NA	NA
1976	1,296	All	NA	NA
1977	1,442	All	NA	NA
(Gap)				
1980	1,754	All	2,036,672	.086
1981	1,817	All	2,068,885	.088
1982	1,998	All	2,096,644	.095
1983	1,815	All	2,112,067	.086
1984	1,822	All	2,123,428	.086
1985	1,660	All	2,137,415	.078
1986	1,644	All	2,156,593	.076

Appendix C5   (*continued*)

Fiscal Year	Class II/III discharges (homosexual)	Branches included	Total forces for included branches	Discharges as % total forces
1987	1,380	All	2,163,578	.064
1988	1,100	All	2,123,669	.051
1989	997	All	2,115,234	.047
1990	941	All	2,043,700	.046
1991	949	All	1,985,500	.048
1992	708	All	1,807,100	.039
1993	682	All	1,705,000	.040
1994	597	All	1,610,400	.037
1995	722	All	1,523,300	.047
1996	850	All	1,471,722	.057
1997	997	All	NA	NA
1998	1,145	All	NA	NA

Note: Data for this appendix are taken from information supplied by the Department of Defense to Congress in 1962 and 1966 and to the general public starting in 1980. Class II and III discharges were those owing to consensual homosexual *conduct* (Class II) and homosexual *tendencies* (Class III).

Appendix C6 Sexual outlaws debarred from entering the United States
by immigration authorities, 1892–1956

Fiscal year	Psych.	Pub. ch.	Crim.	Polyg.	Prost.	Total debarred
1892	NC	1,002	26	NC	80	2,164
1893	NC	431	12	NC	0	1,053
1894	NC	802	8	NC	2	1,389
1895	NC	1,714	4	NC	0	2,419
1896	NC	2,010	0	NC	0	2,799
1897	NC	1,277	1	NC	0	1,617
1898	NC	2,261	2	NC	0	3,030
1899	NC	2,599	8	NC	0	3,798
1900	NC	2,974	4	NC	7	4,246
1901	NC	2,798	7	NC	3	3,516
1902	NC	3,944	9	NC	3	4,974
1903	NC	5,812	1	1	13	8,769
1904	NC	4,798	15	0	12	7,994
1905	NC	7,898	44	3	28	11,879
1906	NC	7,069	205	5	32	12,432
1907	NC	6,866	341	10	19	13,064
1908	NC	4,611	136	6	186	10,902
1909	NC	4,828	273	24	504	10,422
1910	NC	15,540	580	134	496	24,270
1911	NC	15,103	644	57	399	22,349
1912	NC	10,370	592	38	462	16,057
1913	NC	12,264	808	40	621	19,938
1914	NC	22,321	755	31	635	33,041
1915	NC	16,561	276	18	49	24,111
1916	NC	12,130	245	2	754	18,867
1917	3	9,527	257	2	887	16,028
1918	20	3,149	160	4	249	17,297
1919	37	4,348	261	2	125	8,626
1920	38	5,677	355	1	185	11,795
1921	39	6,535	178	16	152	13,779
1922	31	6,128	176	2	210	13,731
1923	55	8,910	364	1	326	20,619
1924	69	8,882	546	2	313	30,284
(Gap)						
1937	28	2,175	215	1	46	8,076

Appendix C6   (*continued*)

Fiscal year	Psych.	Pub. ch.	Crim.	Polyg.	Prost.	Total debarred
1938	29	2,377	200	2	66	8,066
1939	19	2,113	188	1	66	6,498
1940	12	1,356	144	0	33	5,300
1941	4	350	92	2	13	2,929
1942	7	167	70	0	10	1,833
1943	4	100	68	1	6	1,495
1944	15	122	63	0	8	1,642
1945	19	69	87	0	4	2,341
1946	9	37	87	2	3	2,942
1947	44	232	442	0	12	7,435
1948	28	200	367	0	18	7,113
1949	22	215	402	2	31	5,541
1950	49	130	428	3	32	5,256
1951	24	359	610	2	38	5,647
1952	9	52	534	0	29	5,050
1953	14	36	491	0	58	5,647
1954	22	18	196	0	6	3,313
1955	10	11	206	3	124	2,667
1956	1	14	169	0	64	1,709

Note: Data for this appendix are taken from the Annual Report of the Commissioner General of Immigration to the Secretary of Labor, Fiscal Year Ending June 30, 1924, at 128–129; Annual Reports of the Immigration and Naturalization Service for the Fiscal Years 1944, 1946, 1950, 1953, and 1956.

The category "Psych." includes the Immigration Service categories "Constitutional Psychopathic Inferiority" (1917–52) and "Psychopathic Personality Aliens" (after 1952). The category "Pub. Ch." includes the Immigration Service categories "Paupers or Likely to Become Public Charges" and "Surgeon's Certificate of Mental Defect Which May Affect Alien's Ability to Earn a Living." The category "Crim." includes the Immigration Service category "Criminals." The category "Polyg." includes the Immigration Service category "Polygamists." The category "Prost." includes the Immigration Service categories "Prostitutes and Aliens Coming for Any Immoral Purposes," "Supported by Proceeds of Prostitution," and "Aliens Who Procure or Attempt to Bring In Prostitutes and Females for Any Immoral Purpose," categories that after 1924 are collapsed into "Immoral Classes." "NC" means there was no such category for the year in question.

The "Total Debarred" includes all categories, not just the ones outlined in this appendix.

notes

Introduction

1. Mary McIntosh, "The Homosexual Role," 16 *Soc. Problems* 182–193 (1968), reprinted in *Forms of Desire*, 3–42 (Edward Stein ed., 1990); Michel Foucault, *The History of Sexuality*, vol. 1: *An Introduction* (Robert Hurley trans., 1978). The term "homosexuality" did not even enter the English language until 1892. *A Supplement to the Oxford English Dictionary*, vol. 2, at 136 (R. W. Burchfield ed., 1976) (entry for "homosexuality"), analyzed in David Halperin, "Sex before Sexuality: Pederasty, Politics, and Power in Classical Athens," in *Hidden from History: Reclaiming the Gay and Lesbian Past*, 37, 38–39, and nn.1–2 (Martin Duberman et al. eds., 1989).

2. This idea originates in the labeling theory of McIntosh, "Homosexual Role," in *Forms of Desire*, 27–28, and is developed in Michel Foucault, "The Subject and Power," in *Michel Foucault: Beyond Structuralism and Hermeneutics*, 208 (Herbert Dreyfuss and Paul Rabinow eds., 1982); see also Rabinow, "Introduction," in *The Foucault Reader*, 3, 7–11 (Rabinow ed., 1984).

3. Eve Kosofsky Sedgwick, *Epistemology of the Closet* (1990); Janet Halley, "The Politics of the Closet," 36 *UCLA L. Rev.* 915 (1989).

4. See Vern and Bonnie Bullough, *Cross-Dressing, Sex, and Gender* (1993); San Francisco Lesbian and Gay History Project, "'She Even Chewed Tobacco': A Pictorial Narrative of Passing Women in America," in *Hidden from History*, 183.

5. See William N. Eskridge, Jr., "Privacy Jurisprudence and the Apartheid of the Closet, 1946–1961," 24 *Fla. St. U.L. Rev.* 703, 704–707 (1997); Kenji Yoshino, "Suspect Symbols: The Literary Argument for Heightened Scrutiny for Gays," 96 *Colum. L. Rev.* 1753, 1794–1802 (1996).

6. Romer v. Evans, 517 U.S. 620 (1996).

7. Gayle Rubin, "Thinking Sex: Notes for a Radical Theory of the Politics of Sexuality," in *Pleasure and Danger: Exploring Female Sexuality,* 267 (Carole Vance ed., 1984), and in William N. Eskridge, Jr., and Nan D. Hunter, *Sexuality, Gender, and the Law,* 250–259 (1997).

8. Kath Weston, *Families We Choose: Lesbians, Gays, Kinship* (1991).

1. Masquerade and the Law, 1880 – 1946

1. Earl Lind (a.k.a. Ralph Werther), *Autobiography of an Androgyne* (1918) and *The Female-Impersonators* (1922); Louis Sullivan, *From Female to Male: The Life of Jack Bee Garland* (1990) (life of Mugarietta); Lisa Duggan, *Sapphic Slashers* (1999) and "The Trials of Alice Mitchell," 18 *Signs* 791 (1993). Primary documents for Mitchell are reprinted in Jonathan Ned Katz, *Gay American History,* 82–90 (1976).

2. See Allan Bérubé, *Coming Out under Fire: The History of Gay Men and Women in World War II* (1990); George Chauncey, Jr., *Gay New York, 1890–1940* (1994); Lillian Faderman, *Odd Girls and Twilight Lovers: A History of Lesbian Life in Twentieth Century America* (1992); Jonathan Ned Katz, *The Invention of Heterosexuality* (1995); Elizabeth Lapovsky Kennedy and Madeline Davis, *Boots of Leather, Slippers of Gold: The History of a Lesbian Community* (1993); Carroll Smith-Rosenberg, *Disorderly Conduct: Visions of Gender in Victorian America* (1985); Estelle Freedman, "'Uncontrolled Desires': The Response to the Sexual Psychopath, 1920–1960," 74 *J. Am. Hist.* 83 (1987). A detailed account of the law's contribution is William N. Eskridge, Jr., "Law and the Construction of the Closet: American Regulation of Same-Sex Intimacy, 1880–1946," 82 *Iowa L. Rev.* 1007 (1997).

3. N.Y. Penal Code, 1881 N.Y. Laws ch. 676. See also Ill. Rev. Stat., 1845, ch. XXX; Mass. Gen. Stat., 1860, ch. 165; 1872 Cal. Penal Code.

4. 1881 N.Y. Laws ch. 442, §887(4).

5. Chicago Code, 1881, §§1598, 1602–05, 1613. San Francisco's criminal offense ordinances, 1866–1915, are reprinted in Eskridge, "Construction of the Closet," 1127–33 (app. 5).

6. In thirty-five states, there were statutes prohibiting sodomy. Vermont had no statute, but its highest court recognized sodomy as a common law crime. State v. LaForrest, 45 A. 225 (Vt. 1899). Contrast Iowa, whose highest court refused to recognize sodomy as a common law crime in Estes v. Carter, 10 Iowa 400 (Iowa 1860). Iowa had no sodomy law until 1892. Similarly, Ohio had no sodomy law until 1885, Washington until 1893, and the District of Columbia until 1948. The eleven states joining the union after 1881 (North and South Dakota, Wyoming, Utah, Idaho, Montana, Oklahoma, Arizona, New Mexico, Alaska, and Hawaii) all had territorial sodomy laws. Appendix A1 contains references and citations for each state.

7. U.S. Department of the Interior, Census Office, *Report of the Defective, Dependent, and Delinquent Classes of the Population of the United States, As Returned at the Tenth Census,* 506–509, 516–517, 562–563 (1880), excerpted in Katz, *Gay American History,* 57–58.

8. See B. R. Burg, *An American Seafarer in the Age of Sail* (1994); Lillian Faderman, *Surpassing the Love of Men: Romantic Friendship and Love between Women from the Renaissance to the Present* (1981); Jonathan Ned Katz, "Coming to Terms: Conceptualizing Men's Erotic and Affectional Relations with Men in the United States, 1820–1892," in *A Queer World*, 216 (Martin Duberman ed., 1997). On pre–Civil War cross-dressing, see Vern and Bonnie Bullough, *Cross-Dressing, Sex, and Gender* (1993); Katz, *Gay American History*, 209–279.

9. Sarah Seelye, *Nurse and Spy* (1864); Walt Whitman, *Leaves of Grass* (1860 and subsequent editions). See also Mary Livermore, *My Story of the War* (1876) (author and estimated 400 other women passed as men to serve in Union Army).

10. In addition to the sources in note 2 above, see Angus McLaren, *The Trials of Masculinity: Policing Sexual Boundaries, 1870–1930* (1997); Anthony Rotundo, *American Manhood: Transformations in Masculinity from the Revolution to the Modern Era* (1993); Cynthia Eagle Russet, *Sexual Science: The Victorian Construction of Womanhood* (1989); Kevin White, *The First Sexual Revolution: The Emergence of Male Heterosexuality in America* (1993); Allan Bérubé, "Lesbians and Gay Men in Early San Francisco" (San Francisco Gay History Project, draft March 1979).

11. Thomas Mackey, *Red Lights Out: A Legal History of Prostitution, Disorderly Houses, and Vice Districts, 1870–1917* (1987); David Pivar, *Purity Crusade: Sexual Morality and Social Control, 1868–1900* (1973); Ruth Rosen, *The Lost Sisterhood: Prostitution in America, 1900–1918* (1982); Eskridge, "Construction of the Closet," 1112–22 (arrest figures for prostitution in various cities).

12. See Smith-Rosenberg, *Disorderly Conduct*, as well as Rotundo, *American Manhood*; Russet, *Sexual Science*; Joe Dubbert, "Progressivism and the Masculinity Crisis," 61 *Psychoanalytic Rev.* 443 (1974).

13. George Napheys, *The Transmission of Life: Counsels on the Nature and Hygiene of the Masculine Function*, 29 (1871).

14. Havelock Ellis, *Sexual Inversion*, 351–352 (3d ed. 1915).

15. Edward Stevenson (writing as Xavier Mayne), *The Intersexes*, 640 (1908) ("Uranianism in the United States"). Other contemporary accounts are The Vice Commission of Chicago, *The Social Evil in Chicago*, 290, 295–297 (1911); Werther, *Female-Impersonators* (New York); C. H. Hughes, "Homo-Sexual Complexion Perverts in St. Louis," 28 *Alienist and Neurologist* 487–488 (1907); Frank Lydston, "Clinical Lecture: Sexual Perversion, Satyriasis and Nymphomania," 61 *Med. and Surgical Reporter* 253, 254 (1889), excerpted in Jonathan Ned Katz, *Gay/Lesbian Almanac*, 213 (1983) (Chicago); Irving Rosse, "Sexual Hypochondriasis and Perversion of the Genetic Instinct," 17 *J. Nervous and Mental Disease* 795 (1892), excerpted in Katz, *Almanac*, 232 (D.C.). Useful secondary sources are The History Project, *Improper Bostonians: Lesbian and Gay History from the Puritans to Playland* (1998); Chauncey, *Gay New York*; Susan Stryker and Jim Van Buskirk, *Gay by the Bay: A History of Queer Culture in the San Francisco Bay Area* (1996); Bérubé, "Lesbians and Gay Men in Early San Francisco"; Katy Coyle and Nadiene Van Dyke, "Sex, Smashing, and Storyville in Turn-of-the-Century New Orleans," in *Carryin' On in the Lesbian and Gay South*, 54–74 (John Howard ed., 1997); San Francisco Lesbian and Gay History Project, "'She Even Chewed Tobacco': A Pictorial Narrative of Passing

Women in America," in *Hidden from History: Reclaiming the Gay and Lesbian Past,* 183 (Martin Duberman et al. eds., 1989).

16. See Faderman, *Surpassing the Love of Men* (women-affiliated women before 1900); San Francisco History Project, "'She Even Chewed Tobacco,'" 185 (passing women who married other women).

17. Lydston, "Sexual Perversion," 254 (Chicago) and *Social Evil in Chicago,* 296–297 (similar description twenty years later); Werther, *Female-Impersonators,* 146–163, 172–179 (New York); Stryker and Van Buskirk, *Gay by the Bay,* 18 (San Francisco).

18. Sharon Ullman, "'The Twentieth Century Way': Female Impersonation and Sexual Practice in Turn-of-the-Century America," 5 *J. Hist. Sexuality* 573 (1995); Esther Newton, *Mother Camp: Female Impersonators in America* (1979). See also Don Paulson, *A Night at the Garden of Allah* (1996) (Seattle); Chauncey, *Gay New York.* See generally Roger Baker, *Drag: A History of Female Impersonation in the Performing Arts* (1994); F. Michael Moore, *Drag! Male and Female Impersonators on Stage, Screen, and Television* (1994).

19. See generally Ellis, *Sexual Inversion,* 210–212; Coyle and Van Dyke, "Sex, Smashing," 63–65 (New Orleans).

20. San Francisco History Project, "'She Even Chewed Tobacco,'" 188.

21. See D. Michael Quinn, *Same-Sex Dynamics among Nineteenth-Century Americans: A Mormon Example* (1996) (Utah); Chauncey, *Gay New York* (exploring class angle).

22. Nathan Hale, Jr., *Freud and the Americans: The Beginnings of Psychoanalysis in the United States, 1876–1917* (1971); Jann Matlock, "Masquerading Women, Pathologized Men: Cross-Dressing, Fetishism, and the Theory of Perversion, 1882–1935," in *Fetishism as Cultural Discourse,* 31–61 (Emily Apter and William Pietz eds., 1993). Also, Vern and Bonnie Bullough, *Science in the Bedroom* (1994); Faderman, *Surpassing the Love of Men;* George Chauncey, Jr., "From Sexual Inversion to Homosexuality: Medicine and the Changing Conceptualization of Female Deviance," 58–59 *Salmagundi* 114 (1982–1983).

23. Richard von Krafft-Ebing, *Psychopathia Sexualis, with Especial Reference to the Antipathic Sexual Instinct,* 14, 42, 55 (F. J. Rebman trans., 12th ed. 1931 [1st English ed. 1892]); Karl Heinrich Ulrichs, *The Riddle of "Man-Manly" Love* (Michael Lombardi-Nash trans., 1994).

24. Krafft-Ebing, *Psychopathia Sexualis,* 581–585; Havelock Ellis, "The Study of Sexual Inversion," 12 *Medico-Legal J.* 148 (1894–95).

25. George Beard, *Sexual Neurasthenia,* 106–107 (1884).

26. See James Kiernan, "Sexual Perversion and the Whitechapel Murders," 4 *Med. Stand.* 170 (1888) and "Psychical Treatment of Congenital Sexual Inversion," 4 *Rev. Insanity and Nervous Disease* 293–295 (1894); Philip Leidy and Charles Mills, "Reports of Cases of Insanity from the Insane Department of the Philadelphia Hospital," 13 *J. Nervous and Mental Disease* 712 (1886); George Shrady, "Perverted Sexual Instinct," 26 *Med. Record* 70 (1884); P. M. Wise, "Case of Sexual Perversion," 4 *Alienist and Neurologist* 87 (1883) (case study of woman passing as a man who grabbed a female attendant in a "lewd manner").

27. Frank Lydston, *The Diseases of Society (The Vice and Crime Problem),* 37 (first quotation in text), 308–309, 372–373, 394–395 (second quotation) (1906). See Theodore Kellogg, *Textbook on Mental Diseases,* 197–198 (1897).

28. C. H. Hughes, "Postscript to a Paper on 'Erotopathia,'" 14 *Alienist and Neurologist* 731–732 (1895) and "Perverts in St. Louis"; Rosse, "Perversion of the Genetic Instinct" (associating sexual perversions, including cross-dressing, with prehistoric "troglodytes," animals, and people of color).

29. Charles G. Chaddock, "Sex Crimes," in *A System of Legal Medicine*, vol. 2, at 543–547 (Allan McLane Hamilton and Lawrence Godkin eds., 1894). See also W. Travis Gibb, "Indecent Assault upon Children," in id., vol. 1, at 651. See generally Philip Jenkins, *Moral Panic: Changing Concepts of the Child Molester in Modern America*, 28-30 (1998).

30. *Social Evil in Chicago,* 129; *A Report on Vice Conditions in the City of Lancaster, Pa.,* 44 (1913); Ullman, "'Twentieth Century Way,'" 591–595 (California). Similar connections are in Hartford Vice Commission, *Report of the Hartford Vice Commission,* 37 (1913); Philadelphia Vice Commission, *A Report of Existing Conditions,* 5 (1913); see Rosen, *Lost Sisterhood,* 84–85.

31. Quoted in Werther, *Autobiography of an Androgyne,* 24–25.

32. See generally Chauncey, *Gay New York.*

33. Rex v. Jacobs, 168 Eng. Rep. 830 (1817), followed in the early American decisions (Chapter 4).

34. Act of June 11, 1879, §1, 1879 Pa. Public Law No. 156.

35. U.S. Department of the Interior, Census Office, *Report on Crime, Pauperism, and Benevolence in the United States at the Eleventh Census: 1890,* pt I, at 18–20 (1896).

36. Michael Lynch, "New York Sodomy, 1796–1873," described in John D'Emilio and Estelle Freedman, *Intimate Matters: A History of Sexuality in America,* 123 (1988).

37. Eskridge, "Construction of the Closet," 1030 (Boston data).

38. Mathew Michael, Analysis of the Adoption of Oral Sex Laws on Sodomy Arrests for Selected Cities (unpublished paper, August 1997).

39. See Nicole Hahn Rafter, *Partial Justice: Women, Prisons, and Social Control* (2d ed. 1990).

40. Compare the United Kingdom's Vagrancy Act Amendments of 1898, which made it a misdemeanor for men to commit indecent assault, to solicit other men for immoral purposes, or to masquerade in "female attire." See McLaren, *Trials of Masculinity,* 16–17.

41. 1845 N.Y. Laws ch. 3, §6, amended by 1876 N.Y. Laws ch. 1 (codified at 1881 N.Y. Code Crim. Proc. §887[7]). On European regulation, see McLaren, *Trials of Masculinity,* 215–217; Matlock, "Masquerading Women," 49 n.40.

42. Werther, *Female-Impersonators,* 108; see People v. Luechini, 136 N.Y.S.2d 319 (Erie 1912); Magnus Hirschfeld, *Transvestites: The Erotic Desire to Cross Dress,* 277 (Michael Lombardi-Nash trans., 1991) (prison terms of six and nine months for New York men "masquerading" as women in 1904 and 1907).

43. 1873–74 Cal. Amendments 614 (codified, Penal Code §185). See also 1953 Cal. Stat. ch. 32, §18 (codified, Penal Code §650a), making it illegal to appear in public with face concealed by "mask or other regalia" unless concealment was for purposes of "amusement."

44. Nan D. Hunter, "Gender Disguise and the Law," 1–5 (draft 1990); see Hirschfeld, *Transvestites,* 279–297 (gender fraud in Europe stimulated similar laws); Matlock, "Masquerading Women," 45–46.

45. Hirschfeld, *Transvestites,* 276–277.

46. Quoted in Sullivan, *From Female to Male,* 2. See Charles Snyder, *Dr. Mary Walker: The Little Lady in Pants* (1974) (Walker cross-dressed so she could have a professional career); Matlock, "Masquerading Women," 46–54 (similar examples from Europe).

47. Arrest data for St. Louis, 1880–1920, establish that about a third of the cross-dressing arrests were for men in female garb (Appendix C4). Less systematic reports for Boston, Nashville, New York, and San Francisco include male as well as female violators.

48. Compare McLaren, *Trials of Masculinity,* 217 (British masquerade law of 1898 applied against female impersonators soliciting men for sex); Matlock, "Masquerading Women" (first men, then women, who cross-dressed treated as sexually troubled in Europe).

49. San Francisco Ord. No. 819 (June 11, 1903).

50. See Duggan, *Sapphic Slashers,* for an extended account of the Mitchell case and its popular reception.

51. Chicago Code, 1911, §§2012, 2018, 2030, 2031 (Edward Brundage ed., 1911). See also L. A. Ord. No. 68 (February 1883) (regulating "lewd and dissolute" persons).

52. 1860 Mass. Gen. Stats. ch. 165, §28. See also 1875 Wash. Laws 85; 1877 Ill. Laws 87.

53. 1900 N.Y. Laws ch. 281 (recodified in 1910 N.Y. Laws ch. 382). The provision strongly resembles the antisolicitation provision of England's Vagrancy Act Amendments of 1898, which was applied to homosexual solicitation. McLaren, *Trials of Masculinity,* 217.

54. *Report of the Special Committee of the Assembly Appointed to Investigate the Offices and Departments of the City of New York,* vol. 2, at 1429–32, excerpted in Katz, *Gay American History,* 72–73.

55. 1915 N.Y. Laws ch. 285.

56. 1919 N.Y. Laws ch. 502, rewriting §887(4)(b) and adding §887(4)(e) and (f).

57. F. H. Whitin, "Sexual Perversion Cases in New York City Courts, 1916–1921," Bulletin #1480 of the Committee of Fourteen, November 13, 1921, in The Collected Papers of the Committee of Fourteen, New York Public Library, Manuscripts Room.

58. People ex rel. Potter v. Board of Managers of the Wayside House, 196 N.Y.S. 887 (Nassau 1922).

59. 1923 N.Y. Laws ch. 642. For application of §722(8) to homosexual loitering, see People v. Lopez, 7 N.Y.2d 825 (1959); People v. Liebenthal, 5 N.Y.2d 876 (1959).

60. 1891 Cal. Stat. ch. 117, §§5, 7.

61. See Arthur Sherry, "Vagrants, Rogues and Vagabonds—Old Concepts in Need of Revision," 48 *Cal. L. Rev.* 557 (1960); Note, "Use of Vagrancy-Type Laws for Arrest and Detention of Suspicious Persons," 59 *Yale L.J.* 1351 (1950).

62. 1903 Cal. Stat. ch. 201, p. 235, §1, adding Cal. Penal Code §650½ (now §650.5).

63. E.g., Stevenson, *Intersexes* (San Francisco); Ullman, " 'Twentieth Century Way,' " 591–600 (Long Beach).

64. See Stephen Maynard, "Through a Hole in the Lavatory Wall: Homosexual Subculture, Police Surveillance, and the Dialectics of Discovery, Toronto, 1890–1930," 5 *J. Hist. Sexuality* 207 (1994). See also 1917 Pa. Pub. Law No. 1000, §3 (misdemeanor

to solicit or incite to sodomy); 1939 Pa. Public Law No. 872 (raising this offense to felony status).

65. Lawrence Murphy, *Perverts by Official Order: The Campaign against Homosexuals by the United States Navy* (1988); George Chauncey, Jr., "Christian Brotherhood or Sexual Perversion? Homosexual Identities and the Construction of Sexual Boundaries in the World War I Era," in *Hidden from History*, 294.

66. Act of July 9, 1918, 40 Stat. 886, amending Act of May 18, 1917.

67. 1876 N.Y. Laws ch. 122. Similar laws are collected in Appendix A3.

68. 1881 Mich. Pub. Acts No. 260. See also 1885 Mass. Laws ch. 305; 1885 Mo. Laws ch. 146; 1889 Ill. Laws 114.

69. 1881 Ind. Stat. 195–196, §100. See also 1890 Wyo. Laws ch. 73, §87.

70. 1897 Mich. Pub. Acts No. 95. See also 1926 N.J. Laws ch. 172.

71. 1897 Wis. Laws ch. 198.

72. 1907 Ill. Laws 266; 1915 Ill. Laws 368 (codified, Ill. Crim. Code §§109, 100).

73. E.g., 1859 Cal. Stat. p. 297 and 1858 Cal. Stat. p. 204, codified in Cal. Penal Code §§311–314; Ill. Rev. Stat., 1845, §128; 3 Rev. N.Y. Stat. §§77–78, recodified in N.Y. Penal Code, 1881, §317; Act of March 31, 1860, §40, codified at Pa. Penal Code, 1883, title D, §X.

74. 1899 Wis. Laws ch. 198. See also 1900 R.I. Laws ch. 745; 33 Iowa Acts Gen. Ass. ch. 217 (1909); 1910 Mass. Stat. ch. 367; 1911 Conn. Laws ch. 234.

75. Chicago Ords., 1856, ch. XXXVIII, art. I, §6.

76. Regina v. Hicklin, 3 Q.B. 360 (U.K. House of Lords, 1868), followed in United States v. Bennet, 24 Fed. Cas. 1093 (2d Cir. 1879), the leading case construing the Comstock Act.

77. Betsy Erkkila, *Whitman the Political Poet*, 360–371 (1989); David Reynolds, *Walt Whitman's America*, 540–541 (1995).

78. On early homophile literature, see Roger Austen, *Playing the Game: The Homosexual Novel in America* (1977); Jeannette Howard Foster, *Sex Variant Women in Literature* (1956); Byrne Fone, *A Road to Stonewall: Male Homosexuality and Homophobia in English and American Literature, 1750–1969* (1995); James Gifford, *Daynesford's Library: American Homosexual Writing, 1900–1913* (1995). On Stoddard's suppression, see John Addington Symonds, *Male Love*, 151 (John Lauritsen ed., 1983).

79. In England, John Addington Symonds privately printed his essays on the naturalness of same-sex desire, *A Problem in Greek Ethics* (1883) and *A Problem of Modern Ethics: Being an Enquiry into the Phenomena of Sexual Inversion* (1891). Edward Carpenter privately published *Homogenic Love* (1894) but found a publisher for his next work, *The Intermediate Sex* (1907). None of these volumes was published in America, but all were smuggled into this country.

80. Baltimore Code, 1879, art. 51, §1.

81. See Kaier Curtin, *"We Can Always Call Them Bulgarians": The Emergence of Lesbians and Gay Men on the American Stage*, 17 (1987).

82. Id. at 25–42.

83. Detroit Comp. Ords., 1912, ch. 190, §20.

84. Los Angeles Code, 1936, §41.13.

85. Mutual Film Co. v. Ohio Indus. Commn., 236 U.S. 230, 244 (1915).

86. 1921 N.Y. Laws ch. 715 (adding N.Y. Education Law §122).

87. See Vito Russo, *The Celluloid Closet: Homosexuality in the Movies* (rev. ed. 1987).

88. 13 Stat. 50 (1865).

89. Act of June 8, 1872, §148, 17 Stat. 302, amended by Act of March 3, 1873, 17 Stat. 598, codified at 28 U.S.C. §1461. See Heywood Broun and Margaret Leech, *Anthony Comstock: Roundsman of the Lord* (1927); Robert Haney, *Comstockery in America* (1974); James Paul and Murray Schwartz, *Federal Censorship: Obscenity in the Mail,* 18–24 (1961).

90. 30 U.S.C. §1305; see Paul and Schwartz, *Federal Censorship,* 55–63.

91. Act of March 3, 1875, §3, 18 Stat. 477 (prostitutes); Act of March 3, 1891, §1, 26 Stat. 1084 (disease, crime of moral turpitude); Act of February 20, 1907, §2, 34 Stat. 898 (persons *admitting* commission of a crime of moral turpitude). Congress failed to enact a proposal to deport all "immoral or lewd persons." Immigration Service, *Annual Report, 1896,* at 18.

92. Immigration Act of 1917, §3, 39 Stat. 874.

93. Immigration Service, *Annual Report, 1909,* 115.

94. Case of Nicholas P., U.S. Department of Labor, Bureau of Immigration, INS File No. 53429/14, Accession 60A600, Box 869, Records of the INS, Washington National Records Center, Suitland, Maryland. Other INS deportations of people engaging in oral sex or same-sex intimacy are referenced and digested in Eskridge, "Construction of the Closet," 1046–47 n.149.

95. Act of August 3, 1885, §2, 22 Stat. 214.

96. Case of Parthenios Colones, U.S. Department of Labor, Bureau of Immigration, INS File No. 54134/62, Accession 60A600, Box 869, Records of the INS.

97. Case of Ludwig W., INS File No. 53989/31.

98. Senate Report No. 352, 64th Cong., 1st Sess. 4–5 (1916); Public Health Service, *Manual of the Mental Examination of Aliens* (1918), discussed in In re Rochelle, 11 I&N Dec. 436, 440 (Bd. Imm. App. 1965).

99. The transcript of the 1919 Court of Inquiry can be found in the National Archives, Record Group 125, Records of Proceedings of Courts of Inquiry etc., No. 10821-1. See also Murphy, *Perverts by Official Order.*

100. 1919 Court of Inquiry Transcript, 268–269, plus 125 and 398 ("moral degenerates"). Also called "moral perverts," id. at 270, 300.

101. Id. at 375.

102. Murphy, *Perverts by Official Order,* 63–64.

103. "Sodomy" was not a crime under the Articles of War of 1916, although "assault to commit sodomy" was. Like the common law, the *Manual for Courts-Martial, 1917,* para. 443, defined sodomy to exclude oral sex. Congress included sodomy as one of the "miscellaneous crimes and offenses" in the 1920 Articles of War, Act of June 4, 1920, art. 93, 41 Stat. 787, and the *Manual for Courts-Martial, 1921,* para. 443, redefined sodomy to include oral sex.

104. U.S. Senate Committee on Naval Affairs, *Alleged Immoral Conditions at Newport (R.I.) Naval Training Station,* 35–36 (1921).

105. Medical Department, War Department, Army Regulation 40-105, "Standards of Physical Examination for Entrance into the Regular Army, National Guard, and Organized Reserves," §XX, ¶93(a)–(b).

106. Id. §XX, ¶93(p).

107. See Record of Proceedings on a Court of Inquiry Convened at The U.S. Naval Training Station, Newport, R.I., January 22, 1920, at 741. The transcript can be found in the National Archives, Record Group 125, Records of Proceedings of Courts of Inquiry etc., No. 10821-1. See also Murphy, *Perverts by Official Order*.

108. 1921 Senate Report, 129.

109. 1919 Court of Inquiry Transcript, 1360 (first quotation in text), 1956 (second quotation).

110. 1921 Senate Report, 30.

111. Quoted in Murphy, *Perverts by Official Order*, 212.

112. Sigmund Freud, *Three Essays on Sexuality* (1905) and *The Psychogenesis of a Case of Homosexuality in a Woman* (1920). See Nancy Chodorow, *Femininities, Masculinities, Sexualities* (1994); Hale, *Freud and the Americans*, 164–172 (1971).

113. See Nathan Hale, Jr., *The Rise and Crisis of Psychoanalysis in the United States: Freud and the Americans, 1917–1985* (1995).

114. Dr. Paul Bowers, "A Survey of Twenty-Five Hundred Prisoners in the Psychopathic Laboratory at the Indiana State Prison," 33 (no date), attached to Los Angeles Police Department, *Annual Report, 1924*.

115. See Katharine Bement Davis, *Factors in the Sex Life of Twenty-Two Hundred Women*, 247–251 (1929) (half of the unmarried sample experienced "intense emotional relations with other women," and half of that group had physical relations).

116. See Brett Beemyn, ed., *Creating a Place for Ourselves: Lesbian, Gay, and Bisexual Community Histories* (1997) (New York, San Francisco, Chicago, Detroit, Flint, Cherry Grove, 1920s–1930s); Nan Alamilla Boyd, *San Francisco Was a Wide-Open Town: Charting the Emergence of Gay and Lesbian Communities through the Mid-Twentieth Century* (1995); Chauncey, *Gay New York*; Kennedy and Davis, *Boots of Leather* (lesbian community in Buffalo); Faderman, *Odd Girls* (lesbian communities in Harlem and Greenwich Village); Eric Garber, "A Spectacle of Color: The Lesbian and Gay Subculture of Jazz Age Harlem," in *Hidden from History*, 321.

117. See Davis, *Sex Life of Twenty-Two Hundred Women*, 329–394 (women surveyed in 1920s overwhelmingly accepted nonprocreative sex but rejected adultery and premarital sex); Floyd Dell, *Love in the Machine Age* (1930); Margaret Sanger, *Happiness in Marriage* (1926). See generally Christina Simmons, "Purity Rejected: The New Sex Freedom of the Twenties" (Berkshire Women's History Conference, June 1976).

118. Barnett v. State, 135 N.E. 647, 649 (Ohio 1922); see also Berryman v. State, 283 P.2d 558, 565 n.1 (Okla. Crim. App. 1955); [Judge] Morris Ploscowe, *Sex and the Law*, 209 (1951).

119. Freedman, "'Uncontrolled Desires.'" Accord, Jenkins, *Moral Panic*, 46, 49–52.

120. See Appendix C1 (sodomy arrests) and San Francisco Chief of Police, *Annual Reports, 1885–1912* (sodomy arrests increase from two to nineteen; rape from seven to thirty-eight; new categories of "enticing minor to house of ill fame" [1890] and "crime against a child" [1909]); Chicago Police Department, *Annual Police Reports, 1885–1921* (similar, with creation of new felony "crimes against children" and new misdemeanor "contributing to delinquency of children" [both 1909] and average arrests of 120 and 820 persons per year, 1909–1918).

121. See New York City Magistrates, *Annual Reports, 1874–1931* (offenses charged before Magistrates Courts).

122. See Appendix C3 (degeneracy arraignments go up from 554 to 726 between 1935 and 1938); New York City Magistrates, *Annual Reports, 1935–1937* (rape arraignments up from 737 to 904; crime against nature up from 130 to 167; impairing morals of minors up from 257 to 326).

123. Report of the [New York City] Mayor's Committee for the Study of Sex Offenses, 66 (1940).

124. See *Report of the [Michigan] Governor's Study Commission on the Deviated Criminal Sex Offender*, 210–211 (1951) (Table 4) (between 1936 and 1937 rape commitments jump from nineteen to thirty-six, statutory rape from forty-six to seventy-nine, indecent liberties from fifty-five to eighty-eight, and sodomy from thirty-five to fifty-five, with almost as high levels for each crime for the next ten years).

125. 1911 Mass. Laws ch. 595 (amended 1913, 1916, 1919), discussed in Jenkins, *Moral Panic*, 40–41. Massachusetts had also pioneered the idea of incarcerating "habitual offenders" for lengthy periods of time, with allowance for relief if the offender showed reformation. 1887 Mass. Laws ch. 435.

126. The Iowa law requiring sterilization for violent criminals and "moral and sexual perverts," 35 Iowa Gen. Ass. ch. 187 (1913), was found unconstitutional in Davis v. Berry, 216 F. 413 (S.D. Iowa 1914) (three-judge court), but the Supreme Court vacated the judgment on procedural grounds, Berry v. Davis, 242 U.S. 468 (1916). The Supreme Court upheld sterilization laws against due process and equal protection attack in Buck v. Bell, 274 U.S. 200 (1927), and states continued to adopt such laws, e.g., 1929 Mich. Acts No. 281.

127. California Assembly Interim Committee on Judicial System and Judicial Process, Subcommittee on Sex Crimes, *Preliminary Report*, 214–215 (1950). The subcommittee was less confident than the judge. Id. at 51–52.

128. 1941 Cal. Stat. ch. 106, §15.

129. 1935 Mich. Acts Nos. 87–88 (sexual psychopath law); 1929 Mich. Acts No. 281 (procedures for sterilization of "moral degenerates and sexual perverts").

130. Ill. Rev. Stat. ch. 38, §§820, 823–824.

131. William Haines et al., "Commitments under the Criminal Sexual Psychopath Law in the Criminal Court of Cook County, Illinois," *Procs. Am. Psychiatric Assn.* 420, 422–423 (1949).

132. Loitering near a subway toilet was made a crime by 1939 N.Y. Laws ch. 391. Loitering near a school was made a crime in 1929 Cal. Stat. ch. 697. For examples of police harassment of homosexual men under a variety of statutes, see George Henry, *Sex Variants: A Study of Homosexual Patterns*, 57, 154, 166, 200, 280, 364, 409, 433, 444–445, 474, 483–484, 493–494 (1948); Donald Vining, *A Gay Diary, 1933–1946*, at 284–285, 336–338 (1979). Lesbians described in Henry's study had few such encounters with the criminal law.

133. The arrest figures for New York and Los Angeles are taken from each city's annual police reports for the 1940 fiscal year.

134. Allan Bérubé, "The History of Gay Bathhouses," in *Policing Public Sex*, 187–220 (Dangerous Bedfellows eds., 1996).

135. The first police raids against congregations of inverts were around the turn of the century in New York City, targeting Paresis Hall (1896) and the Ariston Hotel Baths (1903). Werther, *Female-Impersonators,* 164; Chauncey, *Gay New York,* 214–216. In 1918 San Francisco police raided the Baker Street Club. Bérubé, "Gay Bathhouses."

136. See the first-person accounts of police harassment of gay men in Henry, *Sex Variants,* and Vining, *Gay Diary, 1933–1946.*

137. Kennedy and Davis, *Boots of Leather,* 64 (Buffalo); David Johnson, "The Kids of Fairytown: Gay Male Culture on Chicago's North Side in the 1930s," in *Place for Ourselves,* 97, 112–113; Allen Drexel, "Before Paris Burned: Race, Class, and Male Homosexuality on the Chicago South Side, 1935–1960," in id. at 119, 132–133 (police tolerated drag balls for black and working-class gays); Rochella Thorpe, "'A House Where Queers Go': African-American Lesbian Nightlife in Detroit, 1940–1975," in *Inventing Lesbian Cultures in America,* 40, 59 (Ellen Lewin ed., 1996).

138. Henry Gerber, "The Society for Human Rights—1925," *One, Inc.,* September 1962, at 10; Katz, *Gay American History,* 581–597.

139. See Chauncey, *Gay New York,* 331–333.

140. Chicago Code, 1911, §§1525–26, 1536.

141. Leonard Harrison and Elizabeth Laine, *After Repeal: A Study of Liquor Control Administration,* 79–80 (1936); e.g., 1934 Cal. Laws, codified at Cal. Bus. & Prof. Code §24200; 1935 Fla. Laws ch. 16774, §1, codified at Fla. Stat. §561.29; 1935 Texas Acts ch. 467, art. 2, §19(A)(7), (B)(16) (revocation if licensee allows conduct that is "lewd, immoral or offensive to public decency"); 1934 Va. Laws 114, codified at Va. Code §4675(25).

142. N.Y. Alcoholic Beverage Control Law §106(6), added by 1934 N.Y. Laws.

143. See Chauncey, *Gay New York,* 338–340, drawing from Record on Review, Gloria Bar & Grill v. Bruckman, 18 N.Y.S.2d 1023 (App. 1940).

144. Id. at 340–342, discussing, e.g., Times Square Bar & Grill, Inc. v. Bruckman, 12 N.Y.S.2d 232 (App. 1939).

145. See Re M. Potter, Inc., New Jersey A.B.C. Bulletin 474, Item 1 (N.J. Commr. ABC 1941) (suspending liquor license because "effeminate" men danced and kissed one another on the premises).

146. Cal. Business and Professions Code §§24200(a), 25601 (1934).

147. Medical books treating homosexuality with comparative dispassion and available in the United States in the 1920s included not just works of Freud and Ellis, but also Joseph Collins, *The Doctor Looks at Love and Life* (1926), and Davis, *Sex Life of Twenty-Two Hundred Women.*

148. E.g., Ernest Hemingway, *The Sun Also Rises,* 20 (1925); D. H. Lawrence, *The Rainbow* (1915).

149. Clemence Dane, *The Regiment of Women,* 337 (1917).

150. See Austen, *Playing the Game,* 59–60; Paul and Schwartz, *Federal Censorship,* 46–48.

151. Paul and Schwartz, *Federal Censorship,* 42, 263.

152. Tariff Act of 1930, §305, 46 Stat. 688, responding to congressional criticisms, 71 Cong. Rec. 4434–35 (1929). See United States v. One Book Entitled *Ulysses* by James Joyce, 72 F.2d 705 (2d Cir. 1934).

153. People v. Friede, 233 N.Y.S. 565, 567–568 (N.Y. City 1929).

154. Vera Brittain, *Radclyffe Hall: A Case of Obscenity?*, 147–149 (1968); Morris Ernst and Alan Schwartz, *Censorship: The Search for the Obscene*, 71–79 (1964) (account by Hall's lawyer).

155. 1927 N.Y. Laws ch. 690, codified at N.Y. Penal Code §1140a(2). See also Los Angeles Code, 1945, §41.02(a) (prohibiting any play or exhibition that "depicts or deals with the subject or theme of sex degeneracy or sex perversion, or sex inversion").

156. On the background of the 1927 law, see Katz, *Gay American History*, 128–139, 881–883; Curtin, "Call Them Bulgarians," 91–104.

157. For lesbian monsters, see Kathleen Millay, *Against the Wall* (1929); Geoffrey Moss, *That Other Love* (1930); Naomi Royde-Smith, *The Island* (1929), discussed in Foster, *Sex Variant Women*. For men as sex maniacs, see Lew Levenson, *Butterfly Man* (1934); Richard Meeker, *Better Angel* (1933); Andre Tellier, *Twilight Men* (1931), discussed in Austen, *Playing the Game*.

158. People v. Gotham Book Mart, 285 N.Y.S. 563 (N.Y. City 1936).

159. Russo, *Celluloid Closet*, 29 *(Salome)*, 57–58 *(Mädchen)*.

160. See Morris Ernst and Alexander Lindey, *The Censor Marches On*, 317 (1940) (reproducing Code); Leonard Leff and Jerold Simmons, *The Dame in the Kimono: Hollywood, Censorship, and the Production Code from the 1920s to the 1940s* (1990); Frank Walsh, *Sin and Censorship: The Catholic Church and the Motion Picture Industry* (1995).

161. William Wright, *Lillian Hellman*, 101 (1986).

162. See Memorandum from the Judge Advocate General to The Adjutant General, October 16, 1931, at 4–6, discussed in Bérubé, *Coming Out under Fire*, 133.

163. Frederick Harrod, *Manning the New Navy*, 196–197 (1978). Bérubé, *Coming Out under Fire*, 330 n.47, found thirty-four cases in the Army between July 1938 and May 1941, suggesting that the rate picked up on the eve of World War II.

164. See Bérubé, *Coming Out under Fire*, 12, discussing "Neuropsychiatric Examination of Applicants for Voluntary Enlistment and Selectees for Induction," Circular Letter No. 19, War Department, March 12, 1941, *War Medicine*, May 1941, at 418–425.

165. See Bérubé, *Coming Out under Fire*, 14–18.

166. War Department, Mobilization Regs. Nos. 1–9, Standards of Physical Examination during Mobilization §20-93(h) ("Sexual Perversions," a subcategory of "Personality Disorders"); see Bérubé, *Coming Out under Fire*, 19–20.

167. Even the homosexuals who confessed their sexual orientation were sometimes excluded for another, make-weight reason by sympathetic physicians. See Bérubé, *Coming Out under Fire*, 26–27; cf. Vining, *Gay Diary: 1933–1946*, at 213–216, 224–227 (cooperative examiner first classified Vining "sui generistic 'H' overt" but was forced to a more explicit reason for rejecting Vining: "homosexualism—overt").

168. TB MED 100 (1944), discussed in Leisa Meyer, *Creating G.I. Jane: Sexuality and Power in the Woman's Army Corps during World War II*, 158 (1996).

169. Bérubé, *Coming Out under Fire*, 33 (citing internal War Department memoranda).

170. War Department Pamphlet No. 35-1, "Sex Hygiene Course, Officers and Officer Candidates, WAAC," May 27, 1943 (Lecture V: Homosexuality), discussed in Allan Bérubé and John D'Emilio, "The Military and Lesbians during the McCarthy Years," 9 *Signs* 759, 761 (1984). See also Meyer, *G.I. Jane*, 158–159.

171. U.S. Army Surgeon General, "Disposition of Overt Cases of Homosexuality," Army Bulletin No. 66, April 1943, pt. E, 83.

172. U.S. War Department, Army Regulation No. 615-368, "Enlisted Men: Discharge—Undesirable Traits of Character," ¶2.b.2½ (as amended April 10, 1945).

173. Bérubé, *Coming Out under Fire*, 146 (Judge Advocate General believed reduced statistics could "reasonably [be] traced" to Circular No. 3).

174. Id. at 147.

175. Lieut. Col. Birge Holt and Capt. Ruby Herman, Report to The Acting Inspector General, July 29, 1944 (available at the National Archives, Record Group 159 [Office of Army Inspector General], File 333.9 [Third WAC Training Center]). See Meyer, *G.I. Jane,* 173–176.

176. See Ellen Ross and Rayna Rapp, "Sex and Society: A Research Note from Social History and Anthropology," in William N. Eskridge, Jr., and Nan D. Hunter, *Sexuality, Gender, and the Law,* 306–309 (1997); Bérubé, *Coming Out under Fire,* especially its discussion of military interrogations; Chauncey, *Gay New York,* especially its discussion of law's campaign against public displays of same-sex affection.

177. Michel Foucault, *The History of Sexuality,* vol. 1: *An Introduction* (Robert Hurley trans., 1978). See analysis by Eskridge and Hunter, *Sexuality, Gender, and the Law,* 262–289.

178. Stevenson, *Imre,* 9, 68–69, 111, 191; see Stevenson, *Intersexes,* 85–87.

179. See Mary Edwards Walker, *Unmasked, or The Science of Immorality* (1878) (Walker passed as a man so she could be a doctor).

180. Reva Siegel, "'The Rule of Love': Wife Beating as Prerogative and Privacy," 105 *Yale L.J.* 2117 (1996).

181. Werther, *Autobiography of an Androgyne,* 135; see id. at 132: brutalizing thugs were encouraged by the law to "look[] upon a fairie as necessarily a monster of wickedness—for why otherwise would the law place upon his sexual conduct a penalty of ten years in state prison?"

182. Stevenson, *Intersexes,* 457–459 (sexual blackmail much bigger problem in Germany and Anglo-American states, where consensual sodomy was illegal, than in France and Low Countries, where it was legal).

183. Ellis, *Sexual Inversion,* 352.

184. See Elizabeth Lapovsky Kennedy, "'But We Would Never Talk about It': The Structures of Lesbian Discretion in South Dakota, 1928–1933," in *Inventing Lesbian Cultures,* 15–39.

185. Werther, *Autobiography of an Androgyne,* 123.

186. E.g., Henry, *Sex Variants,* 115 (Nathan T., robbed by tricks, beaten up when he was an adolescent), 154 (Eric D., complaining about how homosexuals are the ones "preyed upon because they are timid and don't wish to bring in the aid of the law"), 330 (Irving T., robbed and raped by tricks because he and the thugs both knew he had no legal recourse), 474 (Peter R., blackmailed by police for money and, once, for sex); Vining, *Gay Diary, 1933–1946,* at 286–287, 325, 347–348 (author strangled, shaken down, and robbed by tricks; police ineffectual).

187. Werther, *Autobiography of an Androgyne,* 135.

188. Garber, "A Spectacle of Color." See generally George Hutchinson, *The Harlem Renaissance in Black and White* (1995); David Levering Lewis, *When Harlem Was in*

Vogue (1981); Arnold Rampersad, *The Life of Langston Hughes* (two volumes, 1986 and 1988); Steven Watson, *The Harlem Renaissance* (1995).

189. Mrs. Blair Niles, *Strange Brother,* 105 (1931); Gore Vidal, *The City and the Pillar* (1948).

190. In addition to the decisions overturning censorship of *Well of Loneliness* and *If It Die,* see United States v. One Book Entitled *Ulysses* by James Joyce, 72 F.2d 705 (2d Cir. 1934) (Judge Augustus Hand) (the state cannot censor sexual material simply because immature minds could be appalled or corrupted by portions of it).

2. Kulturkampf and the Threatening Closet, 1946–1961

1. *For the President: Personal and Secret Correspondence between Franklin D. Roosevelt and William C. Bullitt,* 513 (Orville Bullitt ed., 1972) (quotations in text). See also Irwin Gellman, *Secret Affairs: Franklin Roosevelt, Cordell Hull, and Sumner Welles,* 236–237 (1995).

2. Samuel Warren and Louis Brandeis, "The Right to Privacy," 4 *Harv. L. Rev.* 193, 195 (1890).

3. John Horne Burns, *Lucifer with a Book,* 105–106, 132–133 (1949). The closeted etching was of a blond man deriving sexual pleasure from both a man and a woman.

4. Marlin Prentiss, "Are Homosexuals Security Risks?," *One, Inc.,* December 1955, at 4.

5. A. E. Smith, "Coming Out," *One, Inc.,* June 1962, at 6–7. See also Samuel Delany, "Coming/Out," in *Boys Like Us: Gay Writers Tell Their Coming Out Stories,* 1, 14 (Patrick Merla ed., 1996) (in the 1950s, black gay culture called men who kept their homosexuality secret from their families "closet queens"); Michelle Duloc and Rene Autil, "Fluff, Buff, and Butch: Spy vs. Spy vs. Yourself," *Vector,* July 1968, at 11 (secret homosexuals were "closet queens" and "lace curtains"). The "mask," however, remained the most invoked metaphor for secrecy about one's homosexuality in the 1950s. E.g., Bob Bishop, "Discard the Mask," *Mattachine Rev.,* April 1958, at 14–16, 21–24; Lisa Ben, "Masquerade," *Vice Versa,* October 1947, reprinted in *The Ladder,* October 1958, at 6–10, 26–29.

6. Roger Austen, *Playing the Game: The Homosexual Novel in America,* 110 (1977) (quoting Burns).

7. Florida Legislative Investigating Committee, Report, *Homosexuality and Citizenship in Florida,* 14 (1964).

8. See William N. Eskridge, Jr., "Privacy Jurisprudence and the Apartheid of the Closet, 1946–1961," 24 *Fla. St. U.L. Rev.* 703, 705–708 (1997), for the gay/straight and threatening/protective dichotomies, drawing from Kenji Yoshino, "Suspect Symbols: The Literary Argument for Heightened Scrutiny for Gays," 96 *Colum. L. Rev.* 1753, 1794–1802 (1996), for the "protective" and "confining" features of the closet.

9. John D'Emilio, *Sexual Politics, Sexual Communities: The Making of a Homosexual Minority in the United States, 1940–1970* (1983). See also Barry Adam, *The Rise of a Gay and Lesbian Movement* (1987); Lillian Faderman, *Odd Girls and Twilight Lovers: A History of Lesbian Life in Twentieth-Century America* (1991); John Loughery, *The Other Side*

of Silence—Men's Lives and Gay Identities: A Twentieth-Century History (1998). For studies focusing on particular local gay communities, see the essays on Chicago, San Francisco, Washington, San Francisco, and Detroit in *Creating a Place for Ourselves: Lesbian, Gay, and Bisexual Community Histories* (Brett Beemyn ed., 1997); the essays on Atlanta, Florida, and Memphis in *Carryin' On in the Lesbian and Gay South* (John Howard ed., 1997); James Sears, *The Lonely Hunters: An Oral History of Lesbian and Gay Southern Life, 1948–1968* (1998); Marc Stein, *The City of Brotherly and Sisterly Loves: The Making of Lesbian and Gay Movements in Greater Philadelphia, 1948–1972* (Ph.D. dissertation 1994, to be published); Susan Stryker and Jim Van Buskirk, *Gay by the Bay: A History of Queer Culture in the San Francisco Bay Area* (1996).

10. Gore Vidal, *The City and the Pillar,* 203–204 (1948).

11. See Allan Bérubé, *Coming Out under Fire: The History of Gay Men and Women in World War Two* (1990); D'Emilio, *Sexual Politics;* Philip Jenkins, *Moral Panic: Changing Concepts of the Child Molester in Modern America,* 52–93 (1998); Estelle Freedman, "'Uncontrolled Desires': The Response to the Sexual Psychopath, 1920–1960," 74 *J. Am. Hist.* 83–107 (June 1987); George Chauncey, Jr., "The Postwar Sex Crime Panic," in *True Stories from the American Past,* 160 (William Graebner ed., 1993).

12. For early articles, see Howard Whitman, "The Biggest Taboo," *Colliers,* February 15, 1947, at 24, and J. Edgar Hoover, "How Safe Is Your Daughter?," *American Magazine,* July 1947, at 32.

13. *Homosexuality and Citizenship in Florida,* 13.

14. Hoover, "How Safe Is Your Daughter?"

15. Carleton Simon, "Homosexuals and Sex Crimes" (Intl. Assn. Police Chiefs, September 1947); see Jenkins, *Moral Panic,* 52–58; Freedman, "'Uncontrolled Desires,'" 94 (when girl kidnapped in Chicago, police rounded up effeminate homosexual men as suspects).

16. Act of June 9, 1948, Public Law No. 80-615, §§101, 103, 62 Stat. 346–347.

17. 1949 Cal. Stat., 1st Extr. Sess., chs. 13–15 (registration, sodomy penalty fifteen years, toilet loitering); 1950 Cal. Stat., 1st Extr. Sess., chs. 34, 56 (child molestation penalty heightened, oral copulation penalty fifteen years); 1951 Cal. Stat. ch. 1200 (child molestation penalty heightened); 1952 Cal. Stat., 1st Extr. Sess., ch. 23 (maximum life penalties for sodomy and oral copulation with minor).

18. 1950 N.Y. Stat. ch. 525, §15, enacted after Governor Dewey vetoed a sexual psychopath bill in 1947 and appointed a sex offender commission to draft more nuanced legislation; 1945 Ill. Laws 677.

19. See generally Appendix A3. Thus, 1943 Fla. Laws ch. 21974 made lewd fondling of girls under fourteen a crime, and 1951 Fla. Laws ch. 26580 did the same for boys. Similar statutes, creating new crimes for sex or lewdness with boys as well as girls, were adopted in Alabama (1955 Acts No. 397), Delaware (1947 Laws ch. 81), Georgia (1950 Laws 387), Idaho (1949 Laws ch. 214), Kentucky (1948 Laws ch. 36), Louisiana (1942 Acts No. 43, arts. 81–82), Missouri (1949 Laws 249), North Carolina (1955 Laws ch. 764), and Texas (1943 Acts ch. 112). Such statutes were later enacted in Arizona (1965 Laws ch. 20), Minnesota (1965 Laws §617.08), and Washington (1961 Laws ch. 65).

20. Miller Act §§201–208, 62 Stat. 347–350, patterned on the sexual psychopath law upheld in Minnesota ex rel. Pearson v. Probate Court, 309 U.S. 270 (1940).

21. Specific statutory references are in Appendix B1. See also Jenkins, *Moral Panic,* 75–93; Karl Bowman and Bernice Engle, "Synopses of Special Sex Psychopath Laws—United States," in *Report on California Sexual Deviation Research,* 41; Alan Swanson, "Sexual Psychopath Statutes," 21 *Crim. L. Comments & Abs.* 215 (1960).

22. California Department of Mental Hygiene, *Final Report on California Sexual Deviation Research* (1954); *Homosexuality and Citizenship in Florida* (1964); *Report of the Illinois Commission on Sex Offenders* (1953); *Report of the Governor's Study Commission on the Deviated Criminal Sex Offender* (Michigan, 1951); *Report of the Minnesota Legislative Interim Commission on Public Welfare Laws: Sex Psychopath Laws* (1959); *Report of the Interim Commission of the State of New Hampshire to Study the Cause and Prevention of Serious Sex Crimes* (1949); Paul Tappan, *The Habitual Sex Offender* (New Jersey, 1953); Bernard Glueck, *Final Report, Research Project for the Study and Treatment of Persons Convicted of Crimes Involving Sexual Aberrations* (New York, 1952–1955); *Report of the Legislative Interim Committee to Study Sex Crime Prevention* (Oregon, 1956); *Sex Offenders* (Pennsylvania, 1951); *The Sex Offender and the Criminal Law* (Virginia, 1951).

23. Tappan, *Habitual Sex Offender,* 28–29. See also Albert Ellis and Ralph Brancale, *The Psychology of Sex Offenders,* 11 (1956).

24. John LaStala (Atascadero inmate in 1955), "Atascadero: Dachau for Queers?," *The Advocate,* April 26, 1972, at 11. "Asexualization" of "sexual degenerate" recidivists was authorized by 1941 Cal. Stat. ch. 106, §15.

25. Jonathan Ned Katz, *Gay American History,* 134–207 (1976) (medical procedures performed on homosexuals, 1930s–1960s).

26. Los Angeles Code, 1955, ch. V, §§52.39 (original law) and 52.38(d) (1950 amendment); 1947 Cal Stat. ch. 1124 (Penal Code §290), amended by 1949 Cal. Stat., 1st Extr. Sess., ch. 34 (Jan. 1950).

27. See "Are You or Have You Ever Been a Homosexual?," *One, Inc.,* April 1953, at 5, 8.

28. Public Law No. 83-85, §202(a)(1), 67 Stat. 90, 92 (1953), codified at D.C. Code §1112(a); see House Report No. 83-514, at 4 (1953); House Report No. 82-538, at 19, 516 (1951); 99 Cong. Rec. 6207 (1953).

29. Note, "Private Consensual Homosexual Behavior: The Crime and Its Enforcement," 70 *Yale L.J.* 623, 635 (1960) (appendix, listing statutes).

30. See Jess Stearn, *The Sixth Man* (1961); Richard Donnelly, "Judicial Control of Informants: Spies, Stool Pigeons, and Agent Provocateurs," 60 *Yale L.J.* 1091 (1951); Note, "Decoy Enforcement of Homosexual Laws," 112 *U. Pa. L. Rev.* 259 (1963); Frank Wood, Jr., "The Homosexual and the Police," *One, Inc.,* May 1963, at 21–22.

31. Philadelphia Bureau of Police, *Annual Report, 1950,* at 31 (morals squad activity); see Stein, *The City of Brotherly and Sisterly Loves.*

32. City of Los Angeles, Police Department, *Annual Report, 1948.* For later data consistent with these early postwar figures, see Jon Gallo et al., Project, "The Consenting Adult Homosexual and the Law: An Empirical Study of Enforcement and Administration in Los Angeles County," 13 *UCLA L. Rev.* 643 (1966). Contemporary accounts of antihomosexual harassment in Los Angeles, Santa Monica, and Long Beach are in Jim Kepner, *Rough News, Daring Views: 1950's Pioneer Gay Press Journalism,* 63–64, 70–71, 100 (1998).

33. See Kepner, *Rough News*, 377–385; Nan Alamilla Boyd, "'Homos Invade S.F.!' San Francisco's History as a Wide-Open Town," in *Place for Ourselves*, 73–96.

34. See Brett Beemyn, "A Queer Capital: Race, Class, Gender, and the Changing Social Landscape of Washington's Gay Communities, 1940–1955," in *Place for Ourselves*, 183–210; David K. Johnson, "'Homosexual Citizens': Washington's Gay Community Confronts the Civil Service," *Wash. Hist.*, Fall-Winter 1994–95, at 50.

35. Contemporary accounts are in Kepner, *Rough News*, 58, 61 (Minneapolis, 1954–1955); 71, 88 (Pittsburgh, 1955); 81 (Sioux City, 1955); 100 (Santa Monica, 1956); 106 (Portland, 1955); 107 (Providence, 1955); 203, 255 (Salt Lake City, 1957–1958); 331–332 (Kansas City, 1958–1959). See also Dal McIntire [Jim Kepner], "Tangents," *One*, February 1958, at 18 (Oklahoma City).

36. See Dal McIntire's [Jim Kepner's] "Tangents" column for these issues of *One, Inc.*: April/May 1956, at 14 (Palo Alto); May 1960, at 19–20 (Ann Arbor). Police stake-outs of public restrooms in Gainesville, Florida, in the late 1950s are described in the Johns Committee Files, Florida Archives, Series 1486.

37. See Sears, *Lonely Hunters* (focus on Florida); *Carryin' On* (Atlanta, Florida, Memphis); Eskridge, "Apartheid of the Closet," 722–724, 727–733 (Miami, Miami Beach, Tampa); Bob Swisher, "One Big Community: Gay Life in Richmond after 1944," *Southern Exposure*, Fall 1988, 29. Contemporary accounts are collected in Kepner, *Rough News*, 49–55, 116–119 (Miami, 1954–1956); 80 (Dallas, 1955); 85 (Charlotte, 1955); 202 (Tampa, 1957); 261–263 (New Orleans, 1958); 335 (Memphis, 335).

38. See Allen Drexel, "Before Paris Burned: Race, Class, and Male Homosexuality on the Chicago South Side, 1935–1960," in *Place for Ourselves*, 119–144.

39. See People v. Earl, 31 Cal. Rptr. 76 (App. 1963) (interracial gay couple spotted committing oral sex by police spying through glass transom into motel room); Laud Humphreys, *Tearoom Trade: Impersonal Sex in Public Places* (1970) (police spying in public toilets); John Howard, "The Library, the Park, and the Pervert," in *Carryin' On*, 107–120 (Atlanta police toilet spying, raids, park surveillance, 1953–1957); Johns Committee Papers (Gainesville police toilet spying, late 1950s).

40. Dale Jennings, "To Be Accused Is to Be Guilty," *One, Inc.*, January 1953, at 11–12. For general allegations of police entrapment, see Wood, "Homosexual and the Police," and Stearn, *Sixth Man*, 168.

41. See Dal McIntire's [Jim Kepner's] "Tangents" column for these issues of *One, Inc.*: December 1955, at 12 (Baltimore); April/May 1956, at 14 (Redwood City); April 1959 (Philadelphia); October/November 1957, at 18–19 (Tampa); December 1961, at 16 (San Francisco), all but the last reprinted in Kepner, *Rough News*, 86–87, 119–120, 203, 329–331. The Yuga ball raid is discussed in Loughery, *Other Side of Silence*, 275–276.

42. Dal McIntire, "Tangents," *One, Inc.*, April 1960, at 15.

43. See Kepner, *Rough News*, 49–55 (Miami), 169–170 (Chicago, Santa Monica).

44. Accounts of various manias can be found in John Gerassi, *The Boys of Boise* (1966); Boyd, "'Homos Invade S.F.!'," 86–87 (San Francisco); Lyn Pedersen [Jim Kepner], "Miami Hurricane," *One Inc.*, November 1954, at 6, reprinted in Kepner, *Rough News*, 49–55; Eskridge, "Apartheid of the Closet," 727–733 (Miami and Tampa).

45. Morris Ploscowe, *Sex and the Law*, 208 (1951). The toilet law was 1939 N.Y. Laws ch. 391, amended 1941 N.Y. Laws ch. 835 (codified, Penal Code §1990a).

46. Los Angeles Police Department, *Annual Report, 1948.*

47. For examples of police harassment, but not arrest, of lesbians in their meeting places for this period, see the first-person accounts in Elizabeth Lapovsky Kennedy and Madeline Davis, *Boots of Leather, Slippers of Gold: The History of a Lesbian Community* (1993) (Buffalo); Eric Marcus, *Making History: The Struggle for Gay and Lesbian Equal Rights*, 8 (1992) (Los Angeles); Joan Nestle, *A Restricted Country*, 38 (1987) (New York).

48. For general accounts of the antihomosexual purges, see D'Emilio, *Sexual Politics; Before Stonewall: The Making of a Lesbian and Gay Community* (PBS, 1984); Johnson, "'Homosexual Citizens.'"

49. See Johnson, "'Homosexual Citizens,'" 49–50.

50. Subcommittee on Investigations of the Senate Committee on Expenditures in the Executive Departments, "Employment of Homosexuals and Other Sex Perverts in Government," app. (December 15, 1950).

51. Bérubé, *Coming Out under Fire*, 262, 354 n.14.

52. Department of Defense, "Discharge of Homosexuals from the Armed Services," October 11, 1949, app. 5 to *Report of the Board to Prepare and Submit to the Secretary of the Navy Recommendations for the Revision of Policies, Procedures and Directives Dealing with Homosexuals* (March 15, 1957) ("Crittenden Report"), implemented in Army Regulation 635-443 (January 12, 1950); SECNAV Instruction 1620.1 (December 10, 1949); Air Force Regulation 35-66 (January 12, 1951).

53. Neil Miller, *Out of the Past: Gay and Lesbian History from 1869 to the Present*, 259, 274–275 (1995); Johnson, "'Homosexual Citizens,'" 50; Jack Tait and Lee Mortimer, *Washington Confidential*, 91 (1951).

54. "Employment of Homosexuals," 3–4 (all quotes in text).

55. Letter from James Hatcher, Civil Service Commn., Investigations Divn., to Donald Webster Cory, May 3, 1951, reprinted in Cory, *The Homosexual in America*, 269 (1951). According to the Personnel Director of the Civil Service Commission in 1963, "persons about whom there is evidence that they have engaged in or solicited others to engage in homosexual or sexually perverted acts with them without evidence of rehabilitation are not suitable for Federal employment." Memorandum from D. J. Brennan, Jr., to W. C. Sullivan, December 24, 1963, "Re: Mattachine Society of Washington," FBI File Number HQ 100-403320, Serial 106. This document, like the other FBI documents referred to, is part of the FBI's Freedom of Information Act (FOIA) release files on the general topic of homosexuality and gay rights.

56. "Employment of Homosexuals," 9.

57. D'Emilio, *Sexual Politics*, 44.

58. Senate Bill 716, 82d Cong., §212(a)(7) (1951), and Senate Bill 2550, 82d Cong., §212(a)(13) (1952); Senate Report No. 81-1515, at 344–345 (1950).

59. Public Law No. 82-414, §212(a)(4), 66 Stat. 163, 182 (1952) (repealed 1990); House Report No. 82-1365, at 47 (1952), reprinted in 1952 *U.S.C.C.A.N.* 1653, 1701 (quoting original McCarran bill); Senate Report No. 82-1137, at 9 (1952).

60. See United States v. Flores-Rodriguez, 237 F.2d 405 (2d Cir. 1956); In re La Rochelle, 11 I&N Dec. 436 (Bd. Imm. App. 1965).

61. Executive Order No. 10,450, §8(a)(1)(iii), 18 Fed. Reg. 2489 (April 29, 1953), codified at 3 C.F.R. 936, 938 (1953).

62. D'Emilio, *Sexual Politics,* 44; Johnson, "'Homosexual Citizens,'" 52–53.

63. Executive Order 10,865, 25 Fed. Reg. 1583 (February 20, 1960), codified at 3 C.F.R. §398 (1959–1963 compilation), and Department of Defense Directive No. 5220.6, §VI.P (December 7, 1966). Eisenhower's previous, and less formal, security clearance exclusionary policy was invalidated for procedural reasons in Greene v. McElroy, 360 U.S. 474 (1959).

64. Marcus, *Making History,* 72, 94–95.

65. E.g., Lait and Mortimer, *Washington Confidential,* 90–98 (contemporary accusation that D.C. was hotbed of perversion); Miller, *Out of the Past,* 270–271 (charges that McCarthy counsel Roy Cohn was gay; threats by Cohn to expose Senator Lester Hunt's son as homosexual, and the senator's subsequent suicide); David Oshinsky, *A Conspiracy So Immense: The World of Joe McCarthy,* 310 (1983) (Drew Pearson suggestion that McCarthy was gay).

66. Chaplain's Presentation (WAVE Recruits), 1953, at 3 (quotation in text); Chaplain's Presentation (Male Recruits), 1953, at 1–2; Indoctrination of Male Recruits on Subject of Homosexuality, 1953, at 5—all reprinted in appendix 23 to the Crittenden Report. See Allan Bérubé and John D'Emilio, "The Military and Lesbians during the McCarthy Years," 9 *Signs* 749 (1984).

67. Army Regulation 600-443, ¶5; also Air Force Regulation 35-66, "Discharge of Homosexuals" (May 31, 1956).

68. D'Emilio, *Sexual Politics,* 46; Bérubé and D'Emilio, "McCarthy Years," 770–774 (reprinting letters from women expelled). Other investigations are discussed in Faderman, *Odd Girls,* 150–155.

69. See Colin Williams and Martin Weinberg, *Homosexuals and the Military,* 46–53 (1971); Crittenden Report, 40 (rate of discharge for women), 51–52 (general rate).

70. See Estelle Freedman, *Maternal Justice: Miriam Van Waters and the Female Reform Tradition,* 267–278 (1996).

71. Cal. Education Code §§13202, 13209 (certificates for state teachers), 24306(a) (state college employees) (West 1960); Cal. Government Code §19572(l) (civil service workers) (West 1954).

72. 1952 Cal. Stat. chs. 389–390, codified at Cal. Education Code §§13207, 12912 (West 1954), and upheld in Sarac v. State Board of Education, 57 Cal. Rptr. 69 (App. 1957).

73. 1951 Cal. Stat. ch. 1482, codified at Cal. Education Code §12105.1–.2 (West 1955).

74. Cal. Business and Professions Code §§2361(d) (doctors), 1680(8) (dentists), 3105 (optometrists), 4350.5 (pharmacists), 7698 (funeral directors and embalmers) (West 1954); Cal. Probate Code §1580(4) (guardians) (West 1954). For an exhaustive list of occupations having immorality exclusions in California and other states, see E. Carrington Boggan et al., *The Rights of Gay People: The Basic ACLU Guide to a Gay Person's Rights,* 211–35 (1975).

75. E.g., Cal. Business and Professions Code §§1000-10(b) (chiropractors), 1679 (dentists), 2383 (doctors), 2685(d) (physical therapists), 3105 (optometrists), 4214 (pharmacists), 6775 (engineers) (West 1954). For an exhaustive list of occupations having criminal offense exclusions in California and other states, see Boggan et al., *The Rights of Gay People,* 211–35.

76. See In re Boyd, 307 P.2d 625 (Cal. 1957) (lawyer disbarred, lewd vagrancy); McLaughlin v. Board of Medical Examiners, 111 Cal. Rptr. 353 (App. 1973) (doctor, fondling of decoy policeman); Marcus, *Making History,* 57 (hairdresser, lewd vagrancy), 149–151 (lawyers and teachers, copulation and lewd vagrancy); Wood, "Homosexual and the Police," 21–22 (doctor, lewd indecency).

77. Florida Legislative Investigating Committee ("FLIC"), Report to Legislature, April 13, 1959, at 4–5, in Florida Archives, Series 1486, Box 1, Folder 21 ("Johns Committee Files"). On Florida's antihomosexual campaign (1954–1964), see Sears, *Lonely Hunters,* 48–84; Eskridge, "Apartheid of the Closet"; James Schnur, "Closet Crusaders: The Johns Committee and Homophobia, 1956–1965," in *Carryin' On,* 132–164.

78. 1959 Fla. Laws ch. 59-404; 1961 Fla. Laws ch. 61-396, both codified at Fla. Stat. §231.28.

79. See FLIC, Revocation Memorandum, in Johns Committee Files, Box 1; Memorandum from William Tanner, Security Officer, to Dr. Gordon Blackwell, President, both of University of Florida, January 31, 1961, at 19–20, in id.

80. E.g., In re Boyd, 307 P.2d 625 (Cal. 1957); State ex rel. Florida Bar v. Kimball, 96 So. 2d 825 (Fla. 1957).

81. Florida Bar v. Kay, 232 So. 2d 378, 379 (Fla. 1970).

82. Jonathan Ned Katz, *Gay/Lesbian Almanac,* 530–531 (1983).

83. "Employment of Homosexuals," 12–13; J. Edgar Hoover, "Role of the FBI in the Federal Employee Security Program," 49 *Nw. U.L. Rev.* 333 (1954); D'Emilio, *Sexual Politics,* 47 (story of B.D.H. whom the FBI followed, interrogated, and harassed for decades to get him to name other homosexuals).

84. *The Ladder,* October 1956, at 2 (quotation). On the history of these homophile groups and their publications, see D'Emilio, *Sexual Politics,* 63–73; Marcus, *Making History,* 32–36, 62–63 (first-person accounts by Mattachine founders Chuck Rowland and Hal Call), 40–41, 50–53 *(One, Inc.* founders Martin Block and Jim Kepner), 111–113 (founders of Daughters New York, Barbara Gittings and Kay Lahusen); Stuart Timmons, *The Trouble with Harry Hay,* 129–53 (1990).

85. Memorandum from Los Angeles Office to FBI Headquarters, December 31, 1953, at 6, in FBI FOIA File HQ 100-403320. The discussion in text is drawn from the FBI Freedom of Information Act files on the Mattachine Society (Files 100-430320 [Headquarters], 100-4588 [Los Angeles], 100-132065 [New York], 100-37394 [San Francisco], 100-33796 [Washington, D.C.]) and the Daughters of Bilitis (File 94-843 [San Francisco]).

86. Memorandum from Special Agent M. A. Jones to Mr. Nichols, FBI Headquarters, February 10, 1956, FBI FOIA File HQ 100-430320; Airtel from Special Agent Malone to FBI Los Angeles and Director, FBI, February 2, 1956, at 3 (in FBI FOIA File HQ 100-430320); Marcus, *Making History,* 52–53 (account by Jim Kepner, one of the staff members harassed). A different account is in Rodger Streitmatter, *Unspeakable: The Rise of the Gay and Lesbian Press in America,* 32 (1995).

87. See Kennedy and Davis, *Boots of Leather* (Buffalo lesbian harassment); Stryker and Van Buskirk, *Gay by the Bay* (San Francisco); Dancel Buring, "Softball and Alcohol: The Limits of Lesbian Community in Memphis from the 1940s through the 1960s," in *Carryin' On,* 203, 215–219; Eskridge, "Apartheid of the Closet," 747–750, and 727–733 (Florida; Miami and Tampa).

88. Interviews with Lisa Ben are in Marcus, *Making History,* 8–12; Streitmatter, *Unspeakable,* 5 (quotation in text).

89. *Juvenile Delinquency (Obscene and Pornographic Materials): Hearings before the Subcommittee to Investigate Juvenile Delinquency of the Senate Committee on the Judiciary,* 84th Cong., 1st Sess., 40–41 (May 24, 1955). For particular focus on the idea that perverted literature depicting cross-dressing and spanking can lead to homosexuality, see id. at 80–85 (Dr. Benjamin Karpman, Chief Psychiatrist, St. Elizabeth's Hospital, D.C.). Other hearings in the juvenile delinquency series focused on sexually explicit or perverse television shows, comic books, and movies.

90. See Austen, *Playing the Game;* Edward DeGrazia, *Girls Lean Back Everywhere* (1992); Jeannette Howard Foster, *Sex Variant Women in Literature* (1956).

91. Quotations in text are from Lawrence Ferlinghetti, "Horn on *Howl,*" in *Evergreen Review,* December 1957, at 145, reprinted in Allen Ginsberg, *Howl: Original Draft Fascimile etc.,* 169–170 (Barry Miles ed., 1986). See Robert Haney, *Comstockery in America,* 34–45 (1974); Dal McIntire [Jim Kepner], "Tangents," *One, Inc.,* May 1957, at 11–12, reprinted in Kepner, *Rough News,* 183–184.

92. Letter from Sen. Alexander Wiley to Arthur Summerfield, Postmaster General, April 28, 1954 (in FBI FOIA File HQ 100-430320, §2).

93. Public Law No. 81-699, 64 Stat. 451 (1950), codified at 39 U.S.C. §3006. In Public Law No. 84-821, 70 Stat. 699 (1956), Congress confirmed that the Post Office had the authority to invoke this impoundment power (albeit for just twenty days) without a hearing or an order from the courts.

94. See Marcus, *Making History,* 51–53 (first-person account by Jim Kepner).

95. 1954 N.Y. Laws ch. 620, §1, amending N.Y. Education Law §122; Los Angeles Code, 1946, §41.13(a) (similar). The Customs Act and Motion Pictures Code are quoted in Chapter 1.

96. See Vito Russo, *The Celluloid Closet: Homosexuality in the Movies,* 115–118 (rev. ed. 1987).

97. See the documentary based on Russo's book, *The Celluloid Closet* (1995) (interview with Vidal).

98. See Loughery, *Other Side of Silence,* 177–180, drawing particularly on the lists in the *Gay Girl's Guide* for 1949 and 1950. For a taste of the expanding scholarship exploring local gay bar scenes, see the chapters on lesbian bars in Buffalo and Detroit and gay bars in San Francisco, Chicago, Washington, and Philadelphia in *Place for Ourselves,* as well as Don Paulson, *An Evening at the Garden of Allah* (1996) (Seattle); David Olson, "The Wonder Years: Chicago Gay Life before Stonewall," *Windy City Times,* June 27, 1996, at 44–47; Ginger Snapp, "Little Codes: The New Orleans Bar Scene in the 1950s and 1960s," *Southern Exposure,* Fall 1988, at 32; Swisher, "Gay Life in Richmond"; Thomas Noel, "Gay Bars and the Emergence of the Denver Homosexual Community," *Soc. Sci. J.,* April 1978, at 59–74.

99. E.g., 1955 Cal. Stat. ch. 1217; Mich. Liquor Control Commn., Admin. Rule 436-3 (Bérubé, *Coming Out under Fire,* 356 n.1); 1949 Tex. Laws ch. 543, §17(h); 1956 Va. Acts ch. 521.

100. 1935 Cal. Stat. ch. 330, §§40, 58, codified at Cal. Bus. & Prof. Code §§24200(a)–(b), 25601; 1935 Fla. Laws ch. 16774, §1, codified at Fla. Stat. §561.29.

101. 1955 Cal. Stat. ch. 1217, overriding Stoumen v. Reilly, 234 P.2d 969 (Cal. 1951).

102. D'Emilio, *Sexual Politics,* 186–188; Kershaw v. Department of Alcoholic Beverage Control, 318 P.2d 494 (Cal. App. 1957).

103. Inman v. City of Miami, 197 So. 2d 50, 51 (Fla. App. 1967), upholding Miami Ordinance No. 5135 (reprinted in Eskridge, "Apartheid of the Closet," 827 [app. 5]).

104. Kennedy and Davis, *Boots of Leather;* Nestle, *Restricted Country;* Buring, "Lesbian Community in Memphis," 210–212, 218–219; Roey Thorpe, "The Changing Face of Lesbian Bars in Detroit, 1938–1965," in *Place for Ourselves,* 165–182.

105. In re Louise G. Mack, [N.J.] A.B.C. Bulletin 1088, Item 2 (November 2, 1955).

106. E.g., Kennedy and Davis, *Boots of Leather,* 74–75 (Buffalo lesbian bars).

107. Interview quoted in Loughery, *Other Side of Silence,* 181.

108. See Stryker and Van Buskirk, *Gay by the Bay,* 31 (San Francisco); Hal Call, "Why Perpetuate This Barbarism?," *Mattachine Rev.,* June 1960, at 14 (New York).

109. For Nazi authorities described in text, see Gunter Grau, ed., *Hidden Holocaust? Gay and Lesbian Persecution in Germany, 1933–45,* at 27–31, 36–37, 64–67, 71–80, 88–91, 109–110, 131–133, 138–150, 151–160, 166–167, 192–199, 264–292 (Patrick Camiller trans., 1993). See also Richard Plant, *The Pink Triangle: The Nazi War against Homosexuals* (1986).

110. Alfred Kinsey et al., *Sexual Behavior in the Human Male,* 659–666 (1948); Kinsey et al., *Sexual Behavior in the Human Female,* 484–487 (1953).

111. Tappan, *Habitual Sex Offender,* 34–35 (1953 survey of state enforcement of sexual psychopath laws).

112. Crittenden Report, 4; Williams and Weinberg, *Homosexuals and the Military.*

113. Foster, *Sex Variant Women;* Gene Damon, "The Lesbian Paperback," *Tangents,* June 1966, at 4–7.

114. *Report of the Illinois Commission on Sex Offenders,* 8–9, 11 (quotation in text); Tappan, *Habitual Sex Offender.*

115. Proposed Model Penal Code, Tent. Draft No. 4, §207.5 (1955). Originally disinclined to this move, the ALI was turned around by Judge Learned Hand's endorsement of the Millian arguments. See Gerald Gunther, *Learned Hand,* 672 n.129 (1994).

116. Proposed Model Penal Code, Tent. Draft No. 4, §207.5, comments, 277–278 (1955); see id. at 207 (power of the state should not be used to enforce "purely moral or religious standards"); Louis Schwartz, "Morals Offenses and the Model Penal Code," 63 *Colum. L. Rev.* 669, 675–676 (1969).

117. Model Penal Code §§213.5 (indecent exposure), 251.1 (public lewdness), 251.3 (solicitation of deviate sexual relations when the actor "loiters in or near any public place").

118. The Wolfenden Report: Report of the Committee on Homosexual Offenses and Prostitution, ¶¶62–76 (1957); see H. L. A. Hart, *Law, Liberty, and Morality,* 13–17 (1963), responding to Patrick Devlin, *The Enforcement of Morals* (1959).

119. Letter from Dr. Charles Bowman, University of Illinois, June 15, 1964, in Johns Committee Files, Box 2, Folder 4. See Appendix A1 for references to the New York and Illinois laws.

120. People v. Randall, 214 N.Y.S.2d 417 (N.Y. 1961). For other lenity decisions, see State v. Vallery, 34 So. 2d 329 (La. 1947) (refusing to enforce law prohibiting "any immoral act" on juvenile); State v. Morrison, 96 A.2d 723 (N.J. 1953) (sodomy law does not include oral sex); Bennett v. Abram, 253 P.2d 316 (N. Mex. 1953) (same).

121. UCLA Project, "Consenting Adult Homosexual and the Law," 770–775.

122. People v. Swald, 73 N.Y.S.2d 399, 400 (Utica 1947); see People v. Feliciano, 173 N.Y.S.2d 123 (N.Y.C. 1958) (requiring actual breach of peace); People v. McCormack, 169 N.Y.S.2d 139 (App. 1957) (requiring actual solicitation); People v. Strauss, 114 N.Y.S.2d 322 (N.Y.C. 1952) (actual breach of peace); People v. Humphrey, 111 N.Y.S.2d 450 (Broome Cty. 1952) (same).

123. *Feliciano,* 173 N.Y.S.2d at 126.

124. People v. Lopez, 164 N.E.2d 720 (N.Y. 1959) (any kind of homosexual solicitation violates the disorderly conduct law); People v. Hale, 168 N.E.2d 518, 519 (N.Y. 1960) (loitering prostitutes law applies to "loitering homosexuals"); People v. Gillespi, 202 N.E.2d 565 (N.Y. 1964) (disguise statute applies to drag queens).

125. McDermett v. United States, 98 A.2d 287 (D.C. 1953), following Dyson v. United States, 97 A.2d 135, 138 (D.C. 1953) (Hood, J., dissenting).

126. Rittenour v. District of Columbia, 163 A.2d 558, 559 (D.C. 1960) (Hood, J.).

127. Crittenden Report, 5–6 (second quotation in text), 46, 55 (first quotation).

128. Id. at 20, 24–26, app. 3.

129. Jennings, "To Be Accused"; Timmons, *Harry Hay,* 163–168.

130. "Your Rights in Case of Arrest," *One, Inc.,* January 1954, at 14; also, an editorial in *One, Inc.,* March 1961, at 4–5.

131. See Appendix C3 (degeneracy versus other offenses); Ralph Slovenko and Cyril Phillips, "Psychosexuality and the Criminal Law," 15 *Vand. L. Rev.* 797, 800 n.9 (1962) (sodomy versus rape); cf. Charles Robinson, "The Raid," *One, Inc.,* July 1960, at 26 (judge complaining that too many homosexual defendants pleaded guilty).

132. Louis Michael Seidman, "Criminal Procedure as the Servant of Politics," in *Constitutional Stupidities, Constitutional Tragedies,* 90–94 (William N. Eskridge, Jr., and Sanford Levinson eds., 1998).

133. Cole v. State, 175 P.2d 376 (Okla. App. 1946); cf. Cole v. State, 179 P.2d 176 (Okla. App. 1947) (affirming conviction on retrial).

134. Woody v. State, 238 P.2d 367, 371 (Okla. App. 1951); also, Berryman v. State, 283 P.2d 558, 565 n.1 (Okla. App. 1955).

135. See, e.g., Kennedy and Davis, *Boots of Leather* (Buffalo butch lesbians); Marcus, *Making History,* 48, 63, 189–190 (drag queens, especially queens of color, harassed in New York, California); Beemyn, "Queer Capital," 194 (D.C. black drag queens arrested and beaten); Drexel, "Before Paris Burned," 139 (black drag queen jailed and lost job for violating Chicago's cross-dressing ordinance).

136. Sherman v. United States, 356 U.S. 369 (1958); Sorrells v. United States, 287 U.S. 435 (1932). The rule may have been more liberal in California, People v. Perez, 401 P.2d 934 (Cal. 1965), but vice squads responded by requiring their decoys to wait for suspects to make the first move. UCLA Project, "Consenting Adult Homosexual and the Law," 701–707.

137. Donnelly, "Stool Pigeons," 1102. Some courts rejected the use of prior convictions, e.g., *Sherman,* 356 U.S. at 375–376, or general reputation, e.g., United States v. Collier, 313 F.2d 157 (7th Cir. 1963).

138. Kelly v. United States, 194 F.2d 150 (D.C. Cir. 1952), extended in Guarro v. United States, 237 F.2d 578 (D.C. Cir. 1956).

139. E.g., Berneau v. United States, 188 A.2d 301 (D.C. 1963) (transvestite prostitute). *Kelly*'s corroboration requirement was found satisfied by a showing that the decoy and defendant were both present at the alleged time and place in Reed v. United States, 93 A.2d 568 (D.C. 1953); King v. United States, 90 A.2d 229 (D.C. 1952).

140. State v. McDaniel, 298 P.2d 798, 800–801 (first quotation in text), 802 (second quotation) (Ariz. 1956).

141. State v. Shively, 176 N.E.2d 436, 439 (Ohio App. 1960); see State v. Huntington, 80 N.W.2d 744, 748–749 (Iowa 1957); State v. Fletcher, 256 P.2d 847, 848–849 (Kan. 1953); State v. Desilets, 73 A.2d 800 (N.H. 1950); Commonwealth v. Kline, 65 A.2d 348, 352–353 (Pa. 1949). See also Willett v. State, 584 P.2d 684 (Nev. 1978).

142. E.g., People v. Giani, 302 P.2d 813 (Cal. App. 1956).

143. People v. Jones, 266 P.2d 38 (Cal. 1954); State v. Sinnott, 132 A.2d 298 (N.J. 1957); Commonwealth v. Tacconelli, 45 D&C2d 654 (Pa. Cty. Ct. 1968).

144. United States v. Phillips, 11 C.M.R. 137, 142 (Military App. 1953).

145. *Kelly,* 194 F.2d at 152, as well as, e.g., *King,* 90 A.2d at 230.

146. *Dyson,* 97 A.2d at 135–137.

147. Freedman, *Maternal Justice,* 272–273, 285, 335–337.

148. United Pub. Workers v. Mitchell, 330 U.S. 75, 102–103 (1947), applied in, e.g., Shelton v. Tucker, 364 U.S. 479 (1960) (invalidating state law requiring teachers to disclose organizational affiliations); Garner v. Board Pub. Works, 341 U.S. 716 (1951) (upholding municipal policy against employing revolutionaries).

149. Konigsberg v. State Bar, Cal., 353 U.S. 252, 273 (1957); Schware v. Board Bar Examrs., N. Mex., 353 U.S. 232, 246 (1957).

150. Harmon v. Brucker, 355 U.S. 579 (1958).

151. Bérubé and D'Emilio, "McCarthy Years"; "ACLU Position on Homosexuality," *Mattachine Rev.,* March 1957, at 7 (reprinting ACLU resolution).

152. Clackum v. United States, 296 F.2d 226, 229 (Ct. Cl. 1960).

153. Dew v. Halaby, 317 F.2d 582, 587 n.10 (first quotation in text) (D.C. Cir. 1963), *cert. dismissed per stip.,* 379 U.S. 951 (1964); see id. at 591 (Wright, J., dissenting) (second quotation).

154. Seymour Krim, "Revolt of the Homosexual," reprinted in *Mattachine Rev.,* May 1959, at 4–5, 9.

155. James Fugaté [James Barr], "Release from the Navy under Honorable Conditions," *Mattachine Rev.,* May/June 1955, at 42.

156. E.g., NAACP v. Alabama, 357 U.S. 449 (1958) (African Americans); Yates v. United States, 354 U.S. 298 (1957) (Communists). See Norman Dorsen, "The Second Mr. Justice Harlan: A Constitutional Conservative," 44 *NYU L. Rev.* 249, 263–268 (1969).

157. United States v. Zuideveld, 316 F.2d 873, 883 (7th Cir. 1963) (Swygert, J., dissenting).

158. The Mattachine Society, Los Angeles, *The Mattachine Society Today,* 1 (1954); D. Griffin, "President's Message," *The Ladder,* November 1956, at 2; Del Martin, "The Positive Approach," id. at 8–9.

159. Lynch's Builders Restaurant v. O'Connell, 103 N.E.2d 531 (N.Y. 1952), followed in Gilmer v. Hostetter, 245 N.Y.S.2d 252 (App. 1963).

160. See Stanwood United, Inc. v. O'Connell, 126 N.Y.S.2d 345 (App. 1953); People ex rel. Fasone v. Arenella, 139 N.Y.S.2d 186 (N.Y.C. 1954).

161. Paddock Bar, Inc. v. Division of Alcoholic Beverage Control, 134 A.2d 779, 780 (N.J. App. 1957) (emphasis in original). Accord, Inman v. City of Miami, 197 So. 2d 50 (Fla. App. 1967); Kotteman v. Gevemberg, 96 So. 2d 601 (La. 1957); In re Freedman, 235 A.2d 624 (Pa. Super. 1967).

162. Stoumen v. Reilly, 234 P.2d 969, 971 (Cal. 1951).

163. These closings were upheld in Nickola v. Munro, 328 P.2d 271 (Cal. App. 1958), and Kershaw v. Department of Alcoholic Beverage Control, 318 P.2d 494 (Cal. App. 1957).

164. Cal. Business and Professions Code §25601, violation of which subjected bar to loss of liquor license, id. §24200(b).

165. Vallerga v. Department of Alcoholic Beverage Control, 347 P.2d 909, 912–913 (Cal. 1959).

166. Morrell v. Department of Alcoholic Beverage Control, 22 Cal. Rptr. 405 (App. 1962); Benedetti v. Department of Alcoholic Beverage Control, 9 Cal. Rptr. 525 (App. 1960); Stoumen v. Munro, 33 Cal. Rptr. 305 (App. 1963).

167. One, Inc. v. Olesen, 241 F.2d 772, 777–778 (9th Cir. 1957), *rev'd per curiam,* 355 U.S. 371 (1958).

168. People v. Ferlinghetti, Decision of October 3, 1957, reprinted in Ginsberg, *Howl,* 173–174.

169. Roth v. United States, 354 U.S. 476, 487–488 n.2 (1957), approving ALI, Model Penal Code §207.10(2) (Tent. Draft No. 6, 1957).

170. One, Inc. v. Olesen, 355 U.S. 371 (1958) (per curiam); see Kepner, *Rough News,* 217–220.

171. Manual Enterprises, Inc. v. Day, 370 U.S. 478 (1962); Kingsley Intl. Pictures Corp. v. Regents, 380 U.S. 684 (1959).

172. E.g., United States v. Zuideveld, 316 F.2d 873 (7th Cir. 1963) (upholding convictions for sponsoring a gay pen-pal club); People v. G.I. Distributors, Inc., 228 N.E.2d 787 (N.Y. 1967) (allowing censorship of magazine displaying nude men).

173. Kameny v. Brucker, 365 U.S. 843 (1961), *denying cert. for* 282 F.2d 823 (D.C. Cir. 1960); see Johnson, "'Homosexual Citizens,'" 55–56.

174. Mattachine Society of Washington, Constitution, art. II, §1(a)–(c).

175. Letter from Franklin Kameny, President, MSW, to Robert Kennedy, Attorney General, June 28, 1962; also, MSW, "Discrimination against the Employment of Homosexuals" (February 28, 1963), both documents in FBI FOIA File HQ 100-403320 (Mattachine Society), §6, Serial 101.

3. Coming Out and Challenging the Closet, 1961–1981

1. John D'Emilio, *Sexual Politics, Sexual Communities: The Making of the Homosexual Minority, 1945–69,* at 152–198 (1983); see Gary Patterson, "Gay Is Good," *Vector,* November 1968, at 5.

2. D'Emilio, *Sexual Politics,* 232. Accounts of the Stonewall riots are in Martin Duberman, *Stonewall* (1993); Dick Leitsch, "First Gay Riot," *The Advocate,* September 1969, at 3; Lucian Truscott, IV, "Gay Power Comes to Sheridan Square," *Village Voice,* July 3, 1969, at 1.

3. See Arthur Bell, *Dancing the Gay Lib Blues: A Year in the Homosexual Liberation Movement* (1971); Donn Teal, *The Gay Militants* (1971).

4. Laud Humphreys, *Coming Out* (1972); *Out of the Closets* (Karla Jay and Allen Young eds., 1972).

5. E.g., Samuel R. Delany, "Coming/Out," in *Boys Like Us: Gay Writers Tell Their Coming Out Stories,* 1, 13 (Patrick Merla ed., 1996).

6. E.g., Gore Vidal, *The City and the Pillar,* 172 (rev. ed. 1965).

7. E.g., A. E. Smith, "Coming Out," *One, Inc.,* June 1962, at 6–7; Barbara Stephens, "The Coming Out of Martos," *The Ladder,* May 1958, at 14.

8. Mapp v. Ohio, 367 U.S. 643 (1961) (fourth amendment, exclusionary rule); Miranda v. Arizona, 384 U.S. 436 (1966) (fifth amendment, self-incrimination); Gideon v. Wainwright, 372 U.S. 335 (1963) (sixth amendment, right to counsel); Pointer v. Texas, 380 U.S. 400 (1965) (sixth amendment, confrontation right); Klopfer v. North Carolina, 386 U.S. 213 (1967) (sixth amendment, right to speedy trial); Robinson v. California, 370 U.S. 660 (1962) (eighth amendment, status crimes).

9. See East Coast Homophile Organizations, *If You Are Arrested,* in FBI FOIA File HQ 100-403320 (Mattachine Society), §6, Serial 117; "*Pocket Lawyer* Ready," *Vector,* September 1965, at 1.

10. See *The Ladder,* May-June 1968, at 22–23. See also People v. Maldonado, 50 Cal. Rptr. 45 (App. 1966) (overturning oral copulation conviction because of *Miranda* violations).

11. 42 U.S.C. §1983 (damage remedy for state violations of constitutional rights); Bivens v. Six Unknown Agents of Federal Bur. Narcotics, 403 U.S. 388 (1971) (damage remedy for federal violations of fourth amendment rights). For damage actions by gay victims, see "Raid Victims to Sue: 'Rights Trampled,'" *Advocate,* Jan. 30, 1974, at 2; Douglas Sarff, "Gay Leaders Cleared," *Advocate,* January 1, 1975, at 3.

12. Bielicki v. Superior Court, 371 P.2d 288 (Cal. 1962), rejected in Smayda v. United States, 352 F.2d 251 (9th Cir. 1965).

13. Katz v. United States, 389 U.S. 347 (1967), and id. at 360–361 (Harlan, J., concurring).

14. See Brown v. State, 238 A.2d 147 (Md. App. 1968); People v. Dezek, 308 N.W.2d 652 (Mich. App. 1981); State v. Bryant, 177 N.W.2d 800 (Minn. 1970); Buchanan v. State, 471 S.W.2d 401 (Tex. Crim. App. 1971).

15. People v. Triggs, 506 P.2d 232 (Cal. 1973). Other states did not follow *Triggs.* E.g., State v. Holt, 630 P.2d 854 (Or. 1981).

16. For cars, see People v. Dezek, 308 N.W.2d 652 (Mich. App. 1981); Honeycutt v. State, 690 S.W.2d 64 (Tex. App. 1985). Most of the adult theater cases arose in Texas. E.g., Leibman v. State, 652 S.W.2d 942 (Tex. Crim. App. 1983); Green v. State, 566 S.W.2d 578 (Tex. Crim. App. 1978).

17. Susan Stryker and Jim Van Buskirk, *Gay by the Bay: A History of Queer Culture in the San Francisco Bay Area,* 41–42 (1996); Eric Marcus, *Making History: The Struggle for Gay and Lesbian Equal Rights, 1945–1990,* at 136–165 (1992) (first-person accounts of the two lawyers and straight woman arrested); Mary Ann Swissler, "San Francisco's Pre-Stonewall Stonewall," *Bay Area Reporter,* December 29, 1994, at 13.

18. See Randy Shilts, *The Mayor of Castro Street: The Life and Times of Harvey Milk* (1982); Sasha Gregory-Lewis, "Building a Gay Politic: The San Francisco Model," *Advocate,* October 8, 1975, at 27, 32.

19. Steven Rosen, "Police Harassment of Homosexual Women and Men in New York City, 1960–1980," 12 *Colum. Human Rights L. Rev.* 159, 164–173 (1980–81); Clayton Knowles, "Cleanup Mapped for Times Square," *N.Y. Times,* February 23, 1966, at 41.

20. Rosen, "Police Harassment," 188. See "Gotham Cops to Be Nicer," *Advocate,* September 12, 1973, at 3; "Koch Accuses Police Here of Harassing Homosexuals," *N.Y. Times,* March 26, 1970, at 30.

21. See William N. Eskridge, Jr., "Challenging the Apartheid of the Closet: Establishing Conditions for Lesbian and Gay Intimacy, *Nomos,* and Citizenship, 1961–1981," 25 *Hofstra L. Rev.* 817, 840–842 (1997) (references for gay-friendlier police regimes established in Washington, D.C., Los Angeles, Chicago, and Denver).

22. William N. Eskridge, Jr., "Privacy Jurisprudence and the Apartheid of the Closet, 1946–1961," 24 *Fla. St. U.L. Rev.* 703, 775–776, 829–838 (1997) (Florida); Robert Fisher, "The Sex Offender Provisions of the Proposed New Maryland Criminal Code," 30 *Md. L. Rev.* 91, 104–111 (1970).

23. Griswold v. Connecticut, 381 U.S. 479, 485–486 (1965) (opinion for the Court); id. at 499 (Goldberg, J., joined by Warren, C.J., and Brennan, J., concurring); id. at 499–502 (Harlan, J., concurring in the judgment).

24. D'Emilio, *Sexual Politics,* 212–213.

25. Eisenstadt v. Baird, 405 U.S. 438, 453 (1972), citing Stanley v. Georgia, 394 U.S. 557 (1969).

26. Doe v. Commonwealth's Attorney, 425 U.S. 901 (1976), *aff'g mem.* 403 F. Supp. 1199 (E.D. Va. 1975). Accord, Wade v. Buchanan, 401 U.S. 989 (1971), *vacating* Buchanan v. Batchelor, 308 F. Supp. 729 (N.D. Tex. 1970) (three-judge court invalidating Texas sodomy law).

27. State v. Enslin, 214 S.E.2d 318 (N.C. App. 1975), *cert. denied,* 425 U.S. 903 (1976). For background, see "'Abominable Crime' Law Heading for Major Test," *Advocate,* November 11, 1974, at 17.

28. See "Sex Bill Passes in Historic Senate Tie-Breaker," *Advocate,* May 21, 1975, at 4.

29. People v. Onofre, 415 N.E.2d 936, 939 (N.Y. 1980).

30. Uplinger v. State, 447 N.E.2d 62 (N.Y. 1983), *appeal dismissed,* 467 U.S. 246 (1984); Commonwealth v. Bonadio, 415 A.2d 47 (Pa. 1980) (oral sex); Commonwealth v. Waters, 422 A.2d 598 (Pa. 1980) (lewd solicitation).

31. See United States v. Harriss, 347 U.S. 612, 617 (1954); Winters v. New York, 333 U.S. 507, 515 (1948); Lanzetta v. New Jersey, 306 U.S. 451 (1939); Anthony Amsterdam, "The Void-for-Vagueness Doctrine in the Supreme Court," 109 *U. Pa. L. Rev.* 67 (1960) (student note).

32. Papachristou v. City of Jacksonville, 405 U.S. 156, 162–163, 169–170 (1972).

33. Harris v. State, 457 P.2d 638, 645 (Alaska 1969); Franklin v. State, 257 So. 2d 21 (Fla. 1971) (per curiam); Commonwealth v. Balthazar, 318 N.E.2d 478 (Mass. 1974).

34. Wainwright v. Stone, 414 U.S. 21 (1973), followed in Rose v. Locke, 423 U.S. 48 (1975) (upholding the application of Tennessee's crime against nature law to cunnilingus).

35. Vagueness challenges were accepted in District of Columbia v. Walters, 319 A.2d 332 (D.C. 1974); City of Columbus v. Scott, 353 N.E.2d 858 (Ohio App. 1975), but rejected in District of Columbia v. Garcia, 335 A.2d 217 (D.C. 1975); State v. Phipps, 389 N.E.2d 1128 (Ohio 1979) (narrowly interpreting challenged law), and in State v. Cota, 408 P.2d 23 (Ariz. 1965); Commonwealth v. Heinbaugh, 354 A.2d 244 (Pa. 1976); State v. Roberts, 421 P.2d 1014 (Wash. 1966).

36. "Denver Free: Months of Legal and Political Maneuvering Pay Off as Police Chief Signs Accord to Halt Harassment," *Advocate,* November 6, 1974; "Dilemma in Denver: As Laws Fall, Arrests Soar," *Advocate,* March 28, 1973, at 15. For another example of police refusal to abide by judicial invalidations of antigay solicitation laws, see "Tampa Police Ignore Court, Go Ahead with Arrests," *Advocate,* March 14, 1973, at 18.

37. In re Lane, 372 P.2d 897 (Cal. 1962).

38. In re Davis, 51 Cal. Rptr. 702 (Cal. App. 1966) (public indecency law); Pryor v. Municipal Court, 599 P.2d 636, 644 (Cal. 1979), relying on Barry Copilow and Tom Coleman, "Enforcement of Section 647(a) of the California Penal Code by the Los Angeles Police Department," *Advocate,* February 14, 1973, at 2–3, 24; "Update: Enforcement of Section 647(a) of the California Penal Code by the Los Angeles Police Department" (1974).

39. 1967 N.Y. Laws ch. 681 (vagrancy law revisions); 1965 N.Y. Laws ch. 1030 (disorderly conduct revisions); *Uplinger,* 447 N.E.2d 62.

40. City of Columbus v. Rogers, 324 N.E.2d 563, 565 (Ohio 1975).

41. City of Chicago v. Wilson, 389 N.E.2d 522 (Ill. 1978); City of Cinncinati v. Adams, 330 N.E.2d 463 (Ohio Mun. 1974); D.C. v. City of St. Louis, 795 F.2d 652 (8th Cir. 1986). Unreported cases are discussed in "Cross-Dress Law Falls," *Advocate,* September 24, 1975, at 10 (Detroit); "Fort Worth Judge Raps Drag Arrests," *Advocate,* December 19, 1973, at 14; "Unconstitutional: Court Voids Miami Beach Drag Bans," *Advocate,* July 11, 1972, at 4.

42. "Toledo's 'Pervert Drag' Law Voided," *Advocate,* November 7, 1973, at 16.

43. Mayes v. Texas, 416 U.S. 909 (1974), denying certiorari to County Criminal Court at Law No. 4, Harris County, Texas. Only Justice Douglas voted to take certiorari. Texas defended the cross-dressing law as protecting the survival of the human race by banning "homosexual disguises." See "Supreme Court Upholds Drag Ban," *Advocate,* April 24, 1974, at 10.

44. Houston Ord. No. 80-2536 (August 12, 1980); "For the Record—Short Takes," *Advocate,* August 20, 1981, at 12.

45. See Rhonda Rivera, "Our Straight-Laced Judges: The Legal Position of Homosexual Persons in the United States," 30 *Hastings L.J.* 799, 908–934 (1979).

46. NAACP v. Alabama, 357 U.S. 449 (1958); Inman v. City of Miami, 197 So. 2d 50, 52 (Fla. App. 1967); "Miami Bar Ordinance Held Void," *Advocate,* January 5, 1972, at 2; "Miami Bars Open Dialogue with Lawmen," *Advocate,* August 16, 1972, at 10.

47. See Eskridge, "Challenging the Closet," 870–873 (San Francisco and New York).

48. One Eleven Wines & Liquors, Inc. v. Division of Alcoholic Beverage Control, 235 A.2d 12, 18 (N.J. 1967). Accord, Kerma Restaurant Corp. v. State Liquor Auth., 233 N.E.2d 833, 835 (N.Y. 1967).

49. Virginia's ABC Board sought to close down Norfolk's Cue Club as a "congregating place for homosexuals," see "Virginia Bar under Seige Because It Caters to Gays," *Advocate,* November 22, 1972, at 14, but retreated in the face of opposition from the Tidewater Gay Freedom Movement, the area's first gay rights organization. Fred Parris, "Virginia Gays Fight Archaic Liquor Laws," *The Blade,* June 1978, at 1.

50. California v. LaRue, 409 U.S. 109 (1972).

51. Randy Shilts, "Big Business: Gay Bars and Baths Come Out of the Bush Leagues," *Advocate,* June 2, 1976, at 37–38.

52. Troy Perry [MCC founder], *Don't Be Afraid Anymore* (1990); "Advocate Survey—Religion: A Guide to the Spiritual Mainline," *Advocate,* October 16, 1976, at 18–19.

53. E.g., Ruth Simpson, *From the Closet to the Courts,* 122–130 (1976) (New York police harassment of Daughters of Bilitis); Cyr v. Walls, 439 F. Supp. 697 (N.D. Tex. 1977) (upholding lawsuit against Fort Worth police antigay spying and name-leaking).

54. *Amending District of Columbia Charitable Solicitation Act: Hearings Before Subcommittee No. 4 of the House Committee on the District of Columbia,* 88th Cong., 1st and 2d Sess. (1963–64); *Mattachine Rev.,* September 1963, at 4–10.

55. State ex rel. Grant v. Brown, 313 N.E.2d 847, 848 (Ohio 1974) (per curiam), *appeal dismissed,* 420 U.S. 916 (1975).

56. In re Gay Activists Alliance v. Lomenzo, 293 N.E.2d 255 (N.Y. 1973); In re Thom (Lambda Legal Defense & Education Fund, Inc.), 337 N.Y.S.2d 588 (App. 1972), *rev'd,* 301 N.E.2d 542 (N.Y. 1973), *on remand,* 350 N.Y.S.2d 1 (App. 1973).

57. E.g., *Lambda Update,* Winter 1985, at 1 (under threat of litigation, Mississippi attorney general granted charters to the Mississippi Gay Alliance in 1985 and the Friends of Lesbians/Gays Mississippi in 1984).

58. Aztec Motel v. State, 251 So. 2d 849 (Fla. 1971), invalidating 1969 Fla. Laws ch. 69-272.

59. Big Mama Rag, Inc. v. United States, 631 F.2d 1030 (D.C. Cir. 1980); Rev. Ruling 78-305, 1978-2 C.B. 172. For the background, see "IRS Reverses Policy on Tax Exemptions," *Advocate,* October 5, 1977, at 11; "IRS Denies Exemption to Pride, Calls Activities 'Detrimental,'" *Advocate,* November 6, 1974, at 27 (quotation in text from IRS); "IRS Grants Tax Exemption to a 'Gay' Group; a First," *Advocate,* September 11, 1974, at 24.

60. Healy v. James, 408 U.S. 169 (1972).

61. Gay Students Organization v. Bonner, 509 F.2d 652 (1st Cir. 1974), followed in Gay & Lesbian Students Assn. v. Gohn, 850 F.2d 361 (8th Cir. 1988); Gay Student Servs. v. Texas A&M Univ., 737 F.2d 1317 (5th Cir. 1984); Gay Lib v. University of Missouri, 558 F.2d 848 (8th Cir. 1977); Gay Alliance of Students v. Matthews, 544 F.2d 162 (4th Cir.

1976) (University of Alabama); Student Coalition for Gay Rights v. Austin Peay Univ., 477 F. Supp. 1267 (M.D. Tenn. 1979); Wood v. Davison, 351 F. Supp. 543 (N.D. Ga. 1972) (University of Georgia).

62. "Recognition for Gay Students," *Advocate,* November 26, 1981, at 10.

63. Fricke v. Lynch, 491 F. Supp. 381 (D.R.I. 1980) (applying *Bonner* to high school prom); Gay Rights Coalition v. Georgetown Univ., 536 A.2d 1 (D.C. 1987) (en banc) (discussed in Chapter 9).

64. See, e.g., Board of Educ. v. Pico, 457 U.S. 853 (1982) (library book-buying); Department of Educ. v. Lewis, 416 So. 2d 455 (Fla. 1982) (university funding); Coleman v. Caddo Parish Sch. Bd., 635 So. 2d 1238 (La. App. 1994) (required curriculum).

65. A Book Named "John Cleland's Memoirs of a Woman of Pleasure" v. Massachusetts, 383 U.S. 413, 418 (1966) (opinion of Brennan, J., joined by Warren, C.J., and Fortas, J.). Three other Justices concurred under approaches more protective of erotic publications. Id. at 421 (Black, J., and Stewart, J., concurring in the reversal); id. at 424 (Douglas, J., concurring in the judgment). Three Justices dissented. Id. at 452 (Clark, J., dissenting) (quoted in text).

66. Mishkin v. New York, 383 U.S. 502, 505 (first quotation in text), 508 (second quotation) (1966); Ginzburg v. United States, 383 U.S. 463, 474 (1966).

67. E.g., People v. Weingarten, 254 N.E.2d 232 (N.Y. 1969) (reversing censorship of "sick" depictions of lesbian relations).

68. Marcus v. Search Warrant of Property at 104 East Tenth Street, Kansas City, Missouri, 367 U.S. 717 (1961); Bantam Books, Inc. v. Sullivan, 372 U.S. 58 (1963); Freedman v. Maryland, 380 U.S. 51 (1965).

69. In May 1969 Clark Polak, the publisher of *Drum*, terminated the magazine after a conviction for violating state obscenity law. Later indicted for violating the Comstock Act, Polak plea-bargained with federal authorities to abandon the pornography business altogether. See "Polak Indicted," *Advocate*, March 1970, at 5.

70. Rodger Streitmatter, *Unspeakable: The Rise of the Gay and Lesbian Press in America,* 58–65, 87–95, 185 (1995). In addition to the pre-Stonewall publications mentioned in the text, new publications included *Come Out* (1969, New York City); *Gay Power* (1969, New York City); *The Gay Blade* (1969, Washington, D.C.); *Gay Dealer* (1970, Philadelphia); *Gay Sunshine* (1970, San Francisco); *Sisters* (1970, San Francisco); *Focus* (1971, Boston); *Lavender Woman* (1971, Chicago); *Lesbian Tide* (1971, Los Angeles); *Amazon Quarterly* (1972, Oakland); *The Furies* (1972, Washington, D.C.); *Lesbians Fight Back* (1972, Philadelphia); *Faggotry* (1972, New York City); *Tres Femmes* (1972, San Diego).

71. See Marilyn Farwell, *Heterosexual Plots and Lesbian Narratives* (1996); Claude Summer, *Gay Fictions: Wilde to Stonewall* (1990).

72. Barry Dank, "Coming Out in the Gay World," in *Gay Men: The Sociology of Male Homosexuality* (Martin Levine ed., 1979).

73. Village Books, Inc. v. State's Attorney for Prince George's Cty., 282 A.2d 126, 134 (Md. 1971), *vacated,* 413 U.S. 911 (1973). For other Maryland decisions, see Hewitt v. Maryland State Bd. of Censors, 254 A.2d 203 (Md. 1969); The B&A Co. v. State, 330 A.2d 701 (Md. App. 1975); Donnenburg v. State, 232 A.2d 264 (Md. App. 1967).

74. United States v. 12,200-ft. Reels of Super 8mm. Film, 413 U.S. 123 (1973); United States v. Orito, 413 U.S. 139 (1973).

75. Paris Adult Theatre I v. Slaton, 413 U.S. 49, 60–61 (1973); Kaplan v. California, 413 U.S. 115, 117 (1973); Miller v. California, 413 U.S. 15, 36–37 (1973), as described in Ward v. Illinois, 431 U.S. 767, 781 n.5 (1977) (Stevens, J., dissenting).

76. E.g., "Adult Bookstore Can't Sell Gay Matter: Judge," *Advocate,* January 30, 1974, at 13; "Problems Already Starting: Porno Producers Gird for Battle," *Advocate,* August 15, 1973, at 11.

77. Hamling v. United States, 418 U.S. 87 (1974) ("Illustrated Report"); Jenkins v. Georgia, 418 U.S. 153 (1974) (*Carnal Knowledge*).

78. Ward v. Illinois, 431 U.S. 767, 771–772 and nn.3–5 (1977) (describing Illinois decisions censoring materials depicting "lesbianism, and sadism and masochism").

79. Coon v. State, 871 S.W.2d 284, 288 (Tex. Crim. App. 1994), following Knight v. State, 642 S.W.2d 180 (Tex. App. 1982); see T.K.'s Video, Inc. v. State, 871 S.W.2d 524 (Tex. App. 1994); Commonwealth v. McCool, 563 A.2d 901 (Pa. Super. 1989).

80. See Michael Bronski, *Culture Clash: The Making of Gay Sensibility,* 160–174 (1984); Randy Shilts, "Plain Brown Wrappers: Peddling Gay Porn by Mail Is a Million Dollar Business," *Advocate,* June 30, 1976, at 16–17.

81. 18 U.S.C. §2252(a) (federal prohibition); New York v. Ferber, 458 U.S. 747, 749 n.2 (1982) (listing forty-seven state laws dealing with child pornography and upholding New York's regulation of nonobscene child porn). See generally Philip Jenkins, *Moral Panic: Changing Concepts of the Child Molester in Modern America,* 118–132 (1998).

82. Vito Russo, *The Celluloid Closet: Homosexuality in the Movies,* 121–129, 173 (rev. ed. 1987).

83. See Russo, *Celluloid Closet;* Andrea Weiss, *Vampires and Violets: Lesbians in Film* (1994); Margaret Blanchard, "The American Urge to Censor," 33 *Wm. & Mary L. Rev.* 741 (1992).

84. See Russo, *Celluloid Closet,* 173.

85. Landau v. Fording, 54 Cal. Rptr. 177, 181–182 (App. 1966), *aff'd,* 388 U.S. 456 (1967).

86. National Museum and Archive, Lesbian and Gay History, compiler, *The Gay Almanac,* 200–201 (1996) (reprinting the "General Principles"); Russo, *Celluloid Closet,* 220–221.

87. E.g., Bob Fosse's *Cabaret* (1972); Sidney Lumet's *Dog Day Afternoon* (1975); Richard Benner's *Outrageous* (1977); Nancy and Peter Adair's *Word Is Out* (1978). See generally *Gay Almanac,* 207–208 (positive gay characters), 208–209 (gay-themed screenplays), 209 (films made by gay directors).

88. See Russo, *Celluloid Closet,* 239–240.

89. There were some local efforts at censoring radio, most prominently Cincinnati's 1981 indictment of radio journalist John Zeh and station WAIF for a humorous program on lubricants and sex toys. *Advocate,* April 2, 1981, at 10. The Greater Cincinnati Gay Coalition established a legal defense fund, and Zeh's ACLU lawyer had the charges dismissed. *Advocate,* October 15, 1981, at 10.

90. Pacifica Found. (KPFK), 30 F.C.C. 147, 149 (1964); cf. id. at 152–153 (Lee, concurring) (doubting gay-themed program is informative; "a microphone in a bordello, during slack hours, could give us similar information on a related subject").

91. *Out in All Directions: The Almanac of Gay and Lesbian Americans,* 124–125 (Lynn Witt et al. eds., 1995); FCC v. Pacifica Found., 438 U.S. 726 (1978) (FCC can ban indecency, "seven dirty words," to protect children).

92. See Edward Alwood, *Straight News,* 69–74 (1996).

93. *Out in All Directions,* 128.

94. Id. at 129.

95. Alwood, *Straight News,* 143–147 (Gay Raiders), 147–154 (Gay Media Action); Kathryn Montgomery, *Target: Prime Time,* 74–100 (1989).

96. See "'Code Is Adequate': TV, Radio Boards Reject Bias Ban," *Advocate,* August 14, 1974, at 20.

97. See "Gay Leaders Go to FCC," *Advocate,* September 21, 1977, at 13.

98. See "FCC Denies Appeal of Antigay Preacher," *Advocate,* April 16, 1981, at 9.

99. E.g., Richard Levine, "How the Gay Lobby Has Changed Television," *TV Guide,* May 30, 1981.

100. Pickering v. Board of Educ., 391 U.S. 563, 564–565 (1968); Robinson v. California, 370 U.S. 660 (1962).

101. McConnell v. Anderson, 451 F.2d 193, 196 (8th Cir. 1971).

102. Acanfora v. Board of Educ., Montgomery Cty., 491 F.2d 498 (4th Cir. 1974).

103. Shelton v. Tucker, 364 U.S. 479, 480–481 (1960) (striking down state law requiring teachers, as condition of employment, to file affidavit listing organizations to which they had been affiliated within preceding five years).

104. Gay Law Students Assn. v. Pacific Tel. & Tel. Co., 595 P.2d 592, 610 (Cal. 1979), construing Cal. Labor Code §§1101–1102.

105. Letter from Franklin Kameny, President, MSW, to Robert Kennedy, Attorney General, June 28, 1962, in FBI FOIA File HQ 100-403320 (Mattachine Society), §6, Serial 88 (quotation); see "News Release from the Mattachine Society of Washington," FBI FOIA File HQ 100-403320 (Mattachine Society), §6, Serial 90X ("homosexual minority" entitled to same rights as other "national minority groups").

106. "U.S. Homophile Movement Gains National Strength," *Ladder,* April 1966, at 4 (reproducing resolution); see MSW, "Discrimination against the Employment of Homosexuals" (February 28, 1963) (similar goals), in FBI FOIA File HQ 100-403320 (Mattachine Society), §6, Serial 101.

107. MSW, "How to Handle a Federal Interrogation," ¶3 (1963), in FBI FOIA File HQ 100-403320 (Mattachine Society) §6, Serial 117.

108. D'Emilio, *Sexual Politics,* 165; Marcus, *Making History,* 122; "Eastcoast Homophile Organization Demonstration in Front of White House" (October 25, 1965), FBI FOIA File HQ 100-403320 (Mattachine Society), §7, Serial 131.

109. Scott v. Macy, 349 F.2d 182, 185 (D.C. Cir. 1965). Chief Judge Bazelon wrote only for himself; Judge McGowan concurred on narrower grounds. Id. at 185.

110. Scott v. Macy, 402 F.2d 644 (D.C. Cir. 1968).

111. Letter from John Macy, Jr., Chairman, CSC, to The Mattachine Society of Washington, February 25, 1966, reprinted in Eskridge, "Challenging the Closet," 966–968; see

Franklin Kameny, "U.S. Government Hides Behind Immoral Mores," *Ladder,* June 1966, at 17 (describing CSC meeting).

112. Norton v. Macy, 417 F.2d 1161, 1167–1168 (D.C. Cir. 1969); see David K. Johnson, "'Homosexual Citizens': Washington's Gay Community Confronts the Civil Service," *Wash. Hist.,* Fall/Winter 1994–95, at 44–47.

113. "U.S. Agency Backs Down on Firing," *Advocate,* November 8, 1972, at 3 (GPO); "Postal Service Dumps CSC's Anti-Gay Policy," *Advocate,* December 20, 1972, at 24.

114. Compare Adams v. Laird, 420 F.2d 230 (D.C. Cir. 1969) (failing to apply *Norton* to security clearance cases), with Gayer v. Schlesinger, 490 F.2d 740 (D.C. Cir. 1973) (remanding for more explanation under *Norton*). See also McKeand v. Laird, 490 F.2d 1262 (9th Cir. 1973); Rivera, "Straight-Laced Judges," 829–837. The Defense Department relaxed but did not abandon its antigay exclusion for security clearances in the mid-1970s. The exclusion survived into the 1990s, e.g., High Tech Gays v. Defense Indus. Security Clearance Office, 895 F.2d 563 (9th Cir. 1990), before it was revoked by Executive Order No. 12,968, 60 Fed. Reg. 40,245 (1995).

115. Society for Individual Rights v. Hampton, 63 F.R.D. 399 (N.D. Cal. 1973), *aff'd,* 528 F.2d 905 (9th Cir. 1975).

116. Singer v. United States Civil Service Commn., 530 F.2d 247, 255 n.14 (9th Cir. 1976), *vacated,* 429 U.S. 1034 (1977) (quoting 1973 guideline); 40 Fed. Reg. 28,047 (1975), codified at 5 C.F.R. §731.202(b).

117. Civil Service Reform Act of 1978, Public Law No. 95-454, §101(a), 92 Stat. 1114, 1115 (1978), codified at 5 U.S.C. §2302(b)(10).

118. See Rhonda R. Rivera, "QueerLaw: Sexual Orientation Law in the Mid-Eighties" (pt. 1), 10 *U. Dayton L. Rev.* 459, 485 (1985), discussing Singer v. United States Civil Service Commn., 530 F.2d 247 (9th Cir. 1976), *vacated,* 429 U.S. 1034 (1977).

119. Unsuccessful challenges to military discharges include Bray v. United States, 515 F.2d 1383 (Ct. Cl. 1975); Nelson v. Miller, 373 F.2d 474 (3d Cir. 1967); Benson v. Holloway, 312 F. Supp. 49 (D. Neb. 1970); Crawford v. Davis, 249 F. Supp. 943 (E.D. Pa. 1966); Unglesby v. Zinny, 250 F. Supp. 714 (N.D. Cal. 1965). Successful due process arguments are reported in Franklin Kameny, "WACs Prevail over Army," *Ladder,* August-September 1969, at 7 (accused women cleared for lack of evidence), and Schwartz v. Covington, 341 F.2d 537 (9th Cir. 1965) (stay order).

120. Champagne v. Schlesinger, 506 F.2d 979 (7th Cir. 1974).

121. Matlovich v. Secretary of Air Force, 591 F.2d 852 (D.C. Cir. 1978); Berg v. Claytor, 591 F.2d 849 (D.C. Cir. 1978). For background, see Mike Hippler, *Matlovich* (1989); Randy Shilts, *Conduct Unbecoming: Gays & Lesbians in the U.S. Military,* 148–149, 176–186, 207–257, 277–288 (1993).

122. Beller v. Middendorf, 632 F.2d 788 (9th Cir. 1980), *rev'g* Saal v. Middendorf, 427 F. Supp. 192 (N.D. Cal. 1977), and two other lower court decisions; 32 C.F.R. pt. 41, app. A (1981), reprinted in William N. Eskridge, Jr. and Nan D. Hunter, *Sexuality, Gender, and the Law,* 372–373 (1997).

123. Rostker v. Goldberg, 453 U.S. 57 (1981).

124. Morrison v. State Bd. of Educ., 461 P.2d 375, 382, 391 (Cal. 1969).

125. Board of Educ. v. Jack M, 566 P.2d 602 (Cal. 1977), probably overruling Governing Bd., Mountain View Sch. Dist. v. Metcalf, 111 Cal. Rptr. 724 (App. 1974) (dismissal of

homosexual teacher based on invalid criminal charge); McLaughlin v. Board of Medical Examrs., 111 Cal. Rptr. 353 (App. 1973) (revocation of doctor's license for private homosexual conduct); Purifoy v. State Bd. of Educ., 106 Cal. Rptr. 201 (App. 1973).

126. E.g., Gaylord v. Tacoma Sch. Dist. No. 10, 559 P.2d 1340 (Wash. 1977); Gish v. Board of Educ., 366 A.2d 1337 (N.J. Super. 1976).

127. See Burton v. Cascade Sch. Dist. Union High Sch. No. 5, 353 F. Supp. 254 (D. Or. 1973), aff'd, 512 F.2d 850 (9th Cir. 1975).

128. National Gay Task Force v. Board of Educ., Okla. City, 729 F.2d 1270 (10th Cir. 1984), aff'd by equally divided Court, 470 U.S. 903 (1985); Aumiller v. University of Del., 434 F. Supp. 1273 (D. Del. 1977).

129. E.g., VanOoteghem v. Gray, 654 F.2d 304 (5th Cir. 1981) (en banc).

130. "Gay Police: Controversy Heats Up," Advocate, October 5, 1977, at 5.

131. See In re Kimball, 301 N.E.2d 436 (N.Y. 1973) (per curiam). Compare State v. Kimball, 96 So. 2d 825 (Fla. 1957) (denying admission to Florida bar because of sodomy conviction), with Florida Bd. of Bar Examrs. v. Eimers, 358 So. 2d 7 (Fla. 1978) (where no evidence of illegal conduct, bar must admit gay attorney).

132. See Rivera, "Straight-Laced Judges," 859.

133. See Cal. Gov. Jerry Brown, Executive Order No. B-54-79, April 4, 1979; N.Y. Gov. Mario Cuomo, Executive Order No. 28, November 18, 1983; Ohio Gov. Richard Celeste, Executive Order No. 83-64, December 30, 1983; Pa. Gov. Milton Shapp, Executive Order, April 1975.

134. 1981 Wis. Laws ch. 112 (March 2, 1982).

135. David Aiken, "Broadest Protection for Gays: D.C. Rights Law Gets Preliminary Nod," Advocate, August 29, 1973, at 5. After the District was granted home rule, the directive was adopted as a statute in 1977, D.C. Code §1-2501 et seq.

136. Compare George Mendenhall, "Gay Cops: An Issue Getting Attention Nation-Wide," Advocate, November 19, 1975, at 14 (few cities willing to hire openly gay cops), with Brett Averill, "On the Beat with Gay Cops," Advocate, May 14, 1981, at 15–17 (New York, Los Angeles, D.C., and Chicago join San Francisco in willingness to hire gay cops).

137. Randy Shilts, "City Rights Laws—Are They Just Toothless Paper Tigers?," Advocate, March 10, 1976, at 6–7.

138. Quoted in Joe Baker, "Anita . . . with the Smiling Cheek," Advocate, April 20, 1977, at 6. See also Anita Bryant, The Anita Bryant Story: The Survival of Our Nation's Families and the Threat of Militant Homosexuality, 145–148 (1977).

139. Cal. Proposition 6, §3(b)(2) (1978), discussed in Nan D. Hunter, "Identity, Speech, and Equality," 79 Va. L. Rev. 1695, 1702–06 (1993).

140. Barbara Gamble, "Putting Civil Rights to a Popular Vote," 41 Am. J. Pol. Sci. 245 (1997).

141. In re Schmidt, 289 N.Y.S.2d 89, 92 (Sup. Ct. 1968), quoting H. v. H., 157 A.2d 721, 727 (N.J. Super. 1959) (granting a husband a favorable divorce because of wife's homosexuality).

142. Fleuti v. Rosenberg, 302 F.2d 652, 657–658 (9th Cir. 1962), vacated, 374 U.S. 449 (1963). Compare Quiroz v. Neely, 291 F.2d 906 (5th Cir. 1961) (lesbians are per se psychopathic personalities under the statute).

143. Act of October 3, 1965, Public Law No. 89-236, §15(b), 79 Stat. 911, 919.

144. Boutilier v. INS, 387 U.S. 118 (1967), applied in Lavoie v. INS, 360 F.2d 27 (9th Cir. 1966), *remanded*, 387 U.S. 572 (1967), *on remand*, 418 F.2d 732 (9th Cir. 1969) (admitted homosexual per se psychopathic, as required by *Boutilier*); Campos v. INS, 402 F.2d 758 (9th Cir. 1968) (same).

145. Babouris v. Esperdy, 269 F.2d 621 (2d Cir. 1959); Wyngaard v. Kennedy, 295 F.2d 184 (D.C. Cir. 1961).

146. In re Labady, 326 F. Supp. 924, 927 (S.D.N.Y. 1971).

147. INS Interpretations §316.1(f)(7) (1976), quoted in "Immigration Department Relaxes Gay Policy," *Advocate*, September 22, 1976, at 10.

148. Letter from John Spiegel, APA, to Leonard Chapman, INS Director, July 17, 1974. This letter and subsequent unpublished materials noted in this section were obtained by the author under the Freedom of Information Act; see Eskridge, "Challenging the Closet," 935–939, for the details of this history. On the APA debates, see Ronald Bayer, *Homosexuality and American Psychiatry* (1987); Gary Alinder, "Gay Liberation Meets the Shrinks," in *Out of the Closets*, 141.

149. Letter from William Foege, Centers for Disease Control (CDC) Director, to Lionel Castillo, INS Commissioner, November 7, 1977; Memorandum from Carl Wack, INS Associate Commissioner, Examinations, to Foege, November 20, 1978.

150. Memorandum from Julius Richmond, Surgeon General, to William Foege, CDC Director, August 2, 1979, reprinted in 56 *Interpreter's Releases* 387 (1979).

151. 8 U.S.C. §1226(d) (1978).

152. Office of Legal Counsel Opinion No. 79-85, for the Acting INS Commissioner, December 10, 1979.

153. Telegraph Memorandum from David Crosland, Acting INS Commissioner, to All Regions, September 8, 1980.

154. Hill v. INS, 714 F.2d 1470 (9th Cir. 1983). Contra, In re Longstaff, 716 F.2d 1439 (5th Cir. 1983).

155. Letter from Lowell Jensen, Acting Deputy Attorney General, to Edward Bennett, Assistant Secretary for Health, April 5, 1984; Letter from Lawrence Farer, Acting Director, PHS Division of Quarantine, to Andrew Carmichael, Associate Commissioner, Examinations, June 8, 1984.

156. Immigration Act of 1990, Public Law No. 101-649, §601(a), 104 Stat. 4978.

157. Compare Del Martin and Phyllis Lyon, *Lesbian/Woman*, 103 (1972), with "Gay Revolution Comes Out," *The Rat*, August 12–26, 1969, at 7 (GLF interview), and Ralph Hall, "The Church, State & Homosexuality: A Radical Analysis," *Gay Power*, No. 14 (undated [1970?]).

158. See William N. Eskridge, Jr., *The Case for Same-Sex Marriage*, chs. 3–4 (1996).

159. Baker v. Nelson, 191 N.W.2d 185 (Minn. 1971), *appeal dismissed*, 409 U.S. 810 (1972), distinguishing Loving v. Virginia, 388 U.S. 1 (1967). Other cases are discussed in Eskridge, *Same-Sex Marriage*, ch. 5 and notes.

160. Singer v. Hara, 522 P.2d 1187 (Wash. App. 1974), rejecting the argument of Note, "The Legality of Homosexual Marriage," 82 *Yale L.J.* 573 (1973).

161. M.T. v. J.T., 355 A.2d 204 (N.J. Super. 1976). Refusing to recognize transgendered marriages were Anonymous v. Anonymous, 325 N.Y.S.2d 499 (Sup. Ct. 1971); Gajovski

v. Gajovski, 610 N.E.2d 431 (Ohio App. 1991); In re Ladrach, 573 N.E.2d 828 (Ohio Prob. 1987).

162. Carrington Boggan et al., ACLU, *The Rights of Gay People,* 103–122 (1975); Julie Lee, "Economics of the Gay Marriage," *Ladder,* April/May 1969, at 12. See also Leonore Weitzman, "Legal Regulation of Marriage: Tradition and Change—A Proposal for Individual Contracts and Contracts in Lieu of Marriage," 62 *Cal. L. Rev.* 1169 (1974).

163. See Rivera, "Straight-Laced Judges," 908 n.657.

164. In re Kaufmann's Will, 247 N.Y.S.2d 664, 674 (first quotation in text) (App. 1964), *aff'd,* 257 N.E.2d 864 (N.Y. 1965); id. at 689 (second quotation) (Witmer, J., dissenting), analyzed in Jeffrey Sherman, "Undue Influence and the Homosexual Testator," 42 *U. Pitt. L. Rev.* 225, 239–248 (1981). For a similar result, but with more evidence of "influence," see Knowles v. Binford, 298 A.2d 862 (Md. 1973).

165. Marvin v. Marvin, 557 P.2d 106 (Cal. 1976), applied to same-sex couples in e.g., Crooke v. Gilden, 414 S.E.2d 645 (Ga. 1992); Whorton v. Dillingham, 248 Cal. Rptr. 405 (App. 1988); Weekes v. Gay, 256 S.E.2d 901 (Ga. 1979) (property passed to decedent's gay lover under theory of implied trust).

166. 1977 Fla. Laws ch. 77-140, codified at Fla. Stat. §63.042(3); In re Adoption of Robert Paul P., 471 N.E.2d 424 (N.Y. 1984). See Sherman, "Homosexual Testator," 254–255; "Developments in the Law—Sexual Orientation," 102 *Harv. L. Rev.* 1508, 1628 (1989).

167. "San Francisco Mayor Says No to Gay Marriage," *Wash. Blade,* January 28, 1983, at 9. See National Gay and Lesbian Task Force Policy Institute, *Gay, Lesbian, Bisexual & Transgender Civil Rights Laws in the U.S.,* 15 (August 1998); Craig Bowman and Blake Cornish, "A More Perfect Union: A Legal and Social Analysis of Domestic Partnership Ordinances," 92 *Colum. L. Rev.* 1164 (1992) (student note); Robert Eblin, "Domestic Partnership Recognition in the Workplace: Equitable Employee Benefits for Gay Couples (and Others)," 51 *Ohio St. L.J.* 1067 (1990) (student note).

168. Stanley v. Illinois, 405 U.S. 645, 658 (1972), applied to gay people in e.g., People v. Brown, 212 N.W.2d 55 (Mich. App. 1973) (lesbian relationship is not sufficient basis to remove child from biological mother). For an example where the state did take away a lesbian mother's children, see In re Tammy F., 1 Civil No. 32648 (Cal. App. August 21, 1973), discussed in Rivera, "Straight-Laced Judges," 887–888.

169. See Kenneth Davidson, Ruth Bader Ginsburg, and Herma Hill Kay, *Sex-Based Discrimination,* 275 (1975); Nan D. Hunter and Nancy Polikoff, "Custody Rights of Lesbian Mothers," 25 *Buffalo L. Rev.* 691 (1976); Rivera, "Staight-Laced Judges," 883–904.

170. E.g., Bennett v. Clemens, 196 S.E.2d 842 (Ga. 1973); Immerman v. Immerman, 1 Cal. Rptr. 298 (App. 1959); Commonwealth v. Bradley, 91 A.2d 379 (Pa. Super. 1952).

171. Schuster v. Schuster, 585 P.2d 130, 133 (Wash. 1978); "Pain and Precedent: Gay Mother Wins Children's Custody," *Advocate,* July 19, 1972, at 6–7.

172. S. v. S., 608 S.W.2d 64, 66 (Ky. 1980). Accord, Jacobson v. Jacobson, 314 N.W.2d 78 (N.D. 1981); Dailey v. Dailey, 635 S.W.2d 391 (Tenn. App. 1981); M.J.P. v. J.G.P., 640 P.2d 966 (Okla. 1982); Roe v. Roe, 324 S.E.2d 691 (Va. 1985).

173. Bezio v. Patenaude, 410 N.E.2d 1207 (Mass. 1980). See Eskridge and Hunter, *Sexuality, Gender, and the Law,* 832–837, for discussion of cases following this approach after 1980.

174. In re J.S. & C., 324 A.2d 90 (N.J. Super. 1974), *aff'd,* 362 A.2d 54 (N.J. App. 1976). Accord, J.L.P. v. D.J.P., 643 S.W.2d 865 (Mo. App. 1982); Roberts v. Roberts, 489 N.E.2d 1067, 1070 (Ohio App. 1985); In re Jane B., 380 N.Y.S.2d 848 (Sup. Ct. 1976); A. v. A., 514 P.2d 358 (Or. App. 1973). For unreported decisions, see Rivera, "Straight-Laced Judges," 892–895.

Part Two. Remnants of the Closet (Don't Ask, Don't Tell)

1. These developments are surveyed in Appendix B2 and in William N. Eskridge, Jr., and Nan D. Hunter, *Sexuality, Gender, and the Law,* chs. 2, 5, 7–10, 12 (1997).

2. Defense of Marriage Act, Public Law No. 104-199, 110 Stat. 2419 (September 21, 1996). As of January 1, 1999, the following states had adopted statutes to prevent any kind of state recognition of same-sex marriages: Alabama, Alaska, Arizona, Arkansas, Delaware, Florida, Georgia, Idaho, Illinois, Indiana, Iowa, Kansas, Kentucky, Maine, Maryland, Michigan, Minnesota, Mississippi, Missouri, Montana, North Carolina, North Dakota, Oklahoma, Pennsylvania, South Carolina, South Dakota, Tennessee, Utah, Virginia, and Washington. See Appendix B3 for references.

3. Bowers v. Hardwick, 478 U.S. 186 (1986).

4. See S. v. S., 608 S.W.2d 64 (Ky. App. 1980); G.A. v. D.A., 745 S.W.2d 726 (Mo. App. 1987); Roe v. Roe, 324 S.E.2d 691 (Va. 1985); and other cases cited in Appendix B3.

5. See Daly v. Daly, 715 P.2d 56 (Nev. 1986). Contra, Christian v. Randall, 516 P.2d 132 (Colo. App. 1973); In re Custody of T.J., 1988 WL 8302 (Minn. App. 1988).

6. In re Appeal of Pima Cty. Juvenile Action B-10489, 727 P.2d 830 (Ariz. App. 1986); Fla. Stat. §63.042(3). Utah's Division of Child and Family Services voted to ban gay adoptions in January 1999. New Hampshire's 1977 bar to adoption by gay people was repealed in 1999.

7. Public Law No. 103-160, §571(a)(1), 107 Stat. 1670, analyzed in Eskridge and Hunter, *Sexuality, Gender, and the Law,* 388–407.

8. See National Abortion Rights Action League, *Sexuality Education in America: A State-by-State Review* (September 1995) (entries for Alabama, Arizona, Georgia, Louisiana, North Carolina, South Carolina, Texas, Virginia).

9. The federal no promo homo rules have been challenged in Gay Men's Health Crisis v. Sullivan, 792 F. Supp. 278 (S.D.N.Y. 1992), and National Endowment for the Arts v. Finley, 118 S. Ct. 2168 (1998).

10. Dillon v. Frank, 952 F.2d 403 (6th Cir. 1992) (gay man harassed by coworkers); Ulane v. Eastern Airlines, 742 F.2d 1041 (7th Cir. 1984) (transsexual); De Santis v. Pacific Tel. & Tel. Co., 608 F.2d 327 (9th Cir. 1979) (discrimination and/or harassment claims by effeminate man, lesbian couple, other gay people); Katharine Franke, "What's Wrong with Sexual Harassment?," 49 *Stan. L. Rev.* 691 (1997) (exhaustive survey of cases). See also 42 U.S.C. §12208 (excluding transsexualism, transvestism, and homosexuality from "disabilities" covered under the Americans with Disabilities Act); 29 U.S.C. §706(8) (F)(i) (transvestites and transsexuals now excluded from previous protection under Rehabilitation Act).

11. Romer v. Evans, 517 U.S. 620 (1996).

12. See Jack Knight, *Institutions and Social Conflict* (1992); William E. Nelson, "Criminality and Sexual Morality in New York, 1920–1980," 5 *Yale J.L. & Humanities* 265 (1993).

13. Cass R. Sunstein, "Sexual Orientation and the Constitution: A Note on the Relationship between Due Process and Equal Protection," 55 *U. Chi. L. Rev.* 1161 (1988).

14. Norton v. Macy, 417 F.2d 1161 (D.C. Cir. 1969); One Eleven Wines and Liquors, Inc. v. Division of Alcoholic Beverage Control, 235 A.2d 12 (N.J. 1967); Morrison v. State Bd. of Educ., 461 P.2d 375 (Cal. 1969).

15. Reva Siegel, "'The Rule of Love': Wife Beating as Prerogative and Privacy," 105 *Yale L.J.* 2117 (1996).

16. Marcus v. Search Warrant, 367 U.S. 717 (1961) (no prior restraints against alleged obscenity); Roth v. United States, 354 U.S. 476 (1957), applied in One, Inc. v. Olesen, 355 U.S. 371 (1958) (per curiam) (lesbian story is not obscene).

17. NAACP v. Alabama, 357 U.S. 449 (1958) (freedom of association); Pickering v. Board of Educ., 391 U.S. 563 (1968) (state cannot penalize employees for public speech).

18. Gay Students Org. v. Bonner, 509 F.2d 652 (1st Cir. 1974) (university cannot censor gay student group).

19. Sherman v. United States, 356 U.S. 369 (1958) (due process right not to be entrapped); Griswold v. Connecticut, 381 U.S. 479 (1965) (right to privacy); Katz v. United States, 389 U.S. 347 (1967) (fourth amendment privacy); Stanley v. Georgia, 394 U.S. 557 (1969); Miranda v. Arizona, 384 U.S. 436 (1966) (right to remain silent).

20. Miller v. California, 413 U.S. 15 (1973) (reformulating *Roth* obscenity test), applied with antigay bite in Hamling v. United States, 418 U.S. 87 (1974); Ward v. Illinois, 431 U.S. 767 (1977).

21. Rose v. Locke, 423 U.S. 48 (1975) (crime against nature law not vague), distinguishing Papachristou v. City of Jacksonville, 405 U.S. 156 (1972); Mayes v. Texas, 416 U.S. 909 (1974) (denying certiorari in cross-dressing case).

22. California v. LaRue, 409 U.S. 109 (1972) (twenty-first amendment gives state substantial authority to regulate expressive conduct within liquor-licensed premises).

23. Beller v. Middendorf, 632 F.2d 788 (9th Cir. 1980) (upholding armed forces' exclusion of person who had engaged in homosexual sodomy in his youth).

24. Bielicki v. Superior Court, 371 P.2d 288 (Cal. 1962) (privacy right to enclosed toilet stall); 1975 Cal. Stat. ch. 71 (repealing consensual sodomy law); Pryor v. Municipal Court, 599 P.2d 636 (Cal. 1979) (lewd vagrancy law cannot be enforced against solicitation for private intimacy).

25. Vallerga v. Department of Alcoholic Beverage Control, 347 P.2d 909 (Cal. 1959) (state cannot prohibit gay people from congregating).

26. *Morrison,* 461 P.2d 375 (Cal. 1969); Board of Educ. v. Jack M, 566 P.2d 602 (Cal. 1977); Gay Law Students v. Pacific Tel. & Tel. Co., 595 P.2d 592 (Cal. 1979) (labor code's prohibition of discrimination on the basis of political speech protects gay people against job discrimination).

27. L. Michael Seidman, "*Brown* and *Miranda*," 80 *Cal. L. Rev.* 673 (1992).

28. See Eric Marcus, *Making History: The Struggle for Gay and Lesbian Equal Rights 1945–1990,* at 147–165 (1992) (San Francisco); Steven Rosen, "Police Harassment of Homosexual Women and Men in New York City 1960–1980," 12 *Colum. Hum. Rts. L.*

Rev. 159 (1980–81); "Chicago Police Order to Curb Antigay Bias," *Advocate,* February 19, 1981, at 9.

29. Randy Shilts, "City Rights Laws—Are They Just Toothless Paper Tigers?," *Advocate,* June 19, 1974, at 6.

30. James Button et al., *Private Lives, Public Conflicts: Battles over Gay Rights in American Communities,* 119–133 (1997).

4. *Hardwick* and Historiography

1. Bowers v. Hardwick, 478 U.S. 186, 188 n.2 (1986).

2. Id. at 192.

3. Id. at 196.

4. Id. at 197 (Burger, C. J., concurring).

5. Al Kamen, "Powell Changed Vote in Sodomy Case," *Wash. Post,* July 13, 1986, at A1; Ruth Marcus, "Powell Regrets Backing Sodomy Law," *Wash. Post,* October 26, 1990, at A3. See John C. Jeffries, Jr., *Justice Lewis F. Powell, Jr.,* 313–330 (1993).

6. Charles Fried, *Order and Law—Arguing the Reagan Revolution,* 81–84 (1991) (inconsistent with precedent); Richard A. Posner, *Sex and Reason,* 341–350 (1992) (factually ignorant); Eve Kosofsky Sedgwick, *The Epistemology of the Closet* (1990) (manipulative); Laurence Tribe, *Constitutional Law* (2d ed. 1988) (inconsistent with precedent); Anne Goldstein, "History, Homosexuality, and Political Values: Searching for the Hidden Determinants of *Bowers v. Hardwick,*" 97 *Yale L.J.* 1073, 1102–03 (1988) (inaccurate); Janet Halley, "Reasoning about Sodomy: Act and Identity in and after *Bowers v. Hardwick,*" 79 *Va. L. Rev.* 1721 (1993) (slippery); Sylvia Law, "Homosexuality and the Social Meaning of Gender," 1988 *Wis. L. Rev.* 187 (antifeminist); Frank I. Michelman, "Law's Republic," 97 *Yale L.J.* 1493, 1496 (1987) (authoritarian); Jed Rubenfeld, "The Right of Privacy," 102 *Harv. L. Rev.* 737 (1989) (authoritarian); Kendall Thomas, "Beyond the Privacy Principle," 92 *Colum. L. Rev.* 1431, 1461 (1992) (violent). See generally Earl Maltz, "The Prospects for a Revival of Conservative Activism in Constitutional Jurisprudence," 24 *Ga. L. Rev.* 629, 645 n.95 (1990), citing thirty-three law review articles and comments criticizing *Hardwick.*

7. Romer v. Evans, 517 U.S. 620, 633–634 (1996).

8. Id. at 641 (Scalia, J., dissenting); accord, John Finnis, "Law, Morality, and 'Sexual Orientation,'" 69 *Notre Dame L. Rev.* 1049 (1994).

9. Edward Laumnann et al., *The Social Organization of Sexuality: Sexual Practices in the United States,* 98–99 (1994) (Table 3.6).

10. Union Pacific Railroad Co. v. Botsford, 141 U.S. 250 (1891), distinguished in Jacobson v. Massachusetts, 197 U.S. 11 (1905) (state has compelling interest in vaccination), and followed in Rochin v. California, 342 U.S. 165 (1952) (state cannot force person to have his stomach pumped).

11. Meyer v. Nebraska, 262 U.S. 390, 399 (1923); see also Pierce v. Society of Sisters, 268 U.S. 510 (1925); Maynard v. Hill, 125 U.S. 190 (1888); Wynehamer v. People, 13 N.Y. 378, 486–487 (1856) (leading case). See generally Washington v. Glucksberg, 117 S. Ct. 2258, 2277–86 (1997) (Souter, J., concurring in the judgment).

12. Buck v. Bell, 274 U.S. 200 (1927); see Stephen Jay Gould, "Carrie Buck's Daughter," 2 *Const. Comm.* 331 (1985).

13. Skinner v. Oklahoma, 316 U.S. 535, 541 (1942).

14. See Ellen Chessler, *Woman of Valor: Margaret Sanger and the Birth Control Movement in America* (1992); William N. Eskridge, Jr., and Nan D. Hunter, *Sexuality, Gender, and the Law,* 3–19 (1997).

15. Poe v. Ullman, 367 U.S. 497, 541 (first quotation in text; emphasis in original), 553 (second quotation) (1961) (Harlan, J., dissenting).

16. Griswold v. Connecticut, 381 U.S. 479, 487 (1965).

17. Id. at 485–486 (opinion for the Court); id. at 499 (Goldberg, J., joined by Warren, C.J., and Brennan, J., concurring); id. at 499–502 (Harlan, J., concurring in the judgment). See generally David Garrow, *Liberty and Sexuality: The Right to Privacy and the Making of* Roe v. Wade, chs. 2–4 (1994).

18. Eisenstadt v. Baird, 405 U.S. 438, 453 (1972) (emphasis in original).

19. Roe v. Wade, 410 U.S. 113, 153 (1973).

20. Carey v. Population Servs. Intl., 431 U.S. 678, 687 (1977) (plurality opinion).

21. Stanley v. Georgia, 394 U.S. 557 (1969), quoting Olmstead v. United States, 277 U.S. 438 (1928) (Brandeis, J., dissenting).

22. Moore v. City of East Cleveland, 431 U.S. 494 (1976) (plurality opinion).

23. Richard A. Posner, "The Uncertain Protection of Privacy by the Supreme Court," 1979 *Sup. Ct. Rev.* 173, 198; Harry H. Wellington, "Common Law Rules and Constitutional Double Standards," 83 *Yale L.J.* 221, 296 (1973). See also Robert Bork, "Neutral Principles and Some First Amendment Problems," 47 *Ind. L.J.* 1, 8–9 (1971), criticizing the whole line of privacy decisions for this reason.

24. People v. Onofre, 415 N.E.2d 936, 939 (N.Y. 1980).

25. John Stuart Mill, *On Liberty,* ch. 4 (1859).

26. Rubenfeld, "Right of Privacy," 777–800; accord, Anita Allen, *Uneasy Access: Privacy for Women in a Free Society* (1988).

27. *Hardwick,* 478 U.S. at 190.

28. Id. at 192–193 and nn.5–7.

29. *Roe,* 410 U.S. at 138–140; id. at 175–176 and nn.1–2 (Rehnquist, J., dissenting).

30. See Goldstein, "History, Homosexuality"; Halley, "Reasoning about Sodomy," 1750–1756 (White cribbed his history of "homosexual sodomy" from a historiographically naive student survey).

31. 25 Henry 8 ch. 6 (1533) was a temporary measure, renewed in 1536 and 1539 and made perpetual in 1540 before it was revoked by Queen Mary in 1553. King Henry's statute was reenacted permanently by 5 Eliz. ch. 17 (1562). See François Lafitte, "Homosexuality and the Law," 9 *Brit. J. Delinquency,* July 1958, at 8.

32. See Rex v. Jacobs, 168 Eng. Rep. 830 (1817) (oral sex between man and boy not within buggery law); Rex v. Wiseman, 92 Eng. Rep. 774 (1716) (anal sex between man and woman is buggery). See William Blackstone, *Commentaries on the Laws of England,* vol. 1, at *215 (1765); Sir Edward Coke, *The Third Part of the Institutes of the Laws of England,* *58–59 (1644).

33. On colonial sodomy laws, see Caroline Bingham, "Seventeenth Century Attitudes toward Deviant Sex," 1 *J. Interdisciplinary Hist.* 447 (1971); Louis Crompton,

"Homosexuals and the Death Penalty in Colonial America," 1 *J. Homosexuality* 277 (1976); Goldstein, "History, Homosexuality," 1082–84 nn.60–65; Robert Oaks, "'Things Fearful to Name': Sodomy and Buggery in Seventeenth-Century New England," 12 *J. Soc. Hist.* 268 (1978); Oaks, "Perceptions of Homosexuality by Justices of the Peace in Colonial Virginia," in *Homosexuality and the Law,* 35 (Donald Knutson ed., 1980). Essential primary documents are reproduced in Jonathan Ned Katz, *Gay/ Lesbian Almanac: A New Documentary,* 66–133 (1983), and *Gay American History* (1976).

34. J. Hammond Trumbull, *The True-Blue Laws of Connecticut and New Haven,* 201 (1879), reprinted in Katz, *Gay American History,* 36–37.

35. See Katz, *Almanac,* 29, 58, 663.

36. See John Winthrop, *History of New England from 1630 to 1649,* vol. 2, at 324 (James Savage ed., 1853), reprinted in Katz, *Gay American History,* 34–35.

37. Coke, *Institutes,* *58–59.

38. E.g., 1827 Ill. Laws, Criminal Code §50; Wis. Rev. Stat. ch. 139, §15 (1849). See Blackstone, *Commentaries,* *215; Coke, *Institutes,* *58–59. Examples of mid-century revisions of earlier state laws include Del. Code tit. 20, ch. 131, §7 (1852); Mass. Gen. Laws ch. 165, §18 (1860); N.C. Rev. Code ch. 34, §6 (1854).

39. See Joel Prentiss Bishop, *Commentaries on the Criminal Law,* vol. 2, at 688 (1858); Joseph Chitty, *A Practical Treatise on Criminal Law,* vol. 2, at *48–50 (5th Am. ed. 1847); Robert Desty, *A Compendium of American Criminal Law,* 143 (1887); John Wilder May, *The Law of Crimes,* 223 (1881).

40. See U.S. Department of the Interior, Census Office, *Report of the Defective, Dependent, and Delinquent Population of the United States, as Returned at the Tenth Census* (1880), excerpted in Katz, *Gay American History,* 57–58.

41. An Act to make further provision for the Protection of Women and Girls, the suppression of brothels, and other purposes, cl. 11, 48 & 49 Vict. cap. 69. See F. B. Smith, "Labouchere's Amendment to the Criminal Law Amendment Bill," 17 *Hist. Stud. (Melbourne),* October 1976, at 165.

42. Prindle v. State, 21 S.W. 360 (Tex. Crim. App. 1893), followed in People v. Boyle, 48 P. 800 (Cal. 1897); Commonwealth v. Poindexter, 118 S.W. 943 (Ky. 1909); Kinnan v. State, 125 N.W. 594 (Neb. 1910); State v. Johnson, 137 P. 632 (Utah 1913); Wise v. Commonwealth, 115 S.E. 508 (Va. 1923); Koontz v. People, 263 P. 19 (Colo. 1927); Bennett v. Abram, 253 P.2d 316 (N.M. 1953).

43. American Law Institute, *Model Penal Code,* Tent. Draft No. 4, §207.5, comments, at 277–278 (1955); see Louis Schwartz, "Morals Offenses and the Model Penal Code," 63 *Colum. L. Rev.* 669, 675–676 (1969).

44. See Chapter 2, plus the transcript of the discussions among Florida's Criminal Code Revision Committee, reprinted in William N. Eskridge, Jr., "Privacy Jurisprudence and the Apartheid of the Closet," 24 *Fla. St. U.L. Rev.* 703, 829–838 (1997) (app. 6).

45. *A Supplement to the Oxford English Dictionary,* vol. 2, at 135 (R. W. Burchfield ed., 1976), credits Charles Chaddock, an early translator of German medical treatises on the subject, for introducing the term "homo-sexuality" into the English language.

46. Halley, "Reasoning about Sodomy," 1756–1765, criticizing Goldstein, "History, Homosexuality."

47. Herring v. State, 46 S.E. 876 (Ga. 1904); Comer v. State, 94 S.E. 314 (Ga. App. 1917); Thompson v. Aldredge, 200 S.E. 799 (Ga. 1939); Riley v. Garrett, 133 S.E.2d 367 (Ga. 1963), clarified in 1968 Ga. Laws 1249, adding Ga. Code §26-2002.

48. See Bernadette J. Brooten, *Love between Women: Early Christian Responses to Female Homoeroticism* (1996); Peter Brown, *The Body and Society: Men, Women and Sexual Renunciation in Early Christianity* (1988); Michael Goodrich, *The Unmentionable Vice: Homosexuality in the Late Medieval Period* (1979). See also Mark D. Jordan, *The Invention of Sodomy in Christian Theology* (1997).

49. See, e.g., Ala. Code pt. 4, ch. 2, art. V (1852); Ill. Rev. Stat. ch. XXX (1845); Mass. Rev. Stat. tit. 1, ch. 130 (1860); Mich. Rev. Stat. pt. 4th, tit. I, ch. 8 (1838); N.Y. Penal Law (1881).

50. E.g., Harvey v. State, 115 S.W. 1193 (Tex. Crim. App. 1909) (charge of oral sex was "too horrible to contemplate," and new legislation is needed to cover "these unnatural crimes"). Cf. John Clelland, *Fanny Hill: Memoirs of a Woman of Pleasure,* 42–43 (Dell rev. ed. 1964) (1749) (bawdy novel describing oral sex).

51. See People v. Hodgkin, 53 N.W. 794 (Mich. 1892); Bishop, *Criminal Law,* vol. 2, at 652–654.

52. See, e.g., 1838 Ark. Acts 121, 122 (sodomy linked with carnal abuse of female children); Ga. Penal Code §§29–38 (1816) (maiming, rape, sodomy, assault listed together); Idaho (Terr.) Laws ch. III, §§44–47 (1866) (carnal knowledge of female child, sodomy, assault, and rape listed together); Ill. Crim. Code §§47–52 (1839) (similar); 1813 N.Y. Laws 408, ¶III (rape, crime against nature, burglary, robbery listed together).

53. All the "model" sodomy indictments reprinted by Chitty, *Practical Treatise,* *48–50, involved allegations of predation by an older man against a minor girl or boy. Most of the reported cases before 1900 involved alleged predation by an adult male against a weaker person. See the cases assembled in notes 58–60 below.

54. See Francis Wharton, *Treatise on the Criminal Law of the United States,* 443 (1852) (also subsequent editions).

55. E.g., Medis v. State, 27 Tex. Crim. App. 194 (1889) (reversing a sodomy conviction because the only witness to penetration was the man being sodomized, a legal accomplice).

56. E.g., Craig v. Boren, 429 U.S. 190 (1976).

57. State v. Williams, 34 La. Ann. 87 (La. 1882); Commonwealth v. Dill, 36 N.E. 472 (Mass. 1894); People v. Hodgkin, 53 N.W. 794 (Mich. 1892); Fennell v. State, 32 Tex. 378 (Tex. 1869); Ex parte Bergen, 14 Tex. App. 52 (Tex. Crim. App. 1883); Williams v. Commonwealth, 22 S.E. 859 (Va. 1895).

58. See Bradford v. State, 16 So. 107 (Ala. 1893) (defendant accused of intercourse with a cow); Collins v. State, 73 Ga. 76 (Ga. 1884) (bestiality); State v. Frank, 15 S.W. 330 (Mo. 1890) (dog); State v. Campbell, 29 Tex. 44 (Tex. 1867) (mare); Cross v. State, 17 Tex. App. 476 (Tex. Crim. App. 1895) (mare); Thomas' Case, 3 Va. 80 (Va. 1812) (mare).

59. Hodges v. State, 19 S.E. 758 (Ga. 1894) (molesting three-year-old boy); Honselman v. People, 48 N.E. 305 (Ill. 1894) (oral sex with fourteen-year-old boy); Davis v. State, 3 Harris & Johnson 154 (Md. 1810) (assault on nineteen-year-old "youth"); Commonwealth v. Snow, 111 Mass. 411 (1871) (seducing a "boy"); Territory v. Mahaffey, 3

Mont. 112 (1878) (seducing a fourteen-year-old boy); Prindle v. State, 21 S.W. 360 (Tex. Crim. App. 1893) (oral sex with an adolescent boy).

60. People v. Hickey, 41 P. 1047 (Cal. 1895) (man-man); People v. Moore, 37 P. 510 (Cal. 1894) (same); Foster v. State, 1 O.C.D. 261 (Ohio Cir. 1886) (gang-raping a man); Lewis v. State, 36 Tex. Crim. App. 37 (1896) (man-woman); Medis v. State, 11 S.W. 112 (Tex. Crim. App. 1881) (men-man).

61. See John Hart Ely, *Democracy and Distrust: A Theory of Judicial Review* (1980); Paul Brest, "The Misconceived Quest for the Original Understanding," 60 *B.U.L. Rev.* 204 (1980); Mark V. Tushnet, "Following the Rules Laid Down: A Critique of Interpretivism and Neutral Principles," 96 *Harv. L. Rev.* 781 (1983).

62. Planned Parenthood of Southeastern Pa. v. Casey, 505 U.S. 833, 855 (1992) (joint opinion).

63. See Kendall Thomas, "Corpus Juris (Hetero)sexualis: Doctrine, Discourse, and Desire in *Bowers v. Hardwick,*" 1 *GLQ* 33 (1993).

64. Jeffries, *Justice Powell,* 515, 518, 521, 523–524, 528–529.

65. See Clellan Ford and Frank Beach, *Patterns of Sexual Behavior* (1951); *The Many Faces of Homosexuality: Anthropological Approaches to Homosexual Behavior* (Evelyn Blackwood ed., 1986); *Ritualized Homosexuality in Melanesia* (Gilbert Herdt ed., 1984).

66. See Alfred Kinsey et al., *Sexual Behavior in the American Male* (1948) and *Sexual Behavior in the American Female* (1953). See also Michael Ruse, *Homosexuality: A Philosophical Inquiry* (1988) (sociobiology).

67. See Evelyn Hooker, "Male Homosexuality in the Rorschach," 22 *J. Projective Techniques* 33 (1958) and "The Adjustment of the Male Overt Homosexual," 21 *J. Projective Techniques* 18 (1957); Sigmund Freud, "Letter to an American Mother" (1935). Modern authorities are collected in *Homosexuality: Social, Psychological, and Biological Issues* (William Paul et al. eds., 1982); *Homosexuality: Research Implications for Public Policy* (John Gonsiorek and James Weinrich eds., 1991).

68. *Evans,* 517 U.S. at 623, quoting Plessy v. Ferguson, 163 U.S. 537, 559 (1896) (Harlan, J., dissenting). *Evans,* handed down May 20, 1996, was delivered 100 years, almost to the day, after *Plessy,* dated May 18, 1896; probably the only reason it was not the same day was that May 18, 1996, was a Saturday.

69. See Christenson v. State, 468 S.E.2d 188 (Ga. 1996); State v. Baxley, 656 So. 2d 973 (La. 1995) (public sex); State v. Gray, 413 N.W.2d 107 (Minn. 1987) (commercial sex); State v. Walsh, 713 S.W.2d 508 (Mo. 1986) (public sex; reserving state constitutional issue); State v. Lopes, 660 A.2d 707 (R.I. 1995) (forcible sex); State v. Morales, 869 S.W.2d 941 (Tex. 1994).

70. *Casey,* 505 U.S. at 848 (joint opinion). See also Michael H. v. Gerald D., 491 U.S. 110 (1989) (Scalia's position that the due process clause protects only those practices, defined at the most specific level, that were protected against state interference in 1868 was rejected by majority of Justices).

71. Washington v. Glucksberg, 118 S. Ct. 2258, 2267–69 (1997).

72. Id. at 2303 (O'Connnor, J., concurring); see id. at 2303–10 (Stevens, J., concurring in the judgment), 2275–93 (Souter, J., concurring in the judgment), 2310 (Ginsburg, J., concurring in the judgment), 2310–12 (Breyer, J., concurring in the judgment).

73. James Wilets, "International Human Rights Law and Sexual Orientation," 18 *Hastings Intl. & Comp. L. Rev.* 1 (1994). See *The Third Pink Book* (Aart Hendriks et al. eds., 1993) for a country-by-country review.

74. Dudgeon v. United Kingdom, 4 Eur. Hum. Rts. Rep. 149 (Eur. Ct. Hum. Rts. 1981); Norris v. Ireland, 13 Eur. Hum. Rts. Rep. 186 (Eur. Ct. Hum. Rts. 1991); Modinos v. Cyprus, 16 Eur. Hum. Rts. Rep. 485 (Eur. Ct. Hum. Rts. 1993). All three sodomy laws have been repealed.

75. See National Coalition for Gay and Lesbian Equality v. Minister of Justice, Constitutional Court of South Africa, judgment of October 9, 1998.

76. In re Toonen, United Nations Human Rights Committee, U.N. Doc. CCPR/c/50/ D/488/1992 (1994).

77. G.A. Res. 2200 A(XXI), December 16, 1966, 21 U.N. GAOR Supp. (No. 16), 999 U.N.T.S. 171, U.N. Doc. A/6316 (1966).

78. Consideration of Reports Submitted by States Parties under Article 40 of the Covenant, U.N. GAOR Hum. Rts. Comm., 53d Sess., U.N. Doc. CCPR/C/79/Add 50, ¶¶2 (second quotation in text) and 9 (first quotation) (1995).

79. American courts can interpret federal law to be consistent with America's international commitments and customary international law, even if not otherwise judicially enforceable. See Murray v. Schooner Charming Betsy, 6 U.S. (2 Cranch.) 64, 118 (1804) (Marshall, C. J.); *Restatement (Third) of the Foreign Relations Law of the United States* §114 (1987). Even non-self-executing treaties "may sometimes be held to be federal policy superseding State law or policy." Id. §115, comment (e); see Toll v. Moreno, 458 U.S. 1 (1982). For an argument that *Toonen* more directly requires overruling *Hardwick,* see James Wilets, "Using International Law to Vindicate the Civil Rights of Gays and Lesbians in United States Courts," 27 *Colum. Hum. Rts. L. Rev.* 33 (1995).

80. See State v. Triggs, 506 P.2d 232 (Cal. 1973) (public toilet); Commonwealth v. Wasson, 842 S.W.2d 487 (Ky. 1992) (solicitation of decoy cop); People v. Dezek, 308 N.W.2d 652 (Mich. App. 1981) (public toilet); *Onofre,* 415 N.E.2d 936 (automobile); People v. Uplinger, 447 N.E.2d 62 (N.Y. 1983), *cert. dismissed,* 467 U.S. 246 (1984) (solicitation); Commonwealth v. Bonadio, 415 A.2d 47 (Pa. 1980) (erotic club); Honneycutt v. State, 690 S.W.2d 64 (Tex. Crim. App. 1985) (automobiles); Leibman v. State, 652 S.W.2d 942 (Tex. Crim. App. 1983) (adult bookstore).

81. See Thomasson v. Perry, 80 F.3d 915 (4th Cir. 1996) (en banc), and Able v. United States, 88 F.3d 1280 (2d Cir. 1996), for discussions of the new policy.

82. See Martha Chamallas, "Consent, Equality, and the Legal Control of Sexual Conduct," 61 *S. Cal. L. Rev.* 777 (1988); Larry Catá Backer, "Raping Sodomy and Sodomizing Rape: A Morality Tale about the Transformation of Modern Sodomy Jurisprudence," 21 *Am. J. Crim. L.* 27 (1993).

83. Schochet v. State, 580 A.2d 176 (Md. 1990); accord, Post v. State, 715 P.2d 1105 (Okla. Crim. App. 1986).

84. See Ralph Hingson et al., "AIDS Transmission: Changes in Knowledge and Behaviors among Teenagers, 1986 to 1988," 85 *Pediatrics* 24 (1990), as well as *AIDS in the Industrialized Democracies: Passions, Politics, and Policies* (David Karp and Ronald Bayer eds., 1992).

85. See Campbell v. Sundquist, 926 S.W.2d 250 (Tenn. App. 1996) (public health amicus brief); Tomas Philipson and Richard Posner, *Private Choices and Public Health: The AIDS Epidemic in an Economic Perspective* (1993).

86. Bottoms v. Bottoms, 457 S.E.2d 102 (Va. 1995), discussed in Chapter 8.

87. See the debate between Judges Silberman and Wald in Steffan v. Perry, 41 F.3d 677 (D.C. Cir. 1994) (en banc), and between Judges Norris and Reinhardt in Watkins v. U.S. Army, 847 F.2d 1329 (9th Cir. 1988), *vacated*, 875 F.2d 699 (9th Cir. 1989) (en banc).

88. Shahar v. Bowers, 114 F.3d 1097 (11th Cir. 1997) (en banc). On Bowers' adultery, see Kevin Sack, "Georgia Candidate for Governor Admits Adultery and Resigns Commission in Guard," *N.Y. Times*, June 6, 1997, at A1.

89. See Powell v. State, 510 S.E.2d18(Ga. 1998).

5. The Sexualized First Amendment

1. "Don't ask, don't tell" was initially implemented by a Defense Department memorandum of July 19, 1993, and subsequently codified in more restrictive form by statute. National Defense Authorization Act of 1994, Public Law No. 103-160, §546, codified at 10 U.S.C. §654. The implementing regulations were issued in December 1993 and are found in Department of Defense Directive Nos. 1332.14.H (separation of enlisted personnel), 1332.30.H (separation of officers), 1304.26 (enlistment). See William N. Eskridge, Jr., and Nan D. Hunter, *Sexuality, Gender, and the Law*, 388–407 (1997), reproducing the legal materials underlying the policy.

2. Rowland's damages judgment was overturned in Rowland v. Mad River Local Sch. Dist., 730 F.2d 444 (6th Cir. 1984), *cert. denied*, 470 U.S. 1009 (1985) (Brennan and Marshall, JJ., dissenting). Selland's case was dismissed in Selland v. Perry, 905 F. Supp. 260 (D. Md. 1995). For other gays-in-the-military cases where such first amendment arguments have been rejected, see Holmes v. California Army Natl. Guard, 124, F.3d 1126 (9th Cir. 1997); Able v. United States, 88 F.3d 1280 (2d Cir. 1996); Thomasson v. Perry, 80 F.3d 915 (4th Cir. en banc 1996); Steffan v. Perry, 41 F.3d 677 (D.C. Cir. en banc 1994); Pruitt v. Cheney, 963 F.2d 1160, 1163–64 (9th Cir. 1991); Woodward v. United States, 871 F.2d 1068, 1071 (Fed. Cir. 1989); Ben-Shalom v. Marsh, 881 F.2d 454, 462 (7th Cir. 1989).

3. See Rankin v. McPherson, 483 U.S. 378 (1987) (protecting an employee in the constable's office for being discharged for saying she hoped President Reagan's next assassin would have better aim); Rutan v. Republican Party, 497 U.S. 62 (1990) (protecting patronage employees even though they were members of the opposing political party).

4. David Cole and William N. Eskridge, Jr., "From Hand-Holding to Sodomy: First Amendment Protection of Homosexual (Expressive) Conduct," 29 *Harv. C.R.-C.L. L. Rev.* 319 (1994). See also José Gomez, "The Public Expression of Lesbian/Gay Personhood as Protected Speech," 1 *J.L. & Inequality* 121 (1991); Carol Steiker, "The Constitutional Status of Sexual Orientation: Homosexuality as a Suspect Classification," 98 *Harv. L. Rev.* 1285, 1295–96 (1985) (student note).

5. See Defense Dir. No. 1332.14.H.1.b(2) (statement of homosexuality creates rebuttable presumption that enlisted person engages in prohibited sodomy). The

statute, however, seems to exclude persons for such statements simply because they are homosexuals. 10 U.S.C. §654(b)(2).

6. Pickering v. Board of Educ., 391 U.S. 563, 568 (1968), applied in Rankin v. McPherson, 483 U.S. 378 (1987); Connick v. Myers, 461 U.S. 138, 140 (1983).

7. In Chaplinsky v. New Hampshire, 315 U.S. 568, 572 (1942), the Court said that some expressive conduct is "of such slight social value as a step to truth that any benefit that may be derived from [it] is outweighed by the social interest in order and morality." *Chaplinsky's* implication that there are tiers of expression was rejected by five Justices in Young v. American Mini Theatres, 427 U.S. 50 (1976) (plurality position on this issue rejected by four dissenters and one concurring Justice); FCC v. Pacifica Found., 438 U.S. 726 (1978) (same). The Court in R.A.V. v. City of St. Paul, 505 U.S. 377, 383–388, 391–392 (1992), further ruled that the state cannot engage in *viewpoint* discrimination when it regulates nonspeech communication such as fighting words, obscenity, and libel.

8. See United States v. Eichman, 496 U.S. 310 (1990) (flag-burning); Texas v. Johnson, 491 U.S. 397 (1989) (flag-burning); National Socialist Party of Am. v. Skokie, 432 U.S. 43 (1977) (marching in uniforms displaying swastikas); United States v. O'Brien, 391 U.S. 367 (1968) (draft-card burning).

9. Wisconsin v. Mitchell, 508 U.S. 476, 489 (1993).

10. See Philip Blumstein and Pepper Schwartz, *American Couples: Money, Work, Sex,* 236 (1983); Morton Hunt, *Sexual Behavior in the 1970s,* at 199, 204 (1974); Edward O. Laumann, et al., *The Social Organization of Sexuality: Sexual Practices in the United States,* 98–99 (1994) (table 3.6).

11. Compare Dennis v. United States, 341 U.S. 494 (1951) (illegal conduct for the Communist Party and its leaders to advocate overthrow of the government), with Scales v. United States, 367 U.S. 203 (1961) (state can penalize only active membership in the Communist Party with intent to further its illegal activity).

12. Barnes v. Glen Theatre, Inc., 501 U.S. 560, 565–566 (1991) (plurality opinion by Rehnquist, C.J., accepting that nude dancing is "expressive conduct"); id. at 581 (Souter, J., concurring in the judgment); id. at 587–588 (White, J., dissenting).

13. Id. at 577 n.4 (Scalia, J., concurring in the judgment). See Dallas v. Stanglin, 490 U.S. 19, 24–25 (1989) (purely recreational dancing is not speech so long as its goal is calisthenic).

14. For different perspectives on the communicative features of sex, see Richard Mohr, *Gays/Justice,* 106–114 (1990); Camille Paglia, *Sexual Personae,* 1–39 (1990); Richard A. Posner, *Sex and Reason,* 111–145 (1992).

15. The proposition in text is hard to test, but the evidence for it is broad: the popularity of romance novels, including lesbian romances, that extol erotic touching as a communication of feelings and love; countless articles in *Cosmopolitan* and other magazines about the importance of kissing, touching, and lovemaking; and the pervasiveness of a communicative approach to sex in mainstream best-sellers, such as Alice Walker, *The Color Purple* (1982).

16. See Thomas Emerson, *The System of Freedom of Expression* (1970); Edwin Baker, "Scope of the First Amendment Freedom of Speech," 25 *UCLA L. Rev.* 964 (1978); Martin Redish, "The Value of Free Speech," 130 *U. Pa. L. Rev.* 591 (1982).

17. Cohen v. California, 403 U.S. 15 (1971).

18. Arthur Aron and Elaine Aron, "Love and Sexuality," in *Sexuality in Close Relationships,* 25, 42 (Kathleen McKinney and Susan Sprecher eds., 1991).

19. Vivienne Cass, "The Implications of Homosexual Identity Formation for the Kinsey Model and Scale of Preference," in *Homosexuality/Heterosexuality,* 39 (David McWhirter et al. eds., 1990).

20. Laud Humphreys, *Out of the Closets: The Sociology of Homosexual Liberation,* 136–141 (1972), drawing from Erving Goffman, *Stigma: Notes on the Management of Spoiled Identity* (1963); *Homosexuality: Research Implications for Public Policy* (John Gonsiorek and James Weinrich eds., 1991).

21. Hurley v. Irish-American Gay, Lesbian, and Bisexual Group of Boston, Inc., 515 U.S. 557, 574 (1995).

22. See Andrew Moffitt, "Still Standing: The Marjorie Rowland Story" (unpublished paper, Yale Law School, 1996) (fascinating account of Rowland's life and her case, drawn from court records and interviews with Rowland).

23. Wooley v. Maynard, 430 U.S. 705, 715 (1977) (state cannot force ideological license plate on Jehovah's Witness); see West Virginia State Bd. of Educ. v. Barnette, 319 U.S. 624 (1943) (state cannot compel children to pledge allegiance to flag); Pacific Gas & Elec. Co. v. Public Utils., 475 U.S. 1 (1986) (state cannot require utility to distribute message it rejects).

24. New York Times v. Sullivan, 376 U.S. 254, 270 (1964); see Alexander Meiklejohn, *Free Speech and Its Relation to Self-Government* (1948) and "The First Amendment Is an Absolute," 1961 *Sup. Ct. Rev.* 245.

25. Gay Law Students Assn. v. Pacific Tel. & Tel. Co., 595 P.2d 592 (Cal. 1979).

26. John C. Jeffries, Jr., *Justice Lewis F. Powell, Jr.,* 521–522 (1994).

27. Sylvia Law, "Homosexuality and the Social Meaning of Gender," 1988 *Wis. L. Rev.* 187; see Elvia Arriola, "Sexual Identity and the Constitution," 10 *Women's Rts. L. Rptr.* 143 (1988); Nan D. Hunter, "Marriage, Law, and Gender: A Feminist Inquiry," 1 *L. & Sexuality* 9 (1991).

28. Lee Bollinger, *The Tolerant Society: Freedom of Speech and Extremist Speech in America* (1986).

29. Kenneth Karst, "The Pursuit of Manhood and the Desegregation of the Armed Forces," 38 *UCLA L. Rev.* 499 (1991).

30. Police Dept. of Chicago v. Mosley, 408 U.S. 92, 97 (second quotation in text), 99 (first quotation) (1972).

31. Id. at 96, quoting Alexander Meiklejohn, *Political Freedom: The Constitutional Powers of the People,* 27 (1948). See Kenneth Karst, "Equality as the Central Meaning of the First Amendment," 43 *U. Chi. L. Rev.* 20 (1975).

32. R.A.V. v. City of St. Paul, 505 U.S. 377, 383 (1992), invoking Chaplinsky v. New Hampshire, 315 U.S. 568 (1942).

33. *R.A.V.,* 505 U.S. at 382.

34. Moffitt, "Still Standing," 5 (reporting Rowland's understanding as to why the assistant principal was not upset initially).

35. National Gay Task Force v. Board of Educ., Oklahoma City, 729 F.2d 1270 (10th Cir. 1984), *aff'd by equally divided Court,* 470 U.S. 903 (1985); Acanfora v. Board of

Educ. of Montgomery Cty., 491 F.2d 498 (4th Cir. 1974); Jantz v. Muci, 759 F. Supp. 1543 (D. Kan. 1991).

36. *O'Brien,* 391 U.S. at 376–377, 384.

37. *Texas v. Johnson,* 491 U.S. at 403.

38. Community for Creative Non-Violence v. Watt, 703 F.2d 586, 622 (D.C. Cir. en banc, 1983) (Scalia, J., dissenting) (emphasis in original), *rev'd,* 468 U.S. 288 (1984). See John Hart Ely, "Flag Desecration: A Case Study in the Roles of Categorization and Balancing in First Amendment Analysis," 88 *Harv. L. Rev.* 1482, 1497–98 (1975).

39. Clark v. Community for Creative Non-Violence, 468 U.S. 288, 297–298 (1984).

40. *Fiscal Year 1993 Defense Budget: Hearing before the House Committee on the Budget,* 102d Cong., 2d Sess. 45 (1992).

41. See *Assessment of the Plan to Lift the Ban on Homosexuals in the Military: Hearings before the Subcommittee on Military Forces and Personnel of the House Committee on Armed Services,* 103d Cong., 2d Sess. (July 21–22, 1993) (testimony of General Powell and Secretary Aspin); *Policy Concerning Homosexuality in the Armed Forces: Hearings before the Senate Committee on Armed Services,* 103d Cong., 2d Sess. (July 20, 1993) (testimony of same officials, accompanied by the other Joint Chiefs of Staff).

42. *Policy Concerning Homosexuality in the Armed Forces: Hearings before the Senate Committee on Armed Services,* 103d Cong., 1st Sess. 618–619 (May 11, 1993).

43. See *July 1993 Senate Hearings* (testimony of General Powell and the Joint Chiefs of Staff).

44. Cf. *July 1993 House Hearings,* 322ff. (testimony and colloquy by Cass Sunstein, rebuking William Woodruff, who opined that don't ask, don't tell raises more substantial first amendment issues).

45. In House hearings several "unofficial" witnesses favoring the military exclusion made arguments that gay or bisexual men were actually unfit for military service, based upon their alleged selfishness, *Policy Implications of Lifting the Ban on Homosexuals in the Military: Hearings before the House Committee on Armed Services,* 103d Cong., 1st Sess. 89 (May 1993) (Colonel John Ripley), or predatory nature, id. at 94–102 (Brigadier General William Weise). That testimony was not embraced by the official policymakers and was rebutted in detail by Gregory Herek, testifying for the American Psychological Association. Id. at 247–261.

46. E.g., Austin v. Michigan Chamber of Commerce, 494 U.S. 652 (1990).

47. Texas v. Johnson, 491 U.S. 397 (1989); Bowers v. Hardwick, 478 U.S. 186 (1986).

48. E.g., Brown v. Glines, 444 U.S. 348 (1980) (upholding Air Force regulation prohibiting distribution of literature without permission of commander); Greer v. Spock, 424 U.S. 828 (1976) (upholding content-based exclusion from military base of political candidates); Parker v. Levy, 417 U.S. 733 (1974) (upholding court-martial of captain for urging enlisted personnel to refuse to go to Vietnam).

49. See Frank I. Michelman, "The Supreme Court, 1985 Term—Foreword: Traces of Self-Government," 100 *Harv. L. Rev.* 4 (1986), criticizing Goldman v. Weinberger, 475 U.S. 503 (1986).

50. Employment Division v. Smith, 494 U.S. 872 (1990).

51. Rostker v. Goldberg, 453 U.S. 57 (1981).

52. Greer v. Spock, 424 U.S. 828 (1976).

53. Anderson v. Laird, 466 F.2d 283, 290 (D.C. Cir. 1972). See also Banks v. Garrett, 901 F.2d 1084, 1088–89 (Fed. Cir. 1990) (dictum that military could not prohibit soldiers from writing legislators in their personal capacities).

54. Waters v. Churchill, 511 U.S. 661, 675 (1994) (plurality opinion). See also cases cited in note 6 above.

55. Acanfora v. Board of Educ., 491 F.2d 498 (4th Cir. 1974) (state cannot discipline teacher for public statements about his sexual orientation).

56. Rankin v. McPherson, 483 U.S. 378 (1987).

57. See Church of the Lukumi Babalu Aye v. Hialeah, 508 U.S. 520 (1993).

58. United States v. Robel, 389 U.S. 258, 263–264 (1967).

59. Korematsu v. United States, 323 U.S. 214 (1944).

60. See *Gays in Uniform: The Pentagon's Secret Reports* (Kate Dyer ed., 1990), whose introduction describes the suppression of the Crittenden and PERSEREC reports.

61. U.S. General Accounting Office, *Defense Force Management: Department of Defense's Policy on Homosexuality* (1992) (*GAO Report*); National Defense Research Institute, *Sexual Orientation and U.S. Military Personnel Policy: Options and Assessment* (Rand, 1993).

62. *May 1993 House Hearings,* 265–270, referring to Samuel Stouffer et al., *The American Soldier* (1949); Edward Shils and Morris Janowitz, "Cohesion and Disintegration in the Wehrmacht in World War II," 12 *Pub. Op. Q.* 280, 315 (1948).

63. *Churchill,* 511 U.S. at 671–675 (plurality opinion).

64. E.g., Terminiello v. Chicago, 337 U.S. 1, 4 (1949).

65. Stouffer et al., *American Soldier,* discussed in *May 1993 House Hearings,* 270–278 (testimony of Prof. David Segal).

66. Morris MacGregor, Jr., *Integration of the Armed Forces, 1940–1965,* at 40 (1981) (polling data); Bernard Nalty, *Strength for the Fight: A History of Black Americans in the Military,* 78 (1986) (same); Richard Dalfiume, *Desegregation of the U.S. Armed Forces,* 189 n.38 (1969) (quotation in text).

67. MacGregor, *Integration of the Armed Forces,* 54; Nalty, *Strength for the Fight,* 100.

68. For the Army's study, see DA Personnel Research Team, A Preliminary Report on Personnel Research Data (July 28, 1951), quoted in MacGregor, *Integration of the Armed Forces,* 441. The study by outside consultants, "A Preliminary Report on the Utilization of Negro Manpower" (June 30, 1951), described in id. at 442, was published as *Social Research and the Desegregation of the U.S. Army* (Leo Bogart ed., 1969).

69. See Allan Bérubé, *Coming Out under Fire: The History of Gay Men and Women in World War Two* (1990).

70. See *GAO Report;* Theodore Sarbin and Kenneth Karols, "Nonconforming Sexual Orientations and Military Suitability" (December 1988), reprinted in *Gays in Uniform,* 3–97; Michael McDaniel, "Preservice Adjustment of Homosexual and Heterosexual Military Accessions: Implications for Service Clearance Suitability" (January 1989), reprinted in id. at 111–135.

71. See Bérubé, *Coming Out under Fire;* Mary Ann Humphrey, *My Country, My Right to Serve: Experiences of Gay Men and Women in the Military, World War II to the Present* (1990); Randy Shilts, *Conduct Unbecoming: Lesbians & Gays in the U.S. Military, Vietnam to the Persian Gulf* (1993).

72. *GAO Report,* 40–41. Cf. *May 1993 Senate Hearings,* 608–609 (General Schwarzkopf testimony that in other armed forces, such as Israel's, open gays are not fully integrated).

73. John Lancaster, "Why the Military Supports the Ban on Gays," *Wash. Post,* January 28, 1993, at A8.

74. *Hate Crimes* (Gregory Herek and Kevin Berrill eds., 1992); *May 1993 House Hearings,* 247–261 (Gregory Herek for American Psychological Association).

75. Compare Paul Cameron et al., "Homosexuals in the Armed Forces," 62 *Psychol. Rep.* 211 (1988) (antihomosexual version of shower-room argument), with Kendall Thomas, "Shower/Closet" (skeptical version).

76. On the psychology of homophobia, see *Bashers, Baiters & Bigots: Homophobia in American Society* (John DeCecco ed., 1985).

77. Shils and Janowitz, "Cohesion in the Wehrmacht," 315.

78. See Mady Wechsler Segal, "The Argument for Female Combatants," in *Female Soldiers: Combatants or Noncombatants?,* 267, 278–281 (Nancy Loring Goldman ed., 1982).

79. See Jennifer Egan, "Uniforms in the Closet," *N.Y. Times Magazine,* June 28, 1998, at 26–31; Diane Mazur, "The Unknown Soldier: A Critique of 'Gays in the Military' Scholarship and Litigation," 29 *U. Cal. Davis L. Rev.* 223 (1996).

80. Foucault is discussed in the introduction to Part One, and in David Cole, "Playing by Pornography's Rules," 143 *U. Pa. L. Rev.* 111 (1995).

81. E.g., Abrams v. United States, 250 U.S. 616 (1919), and Whitney v. California, 274 U.S. 357 (1927) (politically subversive speech can be suppressed), overruled by Brandenburg v. Ohio, 395 U.S. 444 (1969) (state cannot suppress KKK).

82. Feiner v. New York, 340 U.S. 315 (1951) (civil rights speech can be suppressed if it causes a commotion), narrowed by Cox v. Louisiana, 379 U.S. 536 (1965); Beauharnais v. Illinois, 343 U.S. 250 (1952) (white supremacy speech is libelous), essentially overruled by New York Times v. Sullivan, 376 U.S. 254 (1965).

83. For cases where the Supreme Court has tolerated the suppression of gay identity speech, see National Endowment for the Arts v. Finley, 118 S. Ct. 2168 (1998) (allowing federal government to discriminate against lesbian and gay expressive art); S.F. Arts & Athletics, Inc. v. United States Olympic Commn., 483 U.S. 522 (1987) ("Gay Olympics" violates trademark of Olympic Commission); Ward v. Illinois, 431 U.S. 767 (1977) (liberal application of obscenity standard to allow broad state regulation of "lesbianism and sadism and masochism"); and cases listed in endnote 2 of this chapter (allowing armed forces to expel self-identified gay people).

84. See the cases cited in notes 81 and 82 (all overruled or narrowed by subsequent opinions).

85. *Barnes,* 501 U.S. at 575 (Scalia, J., concurring in the judgment); see David Cole, "Sexual Conduct and the First Amendment," *Legal Times,* August 30, 1993, at 23.

86. Dallas v. Stanglin, 490 U.S. 19, 24–25 (1989).

87. On addiction, see Richard Stephens, *The Street Addict Role: A Theory of Heroin Addiction* (1991); Mark Kelman, "Choice and Utility," 1979 *Wis. L. Rev.* 769. On third-party effects of drug use, see Neil McKegany and Marina Barnard, *AIDS, Drugs, and Sexual Risk* (1992); Charles Turner et al., *AIDS, Sexual Behavior, and Drug Use* (1989); Don Des Jarlais and Samuel Freidman, "Shooting Galleries and AIDS," 80 *Am. J. Pub. Health* 142 (1990).

88. See 44 Liquormart, Inc. v. Rhode Island, 116 S. Ct. 1495 (1996); Central Hudson Gas & Elec. Corp. v. Public Serv. Commn., 447 U.S. 557 (1980).

89. Debra Satz, "Markets in Women's Sexual Labor," *Ethics,* October 1995, at 63, 78–79.

90. According to historians, the criminalization of prostitution has contributed to disease and crime, to the disadvantage of female sex workers. See Ruth Rosen, *Prostitution in America: 1900–1918* (1982); Judith Walkowitz, *Prostitution and Victorian Society* (1980). Experience in Europe and Nevada suggests that time, place, and manner regulations are more efficacious than criminalization.

91. Carole Pateman, *The Sexual Contract* (1988); Margaret Jane Radin, "Market-Inalienability," 100 *Harv. L. Rev.* 1849 (1987). See also Elizabeth Anderson, *Value in Ethics and Economics* (1993).

92. *R.A.V.,* 505 U.S. at 382.

93. *Hurley,* 517 U.S. at 579.

94. City of Renton v. Playtime Theatres, Inc., 475 U.S. 41 (1986); Paris Adult Theatre I v. Slaton, 413 U.S. 49 (1973). See also other cases discussed in Chapter 3.

95. Stanley v. Georgia, 394 U.S. 557, 564 (second quotation in text), 565 (first quotation) (1969), quoting Olmstead v. United States, 277 U.S. 438, 478 (1928) (Brandeis, J., dissenting).

96. See New York v. Ferber, 458 U.S. 747 (1982); FCC v. Pacifica Found., 438 U.S. 726 (1978); Ginsberg v. New York, 390 U.S. 629 (1968).

97. See *Out of the Closets: Voices of Gay Liberation* (Karla Jay and Allen Young eds., 1972); Dennis Altman, *Coming Out in the Seventies* (1979); Barbara Ponse, *Identities in the Lesbian World* (1978).

98. *Rowland,* 470 U.S. at 1016 n.11 (Brennan, J., dissenting from the denial of certiorari).

99. Roth v. United States, 354 U.S. 476 (1957), modified by Miller v. California, 413 U.S. 15 (1973); New York v. Ferber, 458 U.S. 747 (1982) (more lenient review for child pornography).

100. *R.A.V.,* 505 U.S. at 383–390.

101. See Scott Tucker, *Radical Feminism and Gay Male Porn* (1983); Jeffrey Sherman, "Love Speech: The Social Utility of Pornography," 47 *Stan. L. Rev.* 661 (1995); Carl Stychin, "Exploring the Limits: Feminism and the Legal Regulation of Gay Male Pornography," 16 *Vt. L. Rev.* 859 (1992). Contra, John Stoltenberg, *Refusing to Be a Man* (1989).

102. Catharine MacKinnon, "Pornography, Civil Rights, and Speech," 20 *Harv. C.R.-C.L. L. Rev.* 1 (1985), followed in Regina v. Butler, [1992] 1 S.C.R. 452.

103. See William N. Eskridge, Jr., "A Jurisprudence of 'Coming Out': Religion, Homosexuality, and Collisions of Liberty and Equality in American Public Law," 106 *Yale L.J.* 2411, 2466–73 (1997).

104. American Booksellers Assn., Inc. v. Hudnut, 771 F.2d 323 (7th Cir. 1985), *aff'd mem.,* 475 U.S. 1001 (1986), quoting West Virginia State Bd. of Educ. v. Barnette, 319 U.S. 624, 642 (1943).

6. Multivocal Prejudices and Homo Equality

1. Romer v. Evans, 517 U.S. 620 (1996); Baehr v. Lewin, 852 P.2d 44 (Haw. 1993).

2. See Yick Wo v. Hopkins, 118 U.S. 356 (1886); Strauder v. West Virginia, 100 U.S. 303 (1879); William E. Nelson, *The Fourteenth Amendment* (1988); Melissa Lamb Saunders, "Equal Protection, Class Legislation, and Color Blindness," 96 *Mich. L. Rev.* 245 (1997); Joseph Tussman and Jacobus tenBroek, "The Equal Protection of the Laws," 37 *Cal. L. Rev.* 341 (1949).

3. Plessy v. Ferguson, 163 U.S. 537 (1896); The Civil Rights Cases, 109 U.S. 3 (1883).

4. David Bixby, "The Roosevelt Court, Democratic Ideology, and Minority Rights," 90 *Yale L.J.* 741 (1981).

5. Brown v. Board of Educ., 347 U.S. 483 (1954); United States v. Carolene Products Co., 304 U.S. 144, 152 n.4 (1938); Louis Lusky, "Minority Rights and the Public Interest," 52 *Yale L.J.* 1 (1942). See generally John Hart Ely, *Democracy and Distrust* (1980).

6. Loving v. Virginia, 388 U.S. 1 (1967). The analytical framework for equal protection after *Loving* is explained in Gerald Gunther, "The Supreme Court, 1971 Term—Foreword: In Search of Evolving Doctrine on a Changing Court: A Model for Newer Equal Protection," 86 *Harv. L. Rev.* 1 (1972).

7. Keyes v. School Dist. No. 1, 413 U.S. 189 (1973) (school segregation); Washington v. Davis, 426 U.S. 229 (1976) (employment).

8. Richmond v. J.A. Croson Co., 488 U.S. 469 (1989); Adarand Constructors, Inc. v. Pena, 515 U.S. 200 (1995).

9. Craig v. Boren, 429 U.S. 190 (1976), followed and applied in Califano v. Goldfarb, 430 U.S. 199 (1977); Orr v. Orr, 440 U.S. 455 (1981).

10. E.g., Reed v. Reed, 404 U.S. 71 (1971).

11. E.g., Michael M. v. Superior Court of Sonoma County, 450 U.S. 464 (1981) (statutory rape by men only); Rostker v. Goldberg, 453 U.S. 57 (1981) (exclusion of women from draft registration).

12. *Evans,* 517 U.S. at 623, quoting *Plessy,* 163 U.S. at 559 (Harlan, J., dissenting). For commentary that has most influenced my thinking, see Akhil Reed Amar, "Attainder and Amendment 2: *Romer's* Rightness," 95 *Mich. L. Rev.* 203 (1996); Daniel Farber and Suzanna Sherry, "The Pariah Principle," 13 *Const. Comm.* 257 (1996); Toni Massaro, "Gay Rights, Thick and Thin," 49 *Stan. L. Rev.* 45 (1996); Louis Michael Seidman, "*Romer's* Radicalism," 1996 Sup. Ct. Rev. 67. For the pre-*Evans* debate, compare Kenneth Karst, *Law's Promise, Law's Expression,* 185 (1993), with Richard Duncan and Gary Young, "Homosexual Rights and Citizen Initiatives," 9 *Notre Dame J.L. Ethics & Pub. Poly.* 93–135 (1995).

13. E.g., City of Cleburne v. Cleburne Living Center, Inc., 473 U.S. 432 (1985) (striking down law disadvantaging mentally disabled because no apparent reason for it but dislike). Contrast Williamson v. Lee Optical Co., 348 U.S. 483 (1955) (presumed health concerns accepted as rational basis for special interest law).

14. *Evans,* 517 U.S. at 632 (first quotation in text), 634–635 (second quotation), quoting Department of Agriculture v. Moreno, 413 U.S. 528, 534 (1973).

15. Bowers v. Hardwick, 478 U.S. 186, 196 (1986).

16. E.g., Lawrence Burtoft, *Setting the Record Straight: What Research Really Says about the Social Consequences of Homosexuality,* 32–35 (1995); *Hardwick,* Amicus Brief of Prof. David Robinson.

17. See Gryczan v. State, 942 P.2d 112 (Mont. 1997); Campbell v. Sundquist, 926 S.W.2d 250 (Tenn. App. 1996); Tomas Philipson and Richard A. Posner, *Private Choices, Public Health: The AIDS Epidemic in an Economic Perspective* (1993).

18. Andrew Koppelman, "*Romer v. Evans* and Invidious Intent," 6 *Wm. & Mary Bill of Rights J.* 89, 138–146 (1997), to which Richard Duncan, "The Narrow and Shallow Bite of *Romer* and the Eminent Rationality of Dual-Gender Marriage," id. at 147, is a response.

19. Elisabeth Young-Bruehl, *The Anatomy of Prejudices,* 32–36, 157–58 (1996).

20. See Stephen Bransford, *Gay Politics vs. Colorado: The Inside Story of Amendment 2* (1994); Robert Nagel, "Playing Defense," 6 *Wm. & Mary Bill of Rights J.* 167, 191–199 (1997) (appendix reproducing key voter information pamphlet).

21. *Evans,* 517 U.S. at 623, quoting *Plessy,* 163 U.S. at 559 (Harlan, J., dissenting).

22. Compare Whaley v. Whaley, 399 N.E.2d 1270 (Ohio App. 1978) (adultery does not disqualify parent from custody otherwise in best interest of the child), with Conkel v. Conkel, 509 N.E.2d 983 (Ohio App. 1987) (same for homosexuality, except that the gay father could not visit the children accompanied by another man).

23. Ward v. Ward, 1996 WL 491692 (Fla. App. 1996) (unpublished).

24. See, e.g., Immerman v. Immerman, 1 Cal. Rptr. 298 (Cal. App. 1959); Bennett v. Clemens, 196 S.E.2d 842 (Ga. 1973); Commonwealth v. Bradley, 91 A.2d 379 (Pa. 1952); Bottoms v. Bottoms, 457 S.E.2d 102 (Va. 1995).

25. *Evans,* 517 U.S. at 633–635.

26. See Lynn Wardle, "The Potential Impact of Homosexual Parenting on Children," 1997 *Univ. Ill. L. Rev.* 833.

27. See Charlotte Patterson, "Adoption of Minor Children by Lesbian and Gay Adults," 2 *Duke J. Gender L. & Poly.* 191 (1995). Leading studies include Patricia Falk, "Lesbian Mothers: Psychosocial Assumptions in Family Law," 44 *Am. Psychol.* 941 (1989); Susan Golombok et al., "Children in Lesbian and Single Parent Households: Psychosexual and Psychiatric Appraisal," 24 *J. Child Psychol. & Psychiatry* 551 (1983); David Kleber et al., "The Impact of Parental Homosexuality in Child Custody Cases," 14 *Bull. Am. Academy Psychol. & Law* 81 (1986); Mary Hotvedt and Jane Barclay Mandel, "Children of Lesbian Mothers," in *Homosexuality: Social, Psychological, and Biological Issues* 275, 282 (William Paul et al. eds., 1982). Competing reviews of the empirical literature are contained in Wardle, "Homosexual Parenting," and Carlos Ball and Janice Farrell Pea, "Warring with Wardle: Social Science, Morality, and Gay and Lesbian Parents," 1998 *Univ. Ill. L. Rev.* 253.

28. E.g., Susan Golombok and Fiona Tasker, "Do Parents Influence the Sexual Orientation of Their Children?," 32 *Dev. Psychol.* 3, 8 (1996) (impossibility of recruiting a random sample of gay parents because of the closetry of most); Charlotte Patterson, "Children of Lesbian and Gay Parents," 63 *Child Dev.* 1025, 1036–39 (1992) (survey of the studies, including those of the author).

29. Mike Allen and Nancy Burrell, "Comparing the Impact of Homosexual and Heterosexual Parents on Children: Meta-Analysis of Existing Research," 32 *J. Homosexuality* 19, 28–30 (1996), correcting for some problems identified by Philip Belcastro et al., "A

Review of Data Based Studies Addressing the Affects of Homosexual Parenting on Children's Sexual and Social Functioning," 20 *J. Divorce & Remarriage* 105 (1993).

30. Richard Green et al., "Lesbian Mothers and Their Children: A Comparison with Solo Parent Heterosexual Mothers and Their Children," 15 *Archives Sexual Behav.* 167 (1986); Golombok et al., "Children in Lesbian and Single Parent Households," 562–567; Rhonda Rivera, "Legal Issues in Gay and Lesbian Parenting," in *Gay and Lesbian Parents,* 199, 226 n.79 (Frederick W. Bozett ed., 1987) (reporting unpublished study).

31. Wardle, "Homosexual Parenting," 852–857, 865–866.

32. Ball and Pea, "Warring with Wardle," 272–308; Baehr v. Miike, 1996 WL 694235 (Haw. Cir. Ct. Dec. 6, 1996) (finding of Fact No. 34 quoted in text).

33. E.g., National Center on Child Abuse and Neglect, U.S. Department of Health and Human Servs., *The Third National Incidence Study of Child Abuse and Neglect* (1996); Carole Jenny, "Are Children at Risk for Sexual Abuse by Homosexuals?," 94 *Pediatrics* 41 (1994). Other studies are reported in Ball and Pea, "Warring with Wardle," 307 n.279.

34. See William N. Eskridge, Jr., and Philip P. Frickey, *Legislation: Statutes and the Creation of Public Policy,* 675–687 (2d ed. 1995).

35. For sexual orientation-neutral statutory constructions that avoid *Evans* problems, see, e.g., In re Guardianship of Kowalski, 478 N.W.2d 790 (Minn. App. 1991) (lesbian partner can be disabled person's guardian); Braschi v. Stahl Assocs., 543 N.E.2d 49 (N.Y. 1989) (passing rent-controlled apartment to "family" member). For an antigay construction that would today raise *Evans* problems, see, e.g., Coon v. Joseph, 237 Cal. Rptr. 873 (App. 1987) (person cannot sue for distress at injury to same-sex partner even though common law spouse can sue).

36. See Nancy Polikoff, "This Child Does Have Two Mothers: Redefining Parenthood to Meet the Needs of Children in Lesbian-Mother and Other Nontraditional Families," 78 *Geo. L.J.* 459 (1990), whose proposal for courts to allow "second-parent adoptions" has been followed by courts in California, the District of Columbia, Massachusetts, New Jersey, New York, and Vermont. See William N. Eskridge, Jr. and Nan D. Hunter, *Sexuality, Gender, and the Law,* 861–868 (1997).

37. See Kenneth L. Karst, "The Pursuit of Manhood and the Desegregation of the Armed Forces," 38 *UCLA L. Rev.* 499 (1991); Eskridge and Hunter, *Sexuality, Gender, and the Law,* 319–407.

38. Rostker v. Goldberg, 453 U.S. 57 (1981).

39. The leading case is Thomasson v. Perry, 80 F.3d 915 (4th Cir. 1996) (en banc), where the majority of the judges interpreted the statutory antigay exclusion narrowly and upheld it against objections by colleagues that the exclusion swept more broadly or was unconstitutional even as narrowly construed.

40. Ariz. Rev. Stat. §15-716(C)(1)-(2) (added 1991). For other policies to similar effect, see National Abortion Rights Action League, *Sexuality Education in America: A State-by-State Review* (September 1995).

41. See Paul Gibson, "Gay and Lesbian Youth Suicide," in U.S. Department of Health and Human Servs., *Youth Suicide Report,* 110 (1989); Donna Dennis and Ruth Harlow, "Gay Youth and the Right to Education," 4 *Yale L. & Poly. Rev.* 446 (1986). See also Nabozny v. Podlesny, 92 F.3d 446 (7th Cir. 1996).

42. E.g., Bethel Sch. Dist. No. 403 v. Fraser, 478 U.S. 675 (1986).

43. Defense of Marriage Act, Public Law No. 104-199, 110 Stat. 2419 (1996).

44. E.g., 142 Cong. Rec. S10,112 (Sen. Boxer) (daily ed. September 10, 1996); id. at H7273 (Rep. Schroeder), H7278 (Rep. Frank) (daily ed. July 11, 1996).

45. E.g., id. at H7482 (Rep. Barr), H7486 (Rep. Buyer) (July 12, 1996).

46. Id. at H7491 (Rep. Canady) (July 12, 1996); also, id. at H7500-H7501 (Rep. Hyde).

47. Id. at S10,114 (September 10, 1996).

48. Watkins v. U.S. Army, 847 F.2d 1329 (9th Cir. 1988), *vacated en banc,* 875 F.2d 699 (9th Cir. 1989).

49. Frontiero v. Richardson, 411 U.S. 677, 685–686 (1973) (plurality opinion). For the Court's similar methodology when evaluating other classifications, see Mathews v. Lucas, 427 U.S. 495, 505 (1976) (nonmarital birth); Massachusetts Bd. Retirement v. Murgia, 427 U.S. 307 (1976) (age); City of Cleburne v. Cleburne Living Center, 473 U.S. 432 (1985) (disabilities); Plyler v. Doe, 457 U.S. 202, 216–217 n.14 (1982) (children of noncitizens).

50. E.g., Alfred Kinsey et al., *Sexual Behavior in the Human Male* (1948) and *Sexual Behavior in the Human Female* (1953); Evelyn Hooker, "Male Homosexuality in the Rorschach," 22 *J. Projective Techniques* 33 (1958) and "The Adjustment of the Male Overt Homosexual," 21 *J. Projective Techniques* 18 (1957); Sigmund Freud, "Letter to an American Mother" (1935). Accord, *Homosexuality: Social, Psychological, and Biological Issues* (William Paul et al. eds., 1982); *Homosexuality: Research Implications for Public Policy* (John Gonsiorek & James Weinrich eds., 1991). See also accounts from disciplines traditionally hostile to homosexuality, Kenneth Lewes, *Psychoanalysis and Male Homosexuality* (1988); Michael Ruse, *Homosexuality: A Philosophical Inquiry* (1988). For accounts from different perspectives of sexual and gender variation across time and cultures, see Clellan Ford and Frank Beach, *Patterns of Sexual Behavior* (1951); *Anthropology and Homosexual Behavior* (Evelyn Blackwood ed., 1986); *Ritualized Homosexuality in Melanesia* (Gilbert Herdt ed., 1984).

51. Adrienne Rich, "Compulsory Heterosexuality and Lesbian Existence," in *Blood, Bread, and Poetry: Selected Prose, 1979–1985,* at 23–75 (1986). See Suzanne Pharr, *Homophobia: A Weapon of Sexism* (1988); Ti-Grace Atkinson, *Amazon Odyssey* (1974); Anne Koedt, "Lesbianism and Feminism," in *Radical Feminism* 246 (1973); *Amazon Expedition: A Lesbian Feminist Anthology* (Phyllis Birkby et al. eds., 1973); *For Lesbians Only: A Separatist Anthology* (Sarah Hoagland and Julia Penelope eds., 1988).

52. 118 Cong. Rec. 9096–9097 (March 20, 1972) (testimony of Prof. Freund).

53. Compare id. at 9315 (Sen. Ervin, invoking Freund to oppose ERA), with id. at 9320–9321 (Sen. Bayh, disputing Freund's analysis). See Note, "The Legality of Homosexual Marriage," 82 *Yale L.J.* 573 (1973).

54. Singer v. Hara, 522 P.2d 1187 (Wash. App. 1974). For other references, see William N. Eskridge, Jr., *The Case for Same-Sex Marriage* (1996).

55. State v. Walsh, 713 S.W.2d 508, 510 (Mo. 1986).

56. See Andrew Koppelman, "Why Discrimination against Lesbians and Gay Men Is Sex Discrimination," 69 *N.Y.U. L. Rev.* 197 (1994) and "The Miscegenation Analogy: Sodomy Law as Sex Discrimination," 98 *Yale L.J.* 145 (1988) (student note); Sylvia Law, "Homosexuality and the Social Meaning of Gender," 1988 *Wis. L. Rev.* 187.

57. Baehr v. Lewin, 852 P.2d 44 (Haw. 1993).

58. *Craig,* 429 U.S. at 198–199.

59. Koppelman, "Sex Discrimination," 255–257; Law, "Homosexuality." See the historical sources in note 74 below.

60. McLaughlin v. Florida, 379 U.S. 184 (1964), overruling Pace v. Alabama, 106 U.S. 583 (1883).

61. United States v. Virginia, 116 S. Ct. 2264, 2280 (1996), quoting Mississippi Univ. for Women v. Hogan, 458 U.S. 718, 725 (1982); see Miller v. Albright, 118 S. Ct. 1428, 1445–46 (O'Connor, J., joined by Kennedy, J., concurring in the judgment), 1449–55 (Ginsburg, J., joined by Breyer and Souter, JJ., dissenting) (1998).

62. Califano v. Goldfarb, 430 U.S. 199, 233 (1977) (Stevens, J., concurring in the judgment), quoted in *Miller,* 118 S. Ct. at 1441 (plurality opinion by Stevens, J.).

63. See Jonathan Ned Katz, *Gay/Lesbian Almanac: A New Documentary* (1983).

64. See, e.g., Joel Prentiss Bishop, *Commentaries on the Criminal Law,* vol. 2 (1858); Joseph Chitty, *A Practical Treatise on Criminal Law,* vol. 2, at 48–50 (5th amended ed. 1847); Francis Wharton, *A Treatise on Criminal Law of the United States* (1852).

65. See Chapter 4 (oral sex); Reva Siegel, "Reasoning from the Body: A Historical Perspective on Abortion Regulation and Questions of Equal Protection," 44 *Stan. L. Rev.* 261 (1992).

66. See Richard A. Posner and Katharine B. Silbaugh, *A Guide to America's Sex Laws* (1996).

67. *Virginia,* 116 S. Ct. at 2276 (citing cases).

68. Baker v. Nelson, 191 N.W.2d 185, 186 (Minn. 1971), *appeal dismissed,* 409 U.S. 810 (1972).

69. See Eskridge, *Same-Sex Marriage,* ch. 2.

70. *Virginia,* 116 S. Ct. at 2276 (citing cases). Possible exceptions include proof of paternity cases and the statutory rape case. After *Virginia* and *Miller v. Albright,* it is not clear that either line of cases retains viability.

71. Stephen Morin and Ellen Garfinkle, "Male Homophobia," 34 *J. Soc. Issues,* Winter 1978, at 29, 31, as well as Mary Laner and Roy Laner, "Sexual Preference or Personal Style? Why Lesbians Are Disliked," 5 *J. Homosexuality* 339 (1980) and "Personal Style or Sexual Preference? Why Gay Men Are Disliked," 9 *Intl. Rev. Mod. Socy.* 215 (1979). For other sources, see Koppelman, "Sex Discrimination," 238 n.157.

72. A. P. MacDonald and Richard Games, "Some Characteristics of Those Who Hold Positive and Negative Attitudes toward Homosexuals," 1 *J. Homosexuality* 9, 19 (1979); see Kathryn Black and Michael Stevenson, "The Relationship of Self-Reported Sex-Role Characteristics and Attitudes toward Homosexuality," in *Bashers, Baiters and Bigots: Homophobia in American Society,* 83 (John DeCecco ed., 1985).

73. Albert Klassen et al., *Sex and Morality in the U.S.: An Empirical Enquiry under the Auspices of the Kinsey Institute,* 241 (1989), quoting A. P. MacDonald et al., "Attitudes toward Homosexuality: Preservation of Sex Morality or the Double Standard?" 40 *J. Consulting & Clinical Psychiatry* 161 (1972).

74. The historiography that has most influenced my thinking in what follows is, especially, that of Carroll Smith-Rosenberg, *Disorderly Conduct: Visions of Gender in Victorian America* (1985); John D'Emilio, "Capitalism and Gay Identity," in *Powers of*

Desire: The Politics of Sexuality, 100 (Ann Snitow et al. eds., 1983); Anthony Rotundo, *American Manhood: Transformations in Masculinity from the Revolution to the Modern Era* (1993); Lillian Faderman, *Surpassing the Love of Men* (1982). For earlier developments along these lines in Europe, see Michael Rey, "Parisian Homosexuals Create a Lifestyle, 1700–1750: The Police Archives," in *'Tis Nature's Fault: Unauthorized Sexuality during the Enlightenment,* 179–192 (Robert Purks MacCubbin ed., 1987); Randolph Trumbach, "Gender and the Homosexual Role in Modern Western Culture: The 18th and 19th Centuries Compared," in *Homosexuality, Which Homosexuality?,* 149, 153 (Dennis Altman et al. eds., 1989).

75. Havelock Ellis, *Studies in the Psychology of Sex: Sex Inversion,* 147–148 (1897). See also Richard von Krafft-Ebing, *Psychopathia Sexualis, with Especial Reference to the Antipathic Sexual Instinct: A Medico-Forensic Study,* 54–55, 382–383 (F. J. Rebman trans., 12th ed., 1931).

76. Especially George Beard, *Sexual Neurasthenia: Its Hygiene, Causes, Symptoms, and Treatment* (1884); G. Frank Lydston, "Clinical Lecture: Sexual Perversion, Satyriasis and Nymphomania," 61 *Med. & Surgical Rep.* 254 (1889). See also references in Chapter 1 and in Katz, *Gay/Lesbian Almanac.*

77. Barnett v. State, 135 N.E. 647, 649 (Ohio 1922). See also Berryman v. State, 283 P.2d 558, 565 n.1 (Okla. Crim. App. 1955), quoting Morris Ploscoe, *Sex and the Law* (1951).

78. See Report of Lieut. Col. Birge Holt and Capt. Ruby Herman to the Acting Inspector General, July 29, 1944, appendix of testimony (Dr. Alice Rost), archived in Record Group 159, File 333.9, National Archives, Suitland, Maryland, and described in Chapter 1.

79. Chaplain's Presentation (WAVE Recruits), 1952, p. 2, app. 23 to *Report of the Board to Prepare and Submit to the Secretary of the Navy Recommendations for the Revision of Policies, Procedures, and Directives Dealing with Homosexuals* (March 15, 1957).

80. Bureau of Public Information, "Miami Junks the Constitution," *One, Inc.,* January 1954, at 16, 19; Lyn Pedersen, "Miami Hurricane," *One, Inc.,* November 1954, at 6.

81. William N. Eskridge, Jr., "Privacy Jurisprudence and the Apartheid of the Closet, 1946–1961," 24 *Fla. St. U.L. Rev.* 703, 827–828 (1997) (app. 5, reprinting Miami's anti-homosexual ordinances).

82. See James Button et al., *Private Lives, Public Conflicts: Battles over Gay Rights in American Communities,* 76–86 (1997).

83. See Michelle Benecke and Kristin Dodge, "Military Women in Nontraditional Fields: Casualties of the Armed Forces War on Homosexuals," 13 *Harv. Women's L.J.* 215 (1990); Karst, "The Pursuit of Manhood."

84. See Richard A. Posner, *Sex and Reason* (1992), analyzed in William N. Eskridge, Jr., "A Social Constructionist Critique of Posner's *Sex and Reason,*" 102 *Yale L.J.* 333 (1992).

85. Cf. Turner v. Safley, 482 U.S. 78 (1987) (prisoners have presumptive marriage right).

86. Richard A. Posner, "Should There Be Homosexual Marriage? And If So, Who Should Decide?," 95 *Mich. L. Rev.* 1578, 1585–86 (1997) (reviewing Eskridge, *Same-Sex Marriage*); see Posner, *Sex and Reason* (pragmatic arguments against gays in the military and same-sex marriage).

87. William N. Eskridge, Jr., and Philip P. Frickey, "The Supreme Court, 1993 Term—Foreword: Law as Equilibrium," 108 *Harv. L. Rev.* 26 (1994).

88. Adarand Constructors, Inc. v. Pena, 515 U.S. 200 (1995) (insisting upon "consistency" and "congruence" across different factual and institutional settings whenever a suspect classification is under review).

89. Alexander M. Bickel, *The Least Dangerous Branch: The Supreme Court at the Bar of Politics,* 169 (1962).

90. *Evans,* 517 U.S. at 631.

91. Seidman, "*Romer's* Radicalism."

92. Vriend v. Alberta, 156 D.L.R. (4th) 385 (Canada Sup. Ct. 1998) (because sexual orientation discrimination is a suspect classification under the Canadian Charter's equality guarantee, provinces have an obligation to include sexual orientation in list of statutory antidiscrimination protections).

93. Samuel Marcosson, "Harassment on the Basis of Sexual Orientation: A Claim of Sex Discrimination under Title VII," 81 *Geo. L.J.* 1 (1992).

94. Bob Jones Univ. v. United States, 461 U.S. 574 (1983). See Gutwein v. Easton Pub. Co., 272 Md. 563 (1974). I owe this reference to Andrew Koppelman.

95. DeSantis v. Pacific Tel. & Tel. Co., 608 F.2d 327 (9th Cir. 1979). Accord, Holloway v. Arthur Andersen & Co., 566 F.2d 659, 662 (9th Cir. 1977); Ulane v. Eastern Airlines, Inc., 742 F.2d 1081 (7th Cir. 1984) (transsexuals); Smith v. Mutual Ins. Co., 569 F.2d 325, 326–327 (5th Cir. 1978) (cross-dressers).

96. Price Waterhouse v. Hopkins, 490 U.S. 228 (1989). See I. Bennett Capers, "Sex(ual) Orientation and Title VII," 91 *Colum. L. Rev.* 1158 (1991) (student note); Mary Anne C. Case, "Disaggregating Gender from Sex and Sexual Orientation: The Effeminate Man in the Law and Feminist Jurisprudence," 105 *Yale L.J.* 1 (1995); Frank Valdez, "Queers, Sissies, Dykes, and Tomboys: Deconstructing the Conflation of 'Sex,' 'Gender,' and 'Sexual Orientation' in Euro-American Law and Society," 83 *Cal. L. Rev.* 1 (1995).

97. See Katharine Franke, "What's Wrong with Sexual Harassment?," 49 *Stan. L. Rev.* 691, 697–698 n.17 (1977) (collecting cases); Dillion v. Frank, 952 F.2d 403 (6th Cir. 1992) (unreported opinion, reprinted in Eskridge and Hunter, *Sexuality, Gender, and the Law,* 926–930).

98. Barnes v. Train, 1974 WL 10628 (D.D.C. 1974), *rev'd,* 561 F.2d 983 (D.C. Cir. 1977). See Miller v. Bank of Am., 418 F. Supp. 233, 236 (N.D. Cal. 1976), *rev'd,* 600 F.2d 211 (9th Cir. 1979). See Marcosson, "Harassment," 19–28.

99. Oncale v. Sundowner Offshore Servs., Inc., 118 S. Ct. 998 (1998); Nabozny v. Podlesny, 92 F.3d 446 (7th Cir. 1996); Dept. of Educ., Sexual Harassment Guidance, 62 Fed. Reg. 12,034, 12,039 (March 13, 1997).

100. See Vicki Schultz, "Reconceptualizing Sexual Harassment," 107 *Yale L.J.* 1683 (1998).

101. The 1996 version of ENDA debated in the Senate is reproduced in Eskridge and Hunter, *Sexuality, Gender, and the Law,* 1165–69.

102. M. V. Lee Badgett et al., *Pervasive Patterns of Discrimination against Lesbians and Gay Men: Evidence from Surveys across the United States* (Natl. Gay and Lesbian Task Force Policy Inst., 1992). See also Jay Brause, "Closed Doors: Sexual Orientation Bias in

the Anchorage Housing and Employment Markets," in *Identity Reports: Sexual Orienta-tion Bias in Alaska* (1989) (18 percent of employers reported that they would fire any known homosexual in their workforces). Such early studies are criticized in Richard Duncan, "Who Wants to Stop the Church: Homosexual Rights Legislation, Public Pol-icy, and Religious Freedom," 69 *Notre Dame L. Rev.* 393, 401–411 (1994). See the next note for a more recent study.

103. M. V. Lee Badgett, "The Wage Effects of Sexual Orientation Discrimination," 48 *Indus. & Labor Rel. Rev.* 726 (1995).

104. See D.C. Department of Human Rights and Minority Business Development, *Annual Activity Reports.*

105. Letter from Gerald Draper, Acting Director, D.C. Department of Human Rights and Minority Business Development, to William Eskridge, Jr., Professor, Georgetown University Law Center, August 15, 1996.

106. Howard Univ. v. Green, 652 A.2d 41 (D.C. 1994) (heterosexual claiming sexual orientation discrimination); Newman v. District of Columbia, 518 A.2d 698 (D.C. 1986); Sartori v. Society of Am. Military Engrs., 499 A.2d 883 (D.C. 1985); Underwood v. Archer Mgmt. Servs., Inc., 857 F. Supp. 96 (D.D.C. 1994) (transsexual has no claim for sexual orientation discrimination but does state a claim for discrimination because of personal appearance); Sondheimer v. Georgetown Univ., 1987 WL 14618 (D.D.C. 1987); Green v. American Broadcasting Co., 647 F. Supp. 1359 (D.D.C. 1986).

107. See Button et al., *Private Lives, Public Conflicts,* 113–116, 123–128; Kevin Sack, "Gay Rights Hurt by Lack of Uniform Protections," *N.Y. Times,* March 28, 1993. See also Norma Riccucci and Charles Gossett, "Employment Discrimination in State and Local Government: The Lesbian and Gay Male Experience," 26 *Am. Rev. Pub. Admin.* 182–185 (June 1996).

108. Randy Shilts, "City Rights Laws—Are They Just Toothless Paper Tigers?," *Advo-cate,* June 19, 1974, at 6.

109. Button et al., *Private Lives, Public Conflicts,* 116–120.

110. *Employment Discrimination on the Basis of Sexual Orientation: Hearings on S. 2238 before the Senate Committee on Labor and Human Resources,* 103d Cong., 2d Sess. 29–30 (Professor Joseph Broadus), 90–93 (Robert Knight, Family Research Council) (1994). See also *H.R. 1863, the Employment Non-Discrimination Act: Hearing before the Subcommittee on Government Programs of the House Committee on Small Business,* 104th Cong., 2d Sess. (1996).

111. *1994 ENDA Hearings,* 44–45; see Chai Feldblum, "Sexual Orientation, Morality, and the Law," 57 *U. Pitt. L. Rev.* 237 (1996) (critically discussing Kassebaum's view).

112. See Janet Halley, "Reasoning about Sodomy: Act and Identity in and after *Bowers v. Hardwick*," 79 *Va. L. Rev.* 1721 (1993).

113. According to the leading national survey, reported in Edward O. Laumann, *The Social Organization of Sexuality: Sexual Practices in the United States,* 98–99 (1994) (table 3.6), 20.4 percent of the female respondents had engaged in anal sex, 67.7 in active oral sex, and 73.1 percent in receptive oral sex. The respondents are not broken down by sexual orientation, but one can reason from this data to the conclusions in text. To begin with, the likelihood that a woman has engaged in any of the aforementioned sexual activities is higher if she is currently married; the main superficial barometer of hetero-

sexual orientation, being married to a man, correlates tightly with these activities. (Similarly, currently married men are more likely to have engaged in anal sex, receptive oral sex, and active oral sex than the average man and much more likely than men who have never been married and are not cohabiting with a woman.) Most forms of anal sex involve a penis, which suggests, a priori, that straight women would be more likely to engage in it than lesbian or (perhaps also) bisexual women.

114. *1994 ENDA Hearings,* 90–93 (Robert Knight).

115. Young-Bruehl, *Anatomy of Prejudices,* 32–37.

Part Three. After the Closet

1. Queer theory starts with the assumption that gender, sexuality, and perhaps even sex are social constructions and not natural givens. Under that assumption, law assumes more critical but also more ambiguous regulatory roles. Leading works of queer theory include Eve Kosofsky Sedgwick, *Epistemology of the Closet* (1990); Michel Foucault, *The History of Sexuality,* vol. 1: *An Introduction* (Robert Hurley trans., 1978); Judith Butler, *Gender Trouble: Feminism and the Subversion of Identity* (1990); Gayle Rubin, "Thinking Sex: Notes for a Radical Theory of the Politics of Sexuality" (1984). Each is discussed and excerpted in William N. Eskridge, Jr., and Nan D. Hunter, *Sexuality, Gender, and the Law,* 250–318 (1997).

2. See Gabriel Rotello, *Sexual Ecology: AIDS and the Destiny of Gay Men* (1997).

3. See *Date Rape: Feminism, Philosophy, and the Law* (Leslie Francis ed., 1996); Martha Chamallas, "Consent, Equality, and the Legal Control of Sexual Conduct," 61 *S. Cal. L. Rev.* 777 (1988).

4. See Robin West, "Jurisprudence and Gender," 55 *U. Chi. L. Rev.* 1 (1988).

5. See Carol Gilligan, *In a Different Voice: Psychological Theory and Women's Development* (1982).

6. See Mari Matsuda, "When the First Quail Calls: Multiple Consciousness as Jurisprudential Method," 11 *Women's Rts. L. Rep.* 7 (1989); Martha Minow, "The Supreme Court, 1986 Term—Foreword: Justice Engendered," 101 *Harv. L. Rev.* 10 (1987); Margaret Jane Radin, "The Pragmatist and the Feminist," in *Pragmatism in Law and Society,* 127 (Michael Brint and William Weaver eds., 1991).

7. Sexual Consent Paradoxes

1. Pat Califia, "Jessie," in *Macho Sluts: Erotic Fiction,* 50 (first quotation in text), 57 (second quotation) (1988).

2. See John Stuart Mill, *On Liberty,* ch. 4 (1859), the intellectual inspiration for both the Model Penal Code and the Wolfenden Report. See Chapter 2.

3. For a survey of state laws generally on the issues discussed in this chapter, see William N. Eskridge, Jr. and Nan D. Hunter, *Sexuality, Gender, and the Law,* ch. 10 (1997); Richard A. Posner and Katharine B. Silbaugh, *A Guide to America's Sex Laws,* chs. 1–5, 7–10, 12 (1996).

4. Va. Code §18.2-61(B) (1998 Supp.). Other states revoke spousal consent when there has been injury, force, or threat of force, see Jaye Sitton, "Old Wine in New Bottles:

The 'Marital' Rape Allowance," 72 *N.C.L. Rev.* 261 (1993) (student comment), and Virginia has created a lesser crime of "marital sexual assault" in such cases. Va. Code §18.2-67.2:1 (1988).

5. Va. Code §18.2-61(A)(i) (1998 Supp.); Bailey v. Commonwealth, 82 Va. 107 (Va. 1886).

6. Heidi Kitrosser, "Meaningful Consent: Toward a New Generation of Statutory Rape Laws," 4 *Va. J. Soc. Poly. & Law* 287, 293–295 (1997); Lani Ann Remick, "Read Her Lips: An Argument for a Verbal Consent Standard in Rape," 141 *U. Pa. L. Rev.* 1103 (1993) (student comment).

7. The Model Penal Code has a crime of "gross sexual imposition," which is based upon nonphysical coercion, MPC §213.1(2)(a) (1980). The commentary indicates that economic coercion could trigger this liability, but there are no reported cases to that effect.

8. Equal Employment Opportunity Commission (EEOC), Guidelines on Sexual Harassment, 29 C.F.R. §1604.11(a)(2). Proposed S.B. 291, 1978 Va. Legis., discussed in Rosemarie Tong, *Women, Sex, and the Law,* 111 and n.70 (1984), would have imposed criminal liability where the defendant abused his "position of authority" to obtain sex from someone subordinate to him, including "occupation[al]" relationships.

9. Posner and Silbaugh, *Sex Laws,* 155–187; Va. Code §18.2-346 (1988).

10. It is statutory rape to have sexual intercourse with a child under the age of thirteen, Va. Code §18.2-61(A)(iii) (1998 Supp.), and it is a class four felony for an adult to have sex with a child between the ages of thirteen and fifteen. Id. §18.2-63. It is a lesser offense if the defendant is also a minor.

11. Id. §18.2-361(A).

12. Id. §18.2-61(A)(ii).

13. See Posner and Silbaugh, *Sex Laws,* chs. 1 (rape) and 3 (age of consent).

14. Oregon v. Hinkhouse, 912 P.2d 921 (Or. App. 1996) (criminal assault and attempted murder); Doe v. Johnson, 817 F. Supp. 1382 (W.D. Mich. 1993) (tortious assault, fraud, battery); C.A.U. v. R.L., 438 N.W.2d 441 (Minn. App. 1989) (tortious fraud); see Kathleen Sullivan and Martha Field, "AIDS and the Coercive Power of the State," 23 *Harv. C.R.-C.L. L. Rev.* 139 (1988). But see Smallwood v. State, 680 A.2d 512 (Md. 1996) (HIV-positive defendant who raped three women not guilty of attempted murder).

15. Va. Code §18.2-366 (1988); Posner and Silbaugh, *Sex Laws,* 129–142.

16. Va. Code §§18.2-344 (fornication), 18.2-365 (adultery) (1988).

17. Va. Code §18.2-361(A) (1998 Supp.); see also id. §18.2-67.1 ("forcible sodomy").

18. Regina v. Brown, [1993] 2 All E.R. 75 (U.K. House of Lords, 1993), appeal dismissed by the European Court of Justice (1997).

19. See Martin v. Commonwealth, 37 S.E.2d 43 (Va. 1946), applied to consensual sadomasochism in State v. Collier, 372 N.W.2d 303, 306 (Ia. 1985).

20. The law in Maryland, which Virginia sometimes follows, is that a woman who says no has nonetheless "consented" to the rape if she says no after penetration has occurred. Battle v. State, 414 A.2d 1266 (Md. 1980).

21. See Carey v. Population Servs. Intl., 431 U.S. 678 (1979); Alfonso v. Fernandez, 606 N.Y.S.2d 259 (App. Div. 1993).

22. See Posner and Silbaugh, *Sex Laws*, 44–64 (age of consent laws).

23. E.g., Doe v. Duling, 782 F.2d 1202 (4th Cir. 1986) (virtually no possibility that heterosexual consenting adults would be prosecuted for fornication).

24. Zysk v. Zysk, 404 S.E.2d 721 (Va. 1990) (fornication law); Bottoms v. Bottoms, 457 S.E.2d 102 (Va. 1995) (sodomy law).

25. For background, see Peter Brown, *The Body and Society: Men, Women, and Sexual Renunciation in Early Christianity* (1988); Michel Foucault, *The Care of the Self*, vol. 3 of *The History of Sexuality* (Robert Hurley trans., 1986).

26. Va. Code §18.2-66 (1988).

27. See Alice H. Eagly, *Sex Differences in Social Behavior: A Social-Role Interpretation* (1987); Brenda Major, "Gender, Entitlement, and the Distribution of Family Labor," 49 *J. Soc. Issues* 141 (1993).

28. American Law Institute, *Model Penal Code and Commentaries*, pt. II, vol. I, §213.1, at 301–303, following James Durham, "Forcible and Statutory Rape: An Exploration of the Operation and Objectives of the Consent Standard," 62 *Yale L.J.* 55 (1952).

29. For critical examinations of postwar rape reforms, see Susan Estrich, *Real Rape* (1987); Catharine MacKinnon, *Toward a Feminist Theory of the State* (1989); Jeanne C. Marsh et al., *Rape and the Limits of Law Reform* (1982); Cassia Spohn and Julie Horney, *Rape Law Reform: A Grass Roots Revolution and Its Impact* (1992).

30. See Diana E. H. Russell, *Rape in Marriage* (1990); Robin West, "Equality Theory, Marital Rape, and the Promise of the Fourteenth Amendment," 42 *Fla. L. Rev.* 45 (1990); Sitton, "Old Wine in New Bottles."

31. People v. Bermudez, 203 Cal. Rptr. 728, 731 (Cal. App. 1984); see Kitrosser, "Meaningful Consent," 307–310.

32. Va. Code §18.2-61(A)(iii) (child under thirteen) and §18.2-65 (adolescent thirteen to fifteen) (1998 Supp.).

33. See Michelle Oberman, "Turning Girls into Women: Re-Evaluating Modern Statutory Rape Law," 85 *J. Crim. L. & Criminology* 15 (1994).

34. See Lisa Granik, "Running in Hermeneutic Circles: Challenging/Embedding Social Hierarchies through Litigation," 188ff. (Yale Law School J.S.D. dissertation, 1997), discussing early workplace sexual harassment cases, e.g., Martin v. Jansen, 193 P. 674 (Wash. 1920) (common law); Corne v. Bausch & Lomb, Inc., 390 F. Supp. 161 (D. Ariz. 1975), *vacated*, 562 F.2d 55 (9th Cir. 1977) (title VII).

35. EEOC, "Guidelines on Discrimination because of Sex," 45 Fed. Reg. 25,024 (April 11, 1980), codified at 29 C.F.R. ch. XIV, §1604, approved in Meritor Savs. Bank v. Vinson, 477 U.S. 57 (1986), following the approach pioneered by feminist consciousness-raising and written up by Lin Farley, *Sexual Shakedown: The Sexual Harassment of Women on the Job* (1978); Catharine MacKinnon, *Sexual Harassment of Working Women* (1979).

36. Posner and Silbaugh, *Sex Laws*, 111–128 (forty-two states and D.C. have laws criminalizing "abuse of position of trust or authority" for specified relationships).

37. FBI, *Crime in the United States 1994*, at 23 (1995) (overall report figures for rape); Bureau of the Census, *Statistical Abstract of the United States: 1995*, at 203 (1995) (table 315); Department of Justice, "Criminal Victimization 1994," *Bureau of Justice*

Statistics Bulletin, April 1996, at 3 (percentage of reported assaults compared with total assaults).

38. See Ronet Bachman and Raymond Paternoster, "A Contemporary Look at the Effects of Rape Law Reform: How Far Have We Really Come?," 84 *J. Crim. L. & Criminology* 554 (1993).

39. Compare Debra Satz, "Markets in Women's Labor," 106 *Ethics,* October 1995, at 63, with Margaret Jane Radin, "Market-Inalienability," 100 *Harv. L. Rev.* 1849 (1987).

40. Judith Lewis Herman, with Lisa Hirschman, *Father-Daughter Incest* (1981); Brenda Vander Mey and Ronald Neff, *Incest as Child Abuse: Research and Applications* (1986); Elizabeth Ward, *Father-Daughter Rape* (1984).

41. See, e.g., Maryland v. Craig, 497 U.S. 836 (1990) (relaxation of defendant's confrontation clause rights when victim is a child).

42. See Pat Gilmartin, *Rape, Incest, and Child Sexual Abuse,* 49, 73–80 (1994).

43. H. L. A. Hart, *Law, Liberty, and Morality* (1963), responding to Patrick Devlin, *The Enforcement of Morals* (1959), responding to Committee on Homosexual Offenses and Prostitution, *The Wolfenden Report* (1957). Analyzing Bowers v. Hardwick, 478 U.S. 186 (1986), as an update of the Hart-Devlin debate is Anne B. Goldstein, "History, Homosexuality, and Political Values: Searching for the Hidden Determinants of *Bowers v. Hardwick,*" 97 *Yale L.J.* 1073 (1988).

44. Andrea Dworkin, "The Root Cause," in *Our Blood: Prophecies and Discourses on Sexual Politics,* 96–111 (1976); Dworkin, *Pornography: Men Possessing Women* (1981); Catharine MacKinnon, "Feminism, Marxism, Method, and the State: An Agenda for Theory," 7 *Signs* 515 (1982); MacKinnon, *Feminist Theory of the State,* 126–154.

45. See Martha Chamallas, "Consent, Equality, and the Legal Control of Sexual Conduct," 61 *S. Cal. L. Rev.* 777 (1988); MacKinnon, "Feminism, Marxism," 533.

46. Gayle Rubin, "Thinking Sex: Notes for a Radical Theory of the Politics of Sexuality," in *Pleasure and Danger: Exploring Female Sexuality,* 267 (Carole Vance ed., 1984); Pat Califia, *Public Sex: The Culture of Radical Sex* (1994).

47. The leading case upholding a criminal conviction for consensual SM is People v. Samuels, 58 Cal. Rptr. 439 (Cal. App. 1967). See also dicta in State v. Collier, 372 N.W.2d 303, 306 (Iowa 1985).

48. Regina v. Brown, [1993] 2 All E.R. 75 (U.K. House of Lords 1993), appeal dismissed by the European Court of Justice in 1997. The case is caustically discussed in Bill Thompson, *Sadomasochism: Painful Perversion or Pleasurable Play?* (1994).

49. See *Against Sadomasochism: A Radical Feminist Analysis* (Robin Ruth Linden et al. eds., 1982), especially Bat-Ami Bar On, "Feminism and Sadomasochism: Self-Critical Notes," id. at 72–82; Hilde Hein, "Sadomasochism and the Liberal Tradition," id. at 83–89; John Stoltenberg, "Sadomasochism: Eroticized Violence, Eroticized Powerlessness," id. at 124–130.

50. Califia, "Feminism and Sadomasochism," in *Public Sex,* 165–174.

51. See Oberman, "Turning Girls into Women"; Frances Olsen, "Statutory Rape: A Feminist Critique of Rights Analysis," 63 *Tex. L. Rev.* 387 (1984).

52. See Susan Moore and Doreen Rosenthal, *Sexuality in Adolescence* (1993); Rubin, "Thinking Sex."

53. Robin West, "The Difference in Women's Hedonic Lives: A Phenomenological Critique of Feminist Legal Theory," 3 *Wis. Women's L.J.* 81, 142–145 (1987).

54. See Michel Foucault, *The History of Sexuality* (three vols., Robert Hurley trans., 1978, 1984, 1986) and "Afterword: The Subject and the Power," in *Beyond Structuralism and Hermeneutics* (Hubert Dreyfuss and Paul Rabinow eds., 1982). Particularly useful applications of social constructionism are Vikki Bell, *Interrogating Incest: Feminism, Foucault, and the Law* (1993); Celia Kitzinger, *The Social Construction of Lesbianism* (1987); Janet Halley, "Sexual Orientation and the Politics of Biology: A Critique of the Argument from Immutability," 46 *Stan. L. Rev.* 503 (1994).

55. Eve Kosofsky Sedgwick, *Epistemology of the Closet* (1990); Kenji Yoshino, "Suspect Symbols: The Literary Argument for Heightened Scrutiny for Gays," 96 *Colum. L. Rev.* 1753 (1996).

56. Compare Edmund White, *A Boy's Own Story* (1982), with Paul Monette, *Becoming a Man: Half a Life Story* (1992), and Califia, *Public Sex*, 11–26.

57. See Jodi Short, "Richard Posner on AIDS, Death, and Immortality" (Georgetown Univ. Law Center, 1993), drawing from Georges Bataille, *The Tears of Eros* (Peter Connor trans., 1989).

58. E.g., Simon Watney, *Policing Desire: Pornography, AIDS, and the Media* (1996); Harlon Dalton, "AIDS in Blackface," 118 *Daedalus* 205 (1989); Linda Singer, "Bodies—Pleasures—Powers," 1 *differences* 45 (1989); Paula Treichler, "AIDS, Homophobia and Biomedical Discourse: An Epidemic of Signification," 1 *Cultural Stud.* 263 (1987).

59. Chris Gosselin and Glenn Wilson, *Sexual Variations: Fetishism, Sadomasochism and Transvestism* (1980); *S and M: Studies in Sadomasochism* (Thomas Weinberg and G. W. L. Kamel eds., 1983); Charles Moser and Eugene Levitt, "An Exploratory-Descriptive Study of a Sadomasochistically Oriented Sample," 23 *J. Sex Res.* 322–337 (1987); Martin Weinberg et al., "The Social Constituents of Sadomasochism," 31 *Soc. Probs.* 379 (1984). See also Bill Thompson, *Sadomasochism*, 116–149; *Leatherfolk: Radical Sex, People, Politics, and Practice* (Mark Thompson ed., 1991).

60. Carol Truscott, "S/M: Some Questions and a Few Answers," in *Leatherfolk*, 15, 16.

61. Id. at 30.

62. E.g., Edward Donnerstein et al., *The Question of Pornography: Research Findings and Policy Implications*, 2 (1987). Going further, but supporting the point in text, is Catharine MacKinnon, "Pornography, Civil Rights, and Speech," 20 *Harv. C.R.-C.L. L. Rev.* 1 (1985).

63. Gosselin and Wilson, *Sexual Variations*, 68–77.

64. David France, "Will Crispo Walk?," *Vanity Fair*, September 1988, at 176; Maureen Orth, "The Killer's Trail," *Vanity Fair*, September 1997, at 268.

65. See Gayle Rubin, "The Catacombs: A Temple of the Butthole," in *Leatherfolk*, 119–141.

66. Mary Koss, "The Scope of Rape: Incidence and Prevalence of Sexual Aggression and Victimization in a National Sample of Higher Education Students," 55 *J. Consulting & Clinical Psychol.* 162 (1987). Similar figures are reported in Diana E. H. Russell, *Sexual Exploitation: Rape, Child Sexual Abuse, and Workplace Harassment*, 283–285 (1984), but disputed in Katie Roiphe, *The Morning After: Sex, Fear, and Feminism on Campus*, 52–55

(1993), usefully reviewed by Wendy Kaminer, "What Is This Thing Called Rape?," *N.Y. Times,* September 19, 1993, at G1.

67. On the rule of lenity, see William N. Eskridge, Jr., and Philip P. Frickey, *Legislation: Statutes and the Creation of Public Policy,* 655–675 (2d ed. 1995).

68. See State v. Collier, 372 N.W.2d 303 (Iowa 1985) (upholding assault conviction of male out-call model coordinator [pimp] who tied up and beat female model); Commonwealth v. Appleby, 402 N.E.2d 1051 (Mass. 1980) (upholding assault conviction when two-year sadistic relationship resulted in severe physical injuries; victim claimed that he had not consented to the repeated beatings); State v. Brown, 364 A.2d 27 (N.J. App. 1976) (upholding assualt conviction of husband who beat his wife when she consumed alcohol, notwithstanding her apparent consent).

69. Cynthia Cotts, "Crispo Calling: A Tale of Sadomasochistic Date Rape" (Yale Law School paper, January 1996) (fascinating account of the Crispo trial, based on printed sources and interviews with participants, including attorneys and one juror).

70. On the high rates of suicide among gay teenagers, see Paul Gibson, "Gay and Lesbian Youth Suicide," in U.S. Department of Health and Human Servs., *Youth Suicide Report,* 110 (1989).

71. See John Preston, "What Happened?," in *Leatherfolk,* 210, 212–213.

72. Felice Picano, *Ambidextrous: The Secret Lives of Children,* 96 (1985) (the shower story and the quotation in text).

73. J. W. Mohr, "A Child Has Been Molested," *Medical Aspects of Human Sexuality,* November 1968, at 43–50; Kenneth Plummer, "Pedophilia: Constructing a Sociological Baseline," in *Adult Sexual Interest in Children,* 221–249 (Mark Cook and Kevin Howells eds., 1981). On America's tendency to lurch from mania to inattention to new mania as regards childhood sexuality, see Philip Jenkins, *Moral Panic: Changing Concepts of the Child Molester in Modern America* (1998).

74. Thore Langfeldt, "Sexual Development in Children," in *Adult Sexual Interest in Children,* 102–120; also, *Children and Sex: New Findings, New Perspectives* (Larry Constantine and Floyd Martinson eds., 1981).

75. In addition to *Ambidextrous,* see Monette, *Becoming a Man;* White, *A Boy's Own Story.*

76. E.g., Philippe Ariès, *Centuries of Childhood: A Social History of Family Life,* 62ff. (Robert Baldick trans., 1962), reports from the diaries of Louis XIII's childhood doctor that adults regularly played with children and adolescents without apparent trauma for any concerned. See also *Male Intergenerational Intimacy: Historical, Socio-Psychological, and Legal Perspectives* (Theo Sandfort et al. eds., 1991).

77. Claudia Konker, "Rethinking Child Sexual Abuse: An Anthropological Perspective," 62 *Am. J. Anthropsychiatry* 147 (1993). On the Melanesian rituals, see Gilbert Herdt, *The Guardians of the Flutes: Idioms of Masculinity* (1981); *Ritualized Homosexuality in Melanasia* (Gilbert Herdt ed., 1984). See generally *The Many Faces of Homosexuality: Anthropological Approaches to Homosexual Behavior* (Evelyn Blackwood ed., 1986).

78. See note 40 above.

79. L. G. Schultz, "The Child Sex Victim: Social, Psychological, and Legal Perspectives," 52 *Child Welfare* 147, 150 (1973).

80. Jacobson v. United States, 503 U.S. 540 (1992).

81. E.g., Mary Kittredge, *Teens with AIDS Speak Out,* 33–39 (1991); Karen Basen-Engquist and Guy Parcel, "Attitudes, Norms, and Self-Efficacy: A Model of Adolescents' HIV-Related Sexual Risk Behavior," 19 *Health Educ. Q.* 263 (1992).

82. See William N. Eskridge, Jr., and Brian Weimer, "The Economics Epidemic in an AIDS Perspective," 61 *U. Chi. L. Rev.* 733, 743–746, 766–768 (1994), and educational theory sources cited therein.

83. See Gilmartin, *Rape, Incest, and Child Sexual Abuse,* 233–235, 252–266; Diana E. H. Russell, *The Secret Trauma* (1986).

84. Kitrosser, "Meaningful Consent."

85. Chamallas, "Consent, Equality."

86. Michel Foucault, *Introduction,* vol. 1 of *The History of Sexuality,* 109 (Robert Hurley trans., 1978) (incest); see Foucault, *Politics, Philosophy, Culture: Interviews and Other Writings, 1977–1984* (Lawrence Kritzman ed., 1988) (child "molestation" as a sexualizing construction).

87. See Lynne Olman Lourim, "Parents and the State: Joining Forces to Report Incest and Support Its Victims," 28 *U. Mich. J.L. Ref.* 715 (1995) (student note).

8. Beyond Families We Choose

1. William N. Eskridge, Jr., and Edward Stein, "Queer Clones," in *Clones and Clones* (Martha Nussbaum and Cass Sunstein eds., 1998).

2. William N. Eskridge, Jr., *The Case for Same-Sex Marriage,* chs. 5–6 (1996).

3. Milton Regan, Jr., *Family Law and the Pursuit of Intimacy* (1993); Jana Singer, "The Privatization of Family Law," 1992 *Wis. L. Rev.* 1443.

4. Kath Weston, *Families We Choose: Lesbians, Gays, Kinship,* 34–35, 43–75 (1991).

5. See the accounts of Bottoms's life in Bottoms v. Bottoms, 457 S.E.2d 102 (Va. 1995), *rev'g* 444 S.E.2d 276 (Va. App. 1994); Stephen Pershing, "'Entreat Me Not to Leave Thee': *Bottoms v. Bottoms* and the Custody Rights of Gay and Lesbian Parents," 3 *Wm. & Mary Bill of Rights J.* 289 (1994).

6. Loving v. Virginia, 388 U.S. 1 (1967); Palmore v. Sidoti, 466 U.S. 429 (1984).

7. *Loving,* 388 U.S. at 12.

8. Zablocki v. Redhail, 434 U.S. 374, 386 (first quotation in text), 387 n.12 and 388 (second quotation) (1978).

9. "State regulation has included bans on incest, bigamy, and homosexuality . . . A 'compelling state purpose inquiry' would cast doubt on the network of restrictions that the States have fashioned to govern marriage and divorce." Id. at 399 (Powell, J., concurring in the judgment).

10. Turner v. Safley, 482 U.S. 78, 95 (1987).

11. Leading judicial decisions rejecting a right to marry for same-sex couples are Dean v. District of Columbia, 653 A.2d 307 (D.C. 1995); Baehr v. Lewin, 852 P.2d 44 (Haw. 1993); Jones v. Hallahan, 501 S.W.2d 588 (Ky. 1973); Baker v. Nelson, 191 N.W.2d 185 (Minn. 1971), *appeal dismissed,* 409 U.S. 810 (1972); Singer v. Hara, 522 P.2d 1187 (Wash. App. 1974). The judicial and attorney general decisions are discussed in Eskridge, *Same-Sex Marriage,* 51–62, with references in id. at 232–233 nn.23–24,

248–249 n.18. An Alaska state trial judge in 1998 declared the same-sex marriage bar a violation of a state constitutional right to privacy in *Brause v. Bureau of Vital Statistics.*

12. Prince v. Massachusetts, 321 U.S. 158, 166 (1944). Accord, Lassiter v. Department of Soc. Servs., 452 U.S. 18, 27 (1981); Meyer v. Nebraska, 262 U.S. 390, 399 (1923).

13. Leading cases include Levy v. Louisiana, 391 U.S. 68 (1968); Labine v. Vincent, 401 U.S. 532 (1971); Trimble v. Gordon, 430 U.S. 762 (1977).

14. Weber v. Aetna Casualty & Surety Co., 406 U.S. 164, 175 (1972).

15. Stanley v. Illinois, 405 U.S. 645, 651 (1972).

16. Editors of the Harvard Law Review, *Sexual Orientation and the Law,* 119 (1989).

17. Smith v. Organization of Foster Families for Equality and Reform, 431 U.S. 816, 844 (1977), applied in Lehr v. Robertson, 463 U.S. 248, 261 (1983), the leading case limiting the *Stanley* principle.

18. Bottoms v. Bottoms, 457 S.E.2d 102 (Va. 1995), applying Roe v. Roe, 324 S.E.2d 691 (Va. 1985).

19. See Bark v. Bark, 479 So. 2d 42 (Ala. App. 1985); Thigpen v. Carpenter, 730 S.W.2d 510 (Ark. 1987); Pennington v. Pennington, 596 N.E.2d 305 (Ind. App. 1992); In re Marriage of Wiarda, 505 N.W.2d 506 (Iowa 1993); S. v. S., 608 S.W.2d 64 (Ky. 1980); Lundin v. Lundin, 563 So. 2d 1273 (La. App. 1990); Hall v. Hall, 291 N.W.2d 143 (Mich. App. 1980); White v. Thompson, 569 So. 2d 1181 (Miss. 1990); T.C.H. v. K.M.H., 784 S.W.2d 281 (Mo. 1989); Woodruff v. Woodruff, 260 S.E.2d 775 (N.C. App. 1979); Jacobson v. Jacobson, 314 N.W.2d 78 (N.D. 1981); M.J.P. v. J.G.P., 640 P.2d 966 (Okla. 1982); Chicoine v. Chicoine, 479 N.W.2d 891 (S.D. 1992); Dailey v. Dailey, 635 S.W.2d 391 (Tenn. 1982); Kallas v. Kallas, 614 P.2d 641 (Utah 1980); Schuster v. Schuster, 585 P.2d 130 (Wash. 1978).

20. *Palmore,* 466 U.S. at 435, applied to gay custody cases in, e.g., S.N.E. v. R.L.B., 699 P.2d 875 (Alaska 1985); Conkel v. Conkel, 509 N.E.2d 983 (Ohio App. 1987). Chapter 6 argues that state rules against lesbian or gay custody or adoption violate the equal protection precepts of Romer v. Evans, 517 U.S. 620 (1996).

21. See, e.g., Lundin v. Lundin, 563 So. 2d 1273 (La. App. 1990); Irish v. Irish, 300 N.W.2d 739 (Mich. App. 1980); T.C.H. v. K.M.H., 784 S.W.2d 281 (Mo. 1989); Woodruff v. Woodruff, 260 S.E.2d 775 (N.C. App. 1979); Conkel v. Conkel, 509 N.E.2d 983 (Ohio App. 1987); A. v. A., 514 P.2d 358 (Or. App. 1973). Such requirements have been rejected in In re Marriage of Birdsall, 243 Cal. Rptr. 287 (App. 1989); Pleasant v. Pleasant, 628 N.E.2d 633 (Ill. App. 1993); State v. Chase, 451 N.W.2d 493 (Iowa 1990).

22. In re Dana, 660 N.E.2d 397 (N.Y. 1995); In re Adoption of Two Children by H.N.R., 666 A.2d 535 (N.J. 1995); In re Petition of K.M. and D.M., 653 N.E. 2d 888 (Ill. 1995); In re M.M.D. and B.H.M., 662 A.2d 837 (D.C. 1995); In re Adoption of B.L.V.D., 628 A.2d 1271 (Vt. 1993); Adoption of Tammy, 619 N.E.2d 315 (Mass. 1994). Second-parent adoptions are allowed in California as well. See generally Nancy Polikoff, "This Child Does Have Two Mothers: Redefining Parenthood to Meet the Needs of Children in Lesbian-Mother and Other Nontraditional Families," 78 *Geo. L.J.* 459 (1990).

23. See Appeal in Pima City Juvenile Action B-10489, 727 P.2d 830 (Ariz. App. 1988) (presumption against gay adoption); Cox v. Florida Dept. Health, 656 So. 2d 902 (Fla. 1995) (remanding challenge to antigay adoption law for factual hearing); In re Opinion

of the Justices, 530 A.2d 21 (N.H. 1987) (upholding antigay adoption law). But see In re Adoption of Charles B., 552 N.E.2d 884 (Ohio 1990) (allowing adoption by gay man).

24. E.g., Vlandis v. Kline, 412 U.S. 441 (1973) (irrebuttable presumption); Reed v. Reed, 404 U.S. 71, 76 (1971). These precepts are discussed in the adoption context in Lehr v. Robertson, 463 U.S. 248, 265–268 (1983), and In re Opinion of the Justices, 530 A.2d 21 (N.H. 1987).

25. E.g., Jones v. Hallahan, 501 S.W.2d 588, 589 (Ky. 1973); see Sidney Buchanan, "Same-Sex Marriage: The Linchpin Issue," 10 *U. Dayton L. Rev.* 541 (1985); Lynn Wardle, "A Critical Analysis of Constitutional Claims for Same-Sex Marriage," 1996 *B. Y. U. L. Rev.* 1, 38–39.

26. Bottoms v. Bottoms, No. CH93JA0517-00 (Va. Cir. Ct. Henrico Cty., September 7, 1993), *rev'd,* 444 S.E.2d 276 (Va. App. 1994), *rev'd and trial court judgment reinstated,* 457 S.E.2d 102 (Va. 1995). Chapter 6 discusses the argument in some detail.

27. Eskridge, *Same-Sex Marriage,* 15–50.

28. E.g., Rev. Louis Sheldon, "Gay Marriage 'Unnatural,'" *USA Today,* December 9, 1996; Dr. Lawrence Burtoft, "Gay Parenting and the Developmental Needs of Children" (Focus on the Family, 1997) (children cannot be healthy if they are not raised by parents of each sex). See generally Traditional Values Coalition Educational and Legal Inst., "Homosexual Marriage Sweeps Nation's Legislatures and Courts" (1997).

29. See Herbert Hovenkamp, "Legal Policy and the Endowment Effect," 20 *J. Leg. Stud.* 221 (1991).

30. Compare J.M. Balkin, "The Constitution of Status," 106 *Yale L.J.* 2313 (1997), which argues that courts should curtail laws creating or perpetuating artificial status distinctions.

31. On the endowment effects undermining women's bargaining position in the workplace and marriage, see Alice H. Eagly, *Sex Differences in Social Behavior: A Social-Role Interpretation* (1987); Brenda Major, "Gender, Entitlement, and the Distribution of Family Labor," 49 *J. Soc. Issues* 141 (1993).

32. Defense of Marriage Act (DOMA), Public Law No. 104-199, 110 Stat. 2420 (1996). Justifications for DOMA were made in *Defense of Marriage Act: Hearing on H.R. 3396 before the Subcomm. on the Constitution of the House Comm. on the Judiciary,* 104th Cong., 2d Sess. (1996); *Defense of Marriage Act: Hearing on S. 1740 before the Senate Comm. on the Judiciary,* 104th Cong., 2d Sess. (1996).

33. 110 Cong. Rec. H7276 (daily ed. July 11, 1996) (Rep. Johnston).

34. Id. at H7278 (exchange between Reps. Frank and Largent).

35. Hadley Arkes, "Questions of Principle, Not Predictions," 84 *Geo. L.J.* 321, 326 (1995); William Bennett, "Leave Marriage Alone," *Newsweek,* June 3, 1996, at 27; Charles Krauthammer, "When John and Jim Say, 'I Do': If Gay Marriages Are O.K., Then What about Polygamy? Or Incest?," *Time,* July 22, 1996, at 102; William Safire, "The Case for Polyandry," *N.Y. Times,* March 18, 1996, at A15.

36. Baehr v. Lewin, 852 P.2d 44 (Haw. 1993), which makes the sex discrimination argument for same-sex marriage discussed in Chapter 6.

37. See J.L.P. v. D.J.P., 643 S.W.2d 865 (Mo. App. 1982); In re J.S. & C., 324 A.2d 90 (N.J. Super. 1974), *aff'd,* 362 A.2d 54 (N.J. Super. App. 1976); In re Adoption of Charles B., 552 N.E.2d 884 (Ohio 1990) (Resnick, J., dissenting).

38. See Robert Barret and Bryan Robinson, "Gay Dads," in *Redefining Families: Implications for Children's Development,* 147, 161 (Adele Eskeles Gottfried and Allen Gottfried eds., 1994); Patricia Falk, "The Gap between Psychosocial Assumptions and Empirical Research in Lesbian-Mother Child Custody Cases," in id. at 131, 142–143; Carole Jenny et al., "Are Children at Risk for Sexual Abuse by Homosexuals?," 94 *Pediatrics* 41, 44 (1994) (heterosexual is 100 times more likely to molest child than is gay person).

39. Pope John Paul II, "Letter to Families" (February 2, 1994), reprinted in 23 *Origins* 637 (March 3, 1994); Richard A. Posner, *Sex and Reason,* 311 (1992); John Finnis, "Law, Morality, and 'Sexual Orientation,'" 69 *Notre Dame L. Rev.* 1051–1053 (1994); Dean v. District of Columbia, No. CA 90-13892, slip opinion at 9 (D.C. Super., December 30, 1991), *aff'd,* 653 A.2d 307 (D.C. 1995).

40. 110 Cong. Rec. H7491 (daily ed. July 12, 1996) (remarks of Rep. Canady).

41. *Roe,* 324 S.E.2d at 694. See also State Dept. of Health v. Cox, 627 So. 2d 1210 (Fla. App. 1993), *vacated,* 656 So. 2d 902 (Fla. 1995); S. v. S., 608 S.W.2d 64 (Ky. App. 1980); Opinion of the Justices, 530 A.2d 21 (N.H. 1987).

42. Amartya K. Sen, *Collective Choice and Social Welfare,* 79–88 (1970). See William N. Eskridge, Jr., "A Social Constructionist Critique of Posner's *Sex and Reason,*" 102 *Yale L.J.* 333 (1992) (Posner's libertarian presumptions tend to be overwhelmed by his pragmatism).

43. Jurisdictions prohibiting surrogacy contracts or declaring them void include Arizona, the District of Columbia, Florida, Indiana, Louisiana, Michigan, Nebraska, New Jersey, New York, North Dakota, Oregon, Utah, and Washington. Surrogacy contracts are heavily regulated in states like Illinois, Kentucky, Maryland, Nevada, New Hampshire, and Virginia.

44. Debra Satz, "Markets in Women's Reproductive Labor," *Phil. & Pub. Aff.,* Spring 1992, at 107 (analyzing the arguments). Compare Lori Andrews, *Between Strangers: Surrogate Mothers, Expectant Fathers, and Brave New Babies* (1989) and Carmel Shalev, *Birthpower* (1989), supporting surrogacy, with Martha Field, *Surrogate Motherhood* (1990), Carole Pateman, *The Sexual Contract* (1988), and Susan Okin, "A Critique of Surrogacy Contracts," 8 *Pol. & Life Sci.* 205–210 (1990), which are critical.

45. See David Orgon Coolidge, "Same-Sex Marriage? *Baehr v. Miike* and the Meaning of Marriage," 38 *S. Tex. L. Rev.* 1 (1997); Elizabeth Fox Genovese, "Better or Worse, Mostly Worse," *Natl. Rev.,* May 6, 1996, at 51–52 (reviewing Eskridge, *Same-Sex Marriage*).

46. The "relational self" is associated with postmodernism, see Regan, *Pursuit of Intimacy,* ch. 4; Coolidge, "Same-Sex Marriage?," 38–40, but the idea might be consistent with, even if subversive of, liberal premises. Compare Amartya Sen, "Behavior and the Concept of Preference," 40 *Economica* 241 (1973) (preferences may be endogenous to the process of choice); Robin West, "The Difference in Women's Hedonic Lives: A Phenomenological Critique of Feminist Legal Theory," 3 *Wis. Women's L.J.* 81 (1987) (for most women, "other-regarding" preferences are often more important than "self-regarding" ones).

47. Richard Bailey et al., "Heritable Factors Influence Sexual Orientation in Women," 50 *Archives Gen. Psychiatry* 217 (1993); Richard Bailey and Richard Pillard, "A Genetic Study of Male Sexual Orientation," 48 *Archives Gen. Psychiatry* 1089 (1991).

Earlier studies include F. J. Kallmann, "Comparative Twin Study on the Genetic Aspects of Male Homosexuality," 115 *J. Nervous & Mental Disease* 283 (1952); E. D. Eckert et al., "Homosexuality in Monozygotic Twins Reared Apart," 148 *British J. Psychiatry* 421 (1986); N. J. Buhrich et al., "Sexual Orientation, Sexual Identity, and Sex-Dimorphic Behaviors in Male Twins," 21 *Behavioral Genetics* 75 (1991).

48. Dean Hamer and Peter Copeland, *The Science of Desire: The Search for the Gay Gene and the Biology of Behavior* (1994) (gay gene theory); Simon LeVay, *The Gay Brain* (1993) (gay hypothalamus theory); John Money, *Gay, Straight, and In-Between: The Sexology of Sexual Orientation* (1988) (prenatal exposure to androgens theory). For critique of these theories, see Edward Stein, *The Mismeasure of Desire* (1999).

49. Important empirical studies include Susan Golombok et al., "Children in Lesbian and Single Parent Households: Psychosexual and Psychiatric Appraisal," 24 *J. Child Psychol. & Psychiatry* 551 (1983); David Kleber et al., "The Impact of Parental Homosexuality in Child Custody Cases: A Review of the Literature," 14 *Bull. Am. Acad. Psychol. & Law* 81 (1986); Mary Hotvedt and Jane Barclay Mandel, "Children of Lesbian Mothers," in *Homosexuality: Social, Psychological, and Biological Issues*, 275, 282 (William Paul et al. eds., 1982); Sharon Huggins, "A Comparative Study of Self-Esteem of Adolescent Children of Divorced Lesbian Mothers and Divorced Heterosexual Mothers," in *Homosexuality and the Family*, 123 (Frederick W. Bozett ed., 1989). Reviews of the empirical literature are contained in Charlotte Patterson, "Children of Lesbians and Single-Parent Households: Psychosexual and Psychiatric Appraisals," 63 *Child Dev.* 1025 (1992); Alisa Steckel, "Psychosexual Development of Children of Lesbian Mothers," in *Gay and Lesbian Parents*, 75 (Frederick W. Bozett ed., 1987). See also Gregory Herek, "Myths about Sexual Orientation: A Lawyer's Guide to Social Science Research," 1 *Law & Sexuality* 133, 156 (1991).

50. Compare Lynn Wardle, "The Potential Impact of Homosexual Parenting on Children," 1997 *U. Ill. L. Rev.* 833 (criticizing progay studies and asserting that children are harmed by gay parenting), with Carlos Ball and Janice Farrell Pea, "Warring with Wardle: Social Science, Morality, and Gay and Lesbian Parents," 1998 *U. Ill. L. Rev.* 253 (criticizing Wardle's antigay presumption as supported by no reliable study and asserting that the cumulative evidence is, so far, strongly in favor of gay parenting).

51. Charlotte Patterson, "Adoption of Minor Children by Lesbian and Gay Adults: A Social Science Perspective," 2 *Duke J. Gender L. & Poly.* 191, 199–200 (1995).

52. Philip Blumstein and Pepper Schwartz, *American Couples: Money, Work, Sex* (1983) (empirical study finding lesbian couples enjoy stable and rewarding relationships, even more so than heterosexual or gay male couples); Susan Johnson, *Staying Power: Long Term Lesbian Couples* (1990) (nonempirical study of 108 lesbian couples, finding great satisfaction); David McWhirter and Andrew Mattison, *The Male Couple* (1983) (similar nonempirical study of gay male couples); Lawrence Kurdek and J. Patrick Schmitt, "Relationship Quality of Partners in Heterosexual Married, Heterosexual Cohabiting, and Gay and Lesbian Relationships," 51 *J. Personality & Soc. Psychol.* 711 (1986) (empirical survey finding equal level of satisfaction among gay male, lesbian, and straight couples, with less among cohabiting couples).

53. Dorothea Hays and Aurele Samuels, "Heterosexual Women's Perceptions of Their Marriages to Bisexual or Homosexual Men," in *Homosexuality and the Family*, 81–100.

54. See David Cole, "Playing by Pornography's Rules: The Regulation of Sexual Expression," 143 *U. Pa. L. Rev.* 111 (1994).

55. See Laura Benkov, *Reinventing the Family: The Emerging Story of Lesbian and Gay Parents* (1994); Eskridge, *Same-Sex Marriage;* Michael Sandel, "Moral Argument and Liberal Toleration: Abortion and Homosexuality," 77 *Cal. L. Rev.* 521 (1989); Carlos Ball, "Moral Foundations for a Discourse on Same-Sex Marriage: Looking beyond Political Liberalism," 85 *Geo. L.J.* 1871 (1997).

56. Lawrence Kurdek, "Relationship Outcomes and Their Predictors: Longitudinal Evidence from Heterosexual Married, Gay Cohabiting, and Lesbian Cohabiting Couples," 60 *J. Marr. and Fam.* 553 (1998).

57. Golombok et al., "Children in Lesbian and Single Parent Households," 562–567.

58. See Richard Green et al., "Lesbian Mothers and Their Children: A Comparison with Solo Parent Heterosexual Mothers and Their Children," 15 *Archives Sexual Behav.* 167 (1986), as well as Rhonda Rivera, "Legal Issues in Gay and Lesbian Parenting," in *Gay and Lesbian Parents,* 199, 226 n.79 (reporting unpublished study comparing children in households having two lesbian parents with those in households having a single female parent, whether straight or lesbian).

59. Paula Ettelbrick, "Since When Is Marriage a Path to Liberation?," in William N. Eskridge, Jr., and Nan D. Hunter, *Sexuality, Gender, and the Law,* 817–818 (1997).

60. Nan D. Hunter, "Marriage, Law, and Gender: A Feminist Inquiry," 1 *Law and Sexuality* 9 (1991). Responding to Hunter is Nancy Polikoff, "We Will Get What We Ask For: Why Legalizing Gay and Lesbian Marriage Will Not 'Dismantle the Legal Structure of Gender in Every Marriage,'" 79 *Va. L. Rev.* 1535 (1995), which is in turn answered by Evan Wolfson, "Crossing the Threshhold: Equal Marriage Rights for Lesbians and Gay Men, and the Intra-Community Critique," 21 *NYU Rev. L. & Soc. Change* 567 (1994–95).

61. See generally Eskridge and Hunter, *Sexuality, Gender, and the Law,* 791–794, 1171–73.

62. On the pathbreaking Danish law, see Linda Nielsen, "Family Rights and the 'Registered Partnership' in Denmark," 4 *Intl. J.L. & Fam.* 297 (1990); Marianne Hojgaard Pedersen [Danish Ministry of Justice], "Denmark: Homosexual Marriages and New Rules Regarding Separation and Divorce," 30 *J. Fam. L.* 289 (1991–92). See generally David Bradley, *Family Law and Political Culture: Scandinavian Laws in Comparative Perspective* (1996).

63. See, e.g., Posner, *Sex and Reason,* 257 (ambivalent evaluation of polygamy from a liberal perspective).

64. See Rhona Mahony, *Kidding Ourselves: Breadwinning, Babies, and Bargaining Power* (1995); Carol M. Rose, *Property and Persuasion* (1994); Amy L. Wax, "Bargaining in the Shadow of the Market: Is There a Future for Egalitarian Marriage?," 84 *Va. L. Rev.* 509 (1998); Joan Williams, "Is Coverture Dead? Beyond a New Theory of Alimony," 82 *Geo. L.J.* 2227 (1994).

65. See, e.g., Elizabeth Joseph, "My Husband's Nine Wives," *N.Y. Times,* May 23, 1991, at A31. See also David Chambers, "Polygamy and Same-Sex Marriage," 26 *Hofstra L. Rev.* 53 (1997).

66. Rose, *Property and Persuasion,* 240–241. Nineteenth-century Mormons made a similar argument. See Lawrence Foster, *Religion and Sexuality: Three American Communal Experiments of the Nineteenth Century,* 193–194 (1981).

67. See Jesse Embry, *Mormon Polygamous Families: Life in the Principle* (1987); Richard Van Wagoner, *Mormon Polygamy: A History* (2d ed. 1989).

68. Van Wagoner, *Mormon Polygamy,* 100 (quoting Sarah Pratt).

69. Eugene Campbell and Bruce Campbell, "Divorce among Mormon Polygamists: Extent and Explanations," 46 *Utah Hist. Q.,* Winter 1978, at 4–23; Embry, *Polygamous Families,* 190–192 (distant relations between fathers and children); Austin and Alta Fife, *Saints of Sage and Saddle: Folklore among the Mormons,* 168–170 (1956) (same).

70. Compare Embry, *Polygamous Families,* 134–140 (tolerable relationships) with Cala Byram, "Prosecute Polygamy, Women Beg," *Deseret News,* July 28, 1998 (abusive relationships). For general but sympathetic accounts, see Irwin Altman and Joseph Ginat, *Polygamous Families in Contemporary Society* (1996); Philip L. Kilbride, *Plural Marriage for Our Times: A Reinvented Option?* (1994).

71. Polikoff, "This Child Does Have Two Mothers."

72. See In re M.M.D. & B.H.M., 662 A.2d 837 (D.C. 1995); In re Jacob, 660 N.E.2d 397 (N.Y. 1995); In re Adoption of B.L.V.B., 628 A.2d 1271 (Vt. 1993).

73. E.g., In re Thomas S. v. Robin Y., 618 N.Y.S.2d 356 (App. Div. 1994).

9. Religion and Homosexuality

1. See Christopher Bull and John Gallagher, *Perfect Enemies: The Religious Right, the Gay Movement, and the Politics of the 1990s* (1996); Nan D. Hunter, "Life after *Hardwick,*" 27 *Harv. C.R.-C.L. L. Rev.* 531 (1992). Leading antigay legal scholarship is apparently inspired by religious concerns, e.g., Richard Duncan, "Who Wants to Stop the Church: Homosexual Rights Legislation, Public Policy, and Religious Freedom," 69 *Notre Dame L. Rev.* 393 (1994); Lynn Wardle, "A Critical Analysis of Constitutional Claims for Same-Sex Marriage," 1996 *B.Y.U. L. Rev.* 1.

2. I started this project in "A Jurisprudence of 'Coming Out': Religion, Homosexuality, and Collisions of Liberty and Equality in American Public Law," 106 *Yale L.J.* 2411 (1997), from which this chapter draws. At the same time, Andrew Koppelman was starting to address similar issues in "Sexual and Religious Pluralism," in *Sexual Orientation and Human Rights in American Religious Discourse* (Martha Nussbaum and Saul Olyan eds., 1997). I view our projects as complementary.

3. See Robert Cover, "The Supreme Court, 1982 Term—Foreword: *Nomos* and Narrative," 97 *Harv. L. Rev.* 4 (1983).

4. See Steven Epstein, "Gay Politics, Ethnic Identity: The Limits of Social Constructionism," 93/94 *Socialist Rev.,* May-August 1987, at 9, reprinted in *Forms of Desire* (Edward Stein ed., 1989), which argues that gay subcultures are akin to ethnic ones.

5. Cover, "*Nomos* and Narrative," 40.

6. Romer v. Evans, 517 U.S. 620, 636 (1996) (Scalia, J., dissenting).

7. Helmut W. Smith, *German Nationalism and Religious Conflict: Culture, Ideology, Politics, 1870–1914,* at 40–41, 54, 62, 79 (1995).

8. See *Evans,* 517 U.S. at 640–643 (Scalia, J., dissenting), discussing and relying on Bowers v. Hardwick, 478 U.S. 186 (1986); id. at 649–653, discussing and relying on Davis v. Beason, 133 U.S. 333 (1890).

9. Gay Rights Coalition of Georgetown Univ. Law Center v. Georgetown Univ., 536 A.2d 1 (D.C. 1987) (en banc).

10. On identity and law, see Kenneth L. Karst, *Law's Promise, Law's Expression: Visions of Power in the Politics of Race, Gender, and Religion* (1993) and *Belonging to America: Equal Citizenship and the Constitution* (1989), as well as Nan D. Hunter, "Identity, Speech, and Equality," 79 *Va. L. Rev.* 1695 (1993).

11. See John Higham, *Strangers in the Land: Patterns of American Nativism, 1860–1925* (1963), as well as the sources in note 12 below. See also Benzion Netanyahu, *The Origins of the Inquisition in Fifteenth Century Spain* (1995).

12. *Nativism, Discrimination, and Images of Immigrants* (George Pozzetta ed., 1991); Les Wallace, *The Rhetoric of Anti-Catholicism: The American Protective Association, 1887–1911* (1990).

13. This was the result of Bismarck's Kulturkampf against the Roman Catholic Church, which the Iron Chancellor abandoned as early as 1878. See Erich Schmidt-Volkmar, *Der Kulturkampf in Deutschland 1871–1890* (1962); Smith, *German Nationalism,* 19–49; Ronald Ross, "Enforcing the *Kulturkampf* in the Bismarckian State and the Limits of Coercion in Imperial Germany," 56 *J. Mod. Hist.* 456–482 (1984).

14. This was the conclusion of the Kulturkampf against the Spanish Jews in 1391, which resulted in exile, expulsion, and massive conversions to Christianity. See Netanyahu, *Origins of the Inquisition,* 127–215.

15. On the Marranos, see Benzion Netanyahu, *The Marranos of Spain, from the XIVth to the early XVIth Century* (2d ed. 1973). On anti-Catholic campaigns in Europe, see Winfried Becker, "Der Kulturkampf als europäisches und als deutsches Phänomen," 101 *Historisches Jahrbuch* 422–446 (1981).

16. Reynolds v. United States, 98 U.S. 145, 164–166 (1878), upholding the Morrill Anti-Bigamy Law, ch. 125, 12 Stat. 501 (1862). On the connection between polygamy and polity, see Maura Strassberg, "Distinctions of Form and Substance: Monogamy, Polygamy, and Same-Sex Marriage," 75 *N.C.L. Rev.* 1501 (1997).

17. On the antipolygamy campaign, see Richard Van Wagoner, *Mormon Polygamy: A History,* 115–122 (2d ed. 1989); Orma Linford, "The Mormons and the Law: The Polygamy Cases," 9 *Utah L. Rev.* 308, 543 (1964–65) (two-part article).

18. Murphy v. Ramsey, 114 U.S. 15, 45 (1885) (disenfranchisement); Clawson v. United States, 114 U.S. 477 (1885) (jury service); Cannon v. United States, 116 U.S. 55 (1885) (criminal cohabitation), sustaining portions of the Edmunds Act, ch. 47, 22 Stat. 30 (1882); Merlo Pusey, *Builders of the Kingdom—George A. Smith, John Henry Smith, George Albert Smith,* 135 (1982) (quoting Apostle Smith).

19. Davis v. Beason, 133 U.S. 333 (1890), and Late Corporation of the Church of Jesus Christ of the Latter-Day Saints v. United States, 136 U.S. 1 (1890), upholding the portions of the Edmunds-Tucker Act, ch. 397, 24 Stat. 635 (1887), that denied the right to vote and that confiscated LDS property, respectively.

20. Martha Sonntag Bradley, *Kidnapped from That Land: The Government Raids on the Short Creek Polygamists* (1993); Jesse Embry, *Mormon Polygamous Families* (1987); Van Wagoner, *Mormon Polygamy,* 192–197.

21. E.g., Boutilier v. INS, 387 U.S. 118 (1967) (immigration law requires expulsion of a bisexual as a "psychopathic personality"); Kameny v. Brucker, 282 F.2d 823 (D.C. Cir.

1960) (state can deny employment to man charged with homosexual "lewdness"). See also state cases cited in Appendix A1.

22. Moore v. City of East Cleveland, 431 U.S. 494 (1976) (civil ordinance prohibiting unmarried people from living together violates right of privacy [four Justices] or takes property [one Justice]); Church of the Lukumi Babula Aye v. City of Hialeah, 508 U.S. 520 (1993) (ordinance regulating animal sacrifice but aimed at a particular faith violates free exercise clause).

23. Brandenburg v. Ohio, 395 U.S. 444 (1969) (advocacy of unlawful action cannot be criminalized unless lawless action is "imminent"); Dunn v. Blumstein, 405 U.S. 330 (1972) (right to vote is fundamental right that cannot easily be taken away); Wisconsin v. Yoder, 406 U.S. 205 (1972) (the state cannot seek to destroy a religious way of life).

24. See *Homosexuality and World Religions* (Arlene Swidler ed., 1993); William N. Eskridge, Jr., *The Case for Same-Sex Marriage* (1996).

25. Gay Rights Coalition of Georgetown Univ. Law Center v. Georgetown Univ., 536 A.2d 1 (D.C. 1987) (en banc). The account in text of *Gay Rights Coalition* is drawn from the judicial opinions and the trial record, but also from the oral history of the case that is being compiled under the auspices of the Georgetown University Law Center's Bisexual, Lesbian, and Gay Students' Association (BiLAGA). See also Walter J. Walsh, "The Fearful Symmetry of Gay Rights, Religious Freedom, and Racial Equality," 40 *How. L.J.* 513 (1997) (account of case by Judge Mack's law clerk).

26. D.C. Code §1-1520(1); see id. §1-2501 (intent of Council).

27. *Gay Rights Coalition,* 536 A.2d at 21 (narrowing statute to avoid requiring recognition), 30–38 (applying statute to require equal access) (opinion of Mack, J.).

28. Id. at 49 (Ferren, J., dissenting in part).

29. Id. at 63 (Belson, J., dissenting in part); id. at 76–78 (Nebeker, J., dissenting in part).

30. Cover, "*Nomos* and Narrative," 12–13.

31. See Congregation for the Doctrine of the Faith, "The Pastoral Care of Homosexual Persons," 16 *Origins* 377 (1986) (letter to Catholic bishops, urging them to exclude from pastoral programs organizations in which "homosexuals" participate "without clearly stating that homosexual activity is immoral"); Bruce Williams, "Homosexuality: The New Vatican Statement," 48 *Theological Stud.* 270 (1987).

32. *Gay Rights Coalition,* 536 A.2d at 49 (Ferren, J., dissenting in part).

33. Bob Jones Univ. v. United States, 461 U.S. 574, 604 (1983).

34. *Gay Rights Coalition,* 536 A.2d at 68 (Belson, J., dissenting in part); see id. at 71–72 (same point for free exercise).

35. Wooley v. Maynard, 430 U.S. 705, 715 (quotation in text), 716–717 (state interests) (1977). *Wooley's* rule against forced speech was derived from West Virginia State Bd. of Educ. v. Barnette, 319 U.S. 624 (1943) (school children cannot be required to pledge allegiance to the flag if inconsistent with their religious belief). See also Pacific Gas & Electric Co. v. Public Util. Commn., 475 U.S. 1 (1986).

36. Compare *Gay Rights Coalition,* 536 A.2d at 67–74 (Belson, J., dissenting in part) (repeated focus on Georgetown's "rights" and terribleness of state "compulsion"); id. at 75 (Nebeker, J., dissenting in part) (similar), and id. at 56–60 (Ferren, J., dissenting in part) (emphasizing the students' statutory rights to "full citizenship" in the university

community), with id. at 31 (opinion of Mack, J.); see id. at 30–39 (detailed analysis focusing on "burdens" and "interests").

37. William N. Eskridge, Jr., *Dynamic Statutory Interpretation*, 185–192 (1994). For a thorough review of the academic literature analyzing Judge Mack's opinion, see Walsh, "Gay Rights, Religious Freedom, and Racial Equality," 530–540. Professor Walsh also makes this intriguing point: the three judges following Mack's accommodationist approach were all black; the four judges taking an all-or-nothing rights approach were all white. Id. at 554.

38. On "coming out," see the discussion in Chapters 2 and 3, as well as Laud Humphreys, *Out of the Closets: The Sociology of Homosexual Liberation* (1972); *Boys Like Us: Gay Writers Tell Their Coming Out Stories* (Patrick Merla ed., 1996); *Out of the Closets: Voices of Gay Liberation* (Karla Jay and Allen Young eds., 1972); A. E. Smith, "Coming Out," *One, Inc.*, June 1962, at 6–7; Kenji Yoshino, "Suspect Symbols: The Literary Argument for Heightened Scrutiny for Gays," 96 *Colum. L. Rev.* 1753 (1996).

39. John Gonsiorek and James Randolph, "Homosexual Identity: Coming Out and Other Developmental Events," in *Homosexuality*, 161, 169 (John Gonsiorek and James Weinrich eds., 1991).

40. See Gay Law Students Assn. v. Pacific Tel. & Tel. Co., 595 P.2d 592, 610–611 (Cal. 1979).

41. Erving Goffman, *Stigma: Notes on the Management of Spoiled Identity* (1963). On the psychological price of suppression, see Linda Garnets et al., "Violence and Victimization of Lesbians and Gay Men: Mental Health Consequences," in *Hate Crimes*, 207 (Gregory Herek and Kevin Berrill eds., 1992); Sue Hammersmith and Martin Weinberg, "Homosexual Identity: Commitment, Adjustment, and Significant Others," 36 *Sociometry* 56 (1973); Gregory Herek, "Stigma, Prejudice, and Violence against Lesbians and Gay Men," in *Homosexuality*, 60; Alan Maylon, "Psychotherapeutic Implications of Internalized Homophobia in Gay Men," 7 *J. Homosexuality* 59 (1982).

42. Paul Gibson, "Gay and Lesbian Youth Suicide," in U.S. Department of Health & Human Servs., *Youth Suicide Report*, 110 (1989). For fictional accounts, see James Baldwin, *Giovanni's Room* (1956); Lillian Hellman, *The Children's Hour* (1934).

43. See Nicholas von Hoffman, *Citizen Cohn* (1988); David Oshinsky, *A Conspiracy So Immense: The World of Joe McCarthy*, 310 (1983); Anthony Summers, *Official and Confidential: The Secret Life of J. Edgar Hoover* (1993).

44. Trudi Alexy, *The Mezuzah in the Madonna's Foot*, 273 (1993), discussed in Chai Feldblum, "Sexual Orientation, Morality, and the Law," 57 *U. Pitt. L. Rev.* 237, 327–330 (1996).

45. See Richard McAdams, "Relative Preferences," 102 *Yale L.J.* 1, 91–104 (1992).

46. One might distinguish Georgetown's masquerade from the students' masquerade: the Roman Catholic *nomos* was in no important way threatened with closetry. Maybe, but the attention to issues of sexual orientation created by the litigation and presence of gay student groups refocused unwelcome attention on the university's—and the Church's—tradition of sexual cloistering, a focus closeted gay priests and officials at Georgetown resented. Moreover, anti-Catholic prejudice remains palpable, and in some ways Georgetown was more politically marginal in District of Columbia politics than traditionally despised gay groups were.

47. Roberts v. United States Jaycees, 468 U.S. 609, 622–629 (1984); accord, Board of Directors, Rotary Intl. v. Rotary Club of Duarte, 481 U.S. 537 (1987).

48. E.g., Roger Fisher and William Ury, *Getting to Yes: Negotiating Agreement without Giving In* (2d ed. 1992); Carol Gilligan, *In a Different Voice* (1982); Melvin Eisenberg, "Private Ordering through Negotiation: Dispute-Settlement and Rulemaking," 89 *Harv. L. Rev.* 637 (1976).

49. Rodney Christopher, "Explaining It to Dad," in *Boys Like Us*, 302–311. For other examples of accommodation, see William Sterling Walker, "January 18, 1989," in id. at 293–301 (mother accepts her son's homosexuality but does not want him sharing food with his nieces and nephews); Paul Caldwell, "Out-Takes," in id. at 270 (author agrees not to tell his brother until the latter graduates from high school).

50. Philip Bockman, "Fishing Practice," in id. at 80.

51. E.g., Essex Hemphill, "The Other Invisible Man," in id. at 176–185.

52. See *Roberts*, 468 U.S. at 633–638 (O'Connor, J., concurring in part).

53. Hurley v. Irish-American Gay, Lesbian and Bisexual Group of Boston, 515 U.S. 557 (1995), *rev'g*, 636 N.E.2d 1293 (Mass. 1994).

54. Id. at 570 (first quotation in text), 573 (second quotation).

55. Id. at 562 (quoting trial court opinion).

56. New York Cty. Bd. of Ancient Hibernians v. Dinkins, 814 F. Supp. 358, 361–362 (S.D.N.Y. 1993).

57. Hurley's various justifications are quoted in *Irish-American Gay, Lesbian and Bisexual Group*, 636 N.E.2d at 1295 and n.8.

58. *Gay Rights Coalition*, 536 A.2d at 31–38 (opinion of Mack, J.). See also Rowland v. Mad River Local Sch. Dist., 470 U.S. 1009, 1011–17 (1985) (Brennan, J., dissenting from the denial of certiorari).

59. *Hurley* Oral Argument, 1995 US Trans Lexis 89, *25.

60. Id. at *42 (Breyer-Darling exchange), *42–43 (Stevens).

61. Smith v. Fair Employment and Housing Commn., 913 P.2d 909 (Cal. 1996); see Religious Freedom Restoration Act, Public Law No. 103-141, 107 Stat. 1488–89 (1993).

62. For criticism of Employment Divn. v. Smith, 494 U.S. 872 (1990), see City of Borne v. Flores, 117 S. Ct. 2157, 2176–85 (1997) (O'Connor, J., dissenting); Church of Lukumi Babalu Aye, Inc. v. Hialeah, 508 U.S. 520, 564–577 (1993) (Souter, J., concurring in part); Michael McConnell, "Free Exercise Revisionism and the *Smith* Decision," 57 *U. Chi. L. Rev.* 1109 (1990).

63. *Smith v. FEHC*, 51 Cal. Rptr. 2d at 742–745 (Kennard, J., dissenting).

64. City of Santa Barbara v. Adamson, 610 P.2d 436 (Cal. 1980).

65. City of Boerne v. Flores, 117 S. Ct. 2157 (1997), invalidating RFRA, 42 U.S.C. §2000bb et seq.

66. *Smith v. FEHC*, 51 Cal. Rptr. at 765–766 (Baxter, J., dissenting).

67. Eskridge, *Dynamic Statutory Interpretation*, 163–164.

68. See Decision 14/1995 on the legal equality of same sex partnerships (Hung. Constl. Ct. March 13, 1995); Attorney General v. M. and H., [1999] S.C.R. (Can. Sup. Ct. March 18, 1999).

69. The 1996 version of ENDA is reprinted in William N. Eskridge, Jr., and Nan D. Hunter, *Sexuality, Gender, and the Law*, 1165–69 (1997).

70. ENDA §§6(a) (exempting "religious organizations"), 17(9) (defining "religious organization").

71. 42 U.S.C. §2000bb-1(b).

72. *Smith*, 494 U.S. at 881–882, distinguishing, e.g., Wisconsin v. Yoder, 406 U.S. 205 (1972), which required the state to allow Amish parents to withdraw their children from compulsory public education.

73. Public Law No. 101-168, §141, 103 Stat. 1267 (1989). An earlier statutory override was invalidated in Clarke v. United States, 886 F.2d 404 (D.C. Cir. 1989), *vacated as moot*, 915 F.2d 699 (D.C. Cir. 1990).

Made in the USA
Lexington, KY
07 June 2011